BRITISH · COLUMBIA · SOCIETY · OF · ARCHITECTS · VANCOUVER · CHAPTER ·

FOUNDED · MCMXI ·

THE MISTRESS ART, ARCHITECTURE, IS A COMPOUND ART AND IS NOT PRODUCED BY

ONE MIND ALONE. IT IS THE PRODUCTION OF MANY MINDS, MARSHALLED BY ONE, INTO

A LANGUAGE ALL ITS OWN, SPEAKING IN STONE, MARBLE OR BRICK, WOOD OR

PLASTER, METAL OR PAINT, SHOWING THE CLOSE UNION OF THE ARTIST'S SPIRIT

WITH THE CRAFTSMAN'S SKILL, SILENTLY WORKING ITS END TO THE WELFARE OF

MANKIND. IS NOT THIS ART A LINK WITH PRIMAL TIMES, WHOSE DECAYING SYMBOLS,

MATERIAL EVIDENCE OF THOUGHT AND PROGRESS, HELP MANKIND TO GAIN A DEEPER

KNOWLEDGE OF THE IMMUTABLE PRINCIPLES GOVERNING THE NOBLEST AND MOST

DIGNIFIED, OR THE MOST ORDINARY CONCEPTIONS OF THIS PRESENT AGE?

ARCHITECTURE IS A SACRED TRUST, AND UPON THE MEN WHO KNOW, LIES THE

RESPONSIBILITY TO HAND ON THEIR KNOWLEDGE, MAKE PERSONAL SACRIFICE OF

CONVENIENCE AND MATERIAL INTERESTS FOR THE BENEFIT OF FUTURE GENERATIONS.

J. Drummond Beatson

Year Book of the British Columbia Society of Architects, Vancouver Chapter,

1913.

BUILDING
THE
WEST

The Early Architects of
British Columbia

compiled and edited by Donald Luxton
revised second edition

TALONBOOKS

Talonbooks
P.O. Box 2076, Vancouver, British Columbia, Canada V6B 3S3
www.talonbooks.com

Typeset in Optima and Trajan and printed and bound in China.

First Printing, Revised Edition: 2007

The publisher gratefully acknowledges the financial support of the Canada Council for the Arts; the Government of Canada through the Book Publishing Industry Development Program; and the Province of British Columbia through the British Columbia Arts Council and the Book Publishing Tax Credit for our publishing activities.

Additional funding was provided by the Canada Millennium Partnership Fund and the Leon and Thea Koerner Foundation. The British Columbia Heritage Trust provided financial assistance to this project to support conservation of our heritage resources, gain further knowledge and increase public understanding of the complete history of British Columbia. The Canadian Art Deco Society was the sponsor for these grants.

Library and Archives Canada Cataloguing in Publication

Building the west : the early architects of British Columbia / compiled and edited by Donald Luxton.

Includes bibliographical references and index.
ISBN-13: 978-0-88922-554-1 (pbk.)
ISBN-10: 0-88922-474-9 (bound)
ISBN-10: 0-88922-554-0 (pbk.)

1. Architects--British Columbia--Biography. 2. Architecture--British Columbia--History. I. Luxton, Donald, 1954-

NA748.B84 2003   720'.92'2   C2003-910124-X

Front Cover: Dominion Building Under Construction c.1909 [Walker/Eveleigh Family]
Back Cover: (top) Chirst Church Cathedral Stained Glass Window [Archives of the Anglican Diocese of British Columbia],
(bottom) Donald Luxton [Mark Mushet Photography]
Title page: B.C. Society of Architects Conference, Victoria, June 1912 [British Columbia Archives F-09372]
Background this page: West End, Vancouver, c.1914 [Elizabeth & Philip Keatley]
Following page: Second Hotel Vancouver under construction [City of Vancouver Archives CVA 647-1]
Contents page: Colquitz (now Wilkinson Road) Jail, Saanich [Jennifer Nell Barr & Colin Barr]
Conventions page: Second Hotel Vancouver [Stuart Tarbuck]

Original book and cover design by Leon Phillips
Graphic production by Leon Phillips, Scott Barrett and Donald Luxton
Graphic revisions (2007) by G. Todd Brisbin (www.iotacreative.ca)

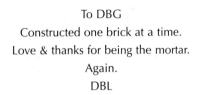

To DBG
Constructed one brick at a time.
Love & thanks for being the mortar.
Again.
DBL

For Carey, Dorothy, Jennifer, Jim, Leon, Scott and Stuart:
It wouldn't have happened without all of you.

And in memory of Terry Reksten, who is sadly missed.

PROJECT DEVELOPMENT BY
Donald Luxton and Stuart Stark

CONTRIBUTING WRITERS

John Adams	Dana H. Johnson
Dennis A. Andersen	Harold Kalman
John Atkin	Joel Lawson
Fiona Avakumovic	Donald Luxton
Catherine Barford	D.E. MacKay
Colin Barr	Donna Jean MacKinnon
Jennifer Nell Barr	Pamela Madoff
Paul Bennett	Edward Mills
Janet Bingham	Dorothy Mindenhall
Edward R. Bosley	David Monteyne
Nancy Byrtus	Carey Pallister
Sister Margaret Cantwell	Terry Reksten
Janet Collins	Martin Segger
Elspeth Cowell	Warren F. Sommer
Jenny Cowell	Ronald Harold Soule
Rosemary James Cross	Jean Sparks
Marco D'Agostini	Allen Specht
Mary E. Doody Jones	Stuart Stark
Helen Edwards	Gwen Szychter
Bruce M. Forster	Julia Trachsel
Gordon W. Fulton	Jana Tyner
Rick Goodacre	Rhodri Windsor Liscombe
D. Bruce Grady	Robin Ward
Maurice Guibord	Drew Waveryn
Christopher J.P. Hanna	Jim Wolf

CONTRIBUTING RESEARCHERS

John Adams, Victoria	Dana H. Johnson, Ottawa
Jennifer Nell Barr, Victoria	Donald Luxton, Vancouver
Scott Barrett, Vancouver	Dennis Minaker, Victoria
Robert Close, Ayr, Scotland	Dorothy Mindenhall, Victoria
Barry Elmer, Calgary	David Monteyne, Minneapolis
Gordon W. Fulton, Ottawa	Carey Pallister, Victoria
Madge Hamilton, Victoria	Stuart Stark, Victoria
Robert G. Hill, Toronto	Jim Wolf, New Westminster

ADVISORY PANEL
John Atkin, Vancouver
Jennifer Nell Barr, Victoria
Michael Kluckner, Langley
Dorothy Mindenhall, Victoria
Carey Pallister, Victoria
Stuart Stark, Victoria
Gwen Szychter, Delta
Jim Wolf, New Westminster

The architects that are covered in this book are those that had begun their work in British Columbia by 1938. The entries on each major architect are listed in chronological order, by the start of their architectural practice in B.C. Within each entry, the first time another architect is mentioned who has their own entry, the name appears in bold. Additional significant architects are listed alphabetically in a separate section beginning on page 450. Known information about the location and status of individual projects in British Columbia are listed under Sources.

A number of abbreviations have been consistently used in this text:

AIA: American Institute of Architects
AIBC: Architectural Institute of British Columbia
BCER: British Columbia Electric Railway
BCIA: British Columbia Institute of Architects
CEF: Canadian Expeditionary Force
CPR: Canadian Pacific Railway
DPW: Department of Public Works
HBC: Hudson's Bay Company
MLA: Member of the Legislative Assembly, Government of British Columbia
MP: Member of Parliament, Government of Canada
RIBA: Royal Institute of British Architects
UBC: University of British Columbia
UVIC: University of Victoria

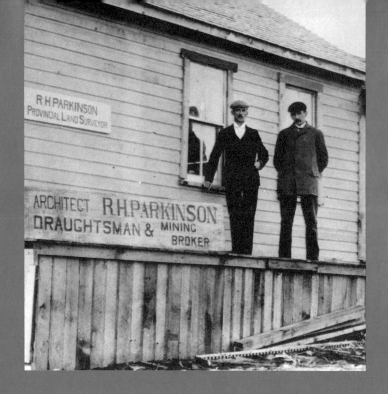

FOREWORD

THE EVOLVING ROLE OF THE ARCHITECT IN A FRONTIER CULTURE

Donald Luxton

The development of early British Columbia was both colonial and commercial, fueled by expansionist militarism and the availability of vast natural resources, but subject to violent swings in economic cycles and outside political interests. European exploration of the Pacific northwest may have begun as early as the voyages of Sir Francis Drake in 1579. Later Spanish and English explorers mapped the west coast and made contact with the native cultures. By the middle of the nineteenth century, the vast potential of these mostly "empty" western lands was well recognized on the increasingly crowded Atlantic seaboard of the continent. Horace Greeley, influential founder of the New York *Tribune*, was exhorting his readers: "Go west, young man, and grow with the country." A momentum of westward settlement began to build, fuelled by an expanding colonial population looking for greater opportunity.

The discovery of coal, enormous stands of timber and other exploitable resources, and a strategic geographic position led to the establishment of two English colonies on the Pacific coast, one on Vancouver Island and the other on the adjacent mainland. The vast interior areas remained a mystery to Europeans until the discovery of gold on the Fraser River in 1858, and in the Cariboo just a few years later. Before this time there had been little need for professionally-designed European-style buildings, but with the gold rushes came major waves of immigration, including a number of architectural practitioners who settled on the coast to meet the needs of the burgeoning new settlements. Several of these architects had been drawn first to the California gold rush, and then moved north seeking richer opportunities. They made only an intermittent living at architecture, and were forced to work at a variety of other pursuits, such as cabinet-making and undertaking, in order to survive on the colonial margin of civilization.

Settlers continued to be drawn by the opportunities offered by these vast unexploited lands. Church, state, military and commercial interests wove a net of connections that tied together these isolated frontier settlements. The trickle of immigration became a flood, as numerous contributing factors led to a mass exodus from Europe, especially from England and Scotland. The population in Great Britain was increasing as more children survived into adulthood due to better sanitation and medical care, but it was the devastating effects of the agricultural depression of the second half of the nineteenth century that finally drove many to seek a new life in the colonies. As transportation became more efficient, access to world markets increased, and British farmers could not compete with the influx of cheap food flooding their country. Mechanized crop farming on the American Prairies caused a dramatic drop in grain prices; British crop farmers could not compete, so they converted to grassland, and invested in milk production. The result was huge milk surpluses, and attempts to produce cheese were frustrated by the ready availability of American product at half the price. Nature itself seemed to turn against the British farmer. The summer of 1879 was marred by constant driving rain that turned the whole countryside into ooze. Crops spoiled and diseases like liver rot became epidemic among sheep, killing millions of them. The rain never really let up until the end of 1882. Then several summers of intense heat followed, and into the early 1890s there were alternating bouts of drought and rain. Many just gave up struggling, and between 1870 and the turn of the century, 700,000 British farmers and farm workers emigrated to start a new life.

R.H. Parkinson, with Harry Parham, at Fairview, B.C., c.1900.

BRITISH COLUMBIA — Product of the Plow Net and Rifle

For adventurous individuals, the British Empire offered limitless opportunities for mobility and professional achievement. With little chance of ever rising to the top in the increasingly rigid society of the Mother Country, the glittering possibilities of the New World proved irresistible to many. Seeing nothing to lose and everything to gain, they set off to the ends of the Empire looking for adventure and fortune. The construction booms in the new towns and cities of South Africa, Australia, New Zealand and western Canada tantalized young architects with the prospects of major commissions. Some, not able to chose a destination, just asked for a ticket for as far as they could go. In turn, the recurring pattern of boom and bust caused them to pull up stakes and continue their pursuit of new opportunities in other places. They were sometimes drawn to these exotic locations by promotional material, such as the products and photographs of British Columbia displayed at the Glasgow Exhibition of 1883, and many were drawn simply by the lure of gold. But despite the boasting and boosterism of the local press, conditions on the west coast of Canada were still extremely primitive, and settlers suffered severe hardships as new communities were carved out of the deep forest and rugged landscapes. Many, finding only hard work and privation, later complained bitterly that they had been misled about the so-called golden opportunities in this new land.

The dream of a transcontinental railway that would unite all of Canada was the catalyst for even more intense settlement. Finally completed in the mid-1880s, it provided the means to move masses of settlers, and the great westward movement reached its height. As the railway had moved west, instant towns sprang up in its path, some almost overnight. New technology such as circular "buzz" saws driven by steam engines, balloon framing, and the standardization of lumber sizes revolutionized the construction industry. The first frontier structures were generally crude, utilitarian shacks that only required the services of a builder, sometimes with highly decorated front facades that caused one western traveller to describe them as "Queen Anne in front and Crazy Jane behind." As settlements increased in size, architectural styles became inevitably more refined, and those made newly rich by the resource industries wanted to boast about their wealth, and leave their mark on this new land. A need arose for those trained in building design, who could provide structures that matched the new wealth and ostentatious aspirations of the burgeoning middle and upper classes. Eager to seek their fortunes in the colonies, droves of British-trained architects started to appear in the new settlements, and many were successful at establishing themselves in a full-time professional capacity.

Who were these early architects that abandoned "civilization" to come to the frontier? Not surprisingly, they were almost exclusively male, white and British, typical of the patriarchal, racially-segregated and hierarchical society from which they had emigrated; it would be many decades before the equality of women and persons of other races was even considered to be a possibility. The crude conditions led to pride in the toughness required for these "real men" to survive and prosper; as reported in the Vernon *News* in 1892: "While there is plenty of room in this country for new-comers who are willing to rough it if necessary and turn their hands to honest work, this is not a good country for useless overfed mamby pamby dudes to come to."

Professional qualifications could not easily be verified, and the first wave of settlement brought an odd collection of those with *bona fide* professional training, as well as master builders equipped with pattern books, competent surveyors and engineers who could also draw building plans, real estate spec- ulators, jerry-builders and ambitious entrepreneurs who later spun off into more profitable pursuits. Often their origins were as uncertain as their fate. Fuelling this volatile mix was a get-rich-quick frontier mentality and a vigor- ous distrust of authority. If these intrepid immigrants had craved stability and regulation they would not have travelled so far to such a wild and untamed area to make their fortune. They had followed the boom trail as far west as they could, and were determined, or forced, to make a go of it here.

Most of the professionally-trained architects came up through the appren- ticeship system that prevailed in Great Britain at the time. Many of them were apprenticed by the age of fourteen or fifteen and emigrated soon after they finished their articles. A surprising number trained with relatives, often their fathers or uncles, as architecture and surveying were generally family pursuits that persisted through generations. This rigorous training in the civilized urban centres of Great Britain often left them bewildered when they arrived on the frontier, where they had to adapt to rapidly changing conditions and accept whatever work – at whatever rate or method of payment – was available. They may have been expecting to find the same types of clients they were used to in the Mother Country, but what they usually found was a bunch of fortune seekers in a big hurry who were liable to offer them a speculative land deal or shares in a business, rather than money, in exchange for their services. Another architect of some description could always be found if they were unwilling to accept the terms offered. This cavalier attitude made it difficult to establish stability in the profession, and flexibility – far more than design ability or professional competence – was the ultimate key to survival.

Beyond obvious commonalities of background and training, these early architects displayed astonishing combinations of drive, determination and individuality, that carried them thousands of miles into the wilderness. They were often transitory, following potential work wherever it showed up, often showing up right after the devastating fires that were common in the hastily-built frontier towns. Some followed the railway to its terminus on the coast; some were intending to pass through but stayed; and some kept right on travelling. Some were rugged individualists who didn't fit into the strict social order of their time. Others were notoriously casual about the conventions of marriage and paternity, and moved frequently to avoid either scandal or prosecution. Some were homosexual, and emigrated to find a less restrictive environment. Some were extremely ambitious and used architecture as a stepping-stone to greater fortunes. Many appear to have had irascible and tenacious personalities, leading to numerous stories of personal conflict. Whatever their personal motivations, these frontier architects retained a professional cachet. As settlements increased in size and sophistication, architects were generally considered business and social leaders, and gained commissions through their connections with churches and fraternal organizations.

In these nascent communities, architecture rarely provided full-time work, and secondary trades ensured survival during the lean periods. Similar to architects in Great Britain, many acted as surveyors and engineers. Some were more generally entrepreneurial, and pursued business opportunities unrelated to their profession. More than one ran for, and won, political office. As a group they retained the status of the comfortable middle class, solidly established, and socially a cut above other immigrants. But until the practice of architecture could be officially regulated, anyone with a pattern book in their hands could, and often did, call themselves an architect. Then – as now – the majority of buildings were constructed without the direct involvement of a professionally-trained architect. Given their common background and outlook, those who had legitimate architectural training were generally collegial, and were anxious to protect their interests through a professional organization which would set standardized fees and provide mutual protection.

During the Victorian era the architectural profession in Great Britain had become more concerned with status and business ethics than with education, leading to the imposition of uniform fees. In 1845 the Royal Institute of British Architects adopted a standardized remuneration figure of five percent of construction costs. The architects in the New World, mostly British-trained, wanted the same type of system, so that some stability could be brought to their practices, as the undercutting of fees was a chronic problem. Seeing common interest in self-regulation, professional groups in British Columbia worked to establish collegial bonds, and in 1891 the *Land Surveyors Act* was passed, regulating the practice of surveying in the province, legitimizing architecture's sister profession. At the same time, architects were pushing for similar legislation, hoping to promote a better standard of design, but also to resist competition from other segments of the building trades. Architects wanted to assume the creative and intellectual role in construction, drawing a clear line between the conception and management of a project and the physical labour that was required to build it.

The first major step to self-organization of the architectural profession was a meeting held in Victoria in 1891. Eleven men were in attendance, with seventeen others represented by proxy, almost the sum total of those who could be considered professional architects in the province. The group agreed to call itself the British Columbia Association of Architects, with the ultimate goal of incorporating on a similar basis as the Ontario Association of Architects; soon after, the name of the association was changed to the British Columbia Institute of Architects (BCIA). In 1892 the BCIA developed bylaws that would have fixed standardized fees at five percent on works above $2,500. For the next two years the BCIA failed in its attempts to persuade the provincial government, which was distrustful of any form of monopoly, to pass legislation that would regulate architecture. By this time the economy was failing drastically, and fraternal feelings among the established architects were strained to the limit. Personal and professional sniping between architects increased as they competed for dwindling amounts of work.

This situation did not change until the economy dramatically improved. In the years after the turn of the twentieth century, the greatest western Canadian boom hit full force. New floods of immigrants surged westward across the country. The might of the British Empire guaranteed the safety and security of the migrating hordes, and ensured that Anglo investors reaped the financial benefits of large scale resource extraction industries. The stupendous boom that lasted from 1908 to 1913 attracted record numbers of new settlers to the coast, including many involved in the building trades, but the situation within the architectural community was chaotic, as many of the new arrivals billed themselves as architects whether or not they had any training or qualifications. Concerned about public confidence as well as their own livelihood, by the fall of 1909 a small group in Vancouver established the British Columbia Society of Architects, and the following year a parallel group was formed in the capital city. For a while the Victoria and Vancouver associations remained separate, but on March 23, 1912 the Architect's Association of Victoria voted to become the Victoria chapter of the BCSA, and the first annual convention of the combined groups was held in Victoria in June, 1912. This seemed to be a real step toward cooperation among architects on a provincial level, but trouble was soon to erupt. It was apparent that the qualifications of prospective members could not be confirmed, and up to 300 men in the province were claiming to be architects. **Andrew Mercer** later wrote that "It is regrettable to record that the ethics of the profession were then observed by some architects more in the breach than in the observance. Many transient and fly-by-night architects and draughtsmen were located in Vancouver and Victoria who had no intention of making their permanent homes in British Columbia. They were here merely to participate in the good times. When dull periods struck the province, they folded their tents and departed. They had no reputation to make or keep up, and, as there was no real power to check or discipline them, the standing of the profession was not very high in those days."

The architectural fraternity was about to split apart on clearly defined lines of self-interest. **R.P.S. Twizell** recalled that "the Society's meetings in the predominant Vancouver Chapter were moderately harmonious during the first year of its life, but after that time until it ceased to function the meetings became increasingly turbulent and noisy. In the fall of 1912 a special meeting was called at the demand of a small group of dissatisfied members after a case became known of flagrant collusion between an assessor and winner of a school competition. The competitor was an officer of the Society and every attempt made to have an enquiry was evaded and finally blocked. This episode and the general prevailing conditions convinced the small group which had requested the enquiry that there was no hope of improvement in the society; they severed from it in March 1913 and formed a club of very limited membership for friendly intercourse among architects."

This small breakaway group of ten men, led by **R. Mackay Fripp**, felt that the inclusive nature and clubbishness of the BCSA served neither their, nor the public's, best interests. They favoured the British and American models for professional organizations, requiring relevant education and office experience as criteria for accreditation. Despite the continued existence and obvious dominance of the BCSA, this group established itself as the Architectural Institute of British Columbia (AIBC). Application for incorporation was made in April 1914, and the search began for other suitable members. The two groups, one large and powerful, the other small and elitist, were deadlocked in their attempts to dominate the profession.

For many, the devastating economic collapse of 1913, and the subsequent outbreak of the First World War, destroyed their careers, dashing any hopes of remaining on the west coast, and many just moved on. During the war the BCSA fell apart, as many members left for overseas, held on in reduced circumstances or left the province seeking work. The upstart, highly-motivated AIBC was kept alive by several active members who filed the yearly returns required under the act. Only the AIBC survived the war. In January 1920 it was announced that both architects and civil engineers would shortly be seeking the passage of private bills calling for professional registration. That April, a bill regulating the profession of architecture was finally passed, after almost thirty years of fractious debate and controversy. This eventual maturation of the architectural community strongly paralleled the taming of the frontier spirit in many segments of the province's social structure. Only a fraction of those who were working as architects in the province before the First World War ever registered with the AIBC.

After the end of the war the economy continued to falter, and then revived briefly before the Crash of 1929. During the early 1930s the profession fell apart, as few architects had any work at all, and most could not afford to pay the AIBC fees. Ironically, the depressed costs of labour and material meant that a few architects – those with the right connections to wealthy clients who saw this as an opportunity to build – remained very busy throughout this period. The general economy revived again briefly in the mid- to late-1930s only to experience the outbreak of another world war in 1939. Stability has never been a hallmark of life in British Columbia, and the recurring cycle of booms and busts continues to rule the architectural profession and all sectors of the economy.

Competition drawings for AIBC Seal, 1920: Maclure & Lort, top; H.L. Swan, centre; winning entry by R.C. Kerr, bottom.

Over time the white, male, British dominance of the profession was progressively diluted, introducing a more egalitarian and Canadian focus. In 1933, **Sylvia Holland** became the first woman to be registered as an architect

H.H. Simmonds, John Porter and F.L. Townley,
AIBC Annual Dinner, 1948

in B.C. The establishment of the School of Architecture at the University of British Columbia in 1946 increased opportunities for local training, and the post-Second World War building boom ensured more stable employment. Women, and persons of other races, although still in the minority, have clearly made steady progress.

The changing nature and complexity of construction has reshaped our view of the role of the architect. Increasingly, architecture is being perceived as a technical pursuit, driven by cost, efficiency and corporate agendas. Perhaps we have lost something over time, for our province's early architects overcame great adversity to produce many sublime and elegant buildings that we cherish and celebrate today as our architectural heritage. These architects shared a common vision, believing in progress, growth, the value of beauty, and the inevitability of their success. All this they needed to accomplish what they did: they built the West.

gold rushes bring european

settlement to the west coast

1

OUTPOST

OF

EMPIRE

Hudson's Bay Company Bastion, Nanaimo

The subject of colonization is, indeed, one of vital importance, and demands much consideration, for it is the wholesome channel through which the superfluous population of England and Ireland passes, from a state of poverty to one of comfort. It is true that the independence of the Canadian settler must be the fruit of his own labour, for none but the industrious can hope to achieve that reward, In fact, idle and indolent people will not change their natures by going out to Canada... But let the steady, the industrious, the cheerful man go forth in hope, and turn his talents to account in a new country, whose resources are not confined to tillage alone – where the engineer, the land-surveyor, the navigator, the accountant, the lawyer, the medical practitioner, the manufacturer, will each find a suitable field for the exercise of his talents.

Major Samuel Strickland, *Twenty-Seven Years in Canada West*, 1852.

By the middle of the nineteenth century, the Hudson's Bay Company (HBC) was taking unprecedented steps in sponsoring the establishment of a colony on Vancouver Island, at the time the most remote and least populated area in the British Empire. In 1843 Victoria was chosen by Chief Factor James Douglas, known as "Old Square Toes," as the site for the HBC's new fur trading post on the west coast. A small community was established, with many of the residents being current or former employees of the Company. In 1846, the boundary between British and American territories was confirmed as the forty-ninth parallel west to the Pacific Ocean, with all of Vancouver Island remaining on the British side. This forced the HBC to abandon its southern operations, based in Fort Vancouver near the mouth of the Willamette River, which was now on American soil, and renew their efforts to consolidate their claims to the strategic western lands north of the forty-ninth, and continue their profitable exploitation of vast amounts of natural resources. In 1849, coal was discovered at the northern tip of Vancouver Island; the HBC established Fort Rupert there and began mining operations. That year, Vancouver Island was established as a British colony, but given the isolation of the area, the lack of population and the difficulty of communication, the HBC was given an administrative lease over the entire colony for ten years. Despite its entrepreneurial nature, the reluctant HBC was being pushed by the British government into the less profitable business of colonization.

When other, richer coal reserves were discovered at Nanaimo in 1852 the HBC relocated the miners from Fort Rupert, and a fledgling settlement was established, guarded by an octagonal bastion constructed in 1853. Thirty feet in height, it was built of hand-hewn logs by French Canadian axemen, Jean Baptiste Fortier and Leon Labine, under the direction of Company Clerk Joseph Mackay. The ground floor provided an office and store for the HBC, while the second floor had an arsenal of two cannons. The third floor, which stepped out over the lower two, was large enough to accommodate all of the original settlers in case of attack. The Nanaimo Bastion is the last surviving fortified tower of the many that the HBC built on the west coast.

The HBC continued to found settlements on Vancouver Island as well as in the mainland territory known as New Caledonia. During this time they were responsible for almost all the significant non-Aboriginal buildings being constructed on the Pacific coast. In 1839 they had established a subsidiary organization, the Puget's Sound Agricultural Company, to undertake large-scale farming operations south of the forty-ninth parallel. This company was expanded into Vancouver Island in an effort to make the HBC fur trading forts self-sufficient. Farms were established at Macauley Point, 1850, and Colwood, 1851, to serve Fort Victoria, and others were established in 1853 at Constance Cove, Esquimalt, and Craigflower Farm on the Gorge. It was resolved in 1853 that a school should be built for the settlers' children, and the following year Craigflower School was completed on a five-acre preserve at Maple Point, opposite Craigflower Farm. It was built with local labour, led by an HBC carpenter, Gideon Halcrow. Lumber was sawn in the farm's mill, and rafted to the site; other components of the building, including the glass, hardware, and foundation bricks, were imported from England. When the framing was completed on September 23, 1854, it was noted the "whole company was in general notoriously drunk." Craigflower Farm was headed by Kenneth McKenzie, an immigrant from Haddingtonshire, Scotland. He built a Georgian-style home, known as *Craigflower Manor*, for his large family and they moved in on May 1, 1856. McKenzie himself likely had a

Fort Victoria, 1860s

major hand in the design, as it is a slightly smaller, wooden version of his stone family home, *Rentonhall,* in Scotland.

The strategic importance of Victoria was also recognized by the Royal Navy, which began to use Esquimalt as a naval station for the British Pacific Squadron. In 1854 the outbreak of the Crimean War focussed attention on the Navy's extensive and mostly undefended supply lines. There were no permanent buildings at the Esquimalt base, and the HBC was asked to construct three wooden hospital buildings at Constance Cove Farm in 1855 to handle potential casualties from the conflict.

In 1856 James Douglas convened the first House of Assembly to meet on British soil west of the Great Lakes. The English settlers and visiting naval officers were having a gradual civilizing influence on remote Fort Victoria, but this relatively peaceful situation changed dramatically when rumours of gold strikes on the Fraser and Thompson Rivers reached Victoria in the fall of 1857. Gold fever reached a "boiling heat" as stories of gold thick in the river beds started to circulate. As reported in *Victoria Illustrated*: "Then came news of gold discoveries in various parts of the country tributary to the struggling settlement, and then the influx of the army of the Argonauts. From California, where they tasted the sweet and bitter of the gold fever, the treasure-seekers, with pick and shovel, poured into Victoria, equipped themselves and passed on in hundreds and thousands to the Fraser... The mad search for riches made the village a city – and one, while the excitement was at its height, of considerable population and constantly changing character." In a four month period in 1858, Victoria's population swelled from just a few hundred to 7,000, with many housed in tents. Within six weeks of the arrival of the first boat full of gold seekers, 225 new buildings were constructed.

The predominantly British fur trade outpost was suddenly swamped with a diverse range of opportunists, many of whom were American and some of whom stayed on in the booming community. The situation was clearly out of control, and it was feared that the area would be overrun, and be claimed again by the United States. The new English Secretary of State for the Colonies, Sir Edward Bulwer-Lytton – also a prolific novelist best remembered for penning the immortal line "it was a dark and stormy night..." – proclaimed the mainland territory of New Caledonia as the Crown colony of

Crimea Hospital Huts, Esquimalt

Victoria in 1858

British Columbia in 1858. Douglas was named as governor of both colonies. Bulwer-Lytton saw the need for a crop of able administrators to assist him, and sent a detachment of **Royal Engineers** who could help establish law and order, provide military protection, build roads and bridges, and survey new town sites.

The single most prominent architectural commission in the growing colony of Vancouver Island would be for the new Colonial Administration Buildings. In anticipation of the expiry of the HBC's ten year lease of Vancouver Island in 1859, the Royal Engineers were asked to draw up plans for several simple frame buildings to be built along Government Street in Victoria. These buildings were never constructed, and **H.O. Tiedemann** received the contract to design a much grander set of administration buildings on the Government Reserve south of the Fort. He provided the plans for five structures, built between 1859 and 1863, consisting of one and two-storey wooden pavilions fitted with both hipped and flat roofs. Tiedemann's inspiration for the buildings' much-criticized decorative timber framing with painted brick infill appears to have been the medieval architecture of northern Germany. The rather unusual design and incongruous stylistic elements attracted much unfavorable comment: the *Colonist* denounced the buildings as a "burlesque on architecture" and the *Gazette* ridiculed them as "the latest fashion of Chinese-pagoda, Swiss-cottage and Italian-villa fancy bird-cages." The latter description stuck and the buildings were thereafter known as the Birdcages.

New Westminster, the new capital of the mainland colony, was incorporated in 1860 as the first city in the new colonies, but Vancouver Island's future seemed assured when Douglas declared Victoria a free port in 1860, a direct challenge to New Westminster. Lighthouses were built at the entrance to Victoria's harbour to improve navigation safety, and the trade routes with San Francisco were stabilized, which cemented Victoria's supremacy in administrative and commercial affairs. Victoria was incorporated as a city in 1862.

Successive discoveries of gold farther and farther inland continued to draw in prospective miners, and Douglas struggled to ensure the consolidation of supply routes and the establishment of new settlements. The contingent of Royal Engineers could not keep up to the demands, and civilian crews were hired to survey and build roads, straining the meagre colonial budgets. With the gold strikes in and around Billy Barker's claims on Williams Creek, the Cariboo Gold Rush began. British Columbia became known as the "Gold Colony."

Missionaries began to appear on the coast, to minister both to the settlers and the Aboriginal peoples. Substantial new churches sprang up in Victoria, the most imposing of which was a prefabricated metal structure imported from England. The first Anglican Bishop to be sent to Victoria, the Rt. Rev. George Hills, was consecrated in February, 1859. At the time, London was enthralled with the technological possibilities that had opened up with the construction of the Crystal Palace in 1851, and the idea of an "iron church" had been publicly discussed. Hill commissioned Samuel Hemming, a London contractor, to build such a building to take with him to his new appointment. During the summer of 1859 the structure, designed to seat up to 600, was assembled of beams of Baltic fir and heavy plates of iron. It was dismantled and packed for delivery by clipper around Cape Horn. The total cost was £1,700, and another £900 for shipping and reassembly. The cornerstone was laid on April 13, 1860, on a site at the far northern edge of the settlement. Redwood panels were installed on the interior, giving a rich, warm appearance. The building was considered a wonder, the finest church north of San Francisco. What was not anticipated was that the drumming noise from heavy rains falling on the metal-clad structure could drown out even the lustiest preacher. The Iron Church served its congregation well, but over time the members outgrew it, and the once remote site found itself in the centre of a bustling downtown. The congregation acquired cheaper land on Quadra Street, and sold the old church to the Hudson's Bay Company, who demolished it in 1913 to build their grand new department store.

When the Royal Engineers were disbanded in 1863, the settlers in New Westminster suddenly felt vulnerable to attack, and sought armed protection. The New Westminster Volunteer Rifles was formed, consisting mainly of the Royal Engineers who had decided to stay. A wooden drill shed was constructed in 1864-65 by the colonial government on a city-owned site, and then leased to the militia unit at ten dollars per annum. The site was cleared by provincial chain gangs, and the final dimensions of the drill shed were sixty-six feet by forty feet, with a lean-to armoury twenty-four by twelve feet.

The two rag-tag colonies continued to grow under pressure from the gold-seekers, and in 1866 they were formally united as the Crown colony of British Columbia, with New Westminster chosen as the first capital city. Permanent settlements were being established, and the first substantial buildings started to challenge the vast natural landscape. In 1870, a Land Ordinance was passed that facilitated the pre-emption of land for those who were male, British and at least eighteen years old.

The boom in economic activity touched off by the gold rushes lasted just a few short years, and a local depression set in. The economy later revived with the promise of a great construction project, a transcontinental railway that would link the Pacific and Atlantic Oceans and unite the British colonies north of the United States. This great dream of nation-building would propel the next wave of settlers to these remote western shores.

The Iron Church, Victoria

Drill Shed, New Westminster

SURVEYORS

Donald Luxton

The professions of architecture, civil engineering and surveying were almost completely interwoven in nineteenth century England. Many of the young apprenticed architects who immigrated to Canada were equally trained, and adept, in all these pursuits, and shifted from the practice of one to the other depending on opportunity and circumstance. In tough times, those who had been advertising as architects in the urban centres might be found leading survey crews in the bush, or relocating to small towns where they took on whatever work was available. Surveying during the earliest settlement of the province was an arduous job, often involving extreme hardship and isolation, but it was an ongoing task, and provided a source of steady income; this was especially true once the surveys began for the transcontinental railway. Many of the early surveyors were, by necessity, accomplished alpinists.

Mapping was one of the primary functions of the first European explorers, and was also an important part of the work of the Hudson's Bay Company. The government office of the Surveyor-General was established at the very beginning of the Colonial era. This appointment was a key position in the administration of Crown Lands, and all original surveys were made under his jurisdiction. Joseph D. Pemberton was the Colonial Surveyor for the HBC from 1851 to 1858, and then was appointed Vancouver Island's first Surveyor-General. The first Surveyor-General of the Mainland colony was Colonel R.C. Moody, commander of the **Royal Engineers**, who was also Chief Commissioner of Lands and Works.

When the Royal Engineers arrived in 1858, many of them were trained surveyors, and their work laid the basis for much of the province's development. In addition to the border survey, they were responsible for establishing the Coast Meridian, the area's first, in 1859. When the Royal Engineers were disbanded in 1863, eight of those who stayed on took up surveying as a full time profession, including John Maclure.

In 1866, Joseph W. Trutch was appointed the first Surveyor-General of the combined colonies. In 1871, under the *Constitution Act*, the

John Maclure

Department of Lands and Works was established, headed by the combined position of Chief Commissioner of Lands and Works and Surveyor-General. **Benjamin W. Pearse** was appointed to the position in 1871, and remained briefly as Surveyor-General after the position was split in 1872. The Chief Commissioner's appointment was considered political, while the Surveyor-General was a civil service position.

Those practising surveying before 1891 were known as "Land Surveyors" (LS). *The Land Surveyors' Act*, passed in 1891, established full regulation of training and registration. In contrast, architecture and engineering were not provincially regulated until 1920, leading to much confusion over who was really qualified. Given the lucrative nature of building during the boom times, the perceived status of architecture, and the lack of professional regulation, there were many surveyors who advertised themselves as "architects" without much to back up their claims. It is now apparent that a number of these are best considered qualified surveyors, as only a few went on to successful architectural careers. An exception was **H.O. Tiedemann**, who initially worked as a surveyor and engineer but then shifted primarily to architecture. Like Tiedemann, **Frederick W. Green** worked on surveys for the Hudson's Bay Company; in addition to his architectural work he was responsible for the original survey of Granville townsite, and later worked in Victoria as City Surveyor. Among the others who alternated between architecture and surveying can be counted **Edward Mallandaine Sr.**, **William S. Gore**, **Henry O. Bell-Irving**, **William H.L. de la Penotière**, **Dennis Harris**, **George Hargreaves**, and **Alan E. McCartney**. The extent of what these early surveyors accomplished is only now being fully appreciated. Despite the increasing specialization that later forced a split, no discussion of early architecture can ignore the initial porosity between these parallel professions.

ABORIGINAL BUILDING

HAROLD KALMAN

The coast of British Columbia – and the entire northwest coast of North America – has been home to Aboriginal peoples who produced a truly remarkable indigenous architecture. Built of massive posts, beams and planks taken from the cedars that grow in the temperate rain forest, the houses of the coastal tribes employed a sophisticated and impressive building technology, while serving highly developed religious and social patterns of living.

Most of the Aboriginal groups occupied permanent villages in winter and lived in either fixed or portable dwellings in the summer – sometimes taking the planks that covered the building-frames from the winter to the summer houses – as they moved about to harvest sea mammals, salmon, other fish and berries. The social structure of the larger villages included a wealthy elite composed of chiefs or nobles, a body of commoners, and a class of slaves, who had been captured, purchased, or born into slavery. The chiefs handed down privileges through a formal gift-giving ceremony known as the potlatch. The plank-houses, as their buildings are called – erected in communities from Alaska to northern California – were essential expressions of a hierarchical culture. The principal groups inhabiting today's British Columbia were the Haida and the Tsimshian in the north (the neighbouring Tlingit lived in what is now the Alaska panhandle); the Kwakwaka'wakw (formerly known as Kwakuitl), Nuu-chah-nulth (Nootka), and Nuxalk (Bella Coola) on the central coast; and the Coast Salish in the south. Each group developed a distinctive version of the plank-house.

Skidegate, Queen Charlotte Islands, 1878

The North

The former appearance of the Haida villages is known through photography. Two types of houses were built. The more common type was the six-beam house, so-called because the building was framed with six large longitudinal roof beams; the other type had only two beams. The magnificent six-beam house, unique among the Haida, was constructed with highly sophisticated joinery. Posts were raised at the four corners, and grooves at their bases received the ends of the wall plates. Massive sloping roof plates, made from cedar planks, were inserted through slots in the corner posts and supported at the centre by pairs of posts, against which the frontal pole was placed. The six beams spanned the depth of the house and rested on the plates, while a seventh beam at the ridge was broken at the middle to allow an opening for the smoke hole. Vertical wall boards were set into grooves on the edges of the bottom and top plates, often with battens securing the joints, and planks or sheets of bark were laid across the roof beams and held down with stones. The exterior walls were left unpainted. Anthropologist George MacDonald has explained that the house functioned both in the secular realm as a dwelling and in the spiritual realm as a ceremonial centre. (Deceased ancestors resided in the house, as well as the living.) Houses were all known by their names. Building a house was a significant event, and its dedication often occurred in conjunction with a potlatch. Most scholars agree that the two-beam house was the earlier form.

The Tsimshian people included three separate entities: the Coast; the Gitksan (upper Skeena); and the Nisga'a (Nass River). Their houses are similar to the Haida, but where they bordered on the interior with the Carrier, the coastal style was used on a more modest scale.

Top: House of Haida Chief Anetlas, Masset, 1884

Centre: *House Where People Always Wanted To Go,* Haina, Queen Charlotte Islands, 1888

Bottom: Carrier Village at Hagwilgate, near Hazelton, c.1915

The Central Region

Kwakwaka'wakw (Kwakuitl) construction is evident in a house-frame at Gwaysadums. The two principal roof beams are supported by pairs of posts at the front and rear; the latter are carved. Two additional beams at the eaves connect the corner posts and also rest on an intermediate support. Rafters, and purlins fashioned from lighter members, are framed on the beams. The walls would have been made from vertical planks and the roof covered with loose planks.

The Nuu-chah-nulth (Nootka), who lived on the west coast of Vancouver Island, built two types of houses: those in the north erected gabled structures with a single ridge beam, while those in the south built shed-roofed houses. As with the other groups, the houses were arranged along the beach.

Top: Kwakwaka'wakw house-frame at Gwaysadums

Left: Coast Salish Village at Quamichan, c.1866

The South

Shed-roofed longhouses were the predominant type among the Salish-speaking groups of southwestern British Columbia. Villages might consist of a single house or many houses. In villages where the buildings were arranged in a row facing the shore, the roof would slope from front to rear. Houses as long as 1,500 feet were observed in the Puget Sound area, in what is now the state of Washington. In 1808 explorer Simon Fraser saw a Musqueam house 800 feet long near the mouth of the river that bears his name, and upriver he visited one nearly as large. The horizontal planks that formed the walls were tied between pairs of poles and were easily removable. The Coast Salish would lash them and the roof planks between their canoes and re-erect them on house-frames set up at the summer camps. Captain George Vancouver observed the "skeletons of houses," at first believing that they were abandoned villages, but then recognizing their role in the annual migration.

Interior Tribes

The principal tribes that inhabited the interior plateau of south and central British Columbia were the Interior Salish, whose economy was based on the yearly runs of Pacific salmon, and the Kutenai, who were primarily hunters; both also gathered fruits and berries. Adapting their way of life and technology to changing climatic and environmental conditions, the Aboriginal peoples were able to survive periods of deprivation. Most of the Plateau tribes on both sides of the present international border occupied semi-subterranean dwellings known as pit houses as their permanent winter residences. This was an indigenous house-form that, for more than 5,000 years, provided an appropriate response to the lifeways and environment of the Plateau Indians. A webbing of spaced rafters was lashed in concentric circles from pit to smoke hole. This supported a snug layer of poles that was thickly padded with pine needles or grass. In the upper Plateau, where rainfall was heavy, cedar bark with the curved side up was laid at this stage. Finally, earth from the original pit was spread over the roof and stamped down, and a notched-log ladder was lowered through the smoke hole. With twenty to thirty people co-operating on the building, a pit house could be finished in a day. The Shuswap, who lived farther north, near today's Kamloops, sometimes used six principal posts and beams rather than four, producing a more conical profile.

At about the same time of initial contact with Europeans, many Plateau Indians discontinued using pit houses and began to build mat houses – lodges built of poles and covered with mats of tule (bulrushes) or with bark and grass. The third house-type found among the Plateau Indians was the tipi. The Kutenai tipi had a four pole foundation, with about fifteen supplementary poles.

The Aboriginal peoples on the west coast did not encounter substantial European contact until the second half of the eighteenth century, somewhat later than on the rest of the continent. The Europeans' motivation for coming to this land was once again commercial: the profits to be reaped from the fur trade and the search for a trade route from Europe to the Orient, the so-called Northwest Passage.

Interior Salish pit house, Nicola Valley, 1903

THE ROYAL ENGINEERS

1858-1863

DAVID MONTEYNE AND DONALD LUXTON

You go not as enemies but as the benefactors of the land you visit, and children unborn will, I believe, bless the hour when Queen Victoria sent forth her sappers and miners to found a second England on the shores of the Pacific.

Government Buildings, New Westminster

With these words the Colonial Secretary, Sir Edward Bulwer-Lytton, dispatched the first contingent of Royal Engineers to tame the wilderness and the wild gold seekers in British Columbia. Bulwer-Lytton was alarmed not only at the "motley inundation of immigrant diggers" that were flooding the area, but also at the possibility that the Americans would attempt to annex the area north of the forty-ninth parallel now that valuable resources had been discovered there. The first priority for the Royal Engineers was to secure the British claim to the area by surveying the boundary with the United States, but they were also charged with surveying lands and roads for public purposes, suggesting a site for the capital city for the newly formed mainland colony, and reporting on the value of mineral resources. Colonel Richard Clement Moody was appointed to command the detachment. The first contingent arrived in mid-1858. A separate detachment arrived in late 1858 with, as Sir Edward continued, a mission "not... to fight against men, but to conquer nature; not to besiege cities, but to create them." This elite body of men laid the foundations for the development of the province. They created one major city, established the location and plan of many smaller but strategically important towns, and determined the major transportation routes that to this day move most people around the Lower Mainland and up into the central interior of the province.

James Douglas, newly-appointed Governor of the Mainland colony of British Columbia, had chosen Derby, near the site of the original Fort Langley, as the site for the new capital, and the Royal Engineers established their first camp there. Rev. William Burton Crickmer of Oxford was assigned as the contingent's chaplain, and he arrived at Derby in February of 1859. Construction began on a church, St. John the Divine, and a rectory, both built of redwood and likely designed by Crickmer himself. Town lots were offered at auction, raising considerable money for the government. Over Governor Douglas's objections, Moody rejected Derby as the site for the new capital, and suggested another site, in a strategic location on an easily defended hill on the north side of the Fraser River, which was a greater distance from the American border and had easier access to Burrard Inlet. Queen Victoria decreed the capital would be called New Westminster. The Royal Engineers prepared a town plan suitable to the ideals of British colonialism: a romantic English plan using a grid intersected by formal gardens and grand avenues delineated Imperial presence on the land and allowed for the capitalist exchange of real estate; church and state reserves established the place of religion and government in the centre of the city; and English street names, gardens, and crescents inspired by Bath and other English cit-

New Westminster, 1860s

ies helped transplant the culture of the Mother Country. Like those of its namesake, old Westminster, the future suburbs across the river would be known as Surrey.

In the spring of 1859, the Royal Engineers began clearing the land for the establishment of New Westminster. Despite the grand plans it was soon obvious that it would be a long time before anything resembling a city could be established, and the site was derisively called the "Imperial stump-field." Upriver, and separate from the capital, the Royal Engineers established their own camp at Sapperton where they constructed barracks, Colonel Moody's official residence (Government House), a school, and a log church. They were mostly simple wood structures, but still appealing to the refined tastes of English visitors such as Lady Franklin and her niece who stayed there in 1861. During her visit, Lady Franklin met John Maclure, whose son **Samuel Maclure** was just a year old. She pronounced Samuel a most perfect baby, suitable for an exhibit.

The plans of many early B.C. towns like Hope, Yale, Lytton, Douglas and Quesnel Forks were laid out by the Royal Engineers. It was hoped that the sale of surveyed town lots would offset the cost of the Engineers' work and make the colony self-supporting. However, after the initial gold rush, economic returns on land development were marginal, and the British Colonial Office refused to continue subsidizing the operations of the Royal Engineers. The order to return home was given on July 8, 1863. Those men that wished to stay were offered a land grant, and over 130 accepted the offer. Only thirty-two officers and men returned to England.

Despite their brief tenure, the impact of the Royal Engineers was immense. They built the first churches on the mainland, based on the style of English country parishes, including ones in New Westminster in 1860, Hope in 1861 (attributed to Captain John Grant, R.E.), and Yale (designed by **Wright & Sanders**) in 1862. Some of these projects were done under the supervision of William Hall, who had trained as a stone mason and had served in the Crimea at the same time as Florence Nightingale, building stone ovens to bake bread for the

Government House, New Westminster

patients. New Westminster's Holy Trinity Anglican Church, 1860, was designed by Captain Arthur Reid Lemprière, who arrived with the third group of Royal Engineers in April, 1859. Lemprière led the small party of sappers who surveyed and built the Boston Bar Trail, from Fort Hope to Boston Bar by way of the Coquihalla River. A career officer, Lemprière, who returned to England in 1863, retired as a Major-General in 1882.

John Clayton White (1835-1907) was the builder for Holy Trinity, and likely had a hand in its design. As White was a Corporal and Lemprière a Captain, the church was attributed to the latter, for obvious reasons of rank. White, an accomplished architect, designed many of the other structures produced by the Royal Engineers in the short period of their stay, which included all types of institutional buildings: assay offices, jails, hospitals, schools (including the first two in New Westminster), and many other structures required by the fledgling settlements. In 1861, White designed Government House, a house in the Picturesque Eclectic style, with bay windows and a verandah, that served as Colonel Moody's residence in Sapperton until his return to England. Governor James Douglas moved into this house briefly until the newly-appointed governor of the mainland colony, Frederick Seymour, arrived in

Hyack Fire Company Engine House on right, New Westminster

1864 to take up residence. Seymour commissioned White to design additions that increased the prominence and grandeur of the house. According to the *Colonist*, this included "a magnificent lofty ball room, with large bow windows overlooking the lawn and the pretty river scenery. At the west end of the ballroom rises an ornamental tower which will much improve the appearance of the Vice-Regal residence from the river, when the shingles on the roof lose their new appearance and darken with age." When the mainland and island colonies were united in 1866, New Westminster was chosen as the seat of government, and this building continued to be used as Government House. After two years of bitter feuding, the decision was made to move the capital to Victoria, and Governor Seymour reluctantly moved into Cary Castle, which he considered "singularly unattractive."

One of White's other known designs in New Westminster was a Museum for the Exhibition of British Columbian Produce, built on Columbia Street near Sixth Street in 1861; James Douglas later gave permission to use this building as the colony's first library. White's design for the Hyack Fire Company Engine House on Columbia Street, 1862, was chosen over the one submitted by Wright & Sanders. St. Mary's Church in Sapperton, 1865, was also designed by White. Built after the contingent was disbanded, it was a rustic wooden version of the Gothic Revival then popular in Britain. White also designed the New Westminster School at Royal Avenue and Sixth Street, 1865, a symmetrical structure with a front portico and cupola. Like many of the other Royal Engineers, White took a discharge and stayed on in B.C. for some time after the disbandment in 1863. In addition to his architectural commissions, he served first as a draftsman for the Lands and Works Department, and then as official artist for the 1865 Collins Overland Telegraph project, which was led by another ex-Royal Engineer, John Maclure. White did not stay long in British Columbia, and died in 1907 at the Berkeley, California home of his granddaughter.

This was not the first or the last time that the Royal Engineers were called on in British Columbia, but it was certainly the most significant. Although their official involvement lasted only a few short years, they had an pivotal impact on the physical development of the fledgling colony.

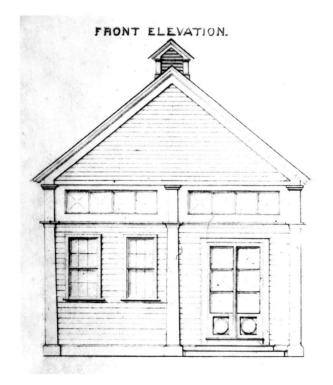

FRONT ELEVATION.

Museum for the Exhibition of British Columbian Produce, New Westminster

Interior of St. Ann's Chapel, c.1873

FATHER JOSEPH MICHAUD
1822–1902

MARTIN SEGGER

In 1858, Joseph Michaud was one of the contingent of helpers recruited in eastern Canada by Bishop Modeste Demers for the fledgling diocese of Vancouver Island. Born in Saint-Louis de Kamouraska, Quebec in 1822, he joined *Les Clercs-de-Saint-Viateur* in 1848 as a Brother. Upon his arrival, Michaud, who had a great interest in architecture, began designing and constructing a small cathedral with California redwood. The cathedral was arranged in symbolic numbers: the eight windows on each side stood for the beatitudes, and the two sections in each symbolized the Old and New Testaments. At the time of its construction it was commented in the *British Colonist* that "On a first examination of the ceiling it appears to be plaster; but when more closely examined the whole vault is found to be constructed of wood so well matched that it is difficult to determine its joints. There are five arches thrown over from the tops of the columns, which are ornamented with flowers carved in wood. Along the top of the ceiling are five circles representing wreaths, within which are several religious devices - the cross, the harp, the initials of Ave Maria – and over the Altar, the Glorypiece gilded like a sun, and in whose centre are the Greek letters Alpha and Omega." Directly behind the cathedral, he also built a residence for the bishop. Both buildings showed the influence of Quebec rural vernacular traditions. Michaud was ordained a priest in the cathedral he had built, and returned to Quebec in 1860.

He was later responsible for the overall scheme, and probably the design details, of St. Ann's Academy, in plans he sent from the mother house in Lachine, Quebec in 1871. Construction of the Second Empire/Quebecois style brick convent was superintended by **Charles Verheyden**, and the scheme was completed in 1886 under **John Teague**. As part of the 1886 construction programme Michaud's cathedral building was put on skids, moved, and joined to the centre of the south side of the Academy. It therefore provided the convent with a large chapel, and was a more economical arrangement than building the new chapel shown in the original design. The development of St. Ann's illustrates how early structures were often adapted over time, to suit both changes in functional requirements and taste. In 1908 **Thomas Hooper** designed a grandiose domed Classical Revival scheme that would have completely replaced the earlier structure, but only the western wing was built, resulting in the current configuration of the building, the subject of a recent restoration programme.

Michaud's Quebec career included a number of churches built between 1860-88, including *Saint-Alphonse*; *Saint-Norbert*; *Sainte-Melanie*; and convents in Rigaud and Lachine, both 1888. However, he is best known for his collaboration with architect Victor Bourgeau on the Cathedral Basilica of *Saint-Jacques-le-Majeur* in Montreal between 1875-94. This was a scaled-down version of St. Peter's, Rome, which Michaud was sent to document and measure in 1871. Michaud was also instrumental in the formalization of architectural education in Quebec through his teaching of the subject at the seminary of *Les Clercs-de-Saint-Viateur* in Jolliette.

Bishop's Palace (centre left) and Roman Catholic Cathedral, Victoria

JOHN
WRIGHT
1830–1915

MARTIN SEGGER
AND DONALD LUXTON

John Wright's life was certainly that of a larger-than-life pioneer figure. After entering into a partnership with George H. Sanders, who moved to Victoria in 1860, Wright dominated the architectural life of the two young west coast colonies. Together, Wright & Sanders soaked up the major governmental, institutional, commercial and domestic commissions. Despite their success in British Columbia, they sought a brighter future in northern California. Then followed a brilliant thirty-year career covering San Francisco's boom years during which the Wright & Sanders partnership produced a stream of large and prestigious buildings for the Bay area. Sadly, the majority of their work was destroyed in the 1906 San Francisco earthquake and fire. It is therefore with some irony that Wright & Sanders's largest architectural legacy is their surviving early work in Victoria.

Wright was born on May 15, 1830 at Killearn, Scotland, a small village near Loch Lomond. His parents died when he was a young child, leaving him to be raised by his grandparents and unmarried aunts. He immigrated to Guelph, Ontario in 1845 to live with cousins, and there he learned carpentry and engineering. There are references to John Wright as a builder and contractor in Guelph, and from 1856-58 he acted as Inspector of Works on the new city hall designed by William Thomas. This may have constituted the major part of Wright's architectural training. In 1858, Wright married Agnes Scott Armstrong, who bore him a large family of ten children.

In 1858, Wright relocated to Vancouver Island. He correctly gauged that, as gold fever and the consequent expanding economy filled the city with transient workers, its shacks and shelters were bound to be replaced with more permanent

structures. On June 24, 1859 he called for tenders for the construction of his first known commission in Victoria, the Wesleyan Methodist Church, a Gothic structure with a one hundred and twenty foot tower. The colonial government became an immediate source of business, and Wright was hired as the contractor for the Fisgard Light House, which still stands at the entrance to Esquimalt Harbour. Wright undoubtedly played a role in the final design, and ever entrepreneurial, patented his design for the interior cast-iron stairs. Designs for a fire company's Hook & Ladder Building in Bastion Square beside the Police Barracks, and a Methodist Church in Nanaimo, soon followed.

In 1860, Wright formed a partnership with George Sanders, who was born in Canada on August 2, 1838 after his family emigrated from England. Wright seems to have acted as the firm's chief designer, and remained more in the public eye. Sanders likely handled most of the business aspects and management of the firm. The partnership was immediately

successful, and lasted until Wright's retirement in 1895. The primary domestic commissions during their first year were a "suburban villa," *Fairfield*, completed for Joseph W. Trutch, on the Douglas estates east of Victoria, and a modest dwelling, *Ince Cottage*, for Sir Henry Pering Pellew Crease in New Westminster. In Nanaimo, the first St. Paul's Anglican (Episcopal) Church, 1861, was designed in the Carpenter Gothic style. The three-storey brick facade of the St. Nicholas Hotel on Government Street, 1862, with its arched second floor windows and ornate Italianate cornice established a commercial idiom that remains a dominant feature in Old Town today. The same year, Wright & Sanders designed a two-storey brick block for druggist, W.M. Searby, on Government Street, embellished with oversize mortars and pestles symbolic of his trade. In addition to their work on Vancouver Island, Wright and the firm received a number of commissions in the mainland colony, especially New Westminster, between 1860 and 1866.

Various strains of Wright's eclectic stylistic palette were evident in major commissions over the next few years. For

Left: St Paul's Anglican Church, Nanaimo

Bottom: Temple Emanu-El, Victoria

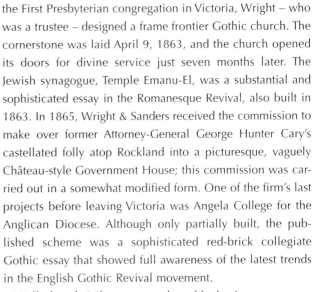

GEORGE HIPSLEY SANDERS

1838-1920

the First Presbyterian congregation in Victoria, Wright – who was a trustee – designed a frame frontier Gothic church. The cornerstone was laid April 9, 1863, and the church opened its doors for divine service just seven months later. The Jewish synagogue, Temple Emanu-El, was a substantial and sophisticated essay in the Romanesque Revival, also built in 1863. In 1865, Wright & Sanders received the commission to make over former Attorney-General George Hunter Cary's castellated folly atop Rockland into a picturesque, vaguely Château-style Government House; this commission was carried out in a somewhat modified form. One of the firm's last projects before leaving Victoria was Angela College for the Anglican Diocese. Although only partially built, the published scheme was a sophisticated red-brick collegiate Gothic essay that showed full awareness of the latest trends in the English Gothic Revival movement.

Well placed civil servants and wealthy businessmen commissioned Wright's architectural skills, and the firm also designed a steady stream of fine residences for Victoria's elite. Although confirmation is difficult, Wright likely provided the plans for *Cloverdale*, 1859-60, for William Fraser Tolmie. Wright & Sanders designed an Italianate villa, *Woodlands*, in James Bay, c.1861, for ex-Hudson's Bay Company official, James Bissett, and the original wing of Point Ellice House, c.1862. Residential work in this style was to reach its apogee in the Richard Carr house of 1863-64.

In 1866, Wright visited San Francisco for the first time. He noted the incredible growth in the Bay area, and in particular the coming of the American transcontinental railroad, scheduled for completion by 1869. In late 1866, Wright and his large family, and Sanders, moved to San Francisco. It proved a canny business decision to relocate their architectural practice. Wright & Sanders were immediately successful in obtaining large commercial and

Angela College, Victoria

institutional commissions, and rapidly became leaders in the local architectural profession. They had a particular talent for winning competitions for institutional projects, starting with the award for the California School for the Blind and Deaf in Berkeley, 1867. The following year, they won the competition for the master plan for the University of California campus at Berkeley, but renounced the commission when they found out the meagre amount of fees being offered. Large scale projects, which often involved years of work for the firm, included the State Asylum for the Insane, Napa, started in 1873 (in its day the largest building of its kind in the United States), the San Francisco Theological Seminary in San Anselmo, 1892-97, and the Pacific Theological Seminary in Oakland, 1893. In their thirty years in the Bay area, they received some 150 commissions, including fourteen churches, and numerous residences in the most ornate, High Victorian, eclectic styles. Their astonishingly flamboyant 1878 Nob Hill mansion for railway magnate Mark Hopkins was significant for marking a radical departure from the Italianate styles prevalent in California at the time. The firm also embraced the popular Richardsonian Romanesque, and produced some superb examples of the style, such as the Pacific Mutual Life Insurance Company Building in San Francisco, 1891.

Wright's reputation supported his interests and crucial role in promoting the professionalization of architectural practice in California. When the Pacific Coast Association of Architects was formed in 1881, he was elected unanimously as first

president. When it was reorganized the following May as the San Francisco Chapter of the American Institute of Architects, Wright was re-elected president,. When Wright's term ended in 1884, Sanders was made a trustee, and later served as president from 1888-94.

Despite being self-educated, Wright maintained throughout his life a keen interest in the education of the younger generation, a number of whom, like Bernard Maybeck, worked or apprenticed in his office. This was also evidenced by Wright's sponsorship of students in architecture and draftsmanship. Students were welcome to peruse his private architectural library, which was apparently the largest and most complete on the coast. In 1885, Wright displayed similar generosity when he refused payment for the design of the St. Francis Roman Catholic Technical School, devoted to the vocational education of orphaned and impoverished girls. Sanders also remained involved with the educational efforts of the AIA, and was in charge of their drawing classes throughout the 1880s and 1890s.

From their California offices, Wright & Sanders maintained their contacts with Victoria. Correspondence between Wright and Henry Crease for additions to his Fort Street house, *Pentrelew*, discussed the suitability of adapting a design from A.J. Downing's *Country Houses*, and reveals the generally conservative nature of Wright & Sanders's work, relying on the pattern books, catalogues and standard architectural texts of the Victorian period. Wright also provided the unexecuted design for a new *Ince Cottage* in New Westminster for the Crease family, that clearly reflected the influence of Downing's pattern book designs. Wright's connections continued to bring him back to Victoria. To the chagrin of local architects, Wright & Sanders were chosen in 1890 by the directors of the Canada Western Hotel Company to design a grand new hotel, and Wright travelled to Victoria to meet with them. The proposed site was at the corner of Government and Broughton Streets, facing the Inner Harbour. Later that year, the plans were ready. By the following January, the excavations were complete, and the company president went to San Francisco to confer with the architects as to best method of letting building contracts. The company was short of funds, and wanted to issue more shares, but the project dragged on through 1892 when it was finally abandoned at the time of the local smallpox outbreak. The site was later sold to the federal government as the location

WRIGHT & SANDERS,
ARCHITECTS,
OFFICE—Corner Yates and Langley Sts.

VICTORIA, V. I.

Carr House, Victoria

Ince Cottage, New Westminster, plans sent by Wright & Sanders from San Francisco

for the new Post Office, a decision protested by Victoria City Council as they felt it was too far from the business district.

John Wright's wife, Agnes, died in 1890. Wright carried on working for another five years, retiring in 1895 with substantial wealth. The rest of his life he devoted to travelling, to his large family and to mentoring talented young architects, whom he sometimes sponsored for studies abroad. John Wright watched as much of his life's work was consumed in the fires that followed the great San Francisco earthquake, or was dynamited to stop the spread of conflagration. In the summer of 1915 Wright decided to visit Canada again. He became ill while crossing from Seattle to Victoria where he intended to meet friends *en route* to Ontario. He died in the Jubilee Hospital on August 23, 1915.

The Wright & Sanders office remained open until 1900, and then Sanders advertised himself as being in independent practice in 1901. While in San Francisco, Sanders had married Wright's sister-in-law, Euphemia Armstrong. Sanders was widowed when Euphemia died in a tragic ferry boat accident on San Francisco Bay in 1868. His second wife, Emma, also predeceased him. Undoubtedly, Sanders had an influence on the architectural career of his nephew, George A. Applegarth (1875-1972). At the age of eighteen, Applegarth dropped out of Oakland High School to work as a draftsman for Wright & Sanders. In 1902, Applegarth hopped on a whaling boat with his best friend and school chum, Jack London, later a famous author. When they reached Paris, Applegarth disembarked to attend the *École des Beaux-Arts*. Recognizing the need for architects to rebuild the city after the 1906 earthquake and fire, he returned to San Francisco after graduation in 1907. His creative talents were immediately appreciated and his classical influence would have an impact on the city's rebuilding. The most famous of Applegarth's buildings in San Francisco are the Spreckels mansion, designed in 1913 with partner Kenneth MacDonald, and the Palace of the Legion of Honor in Lincoln Park, opened in 1924. George Sanders moved to Berkeley about 1914. He died on January 24, 1920 at the age of eighty-one following an illness of several months, at the home he shared with a stepdaughter. To the end of his life, Sanders was remembered by his friends in Victoria.

Of Wright & Sanders's California work, only a few early churches survive, along with the Lick Observatory, built in the 1880s on Mount Hamilton in the Diablo Range east of San Jose, and the recently-restored San Francisco Theological Seminary. In Victoria, a number of Wright & Sanders's buildings form the core of the City's protected architectural heritage. Richard Carr House and Temple Emanu-El are federally designated historic sites. Carr and Point Ellice houses are operated as provincial heritage attractions. *Woodlands*, Angela College, and *Fairfield* are municipally designated heritage sites. The early work of Wright & Sanders in Victoria was a strong and convincing demonstration of the architectural talent that would mature and flourish after their departure for California.

Canada Western Hotel, Victoria

HERMANN OTTO TIEDEMANN
C.1821–1891

MARY E. DOODY JONES AND
CHRISTOPHER J.P. HANNA

H.O. Tiedemann was a successful architect, surveyor and civil engineer. His career as an architect spanned over thirty years and included some of the most notable commissions of nineteenth century Victoria. Tiedemann's work encompassed a wide variety of structures, from coal wharves to Gothic cathedrals. He was born about 1821 in Althammer village, also known as Trahhammar ("Trah's Forge"), located in the midst of an Upper Silesian mining area in Prussia, that is now part of Poland. Most likely he learned surveying and civil engineering at a German trade school. Arriving at Victoria in May 1858, Tiedemann was immediately hired as a surveyor and draftsman by Joseph D. Pemberton, Colonial Surveyor for the Hudson's Bay Company. Pemberton found Tiedemann to be "a finished Artist and an accurate Surveyor." The 1859 Official Map of Victoria included Tiedemann's sketches of the city, and in 1860 his panoramic sketch of Victoria was published as a large coloured etching. Tiedemann was employed by the Colonial government between 1859-62, during which time he drafted the plans, based on Pemberton's specifications, for the Fisgard Light House, 1860, at the mouth of Esquimalt harbour. **John Wright** was hired as the contractor for the project, and the two men may have jointly influenced its final design. Tiedemann's best known commission during his government tenure was for the complex of five wooden Colonial Administration Buildings in Victoria, begun in 1859. Their much-criticized decorative timber framing with painted brick infill was probably inspired by the vernacular architecture of northern Germany. The buildings soon became known as the "Birdcages," after a newspaper editor labelled them "the latest fashion of Chinese pagoda, Swiss cottage and Italian-villa fancy bird-cages."

On August 13, 1861, Tiedemann married Mary Bissett, of Lachine, Quebec, who had arrived in Victoria the previous year with her family; her brother, James, was a Hudson's Bay Company officer. Close to the Bissett family property in James Bay, Tiedemann built a new house in the Italianate style popular in early Victoria. Following his resignation from government service, Tiedemann advertised himself, in early 1862, as an architect and civil engineer, but his only known commission at that time was a wharf. Alfred Waddington soon hired him to survey a road from rugged Bute Inlet to the Fraser River. Tiedemann completed the survey in July, 1862 and reported being "reduced almost to a skeleton, unable to walk," due to lack of supplies and desertion by his Aboriginal guides. On January 12, 1863 he became a naturalized citizen.

Tiedemann worked as a surveyor on mining and public work projects until 1867, when he secured another architectural commission, for the second Holy Trinity Anglican Church in New Westminster. Built in the "pure Gothic" style desired by the clients, Holy Trinity was of cross-axial design with a semi-octagonal apse. The contract for its construction was

The Birdcages, Victoria

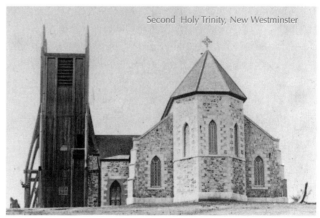

Second Holy Trinity, New Westminster

awarded to **Thomas Trounce**, and its walls were built of imported Salt Spring Island sandstone. The next year, Tiedemann designed St. Andrew's Presbyterian Church, Victoria. Built of brick, it had round-topped doors and a semi-circular apse window. **E. Mallandaine Sr.**, who had lost the design competition, denounced Tiedemann's Romanesque elements as "the rudest travesty of Gothic" and "certainly calculated to kill George Gilbert Scott, should he ever see it." The church board members threatened to fire Tiedemann over construction problems and his failure to consult with them. The structure demonstrated poor acoustics and required remedial repairs. Tiedemann's next important project was Victoria's second Christ Church Cathedral, 1872. While in England, Anglican Bishop George Hills had commissioned plans for a stone structure from the British architect Benjamin Ferry, a member of the Ecclesiological Society and a follower of A.W.N. Pugin. Ferry's High Victorian Gothic design, flanked on both sides of its entry by "massive and lofty towers," proved to be far too expensive, so a modest wooden structure was commissioned from Tiedemann. While this building was again criticized, most commentators regarded the structure as a good compromise, given the congregation's limited finances.

In the early 1870s, Tiedemann worked as a chief surveyor for the Canadian Pacific Railway Survey. In spite of his own previous suffering in the bush, he was a harsh overseer. When a man became lost on a survey near Bute Inlet in 1872, surveyor **George Hargreaves** recorded in his diary that Tiedemann stated "anyone who gets lost deserves to die" and that "he will go on if half his party are lost which does not improve the feelings of the men towards him, at all times not very amicable." A comment in the Colonist of August 12, 1867, builds on this description of his belligerent character: "Mr. Tiedemann appears to be rather a funny man; he 'guys' [ridicules] some of the leading merchants here pretty badly."

Tiedemann's only architectural commissions during the mid-1870s were a bell tower for the Tiger Fire Company, 1874, the Jacob Sehl factory, 1874, and the William McNiffe store, 1875. In 1878, Tiedemann designed nine structures, and at least four-teen in the following four years. His commercial buildings ranged in style from the very austere, such as the Bossi & Giesselmann store, 1878, to more ornate examples with cor-

Court House, Victoria

belled cornices and banding, including R. Rocke Robertson's law offices, 1878, and Roderick Finlayson's warehouse, 1881-82. Buildings displaying an array of disproportionate Italianate elements were: the John Wilson store, 1878; the Indian Department office, 1882; the S.J. Pitts warehouse, 1882; and the Finlayson Building on Pandora Street, 1882, with its window hoods joined to string courses on both stories. Victoria's worst example of High Victorian excess was Tiedemann's Canadian Pacific Navigation Company office, 1884, with the front façade covered by an incongruous assemblage of high-relief shapes and asymmetrical patterns. His most attractive commercial buildings were a store for Elijah Howe Anderson, Johnson Street, 1881, with restrained decorative treatment, and the three-storey brick Italianate Angel Hotel, 1890. Other projects included R.P. Rithet's Outer Wharves at Shoal Point, 1882, and a sixty-room addition to the first Driard Hotel, 1883. Tiedemann's designs for Sehl's factory and Pitts's warehouse included two of the first patent elevators in Victoria.

His last important public commission was the new Victoria Court House, won through a competition in 1887. Reportedly based upon a Munich court house, Tiedemann's design blended Italianate and Romanesque styles, with horizontal masonry and string courses contrasted with vertical bays and towers. As Tiedemann was ailing at the time, **S.C. Burris** took over as supervising architect. Design flaws and poor acoustics necessitated alterations soon after its completion in 1889.

While Tiedemann was a competent architectural designer and engineer who utilized new building technologies, the eclectic and incongruous styles of some of his buildings damaged his reputation as an architect. He died at his home on September 12, 1891, survived by his wife and three sons. In recognition of his surveying activities, Mount Tiedemann, Tiedemann Glacier and Creek, near Bute Inlet, and Tiedemann Island in southeast Alaska, are all named after him.

Second Christ Church Cathedral, Victoria

Map of Victoria, 1859

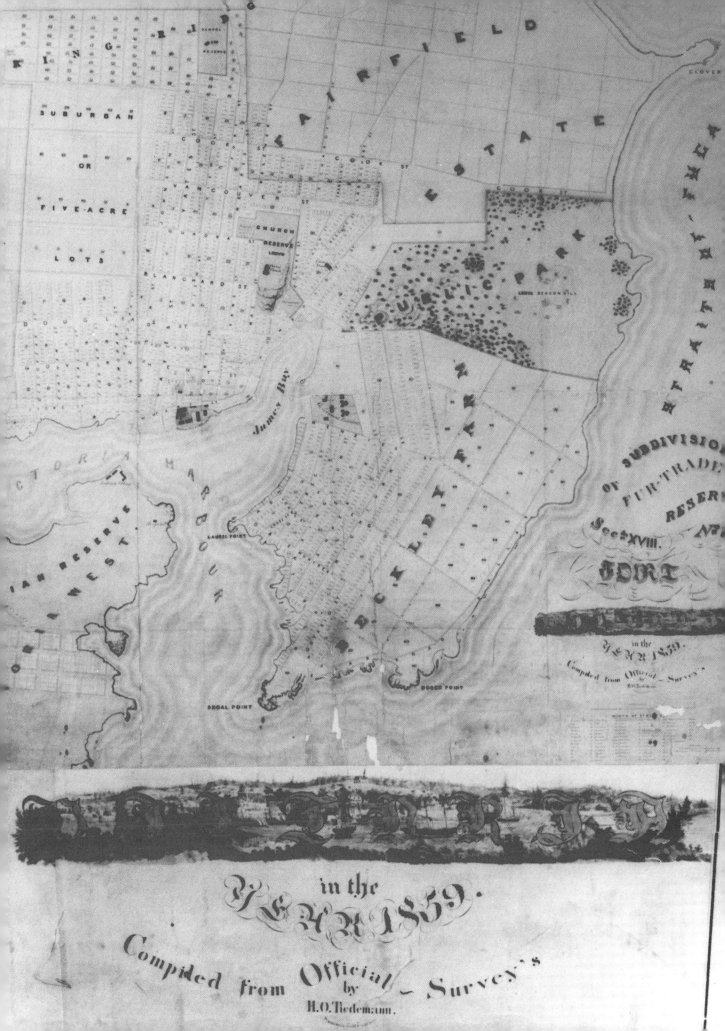

THOMAS TROUNCE

1813–1900

STUART STARK

Thomas Trounce was one of the pioneer Cornishmen who contributed much to the life of early British Columbia. Born at Tregero Farm, Veryan, Cornwall, United Kingdom, Trounce later spent five years in London. Then, with his wife, Jane, he departed for New Zealand in 1841 and arrived, via the SS *Clifford*, on May 11, 1842. Trounce worked in New Zealand as a carpenter and joiner. He caught "gold fever" during the 1849 California gold rush, and arrived in San Francisco on June 1, 1850. Trounce worked there as a builder until 1858, when another gold rush in British Columbia's Fraser River valley worked its magic. Trounce, who "wanted to live under the British flag," stayed in Victoria, where he first lived in a tent on

Government Street, and worked as a builder. When the HBC sold off the land that provided access to his property, he established Trounce Alley in 1859, a convenient thoroughfare between Government and Broad Streets. Trounce had some means, and owned other property in both Victoria and Esquimalt. By 1859, Trounce had built a frame house on Kane Street, and by 1861 had built *Tregew* in James Bay, one of the first stone houses in British Columbia. Italianate in style, *Tregew* was built of random rubble stonework with walls two feet thick. The ceilings on the main floor were eleven feet high and embellished with simple plaster mouldings, and the fireplaces had horseshoe-shaped cast iron grates decorated with flowers. Most of Trounce's known buildings were of masonry construction, an influence from his Cornish background. Although he certainly designed buildings from his first arrival in Victoria, Trounce also continued to act as a contractor, notably for the construction of the St. Nicholas Hotel for architects **Wright & Sanders** in 1862.

Trounce was a favourite of Admiral Hastings, Commander-in-Chief at the Royal Naval Dockyard, and also developed a comfortable relationship with Paymaster Sidney Spark. From 1866 he was brought in to do the estimates for all work, which were then sent to London for approval. Spark was then supposed to tender the work but usually it was just given to

Armadale, Victoria

Tregew, Victoria

Trounce. This changed when a new Paymaster put an end to "irregularities" and instituted tendering procedures. Trounce's activities at the Dockyard resulted in his best known building, St. Paul's Anglican Church in Esquimalt. Built in 1866, the Gothic-style wooden church is twenty-six by fifty feet in size, with a modest transept, and sixty-four feet to the top of its steeple. Associated from the beginning with the Royal Navy, the church was built with an Admiralty grant, and located on the rocky shoreline just outside the gates of the Dockyard; by 1904, the church was moved to a new site away from the potential damage of gunnery practice and storms. Trounce designed other churches including an extension to First Methodist Church in Victoria in 1872, and in 1874 a "Church and Day School for the use of the Indians" on Herald Street, Victoria. In 1867 he was awarded the contract to build Holy Trinity Church in New Westminster, designed by **H.O. Tiedemann**, and opened for services the following year.

Trounce's most productive years, architecturally, were the 1870s. He built his largest and most impressive buildings during that period, including *Armadale*, the substantial residence of Senator William John Macdonald, named after the seat of Lord Macdonald in Skye and built on about twenty-six acres in James Bay in 1876-77 for $12,000, an enormous sum in those days. Trounce designed at least a dozen other substantial dwellings in this decade, in addition to what was probably his largest commission, the Hirst warehouse and docks in Nanaimo. This two-storey stone warehouse had a restrained classical frontage, and although much altered still serves as part of the Harbour Commission Building in Nanaimo. In Victoria, Trounce's 1879 Weiler Warehouse still stands at the corner of Broughton and Broad Streets. Trounce continued his architectural practice throughout the 1880s, designing

such buildings as Morley's Soda Works on Waddington Alley, and a number of dwellings. Trounce continued to design smaller buildings well into old age, with his last known commission being a two-storey store and additions to its stables in 1891-92.

Trounce was well known for his horticultural interests, and in 1874 dropped off a basket of fruit at the offices of the *Daily Colonist*, which noted: "To Thomas Trounce Esq. We are indebted for a basket of the largest, prettiest and best flavoured peaches we have had the pleasure of trying in this or any other country. They were grown in the fine garden attached to that gentleman's residence at James Bay." In 1885, he sent off a basket of apples to the Colonial and Indian Exhibition in London and was awarded a prize for his exhibit.

Trounce served as alderman on Victoria City Council from 1874-77, and in 1885 became a Grand Master of Masons. His wife, Jane, who had travelled the world with him, died in 1888. Shortly after, Trounce, at the age of seventy-six, married Emma Richards, a widow twenty-seven years younger, and they honeymooned in Australia. Emma was Methodist like her husband, and they attended the nearby James Bay Methodist Church. Trounce died on June 30, 1900, after an illness of two weeks. Emma lived until the age of sixty-four, and died in 1902. *Tregew* survived demolition attempts by developers until 1967, when it was replaced with a forty-four-suite apartment building.

Trounce's success was partly based on being in the right place at the right time, and also on his ability to move between contracting and architecture. His buildings were generally competent, workman-like structures, and those that survive are rare examples of British Columbia's earliest architecture.

THOMAS TROUNCE,
ARCHITECT AND BUILDER,
CORNER DOUGLAS AND KANE STREETS,
VICTORIA, V. I.

RICHARD LEWIS
1824–1875

CHRISTOPHER J.P. HANNA

Though it is difficult to determine the full extent of his practice, Richard Lewis achieved some success as an architect in colonial Victoria, and his known works included some of the city's most impressive commercial structures. Born in London, England, in 1824, Lewis apparently spent several years in Scotland before immigrating to Chile in 1853-54, and then in 1855 to San Francisco where he reportedly worked as a builder and architect. Lewis's architectural training is unknown, but his numerous other pursuits suggest it was of a practical rather than a theoretical nature.

During the Fraser River Gold Rush of 1858 he came north to Victoria. Lewis apparently did not enjoy much financial success during the early years of his career. He probably served as builder, if not architect, for a number of the buildings erected in Victoria between 1858 and 1860. Though Lewis fitted out the first Masonic Hall in 1860, such work he obtained in the building industry was insufficient to support him and he turned to cabinetmaking and, like several other architects and builders of early Victoria, undertaking. He completed an order for furniture for the new Colonial Administration buildings in April 1860. Lewis also imported Victoria's first hearse in the summer of 1860. Despite these efforts he had to admit that same year to a serious want of money.

Things changed during the business boom that followed the 1861 discovery of gold in the Cariboo district, when Lewis designed most of the commercial structures erected for the merchants of Wharf Street, then the leading business thoroughfare in Victoria and known as "Commercial Row." Lewis's seven buildings there were erected in two stages, the first four with cast iron fronts from San Francisco and the last three with brick arcading on the street frontage. Befitting structures located in the principal wholesale and warehouse district of early Victoria, large steel shutters and doors on the fronts of the buildings provided both easy access to the interiors of the buildings and security against fire or theft of their contents. In 1862 Lewis designed two one-storey brick stores in the Italianate style for local saloon owner, Thomas Golden, and their completion created the largest assemblage of commercial buildings designed by one architect in colonial Victoria. Unlike the rather vague stylistic references in the rest of Commercial Row, Lewis made greater use of Italianate design elements in Golden's two buildings which were among the best local commercial examples of this style of architecture.

Other commissions during this period included several residences, a number of smaller commercial buildings, and some cisterns for the fire department. In late 1863 Lewis designed a two-storey block of four brick stores on Wharf Street for Captain James Murray Reid. The brick arcading was mirrored above by round-headed windows, while brick pilasters and banding gave the façades a regularity in spite of the irregular shape and slope of the lot. In 1864 Lewis designed a fireproof brick warehouse with a stone basement on Wharf Street for merchant, J.J. Southgate, and supplied estimates for repairing Craigflower School. The following year Lewis designed a brick hospital on Collinson Street for the Sisters of St. Ann, a two-storey frame residence at Fort and Pemberton Streets, a hall for the Odd Fellows on top of the southernmost store in Commercial Row and the two-storey brick and stone White Horse Tavern at the corner of Humboldt and McClure Streets.

The end of the Cariboo gold rush boom in the mid-1860s brought a great decline in building activity in Victoria and Lewis was one of those who fell upon hard times. By 1867 he applied, unsuccessfully, for appointment as Inspector of Weights and Measures for Victoria, or any other vacant position, as his business as an architect and builder was at a standstill. During this period of his life Lewis became rather depressed and at one point during a minor illness managed to convince himself that he was about to die, although he reportedly recovered from this conviction because he could not bear to have his competitor in the undertaking business succeed in burying him. Lewis secured another architectural commission in 1869 when he designed and erected a second building for J.J. Southgate at the corner of Government and Fort Streets. A brick store erected on Fort Street in April 1871 was his last known architectural commission, but among his papers

Bottom: Richard Lewis as Worshipful Master of Golden Gate Masonic Lodge No. 30, San Francisco, California

at the time of his death was a set of house plans for Henry Slye Mason. Lewis was an enthusiastic member of the Masonic order and held a number of offices in the Victoria lodges. He was also a member of the Odd Fellows Lodge, a volunteer fireman of the Deluge fire company, a member of the Pioneer Society, a member of the City of Victoria's Board of Variance and was elected as a city alderman several times in the 1860s-70s. Following the resignation of William J. MacDonald, Lewis was appointed Mayor for the remainder of his 1872 term, but he did not seek re-election.

The death of Lewis's wife, Christina, at the age of thirty-six in June 1864, was followed by his marriage in January 1865 to Jeanette Mitchell, the daughter of a Scottish ironfounder. Lewis had one daughter by his first wife and two daughters and a son by his second. All the children outlived Lewis, who died on New Year's Day, 1875. Buried in Ross Bay Cemetery with Masonic rites, Lewis was given a funeral described as the largest that had ever taken place in Victoria up to that date, with large numbers of Masons, Odd Fellows, firemen, Pioneer Society members and the general public forming his cortege. Lewis's wife continued to operate his undertaking business for several months before selling it to Thomas Storey, another contractor and builder in early Victoria.

FREDERICK WALTER GREEN
C.1821–1877

DOROTHY MINDENHALL AND
CAREY PALLISTER

F.W. Green was more prominent as a surveyor and a civil engineer than as an architect. Best remembered for his survey of what is now Gastown in Vancouver, he also designed one of Victoria's earliest architectural oddities, Cary Castle. Green was born in Yorkshire, England, arrived in Victoria in June 1858, and by July had entered into partnership with Lammot & Freeman "Surveyors, Engineers, Draftsmen," offering to prepare architectural plans and maps, and to undertake machine drafting. Green was hired by the Hudson's Bay Company to map the area around James Bay in 1861. In 1862 he designed a stone residence for George Hunter Cary, who had taken a notion to build himself a small castle. The brilliant but controversial Cary served as Attorney-General of both colonies and was also politically active, but signs of mental unbalance became quickly evident and he was lured back to England with a contrived telegraph announcing his appointment as Lord Chancellor. His detractors had dubbed his eccentric home "Cary Castle," a name that stuck long after his departure.

In October 1862, Green offered his services to the newly formed City Council, and was elected City Surveyor over five other applicants, including **H.O. Tiedemann**. His building work in the 1860s was mainly wharves, warehouses and stores, mostly in Victoria, although he did build a sawmill building and an engine/boiler house at Burrard Inlet for Edward Stamp in 1865, possibly with William Oakley, Architect and Surveyor, with whom he had formed a partnership at the beginning of that year. In 1864 Cary Castle was acquired as his

**FREDERICK WALTER GREEN,
CITY SURVEYOR,
Architect and Civil Engineer,**
Cor. Broughton and Government Sts.

official residence by Governor Arthur Kennedy, who desired substantial modifications. Although Green and Oakley went to see the Governor in 1865 to request permission to prepare plans and estimates, "as Mr. Green was the architect of the original edifice," **Wright & Sanders** had already been chosen to do the work. Throughout the 1860s Green led survey parties to Newcastle town, the Queen Charlotte Islands, Burrard Inlet, and the Rockies; he was, reputedly, "well liked by his men." He prepared coloured drawings, elevation and sectional plans of Race Rocks Light House for the use of the Light House Commissioner in 1869, possibly in preparation for the erection of a fog bell tower in July 1870. In 1870, he was involved in surveys around Burrard Inlet, and was responsible for the original survey of Granville townsite, later known as Gastown, Vancouver's birthplace. After the 1886 fire which destroyed the young settlement, four of his survey posts still remained in place from which it was possible to re-establish the townsite.

As City Surveyor for Victoria, Green was involved with the construction of the Victoria Water Works at Beaver Lake, which began in 1873. His sudden death at the age of fifty-six on October 30, 1877 was, according to Councillor Robert Beaven, "accelerated by catching a severe cold while in execution of his duty" at the Water Works. He was given a lavish funeral attended by the Mayor and Council, and many members of the Legislative Assembly. City Council voted three months salary, in compensation for his untimely death, to be given to his widow and surviving daughter.

Original appearance of Cary Castle, Victoria

DAVID WILLIAM GORDON

1832–1893

DONALD LUXTON

It was likely Dunsmuir who persuaded Gordon to run for a seat in the Legislative Assembly, which he won in 1877. In August 1882, Gordon was elected to the House of Commons, and was re-elected by acclamation in 1887. Emma died in 1882, and four years later, his children now grown, Gordon married Statora Catherine "Kitty" Shepherd, and they had three children. Gordon acted as a contractor throughout his time in public office, and continued to provide plans, including the design for additions to the first Nanaimo Court House, 1884. Gordon advertised himself variously as an architect and builder right up until the time of his death, on February 19, 1893, just days before his sixty-first birthday. The Provincial Legislature was adjourned so that Premier Theodore Davie and other MLAs could attend his lavish funeral.

Better remembered as a politician, D.W. Gordon was also one of the first private contractors in Nanaimo, and in the manner of many early builders, offered design services as well. Born February 27, 1832 at Camden, Kent County, Ontario, he was a descendant of United Empire Loyalists. After an education in the Kent County Public Schools, Gordon served his apprenticeship with Fisher & Smith, contractors in Wallaceburg, after which he worked as a builder and joiner until he left for California in 1856 to take part in the "gold mining excitement." In 1858 he was lured north by the Fraser River Gold Rush, but returned to California the following year.

About 1862, after a brief stop in Victoria, Gordon moved to the small but growing community of Nanaimo. Upon his arrival he entered into a partnership with contractor Jacob Blessing. Among their many projects were a prominent house for Captain William H. Franklyn, c.1862; the Vancouver Coal Company's offices and Mine Manager's House on Haliburton Street, 1860s; and the Mechanic's Institute Hall on Bastion Street, 1864-65. Gordon almost certainly designed as well as built these buildings. In 1864 he married Emma Elizabeth Robb; they had five children, a son and four daughters. Gordon rapidly became established as one of the city's leading businessmen. He became close friends with Robert Dunsmuir, who was growing rich on the profits from his coal business. About 1876 Dunsmuir commissioned Gordon to design and build his new home, *Ardoon*, on Albert Street. It was the most luxurious residence in Nanaimo, and Dunsmuir hosted many important guests there such as Sir Charles Tupper, Canada's Minster of Railways, and the Marquis of Lorne, Governor-General of Canada.

His life has been one of earnest, energetic and practical work, and he was stricken down while in harness, for his attention was given to matters of duty incident to his position as member for Vancouver Island District in the Dominion House of Commons, up to within a few days of his death.

Nanaimo *Free Press*, February 20, 1893, p.1

Ardoon, Nanaimo

JAMES KENNEDY
1817–1902

DONALD LUXTON

James and Caroline Kennedy were among the earliest settlers of New Westminster. Although he was one of the Royal City's first architects, like most other pioneers James Kennedy had to work at a variety of occupations to support his family. Born December 9, 1817 in Ballymena, County Antrim, Ireland, he received a thorough and practical training in architecture before leaving for North America in 1839. Restless and in search of opportunity, he settled and practised briefly in Rochester, New York, and then in the late 1840s moved to Whitby, Ontario, as his "inborn love of the old flag and of British institutions led him to bend his steps towards Canada." Hearing reports of the gold fields, he shipped out from New York in 1852 for a six month sea voyage to Australia. Staying for a year, he returned to Whitby, where he married Caroline Stone in 1854. Five years later, in the spring of 1859, they started by way of Panama for the west coast, arriving in New Westminster on April 3, where Mrs. Kennedy was noted as being the first white woman settler. The "Royal City" in the 1860s was a fledgling community of pioneer construction, although some finer structures had been built by the **Royal Engineers**, and **Wright & Sanders** are also known to have received a number of local commissions.

In the 1860s the Kennedys pre-empted a total of 455 acres in what is now known as Kennedy Heights in North Delta. In 1861, under contract to the Colonial government, Kennedy cut a ten foot wide trail from Brownsville to Mud Bay, which mostly followed the higher contour of the escarpment in North Delta. This trail proved to be a vital communications link, especially from the United States, and was used to transport goods and people from ships landing in Mud Bay. By 1863

Kennedy was advertising his services as an architect. Kennedy's practical experience was invaluable, and he was hired by the provincial government to supervise the final construction of the Lunatic Asylum, the plans for which had been provided by **A.J. Smith** of Victoria in 1875. Kennedy acted in a similar capacity for the Federal Government for the New Westminster Post Office. He was the architect for P. Arnaud's second Colonial Hotel on Columbia Street, built 1875-76 but lost to fire in 1883, and also designed the workshops at the Penitentiary in 1881. As the city grew, he received commissions to design several business blocks, such as the Webster Block, a substantial and finely detailed three-storey brick block on Front Street completed in 1887, and the Powell Block, a brick building with three storeys fronting Columbia Street and five storeys facing Lytton Square, built at a cost of $30,000 in 1889. Kennedy's sons published the *Daily* and *Weekly Columbian*, and James sometimes contributed articles for publication.

In 1898, a disastrous fire destroyed much of New Westminster, including all of James Kennedy's downtown buildings. By this time he had retired, and his only known participation in the reconstruction was a design for a two-storey frame building for The Columbian Printing Company. James died at home on November 23, 1902, and was buried in the Odd Fellows Cemetery in Sapperton, with seven of his sons as pall bearers. Caroline died on February 20, 1923, aged eighty-eight.

Powell Block, New Westminster

Work was going on at the hotel, and once again I found my early education useful. The building had a Mansard Roof, with a number of circular roofed dormer windows on each side; which four of us were set to roof with tongue-and-groove flooring. Rather an awkward little job. However, instead of cutting each piece separately, scribing them to bevels which changed with every piece, as the other fellows were doing, I thought I could do it in more scientific fashion. Accordingly I laid down a strip of flooring on some of the lower joists and took the measurements and bevels I required. Then bearing in mind one of the first lessons in drawing which I had received from the old Polish Count in Derry some years before – i.e. "Given any three points, to find the centre of a circle which will pass through all of them." I found my centre and drew the correct segment for each of my five windows, and also the greatest and least of the bevels required also.

*I was just about ready to commence cutting when **Mr. Kennedy** the architect came along. "Tut-tut," said he, "you can't lay any flooring until we get the roof on." "I'm not laying flooring" I replied. "These are for sheathing the dormer window roofs." "Oh, nonsense," he said, "you can't cut them down here." "Excuse me," I said, "I'm quite sure I can do so, and do it correctly, too." Then I showed him my calculations, and with some reluctance I was allowed to go ahead, and done so. The result was that they fitted perfectly; nothing to do but nail them into place, and I had all of my five windows covered before any of the other fellows had got their second one finished; and a better job besides. This was quite a feather in my cap, besides one or two other short cuts I was able to show them, and I became rather a favourite of the old man, and got my full share of any work going on in town thereafter.*

Excerpt from **John Baptist Henderson**, *The Story of an Old Timer of B.C.*, pp.22-24.

EDWARD MALLANDAINE, SR.

1827–1905

JOHN ADAMS

Edward Mallandaine's career was a kaleidoscope of constantly changing fragments. Throughout his life he wanted to practise architecture, and actually managed to do so on and off beginning in the 1850s. However, between architectural commissions – or sometimes concurrently with them – he took on other work to put bread on his table. These pursuits were numerous and varied: book-keeping, drafting, land surveying, estimating and quantity surveying, drawing, gold mining (in Australia and British Columbia), brick making, funeral arranging, farming (on Salt Spring Island), teaching, compiling city directories, debt and tax collecting, law copying, writing from dictation, inventing, serving as military paymaster, map making and building contracting.

Mallandaine was born in Singapore in 1827, the son of the military commander of the Straits Settlements. In 1832 his mother died while the family was returning to Kent, England. By 1836 his father had lost his money and the family moved to France where living was cheaper. They settled in Brittany where at age ten Edward attended school for the first time. He excelled in languages and drawing. When he was seventeen he was apprenticed to a London firm to learn bookkeeping. In 1846 he became an articled pupil to Mr. Stow, District Surveyor for St. Giles Camberwell in London, whom he accompanied to inspect buildings under the provisions of the *Metropolitan Buildings Act.* Mallandaine learned about design and construction mainly through first-hand experience copying architectural drawings, and assisting in inspections and quantity surveying. He was admitted as a student at the Royal Institute of British Architects, served as an assistant to T.C. Robinson, architect in Wolverhampton, and then in the office of W. Tress, architect for the South Eastern Railway.

He interrupted his architectural career to mine for gold in Australia in 1852 and 1853. While there he was employed in Melbourne briefly as a draftsman. Poor results from mining, an ankle injury, and the lure of a young woman back in London made him return to England in 1854. He found work as a quantity surveyor and architectural assistant, and was an "influential" member of the London Architectural Association. In 1855 he married Mary Smith at St. Giles Cathedral, but was devastated when his wife and their baby girl died, prompting him to follow another gold rush, this time to British Columbia, via New York, Panama, and San Francisco, in 1858. His efforts to reach the Fraser River gold fields failed, and so he settled in Victoria.

Mallandaine had hoped to set up an architectural practice in British Columbia after he arrived in 1858, but spent the first two years at other pursuits, most frequently teaching, and returned to architecture whenever the economy improved and prospects brightened. He dabbled in the field as early as 1860 when, probably through the influence of his teaching partner J. Silversmith, he was awarded the contract to design and construct a fence around the Jewish Cemetery in Victoria. However, Mallandaine is best known for his work in the 1860s-70s producing the first city directories in what is now British Columbia. In 1863 he opened his first professional office as an "architectural assistant" and the following year received a commission to design a three-storey brick building on Store Street for T.J. Burnes. At this time, although he entered many competitions and prepared plans, few architectural commissions came his way.

When an economic slump hit British Columbia in 1864 Mallandaine was again obliged to earn his livelihood as best he could. He took part in the 1864 Leech River Gold Rush near Sooke, and in 1866 went to Portland, Oregon briefly in search of architectural work, but found that only drafting jobs were available. He married again, to Louisa Townsend in 1866, and they had five children. One of them, **Edward Mallandaine**, **Jr.**, later practised architecture on the coast before moving to Creston.

By 1871 Mallandaine had found temporary work surveying in the Fraser Canyon for the CPR, the first of three times he was employed on the railway surveys. In 1872 he drew the plan for Ross Bay Cemetery and probably influenced its layout as a Victorian rural cemetery. That year he also provided the plans for the first public school in Nanaimo, built in 1873 by **Bruno Mellado**. He also prepared plans in 1872 for a school at Cedar Hill, and a lunatic asylum in Victoria, the design of which was condemned in the *Colonist* on October 4, 1872, and roundly defended by Mallandaine the following day. The next year he designed St. Mary the Virgin Church in Metchosin. In 1874 he was on the temporary payroll of the Lands and Works Department as a draftsman, copying maps and plans. When the position of chief draftsman became available, **W.S. Gore** was appointed, and Mallandaine complained bitterly in his memoirs that it was not based on merit, but was purely a political decision.

Again seeking his fortune, in 1875 he was off to the gold rush in the Cassiar District. In 1876 he unsuccessfully sought architectural work in San Francisco. Although he designed numerous houses on speculation, no commissions were awarded to him there.

On his return to British Columbia in 1876 he began one of his most productive periods, beginning that year with a church in Comox and a teacher's residence at Cedar Hill, followed two years later by a new wing for the Nanaimo Public School, a ward for the Royal Hospital in Victoria and a small chapel at the Naval, now Veterans, Cemetery in Esquimalt. He formed a partnership in 1879 with John McDowell, a carpenter and mechanic, apparently in the hope that the combination of his design skills with McDowell's construction expertise would yield more commissions. The notion, however, proved overly optimistic and the partnership soon ended. In 1880 Mallandaine designed a small house for the Fawcett family in James Bay, one for his own family on Simcoe Street, and a plan for the churchyard at St. Stephen's Church, Saanichton.

Following another abortive attempt to seek architectural work in Portland in 1882, Mallandaine returned to Victoria and in 1884 prepared plans for the Chinese Theatre on Cormorant Street, laid out St. Mary's Cemetery in Metchosin, and designed *Marifield*, a modest cottage in James Bay for Bishop and Mrs. Cridge. In 1886 he designed a small house for Skene Lowe at the corner of Simcoe and Government Streets, and St. Luke's Anglican Church in Saanich, 1888. A surviving commercial project is the London Block on Broad Street in Victoria, 1892.

Around this time his son, Edward Mallandaine, Jr., began to practise architecture in both Vancouver and Victoria. Although father and son did not enter into a formal partnership it is likely they did collaborate during the 1890s, and by 1897 they even shared office space in Victoria. Some confusion arises in trying to specify attributions to either father or son or both in the years 1892-98. Around this time several extant houses were designed by one or both of the Mallandaines in Victoria.

Edward Mallandaine Sr. continued to practise architecture almost until his death on April 4, 1905. His career as an architect was frustrated by competition, and produced no famous monuments. However, some notable survivals, particularly a number of picturesque rural Anglican churches on Vancouver Island and several cemeteries are a commendable legacy.

Public School, Nanaimo

DOROTHY MINDENHALL AND
CAREY PALLISTER

James Syme played a small but pivotal role in the development of British Columbia's salmon canning industry as well as pursuing various artistic and architectural endeavours. Born in Edinburgh in 1832, he was drawn by the lure of gold, and lived in San Francisco from 1859-62. He passed through Victoria on his way to the Cariboo gold rush in 1862, and returned to the coast two years later seeking business opportunities. Showing his artistic talent, in 1864 he executed a plaster relief portrait of Sir James Douglas. His earliest known, and most prominent, architectural commission appears to have been the New Westminster home of Captain William Irving, 1865, described in a contemporary account as being in the "mixed Gothic" style. With its elaborate wall dormer, verandahs, and gingerbread bargeboards, it bears a striking resemblance to contemporary pattern book designs. Irving's

daughter recalled that Syme "was the architect and builder of our house. He was a Scotsman and highly educated and he and father were great friends." **Thomas W. Graham** acted as the contractor, Syme executed the elaborate interior plaster work, and Thomas Stoddard was the painter and finisher.

Syme became intrigued with the potential of the vast unexploited Fraser River salmon runs. In 1866, he began canning small amounts of salmon, the first time that this had been done on the B.C. coast, and publicly exhibited his product at New Westminster. Despite its innovations, Syme's canning operation lacked capital, and lasted only two years. The local depression that set in after the union of the two colonies, and the end of the gold rushes, drove Syme back to San Francisco in 1869 to resume the interior decorating and ornamental plastering business he had left seven years previously. He returned to Victoria by 1874 and on October 11, four of his "fine art" prints were presented in a show and subsequently raffled. After this he turned again to architecture. His first contract was a large one, the original St. Joseph's Hospital, in 1875 (**John Teague** later added a third floor). He also entered the competition to design City Hall but came in second after Teague. In 1876 he designed a house for John Graham, *Barossa Lodge*, on Simcoe Street, "furnished with hot air apparatus" and "patent water closets;" Syme and his wife,

St. Peter's Catholic Church, Nanaimo

Janet, also lived at the Graham home until their deaths. When Lord Dufferin, the Governor-General of Canada, and Lady Dufferin visited Victoria in 1876, the streets were adorned with arches designed by Syme, including three for the Chinese community. The following year he designed St. Peter's Catholic Church in Nanaimo. A surviving landmark is the house Syme designed for Scottish-born merchant, Alexander Blair Gray, built overlooking James Bay in 1877. It represented an early foray into the Italianate style, with a symmetrical front façade and an adapted Palladian window above the entry. "Social, almost to a fault," Syme was also a member of the Union Hook & Ladder Co. No. 1. He died on April 19, 1881, at the age of forty-nine, and was buried in Ross Bay Cemetery. His wife, Janet, died two years later on June 23, 1883.

Cottage Residence, Design No. 7,
Calvert Vaux, *Villages and Cottages*, 1864

To him nature has been kindly in the dispensation of her gifts; though in the tranquil flow of ordinary existence his capabilities did not appear in very marked relief, still they did not "fust in him unus'd" and his ingenious and active spirit played its useful part of measured power in the economy of human progression.

Victoria *Daily Colonist*, April 21, 1881, p.2.

Irving House, New Westminster

VICTORIAN PATTERN BOOKS

STUART STARK

A common public misconception is that all of our buildings were designed by local architects. In fact, many of our most delightful heritage structures owe their designs and layout to pattern books. The rapid growth of settlements required expedient methods of construction, and pattern books arrived at the same time as new technology such as balloon framing and steam-driven power tools. Sometimes there were just not enough architects to handle all the available work, and competent builders, armed with pattern books, fulfilled their role.

Published books of building plans have been used for centuries. Marcus Vitruvius Pollio was a Roman architect whose *Ten Books of Architecture* outlined appropriate styles for public and private buildings, and discussed decoration and construction methods. The Renaissance architect Andreo Palladio wrote his *Four Books of Architecture* in 1570.

Illustrated with woodcuts, his books, like those of Vitruvius, offered information on architecture and design. By the nineteenth century, J.C. Loudon's *Encyclopaedia of Architecture* (London, 1833, with reprints), was a comprehensive and definitive work which would have been well known to many of British Columbia's early architects. The *Encyclopaedia* was full of practical information on construction, and contained many designs for model cottages, villas and farm buildings along with their fixtures and fittings. With inexpensive printing and ease of distribution through ever more efficient mail services, architectural pattern books reached their greatest popularity in the late 1800s and early 1900s, and were a major influence on British Columbia's architectural development.

Pattern books were used for several purposes. Many evolved from promotional books by well-known American architects like Calvert Vaux (1824-1895) or Andrew Jackson Downing (1815-1852). Their compact books of the 1840s, 1850s and 1860s, such as Downing's *The Architecture of Country Houses*, 1850, provided brief descriptions of homes and other structures, such as churches or barns, as well as

RESIDENCE OF CHAS. KEITH,
GREENFIELD, MASS.

Murray Residence, New Westminster,
Clow & Maclure

an accompanying line illustration of the building. Sometimes the perspective drawings were supplemented by a floor plan along with helpful hints and recommendations for good construction, appropriate house styles and good taste in interior decoration. These promotional books were originally intended to capitalize on the author's well-known name and reputation, while providing inspiration and guidance for contractors and homeowners in rural areas, who did not have ready access to architectural services.

From the 1860s to the 1890s, the role of pattern books had become clearer. Large-scale pattern books, up to eleven by fourteen inches in size, were published by American architects such as A.J. Bicknell and W.T. Comstock and were widely distributed. These books usually gathered plans from several architects, and not only provided very detailed elevations and floor plans – often with an accompanying perspective illustration – but also provided scale drawings of architectural details. These illustrations were no small boon to contractors and builders, who used them shamelessly to copy well-designed details and apply them to their own buildings. The late Victorian period, with its propensity for fanciful exterior woodwork

Roslyn, Victoria
George F. Barber Plan No. 60

and other elaborate detailing, was well serviced by these books, disseminating big city styling across North America. Pattern book authors were clear in their intention that a home's appearance should reflect the owner's financial and social status. Cultural values and social context were being authoritatively articulated, often from a high moral stand-point, in the increasingly detailed text that accompanied the illustrations. The period of the railway boom also coin-cided with an explosion in mass communication and the development of a print culture, based on improved printing technology, a developing postal service, and lowered shipping rates for books and magazines, allowing for far and wide distribution of the now more inexpensive pattern books.

It wasn't only details that were copied by builders. Whole buildings were duplicated directly out of pattern books and magazines of the day, such as *Scientific American's Architects and Builders Edition*. It was common for a building design to be copied by a homeowner or contractor, and to be con-structed across the continent, far from its original place of design. Sometimes these designs would be almost out of fashion by the time they were built, presumably with the homeowner having set his mind on a particular house design, and then keeping the plans for several years until circumstances finally allowed construction. One example of this situation survives in Esquimalt. A beautiful mansard-roofed home was built for Captain Victor Jacobson in 1893. For many years it was regarded as a unique home, having been built with a tower so the captain could watch for ships from his seaside location. Further research revealed that the home had been built from plans prepared by C. Graham & Son, Architects in Elizabeth, New Jersey, and printed in an 1873 pattern book published by Bicknell. Many other matching houses from these particular plans had been built along the west coast of North America. Some were exact copies of the Victoria house, some had the plan reversed, while others were adapted slightly while being built, and differ only in detailing.

In Vancouver, it was reported in 1888 that a substantial house was being built for Mr. Ford from a design in the popular American pattern book *Shoppell's Modern Houses*, published by the Cooperative Building Plan Association of New York. In Victoria, *Roslyn* was built on the Gorge water-front for Andrew Gray in 1890, based on Plan No. 60 by George F. Barber; houses from this same flamboyant plan appeared across the United States, including a surviving example, the Samuel Spitler House, built in 1894 in Brookville, Ohio. Barber (1854-1915), an architect based in Knoxville, Tennessee, led the transition from the use of pat-tern books to mail-order designs, and exhorted his custom-ers to "keep writing till you get just what you want... Don't be afraid of writing too often." Between 1888 and 1912,

Barber published twenty-three books of house plans, and sent out countless sets of plans by mail; by 1900 he was boasting that his firm had fifty employees, and even offered prefabricated homes that could be shipped by rail.

Architects also used plan books for inspiration. Often plan book designs would show up in a house by an architect, altered, and undoubtedly improved, but the trained eye can often spot its origins. Perhaps the impetus was a client want-ing something similar to a design they had already seen, and were therefore able to visualize the final result. Possibly the early architects were using plan books for inspiration, but also as a selling tool for clients. An example is a house in New Westminster designed by **Clow & Maclure** for local decorator, Charles Murray in 1890. Its inspiration was a pat-tern book design, based on a house built in Greenfield, Mass. and published in the August 1888 *Scientific American, Architects & Builders Edition*. The Murray residence was later purchased by Walter R. Gilley and named *Rostrevor*. After being renovated many times it was restored in the 1990s to its original design and is now a municipally desig-nated property.

Pattern books made home design easy. They espoused the desirability and joy of home ownership, and dispensed practical advice on all aspects of interior layout and deco-rating, site planning and gardening and other matters of appropriate taste and appearance. Using these books, competent builders lacking in design skills could construct attractive homes for their clients, knowing that the finished result would be attractive and fashionable. Looking around our cities today, we can be grateful for such an architec-tural legacy.

Captain Jacobson Residence, Esquimalt

FRONT VIEW

C. GRAHAM & SON,
ARCHITECTS,
ELIZABETH N.J.

the promise of a transcontinental railway

rings British Columbia into Confederation

2

CANADA

ON THE

PACIFIC

On every side the sound of the hammer and trowel is heard. Not even in the days of '62, which we have been accustomed to refer to as "palmy," was there so much building undertaken. The structures of that period were of a transient, shell-like character, exactly in keeping with the ideas of the immigrants who came to dig gold, make their fortunes in a few months, or years at farthest, then flit away to some more congenial clime to spend their money. The buildings of the present day are of a more substantial kind... The one-storey straggling structures, devoid of paint or adornment of any kind, lined with calico and paper, and conspicuous for their tumble-down look, are about to give way to handsome brick edifices that will be ornaments to the city.

Victoria *Daily British Colonist,* July 9, 1875, p.2.

Dorothy
Mindenhall
and
Donald
Luxton

CLAUSE 11: The Government of the Dominion undertakes to secure the commencement simultaneously, within two years from the date of the Union, of the construction of a railway from the Pacific towards the Rocky Mountains, and from such point as may be selected, east of the Rocky Mountains, towards the Pacific, to connect the seaboard of British Columbia with the railway system of Canada; and further, to secure the completion of such railway within ten years from the date of the Union.

The Terms of Union, May 16, 1871

British Columbia's entry into Confederation was almost inevitable, given the shifting balance of power on the Pacific. The British Colonial Office was indifferent, at best, to the remote colony, and although the British recognized its strategic importance they were unwilling to continue financial support. Unease over the turmoil that followed the American Civil War, the American purchase of Alaska in 1867, the end of the Hudson's Bay Company's local dominance, and faltering economic returns were all contributing factors to a final resolution of the issue. In 1867 the British Parliament passed the *British North America Act*, which contained a provision for British Columbia's entry into the new Dominion.

The future of the colony was, however, of great concern to the many British capitalists who had extensive investments in many different enterprises, including the financial bonds of the colonial government. As relationships between Britain and the United States worsened, there was renewed pressure to strengthen Anglo interests in the New World. From London there were calls for the construction of a drydock at Esquimalt and a railway that would span the continent, key projects that would benefit and enhance Britain's world-wide interests in trade and Empire.

In 1870 the federal government purchased the North-West Territories from the HBC; this vast tract of land contained what later became the provinces of Alberta, Saskatchewan and Manitoba. The Red River rebellion led to Manitoba being granted limited provincial status in 1870, but the territories between B.C. and Manitoba would not achieve provincial status for several more decades. British Columbia, however, joined Confederation in 1871 in exchange for relief of its substantial debt, a promise that was kept, and for the completion of the transcontinental railway within a decade, a target destined to be missed.

Despite laments for the passing of the British social order, it was generally recognized that affiliation with Canada would bring new political, economic and professional opportunities to British Columbia. Unlike the short-lived boom of the gold rush era, it was hoped that the railway would bring long-term prosperity and stability. The stage was now set for an unprecedented golden era, based on the exploitation of vast and untapped natural resources. British Columbia would be a full partner in Confederation, and nothing could dim the bright prospects for the Pacific province. To attach this far-flung colony to the distant Dominion was seen as an heroic act of nation-building. Surveys for the railway started the day that B.C. entered Confederation.

The federal government hoped to demonstrate its presence, both administrative and physical, through the imposition of new institutions, which required monumental structures unlike any yet seen on the west coast. In 1871 the Minister of Public Works, Hector-Louis

Langevin, travelled to British Columbia to tour the newest addition to the Dominion. This was the same year that the Chief Architect's Branch was established in the Federal Department of Public Works (DPW), to develop the infrastructure of the vast and rapidly growing young country. Langevin recognized the need to recruit new talent, and Thomas Seaton Scott (1826-1895) was hired in 1871 to head the new branch. The following year Scott petitioned for, and received, the title of Chief Architect, denoting not so much his preeminent position as architect but the fact that he controlled the largest public construction budget in the country. Born at Birkenhead, England, Scott had immigrated to Montreal in the mid-1850s. He became best known for his work in the Gothic style, which included churches in Ontario and Quebec, and his 1874 design for the Mackenzie Tower on the West block of the Parliament Buildings in Ottawa. The responsibilities of the new Chief Architect included, in addition to the design of new structures, a whole range of activities related to the federal building inventory. There was a complex relationship between the Branch and its "clients," the other government ministries. Given the combination of political influence and public policy, the Branch was an easy target for allegations of the waste of public money. For some, every embellishment on a public building was shocking profligacy, while others decried the lack of beauty and refinement. Government architecture generally followed, rather than set, trends, and often fell short on inspiration.

As Chief Architect, Scott directed the post-Confederation building programme, which established an architectural image for the new Dominion. Immediately after his appointment he took a tour of major cities in the United States, and as a result enthusiastically embraced the Second Empire style as being most appropriate for public buildings. Popularized during the reign of French Emperor Napoleon III, 1852-70, this style achieved wide-spread acceptance in America. With their ornate detailing, symmetrically composed facades and characteristic mansard roof, these buildings projected an air of confidence, prosperity and stability. Tending towards the monumental, they satisfied the need for government buildings to distinguish themselves from the crude buildings usually seen in frontier communities; in more urban settings, the scale of the building could be enlarged, and the ornament more lavishly applied. The mansard roofs also provided a contrasting symbol to the Gothic church spires that punctuated the growing new settlements, and provided a clear separation between secular and religious authority.

For the first few years after Confederation, the new Branch was mostly busy with the inventory and consolidation of its inherited assets. Significant new buildings were planned for the major revenue-generating federal departments, notably post offices, customs houses, and inland revenue facilities. As communities became more established, whole new categories of buildings were erected for military, immigration, quarantine and judicial purposes. In the larger cities, local architects were hired to design and supervise these new buildings, although they had to adhere to strictly prescribed requirements. For more modest structures, Scott's staff provided the designs. Given the distances involved, budgetary priorities, and the lack of more sophisticated construction capabilities on the frontier, there was clearly a distinction between the way buildings were designed for western and eastern Canada.

Construction of the first Dominion buildings in the new province of British Columbia was fraught with seemingly interminable delays and difficulties due to the complexity of the administrative arrangements and the difficulty of communication. The bureaucratic habits of the DPW seriously hampered work on the west coast because virtually every action by a resident architect had to be approved by headquarters. In the days before the arrival of the railway, this entailed a slow-moving river of correspondence, first within the department concerned (Justice, Post Office, Inland Revenue, etc.), and then between local DPW staff and DPW headquarters. Those outside the process were enormously frustrated as they continued to wait for action on these new and much needed facilities. On August 6, 1872 the *Colonist* reported that the architect and plans for a General Post Office and Custom House would arrive on next mail steamer, the buildings to be of stone, two storeys in height, with mansard roofs. It was rumoured that the post office would be built on Government Street and the Custom House on the site of the Police Barracks. During the following two months it was reported that **Edward Mallandaine Sr.** was preparing plans for a new Custom House and Post Office, with a cut

T. Seaton Scott

stone front in Italian style, rusticated ground floor, and a central door of Palladian character "subject to approval of Dominion authorities."

In October 1872, **Benjamin William Pearse** took over as head of the British Columbia office of the Department of Public Works, and until 1879 was responsible for the supervision, and often design, of these federal building projects. The 1870s represented a brief period of expansion for marine hospitals throughout the new country of Canada, paid for by a tax levied on shipping tonnage. These specialized facilities were intended to relieve local hospitals of the responsibility of caring for non-resident sailors. Victoria, growing in importance as a shipping centre, was designated as the site of one of these marine hospitals. Pearse prepared the plans in 1872 and construction started the following year on the Songhees Reserve to the northeast of the existing Lunatic Asylum. The first federal building on the west coast, the Marine Hospital remained in active use for only a few years, and burned down in 1914.

When Pearse received his appointment in 1872, Mallandaine's plans for the post office were abandoned and Pearse prepared a revised set of plans. In June of 1873, Scott was able to report that a new building was under construction in Victoria that would house the post office, savings bank and customs, Public Works, and Indian Affairs, with foundations of stone and walls of brick, arranged in such a manner that it could be sold easily if more space was needed. Pearse was also the architect of this structure. On June 27, 1873, an editorial in the *Colonist* railed against what the federal government was up to, claiming that these buildings were cheap, that there was too much talk and too little action, that workmen were fed up with waiting to get on with the job and leaving town, and that these buildings were falling "short of the just expectations of the people." By July, work on the post office had been halted, awaiting new plans for interior arrangements being sent from Ottawa. These changes were necessary as the Federal Government was now

Post Office (centre), Victoria

determined to erect a separate Custom House at the foot of Broughton Street instead of accommodating that department in the post office building. The post office was finally opened in September of 1874, but its troubles did not end there. In the Chief Architect's Report of June 30, 1880, it was noted that the front facade of this building was built of poor quality stone, and it had been decided to demolish it and reconstruct it in a more solid manner. The contract for the reconstruction of facade and interior alterations, according to the plans of **H.O. Tiedemann**, was awarded to **Smith & Clark** of Victoria. When the work was started, reinforcing rods intended to brace the structure were found buried in the ground, giving rise to further accusations that the original contractors were guilty of shoddy workmanship, but in the end the public appeared to be pleased with the rebuilt structure. The *Colonist* considered the changes, described as being in the "Eastlake" style of architecture, as having "strikingly beautiful proportions...one of the handsomest buildings on the coast."

One of the new federal responsibilities was also defence, and it was considered essential to provide a proper military facility on Vancouver Island for protection of the western gateway to the Dominion. Nothing happened until three years after Confederation, when Ottawa provided plans for a drill shed in Victoria. In 1867 the government had commissioned standardized plans for three sizes of wooden drill hall – small, medium and large – from Walter Moberly, an engineer for the Northern Railway of Canada; the Victoria drill shed was a variation on the medium-size standard plans. Located on Menzies Street behind the Birdcages, it was a wooden structure, 110 feet long, and thirty-five feet wide, with a two-storey high central section lit with banks of clerestory windows. Vertical

Drill Shed, Victoria

board-and-batten siding was used as cladding. This structure soon proved to be inadequate and was demolished when a new masonry drill hall was built just two decades later.

In 1866, Victoria had lost its status as a free port, and the colonial government reinstated the collection of customs duties. The federal government assumed this responsibility after Confederation, and construction began on a brick and stone Custom House on Victoria's inner harbour, designed by Scott's office in the Second Empire style in 1873. Although it was impressive in the context of its frontier setting, it was clearly the poorer country cousin of the structures being designed for eastern cities. The contract was awarded on April 30, 1874 to **Smith & Clark**, and construction was supervised by **H.O. Tiedemann**. Although the building was completed in 1875, the offices, including facilities for the Internal Revenue, Marine, and Fishery departments, were not fully occupied until June the following year.

Another sign of the federal presence was the construction of a secure institution in which long-term prisoners could be held, similar to those facilities underway in Stony Mountain, Manitoba and Dorchester, New Brunswick. New Westminster was chosen for two reasons: to compensate it for the loss of status as the province's capital, and the availability of a suitably large, government-owned plot of land. Wags in Victoria noted that its proximity to criminal activity would save the expense of transporting prisoners to Vancouver Island. The plans were prepared by **Canadian Department of Justice staff**. After three years of construction, and then standing empty for eighteen months after completion, it was finally opened in 1878. The finished building was roundly criticized. The plans were copied from those prepared for a flat site in Manitoba, and had not been adapted for this hillside location. The foundations prevented drainage of the gravelly soil, and the lower level was soon saturated. The upper storey remained unfinished, and was used for storage of "an immense number of double or weather windows, which are not required in this climate, a fact that must have been well known to the architect in charge of construction." For years, the administrative section of the building was considered to be grossly larger than necessary, while the cellblock was too small. Despite its initial problems the building still stands today, renovated for commercial use.

Just as the federal presence became manifest in the west, the political tides in Ottawa shifted. Sir John A. Macdonald's Conservative government was defeated in 1873 by the Liberals under Alexander Mackenzie, who had called the railway contract "a bargain to be broken." When the Liberals formed the new government in January, 1874, the railway was put on hold, and Mackenzie – a parsimonious ex-contractor who had been hurling charges of waste and corruption at the DPW – retained the Ministry of Public Works for himself. The Branch was forced to rely on more meagre resources, and started to undertake more designs in-house as a measure of economy, which led to the development of standardized plans that could be repeated in different parts of the country.

Throughout the 1870s British Columbians continued to express wide-spread dissatisfaction with the results of Confederation. There was serious question about how many people were actually benefitting from the connection with Ottawa. A whole new network of politicians and civil servants was now in place, and deficits had reappeared in the public accounts. The complaints continued until Macdonald's Conservatives were swept back into power in 1878, ushering in a grand new era of national

Federal Building and Post Office, New Westminster

expansion. The railway was back on the agenda, and two years later a blast of dynamite signalled the start of construction.

In the meantime, there had been an intense rivalry between Vancouver Island and the mainland for the terminus, but the matter was settled when the Fraser Valley route was chosen for the railway. Port Moody was chosen as the "end of steel," setting off frantic land speculation. The *Federal Free Homestead Act*, passed in 1874, allowed land grants to settlers if they were able to meet certain stringent conditions, including clearing and cropping of acreage. As part of its bargain with the federal authorities, the province was asked to grant a strip of land twenty miles wide on each side of the rail right-of-way, to be used for settlement purposes. When the 11,000,000 acres of the "Railway Belt" was finally surveyed, some of this land had already been disposed of, and much of the rest was found to be rocky and infertile, so a further block of 3,500,000 acres in the Peace River country was transferred to the federal government as compensation. In 1872 the province had passed the *Municipalities Act*, and many of the Fraser Valley communities petitioned for municipal incorporation in anticipation of the impending rush of settlement, including Chilliwack and Langley in 1873, Maple Ridge in 1874, and Delta and Richmond in 1879. The province had also passed the *Schools Act* in 1872, allowing for the introduction of a truly public, non-religious, school system.

In an effort to mollify the malcontents on the Island and quell talks of secession, enormous concessions, including one-fifth of Vancouver Island's land area, control of the coal fields on the Island's east coast, and $750,000, were given to Robert Dunsmuir in 1883 to build a rail line between Esquimalt and Nanaimo, which was rushed to completion by 1887. Dunsmuir's financial backers were the American railway magnates Huntingdon, Hopkins, Stanford and Crocker of San Francisco. Victoria remained the provincial capital, locked in place a few years later with an elaborate new Parliament Building. The construction of the Esquimalt drydock gave some stability to the Island's economy, but to those with open eyes the future now clearly belonged to the mainland.

As the country's population expanded over the next few years, so did the requirements for new and ever larger institutional buildings, and the DPW was

THE CANADIAN DEPARTMENT OF JUSTICE

DANA H. JOHNSON

Researchers often work under the misunderstanding that the central government's Department of Public Works (DPW) always prepared the plans for federal projects in British Columbia. In fact, this has been the practice only since 1962, when other departmental architectural services were disbanded. Between the completion of the British Columbia Penitentiary at New Westminster in 1877 and the transfer of architectural responsibilities to DPW in 1962, design work at federal correctional institutions in the province was under the control of the architectural staff of the Department of Justice, and the initial plans and appearance of federal institutions at New Westminster, William Head, Agassiz and Abbotsford were determined by Justice Department architects.

Having an in-house design staff achieved three clear objectives. First, it permitted the department to organize its institutions in keeping with its own correctional philosophy. Furthermore, it allowed the department to control the construction process, because it released the department from the Public Works practice of public tendering, and encouraged the construction of buildings by inmate labour through vocational training programs, albeit at the price of lengthy construction periods. Finally, Justice Department designs were less expensive than those by DPW because the former's staff paid even less attention to contemporary aesthetic standards than DPW architects did.

Though DPW architects claimed the credit for their authorship, the plans for the original sections of the British Columbia Penitentiary at New Westminster were prepared by Justice Department staff members, Thomas Painter and James Adams of Kingston Penitentiary. After DPW handed over the completed prison building in 1877, further design work at the site was carried out by Justice Department staff architects. Starting in the 1880s, they planned residences for the warden and the accountant, separate quarters for married and single staff, and a new wharf and combined bakery and laundry. The first major expansion of the institution came in 1904, when inmates began construction of two Justice-designed projects: a long narrow fireproof shops building, 1904-09, and a much-needed north wing, with 116 cells, 1904-05. To these were added the east cell-block, 1911-15; a combined kitchen, chapel and hospital, 1916-19; a laundry, 1922-24; a new administration building and gatehouse, 1924-29; a boiler house, 1930-31; and the west cellblock, 1932-38. The enclosing walls with corner towers were started in 1908 and completed in 1928.

The work of Justice Department architects was not limited to the New Westminster prison site. At the turn of the century, they designed a satellite prison at Convict Island on Pitt Lake, where inmates cut stone for institutional use. When large-scale civil disobedience by the Sons of Freedom Doukhobors wracked the province in the 1930s and the 1950s, Justice Department architects responded by establishing special temporary prisons adjacent to the New Westminster facility for those members convicted of crimes. In the 1950s, over-crowding forced the Justice Department to convert the former immigration station at William Head, near Victoria, to prison use, and when new institutions were forecast at Agassiz and Abbotsford in the early 1960s, in-house plans were drawn up, though Public Works supervised the actual construction.

Advances in correctional thinking have meant that very little of the extensive work done by Justice Department architects in British Columbia remains intact. The highly specialized character of their efforts ensured that this group of designers – whose associations with specific projects were hidden by the departmental practice of not always signing drawings – would have little, if any, impact on the architectural character of the province. Nevertheless, the staff of the Department of Justice deserves to be mentioned in the history of architectural design in this province.

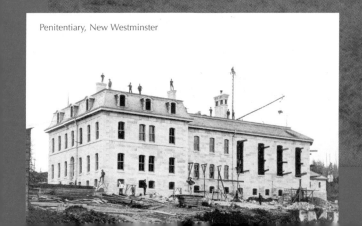
Penitentiary, New Westminster

hard-pressed to keep pace. Under newly re-appointed Minister Langevin, the Department set out to reflect the best architecture of the communities they were building in, but the designs provided for western settlements still fell short of the mark, both in size and prominence. The frontier settlements were growing so rapidly that by the time the federal buildings were finished, they were completely obsolete. Construction finally started on a much-needed Federal Building and Post Office in New Westminster. Plans for this modest and mostly unadorned example of the Second Empire style, among the last to be issued during Scott's tenure, were provided in 1881. Construction, which cost $17,000, dragged on until 1883; the building was lost in the Great Fire of 1898, necessitating a much larger replacement that finally reflected the city's status and population.

Thomas Fuller (1823-1898) succeeded Scott as Dominion Chief Architect in 1881 and during his fifteen-year tenure supervised the design of over 140 buildings across the country. The federal government was now determined to

Thomas Fuller

raise its profile through an ambitious building programme that would establish a national architectural identity, and Fuller, with his international reputation and experience with public buildings, was a natural choice for the job. He had received his architectural training in England, followed by a brief period working in the Caribbean, and then returned to England for several years. He immigrated to Canada in 1857 and set up a partnership with Chilion Jones in Toronto. The firm won two important competitions, the first in 1859 for the central portion of the new Houses of Parliament in Ottawa, and the second in 1863 for the New York State Capitol in Albany. Fuller later moved to New York state, working on the Capitol. In 1871 Fuller and Augustus Laver won the competition for the new city hall and law courts in San Francisco, and for a while they were considered to be in the vanguard of American architecture. Fuller was one of the early members of the American Institute of Architects, and served as its Vice-President from 1874-78. Under Fuller's leadership the Chief Architect's Branch began to explore the complex picturesque eclecticism of the late Victorian era, defining a new character for federal architecture in Canada. Accompanying the plans that's Fuller's office sent out from Ottawa was a new sophistication and sense of purpose that helped pull these rag-tag frontier settlements into a more cohesive urban form.

Post Office, Nanaimo

INDIAN AFFAIRS

DANA H. JOHNSON

In 1875, the Canadian government implemented a policy of restricting Aboriginal peoples to reserves. This approach required the construction of facilities, such as offices and houses for federal officials, farm buildings, schools and council houses, which would contribute to the explicit purpose of the reservations policy of assimilating Aboriginal peoples to the cultural values of the dominant culture. Architecture was to be an important component in this process of assimilation, for the design of buildings helped to convey the very cultural values which the government hoped Aboriginal peoples would adopt.

Matters relating to Aboriginal peoples have been lodged over time in various ministries: Interior; Northern Affairs; and National Development, Indian and Northern Affairs. Departmental annual reports and records indicate that Indian Affairs and private architects prepared plans for over 1,200 projects across the country before 1962, when the Department of Public Works took over all federal responsibilities for design. These projects included a wide variety of building and engineering works and were located on the thousands of reserves across the country. Roughly fifty of these projects were planned to serve the scattered Aboriginal peoples of British Columbia.

To make their jobs easier, Indian Affairs architects depended heavily upon standard plans in constructing buildings across the country, in the same way that other departments with their own design staffs did. In contrast to most departments in the late nineteenth century, the agencies responsible for Indian Affairs had very small staffs. As a result, they did not hesitate to hire private architects to work under departmental guidance in preparing plans, especially for large projects, such as Native residential schools.

The earliest plans to survive in departmental records appear to be those for a house for the resident Indian agent at Alert Bay, prepared by departmental architect W.A. Austin in 1887. A note on the plan indicates that a duplicate was used two years later for a building at Metlakatla. The largest group of plans was created by private architects for Native residential schools: there are extensive sets prepared by Vancouver architects **E.E. Blackmore** and Charles F. Perry, and a smaller group by Yale architect W.W. Barley for the Church of England residential school there. **G.W. Grant** contributed a set of plans for a mission school at Ahousat in 1904.

After 1900, plans were usually prepared in-house by the departmental architect, Robert M. Ogilvie, rather than by private firms, and were most often derived from standard plans. Ogilvie's proposals for day schools in Port Essington, Kitimat and Metlakatla, all prepared in May-June of 1906, were strikingly similar. His plans for a teacherage for the Chilliwack School at Skwak were borrowed from a standard plan, and those he prepared for the Kuper Island residential school in 1914 followed a formula which he had developed some years before and had already utilized elsewhere. (In the latter case, the department also obtained a second set of plans from the Nanaimo architect, **W. A. Owen**). Later departmental architects, Denis Chené and R. Guerney Orr, followed Ogilvie's lead in utilizing standard plans for designs for boarding schools at Sechelt, 1920, the Coqualeetza Institute at Sardis, 1923, and Kamloops, 1923-28.

In spite of the appointment of active professional departmental staff, private architects were still hired for many projects. When plans were required for a new residential school at the St. Eugene Mission, near Cranbrook, the department turned to a private Ottawa architect, Allan Keefer (though later additions were planned by departmental architects), and those for an addition to the mission school near Chilliwack in 1907 were prepared by the Vancouver firm of **Hooper & Watkins**. Fort George contractor, John Bronger of Bronger & Flynn Construction, provided plans and elevations for a new church and seventeen nearly identical houses at #2 and #3 reserves near that community in 1913. **S.M. Eveleigh** was hired in 1931 to design St. Bartholomew's Hospital in Lytton.

Except for those who attended Native residential schools, many Aboriginal peoples in British Columbia probably never saw a structure designed by (or under the guidance of) an Indian Affairs architect. The assimilative value of the architectural designs was likely considerably less than government policies intended. None the less, the efforts of departmental architects to design buildings which were both functional and instructive in the values of the dominant culture remain a part of the story of European–First Nations relations in Canada.

BENJAMIN WILLIAM PEARSE

1832–1902

DOROTHY MINDENHALL AND DONALD LUXTON

Although better remembered as a colonial administrator and an exceptionally competent surveyor, B.W. Pearse also provided designs for buildings when required. Born January 19, 1832 in Devon, England, he was apprenticed to a civil engineer in London. In 1851 he was the successful respondent to an advertisement placed in the London *Times* by J.D. Pemberton for an assistant engineer and surveyor for the Hudson's Bay Company on Vancouver Island. He arrived in Fort Victoria that November, at the age of nineteen, was apprenticed to Pemberton, and then became his assistant. In 1855 he was transferred from the employ of the HBC to the colonial government, retaining his position of assistant surveyor, and rapidly becoming a central figure in both the social and political life of the growing settlement. With knowledge gained from his surveying duties, Pearse also bought large tracts of inexpensive land, worth a small fortune after the Gold Rush of 1858. This allowed Pearse to build an impressive stone house, *Fernwood*, in 1859-60. He married Pemberton's cousin, Mary Letitia Pemberton, in 1862, cementing his position in Victoria's social and political hierarchy. Pearse acted successively as Surveyor-General for the Vancouver Island colony, 1864-66, Assistant Surveyor-General to the united colonies, 1866-71, and Surveyor-General, 1871-72. He also served as Chief Commissioner of Land & Works from August to November 1871, but was replaced after the provincial election.

In October 1872, he resigned as Surveyor-General to take over as head of the British Columbia office of the Federal Department of Public Works. In this capacity he was in charge of the first federal buildings to be built on the west coast. Pearse designed, and supervised the construction of, the Marine Hospital and the Post Office in Victoria, both 1873-74. He also supervised the construction of the Custom House, Victoria, 1873-75, and the federal penitentiary in New Westminster, 1874-78, from plans sent from Ottawa. He resigned from the Department of Public Works in 1879.

These earliest federal buildings had been criticized as "cheap," and construction was often delayed, sometimes taking several years, frustrating everyone. Pearse later recalled that Ottawa had treated the province "in a most scurvy manner," taxing heavily but building only minimal structures in "paltry little places, in exchange for votes." By the time he made these remarks in 1900, however, B.C.'s strategic importance had been recognized and the quality of federal buildings had been steadily improving.

His first wife died in 1872, and Pearse married a second time, to Sara Jane Palmer in 1876. He died on June 17, 1902 at the age of seventy, a wealthy and respected man. In his will he bequeathed $10,000 "towards the establishment of a university or other institute for higher education in Victoria." Pearse also was a generous donor to the Victoria Public Library, the Royal Jubilee Hospital, and the B.C. Protestant Orphans Home.

Marine Hospital, Victoria

JOHN TEAGUE
1835–1902

DOROTHY MINDENHALL AND
CAREY PALLISTER

Over a span of thirty years, John Teague can be credited with the design of approximately 350 buildings, a remarkably prolific accomplishment given the cyclic nature of British Columbia's economy. Although he was cognizant of the latest technological advances in construction and the building trades and employed them when appropriate, his buildings cannot be said to have introduced any innovations of style. Teague established a stable and long-term practice at a time when architecture was usually an intermittent occupation. His success must be attributed to a number of factors: skill in understanding the requirements and the wishes of his clients; organizational abilities; hard work; and his technical mastery in rendering drawings.

The eldest son of mine agent, John Teague, and Anna Tonkin, he was born on June 3, 1835 in Redruth, the centre of the tin and copper mining district of Cornwall. He was sent to Trevarth House Grammar School near Redruth, which had been established by mine managers to train their sons for the increasingly skilled mining industry. There he learnt mapping, linear and perspective drawing, surveying and mathematics, as well as Latin and natural history – skills which equipped him for a successful career in architecture; after the Grammar School Teague apprenticed as a cabinet-maker. Leaving Cornwall in 1856 he travelled to North America and spent some time in the gold fields of California before joining the rush to the Fraser River. After two seasons searching for gold, he settled in Victoria in 1860, set up in business as a carpenter and undertaker, married and had a family, and became, eventually, the city's most prolific architect of the nineteenth century.

On July 17, 1863 John Teague married Emily Birt Abington

who had arrived in Victoria, with her sister Catherine, on the brideship *Tynemouth*. John and Emily had six children, two of whom died in infancy. In 1865 Teague and Phillip Swigert formed the undertaking firm of Swigert & Teague. Competition was fierce – the main competitor being **Richard Lewis** – so Swigert & Teague branched out into construction and are known to have built two brick buildings. Their business ran into trouble in the economic downturn of 1867, independent financial administrators were brought in to manage the company on behalf of the creditors, and Teague was ousted the following January. Ironically, Swigert died in October 1868 of smallpox probably contracted "in connection with his professional duties," and the firm's assets were auctioned off.

Teague returned to carpentry and construction, gradually building up his business until, in 1873, he began advertising himself as an architect. He consolidated his position as a significant architect in Victoria by winning the approval of the building committee and congregation of the Reformed Episcopal Church for his designs for their new church. His plans, which were accepted over those of **H.O. Tiedemann** and **Edward Mallandaine, Sr.**, were in Carpenter Gothic style, a typically North American treatment of the Gothic Revival style of church architecture. The exterior cladding of vertical board-and-batten; doors and windows with pointed Gothic arches; wooden window tracery; the rose window; and the original exterior grey paint colours all pointed to Teague's understanding both of the ideas of the Gothic Revival in church architecture and of the work of American architects concerning appropriate form for wooden buildings. The Church of Our Lord has been carefully maintained by the congregation and, in 1998, was declared a National Historic Site.

While the Church of Our Lord was under still construction, during 1875, Teague was busy with other projects: a new audit office, and alterations to the supreme court for the provincial government; his competition entry for the Victoria city hall; various cottages, villas, and business blocks in brick and in wood; and a number of buildings in the Royal Naval Dockyard and Hospital at Esquimalt. For the following twenty years Teague followed only the profession of architecture and he never entered into a partnership – his experiences in the firm of Swigert & Teague had been a salutary lesson. Although most of his projects were in and around Victoria, he was working elsewhere, for example: the Occidental Hotel in Nanaimo,

City Hall , Victoria

1886; the Masonic Lodges in New Westminster, 1887, and Nanaimo, 1894; and a two-storey frame store in Vernon for W.F. Cameron, Vernon's first mayor, in 1892.

Victoria City Hall, 1878-91, now a National Historic Site, is perhaps the building for which he is best remembered. He won the design competition in 1875 with an elaborate Second Empire plan alluding to the style of the Federal Custom House, then nearing completion on Wharf Street. He submitted his entry under the motto "Work And Win," an apt epithet for this tireless worker, and one of which he was obviously fond as he used it again in his competition entry for the Provincial Royal Jubilee Hospital in 1887. Teague employed the Second Empire idiom, with varying levels of ornamentation, for most of his institutional commissions such as the Royal Jubilee Hospital, Victoria Public School, and the Masonic Temple.

Rose Villa, Victoria

Over half of Teague's buildings were residences and ranged from frame cottages to mansions, the most prestigious of which was *Burleith*, 1891, for James Dunsmuir. His designs were in the fashionable style of the day – Italianate and later Queen Anne eclecticism. For his many commercial buildings Teague usually employed the Italianate style with varying degrees of ornamentation, for example the Oriental Hotel, 1883 (addition 1888); Thomas Shotbolt's drug store, 1876; and law offices for the Honourable Theodore Davie, 1885. He did venture at least one very eclectic essay in what might broadly be called the Queen Anne idiom in his Reynolds Block built for the Canadian Pacific Land & Mortgage Company at the corner of Douglas and Yates Streets, 1889.

Although he designed a number of buildings in Chinatown, only a few can be securely identified: the Chinese Consolidated Benevolent Association building, 1885; a building for Look Den at 534 Pandora Avenue, 1884; a mixed-use building on Fisgard Street for Michael Hart, 1891; and a livery stable and carriage repair shop on Herald Street, also for Michael Hart, 1891. These last two buildings have recently been the subject of a sympathetic restoration and are now, with renovated tenements connecting them through the block, a condominium/small business complex.

Over the years Teague had a number of institutional clients for whom he designed and superintended construction of many buildings: the Royal Navy, for which he was responsible for all the buildings at the Dockyard and Hospital for over fifteen years; the Sisters of St. Ann; the B.C. Land & Investment Agency; and the City of Victoria. For the navy he was responsible for, in addition to the early wooden buildings, the Storekeeper's House (now the Admiral's House, HMCS *Dockyard*, 1885), and a cluster of seven brick buildings at the

Odd Fellows Hall, Victoria

Reynolds Block, Victoria

Naval Hospital 1888-91 (now in Museum Square, HMCS *Naden*). The Admiral's House is generally Georgian in plan, with Italianate decorative details; in massing and in details such as the plat stringcourse that marks the level of the first floor, a hipped roof, and tall chimneys, it resembles Naval Commissioner's Houses found in British yards. The naval hospital is laid out as a pavilion-plan hospital, based on ideas published by Florence Nightingale in *Notes on Hospitals* in 1863; she developed these ideas after seeing the military hospital at Scutari, Turkey, during the Crimean war, where more soldiers died of unsanitary conditions than of battle wounds. For the Sisters of St. Ann Teague designed the convent in Nanaimo, 1879; the east and central bays of the main convent in Victoria, 1886, following the style set by **Father Michaud**, architect of the first wing; and major additions to St. Joseph's Hospital in 1888.

The early 1890s were Teague's most prolific years. In 1891, after visiting San Francisco to study the latest in architectural style, he designed the Driard Hotel for Messrs. Redon & Hartnagle. This was probably his finest work and, in its heyday, the most prestigious hotel north of San Francisco. The lingering affection for the picturesque in commercial buildings was handled with restraint and aplomb.

Teague involved himself in civic activities: he served the city both as a councillor and mayor; he acted as surveyor and valuator for the Vancouver Island Building Society; he was involved in the early attempts to form an association to regulate the profession of architecture in B.C.; and he was an active and enthusiastic member of the Masonic Lodge. In 1885 he was elected councillor for the Johnson Street ward but did not

run for election the following year citing pressure of work. Emily Teague died in 1892 and John, with a daughter and young son still at home, soon married again. On December 28, 1892, a mere six months after the death of his first wife, the fifty-seven year old Teague married the fifty-year-old spinster, Eliza Lazenby. John and Emily's daughter, Catherine, later

BC Land & Investment Agency Ltd. House, Victoria, 1892

married **John Graham Brown**, a Scot who eventually became Dominion Government Architect for British Columbia.

In a landslide victory in 1894 Teague was elected Mayor and in 1895 he won a second term. His mayoralty occurred at a lean time as both the worldwide depression and the loss of trade to Vancouver began to adversely affect the economic life of the city. Teague's second term as mayor of Victoria was gruelling; he applied himself to the task of running the city as diligently and tirelessly as he had pursued his architectural practice in earlier times. But, by this time, few architectural commissions were available and new architects, notably **F.M. Rattenbury** and **Samuel Maclure**, were attracting the attention of commissioners. In failing health, he did little work after 1895 and died on October 25, 1902; he was buried in the family plot in Ross Bay Cemetery.

A PRACTICAL MAN: It can be seen at a glance that Mr. Teague wastes no words on professions or promises. His address is a business address from first to last. The address is characteristic. It shows the nature of the man and the bent of his mind. Mr. Teague is a man of affairs. He has no hobbies and does not bother his head about fads. He is a worker rather than a talker or writer. This is the kind of man the citizens ought to have to manage their city's affairs.

Victoria *Daily Colonist*, January 6, 1894, p.4

Driard Hotel, Victoria

ANDREW JOHNSTON SMITH
1840–1899

DOROTHY MINDENHALL AND
DONALD LUXTON

Until William S. Gore was hired as chief draftsman in 1875, the Provincial Department of Lands and Works hired local architects to prepare plans for government projects. In the building boom that followed Confederation in 1871, there were few available who could take on the work; although not specifically qualified as an architect, A.J. Smith, a well-known Victoria contractor, competent and familiar with local conditions, was retained to design several prominent buildings in the mid-1870s. Born in Edinburgh in 1840, Smith came to Victoria via Panama in 1862. He worked as a carpenter until 1864 when he took charge of a sawmill at Freeport on Puget Sound, and then returned to Victoria in 1865 where he worked in steamboat contracting. Smith later took over management of the Hastings Sawmill Company on Burrard Inlet, and in 1869 went to San Francisco to undertake sawmill work, returning again to Victoria in 1872. His first major contract after his return was for the construction of the second Christ Church Cathedral, designed by **H.O. Tiedemann**. In 1872 he entered into a successful partnership with fellow Scot, Graham James Clark; Smith & Clark built the Public School House in Victoria, 1875, and were involved in numerous projects at the Royal Naval Dockyard. In addition to his activities as a builder, Smith was retained as the architect for alterations to the House of Assembly, Victoria in 1873 and for the new Yale Court House in 1874, both now demolished.

Smith provided the plans in 1875 for the Provincial Lunatic Asylum in New Westminster, a site chosen so that the staff of the nearby penitentiary could provide assistance in times of emergency. Work commenced under the supervision of Charles McKeivers Smith (the brother of Amor de Cosmos) with bricks made at Langley. By 1876 there were new contractors on the project, **Thomas MacKay** and Alexander Robert Kennedy; the work was supervised by **James Kennedy**. Completed in 1878, the Asylum stands today within a complex of later additions.

Clark died November 7, 1884 at the age of forty-six, but the business was so well known that Smith opted to keep the name Smith & Clark. The *Northwestern Review* of July 1891 stated "Mr. Clark died about six years ago, and the business was assumed by Mr. Smith, who is now the sole proprietor of the Fort Street planing mills. Many of the finest buildings in the city have been erected by this firm, amongst which may be mentioned the customs house, post office, central schools, Bank of British Columbia, law courts, numerous business blocks and a large number of suburban residences." Smith, who also served as an alderman for six years, died at the age of sixty on September 21, 1899.

Provincial Lunatic Asylum, New Westminster

WILLIAM
DUNCAN
1832–1918

DONALD LUXTON

One of the most remarkable churches ever built in British Columbia was designed by an early Anglican missionary with no architectural training. In 1857, William Duncan was sent by the Church Missionary Society of England to work among the Tsimshian Indians at Fort Simpson. Five years later, with a dream of "aboriginal restoration," he led a small group of his native followers away to the site of the Tsimshian's old village, where they established a Christian community, Metlakatla, based on English precedents. In a short time they created an imitation of a "civilized" village. Duncan tried to emulate European customs but at the same time isolate his community from "harmful" outside influences, and developed a policy of self-sufficiency, including the establishment of local factories and industries. He also made numerous extended trips to England to learn various trades, such as the technical aspects of construction.

The centrepiece of the settlement, to be set dramatically on a hill above the rest of the buildings, was a large church that could hold the entire population of Metlakatla. In 1867 Duncan hired **Edward Mallandaine Sr.** to draw plans for his church, but he was most dissatisfied with the preliminary drawings, writing back to Mallandaine "Your design is altogether too grand and your working plan quite unintelligible to an amateur like myself." Duncan wanted a plain building "free of complications of grandeur which the building you have designed presents... The bare circumstances of a remote Indian village should have been sufficient for you to guard against extravagance in your work." Duncan returned the drawings and refused to pay Mallandaine's "unreasonable" fee.

Duncan decided to take on the project himself, and drew up eight different sets of plans, based on images from various British publications. The men of Metlakatla and Fort Simpson had learned their carpentry skills in Victoria, and Duncan consulted with them on the final plans during the fall and winter when the fishing season was closed. The foundation stone was finally laid on August 13, 1873 by Lieutenant-Governor Joseph W. Trutch. Massive timbers were used to build the structure. There was little applied or carved ornament, and the power of the building was vested in the simplicity and clarity of its structural expression. Substantial buttresses were required to support the enormous roof, and the sheer massiveness of the structure was relieved with bristling dormers, oversize roof cresting and a belfry with crenellated parapets. At the time of its dedication in 1874 it was reputedly the largest church north of San Francisco and west of Chicago. With Duncan in firm command of every aspect of its development, Metlakatla became a world-famous model for the treatment of Aboriginal peoples.

In 1887 Duncan split with the Church Missionary Society over his refusal to accept ordination and to allow his people Holy Communion. Also at odds with the provincial and

St. Paul's Church, Metlakatla (below and opposite page)

federal governments over the issue of land ownership, the combative Duncan went to Washington, D.C, in 1886 to build support for moving his settlement to Alaska. One of the first people he met was Henry Solomon Wellcome, who was writing a book about Metlakatla. Wellcome, who made a fortune when his pharmaceutical business Burroughes Wellcome & Co. introduced the gelatin-coated medicine capsule to the British market, became one of Duncan's strongest allies. The United States was reluctant to accept Indians from another country, so Wellcome organized a campaign to build public support. The American press was delighted to take up Duncan's cause, as the United States and Canada were involved in a dispute over the boundary between British Columbia and Alaska. After a meeting with President Grover Cleveland, Duncan returned to Canada, and in 1887 moved to Annette Island in Alaska with 600 of his followers and established New Metlakatla. The old community continued, but most of their existing buildings, and their landmark St. Paul's church, were destroyed by fire in July, 1901.

Wellcome continued to be involved in New Metlakatla's affairs, which turned into a curse for Duncan. In 1901, the forty-eight-year-old Wellcome married twenty-one-year-old Syrie Barnardo, daughter of the famous Dr. Thomas John Barnardo, the renowned benefactor of London's slum children who shipped thousands of "Home Children" to the colonies. The Wellcomeses' marriage was a tragic mistake; Syrie had a string of lovers, and in 1910 separated from her husband. In 1911, while still legally married, she initiated a liaison with author William Somerset Maugham, and despite his ambivalent sexual proclivities conceived his child. Maugham reluctantly married Syrie after her divorce, and they stayed together for ten miserable years. Syrie Maugham went on to fame as a noted interior designer, but had to endure the bitter words about herself in Maugham's autobiographical writings. Wellcome writhed in agony over the public humiliation of his messy divorce, and took up Duncan's cause with frightening vigour when he ran into the same problems with American authorities that he had in Canada. The obsessed Wellcome threw his fortune into rehabilitating Duncan's now tarnished reputation by trying to disprove allegations of business and financial mismanagement and sexual misconduct. Vast sums of money were spent in pursuit of the so-called Metlakatla Case, which constantly annoyed government authorities and prevented any resolution of Duncan's difficulties. Duncan died in 1918, but Wellcome refused to let go of the issue, and continued to battle the United States Government until his death in 1936, by which time the original purpose of his crusade had long since been forgotten.

WILLIAM
SINCLAIR
GORE

1842-1919

DOROTHY MINDENHALL AND
DONALD LUXTON

W. S. Gore, in his capacity as a civil servant, had among many other duties responsibility for supervising competitions, tenders and construction, and occasionally even designing, provincial buildings. Descended from the Earls of Arran, his father, William Gore, a civil engineer, came with his bride to Ontario in 1841, and their son, William, was born in London, Ontario, on June 29, 1842. Young William was sent back to Ireland to attend public school, and then returned to attend grammar school at Barrie, Ontario. He took a course in civil engineering at the University of Toronto, and then served his articles in Bowmanville. After he obtained his commission in 1864 he worked on railway construction in the western United States, and while in Iowa he met and married Jennie Blodgett.

When the Dominion government took over control of the North West Territories from the HBC, Gore was employed to survey the lands lying west of Fort Garry (near present-day Winnipeg). After a brief period working in the United States, he moved to Victoria in 1875, and was hired by the provincial government to complete surveys of the north end of Vancouver Island and the North Thompson River.

In December, 1875, Gore was appointed chief draftsman in the Department of Lands and Works. The 1877 *Sessional Papers* list him as a Draftsman, Land Office at an annual salary of $1,600; he was the only draftsman listed at the time. In 1878 he was appointed Surveyor-General of B.C., and in April 1891 he was promoted to Deputy Chief Commissioner of Lands and Works, a position he held until his retirement in 1905. He was also Gold Commissioner and Water Commissioner for B.C. In 1888 his younger brother Thomas Sinclair Gore, also a professional surveyor, moved to Victoria.

Although he called for many tenders on behalf of the province, it is difficult to determine which projects William Gore actually designed. He is known to have designed a public school at James Bay, 1883, and may have done work on other schools; he also designed the Provincial Gaol on Topaz Avenue, 1885-86. In general, though, his role seems to have been supervisory and managerial. Most significantly, he developed the specifications for the competition for the new Parliament Buildings, won by **F.M. Rattenbury**, and guided their construction through to completion.

Gore retired in 1905, remaining active in a number of hobbies and interests including boat-building and design. From 1916 he was in declining health; he died on April 11, 1919, and was cremated three days later in Seattle, as there was no crematorium in Victoria at the time. His widow went to Mexico City to live with their son, Thomas, an architect. Their other son, Arthur, remained in Victoria, where he worked as a draftsman and mathematical instrument dealer.

Provincial Gaol, Victoria

McKAY & TURNBULL

WILLIAM TURNBULL
1842-1912
THOMAS McKAY
1842-1887

JIM WOLF

St. Louis College, New Westminster

Thomas McKay and William Turnbull were important architects and building contractors who are credited with the design and construction of some of the most prominent Catholic buildings in New Westminster. McKay, a native of Osgoode, Ontario, travelled to California in 1867 and came to British Columbia by 1877. One of his earliest projects was his role as one of the contractors called in to finish, with his partner, Alexander Robert Kennedy, the Provincial Asylum during its four year construction fiasco. This partnership was also credited with construction of the landmark Second Empire-style St. Ann's Convent, built in 1877. Although his obituary credits him with the design of the convent, other sources credit his later partner William Turnbull. Born in Newcastle, England, Turnbull emigrated to Oakland, California before coming to New Westminster in 1876. He was a skilled builder by trade who would be appointed as New Westminster's first Building Inspector in 1911 only to die a year later at the age of sixty-nine. McKay & Turnbull are listed as partners working together in 1886 as both the designers and contractors for St. Peter's Roman Catholic Church in New Westminster, a highly detailed early Gothic Revival structure completed in 1886. They were also responsible for St. Louis College, a prominent Second Empire structure built in 1886.

While McKay was living in New Westminster at the Arlington Hotel and working on the construction of St. Mary's Hospital under the direction of **Mother Joseph**, tragedy struck. In the early morning of January 15, 1887 a fire broke out in the

hotel's lower floors, and McKay and two other men were trapped in their upper storey rooms. With his clothes on fire, he jumped to his death, to the horror of bystanders. The *Mainland Guardian* said of his passing "Poor McKay. He was a thoughtful, peaceable citizen and a very clever man. He prepared the plans for the Convent, the College and St. Peter's Church and he superintended the erection of these three fine buildings." Ironically his death also led the local press to launch a debate on building safety and the responsibility of owners, architects and builders. One editorial declared that there were hotels in New Westminster "constructed according to plans prepared by architects that are the most dangerous deadfalls in town." Thomas McKay was buried in the Roman Catholic section of the Fraser Cemetery and mourned by a large circle of friends.

William Turnbull

St. Ann's Convent,
New Westminster

ALAN EDWARD McCARTNEY

1852–1901

PAUL BENNETT

A.E. McCartney was a pioneer who contributed much to the settlement of the Lower Mainland. Born in the West Indies in 1852 of Irish descent, his father was probably stationed there with the Colonial Office. Alleged by some to have "dark blood" and "dark woolly hair," McCartney moved to New York, and then Montreal. He arrived by ship at New Westminster in approximately 1880, and was awarded a 600 acre land grant, primarily in the North Vancouver area but stretching as far as Pemberton Meadows. Officially employed as an engineer, although described by one relative as a "tally man," at Hastings Mill as early as 1882, McCartney also undertook numerous surveys and maps, including the first official map of the District of North Vancouver. McCartney Creek, now part of the Seymour River watershed at the east side of North Vancouver, bears his name today.

His first documented architectural project was the design of All Saints' Church, Ladner, 1881. McCartney was referred to in the Church minutes as an architect, living in New Westminster, providing a clue that he had previous training and experience. As the first Anglican church built after the 1881 incorporation of the Diocese of New Westminster, this was an important commission. The property was deeded by founding parishioner and settler, William H. Ladner. Bishop Acton Sillitoe was deeply impressed with the devotion of the locals, many of whom travelled by boat to the parish's initial school house location. All Saints' was an attractive wooden Gothic building with a very steep gable roof and a gabled side entrance. When the builders balked at shingling the steep roof, Ladner, who was also the local Justice of the Peace, sentenced a drunken offender to undertake the work. A strikingly similar design, with the addition of a tower, was likely prepared by McCartney in 1884-85 for Christ Church Anglican in Surrey Centre, or else his design was just copied.

In 1886, McCartney was very briefly in partnership with Paul Louis Françoise-Xavier Marmette (1859-1952), a civil engineer who worked for the CPR Land Department. In 1886, they called for tenders for the Church of Our Lady of the Rosary on Richards Street, which was completed the following February. McCartney designed additions and alterations in 1889, that enlarged this church at a cost of $5,000. In 1887, McCartney was retained to design the first building at the new City Hospital, Vancouver, located on a large lot at the southeast corner of Cambie and Pender Streets. Officially opened September 22, 1888, the Board of Health Chairman Dr. Lefevre commented that the facility was "one of the best equipped hospitals on the Pacific coast." In the 1890s other buildings were added to the site, and the hospital later moved to a new site in Fairview developed in the early 1900s. McCartney designed the short-lived one-storey brick Condell Block at the southeast corner of Homer and Cordova Streets, 1888, owned by Loyalist descendant, J. Condell, the father of financier and real estate developer, T.H. Condell. It was

All Saints' Anglican Church, Ladner

erected at a cost of $4,000, and when it was complete McCartney moved his office there. Typical of the rapidly expanding city, this building was demolished by 1892.

Other members of the McCartney family had also settled in Vancouver, and made their own mark on the early settlement. His brothers included William Ernest and Frederick C. McCartney, who together operated Vancouver's first drug store on Abbott at Water Street beginning in 1886. Their 1888 advertisement noted that their shop was a "depot for Crinivine, the infallible hair restorer." Frederick was said to have curiously disappeared at some point, and William moved to Kamloops. With his wife, Fanny (Mann), Alan McCartney had seven children, all males, only three of whom survived childhood. Fanny was an accomplished musician who taught the boys music at home. Their son, William Edward, became a "moving picture projectionist" while another son had an electrical business, and the third son moved to Oregon.

McCartney was also active in the public affairs of the District of North Vancouver, which at the time of its incorporation in 1891 extended from Howe Sound on the west to the North Arm of Burrard Inlet on the east. He was instrumental in the survey work necessary to build the roads that allowed the area to develop. McCartney was elected to the district's second Council in 1892, and served until his unexplained resignation early in 1895, after which he acted as municipal engineer. McCartney also served as a member of first council of the B.C. Institute of Architects, formed in 1891. Busy with other activities, his architectural career had effectively ended by 1892.

After a seven week illness, McCartney died of consumption early in the morning of May 8, 1901 at forty-nine years of age. The funeral was held at his home and he was buried in Vancouver's Mountain View Cemetery.

Church of Our Lady of the Rosary, Vancouver (top and bottom)

N. S. Hoffar

NOBLE STONESTREET HOFFAR

1843–1907

DAVID MONTEYNE

For several years following Vancouver's Great Fire of 1886, Hoffar was the city's most prolific architect. Many of his commercial blocks still stand in Gastown, as evidence of that boomtown era. The buildings also bear witness that, after years of wandering, Hoffar finally found a home in Vancouver. He was born to Mary Ellen (Stonestreet) and Ancius M. Hoffar in Washington, D.C. on December 12, 1843. As the second oldest in a large Catholic family of nine children, it was necessary for Hoffar to seek his fortune. Luckily, his dentist father could afford to provide a good education first, and Hoffar attended the Jesuit-run Georgetown College in his hometown of

Washington, D.C., where he completed Bachelor's and Master's degrees. It is probable that he was being groomed for the priesthood, but Hoffar had a wanderlust, and left his family in the 1860s, apparently visiting New Orleans, Panama, and New York before heading to the west coast.

Arriving in San Francisco by 1868, Hoffar taught bookkeeping and elocution at the Jesuit college for a year. Attracted by stories of fortunes made, he soon went to the rugged frontier mining country of Hamilton and Pioche City in Nevada, first as a deputy magistrate. When his employer lost the judiciary election, Hoffar moved on and for a time mined his own claims, writing to his family "If I intend to follow mining and expect to make anything out of it, you know I must follow the excitements." This proved unprofitable, so he was forced to take low paying office work with a mining company. As he wrote home: "What else could I do? Here up in the mountains, without a cent, not enough to grub me to the mouth of the canyon." Later, he complains that "here of course brains are below par for I do not get as much as the laborers in the mine." The surviving letters written home by Hoffar charted an ever decreasing hope of making his money and going home, but his strong ties with his family kept him going through bad times. He made light of his "straightened circumstances" with comments like "I am a good cook now, and very willing to cook when I can get anything to cook." In Pioche in 1870 he was living with a doctor, helping with amputations and also undertaking rudimentary dental work, and wrote home to his

DUNN BLOCK.

MILLER BLOCK.

Hospital Addition, Nanaimo

father, asking him to send any of his old instruments. Hitting the mining trail again, he reported killing a large cinnamon bear that blocked his path, driving a pick into its brain and knocking it down a three hundred foot cliff. Particularly touching is a letter home to his dog Jack, in which he advised his pet – no doubt self-referentially – that in the west one has to keep running "if you don't want to be cooked up into a stew."

Unsuccessful at mining, by 1872 Hoffar returned to teach in San Francisco where his education was an advantage. He also began teaching himself architecture and engineering in his spare time. About 1873, Hoffar fully immersed himself in this new interest by undertaking a three-year apprenticeship in the building trades. Upon completion, his first independent work was a two-year government surveying contract in Utah. From here, Hoffar's would be a continuous migration northward; the first stop was in Baker City, Oregon, where in 1878 he married Annie Odom who had migrated west from St. Louis. The newlyweds did not tarry: they lived in Walla Walla and Seattle, Washington. Hoffar designed at least one building in Seattle, the Bell's Hotel, before arriving in Victoria in 1883, in time for their fourth child to be born a Canadian.

Short stints in Victoria, Nanaimo, where he built an addition to the hospital as well as other large structures, and New Westminster, where he erected several buildings, brought him to Vancouver in 1886, just before the Great Fire. The disaster, of course, presented Hoffar with an ideal opportunity. The field of architecture in eastern North America had just begun to experience the tremors of coming professionalization; in B.C., registration or architectural education were unheard of. This

situation suited people like Hoffar who had a broad range of experience, but no official architectural training. Depending on the client, Hoffar would have been comfortable acting as architect, general contractor, or, no doubt in many cases, both.

After the inferno, Vancouver's city by-laws and common sense dictated that buildings should be of more fireproof construction. Hoffar designed some of the city's earliest brick structures, including two adjacent buildings on Cordova Street, the Springer-Van Bramer Building, 1888, and the Horne Block, 1889, a highly ornamented Italianate commercial building that once boasted an elaborate cupola above the Juliet balcony on its southwest corner. He submitted an unsuccessful entry in the 1889 competition for the new City Market, apparently not grand enough for the growing city; a much more elaborate design by **Sansom & Dawson** was chosen. Hoffar also designed other buildings for real estate developer, J.W. Horne, including a second Horne Block on Cambie Street, 1891, unusual for its arcaded ground floor, with recessed storefronts behind cast iron columns, and a lower level of retail stores below street level. Commissions abounded through the end of the decade as two-, three- and four-storey business blocks, hotels and single family homes were rapidly built. These eclectic buildings all share the zest for ornament, particularly along cornices and around windows, that defines the Italianate style popular at the time. Hoffar's most prominent extant work is the Dunn-Miller Block on Carroll Street (now home of the Army & Navy department store), which long-time city archivist, Major J.S. Matthews, claimed was "at the time it was built, in 1889, the largest, most pretentious, and important building in Vancouver." Hoffar also designed Thomas Dunn's grand residence, located at the intersection of Georgia and Thurlow Streets, 1889. The "elegant and spacious" eighty-room Hotel Metropole on Abbott Street, started in 1891 and completed the following year, was distinguished by the use of round-arched

Hoffar Residence, Vancouver

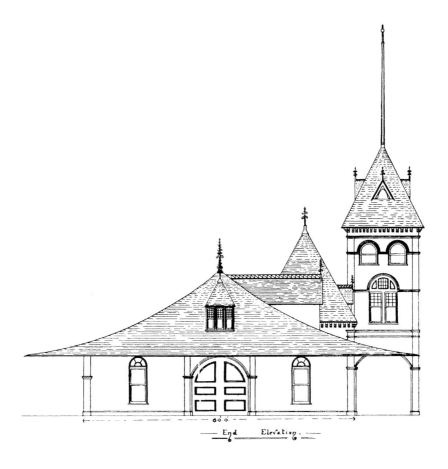

Competition plan for City Market, Vancouver, 1889

Court House and Second Horne Block (right), Cambie Street, Vancouver

Court House and Second Horne Block (right), Cambie Street, Vancouver

structural openings and projecting bartizan turrets. These varied commissions certainly prepared him for his most imposing project, the Court House addition of 1893-95.

The first Court House at Hastings and Cambie Streets had been designed by **T.C. Sorby** and completed in 1890, but Vancouver's exponential growth soon demanded a much larger facility. Hoffar designed a Palladian addition with a grand staircase and portico facing Hastings Street. A large raised cupola was topped by a statue of Justice, and there was more than a hint of the classical monumentality so prevalent in Hoffar's hometown of Washington, D.C. The Court House addition was quite controversial at the time, because the British-born and trained architectural establishment – a small group of men including Sorby and **R. Mackay Fripp** – took offence at Hoffar's untrained American pomp. This prejudice may also explain why Hoffar's prolific practice was ignored by *Canadian Architect & Builder*, the Toronto architectural journal that regularly published designs by Fripp, who acted as their west coast correspondent, and even mistakenly attributed the Court House addition to him.

Hoffar lost money in the recession of the mid-1890s, and he found little work in architecture. By 1906 the elderly Hoffar was employed by the United Supply and Contracting Company as architect and superintendent of the buildings the company

was erecting for the Grand Trunk Pacific Railway in Prince Rupert. Conditions were difficult, especially for someone his age, and in one letter home he professed homesickness, and that "I would be all right here were it not for the cramped quarters at night and cold drafts – I feel pretty good only a bad cold and pains in my chest." He fell ill in October the following year, and after a few weeks returned to Vancouver, where he passed away at home on November 12, 1907. The Prince Rupert *Empire* noted that "He was one of the early settlers of Vancouver, and few men were better known in that city than 'Dad' Hoffar. He has crossed the divide and may he take the right road when he comes to the place where the road forks."

His two sons would soon make names for themselves in the design and manufacture of seaplanes and boats. By the time of Noble Hoffar's death the family was living in Mount Pleasant at Main and 12th. For several years, though, they had lived in a grand, turreted Queen Anne house that Hoffar had built on the downtown corner of Georgia and Seymour just after the Great Fire. This prominent site is symbolic of the central role he had played in pioneer Vancouver society.

SAMUEL CYRUS BURRIS

BORN 1848

STUART STARK

Kains Residence, Victoria

S.C. Burris appeared on the architectural scene in Victoria with no fanfare. He was born in Ontario of an Irish father and a Scottish mother. The Burris family in Canada primarily came from Nova Scotia, where the name Burris was derived from the English name Burrows. Burris was first noted as a cabinet-maker in Victoria in 1879. He specialized in making and repairing office furniture, at moderate prices, and he kept "Flower Trains of all designs on hand." In 1880 he bid unsuccessfully to build a fence around Ross Bay Cemetery. In 1883 Burris was busy as an architect, designing a house for A. Allen and a conservatory for *Armadale*, the residence of Senator Macdonald; the conservatory was later enlarged by **T.C. Sorby** in 1888 for $1,500. He also designed a two-storey home, complete with a marble mantlepiece, for J.H. McLaughlan in 1883, that still stands at the northeast corner of Pandora and

McLaughlan Residence, Victoria

Fernwood. After the second Colonial Hotel on Columbia Street in New Westminster was lost to fire in 1883, Burris provided the plans for the replacement, a handsome three-storey brick structure with a ground floor arcade and projecting second storey bays. In turn, this hotel was destroyed by fire in 1898. In 1885, in partnership with **William H.L. de la Penotière**, Burris worked on the Victoria Club Rooms.

A noteworthy commission came in 1886, when he was asked to design a new home for the Premier of British Columbia, the Hon. William Smithe. Located close to the Parliament Buildings, the $9,000 home was two storeys in height, with ten rooms finished lavishly with oak mantelpieces and the best Minton tile hearths and facings. Plaster cornices and centres were in all of the principal rooms and special care had been taken with the heating and sanitary arrangements. The *Daily Colonist* commented that "the design is by S.C. Burris... and is evidence of his good taste and judgement." Regrettably, Premier Smithe died before he was able to move into his home, which must have been a blow to Burris's career.

Burris continued with his architectural practice, building a substantial $7,000 home for L.G. McQuade on Vancouver Street in 1888, and in that same year he sold his "real estate and architectural practice" to Mr. F. Bourchier. Having sold his business, Burris nevertheless continued to design buildings, notably: a glazed conservatory at Cary Castle (Government House), 1888; a three-storey brick warehouse on Broughton Street, 1889; and a house for Surveyor-General Thomas Kains on Dallas Road, 1889. He moved his office to the Burns Block in Bastion Square where he was close to his work as Supervising Architect for the new Law Courts, which had been designed by the ailing **H.O. Tiedemann**. He also designed a residence, *Aldermere*, for Dr. E.C.B. Hannington at Millstream near Langford, in 1889.

At the same time, Burris was occupied in a related business

Smithe Residence, Victoria

venture. In partnership with John Watson Keller, Burris had been operating a pottery company, unfortunately completely destroyed by fire on December 29, 1889. Though the business premises were rebuilt in 1890, it was soon after reorganized as the British Columbia Pottery & Terra Cotta Company with William Herbert Bainbridge acting as Secretary *pro-tem*. The company, with its works at Constance Cove in Esquimalt and an office downtown, produced all manner of sewer pipe and drain tile, chimney tiles and tops, and they proudly noted in their advertisements that ornamental work for buildings was a specialty. In the form of decorative red terra cotta, this ornament was used to good effect in *Jolimont*, an Oak Bay house designed for Bainbridge by Burris in 1892. Each of the four

chimneys was decorated with floral terra cotta blocks, and the firebricks in the six fireplaces were also stamped CONSTANCE, for the works at Constance Cove. Burris stayed on at the Company as manager, and in 1894 he was listed as living at 62 Queen's Avenue, sharing a house with five other men. His architectural experience continued to be useful, as, according to permit records, he was working on installing plumbing into houses he had previously designed.

In 1896 Burris left Victoria for Trail, where he had an office until he relocated to Vancouver in 1899. He is not known to have ever married and no record of his death can be found. What happened to him is unknown.

Jolimont, Oak Bay

HARRIS & HARGREAVES

PARTNERSHIP 1884–1888

**DENNIS
REGINALD
HARRIS**

1851-1932

MARY E. DOODY JONES

Dennis Harris and George Hargreaves belong to that group of hardy pioneers who endured much in the wilderness and contributed their skills to make British Columbia a place attractive for settlers. They came to British Columbia with abundant energy and technical skills, and were willing to try many occupations. As surveyors and civil engineers, they possessed enough skills to dabble in building design, but are best known for their maps and surveys. They proved themselves to be competent architects, working in a variety of styles that reflected the requirements and aspirations of their clients.

Hargreaves was born and educated in Manchester, England. He arrived in B.C. on July 2, 1862, as a gold seeker and tried to reach the Cariboo, but turned back after hearing the discouraging accounts of those returning. Hargreaves turned to surveying to earn his living, and spent much time during the 1860s-70s in the bush, where the life was one of continued hardship and deprivation in return for poor pay. His 1872 journal of the CPR's Bute Inlet Survey contains ironic comments on personal sufferings, including dysentery where one "cannot eat supper but part with what little is in me both ways." A life-long bachelor, he moved to Victoria in 1882.

Dennis Harris was born in Winchester, England on February 3, 1851. He immigrated to Canada in 1869, and in the 1870s worked as a civil engineer surveying the CPR route in B.C. In 1882-83 he was the City Engineer in Victoria. Harris's per-

sonal life was very different from that of George Hargreaves. Harris gained both a wife and social distinction in 1878 when he married Martha, the youngest daughter of the late Sir James Douglas. The couple were leaders in the cultural scene, and they had seven children of whom two boys and two girls survived to adulthood.

The significant architectural period for both men began with their partnership in 1884, a year which brought four commissions. Two were stores on Government Street, one for jeweler, Charles Redfern, and one for British property investor, Thomas Galpin. The Union Club, at the corner of Courtney and Douglas Streets, was their most impressive commission. The basement had service rooms; the main floor had club rooms; and the second floor had seven chambers for members. The eclectic facade was described in the *Colonist* of June 1, 1884 as a "sort of composite, in which the French style largely dominates." The building was ornamented with string courses of black-painted brick, with black mortar used for pointing the red brick.

In 1884 Harris & Hargreaves also designed a "commodious" wooden two-storey residence, measuring fifty-three by forty feet, at Michigan near Douglas Street, for David Leneveu, a feed merchant and charter member of the Union Club. The simple Victorian structure, with a front bay window and a

Union Club, Victoria

pentagonal angular arch over its front porch, was set on two large lots. Eclectic features of this house included diamond-shaped windows underneath the eaves, pointed window heads, and large front window panes for a conservatory. In 1885 Harris & Hargreaves transformed an 1860s colonial bungalow into a twenty-two room mansion, *Fernhill*, for MLA Charles E. Pooley. The resulting eclectic structure had Gothic Revival and Italianate elements, combined with battlements, parapets, and towers, probably influenced by Elizabeth, Pooley's wife, whose father, William Fisher, had earlier built the wooden "Fisher's Folly" in Esquimalt with similar references from an ancestral house.

Between 1885 and 1887 more buildings and additions were done for the 1000 block Government Street, including the Hamley Building at the corner of Broughton Street. Both partners continued surveying during this period. By 1888, the partnership dissolved and Hargreaves continued his surveying career full time. Harris worked in a variety of businesses, including a real estate partnership, begun in 1890 and sold by 1900. He took an extended trip to England that year to open "a London office where fresh and reliable information in regard to British Columbia will be supplied to all applicants." In 1913 Harris prepared plans of Victoria Harbour as a basis for further modifications. He also found time to be on city council 1887-89 and 1893-94, and by 1889 he was listed as a Justice of the Peace. Harris worked until close to his death in 1932, at age eighty-one.

In contrast to his partner, Hargreaves did not seem to have political ambitions, nor as active a social life, though he was a member of the Pacific Club. Hargreaves was known for his work in the church and, like his partner, was a faithful

GEORGE HARGREAVES
1825-1910

Geo Hargreaves

member of the Reformed Episcopal Church. In spite of, or perhaps because of, his early privations, Hargreaves was strong enough to continue working well into his old age. Two weeks before his death, in spite of health problems, he was laying survey cables for the Union Bank in Trounce Alley. Aged eighty-one, he died in 1910 with no relatives in Victoria, but "a host of friends."

Galpin and Redfern Blocks, Victoria

CHARLES E. APPONYI

CAREY PALLISTER AND
MARY E. DOODY JONES

Before coming to Victoria in 1884, C.E. Apponyi, an architect of Hungarian descent, had worked in Denver, Colorado, and in Sacramento and San Francisco. In Denver in 1875 Apponyi met a remarkable woman, Flora Haines. Born July 12, 1855 in Wisconsin to John P. Haines and Mary Avrill, she was university-educated and supported herself as a journalist and a writer. They married that same year and had three children, May, Victor and John; the latter died in childhood. The marriage did not last and in 1886, after being mistreated and abandoned by her husband, Flora divorced Charles. She then married John Loughead and they had two sons Malcolm and Allen. The three boys, Victor, Malcolm and Allen, were all mechanically inclined and had an interest in aviation. Victor became a writer like his mother and published *Vehicles of the Air* in 1909. His brothers went on to found the Lockheed Aircraft Corporation. They officially changed the spelling of their name in 1926.

From 1884-85, Charles Apponyi was living in Victoria and designed two significant buildings. The first was the Victoria Theatre, "the largest and costliest building" of 1885, costing close to $60,000. The thousand-seat theatre, three storeys in height, was "of brick with cement finish and in the Tuscan order of architecture." The overall design was an eclectic mix of three rather old-fashioned styles, given that in 1885 the Romanesque Revival was well underway. Mainly inspired by Italianate *palazzi*, each floor was delineated with different window treatments and pilasters. But there were also Gothic Revival features, particularly in the ground floor windows and the window treatment in the central bay. As well, certain classical elements were present such as the central pediment. The final result, however, was a handsome and impressive building.

Robert Dunsmuir, Chairman of the Victoria Theatre Co., personally accepted the plans on November 11, 1884, and tenders were called for the following March. Labour shortages and two court cases marred the construction. The first involved contractors Jones & Williams whose workmanship, according to the architect, was not up to standard, so their pay was withheld. This case ended up at the Supreme Court. The other case, settled in municipal court involved an altercation between Apponyi and fellow architect **Edward Mallandaine Sr.**; "C.E. Apponyi (Defendant) charged by Mallandaine (Plaintiff) with using threatening language. Prosecutor swore that the defendant called upon him last Saturday and accused him of writing

in an evening newspaper a letter headed 'Macaroni, the man with no brains' and at the same time threatening to horsewhip him, deeming the letter as casting aspersions upon him. The Defendant, Apponyi, was bound over for the sum of $50 and to be of good behavior."

Under the direction of Apponyi, the sewer for the Victoria Theatre was hooked up illegally so the theatre people said that they simply wouldn't use the bathrooms until the situation was rectified. In October 1885, Apponyi also took charge of designing the decoration of the new theatre for the visit of the Governor-General of Canada Sir Henry Charles Keith Petty-Fitzmaurice, 5th Marquess of Lansdowne; to achieve his desired effect he used 250 candles.

James K. Nesbitt claimed in 1945 that the architect's name could still be seen hand carved in the main View Street entryway even after the theatre, along with the adjoining Driard Hotel, became Spencer's Department Store. The structure was demolished in the 1980s to make way for the Eaton's Centre mall.

Apponyi's second commission was a grand home for the well-known furniture manufacturer, Jacob Sehl. Built in 1885 on Laurel Point with a commanding view of the harbour, the house was designed in the popular Gothic Revival style with bay and cantilevered windows, false shaping above the windows, finials and gothic decorative elements including ridge cresting, quatrefoils and scrollwork. A square cupola, more Second Empire than Gothic, graced the north end of the house taking full advantage of the view. The Sehl mansion, which cost $34,000, also featured a lavish interior with grand staircases, and was surrounded by a terraced garden. Unfortunately, it burned down in 1894 and Sehl's wife, Elizabeth, who never got over the shock, died six months later.

On July 8, 1885, The *Colonist* reported that Apponyi had been "dragged from retirement" and that he had won the competition for the Colorado State Capitol, although there is no evidence that his project was ever built. After leaving Victoria in 1885, Apponyi returned to San Francisco. In 1890 he won a $250 prize and the design competition for the Salt Lake City Municipal Hall. Construction began in the fall of that year and after sinking $20,000 into the building, it was deemed that both the site and the plans were unsuitable because "there seems to have been many questions regarding the safety of Apponyi's design as well as the actual costs, which appeared to have been underestimated." Apponyi was dismissed, and a new site and new architects were found.

The following news item appeared in the *Colonist* on October 19, 1893: "Apponyi, who designed and built the Victoria Theatre... has been arrested in San Francisco for the embezzlement of $2,000 from Mrs. Lucy Gibson, a widow." To date, this is the last known mention of Charles Apponyi, who seems to have been plagued with personal and professional problems throughout his life.

94   **Building the West**

Sehl Residence, Victoria

Sister Joseph of the Sacred Heart

MOTHER JOSEPH OF THE SACRED HEART

1823-1902

SISTER MARGARET CANTWELL

Mother Joseph, in her years of planning, building, and supervising, inspired workmen to achieve the buildings she believed important for ministry, buildings she planned and at which she often, personally, laboured. As founder of the Sisters of Providence missions in the west, she triumphed over many hardships and physical and financial challenges to establish a network of charitable services, including some of the first schools and hospitals in British Columbia, Washington, Oregon, Idaho and Montana. A towering figure in the history of the settlement of the Pacific Northwest, Mother Joseph was intimately involved in the design and construction of many of these seminal buildings.

She was born Esther Pariseau, on April 16, 1823, in St. Elzear, Quebec, and received her early training in carpentry from her father, who owned a carriage shop. Although she was a girl, he encouraged her propensity with hammer and saw, shared with her his own insights about human nature and quality work, and soon realized that few, if any, could ever rival his daughter in understanding tools and structural procedures.

After entering the Sisters of Providence novitiate in Montreal just after Christmas 1843, she learned of the Pacific Northwest missions and longed to go. In 1856, with four other sisters of her community, she left Montreal for Fort Vancouver, Washington Territory. Within a few months, she was renovating a small wooden building that would serve as their home. In the 1860s she pioneered in establishing health care and educational facilities in the area, and struggled to pay the accrued debts by begging at mines. Her ministry reached north of the border into British Columbia, and some of the major accomplishments that resulted from her faith in God, her trust in her co-workers, and her great love for the people she had come west to serve, included hospitals in Vancouver and Cranbrook, a school in the Kootenays, and an orphanage in New Westminster, all built between 1885-1901. Construction began in 1886 on St. Mary's Hospital, in New Westminster; during the course of construction the contractor, **Thomas McKay**, was killed in a hotel fire, and all his papers lost. Mother Joseph came from Vancouver, Washington to personally finish the hospital, which opened on May 24, 1887.

Jean-Baptiste Blanchet (1839-1913) played a considerable role in a number of Mother Joseph's projects, acting for years as her architectural assistant and *confidante*. Born in Cacouna, Temiscouata County, Quebec, he arrived at Fort Vancouver, Washington in 1866 with his great-uncles Archbishop F.N. Blanchet of Oregon City, and Monsigneur A.M.A. Blanchet, Bishop of Nisqually. Jean-Baptiste Blanchet worked for the western missions in a number of capacities but showed a facility for carpentry and architecture. Mother Joseph "was not long in perceiving that a veritable treasure had been sent in the person of this able and virtuous young man," and often left him in charge of supervision while she continued with projects in other areas. He called for tenders, and was likely the designer, for the first St. Paul's Hospital in Vancouver, 1894.

In 1900 Mother Joseph, at the age of seventy-seven, planned and supervised her last architectural work, an orphanage in New Westminster to replace one earlier lost to

St. Mary's Hospital, New Westminster

fire. Mother Joseph, in a letter to Mother Antoinette, Superior General, July 9, 1900, pleaded "I ask you, Mother, to grant the favour of this beautiful name, Providence Orphanage. It is probably the last 'child' I will have the honor of holding over the baptismal font." The plans were drawn by Jean-Baptiste Blanchet for a four-storey brick building with a frontage of 141 feet. The contract for construction was let to H.J. Williams of New Westminster, and it was completed in 1901.

Artistically gifted as well, Mother Joseph adorned her buildings, particularly the chapel of Providence Academy, with her beautiful woodcarvings. Her career as an architect ended only with her death in 1902. In 1980, a kneeling statue of Mother Joseph, fittingly surrounded by her carpentry tools, was presented by the State of Washington to the Congress of the United States and placed in the National Statuary Hall in the Rotunda of the Capitol.

She had the characteristics of genius: incessant works, immense sacrifices, great undertakings; and she never counted the cost to self... God had endowed her with talents rarely found in a woman. She excelled not only in feminine arts, from the most ordinary to the finest, but she was also skilled in works considered the domain of men.

Mother Mary Antoinette,
letter to the Sisters of Providence community,
January 24, 1902.

Providence St. Geneviève Orphanage, New Westminster (below and opposite)

expansion and consolidation

of settlements in the Imperial Age

3

HOTEL VANCOUVER IN 1887

THE
COMING
OF STEEL

Two good genii named Enterprise and Improvement perform feats as
wonderful as those related in the Arabian Nights. They reclaim the wilderness literally, making it blossom as the rose. They build a few houses on a virgin tract; next year they build a few more... the fifth year a
still greater number, and establish a water supply, a sewage
system and gas works, and so on, until a populous town extends
through the valley and climbs up the side of the hills. A distant
mountain top, outlined against the sky, is all that is left of the
virgin tract.

R.W. Shoppell, 1887

WHAT
PLUCK
AND
ENERGY
CAN
ACCOMPLISH

Donald
Luxton

I hear the tread of pioneers,
Of Cities yet to be,
The first low wash of waves which soon
Shall roll a human sea.
The rudiments of Empire here
Are plastic yet and warm,
The chaos of a mighty world
Is rounding into form.

Nanaimo *Free Press*, February 20, 1893, p.1.

After years of controversy, foot-dragging and political maneuvering, on November 7, 1885, Donald A. Smith, the chief financier of the Canadian Pacific Railway, drove the Last Spike at the isolated mountain town of Craigellachie, British Columbia. The first passenger train on the "Imperial Highway" arrived in Port Moody on July 4 of the following year, but the CPR had already come to the conclusion that their needs would best be served by the establishment of a deep-water port, and Burrard Inlet was the obvious choice. In exchange for extending the line to the tiny settlement of Granville, the province gave the CPR a generous and wholly unnecessary land subsidy of 6,000 acres. To gild the lily, private land-owners along the waterfront donated a one-third interest in their property to ensure that the CPR would build railway docks on Burrard Inlet. New Westminster was connected to the CPR's main line in 1886, setting off an explosion of building activity, with new brick blocks being built one after another along Columbia and Front Streets. With the intention of making their line even more profitable through the development of a tourism network, the CPR began an extensive building campaign across Canada of luxury railway hotels and landmark stations. Sir William Van Horne declared that "Since we can't export the scenery, we shall have to import the tourists."

The progressive western march of the railway had created a momentum of settlement, and promoted the establishment of an economy based on the exploitation of natural resources. The province's seemingly unlimited potential was widely publicised throughout Eastern Canada, the United States, and Great Britain. Many restless settlers followed the railway in the 1880s, seeking their fortunes throughout the western lands. Towns sprang up along the new rail line, which allowed ready access to the agricultural land of the Prairies, large ranches in B.C.'s interior, new mineral claims, endless stands of untouched timber, and the vast fish stocks of the Pacific. The infrastructure for permanent settlements was established, and a new crop of immigrant architects found a bustling frontier economy eager for their talents.

Granville was incorporated as the City of Vancouver on April 6, 1886. The rag-tag settlement was annihilated by the Great Fire just two months later, which provided an excuse to build bigger and better masonry structures more appropriate to its new status. The blasting of stumps and the noise of hammering was heard night and day. "Terminal City" rose like the Phoenix in time for the arrival of the first passenger train, pulled in by Engine #374 on May 23, 1887, the eve of the celebration of Queen Victoria's Golden Jubilee.

First City Hall, Vancouver

Vancouver's growth was explosive, and architects and builders struggled to keep up with the demand. As stated in a CPR promotional pamphlet in 1887: "The city is new indeed; only one or two of its many buildings were here twelve months ago – a forest stood here then. The men who built the town could not wait for bricks and mortar, and all of the earlier houses were built of wood; but now many solid, handsome structures of brick and stone are going up, and there is more of a come-to-stay look about it all." Expediency was the order of the day. The useful life-span of a building could be quite short, and if it wasn't large enough it would quickly be added to, moved out of the way, adapted to a new use, or demolished and rebuilt. An example was Vancouver's first city hall. Immediately after the fire the City rented quarters in an Oppenheimer Brothers warehouse at Powell and Carrall Streets, but a modest frame city hall building on Powell Street, designed by John P. Lawson, was completed by September 1886; Lawson (c.1833-1896), the City Engineer from 1886-90, was also responsible for the layout of Mountain View Cemetery in 1887. Almost immediately after the completion of City Hall, **W.T. Whiteway** was hired to expand it with additions, completed in 1887. The new accommodations were derided in the local press: "The new Council Chamber looks as if it had been built for the express use of the members, and says plainly that the ratepayers are not wanted here. Possibly the want of funds, or a violent fit of economy, is the cause of the cramped dimensions. There is not space even for a supply of fresh air. When the popular habit of smoking is added, the non-smokers in defence of the principles of health of body and soundness of mind, might fairly protest against all artificial methods of vitiating the atmosphere." The following year **Mallandaine & Sansom** were hired to expand the building again, even more extensively this time. This utilitarian structure served as City Hall only until 1898, after which it was used as the Police Station. The city government moved to "temporary" quarters on the second floor of the Market Building on Main Street, where it remained for several decades.

As settlements increased in size, building types and styles became more refined, and those made newly rich by the burgeoning resource industries wanted to boast about their wealth. The result was that many architects, while providing functional space, also dressed the facades in overblown, fashionable styles with fanciful ornamentation, designing astonishingly inventive symbolic pastiches that were inspired by, and demonstrated, colonial ambitions. Drawing on historical motifs to increase their legitimacy, these facades became backdrops, essentially stage sets, for the evolving settlements. Solid commercial structures and sprawling dwellings demonstrated ambition, greed, pride and hubris, anchored and watched over by the ever-present highest point in town, the church spire. Ornate residences designed in the newly popular Queen Anne and Italianate styles conveyed values of social refinement, hospitality and graciousness, and attested to their owner's character and refinement. The development of these detached single family dwellings in suburban areas – surrounded by landscaped lawns and like-minded Christian neighbours – epitomized the family as the central unit of the newly-genteel society, and gave concrete manifestation to shared cultural values, demonstrating how far the crude frontier towns had evolved in just a few short years.

The flow of capital that enabled the rapid maturation of the frontier communities was very different than the banking and investment system that we know today. The earliest settlers arrived before financial institutions could be established. Speculative land development happened quickly and with little regulation, and those who took risks could make quick profits, which suited admirably the aspirations of those who had moved this far to make their fortune. Much early development was backed by British investment, as the great majority of the western settlers had ties to the Mother Country, and despite potential risks, overseas investments were often surprisingly lucrative. At this time of Imperial expansion, there was a general sense of optimistic entrepreneurialism, fuelled by seemingly unlimited available land and natural resources. The completion of the transcontinental railway, and the linkage of world-wide trade routes, seemed to promise a continuing flow of good, solid profits.

In this overheated atmosphere, banking became very competitive. No one could predict which of the instant settlements along the railway would survive. In the early 1880s, banks fought for the opportunity to be the first to establish in potentially stable settlements across western Canada, sometimes opening up for business in hastily-built log structures or shacks. Within a few years, every sizable settlement boasted at least one major bank, usually housed in an ostentatious Italianate structure that was one of the largest

Glacier House, Glacier, B.C.

FINANCING THE VICTORIAN HOME

DOROTHY MINDENHALL

For immigrants all over the world, owning land and their own home was their most cherished objective; these possessions signified that they had succeeded in their new country, and were markers of prestige, acceptability, and respectability – but borrowing money to pay for housing was not the easy matter it is today.

Wealthy businessmen, professionals, and government officials were able to buy and build without recourse to borrowing; but for the middle- and working-class often the only way to achieve these goals was to borrow money. Land and home ownership were so important to the middling sort that they would save and borrow to finance these possessions to the extent that they would not agree to diverting money to pay municipal tax increases to finance the supply of services such as sewer and water. Banks in Canada were forbidden by the 1871 *Bank Act* from selling mortgages, a situation that remained until 1954, so other sources of funding had to be found if the immigrants' dream of a home of their own was to be realized. As soon as they had the money, they would either build their own home – sometimes based on a pattern book design – or purchase a speculatively-built house. Lower- and middle-class housing was less likely to be architect-designed or custom-built.

In Victoria, the Vancouver Island Building Society, incorporated in 1884, was one source of funds for mortgages. More like a credit union than a bank, the building society accepted the savings of its members and from time to time held a "draw" or lottery to decide which members would be given a mortgage. As the debts were repaid, money became available for other members to obtain loans for land and homes, which they often built themselves. This was a "terminating" society – once all the members had a mortgage and obtained their own home, it was wound up. Balloting for mortgages gradually fell into disrepute as it "attracted gamblers as well as genuine house-buyers."

In the second half of the nineteenth century a massive amount – billions of pounds – of British capital was invested abroad. One reason for this outflow was the decreased demand for capital investments in Britain where, after nearly a century of industrialization, the economy was growing at a slower pace and there was little demand from industry; as well, the birth rate was falling so there was decreased demand for capital investment in housing. A new class of investor – the "reformed gentlemanly class" – emerged in wealthy industrial Britain and investing in the empire and beyond was considered a profitable opportunity. Thomas Dixon Galpin, of the London publishing house Cassells, Petter, Galpin & Co., was a member of this new class; he began investing in British Columbia land using the Victoria firm of Allsop & Mason to manage his transactions. Ultimately this became the British Columbia Land & Investment Agency, Ltd., with headquarters in London, England, and offices in Victoria, Vancouver and Nanaimo. Through this agency, and its affiliate the Canadian Pacific Land & Mortgage Company, capital from Britain was used, on behalf of the investors, to lend as mortgages, as well as to buy land to be leased for income, and construct buildings to be rented for income.

Large amounts of British money for investment in mortgages, land, and buildings continued to flow to Canada until the economic collapse that preceded the First World War.

buildings in town. There were dozens of competing chartered banks, including the now-disappeared Molson's Bank, Merchant's Bank of Canada, Union Bank, and the Bank of British Columbia, but over time they merged their assets and consolidated into the few larger conglomerates still in existence today.

The chartered banks, however, were only a small part of the financial web of investment. Forbidden by Dominion law to speculate in real estate, they had no role to play in the provision of chattel mortgages, which were often privately held. The administration of personal accounts and estates was also handled by trust companies, which usually paid more interest on deposits and charged less for loans than the banks. Trust companies and insurance brokers also acted as conduits for vast amounts of foreign – primarily British – and domestic investment capital. This enormous influx of investment helped provide the infrastructure for the development of the rapidly expanding province, and enabled the spectacular growth of numerous communities, many of which seemed to appear almost overnight.

Some entrepreneurs arrived with their own capital, that they used to speculate on the future of these virtually empty new western cities. One

example was English-born real estate speculator, Harvey Hadden, who arrived in Vancouver in the city's very early days. He had been travelling in the United States, making purchases of real estate in different cities, and was taking the boat from Seattle to Vancouver when he fell into conversation with another man, who mentioned to Hadden that it was a "peculiarity of community development, especially in the cities of the North-west, that the first street up from the waterfront invariably became a wholesale thoroughfare and that the second street usually developed as the retail district centre." Hadden arrived on a Sunday, and was thoroughly unimpressed with the sleepy city, but applying the logic he had just learned, found the property at the northeast corner of Granville and Hastings Street, two blocks up from the water, to be of the most interest. Deciding not to pursue it any further, he booked his passage by rail back east. He met a man from Boston in the train's smoking compartment, and when Hadden told him that he had not been much taken with Vancouver, he was told in no uncertain terms that he was mistaken, and that the Terminal City had the best prospects in the Canadian West. Hadden got off the train at Sicamous, and returned to Vancouver to talk to a real estate agent. He purchased the lot he was interested in for $25,000, but afterwards was told that as the agent tagged him as a "green Englishman," $5,000 had been added to the purchase price. This was of no great concern to Hadden, for when he sold the lot to the Royal Bank in 1913, it was considered the most valuable piece of property in Vancouver. This was just one of the lots Hadden acquired, and he returned to England after acquiring $50,000 in property, and this turned out to be just the first of his buying trips to Vancouver. Over the next several decades, Hadden returned a number of times to buy more lots, usually hiring his friend, **S.M. Eveleigh**, to design a building for them so that they would not sit empty and lose value. After this chance encounter on a train, Hadden went on to become one of the wealthiest land holders in early Vancouver.

Many in the architectural profession slavishly devoted themselves to catering to the needs of the newly arrived and rich entrepreneurial classes. Their bombastic and fanciful designs boasted of newly-acquired wealth, well-suited to the frontier antecedents of the emerging urban centres. Providing a counterpoint was an emerging school of design that promoted the evolution of a local architecture, rooted in the local landscape and natural materials, reflecting the growing influence of the Arts and Crafts movement. This split was illustrated by the withering comments of an anonymous writer, almost certainly **R. Mackay Fripp**, who took a swing at nearly everybody in his description of Victoria's buildings in 1899:

> The Five Sisters Block (**Sorby & Wilson**, 1890-91) though not exactly a new building is one of the more recent improvements, a plain red brick building with mansard roof, with refined detail throughout, marred by its execution in painted metal, a hopelessly lifeless material to design in. The Bank of British Columbia (**Warren H. Williams**, 1885-86) though not lacking a certain degree of dignity is rendered trivial by its overload of cement and metal ornament, some of which is flimsy; the style is a conventional style of Italian; the Driard Hotel (**John Teague**, 1890-91) from its size and importance as an hostelry next commands attention, which its architectural merits could not earn for it; the Board of Trade Building (**A. Maxwell Muir**, 1892) and the new home of the Colonist newspaper (**Thomas Hooper**, 1897) are attempts in that species

PROVINCIAL LAND SURVEYORS

FROM 1891

DONALD LUXTON

The profession of surveying was recognized and regulated decades before either architecture or engineering. *The Land Surveyors' Act* of 1891 established a government-appointed Board of Examiners, which included the Surveyor-General, charged with the admittance of new members, and the discipline of members guilty of negligence or corruption. Those practising in accordance with the Act were authorized as "Provincial Land Surveyors" (PLS). This Act was replaced by the *British Columbia Land Surveyors' Act* of 1905, which established the Corporation that still regulates the profession. Those recognized under the Act were now designated as "British Columbia Land Surveyors" (BCLS).

Once registration was in place, surveyors gained professional prestige not enjoyed by architects or engineers. Many of the new surveyors, especially in smaller towns, remained flexible in how they promoted themselves, and their new status led them to dabble in architecture. Although their names turned up as architects, their actual output of building designs was likely minimal, as the bulk of their work was undoubtedly surveying, civil engineering, or contracting – more valuable and marketable skills on the evolving frontier. This was especially evident in the early 1890s, likely a response to rapid expansion in smaller towns at the time. Examples included John Abraham Coryell (1861-1912) and John Purvis Burnyeat (1855-1923), both Provincial Land

Frederick Bernard Pemberton

John Purvis Burnyeat

Surveyors in Vernon, who advertised as architects for just one year, in 1891. **Robert Henry Lee** (1859-1935) of Kamloops, although primarily a surveyor and civil engineer, also advertised his architectural skills for many years. Frederick Bernard Pemberton (1865-1947) advertised as an architect in Victoria, 1892-93; William Alfred Bauer (1867-1932) advertised as an architect in 1893 in Vancouver; and Arthur Oliver Wheeler (1860-1945) was listed as an architect in Armstrong, 1893-94. The economic recession of 1893, and a rising desire among the province's architects to achieve their own registration, ended this apparent cross-over between the professions. However, many of these men were technically competent in both fields, an example being Alfred Harold Green (1879-1941), who turned to design and contracting in and around Nelson to support himself when survey work was slow.

Over time the professions became increasingly specialized. By the time architecture and engineering were finally regulated in 1920, the cross-over had ended, even though these pursuits remained complementary.

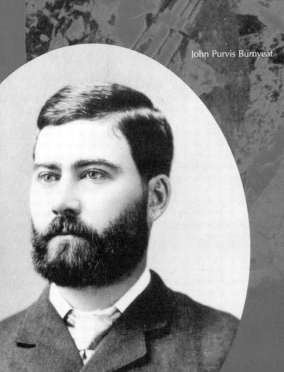

The federal government recognized the need to expand and consolidate
its presence in the booming new West. Landmark structures were started in
the key cities, providing immediately recognizable symbols of a federal
presence. This was evident in the designs for new post offices, executed in a
distinctive blend of Gothic Revival, Neo-Romanesque and Second Empire
forms, punctuated by masonry gables and on the more prominent examples,
tall clock towers. Plans were provided by Thomas Fuller for structures
throughout British Columbia, including imposing stone post offices for
Nanaimo, 1882-84, Vancouver, 1889-92, and Victoria, 1894-98, each one
grander than the last. The contract for the Vancouver Post Office was signed
with local contractor A.E. Carter in August, 1890. When Carter was unable to
finish the work, **C.O. Wickenden**, the local supervising architect, called for
new tenders in September, 1891. The project was taken over by Thomas
Tompkins of Brockville, Ontario, and finally completed in 1892. This was the
city's first purpose-built general post office, and was located in the heart of

Molson's Bank, Vancouver

the burgeoning new business core at Granville and Pender Streets. It was faced with stone, three storeys high with a basement, and eighty-one by sixty-four feet in dimension. When the new post office was opened a block away in 1910, this building was gutted, and fitted up to accommodate other government offices, sold in 1925, and demolished the following year.

Vancouver was booming, and confidence in the new city was being demonstrated through English and eastern Canadian investment. Business connections sometimes brought sophisticated architectural designs to this brand new city. One example was the landmark Bank of Montreal Building, built at the corner of Granville and Dunsmuir Streets, 1892-93. The plans were sent out by a Montreal architectural firm, Taylor & Gordon, the partnership of Sir Andrew Thomas Taylor (1850-1937) and George William Hamilton Gordon (c.1854-1906). **C. O. Wickenden** acted as supervising architect for the project. Taylor was a Scot who trained and practised in England before he and Gordon set up an office in Montreal, where Taylor's maternal uncle, George Drummond, was a leading industrialist. Their practice was very successful, and they worked extensively for McGill University and for the Bank of Montreal, designing their branch offices across the country. Taylor & Gordon also designed the branch office for the Molson's Bank, 1897-99, built with dark stone shipped from Calgary and supervised by **W.T. Dalton**, which stood at the northeast corner of Hastings and Seymour Streets. Many other grand commercial blocks started to appear along Granville and Hastings, which were developing as the great commercial strips of Vancouver. The suburban areas surrounding Vancouver were also growing, with Coquitlam and the District of North Vancouver being granted municipal incorporation in 1891, and Burnaby and South Vancouver the following year.

Victoria was feeling left out by all the building activity on the mainland, and steps were taken to enhance some of the city's institutional structures. When the City Council was discussing the possibility of a new drill hall in 1890, Alderman Wilson commented that "the Dominion buildings in Victoria were the shabbiest government buildings in Canada." After Council approved the payment of $5,000 towards the construction of the new drill hall, plans were provided by the Militia Department for a large structure for the 5th British Columbia Artillery Regiment, to satisfy the need for the expanding militia. The Militia Department did not become responsible for its own design

Post Office, Vancouver

Drill Hall, Victoria

and construction until 1884, when Henry James, an engineer with the DPW, was transferred to the newly established Engineering Branch of the Department of Militia and Defence; when James died in 1893, design responsibilities reverted to the DPW. James provided the design for the Victoria Drill Hall, the exterior of which reflects the Romanesque Revival, with round-headed arches capping the window bays. Tenders were called in March, 1892, and the existing drill shed, built in 1874, was demolished by June. Work proceeded slowly, and the new facility didn't open until January of 1894.

Despite the uncertain economic prospects in 1892, few appeared willing to give up the optimistic dream of unlimited western expansion. In one year, between 1891 and 1892 the number of architects advertising in the Williams *B.C. Directory* almost doubled, from twenty-six to forty-six. Great deposits of minerals were found throughout the Boundary country and the Kootenays, and the province's timber displays had attracted much attention at the 1893 Chicago World's Fair. The existing provincial government buildings, the much derided "Birdcages," were now considered woefully inadequate, and nowhere near pretentious enough as a symbol of the province's increasing prominence. Notice of an anonymous competition was given on June 16, 1892, and by the time it closed on September 30, sixty-two contenders had entered. Nineteen individuals or teams from British Columbia entered, sometimes with more than one scheme, and the remaining entries came from Eastern Canada and the United States. Five designs were chosen as finalists, including two local architects, **T.C. Sorby** and **F.M. Rattenbury**, a rank twenty-five year old newcomer. After the submission of refined schemes, in March of 1893 Rattenbury's Free Classical design was chosen as the winner. This was a stinging blow to the more established architects, and it ignited personal rivalries that would dog Rattenbury for the rest of his career. Called "a building which should furnish a theatre for the great deeds of legislators and administrators unborn," it was criticized by many as an outrageous extravagance, but over time Rattenbury's design has come to be recognized as British Columbia's finest example of architecture.

Just when it looked as though the local economy was going to stabilize, things fell apart. A smallpox epidemic broke out in Victoria in June, 1892, and port activity was curtailed due to quarantine regulations. The epidemic affected all aspects of life in Victoria, including the service industries; the Hotel Driard began serving meals *table d'hôte* to decrease the number of employees and diminish the chances of infection. The Federal DPW started planning a quarantine station at William Head, just outside Victoria, which went to tender in April 1893. By the time that construction started on the Parliament buildings, indications of economic recession were in the air. Global gold production dropped dramatically, and western currencies, based on gold reserves, faltered. By the end of 1893, a full-scale bank panic was underway in the United States, and the abundance of silver on the world market enabled gold to be purchased in the United States at favourable rates, leading to a gold drain and fears that supplies of gold would be insufficient to back the circulation of bank notes. Capital from American sources dried up, and investor confidence evaporated. The boom went bust, suddenly and completely. Real estate speculation collapsed and foreclosures were common. 'Disaster was added to misery' when the record winter snows melted in May 1894, causing devastating flooding throughout the Fraser Valley.

Good feelings among the established architects waned. Personal and professional sniping began as they were thrown into fierce competition for the few remaining scraps of work. There was not much good news at the British Columbia Institute of Architects' annual meeting held December, 1893, and Vice-President **R.R. Bayne** reported that "a period of unexampled dullness has prevailed in our profession... Before we meet again, gentlemen, let us hope that things may improve with us all, and that we will be all busy men as now too many of us are idle men." In spite of the recession, in 1894 a new post office for Victoria was finally announced, to be designed by Thomas Fuller. Incensed that the design work would not be done locally, the BCIA sent a letter to Ottawa asking instead for a design competition to be held: "It is argued that something more likely to meet the requirements of the city would be obtained by this means, both as to materials and convenience, and also plans more likely to fulfil modern requirements than the stereotyped works of one man alone." Despite these sentiments, Fuller's design was a triumph, arguably the best federal structure built in B.C. in the nineteenth century. A stupendous masonry creation, it was a landmark on the Inner Harbour, providing an apt counterpoint to the rising Parliament Buildings and the other bookend for the future Empress Hotel. **A.J. Smith** was the contractor, with work first supervised by F.C. Gamble, C.E., resident DPW engineer, until 1897, and then by **William Henderson**, resident DPW architect. This landmark was replaced by a banal modern building in 1956, since tarted up with historical elements in a graceless attempt to make it fit into its historical context.

Hard times continued for the next few years, and relief did not occur until international conditions improved. In addition to the Victoria Post Office, a few larger government projects were undertaken due to the reduced costs of labour and material. New Westminster's original drill hall was damaged in an earthquake, and a new structure, which still stands today, was built according to standardized federal specifications. F.C. Gamble designed the massive wooden structure and supervised its construction. This was, however, an exception to the general malaise of the mid-1890s.

It was reported in the *Canadian Architect & Builder* that 1895 had been: "an exceedingly dull year in British Columbia, except perhaps in the mining centres, and in common with the rest of the country the cities have not progressed to any marked degree. Building operations have been backward and there has been a great scarcity of employment. Both materials and wages are down in price, and the trade generally is much depressed... there has been great stagnation, any buildings erected having been of the cheaper class." Vancouver had been subject to constant fluctuation in the construction industry, but by March 1896 at least half the city's carpenters were chronically unemployed, and even those working were receiving less than the standard wages.

The Kootenay mining booms that started soon after, and the Klondike gold rush snapped the local depression. By 1898 the province was roaring again. One bitter lesson that local industries learned from the hard times was that cooperation might be a better business strategy than rampant competition. The movement had already begun towards the great business consolidations in the lumber, mining and fishing industries in British Columbia, that in the early twentieth century would result in some of the largest industrial plants in the world.

Post Office, Victoria

BRUCE PRICE
1845-1903

JANA TYNER

Bruce Price, considered one of the most fashionable American architects of the later nineteenth century, had impeccable connections, and moved in exclusive social circles. The CPR chose Price as architect for a number of their buildings, attesting to his ability to encapsulate the goals of financiers and speculative interest parties. Born in Cumberland, Maryland on December 12, 1845, Bruce Price practised briefly in Baltimore before opening an office in New York City in 1877. As further affirmation of his social connections, Bruce Price was the father of Emily (Price) Post, the famous authority on American etiquette.

During the late 1880s and 1890s, Price designed a number of buildings in Canada. Of particular note were a train station and two hotels for the Canadian Pacific Railway: the Windsor Station in Montreal, 1888-89; the Banff Springs Hotel in Banff Springs, Alberta, 1886-88; and the Château Frontenac, 1892-93, in Quebec City. In the latter, Price refined what would become known as the Château style, which looked to sixteenth-century French castles as precedents. For over thirty years following the construction of the Château Frontenac, this style would follow the CPR across the country, and can be seen in British Columbia in Victoria's Empress Hotel (by **F.M. Rattenbury**, 1904-08), and the third Hotel Vancouver (by **John S. Archibald**, Architect and John Schofield, Associate Architect, 1928-39). All of these luxury hotels are characterised by extensive stone and brick masonry, steeply pitched roofs, tall chimneys, prominent turrets, and ornate dormer windows.

In Vancouver, Price was the architect of several imposing buildings constructed between 1886 and 1889. In 1885, the CPR received over 6,000 acres of land in central Vancouver from the British Columbia government in return for relocating their planned railway terminal from Port Moody. Situating the terminus at the foot of Granville Street, the CPR developed the adjacent land to become the centre of the new city, selling off parcels as it became profitable. The CPR was determined to solidify its plans for the new City of Vancouver, at the time a *tabula rasa*. They envisioned Granville Street, running south from the train terminal, as the main avenue of commerce. This included construction of the first Granville Street Bridge in 1888, and the surveying of the downtown grid system with Granville Street as the major north-south axis. The CPR chose Bruce Price to prepare plans for some of the key structures in their instant metropolis. These included the Van Horne Block, with thick ground floor walls built of granite from the CPR quarries, and "cream-coloured brick... brought in detachments from the St. Boniface brick yards opposite Winnipeg." The New York Block was faced and trimmed entirely with granite, and the *Daily World* trumpeted that it was "certainly the grandest building of its kind yet erected here, or for that matter in the Dominion." Price also designed the Crewe Block, built of brick and granite, with sixteen inch pilasters running the height of the three-storey structure. At the corner of Georgia and Granville Streets, the four-storey, granite-faced Sir Donald A. Smith Block was also designed by Price, as was the unique CPR "Double Cottage B," built 1886-88 of dressed stone and brick, with the upper portion finished in shingles; one half of this duplex was occupied by J.M. Browning, the CPR Land Commissioner. The buildings themselves, while imposing relative to others erected at the time, show little of Price's talents, and his plans at least for the Van Horne Block were "considerably altered," likely to conform to the rather primitive local conditions. With the demolition in 2001 of the Crewe Block, all of Price's Vancouver work has now been destroyed. Price was made a Fellow of the American Institute of Architects in 1890. He died in Paris, France on May 29, 1903.

CPR "Double Cottage B", Vancouver

Van Horne Block, Vancouver

New York Block, Vancouver

Artistically inventive, Price was socially conservative. Charming, attractive and respected, he met clients at the posh clubs of New York City, where he established a practice in 1877.

Arnold Lewis, *American Country Houses of the Gilded Age*, p. 19.

EDWARD MALLANDAINE, JR.

1867–1949

JOHN ADAMS

Edward Mallandaine, Jr. was the son of one of British Columbia's earliest architects, and like his father had a varied career only partially based on architecture. Ranging from the coast to the Kootenays, he tackled different business pursuits in order to make a living. Born in Victoria on June 1, 1867, he was the oldest child of Louisa and **Edward Mallandaine, Sr.** By his own admission he had a tempestuous youth and once during a prank accidentally set fire to the James Bay Bridge. He attended Victoria Central School, and then went to Portland, Oregon, High School from which he graduated in 1885. A noted athlete in his youth, he excelling at boxing and sculling. Upon graduation he wanted adventure and headed east on the partially constructed Canadian Pacific Railway to take part in quelling the Riel Rebellion, but when he got to Golden, B.C. he learned that the skirmish had ended. Subsequently he stayed in the area and operated an express business between Farwell and Eagle Pass.

In 1886 Mallandaine, Jr. moved to the infant city of Vancouver where he was present at the time of the Great Fire. Immediately after the conflagration the city experienced a building boom and Mallandaine remained for a few years, working as an architect. He had studied architecture and engineering under his father and possibly others, but seems to have had no formal training in the subjects. From 1886-89 he was in partnership with **C. Wyndham H. Sansom**. The year 1888 was particularly productive for them, as they designed an extension to the Byrnes Block on Maple Tree Square; a commercial block for Frank Granville; the City Morgue on Pender Street; an extension to the first Vancouver City Hall on Powell Street; a school on Main Street; and a house for James Harney. Following a brief stay in Victoria, Mallandaine Jr. went to Seattle after the 1889 fire and practised architecture there during 1890-91. By 1892 he returned to Victoria, maintaining an independent architectural practice at first, but by 1897 he and his father shared an office. In 1892 he submitted an unsuccessful entry in the competition for the new Parliament Buildings in Victoria, and his drawing shows more than a passing familiarity with British architectural antecedents. During the mid-1890s a long list of houses on Fort, Courtenay and View Streets were designed by one or the other of the Mallandaines, but some confusion arises in attributions. In 1894 Mallandaine Jr. married Jean Ramsay; the couple had no children.

Due to ill health he left Victoria and joined the surveying staff of the CPR in 1898, going to the East Kootenay where he spent most of the rest of his life. He worked as a civil engineer on the Bedlington & Nelson Railway and in 1898 was instrumental in founding the town of Creston. In 1908 he helped found the Creston Board of Trade, but by 1911 resided in Cranbrook where he served as land agent for the CPR in charge of tie and timber limits. In 1911 he moved to Windermere to take charge of the Columbia Fruit Lands, and then moved back to Creston. During the First World War he served overseas as Colonel of the Kootenay Regiment and later with the Canadian Forestry Corps. Following the war he left the CPR and settled permanently in Creston.

He took an active part in Creston business and community endeavours, and had the distinction of being the town's first postmaster, coroner and Justice of the Peace. He was elected to the Board of School Trustees, was founding President of the Creston Valley Hospital in 1930, was elected Reeve in 1936-38 and 1939-41, and served as Stipendiary Magistrate until 1948. In between these civic duties he operated the Goat Mountain Waterworks, sold real estate and fire insurance, operated a fruit ranch, and maintained his architectural career in some small capacity. He died in Creston on August 3, 1949.

He has taken a prominent part in practically every project looking to the development of the Kootenay districts, along the lines of general progress, and in all of his business, social and public connections he has stood as a man among men, respected by all for the sterling worth of his character.

British Columbia Pictorial Biographical, 1914, Vol.II, p.765.

Proposed New Government Buildings.
Victoria B C.
1892.

William
Tuff
WHITEWAY
1856-1940

JOHN ATKIN

W.T. Whiteway was born April 30, 1856 in Musgrave, Newfoundland, but didn't remain there long before setting out for the west coast of Canada. Between 1882 and 1902 he practised architecture in Vancouver; Port Townsend, Washington; Victoria; Halifax; and St. John's, Newfoundland before settling once again in Vancouver. Whiteway's name is largely remembered in Vancouver as the architect of record for one of the city's most recognizable buildings, the World (Sun) Tower at Beatty and Pender Streets.

Victoria was Whiteway's first stop on the west coast in the early 1880s; then he moved to Vancouver in 1886 and completed the designs for one of the city's first brick buildings, the Ferguson Block, Fire Hall No. 1 on Water Street and additions to the first City Hall, all in 1886-87. At the same time, the San-Diego-Coronado building boom was occurring, and

Whiteway relocated to San Diego in 1887. He is known to have designed at least two residences there, but his wife, Elizabeth, pregnant at the time of the move south, died there while giving birth. In 1888, Whiteway moved back up the coast to Port Townsend and established a partnership with Julius C. Schroeder, who had also been in San Diego during its short-lived boom. Together they designed a number of significant buildings in that city including First United Presbyterian Church. At least six of their buildings in Port Townsend have survived.

In 1892, Whiteway departed for the east coast once again. But before leaving he found time to design the Duck Block on Broad Street in Victoria for Simeon Duck. Back east his first stop was St. John's where he submitted drawings for the proposed court house in that city. The design was accepted but it would be another eight years before construction would begin. In the meantime Whiteway moved across the water to Halifax and established a practice. One of his first projects was the Gordon & Keith Building on Barrington Street, 1896-97. This Romanesque structure was virtually identical to Whiteway's design for the Duck Block on the other side of the country. In 1897 he went into partnership with William T. Horton. Along with commercial buildings they undertook the design of a number of residences, including the city's first Queen Anne design.

Vancouver High School

City Market, Vancouver

When construction began in 1900 on the long awaited court house in St. John's, Whiteway stopped in briefly to check on its progress before once again returning to Vancouver. Whiteway wasted no time in establishing an office. Building records show that he was prolific, and he soon received some very substantial commissions such as a new department store for Woodward's on Hastings Street, 1903; the Kelly Douglas warehouse on Water Street, 1905, considered the city's first "skyscraper;" the Woods Hotel at Hastings and Carrall Streets, 1906; and a new City Market on Main Street, 1906-08. The market building was a full blown fantasy of glass and turned wood that sat on pilings on the edge of False Creek. Its entrance with its twin towers and large arched glass window was reminiscent of either a Victorian train station or exhibition hall. The building wasn't the success it was meant to be, but lasted until the 1920s when it was consumed by fire.

In addition to this commercial work, Whiteway specialized in the design of schools. He provided the plans for at least six schools for the Vancouver School Board, one of his earliest being the Vancouver High School at 12th Avenue and Oak Street, 1903. It was a large Neoclassical edifice with a central pediment and a columned entrance, topped off with a central cupola. Later in its life, when it was being used as the King Edward campus of Vancouver Community College, it was destroyed in a spectacular fire. Today, only the beach cobble school yard wall remains. His extant school designs in the Vancouver area included the almost identical Lord Roberts and Admiral Seymour schools in 1907, and the MacDonald School on East Hastings, 1906. Whiteway was also chosen to design a large new three-storey brick public school in Kamloops, 1906-07, originally intended to have an ornate tower that was deleted due to cost. On Vancouver Island he designed the impressive Duncan Elementary School in 1913. The building received enthusiastic notices in the Cowichan *Leader* newspaper, which noted that the architect was an expert in school design.

Hotel for Leon Melikov, Vancouver

Storey & Campbell Building, Vancouver

His commercial commissions continued with the design of the Holden Building on Hastings Street, adjacent to his earlier Woods Hotel. This was a fairly typical office building of the period, but built at a time when the area's fortunes were moving west with the centre of the business district, and today it appears isolated from its older and lower neighbours. Other designs by Whiteway during this boom period included the Commercial Hotel in Hope, B.C., 1910, and a warehouse for Storey & Campbell on Beatty Street, 1911.

Whiteway most impressive building was the World Building, designed in 1912 for newspaperman, businessman and Mayor, Louis D. Taylor. This impressive building – once the tallest in the British Empire – with its distinctive copper roof and its famous nine terra cotta maidens holding up the cornice line, anchors the corner of Beatty and Pender Streets. Its podium and tower design reflects the Woolworth's Building in New York City and the Smith Tower in Seattle. Yet Whiteway's achievement might not be of his own hand. In a 1972 interview conducted by Harold Kalman with the architect **G.L.T. Sharp**, it was suggested by Sharp that the original design for the World Building was not actually Whiteway's: "[Taylor] came and asked me to give them a sketch, which I did. Next thing I know its been handed on, you see. So I went after him... I think he gave me three hundred dollars for it."

Ten years later Whiteway was in trouble with the Architectural Institute of B.C. because he collaborated on a building with the unregistered **W.H. Chow.** In the same year he was struck from the register for arrears in his fees and wasn't reinstated until 1924. His troubles with the AIBC continued when he sent a letter in March 1926 to purchasers of lots in the exclusive Shaughnessy Heights subdivision suggesting that they hire him to design their new houses because he would do the job for 2% less than architect's scale and not charge for the initial consultation; he was called before the Council of the Institute for this attempt at undercutting the recommended fee structure. During the late 1920s Whiteway was busy designing a number of brick-faced walk-up apartment blocks in the West End of Vancouver, including three on Haro Street built in 1927: the St. Margaret for J.J. Perrigo; The Normandie for Gordon Drysdale Ltd.; and Viola Court for George Canary. Like many other architects after the onset of the Depression, he was struck from the AIBC register for non-payment of fees. His last years were spent in quiet retirement at his Barclay Street residence. He died in Vancouver on October 9, 1940.

Holden Building, Vancouver

*Vancouver must be reckoned among the great
progressive capitals of commerce of the Dominion,
for the architecture, and particularly that part of it which
one sees in the business district, and especially that of
recent construction is notably striking and remarkably
modern and effective. A large number of these recent
improvements are the creation of Mr. W. T. Whiteway,
one of the leading architects of the city.*

Greater Vancouver – Illustrated, c.1907, p.212

World Building, Vancouver

Public School, Kamloops

HENRY OGLE
BELL-IRVING
1856–1931

DONALD LUXTON

Although he is well-remembered as one of the province's most successful and influential businessmen, one aspect of H.O. Bell-Irving's talents has been largely forgotten. Among his many other pursuits he was one of Vancouver's first architects. The eldest son of a wealthy Scottish laird, Henry was born at the ancestral home, *Milkbank*, near Lockerbie, on January 26, 1856. His father suffered heavy financial losses just before his untimely death in 1864. Educated as an engineer in Karlsruhe, Germany, young Henry immigrated to Canada in 1882 to seek his fortune, with the hope of winning back title to the family estate. He found immediate employment with the CPR as an engineer and surveyor on construction of the railway west of Winnipeg. Working his way through the Rocky and Selkirk Mountains, he arrived at Burrard Inlet in October, 1885. In the public excitement of the extension of the railway twelve miles further west from Port Moody to Granville, Bell-Irving found a ready market for his practical skills. Artistic and versatile by nature, he had a flair for drawing that translated into a sideline in architecture.

Bell-Irving borrowed money to return briefly to England in February, 1886 to marry his betrothed, Maria Isabel del Carmen Beattie, known as Bella. They had met twelve years earlier in Lucerne when he had been studying in Germany. The newly-married couple returned by ship to New York, by railway to San Francisco, by steamer to New Westminster, and by oxcart to New Brighton on Burrard Inlet, where they took up residence at Black's Brighton House Hotel. As Bella entered the hotel she tripped over a corpse on the floor, but was told by a logger at the bar not to worry about hurting him, as he was already dead. Her reaction can only be imagined.

Henry Bell-Irving's faith in the new settlement remained unshakable. He rowed three miles each day to his new architectural office in Gastown. The conditions seemed appalling to his new bride, but she assisted the business by writing building specifications in meticulous calligraphy. Vancouver, a struggling backwater of 700 residents, promptly burned down, and although his office and drawing instruments were lost in the fire, Bell-Irving threw himself into the city's rebuilding. Working at first with Walter Gravely, he designed some of the first homes built after the fire. On his own he provided designs for residences for J.M. Spinks on Hastings Street, and for Captain R.G. Tatlow on Pender Street, both 1888. The same year he also designed the Bell-Irving Block at Cordova and Richards Streets, a two-storey brick block of three stores with offices above, fitted with electric light and gas.

Bell-Irving quickly realized the potential in the export of the province's vast resources, and actively pursued many commercial ventures. With Tatlow, who later became the provincial Minister of Finance, he established a grocery and general store on Water Street, and subsequently formed an import-export company with R.H. Paterson. In 1889 Bell-Irving & Paterson chartered the sailing ship *Titania* from the Hudson's Bay Company to bring over the first direct cargo from London to Vancouver, but the return voyage was more significant, as Bell-Irving had arranged to send back a full load of canned Fraser River sockeye salmon, the first such shipment to reach England. Recognizing the enormous amount of salmon available, he quickly acquired options on a number of canneries, and in 1890 established the Anglo-British Packing Co. Ltd., a large conglomerate of cannery companies backed by English financing, that by the following year was the world's largest packer of sockeye salmon. He is credited with making the name 'Sockeye' famous by shipping quantities of the fish to the U.S. forces during the Spanish-American War in 1898. Influential in business, he also found time for public life, and was elected as an alderman in January, 1888. He was the first chairman of the Vancouver Board of Works, and was responsible for the construction of the road around Stanley Park.

Although he made enough money to regain title to his ancestral home, he realized that his roots in this new land were now deeply embedded, and in 1895 he relinquished his claim to *Milkbank* to a cousin. Henry and Isabel began a large family, establishing a dynasty that is still prominent today. By 1907 he was able to build a grand family home, *The Strands*, in the West End, with a large central hall featuring a massive stone fireplace surmounted by a stag's head. *The Strands* was the original name of *Milkbank*, the Bell-Irving ancestral home in Scotland. Bell-Irving died on February 19, 1931. Although his entrepreneurial accomplishments remain legendary, his brief architectural career demonstrated his willingness and ability to tackle almost any challenge presented in a pioneering frontier environment.

The next new building is the Bell-Irving brick block, close to Richards Street. This block has a frontage of sixty-nine feet, divided into three stores twenty-three by sixty, well lighted both in front and rear. Stairs lead up from Cordova street on one side of the building to a landing from which well lighted offices branch off. A skylight supplies plenty of light from above. The roof has been sheeted over with patent tarred roofing. Fitted with electric light and gas. Mr. H. Bell-Irving, owner and architect. Estimated cost $10,000.

Vancouver *Daily World*, December 31, 1888, page 4.

Bell-Irving Block, Vancouver

ELMER H. FISHER

C.1844–C.1905

DONALD LUXTON

Elmer Fisher was one of a number of restless architects who followed the frontier westwards and lived a vagabond existence, never quite setting down roots, but rather chasing opportunities wherever the economy was booming. Either aggressive in his pursuit of clients, or very skilled at self-promotion, Fisher had a knack for showing up ahead of where rail tracks were being laid, or just after the disastrous fires that plagued pioneer settlements, sometimes even before the ashes had cooled.

The accounts of his life and professional background appear to have been mostly fabricated by Fisher himself, and are notoriously unreliable. Likely he changed his name, at least once.

Virtually nothing is known about his origins and education, although he claimed to have been born in Edinburgh about 1840 – even though Elmer was a most unlikely Scottish name – and arrived in the United States at about the age of seventeen. The 1880 census records indicate that he was more likely born in Massachusetts about 1844 to Scottish parents, although census information was provided by the subjects so Fisher again may have provided false information; he was also listed as married at the time. He claimed to have fought in the Civil War in the 25th Massachusetts Volunteers, and to have been wounded in the siege of Richmond, but no evidence can be found to support this. Between 1874 and 1886 he moved between Minneapolis (where he worked as a cabinet maker), Denver (where he worked as a "band sawyer" and by 1883

E. H. FISHER,
ARCHITECT,
DeCosmos New Block, Government St.,
VICTORIA, B. C.

P. O. Box 474.   fe6 1y

---

was listed as an architect) and Butte, Montana. He arrived in Victoria by February 1886, and lost no time in setting up an architectural practice. Keeping his options open, a sensible move given the imminent arrival of the transcontinental railway, Fisher was the only architect to advertise his services in Vancouver newspapers in early 1886.

From this point on, Fisher rode the crest of the development boom in the West. Vancouver's Great Fire of 1886 provided the opportunity for several commissions, notably the Alhambra Hotel (Byrnes Block) fronting onto Maple Tree Square, 1886-87. In 1886 he designed a new commercial arcade in Victoria for David Spencer. The following year he was responsible for Wille's Bakery on Victoria's Lower Johnson Street, the Goldstream Hotel for James Phair, and the Pimbury Building in Nanaimo. The striking Bank of B.C. building in New Westminster, 1887, was also a Fisher design, as was Nanaimo's second Court House, a plain boxy two-storey wooden structure with flanking wings, distinguished only by an ornamented porch and "Gothick" windows on the front facade. Although Fisher rarely undertook residential commissions, he designed a pair of houses for pioneer Victoria druggist A.J. Langley, built by **George Mesher** in 1887. Enlivened with picturesque and complex rooflines, corner verandahs, and extensive scrollcut ornamentation, these identical houses still stand on upper Fort Street. Fisher was known to copy residential designs directly from plan books such as the *Scientific American's Architects & Builders Edition*, and these houses, with their "cottage" roofs bear more than a passing resemblance to pattern book illustrations of the era.

In May 1888 Fisher entered into a year-long partnership with **William Ridgway-Wilson**, a recent arrival in Victoria, and together they designed several prominent structures in Victoria, including the W.G. Cameron Building, and the Craft & Norris Block, both from 1888. This latter building, along with the Byrnes Block and the Bank of B.C., are similar Italianate designs with imposing beveled corner entrances. During his time in B.C., Fisher was responsible, alone or with Wilson, for at least twenty buildings in its four main cities.

The ever restless Fisher was also travelling further afield to search for larger commissions, and turned his attention to Port

White House, Victoria, Fisher & Wilson, 1888.

Townsend, Washington, which was another anticipated terminal of a transcontinental railway; Fisher designed a number of major structures there. By November 1887 Fisher had also established an office in Seattle, and was the leading architect in the city by the time of the 1889 fire, which levelled thirty square blocks of the city's business core. Once again, his timing was excellent, as he had abandoned his Victoria practice by April of that year.

His Seattle practice was extremely successful. Fisher appears to have exaggerated his achievements in other cities, although none of his clients seemed to care as long as he produced results, which he did. No one was going to check his credentials when there was a city to rebuild. After just two years of work he was able to leave a magnificent legacy of impressive structures in and around Pioneer Square, and he was instrumental in establishing the Romanesque Revival vernacular in the area, exemplified by the robust Pioneer Building of 1889-91.

In the Victoria *Daily Colonist*, May 20, 1890 it was reported that Fisher, "formerly of this city, came over from Seattle via Vancouver on Sunday night, and went out to Shawnigan Lake for the benefit of his health. During the past year Mr. Fisher has had in charge $2,500,000 worth of buildings in Seattle, and the great strain on his mental powers has necessitated a rest." After executing dozens of large commissions, Fisher appears to have lost interest in architecture, and in 1891 abandoned his practice to run the Abbott Hotel in Seattle. He invested heavily in unsuccessful business ventures, and "went bust" in the general economic collapse of 1893.

Fisher's personal life was also plagued with problems. Sometime before he left Denver in 1885, he had taken as a mistress Mary H. Smith, whom he later testified was "a woman of unchaste life." They apparently entered into a verbal agreement to live together as man and wife, but were never formally married. They moved to Butte, and then on to Victoria, where Fisher abandoned her when he moved to Seattle. In 1893 he married widow Charlotte Mollie Willey, and a furious Smith filed a breach of promise suit claiming $10,000 in damages. While in Victoria Fisher introduced her as his wife to avoid scandal, and he claimed that although they had sexual intercourse in Colorado, he had paid her a "pecuniary compensation." The case became a *cause célèbre*, but was resolved in Fisher's favour when the jury concluded "that he had paid the woman many times over the price of her shame." Despite the favourable conclusion for Fisher, he was publicly disgraced, which may have contributed to the failure of his attempts to restart his career in Seattle. By the mid 1890s he gave up and moved to Los Angeles. Never again successful in architecture, he ended up working as a carpenter, and as an outside supervisor for architect John Parkinson. Fisher died in obscurity about 1905, but his place of death and burial are, like his birth, unconfirmed.

House for A.J. Langley, Victoria

Bank of British Columbia, New Westminster

THOMAS CHARLES SORBY
1836–1924

HAROLD KALMAN

It is fascinating to observe the conflict that can arise between an architect's natural design tendencies and the environmental situation to which he/she may be exposed. This conflict is particularly evident in the case of T.C. Sorby, an English architect who abandoned a first career in Britain, arrived in Canada in middle age, and then moved to British Columbia, intent on bestowing his sophisticated architectural talents on the young community of Vancouver – only to watch his career flounder as he was unable to adapt to the pioneer environment. In his final phase of work, at Victoria, he succeeded in forging a compromise between the sophistication of his European career and the freshness of the new West.

Sorby was born in 1836 near Wakefield, Yorkshire. He visited London at the age of fifteen to see the Great Exhibition, and decided then and there to travel in continental Europe and become an architect. A decade later he entered private practice in London, where he sought fame and fortune on the bureaucratic ladder. In 1866 he was appointed Surveyor (i.e. architect) of County Courts for England and Wales, and also Surveyor to the Metropolitan London Police and Police Courts. In the three years he held the former post, he designed court houses for eleven English cities, most of them competent exercises in the Italian Renaissance Revival style. He was fluent as well in the Gothic Revival and Queen Anne styles, and designed a number of fine public buildings, churches, and private residences in these eclectic manners.

Sorby chose to drop his English practice and immigrate to Canada at the age of forty-seven, disembarking at Quebec in May 1883. He soon found work in Montreal with a leading corporate employer, the Canadian Pacific Railway, for whom he designed a number of innovative stations (including those at Peterborough, Yorkville, and Port Arthur in Ontario) and hotels (in Montreal and Algoma Mills, Ontario). While in Montreal he also produced designs for a variety of institutional and residential clients, but it seems that few of the buildings were executed. Records suggest that he had a prickly personality and a knack for alienating his clients.

The next phase of Sorby's career took him to British Columbia. With the completion of the transcontinental railway in November 1885, the CPR promoted tourism through the Rocky Mountains in order to stimulate passenger traffic. Dining cars – required to serve the travellers – were too heavy to haul economically up the steep mountain grades, so the company built "dining stations" with hotel rooms in the mountains of British Columbia. Sorby designed three: the Glacier House at Glacier, the Mount Stephen House at Field, and the Fraser Canyon Hotel in North Bend. The Glacier House, which became a popular resort, was aptly described by a visitor as "a very artistic building of the Swiss chalet type." Its two-storey timber frame was covered with yellow drop siding and brown shingles. The combination of local materials and picturesque gabled Alpine design were perfect for the sublime mountain landscape.

The Laurels, Victoria

Sorby arrived in Vancouver in the spring of 1886 – a man of fifty, with a generation of architectural practice, most of it in Britain, under his belt. His unquestioned experience and sophistication, however, were not what the infant city was looking for, and he was continually forced to simplify his ideas, in order to meet local tastes, budgets, and demands for expediency.

He quickly obtained several prestigious commissions. The CPR retained him to design the Lady Stephen Block on the north side of Hastings Street, named for the wife of the railway's President, Sir George Stephen. His houses for company employees included one for Harry Abbott, General Superintendent of the Pacific Division, a half-timbered structure on Hastings Street, west of Granville, on the edge of the bluff overlooking the tracks and station. Sorby was the architect as well of the first Court House, 1888-90, located in today's Victory Square, and the Bank of British Columbia at Hastings and Richards, 1889-91, which is still standing. Both underwent considerable simplification between the initial conception and the final execution. He also designed a store for the Hudson's Bay Company, on Cordova Street, a plain one-storey wood structure that was not without its charms, with repeated gables and attractive shingle work, but which had no pretension to traditional "high style."

What might have been Sorby's most significant Vancouver project was the CPR's first Hotel Vancouver. The design went through several stages, each further removed from European models. The first displayed grand "Jacobethan" gables and bay windows, which were simplified somewhat in an alternative Italianate elevation. The designs were being completed when, on June 13, 1886, Vancouver suffered its Great Fire. The young city – and Sorby's drawings – were lost to the flames. Sorby hurried down to San Francisco to buy new drawing instruments, and returned to find the city quickly rebuilding. The hotel underwent another re-design (the working drawings are dated June 1886), and what emerged at the opening in May 1887 was a wholly unornamented five-storey brick-and-stone building. Although its grand scale led the press of the day to praise it as "magnificent" and an "unexcelled hostelry," a later journalist described it more accurately as "a sort of glorified farmhouse," a pragmatic response to the needs of a young, frontier community. Sorby himself was embittered by what he viewed as the CPR's stinginess. As his plain hotel was being demolished in 1913 to be replaced by the somewhat Mediterranean "new" Hotel Vancouver, he indignantly recalled in a Victoria newspaper: "[The bricks on the lower storey] were so soft... that they were obliged to cement the whole storey to secure a decent face. Every bit of decoration was left out. The roof was covered with the cheapest tinned iron shingles and leaked like a sieve, at which time they [the CPR] called me in to finish the work."

The same reductive process occurred with the CPR station. Sorby produced a design for a picturesque, multi-gabled and turreted concoction not unlike his Ontario depots of a few years earlier. But when the first train arrived, the station had become the simplest of frame structures, hidden beneath a plain roof. It is even uncertain whether it was Sorby or a civil engineer who worked for the CPR Land Department, Paul Louis Françoise-Xavier Marmette (1859-1952), who was responsible for the executed structure.

Competition entry for the Parliament Buildings, Victoria

A comparison of these Vancouver buildings with Sorby's English work of only a decade or two earlier reveals an enormous change in his architectural style, from mainstream historicist revivalism to an almost rustic simplicity. Sorby seemed not to have accepted the constraints of frontier pressures graciously, and Harry Abbott and CPR General Manager William Van Horne quickly lost patience with him. The unhappy architect was dismissed from company service, and late in 1888 he crossed the Strait of Georgia to settle in Victoria, where he remained for the rest of his long life.

The capital city was older, more established, and more worldly than upstart Vancouver – it had long passed the pioneer phase – and Sorby was evidently more comfortable there. In Vancouver, his architecture had undergone a rebirth; in Victoria, it achieved a new maturity. He came to work with, rather than in opposition to, the styles of his time and place, although he continued to insert English ideas from his first career. He designed two substantial masonry commercial buildings on Government Street, the Five Sisters Block, 1890-91 (with **W. Ridgway-Wilson**, with whom he was briefly in partnership), and the Weiler Block, 1898-99. Both exhibited restrained classical detailing, perhaps more so than their home-bred neighbours, but they fit in and were widely admired.

Among Sorby's fine residential designs was *The Laurels* on Rockland Avenue, a picturesque and eclectic house, featuring an entrance tower, for wealthy businessman Robert Ward. The local press didn't quite know what to make of it, reporting that "the principal feature of the front is the large Moorish window, above which are graceful balconies. The general style is 'Ionic.'" Today its style would be described as the Queen Anne Revival of the northwest region, in the same family as its peers, although somewhat more ornamented.

Sorby tried his hand at grander projects as well, but fell short of the mark. He placed second to **F.M. Rattenbury** in the competition for Victoria's Parliament Buildings, and then submitted an unsuccessful design for Government House. He also submitted an entry in the competition for two new Victoria schools in 1893. The *Colonist* noted his overseas sources: "Mr. T.C. Sorby's design was planned broadly upon the lines laid down by the School Board of London... The style is Queen Anne, somewhat after the manner of the London Board Schools. This plan is radically different from all others." The competition was judged by **R. Mackay Fripp**, and the designs of **Soule & Day** and Ridgway-Wilson were chosen as the winning entries. Sorby also prepared an unsuccessful competition entry for the state capitol at Olympia, Washington. From about 1896 until his death, he spent much of his time contriving and promoting an ambitious plan for improving Victoria's inner harbour. He wrote endless letters to the paper in support of his project, and travelled to Ottawa to argue for its adoption, but to no avail. Sorby died in 1924 at the age of eighty-eight, still secretary of the Inner Harbour Association, but his architectural career had been largely forgotten. He was buried in Ross Bay Cemetery.

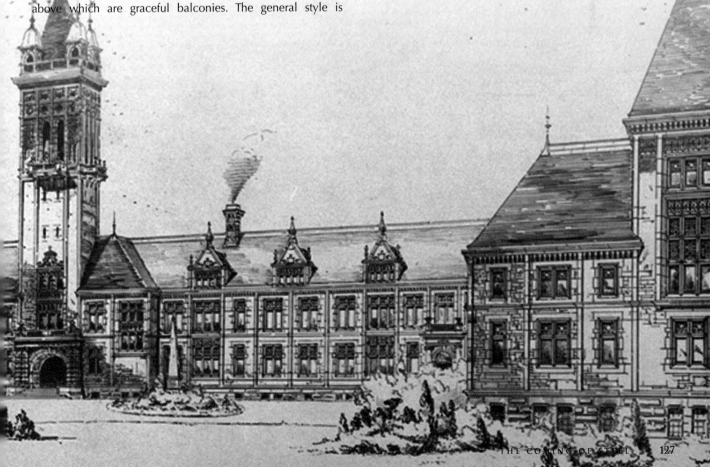

GEORGE WILLIAM GRANT
1852–1925

JIM WOLF

George William Grant's prodigious architectural accomplishments can be measured not only by the number of commissions he received, but also by the prominence of the structures he completed in Vancouver and New Westminster. Born in Pictou, Nova Scotia on December 14, 1852, he was the son of Nova Scotia-born farmer Alpin and Eleanor (Braden) Grant. His early education took place in public schools and the Pictou Academy, but it was through his apprenticeship in the building trades that his interest and pursuit of a career in architecture began. An early account of his life reported: "It was necessary for him to earn his own way and through hard work and close economy he saved the sum that enabled him to take up the study of architecture." After completing his studies Grant found little work as an architect in Nova Scotia and therefore continued to "act as superintendent of building and construction work." Grant married Olive Burris, a native of Nova Scotia, in the town of Musqudoboit in 1876. Although the couple did not have children, they adopted a niece, Yaney, whom they raised as their own.

In 1885 he took a chance to go west and seek employment in his chosen field. Grant's journey across the continent was made by the Northern Pacific Railroad to Portland, Oregon via Tacoma, Washington and then directly to Granville by boat, where he must have been disappointed to find the "only vestige of civilization" was the Hastings Sawmill. He promptly moved to Victoria, where he began working again as a superintendent of construction. The arrival of the transcontinental railway inspired Grant to set up a Vancouver office in the spring of 1887, but it was in New Westminster, experiencing a boom as a result of its connection to the main line of the CPR

in 1886, that Grant found a setting in which to achieve great things. In 1886-87 he completed nine projects in the Royal City documented to be worth $90,000, including the Queen's Hotel on Columbia Street, 1887. The Masonic and Odd Fellows building was notable for its sophisticated style and immense size, completed in concert with John Teague for $35,000. Also of importance was *Hillcroft*, a spectacular wooden mansion designed for lumber baron John Hendry in Nova Scotia's vernacular Second Empire style, built in 1886 with a wing added two years later.

Grant appears to have all but abandoned his office in Vancouver as the number and size of the commissions offered to him in New Westminster was tremendous. Between 1888-92 Grant designed and supervised 117 projects with a construction value of $919,000. These included landmark public structures such as major additions to the Provincial Asylum Building, 1889; the first Provincial Exhibition Building in Queen's Park, 1889; the Provincial Court House, 1891; and the City Library 1891. His residential commissions ranged from the most humble frame cottages to the elaborate Queen Anne-style mansions of H.V. Edmonds, 1889 and A.E. Rand, 1891, and substantial additions to the home of prominent salmon cannery owner, Alexander Ewen, 1890. Some of the province's largest commercial structures were designed by Grant for New Westminster's Columbia Street and included the Douglas-Elliot Block and the Harris-Dupont Building, both 1891. He was responsible for some of the city's more elaborate churches, and also provided the designs for St. Andrew's

Hillcroft, Hendry Residence, New Westminster

Presbyterian Church, Ladner, 1891-93. Grant's success appears to have been tied not only to his skill in design but also directly to his expertise in building construction. It was reported that "he superintended the construction of all of the buildings which he designed." This ability provided the extra confidence that many of his clients appreciated.

In 1891 *The Daily Columbian* remarked: "A well known and successful, as well as reliable architect, engaged in this interesting and useful branch of art is Mr. G.W. Grant. His business has assumed immense proportions. He stands at the head of his profession in public building architecture, being a man of unquestionable skill and ability in his line, an expert draftsman and devoting close personal attention to every detail. He has in the nature of things, built up an extensive and influential patronage, having designed the leading and most noted buildings in the city, besides many throughout the province. Ample evidence of his skill can be found on every hand. He certainly occupies an enviable and seldom surpassed position in his business. Mr. Grant is in every sense of the word, New Westminster's leading architect."

The recession that followed in 1892 was felt by Grant perhaps a little harder after the success that he had enjoyed as one of the province's most prominent and prolific architects. His New Westminster office was closed and Grant spent more time in

Masonic Temple, New Westminster

Provincial Exhibition Building, Queen's Park, New Westminster

Court House, New Westminster

design of these blocks are typical of Grant's work, which showed a preference for the Romanesque style. Grant also designed the Carnegie Public Library at Hastings and Main, 1900-03. This prominent structure, with its landmark domed corner entrance, brought Grant much critical praise and many more clients.

In 1903 Grant accepted former employee, **Alexander E. Henderson**, as a partner. This move may have been the only way Grant could keep pace with the number of commissions in his office. The largest was for the new City Hospital, Vancouver, built at a cost of $160,000. Known today as the Heather Pavilion, although obscured and altered by later additions, it is slated for partial restoration. This grand building in Romanesque style was the last of Grant's large public structures. In the following years, Grant and Henderson designed a large number of commercial buildings, apartment buildings and residences. In 1912, at the height of the construction boom, H.T. Cook was added as a partner to the firm. During this period, the firm exhibited stylistic versatility, completing eclectic residential structures combining late Queen Anne and Classical Revival styles and also some exceptionally refined Arts and Crafts-styled residences.

With the advent of the depression and the First World War, Grant's once proud office suffered a terrible loss of income. Despite his long connection with British Columbia, in 1914 he moved to the warmer climate of California, where he is known to have designed a few houses. He died in Bellflower, California on November 7, 1925.

Vancouver trying to find work. The West End (later Dawson) School was designed by him in 1892 for the Vancouver School Board, to which he was later elected as a Trustee. He shared an office and partnership out of convenience with **T.E. Julian** in 1893-94. A residential commission from this period was a grand house designed for Thomas E. Ladner in Delta in 1894. The salmon canning industry provided Grant a number of commissions for the wharves and buildings of fish packing plants in 1897, including the Automatic Can Co. at New Westminster and the Phoenix Cannery at Steveston.

Grant's temporary lull in business ended dramatically when September 11, 1898 dawned on the smoking ruins of New Westminster's downtown core. Grant was soon on the scene and pressed into service by former clients who needed his immediate assistance. He set up an office in the surviving Burr Block and got to work. Of the reconstruction that took place in 1899, Grant received seventeen major commissions totalling $261,000. He redesigned and restored structures that survived with only their walls intact, such as the Court House, Holy Trinity Church, and the Masonic Block, and also designed new replacement blocks for commercial property owners on Columbia Street, much reduced in scale and opulence from the pre-fire buildings.

With the Klondike and Kootenay mining booms the general economy had picked up, and Grant was also extremely busy in Vancouver, where he also served as the city's License Commissioner between 1898-99. In addition to a number of residences he received some substantial commissions such as the Romanesque Revival Leckie Block on Granville Street, 1898-99, which housed the Imperial Bank, faced with rusticated "fine white stone" from Gabriola Island. Another project at this time was the refined brick and terra cotta Walker (Ormidale) Block, 1900, on West Hastings Street. The exterior

Carnegie Library, Vancouver

Leckie Block, Vancouver

Walker (Ormidale) Block, Vancouver

*He thoroughly understands every phase of the
business, both theoretically and practically, and his
knowledge and power have enabled him to combine
utility, convenience and beauty in a harmonious whole.*

Howay & Schofield, *British Columbia Biographical*, Vol. III, p.804

G. W. Grant,

ARCHITECT,

NEW WESTMINSTER, B. C.

City Hospital, Vancouver

WILLIAM RIDGWAY-WILSON
1862–1957

ROSEMARY JAMES CROSS

Colonel Ridgway-Wilson was a prolific and surprisingly versatile architect. He designed many impressive residences still standing today, and was also responsible for numerous commercial buildings and for several grand military and institutional landmarks. Wilson was born in Hong Gow, China on July 24, 1862, and his family moved to England soon after. He began serving articles in the office of Bromiton Cheers, a Liverpool architect, as early as age thirteen, and later moved to London to work as assistant in the offices of architects, Searles & Hayes, and also with the "legendarily fat" Sir Horace Jones (1819-1887), London City Architect. During his

time in London he passed examinations at the South Kensington Science and Art school, which allowed him to lecture on building construction, and to pursue studies at the Royal Academy.

At the end of 1887, Wilson arrived in Victoria and set up his practice. In May 1888 he entered into a short-lived but productive partnership with the experienced and well-travelled frontier architect, **Elmer H. Fisher**, and they completed buildings in Victoria and Vancouver between 1888-89 before Fisher left for Seattle. In 1889, Wilson was hired by John Mahrer to design the Nanaimo Opera House, a three-storey, brick-faced Italianate structure that seated up to 600 persons. The same year he designed the Queen Anne-style residence for banker Alexander A. Green, named *Gyppeswyk*, the Saxon name for Green's birthplace, Ipswich. *Gyppeswyk* survives today as part of the Victoria Art Gallery. In 1890-91, Wilson had a short-lived partnership with **T.C. Sorby**, and they provided the designs for the Begbie Block in New Westminster, 1890-91, and a commercial block for the five daughters of Sir James Douglas, which became known as the Five Sisters Block.

In 1889, Wilson had married Flora Alexandra Jenns, daughter of Reverend Jenns of St. John the Divine Church. This was the old iron church that was replaced by the present Hudson's Bay Company department store. When the church sold their property to the HBC, Wilson designed a new Gothic Revival St. John the Divine in 1912, of dark brick with contrasting

Glenelg, Victoria

light stonework. His funeral would be held in this church forty-five years later.

From 1892, Wilson operated as a sole practitioner, and his career took off with numerous grand houses, commercial blocks, and large institutional projects to his credit. His early institutional projects included Victoria's South Park School, 1894, inspired by the contemporary school architecture of London. The passage of the revised *Public Schools Act* in 1891 transferred control of educational funds to local school boards, and rapid population growth put a great deal of pressure the boards, to provide more classroom space. On May 11, 1893 the Victoria School Board announced a competition, open to Victoria architects, to design two graded elementary schools, in the North and South Wards. The rules specified brick construction, with stone foundations and slate roofs, with each school containing eight classrooms. A total of twelve entries were received, and the Board, unable to make a decision, asked Vancouver architect, **R. Mackay Fripp**, to act as judge. Fripp awarded the highest honours to Messrs. **Soule & Day's** entry, which was assigned to the North Ward site. The rest of the entries were considered "fairly level in merit," and **S.M. Goddard** was awarded a qualified second place, and Wilson placed third. The School Board, however, preferred Wilson's interior layout, and chose his design for the other school, which survives today as South Park School. Wilson also undertook the isolation hospital at Royal Jubilee, 1893, and alterations and additions to the Provincial Asylum in New Westminster in 1897-98. Victoria West School, 1907-08, and additions to Lampson Street School, Esquimalt, 1913, followed later in Wilson's career.

Commercial projects of interest included his Italianate designs for Chinese clients in Victoria's "Chinatown," such as the Loo Tai Cho Building, 1893. Wilson, in addition to being the architect for the B.C. Land & Investment Agency from 1894 on, designed many buildings like the two-storey Porter Block, 1897, and Mahon Block, 1907, in Victoria. The W. & J. Wilson

South Ward School, Victoria

Building, 1912, is a remarkable exercise in restrained Classicism, with two ornate pilasters serving as bookends to a wall of glass display windows, the entire structure capped by a simple cornice. Examples of his diverse residential work in Victoria include: *Schuhuum*, a large Tudor residence, built for Hewitt Bostock, 1894; the Charles Spratt Residence on the Gorge, 1894, later the home of Premier McBride who named it *Glenelg*; a two-storey brick house for Dr. Charles F. Newcombe on Dallas Road, 1907-08; a grand turreted house on Rockland Avenue for Dr. Jones, 1908; and *Lotbinière*, also

Below, *Gyppeswyk*, Victoria. Right, William Ridgway-Wilson.

St. John the Divine, Victoria, under construction

Ridgway-Wilson and his four sons c.1916.

for Charles Spratt, on Lotbinière Avenue, 1909. In 1899, Wilson built his own Arts and Crafts-influenced home on the Gorge, with distinctive jerkin-headed roofs and elaborate coursed shingle siding.

Wilson joined the militia in 1899, and two of his last major commissions were related to his military contacts. He provided plans for both the Victoria Drill Hall, now the Bay Street Armoury, Victoria, 1913-15, and the Colquitz Jail, on Wilkinson Road in Saanich, 1914. These two large structures maintain the Victorian aesthetic prevalent through Wilson's career, their crenellated tops and towers giving a picturesque Gothic interpretation to these institutions of discipline. Wilson achieved the rank of Colonel, and during the First World War was in charge of the internment of enemy aliens on the west coast. At first, the aliens were kept in the Saanich prison that Wilson himself designed, and later they were moved to an Internment Camp in Vernon, of which Wilson became the commander.

After the outbreak of war in 1914, Wilson went into partnership with **Alexander Robert Hennell**, an association that lasted until 1918. Hennell carried on the architectural business while Wilson went into the army full-time. By the 1920s Wilson was approaching retirement age and took on smaller projects, although he did not officially retire until 1940.

Ridgway and Flora had five children: Basil, Guy, Percy, Hebden, and Daisy. His grandchildren, who all called him "Pop," were expected to stand when he entered the room. They remember his military bearing and declare that he marched everywhere, never merely walked. He had a bad habit of jay-walking, as he believed it his right to step off the curb wherever and whenever it suited him. Asked to give away his granddaughter Barbara, at her wedding, he was willing but declared, "I have to get to a cricket match that day." She arranged a morning service and wedding breakfast to accommodate his plans, and afterwards the groom drove him to the match which he was attending not as a player, but merely as a devoted spectator.

Despite these stiff characteristics of an English-born military officer, the present writer remembers his friendly piercing eyes and his smart, straight bearing. In 1927, the Wilsons moved in with their son Basil; Flora died in 1939. Wilson continued to be seen daily climbing the stairs from the fifth floor of the Royal Trust (Union) Building to the roof-top quarters of the British Empire Club of which he was a member. He died on February 21, 1957 at the age of ninety-four, and was interred in the family plot in Colwood Burial Park.

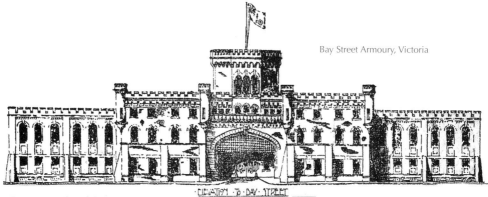

Bay Street Armoury, Victoria

WILLIAM BLACKMORE
1842–1904

DONNA JEAN MacKINNON

One of Vancouver's earliest and most prolific architects, William Blackmore was a successful transplant to pioneer society. Born in England, the son of William and Jane Blackmore, he trained as an architect before he immigrated to Winnipeg about 1878. There he was married to Susan Lavina Cornish of Ontario who was the sister of Winnipeg's first mayor. They had four children, three boys and one girl. Their second son, **Edward Evans Blackmore** also become a prominent architect in Vancouver.

An enterprising man, Blackmore embarked on a number of entrepreneurial projects when he first arrived in the city, purchasing a share in a mine on Seymour Creek in North Vancouver and a section of the mud flats of False Creek east of Main Street. His early architectural projects in Vancouver included a number of buildings erected in 1888: a grand house for C.D. Rand; Fire Hall #2; and the modest first St. Andrew's Presbyterian Church on Melville Street. These were followed by the landmark Manor House at the southwest corner of Howe and Dunsmuir Streets for Joseph Couture, known for most of its life as the Badminton Hotel; the First Congregational Church on Georgia Street; and the Vermilyea Block on Granville Street, all 1889. On May 25, 1890, his impressive new St. Andrew's Presbyterian Church was opened at the corner of Richards and Georgia Streets. In 1891, he designed the impressive Larrabee School in Bellingham, Washington, where he maintained an office for a brief period of time. From then on, he designed a steady stream of buildings, despite the slowdown in Vancouver's economy in the early 1890s.

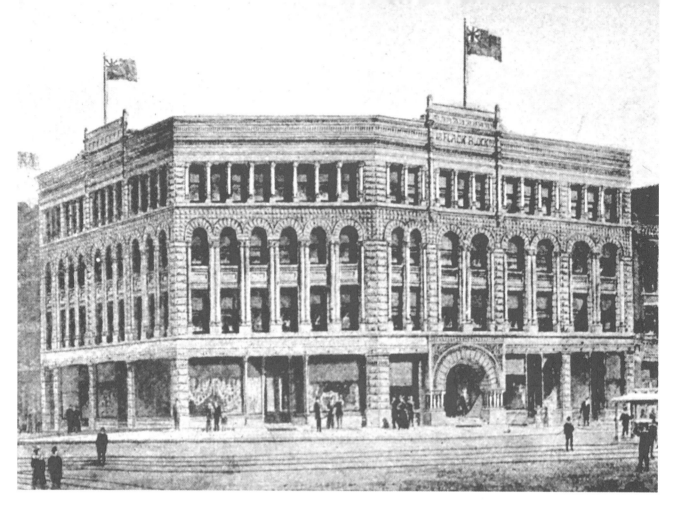

Blackmore had established himself as a designer of commercial blocks, churches and public buildings, as well as designing numerous houses in the West End, indulging the fashion of affluent clients such as John Hendry, the founder of the B.C. Mills Timber & Trading Company conglomerate. In 1899, Blackmore designed a commercial building for Thomas Flack, who had "struck gold" in the Klondike and wanted an impressive building to bear his name. Blackmore's output during the last part of the decade also included a few churches and schools, including the new East End School, 1897. Blackmore's design for the "monster" Fairfield Block, 1898, was thoroughly savaged by the anonymous B.C. Letters correspondent (undoubtedly **R. Mackay Fripp**) in the *Canadian Architect & Builder*, July 1899: "The Fairfield Block is a plain, four-storied erection without any peculiar claims to our attention, being simply a series of bands of brick alternating with stone—rock-faced, of course... The worst features are the entries, which are extremely elementary in conception." Fripp neglected to mention that he had used the same banded brick and stone treatment in his own earlier work. In retrospect, Fripp's comments appear personally motivated, as the Fairfield Block was a very impressive structure, and its exuberance epitomized the boisterous Klondike era. Had it survived it would have been much appreciated today.

Another of Blackmore's landmark projects was the Wesley Methodist Church, 1900-04, which stood at the corner of Burrard and Georgia Streets, originally designed as a masonry structure, but executed in wood. Its Greek cross plan and square central tower bore an obvious resemblance to Henry Hobson Richardson's renowned Trinity Church in Boston, built 1872-77.

In 1901, Blackmore took his son, "Ted" Blackmore, into partnership, and they are jointly credited with several buildings, including an addition to the Sacred Heart Academy and a B.C. Electric Railway office and substation. William Blackmore died at the age of sixty-two on August 10, 1904. He had been an executive member of the Terminal City Club, a men's social and professional club, and served the city as alderman for Ward One in 1902. He was an avid sportsman, and in 1900 was on the executive committee of the Vancouver Bicycle Club.

East End (Strathcona) School, Vancouver

Wesley Methodist Church, Vancouver

(top left) Flack Block, Vancouver

(bottom left) Fairfield Block, Vancouver

THOMAS
HOOPER
1857–1935

DONALD LUXTON

The story of Thomas Hooper echoes the boom and bust cycle of British Columbia's resource-based economy. He had one of this province's longest-running and most prolific architectural careers, but until recently the extent of his accomplishments was virtually unrecognized. He designed hundreds of buildings, travelled extensively in pursuit of numerous institutional and commercial commissions, and made and lost four fortunes. At one point he had the largest architectural practice in western Canada, with offices in three cities, but the First World War and the Great Depression conspired to end his career prematurely. He died a pauper, and was buried in an unmarked grave.

Born in Hatherleigh, Devon, England on March 2, 1857, he was the sixth of eleven children of John and Susan Hooper. Young Thomas was exposed at an early age to the building trades. His uncles, Samuel and James, were both architects and surveyors to the Duchy of Cornwall, and family members had been masons for many generations. John Hooper brought his wife and children to London, Ontario in 1871, and after Thomas completed his schooling he was apprenticed for four years as a carpenter and joiner to J.M. Dodd & Sons. The opening of the west tempted the Hooper family to move to the boomtown of Emerson, Manitoba in 1878. There, Thomas

Hooper married Rebecca Johnson on June 21, 1879; their only child, a daughter, was born in 1880, but died at the age of four months. When it became clear that the railway was going to pass through Winnipeg rather than Emerson, Thomas moved there, and worked as a contractor; later he engaged in architectural work with older brother, Samuel, who in addition to his private architectural practice and work as a sculptor, became, in 1907, the first Provincial Architect of Manitoba.

Thomas Hooper decided to push farther west, and arrived in Vancouver in July, 1886, having walked the last 500 miles to the west coast. His timing was fortuitous, as he arrived in Vancouver just one month after the great fire that had destroyed the burgeoning new community. Hooper worked as Provincial Supervisory Architect from 1887-88, and also established his own practice in 1887. His first projects in Vancouver included several houses, a Chinese Mission church, a commercial block for R.V. Winch, and his largest early commission in Vancouver, the Homer Street Methodist Church, 1888-89. This was the first of many commissions that he received from the Methodists, and marked the beginning of a long association with Ebenezer Robson, a pioneer missionary and brother of B.C. Premier John Robson. As a result of these connections, Hooper was chosen to design the Wallace Street

Protestant Orphans' Home, Victoria
Thomas Hooper standing sixth from left

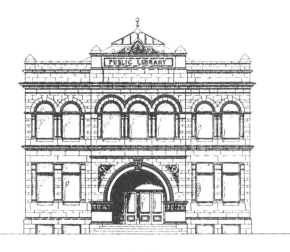

— YATES ST. ELEVATION —

Competition drawing for the Victoria Public (Carnegie) Library, Victoria

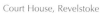

Court House, Revelstoke

Methodist Church in Nanaimo, and the Metropolitan Methodist Church in Victoria, and in 1889 was sent back east by the church elders to tour the new trends in church architecture, where he was exposed to the Romanesque Revival style popularized by H.H. Richardson.

While the Metropolitan Methodist Church was under construction, Hooper shifted the focus of his activities to the more established city of Victoria. From this point on, Hooper maintained offices in both cities, and his practice flourished. He maintained close friendships with many clients, including department store merchants, David Spencer and his son Christopher, and businessmen, R.V. Winch and E.A. Morris, for each of whom he designed a series of buildings.

Always looking to expand his practice, in 1890 Hooper established a partnership in Victoria with **S.M. Goddard**. Although the firm was dissolved in June the following year, together they designed several prominent buildings, including the Wilson & Dalby Block in Victoria, and an Indian Mission School in Port Simpson. In 1891 Hooper also started a short-lived association with a Mr. Reid in Nanaimo, a partnership that produced only one known building, a shopping arcade for David Spencer. In 1893, Hooper won the competition for the Protestant Orphans' Home in Victoria, the design of which is almost a direct quote of Henry Hobson Richardson's Sever Hall at Harvard, 1878-80. Although smaller in scale, Hooper echoed Richardson's symmetrical massing, simple use of red brick, and semi-turrets flanking a round-arched central entry.

Hooper's career suffered during the general depression of the mid-1890s, but flourished again starting with the boom years of the Klondike Gold Rush. He acquired a reputation as a solid and astute businessman who understood the needs of commercial clients, and his office turned out numerous handsome, and sometimes innovative, structures. The front facade of his warehouse for Thomas Earle, Victoria, 1899-1900, is one of the earliest local examples of a glass curtain wall, demonstrating Hooper's awareness of developing trends in architecture in Eastern Canada and the United States.

By 1902 he formed a partnership with **C. Elwood Watkins**, who had entered his office as an apprentice in 1890. Among the many projects that the firm undertook at this time were the successful competition entry for the Victoria Public Library, 1904; the campus for University Schools Ltd. in Saanich, 1908; additions to St. Ann's Academy in Victoria, designed 1908; and many projects in Vancouver including the Odd Fellows Hall, 1905-06; the B.C. Permanent Loan Co. Building, 1907; and the landmark Winch Building, 1906-09.

After the partnership with Watkins ended acrimoniously in 1909, Hooper concentrated on large-scale commercial and institutional projects, advertising himself as a specialist in steel-framed structures. This was the most prolific period of Hooper's career; his work ranged from the magnificent residence *Hycroft*, 1909-12, for A.D. McRae – the most

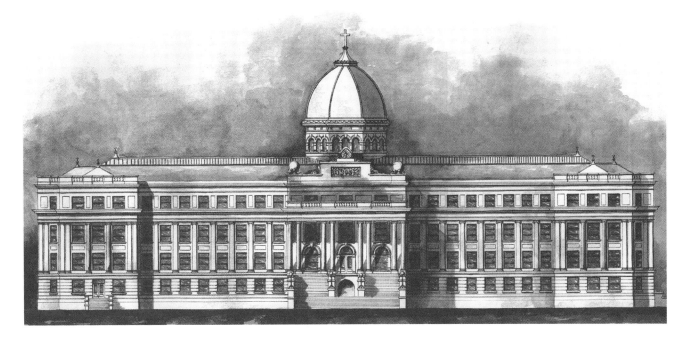

1908 concept drawing for St. Ann's Academy, Victoria

imposing mansion in the CPR's new suburb of Shaughnessy Heights in Point Grey – to court houses, churches, and numerous warehouses and commercial buildings throughout the province. Another grand Shaughnessy residence was *Greencroft*, for Hugh McLean, 1912, with a mixture of Arts and Crafts and Shingle style elements that resembles a baronial hunting lodge, a very unusual departure for Hooper's work; the plans are signed by John M. Goodwin, who possibly took direction more from McLean than Hooper. Other significant projects during the boom years included a tobacco shop for E.A. Morris in Victoria, 1909; the classically-inspired Chilliwack City Hall, 1910-12; the Vancouver Labor Temple, 1910-12; additions to the Vancouver Court House, 1910-12; the Vernon Court House, 1911-14; the Revelstoke Court House, 1911-13; ice arenas for the Patrick Brothers in Vancouver and Victoria, 1911-12; the Tudor Revival mansion *Lyndhurst*, for P.R. Brown in Esquimalt, 1913; and a number of

Proposed Dominion Stock & Bond Building, Vancouver, 1910

Winch Building, Vancouver

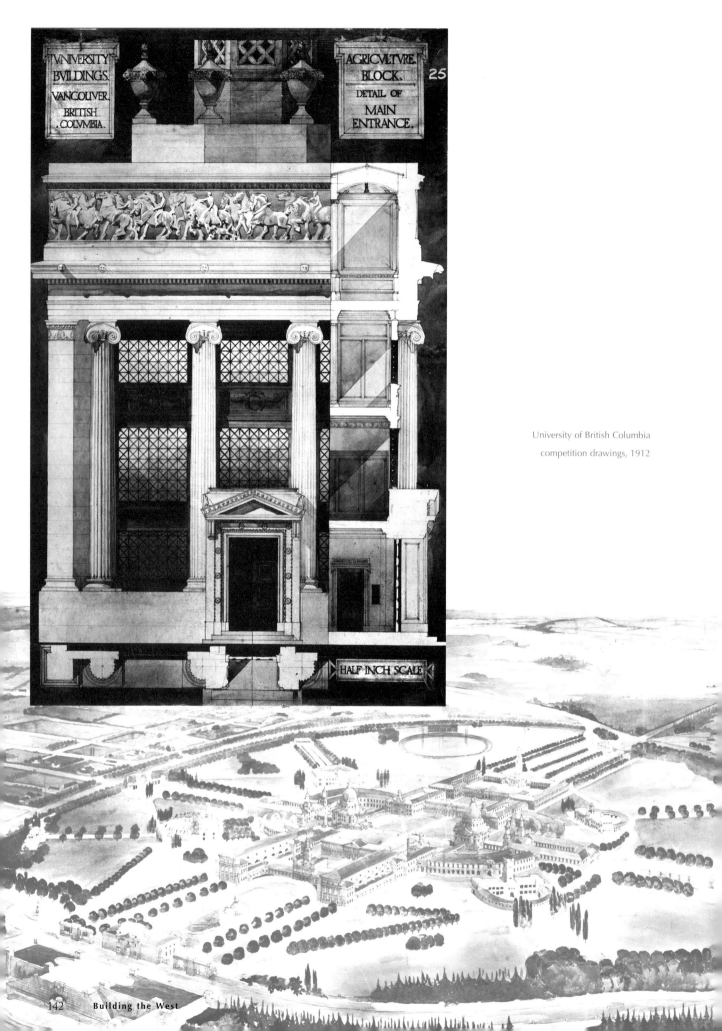

UNIVERSITY BUILDINGS. VANCOUVER BRITISH COLUMBIA.

AGRICULTURE BLOCK. DETAIL OF MAIN ENTRANCE.

25

HALF INCH SCALE

University of British Columbia
competition drawings, 1912

Mr. Hooper, who is one of the leading architects...
Victoria Illustrated, p. 90.

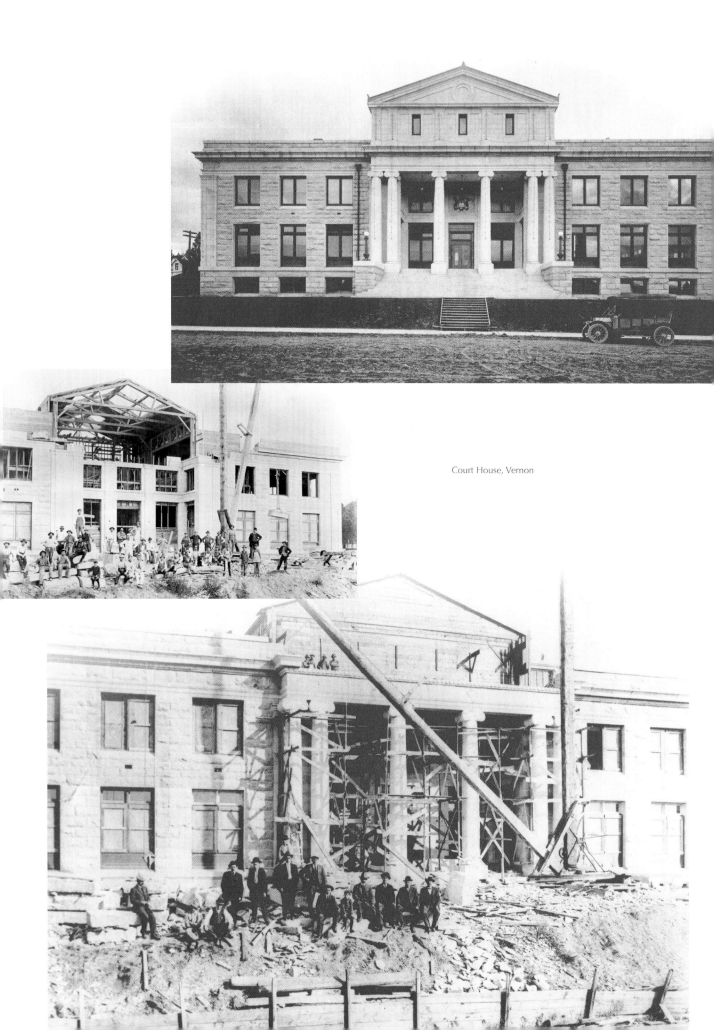

Court House, Vernon

B.C. commissions for the Royal Bank. One of these, the Royal Bank on Government Street in Victoria, 1909-10, has a facade designed by acclaimed New York architects Carrère & Hastings, architects of many landmark buildings including the Beaux-Arts New York Public Library, 1911. This was not an isolated connection – Carrère & Hastings also provided designs for Royal Bank projects in Winnipeg, Alberta, New York and Port of Spain, Trinidad – but indicates the importance of the Victoria commission within the context of British Columbia.

Hooper's office prepared an elaborate submission for the 1912 competition for the new University of British Columbia. His grand *Beaux-Arts* scheme was a beautifully rendered concept that completely disregarded the implicit directions for a free rendering of either a Late Tudor, Elizabethan or Scottish Baronial style. Hooper's designs were so at odds with what was asked for that it was singled out for especially vicious criticism, the judges – including **Samuel Maclure** – stated "it is not desired to erect palaces... the style is frankly classical of a palatial nature... It appears, therefore, that the practical issues such as appropriate planning and cost of erection have been sacrificed to grandiose and pictorial effects." A current assessment of the competition indicates that, in fact, Hooper's entry would likely have produced the most interesting campus, and his personal disappointment at losing this important commission can only be imagined.

The general economic downturn of 1913 caught the booming province by surprise. Many proposed projects were stuck at the planning stage and were eventually abandoned. After an unsuccessful attempt to establish an office in Edmonton, and a failed entry to the Vancouver Civic Centre competition in 1914, Hooper, seeing no future in British Columbia, left in 1915 to try his luck in New York City. Prospects looked brighter there as America was staying out of the European conflict, and Hooper's favoured *Beaux-Arts* style was all the rage, spearheaded by leading firms with all the right social connections such as McKim, Mead & White. He formed a partnership, and was beginning to establish his reputation, when America's entry into the Great War in 1917 choked off any further commissions, and his career was effectively ended. He remained in New York, travelling regularly to Europe with Christopher Spencer on his buying trips, but finally ran through his money and returned penniless to Vancouver in 1927. With the assistance of his family he tried to reestablish his practice. He formed a brief partnership with **Robert Wilson**, who had previously been his office manager, and they are known to have designed one apartment building together in 1928. Hooper also consulted on the design of the Benjamin Franklin Hotel in Seattle (opened 1929, Earl Roberts, Architect), but the Crash of 1929 and the ensuing Depression ended any further attempts to find work. Along with many others he withdrew his membership from the AIBC in 1931, and lived with family members until ill health forced his entry into an Old Folk's home. Hooper died January 1, 1935, and was buried in the family plot of his relatives, the McCauls, in Mountain View Cemetery in Vancouver.

Hooper's importance to the profession in British Columbia lies in his introduction and promotion of new styles of architecture, and his continual development and improvement of commercial building types. In the early 1890s he was involved in the earliest attempts to have the profession officially recognized, and for decades ran large offices that trained a generation of young designers, including C. Elwood Watkins and **J.Y. McCarter**. Hooper was highly regarded by other architects for his business acumen, his personal drive, and his considerable design skills. Along with **Francis Rattenbury**, he was respected by many contractors as the most accomplished and competent of the local architects.

Lyndhurst, Esquimalt

Signature: *Chas. H. Clow*

CHARLES HENRY CLOW

1860–1929

JIM WOLF

Charles H. Clow figures prominently in British Columbia's early construction history, despite a life marred by personal tragedy. He was born in 1860, the son of master carpenter Ambrose Clow of Ayr, Ontario. In 1864, the family moved to Detroit, Michigan, where they lived until 1883, and then moved west to New Westminster. Here both father and son took an active part in contracting, and constructed some of the city's most prominent buildings as part of a company named Murray, Clow and Lord. In 1884, Charles married Jessie McFadden, a native of Detroit, who had travelled west to join him.

Clow left the family contracting business in 1887 when he formed an architectural partnership with New Westminster native son, **Samuel Maclure**. It is not known what formal training Clow had received in architecture apart from his contracting apprenticeship with his father. However, he was described in 1892 as an architect of "well-known experience and ability... [being] more or less interested in building operations all his life." In 1887 Maclure had just returned from his studies in Philadelphia and a brief sojourn in Victoria. The partnership may have been born in the interests of combining Maclure's newfound design skills with Clow's practical construction knowledge, and was very successful from the outset. They concentrated on residential design, and received commissions from some of the city's most prominent families. Several of their earliest projects were adapted from architectural pattern books, and were notable for their introduction of the Queen Anne style to New Westminster; prior to this, residences had usually been built in the Gothic and Italianate styles. Other projects of the firm that received considerable

notice and praise were the Royal Columbian Hospital in Sapperton, 1889, and the YMCA Block at Church and Columbia, 1890, "a very handsome building and is fitted up with all the modern appliances."

Clow's partnership with Maclure was dissolved by March, 1891, but although he continued to design buildings he became pre-occupied with family matters and the establishment of a small farm near Cloverdale in Surrey. As the recession of the mid-1890s took hold, Clow spent more of his time with his family. In 1895 Jessie Clow became ill as the result of a serious pulmonary complaint and was advised by her doctor to return to her old home in Detroit. With her three daughters by her side, she made the journey home and wired her safe arrival back to her husband. Three days later Clow received the tragic news of her death. After a trip to Detroit where he placed his three infant children in the care of relatives, Clow returned to New Westminster. He established a new home and office in the Odd Fellows Block. This was an important fraternal organization in the city and provided much assistance to Clow in his career. He was a charter member of the Odd Fellows Lodge No.13 and this group provided him with many important commissions. Not only was Clow the direct recipient of the commissions for Lodge buildings, but many of his clients were also fraternal associates.

These connections proved especially important to Clow when he became homeless as a result of the Great Fire of New Westminster in September 1898. Clow lost all of his possessions in the fire, including his library of books and plans, drafting tools, and office furniture; he received only two blankets and $50 from the fire relief committee. Thanks to his

Royal Columbian Hospital, New Westminster

fraternal connections, he was given several important commissions and was back in business within a few months. In fact, he had so much work that he took on a partner, young Daniel Welsh, a native of New Westminster, from 1899-1904.

The fire created opportunities for new commissions, including the reconstruction of the Reformed Episcopal Church, 1899. During the building boom prior to 1913, Clow once again enjoyed popularity among the prominent families of New Westminster. Residential designs by Clow mixed the popular elements of Classical Revival and Craftsman styles. His house interiors achieved a refined state of modern Arts and Crafts elegance, incorporating built-in furniture, inglenooks, grand stair halls, and art glass. Another project was a new YMCA Building on Royal Avenue, 1910. Between 1910 and 1912 he employed newly-arrived and talented young **Joseph F. Watson** in his office.

During this busy period Clow decided to return to his ranch in Cloverdale. As Surrey's first resident architect, Clow received a number of prominent commissions. At Cloverdale, his fraternal connections provided him with the commission to design and supervise construction of the Odd Fellows Hall in 1904. This unique lodge temple building, although small, was rendered monumental through Clow's clever employment of decorative wood exterior details. In 1912 he designed the Arts and Crafts-style Surrey Municipal Hall at Cloverdale, which was Surrey's most prominent architectural landmark of the time, and which still stands today as a municipally-designated heritage building. In addition, Clow was hired as early as 1910 as the Surrey School Board's architect, a position he retained well into the 1920s.

In 1913 Clow married Christiana Gordon Davidson and they spent the war years farming their property on Clow Road in Surrey near Sullivan Station. Sadly, Christiana died in 1918 and Clow all but retired to his farmhouse, where he lived as a recluse. After a short illness he died at Saint Mary's Hospital in New Westminster on July 7, 1929, and his fellow lodge members ensured that he was buried in the Odd Fellows Cemetery with full ceremony. His obituary noted that Clow was "of a quiet retiring nature and was not conspicuous outside his lodge and profession, though he was for many years a member of the choir of St. Andrews (Presbyterian) church." When Clow's $2,500 estate was probated a year after his death, it was discovered that he had stock certificates hidden among his book collection valued at over $10,000. The members of the Odd Fellows Lodge became the grateful beneficiaries.

Clow Residence, New Westminster

Idlewild, New Westminster

YMCA, New Westminster

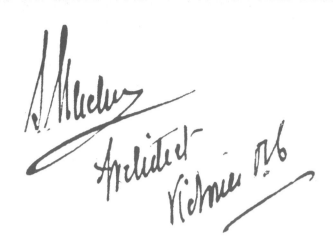

SAMUEL
MACLURE

1860–1929

PERSONAL BIOGRAPHY BY JANET BINGHAM

The name of architect Samuel Maclure is synonymous with the predominantly Tudor Revival style of his domestic architecture. This naturally leads to the assumption that Maclure's background and training were of English origin. In fact, as the Vancouver *World* of 1897 stated, Maclure was "British Columbian to the marrow bone." His father, John Cunningham Maclure, of Wigtonshire, Scotland, was a surveyor in the party of **Royal Engineers** sent to the Mainland Colony of British Columbia in 1858. His mother, Martha McIntyre from Cookstown near Belfast, followed her husband to the new colony. Their first son, Samuel, was born on April 11, 1860 in the Royal Engineers' camp at Sapperton, near New Westminster, B.C.

After the Engineers were disbanded, John Maclure took his family up the Fraser River, in 1868, to settle on 150 acres which he was awarded by the British Government. He chose his land on the south bank of the river at Matsqui, near the Sumas border, in order to create a telegraph repeater station to send news emanating from the United States to the rest of the province. The main room of the Maclure family's pioneer cabin became an important repeater station. John Maclure taught his five children, including Samuel, to operate the telegraphic key and as time went on Samuel, his brother Charles and his sisters, Sara and Susan, all operated telegraph stations in various parts of the province.

Young Samuel grew up enjoying the freedom of completely unspoiled natural surroundings at *Hazelbrae*, the family homestead. There were fish to be caught in nearby streams and each Maclure son was allowed at the age of twelve to shoot game for their mother to cook. For a few years Samuel attended the local school, but soon outgrew this and was encouraged to apply for a final two years of high school in Victoria. There he began to take a serious interest in art, demonstrating a surprising talent. Since Maclure longed to study art in Germany, he worked to raise the funds as a telegrapher at Granville (Vancouver) from 1880-81 and as a Government Agent in New Westminster in 1882. He also foolishly speculated in land at Port Moody and lost much of his investment. Unable to afford European training, he left for Philadelphia in May, 1884 to attend the Spring Garden School of Art, where he could stay at the home of an aunt. Maclure's year away from home was in his words "a heavenly time." He had never seen such paved roads and sidewalks, tall ornamented buildings or city squares and parks. The buildings of the great cities of the United States, including New York, had a tremendous impact on him and created his interest in pursuing architecture.

He returned home, in June, 1885, to assist his family financially, and worked briefly as a telegrapher in Duncan. Frequent visits to Victoria however, led to his romance with Margaret Catherine (Daisy) Simpson with whom he eloped to New Westminster. In the 1890s, New Westminster was a booming commercial centre, the main distribution point on the Fraser River. Maclure's need to earn a living led him to try his hand at drawing architectural plans. The couple's first daughter, Catherine, was born in 1890. In 1891 the Maclure's second child, Helen, was born but she died shortly after birth. This sad event may have prompted the family's move to Victoria to be closer to Daisy's parents. The Maclures both became involved with Victoria's artistic community – Daisy, an excellent musician, giving recitals, and as a painter herself, becoming well known for her miniature portraits of the local Aboriginal people. "Sam" Maclure gave classes in painting, which were attended by the leisured class, mostly women. All this exposure of their talents was helpful in the establishment of an architectural career for Maclure. Two more children were added to the family during their early years there, Barbara born in 1892 and Merione born in 1896.

When the Maclures settled in Victoria it was still the largest city in the province and money was available for investment. Samuel Maclure's first commissions of note were for prominent businessmen. On several occasions he worked closely with **F.M. Rattenbury**, with whom he shared office space. By 1907 his reputation for designing exceptionally beautiful homes led to his largest commission, as the architect of *Hatley Park* on the outskirts of Victoria. His client, Lieutenant-Governor of the province, James Dunsmuir, gave Maclure a free hand in planning this forty room house/castle, and the opportunity to travel to Europe to choose furnishings, his first and only trip abroad.

Recognition of his talent was spreading, and he opened a branch office in Vancouver with his young partner, Cecil Croker Fox, in charge. Frequent trips to the Mainland to check

Maclure's Victoria office; Ross Lort on the right, possibly Cecil Croker Fox on the left

up on work in progress gave Maclure the opportunity to also visit the old family homestead in Matsqui. There his brother, Charles, was establishing a brickmaking industry using local fireclay. Maclure became involved in the planning of Clayburn, the small surrounding village.

Praise for Samuel Maclure's architecture appeared in international magazines and periodicals throughout his forty year career. During this period it is estimated he designed close to five hundred structures, most of which were houses. An article in the American publication, *The Craftsman*, called a Victoria house of 1908 "absolutely suited to its environment," while the popular *British Country Life* featured another of his masterpieces in photos and text. A Paris journal in the twenties called Maclure "this noteworthy artist" and went on to say that he was "gifted with an original, inventive, pliable and trustworthy genius." Requests for him to design houses took him to Lytton, Armstrong and Summerland in B.C., and to Edmonton and Toronto, and Ellensburg, Washington, where he designed a large bungalow for a Scottish merchant. Many of his clients, usually those with an English background, preferred his Tudor Revival style. Maclure had absorbed many stylistic influences, however, and was able to adapt his use of indigenous materials with remarkable versatility.

With the advent of the First World War the pace of building slackened. Three young men close to Maclure enlisted. Douglas McLagan, the only son of his eldest sister, Sara, was killed in action, as was Cecil Fox. **Ross Lort**, who had also trained with Maclure, returned from the war unscathed, and in 1920 headed the vacant Vancouver office. The Maclure & Lort partnership survived under his management, though clients were fewer than in prewar times, and houses were less extravagantly planned. Debts began to haunt Maclure and he would often sell a hastily executed watercolour to pay bills. Poor health plagued him throughout the following years, and he

died after a short illness on August 8, 1929.

It was not until the 1970s that Maclure's work came into focus. Leonard Eaton, an architectural historian from the University of Michigan, was surprised during a visit to Victoria by the number of houses designed in a very distinctive style, with dark, half-timbered motifs. He declared this the work of a major artist who deserved to be part of the Canadian heritage. Many of Maclure's buildings have now been recognized as masterworks of design, and are cherished as part of British Columbia's heritage.

All his life Sam found an absorbing interest in the beauties and natural surroundings of British Columbia, and to the very end he retained in his charming water colour sketches an unfailingly accurate perception of the colouring and arrangement of things around him.

Ross Lort, RAIC *Journal*, April, 1958, p.114.

Daisy and Samuel Maclure and their three daughters, Victoria c. 1899

SAMUEL MACLURE

PROFESSIONAL BIOGRAPHY BY JIM WOLF

Temple Building, Victoria

The life and work of Samuel Maclure were inextricably connected with British Columbia's early history and prominent residents, and his name is legendary. Several of his buildings are among the best known and loved in the province. The architectural achievements of this native son have been chronicled in many books and articles that attempt to define his fascinating career. One of the most remarkable aspects of Samuel Maclure's success was that his training was more practical than formal. In 1887 he began working as an architect in partnership with the young building contractor and architect **Charles Henry Clow** in New Westminster. They received many local commissions for residences as the City's population grew because of its connection to the Canadian Pacific Railway in 1886. The firm relied extensively on pattern books for inspiration to create their Queen Anne-styled residences. However, their design talent evolved through experience and was rewarded with two of the city's largest commissions, the Royal Columbian Hospital, and the YMCA Block. In a competition to design the City's Library, Clow & Maclure's design submission won first prize; however, they lost the commission to rival **George W. Grant**, despite an aggressive battle by their fellow architects to reverse the decision based on improper competition procedures.

In 1891 Maclure started a new partnership with **Richard P. Sharp**, a talented and experienced English architect. Together they excelled at designing residences based primarily on the Victorian British Arts and Crafts style. They lavished attention on their functional and beautiful interiors, utilizing B.C. native woods extensively. In this brief period Maclure clearly learned much from Sharp, developing a signature style that would carry him successfully through his early career.

Maclure's relocation from New Westminster's failing economy to more stable Victoria in 1892, and the establishment of his solo practice, began auspiciously with a commission to design the Temple Building for Robert Ward and Company. Completed in 1893, its design was influenced by the work of American architects, H.H. Richardson and Louis Sullivan, and was recognized at the time for its inspired and vigorous execution. This success boosted his reputation, which grew among wealthy and influential clients. One noteworthy residential commission was *Ruhebuhne*, built 1895-97 for prominent politician and financier, A.C. Flumerfelt, which

Vancouver World Building, Vancouver

Ruhebuhne, Victoria

Bank of Montreal Manager's Residence, Vernon

was Tudor Revival in style and designed on an extravagant scale. Maclure's residential style had become increasingly American in spirit following his return from a tour of the largest of its eastern cities in 1897. During this period Maclure also became an admirer of the work of Frank Lloyd Wright, with whom he later corresponded. Maclure's style was widely recognized as artistically unique. It garnered a national audience in 1899 when a number of his buildings were featured in the *Canadian Architect & Builder.*

As the economy improved at the turn of the century, Maclure's talent was put to the test with larger and more prominent commissions garnered from wealthy Victoria society. He also designed smaller homes similar to the new bungalow home he built for his own family on Superior Street, 1899. It was featured in the Victoria Tourist Association leaflet and copied in the widely distributed magazine, *Beautiful Homes of America.* This resulted in a large number of local commissions and inquiries from as far east as Buffalo, New York. The "Maclure Bungalow" was not to be confused with the popular California Bungalow house form, of which Maclure was an outspoken critic. He felt it simply did not fit into British Columbia's rugged landscape.

During this time Maclure recognized the opportunity for additional commissions in Vancouver, as it began to eclipse Victoria as the province's metropolis. He established a brief partnership with **J.E. Parr** in 1897 and then joined fellow Victoria architect, **C.J. Soule**, in an office from 1898-99. It is yet unclear what commissions were undertaken by these two partnerships. Soule was involved, perhaps in a supervisory role, in Maclure's design for the Strathcona Lodge at Shawnigan Lake in 1900. Maclure was clearly on his own by 1900, when he received a plum commission to design *Gabriola*, a grand sandstone mansion for sugar baron, Benjamin Tingley Rogers, on Davie Street in Vancouver's West End. The completion of this landmark structure provided Maclure with widespread press coverage and elevated his reputation throughout the province.

Maclure's prominence and skill in residential design led to his appointment by the provincial government for the design of the new Lieutenant-Governor's home, with **F.M. Rattenbury** as supervising architect. In this commission it is widely surmised that Rattenbury was responsible for the design. However, Maclure's signature style was seen throughout the beautiful interior and its decorations – on which he collaborated with artist **James Bloomfield** – which paid homage to British Columbia's natural flora and the art of its Aboriginal people in wall murals and stained glass.

Through these landmark residential projects Maclure's fame spread, and in 1900 he took on a young English assistant, Cecil Croker Fox. Born in Falmouth, England in 1879, Fox had attended Malvern School, and then moved to London where he was a student of the famous Victorian architect, Alfred Waterhouse. Fox entered the very select practice of C.F.A. Voysey (1857-1941), a gifted architect and one of the leading proponents of the British Arts and Crafts movement. Yet in spite of his work being popular and well-publicised he only employed two or three draftsmen at a time, and Fox would have worked under Voysey's close supervision. Fox spent two years under Voysey, until in 1898, accompanied by his father, he left England for Victoria. Fox joined Maclure's office and soon the two men had established a common architectural aesthetic and working relationship. Maclure's architectural skills were in great demand not only in Victoria, where he lived, but also in the Lower Mainland, and in 1905 he had so much work on hand that he opened a Vancouver office with Fox as his partner-in-charge.

Maclure's greatest achievement came in 1907 with the commission to design *Hatley Park*, for which he was solely responsible. This palatial estate residence for James and Laura Dunsmuir was said at the time to be the finest home in Canada. In this mammoth project Maclure was assisted by English draftsman, **Douglas James**. He was also funded by the Dunsmuirs to travel to Europe, to locate and purchase furnishings and to satisfy his long held dream to see its art and archi-

Hatley Park, Colwood; rendering by P. Leonard James

Overlynn, Burnaby

tecture. The completion of *Hatley Park* coincided with professional tragedy when the Five Sisters Block in Victoria was destroyed by fire in 1910, eliminating his valued studio, library and historically valuable record of commissions.

Maclure's chosen idiom of the medieval half-timbered Arts and Crafts home received much attention as the style of choice for the elite of both Vancouver and Victoria. Despite trying "time after time to break away from" the Tudor idiom and experimenting with rough cedar siding and stucco, Maclure was typecast, and clients continued to demand his half-timbered house. Fox's experience and knowledge, however, helped infuse Maclure's work with a more modern English style, and brought an entirely new aspect to the character of their designs. Perhaps the change was best described in *Canadian Architect & Builder* in 1908, describing the Victoria residence of Alexis Martin designed by Maclure: "The blending of English taste with that which is characteristic of the architecture of our own Pacific Coast has an effect of quiet sumptuousness, combined with straight-forward utility." Fox not only brought the Voysey aesthetic to the partnership, but also knowledge of the best English architectural supply firms, giving their designs an elegant refinement rarely seen in British Columbia. Maclure also did his best to improve the development of artists and crafts people in British Columbia by supporting the fledgling Vancouver Arts and Crafts Society, established in 1900, and founding with other artists the Victoria-based Island Arts and Crafts Society in 1909. Early in his career Maclure had developed an intimate knowledge of the use of local woods and stone and of the ability of local firms to manufacture, install and finish the finest cedar, fir and maple

interior fittings to his own designs. He also cultivated local talent such as wood carver, George S. Gibson to create interior decorations, inspired from the native landscape in the best Arts and Crafts tradition. Maclure's artistic development became focused on interior layout and the decoration of his designs which became ever more refined. He achieved extraordinary spatial arrangements in many residences by incorporating double-height, galleried central halls, which became one of his trademarks. His hobby of gardening also became part of his practice as he expertly drew many landscape designs, including several elements of the famous Butchart Gardens in Central Saanich.

The booming economy of 1911-13 and the creation of new residential districts such as the Uplands in Victoria and Vancouver's Shaughnessy Heights created an unprecedented growth in the construction of homes for wealthy British Columbians. Maclure & Fox were at the height of their success and influence, and between 1909-15 the Vancouver office alone received almost sixty commissions, including several country clubs, two private schools and a host of large residences. Two adjacent residences facing The Crescent in Shaughnessy Heights demonstrate Maclure & Fox stylistic range, the Dockrill Residence, 1910, with its emphatic half-timbering, and the Walter C. Nichol Residence, 1912-13, more evocative of the British Arts and Crafts movement. Fox also left his particular stamp on the Huntting House in Shaughnessy Heights, 1911-13, by creating a design with unmistakable Voyseyan elements: an extraordinarily low front double gable effect with rows of casement windows stamped out of the rough stucco facade – not only Voysey trademarks but an imitation of the great architect's own home, *The Orchard*, at Chorley Wood, Hertfordshire, England, built 1900.

Maclure's reputation and client base spread beyond British Columbia in this prewar period. Both national and international design periodicals profiled his designs. From his connections with wealthy patrons came other non-residential commissions, such as the Vancouver Golf Club in Coquitlam, and private schools in Vancouver that emulated Maclure's residential design aesthetic. Commercial projects were rare but included elegant buildings such as the $100,000 B.C. Electric Railway Company station in New Westminster, designed with Fox in 1909, and the Jones Building of Victoria, 1912. Now at the height of his success, Maclure regarded his appointment as one of the assessors to determine the winner in the 1912 University of B.C. competition one of the highest compliments of his career.

The 1913 recession and the outbreak of the First World War brought significant change to Maclure's practice. The Vancouver office closed in 1915 when Cecil Fox returned to England to enlist, serving as a lieutenant with the 12th Battalion of the East Surrey Regiment. Tragically, he was killed in action in France on September 15, 1916. After the war **Ross Lort**, a long time Maclure apprentice and draftsman, was made a full partner, and the Vancouver office came under his direction from 1920-23. An example of the firm's work at this time is an Arts and Crafts bungalow for C.B. McAllister on Connaught Drive in Shaughnessy, 1920, designed at a much more modest scale than the great prewar projects.

During the 1920s Maclure maintained a busy practice in Victoria where from time to time he collaborated with other architects. His designs followed a national trend towards smaller and more economical residences, reflecting the reality that most families now lived without servants. A change in popular tastes finally let Maclure experiment with the symmetrical and classical Georgian Revival style, and the English Cottage style, featuring roughcast stucco exteriors. However, his Tudor Revival designs remained popular.

The pleasure of designing yet another elaborate residence eventually came Maclure's way in 1924. This was to be a summer home, called *Miraloma*, at Sidney, on Vancouver Island, for Lieutenant-Governor Walter C. Nichol, for whom Maclure & Fox had previously designed a grand Shaughnessy mansion. This unusual commission, completed in 1926, brought out all his artistic ability. Described as "an extremely powerful statement in wood," the house was entirely clad in undressed Douglas Fir, creating a completely unique rustic exterior.

When Maclure died in 1929, the City of Victoria mourned the passing of one of their most remarkable citizens and a great Canadian artist. His body was cremated and the ashes spread at his childhood home at Matsqui Prairie by his brother, Charles, and Ross Lort. Daisy Maclure hoped to continue her husband's practice by reopening the Victoria office with architect Wallace Deffett in charge and Ross Lort heading up a new Vancouver office. However, this attempt failed due to the lack of family finances and the Great Depression. As a result the firm's drawings were transferred to Lort, who knew their value and ensured their survival. Through these records and many surviving buildings the artistic genius of Maclure is revealed as a true legacy of architectural achievement.

B.C. Electric Railway Co. Station, New Westminster

LEONARD BUTTRESS TRIMEN

1846–1892

CAREY PALLISTER AND DOROTHY MINDENHALL

L. Buttress Trimen immigrated to Victoria by June 1887, soon after his arrival he obtained some substantial commissions in the execution of which he demonstrated confidence, skill, and an understanding of current ideas in building design. The evidence of his buildings suggests a confidence and assurance born of experience and training, although little is known, at present, of his early life. He was born in London, England in 1846, son of Andrew Trimen and Mary Buttress. In 1872 he married Susannah Mary Chaille at Isleworth, west of London and they had three children.

One of his earliest works in Victoria was the north-west wing of Victoria City Hall, 1888, in which he, of necessity, followed the style of the existing building but included design details – subtly altered window heads, more ornate eaves brackets, and a baroque treatment of the dormers – to give this wing his personal stamp. When the congregation of St. Andrew's Presbyterian Church outgrew their building on Courtney Street (1868, by **H.O. Tiedemann**), Trimen designed a new one for them on Douglas Street at Broughton, 1889-90. He employed

St. Andrew's Presbyterian Church, Victoria

the Scottish Baronial style, appropriate for a congregation which adhered to the Scottish origins of the denomination, but added architectural elements, such as polychrome brickwork and a diaper-patterned roof, that demonstrate his awareness of the ideas of the Gothic Revival architects in England at the middle of the nineteenth century. He obtained a number of commissions from the family of wealthy and prestigious coal baron, Robert Dunsmuir. In 1890 he designed a residence, *Mount Adelaide*, for Henry Croft and his wife, the former Mary Dunsmuir. It was a Tudor Revival-style mansion with half timbering on the second storey, patterned timbering in the gables, overhanging eaves, and an open tower, rectangular in plan. For Dunsmuir's daughter, Emily Ellen and her husband, Northing Pickney Snowden, Trimen designed a grand "Elizabethan" house on the Gorge, *Ashnola*, 1889. For Joan Dunsmuir, the widow of Robert Dunsmuir, he designed a lodge and gateway for *Craigdarroch Castle* in 1891.

His commercial work included two buildings on Johnson Street in 1890 for Henry Saunders, the Colonial Metropole

Saunders Groceries, Victoria

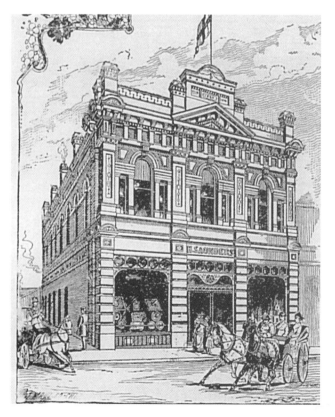

Colonial Metropole Hotel, Victoria

Bushby Block far right, Hamley Block adjacent; New Westminster

Hotel, and a grocery and liquor store farther up the street. The central portion of the hotel is plain but with elaborate Eastlake decoration along the cornice line and on the pilasters; the east wing has a mixture of styles, including Italianate shallow arched window heads and false quoins, with decorative capitals on the second floor and, on the third floor, flat headed windows surmounted with crown mouldings. For Saunders's store Trimen designed in the Free Classic style. The original building had a pedimented central bay, rusticated pilasters at street level, and a decorative cornice. When it was built it reputedly had the largest glass windows in the city. Trimen's other works included: a three-storey brick block for the Brackman-Ker Company on Government Street, 1889; five stores on Johnson Street and two on Oriental Alley for E.H. Anderson; a flouring mill and warehouses for the Mount Royal Milling Company, 1890, for which he employed polychrome brickwork as he had in St. Andrew's; a brick building near Johnson Street for Powell & Currall, 1891; and residences for Mr. Caton, 1888, and for Frederick Elworthy in James Bay, 1890. In 1888-89 he designed two adjacent business blocks on Columbia Street in New Westminster, the Hamley and Bushby Blocks, both built 1888-89, and both destroyed in the Great Fire of 1898.

Sadly, Trimen's career in Victoria spanned fewer than five years. Having executed over twenty commissions in the short time he had been in the city, he died, in 1892, at the age of forty-six, and was buried in Ross Bay Cemetery.

Bushby Block, New Westminster

ROBERT
MACKAY
FRIPP
1858–1917

EDWARD MILLS

In March 1888, a young English adventurer disembarked from a ship on the Vancouver waterfront. Within days of his arrival, R. Mackay Fripp placed an advertisement in the *Daily Herald*, offering his services as an experienced architect and "lessons and instructions in practical drawing and various branches of the building trade." So began the intermittent local career of one of British Columbia's most intriguing early architects. Fripp's life and career epitomizes the unique set of circumstances that existed for young British-born professionals during the High Victorian era. Vancouver represented yet another stop in a journey that began with his departure from London and which would continue with subsequent travels to various parts of the world. Above all else he valued drawing and education, which pulled him restlessly between centres of creativity such as Toronto, London and Los Angeles, as well as to sites of opportunity like Auckland and Vancouver.

Born December 16, 1858 in Clifton, Gloucestershire, Robert Mackay Fripp was one of twelve children of George Arthur Fripp, a prominent English watercolourist favoured by Queen Victoria. His family background included a long line of architects out of Bristol. Two of his brothers, Charles and Thomas, pursued successful artistic careers, the former as a globe-travelling artist-correspondent for London's *Graphic Magazine* and the latter as an important pioneering British Columbia landscape artist and founding President of the British Columbia Society of Fine Art. Following private tutorage with his father, Robert was sent to Berkshire to article in the architectural firm of J.S. Dodd. During his three years in Berkshire, young Fripp was directly exposed to the Arts and Crafts theories of Richard Norman Shaw and William Morris.

These influences shaped Fripp's aesthetic views about art and architecture, and imbued him with a lifelong belief in the architect's role as an educator, so much so that in later life he combined his architectural practice with active involvement as a lecturer and organizer of artistic and professional organizations. Following this, in 1879-80 he worked in the office of Sir Horace Jones, London City Architect.

Possibly spurred on by the colourful life of his older brother, Charles, Robert Fripp struck out on a prolonged journey that took him through Europe, South Africa, eastern India, Tasmania and Australia. In 1881 he ended up in Auckland, New Zealand, where he was first employed by William F. Hammond. He later worked as a draftsman for Sir William Fox, and taught architecture classes at the Auckland Society of the Arts. Fripp set up his own practice in Auckland, and on February 27, 1887, married Christina Nichol. In early 1888, he boarded a ship and set off for Vancouver where he met up with Charles. Robert's time in Auckland had been very busy and productive, and he must have had high expectations that this growing new city would provide rich opportunities for an experienced architect. The brothers formed an architectural partnership, and achieved

Proposed business premises, Vancouver

immediate success, including commercial blocks for A.G. Ferguson, 1888, and Harry Abbott, 1889, but Charles left Vancouver in 1889.

R. Mackay Fripp was a man of diverse interests and strong convictions, particularly with regard to the social importance of art and architecture. His commitment to the aesthetic tenets of the British Arts and Crafts movement extended well beyond his architectural commissions, and indeed his published drawings demonstrated a much higher quality of design than he was able to achieve in this frontier context. He was also one of the few architects in either Vancouver and Auckland to seek RIBA membership. From 1894 onwards, he aired his strongly critical views on the state of art and architecture in British Columbia in a series of letters and articles that appeared in national publications. His adventuresome spirit found him forming an expedition with four friends and native guides to discover the headwaters of the Capilano River in 1890. He

The Bungalow, Vancouver

A.J. Dana Residence, Vancouver

Proposed Masonic Temple

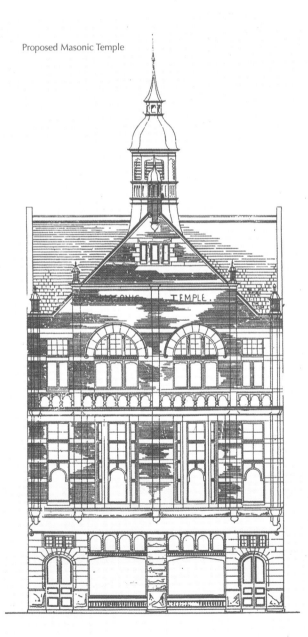

A.G. Ferguson Block, Vancouver

lectured to Chautaquas and various Arts and Crafts organizations on art, archaeology and architecture, and served as founding President of the Vancouver Arts and Crafts Society in 1900. In 1910, he was named a fellow of the Royal Society of Arts. In a dramatic and public split with the B.C. Society of Architects in 1914, Fripp led the breakaway group of ten men

British Columbia Land & Investment Agency Building, Vancouver, 1892

wards, Fripp acquired a waterfront lot nearby on Coal Harbour, on which he built a modest half-timbered frame house for himself. Fripp's most notable residential designs from this phase were a rambling Elizabethan cottage built for A.J. Dana, the CPR's first purchasing agent, 1889, and *The Bungalow*, built in 1890 for sugar magnate, Benjamin Tingley Rogers, unique in showing the influence of the sprawling New Zealand villa with surrounding verandahs that was common in Auckland.

Fripp entered briefly into a partnership with English-born architect Herbert Winkler Wills (1864-1937). Educated in London, Wills left for New York to work in the offices of McKim, Mead & White and Henry Vaughan in Boston, before returning to London. He next moved to Hong Kong, where he worked in the Public Works department for three years before relocating in British Columbia. In January 1892 Fripp & Wills set up offices in Vancouver and New Westminster, but later that year they submitted separate entries to the competition for the Parliament Buildings, Fripp on his own and Wills in association with **J.G. Tiarks**. The downturn in the local economy by the following year undoubtedly contributed to Wills's decision to return to Great Britain, where he achieved moderate professional success.

Fripp was briefly active in Vernon. W.W. Spinks, Judge of Court for the County of Yale, moved from Kamloops to Vernon in 1892, and commissioned Fripp & Wills to design a grand new home, which he took possession of in April, 1894. In July 1893 the Bank of Montreal commissioned Fripp to design a new branch office in Vernon. Although the building was moved in 1909 and altered, it is still extant. Fripp was also involved with Lord Aberdeen's ranching and orchard investments in the area. Aberdeen's manager at his Guisachan Ranch, Coutts Majoribanks, had a rambling house built by a local contractor in 1891. Aberdeen's solicitor was sent out in 1892 to see why these investments were failing, and expressed his surprise that no architect had been employed on the design

that founded the British Columbia Institute of Architects, the group that ultimately became the current Architectural Institute of B.C.

There were three phases in Fripp's architectural career in British Columbia that were interrupted by work and travel in other parts of the world. His first Vancouver practice began in 1888 and lasted until 1896. During this period Fripp secured numerous commissions from prominent local and absentee investors and businessmen, including two prominent English investors, the Marquis of Queensbury and Thomas Dixon Galpin, the London-based manager of the B.C. Land & Investment Agency.

Although Fripp profited from the early demand for conventional commercial blocks in downtown Vancouver, he found greater opportunity to indulge in his passion for British Arts and Crafts aesthetics through a series of residential and institutional commissions. This began with a half-timbered clubhouse in Coal Harbour designed with his brother, Charles, for the newly-established Vancouver Boating Club, the precursor of the Vancouver Rowing Club, in March 1888. Shortly after-

Provincial Home, Kamloops

Bank of Montreal, Vernon

Spinks Residence, Vernon

of the house. When tenders were called late in 1892 for Aberdeen's large jam-canning factory in Vernon, the plans were prepared by Fripp. With all these projects in hand, on July 6, 1893 Fripp announced his intention to open an office in Vernon. These plans never materialized, as the local economy slumped at the time along with the rest of the province.

Fripp's largest commission of the period was the Provincial Home constructed near downtown Kamloops. This rambling institution for "aged, indigent and infirm persons," commonly known as the Old Men's Home, was designed in 1893-94, and opened in 1895. Complete with a large dining room, sitting and smoking rooms, and dormitories, it was set on 320

acres with an established orchard and extensive surrounding gardens. Fripp's first British Columbia phase drew to a close during the economic doldrums of the mid-1890s. Obviously disappointed with what was happening in British Columbia, in 1896 he returned to Auckland, New Zealand where he revived his former practice. He remained there for two years, and his residential work showed a new maturity, such as the shingled Bloomfield House in Parnell that overlooked the Waitemata Harbour. He formed a brief partnership with George Selwyn Goldsboro' in 1898, before sailing back to British Columbia.

The second phase in Fripp's British Columbia career extended from 1898 to 1901 and was divided between Victoria and

Competition drawing for State Capitol, Olympia, Washington

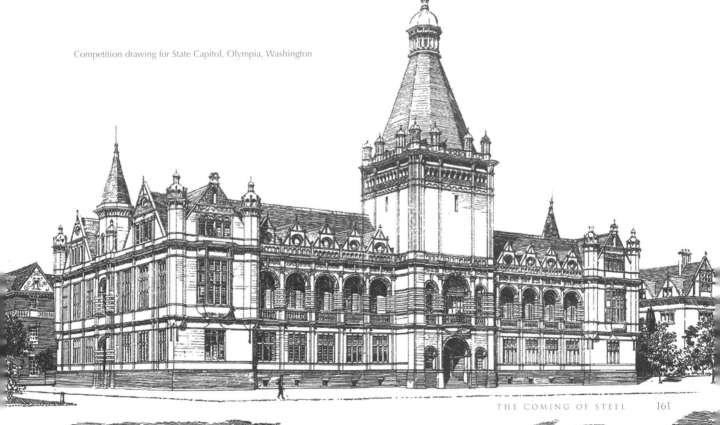

Vancouver. During this period he became increasingly committed to the cause of the Arts and Crafts movement. In his letters to the *Canadian Architect & Builder*, he railed against the mediocrity of prevailing architectural standards in British Columbia. Convinced that it was the duty of architects to elevate public taste in design, he proceeded to found an Arts and Crafts society in Vancouver "based upon similar lines to the now famous Arts and Crafts Society of London, founded by the late Mr. William Morris." Fripp's crusading zeal failed to attract much interest beyond a small circle of English-trained architects and artisans, and his dwindling number of architectural commissions suggests that his strident idealism drove a wedge between him and his prospective clientele. In late 1901 Fripp departed for England. He appeared briefly in Toronto, and his passion for the Arts and Crafts movement was clearly undiminished. This passion led him, in 1905, to strike out for Los Angeles, California, then the centre of the burgeoning American Craftsman movement. He had his office in the same building as **Charles and Henry Greene**, its most celebrated exponents. Fripp produced plans for modest bungalows in the Craftsman style, but also larger residences, including one for Dr. W.T. MacArthur in Los Angeles, 1905-08.

In 1908 he returned to Vancouver to begin the third and final phase of his British Columbia career. By that time Vancouver was on the brink of another major construction boom, and prevailing tastes had moved closer to the aesthetic ideals that Fripp had been championing for a decade or more. Fripp rode the crest of this favourable climate which continued until 1914. His output during this period was prolific and consisted mainly of residential designs which ranged from modest California bungalows to stately Tudor Revival homes in Shaughnessy and Point Grey. The most intriguing aspect of this phase in his career lay in his introduction of Craftsman design elements to Vancouver. This is especially well-illustrated by the 1910 S.B. Snider residence located in Kitsilano Point, in which the influence of the Greene Brothers is revealed through Fripp's bold use of heavy timber structural elements. This design anticipated the profusion of California bungalows that appeared throughout the lower mainland during the following decade. Commissions from this period include residences in Shaughnessy Heights for F.W. Morgan, 1912; Victor Spencer, 1913; and George Walkem, 1913-14, and in Point Grey a large home for H.A. Stone, 1913. For the South Vancouver estate house, Oakhurst, designed for Charles Gardner Johnson in 1912, Fripp combined river rock and locally cut logs to create an exemplary model of Arts and Crafts design. He also designed a low-slung and still extant bungalow for Henry Ramsay at Burnaby Lake, 1912. For the First Unitarian Church in Fairview, Vancouver, Fripp designed a simple but evocative structure, 1912-13. A prominent apartment block, Grace Court, designed for Dudley D. Hutchinson and built 1912-13, still stands in the West End.

Fripp's legacy of built work exists in three countries. Perhaps the most fascinating aspect of Fripp's career lies in his role as a direct transmitter of architectural ideas which he gained firsthand in England, New Zealand and California, and then introduced into British Columbia. He died in Vancouver on December 16, 1917, and was buried in the family plot in Mountain View Cemetery.

Grace Court, Vancouver

EDWARD McCOSKRIE

1822–1893

BARRY ELMER AND DOROTHY MINDENHALL

Originally from England, Edward McCoskrie immigrated to Canada in 1870 to settle first in southern Ontario, then moved to Manitoba several years later, and subsequently to Winnipeg. He established one of the earliest architectural and engineering practices on the Prairies. McCoskrie followed the Canadian Pacific Railway, providing architectural services in the pioneer boom towns as they sprang up. He opened offices successively in Brandon, Regina and Moose Jaw.

In 1884 he established an office in Calgary, and in his capacity as Town Engineer designed the first municipal buildings, including a town hall and a fire station. He practised briefly in Vancouver, 1888-89, but relocated to Victoria in late 1889, likely to be near his son, Captain Edward McCoskrie, a merchant mariner born in England in 1852. In October 1890 McCoskrie began to advertise himself as an Architect, Civil and Sanitary Engineer, Building Surveyor, and General Valuator paying "special attention to churches, schools and public buildings, and to elevators, bridge, railway, hydraulic and sanitary works generally." One of his early patrons was William Jensen for whom he designed a terrace of six houses on Superior Street in 1890, three stores on Dallas Road, 1891, and the waterfront Hotel Dallas, at the corner of Dallas Road and Simcoe Street, 1891. The Dallas was the first of the "seaside" hotels in Victoria, and was lavishly appointed both inside and out. This handsome structure, with projecting bays and a central tower, stood until it was destroyed by fire in 1928. Other known commissions included: a frame residence on Quadra Street for E. Conlin, 1891; an unbuilt project for a hotel in Nanaimo for A.R. Johnstone & Co., 1891; and a frame building on Blanshard Street for the St. Andrew's & Caledonian Society which opened in June 1892, now demolished. In June 1891 he entered into partnership with **S.M. Goddard**, who had recently dissolved his partnership with **Thomas Hooper**, but no joint commissions for McCoskrie & Goddard have been identified. In June 1891 McCoskrie attended the first organizational meeting for the B.C. Institute of Architects. He died at his son's house at the age of seventy-two on June 5, 1893, and was laid to rest in Ross Bay Cemetery.

Hotel Dallas, Victoria

CHARLES OSBORN WICKENDEN
1851–1934

CATHERINE BARFORD

C.O. Wickenden was one of Vancouver's first architects, and also helped introduce the Romanesque Revival Style to the west coast. Wickenden had a wide-ranging career before settling in Vancouver. Born near Rochester, Kent in 1851, the son of Thomas and Maria (Harris) Wickenden, he articled in London with Peck & Stephens, and practised in that city before immigrating to New York. He then moved to St. John, New Brunswick in 1876, where his commissions included Acadian College in Wolfeville, Nova Scotia. In 1881 Wickenden began the westward trek to the booming city of Winnipeg, which was

attracting a number of architects at the time. His commissions there included the Provincial Offices, Christ Church, the court houses in Winnipeg, Brandon and Neepawa, and numerous other buildings for private businesses including the Hudson's Bay Company. By the end of 1888 he had announced that he was moving to Victoria, but ended up that December in Vancouver. In 1889 he returned briefly to Winnipeg to marry Maud Underhill.

Wickenden was one of only a handful of qualified architects in Vancouver at the time. The city was expanding explosively following the devastation of the Great Fire and the arrival of the transcontinental railway, and Wickenden launched immediately into a number of important commissions, including the Lefevre Block (also known as the Empire Building), 1888, the Innes-Thompson Block, 1889, and Vancouver's oldest surviving church, Christ Church Cathedral, 1889-95. Wickenden's trademark style for commercial buildings was the Romanesque Revival, with which he helped establish the character of early Winnipeg and Vancouver business districts. Christ Church, on the other hand, is a traditional Gothic Revival building, distinguished by a hammer-beam gable roof.

In 1891, Wickenden supplied the designs for the extant but now greatly altered Kalamalka Hotel in Vernon, and the sand-

Christ Church, Vancouver

Bank of British North America, Vancouver

stone Hudson's Bay Company store at Calgary. He was well connected with the federal Conservative government of the day, and generally enjoyed their Vancouver patronage. He supervised construction of Vancouver's first purpose-built general post office at Granville and Pender, designed by Thomas Fuller and the Federal Department of Public Works. In the 1890s he continued to do work for the Hudson's Bay Company in Calgary and Winnipeg, as well as the Hudson's Bay Store in Vancouver at Granville and Georgia; the plans had been sent to London for approval in 1891, and the building was completed in 1893. He also designed the HBC Warehouse on Water Street in 1894. While **S.M. Eveleigh** was working in his office in 1894-95, Wickenden designed The Arcade, an unusual structure located across the street from the Vancouver Court House. Another prominent project was the stone-clad Bank of British North America on Hastings Street, 1891-93, described by **R. Mackay Fripp** in the *Canadian Architect & Builder* as "*a severer type of Italian, dignified but cold in effect.*" Wickenden also provided the design for the Bank of British North America in Rossland, 1897, built in response to the mining boom in the area. From 1901-02 he served as Reeve of North Vancouver, and one of his last known designs was the municipal hall in the District of North Vancouver, 1903. Wickenden was a founding member of the Council of the British Columbia Institute of Architects, 1891-94, and served as its second President. He retired from the practice of architecture about 1914, died in Vancouver on December 7, 1934, and was interred at Ocean View Burial Park in Burnaby.

Hudson's Bay Company Store, Vancouver

The Arcade, Vancouver

JOSEPH HENRY BOWMAN
1864–1943

JIM WOLF

Joseph H. Bowman's long career embraced many stylistic changes and technological advances, including the design of prefabricated buildings. He was born in London, England in 1864, and acquired an early interest in architecture through his father, William B. Bowman, who was a master builder in London. His early education was at the Sir Walter Singen School in Battersea, London and was supplemented by an architectural course in the department of science and art at the South Kensington Museum. He worked initially as a draftsman with designer, William Rendall, for two years before joining his father's construction business.

In 1888 he chose to come to Canada and was immediately employed by the Canadian Pacific Railway. However, instead of drafting in a comfortable office, he was shipped out west to work on construction of the railway in the wilderness of the Rocky Mountains. After a few months he "resigned his position" at Donald, B.C. when he found temporary employment in building construction. Instead of returning to the refinements of eastern Canada, Bowman continued westward, moving to Vancouver in September, 1888. "At this time he had few assets beyond his ability in his profession and his unwavering determination, but applied himself to any work he could find." One of his first jobs was to build, along with **Baynes & Horie**, the rustic entrance arch to Stanley Park at Lost Lagoon, a prominent landmark in early Vancouver that was designed by another young, recent immigrant architect, **Sydney Morgan Eveleigh**.

Amid the work on a variety of commissions, Bowman became increasingly involved with Vancouver society, and in 1892 he married Gertrude Mann. As newlyweds, they eagerly took advantage of an 1894 provincial government sale of land on the tramline in South Vancouver's Central Park district. Here they farmed a six-acre parcel and raised seven children: Ethel, Dorothy, Phyllis, Evelyn, Sidney, Irene and Margery. The Bowmans were active members of the Central Park community, which spanned the boundary into the Municipality of Burnaby. They were founding members of St. John the Divine Anglican Church, designed by Bowman in 1899 and redesigned by him after a fire in 1905.

In 1897 Bowman found employment as a draftsman with the **B.C. Mills, Timber and Trading Company**, based at the old Hastings Mill on Vancouver's waterfront. Headed by John Hendry, this was the largest company in the province. This position afforded Bowman an opportunity to develop his skills in the wood manufacturing industry. In 1904 the company started the production of prefabricated homes and buildings developed by inventor, Edwin C. Mahoney. It was in this famous B.C. enterprise that Bowman's architectural skill was put to the test, and where he designed buildings using Mahoney's prefabricated wall system. These homes and buildings were produced by the thousands for export across B.C. and western Canada; Bowman's designs exploited popular vernacular architectural styles and forms.

Bowman left Hendry's employ in 1908 and began his own architectural practice. His style matured, showing the influence of the Arts and Crafts movement. Many of his residential designs, such as the elegant 1912 home for J.H. Alexander on

Mahoney Residence, Vancouver

Cypress Street in Point Grey, employed the popular California Bungalow form. He also favoured the use of the Tudor Revival style for more elaborate buildings, such as his design for the Port Moody City Hall in 1914. Bowman's reputation at this time was highly regarded, and a prominent biographical dictionary stated: "His present position among the men of marked ability and substantial worth in this community has been achieved through earnest and well directed labour, for he has steadily worked his way upward to prominence, the structure of his life standing upon the firm foundation of honor, integrity and upright dealing."

Bowman specialized in school buildings and was the school board architect for both South Vancouver and Burnaby. One of his first designs for Burnaby was a utilitarian two-storey school that could be built with two classrooms and later expanded to eight rooms as the district's school population grew; five schools from this design were built in 1908, and then four others in modified versions between 1910-16. For the South Vancouver School Board, on which he had served as a founding trustee, Bowman designed and supervised construction of the Selkirk and Tecumseh Schools, 1910-12. Young English architect, **J. T. Alexander**, assisted Bowman in his office during this period. Shortly after, **Harold Cullerne** was brought into the busy office. One of Bowman's largest school buildings is the Classical Revival-styled Gilmore Avenue School in North Burnaby; the central four-room block was built 1915-16. Bowman also designed a number of schools in Richmond, including the handsome General Currie School of 1919.

In 1919, Cullerne and Bowman formed a partnership that lasted until Bowman retired in 1934. The firm continued to specialize in school design, and their subsequent projects included Robertson Elementary School, Chilliwack, 1921; the north wing to Gilmore Avenue School, 1921-22; Seaforth School, Burnaby, 1922 (since relocated to Burnaby Village Museum); Burnaby North High School, 1923; and Chilliwack Central Elementary School, 1929.

Robertson Elementary School, Chilliwack

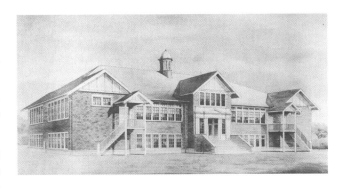

Burnaby North High School, Burnaby

After retirement, Bowman kept busy with a number of pastimes. He was made a life member of the AIBC, was a charter member of the Dickens Fellowship and an active member of the Vancouver Pioneers Association. He took a keen interest in the founding and development of the Bursill Institute of East Collingwood, Vancouver, as its founder, writer J. Francis Bursill, was a close friend. This group set up the first cultural organization in Collingwood, establishing a free library and vagabond club. After a long illness, Bowman died at home in Vancouver on May 10, 1943 at age seventy-nine.

Roe Residence, Port Moody

He is today one of the foremost architects in the city, controlling an extensive and representative patronage, and his individual success is well deserved, supplementing as it does valuable work along public lines.

Howay & Schofield, *British Columbia Biographical*, Vol. III, p. 92

JOHN
GERHARD
TIARKS
1867–1901

STUART STARK

Good family and social connections undoubtedly contributed to J.G. Tiarks's success in life. He was confident, self-assured, energetic and opinionated, and he achieved much in his short life, erecting over seventy-five buildings in the course of a thirteen-year career. Tiarks's grandfather, Reverend Johann Gerhard Tiarks moved to England from Jever (now in Germany) in 1820. The Rev. Tiarks became Chaplain in 1827 to HRH The Duchess of Kent, the mother of the future Queen Victoria. He married Emily, the well-connected daughter of the Phipps family in 1825, and they had three children, one of which lived to adulthood. That son, John Gerhard Tiarks, also took Holy Orders, and was Rector of Loxton in Somerset. In 1863, he married Anne Condron of Macclesfield, England. They had two sons, one of whom died as an infant, and the other, named after his father, grew up to travel to Canada and work as an architect.

John Gerhard Tiarks was born March 12, 1867 in Macclesfield. His architectural training was based in the town of Weston-Super-Mare, where he articled with the firm of Messrs. Hows, Price and Wooler, and claimed experience with "villas of the better class and residences of country gentlemen and in all detail of church design." He left Liverpool on June 6, 1888 on the steamer *Parisian* and arrived in Quebec City ten days later. He continued on the *Parisian* to Montreal, visited Ottawa, Toronto, Hamilton, and Niagara Falls, took the CPR steamer *Alberta* on the Great Lakes to Port Arthur (Thunder Bay), and then continued across Canada on the Canadian Pacific Railway, with a two day stop in Winnipeg. Tiarks arrived in Vancouver by rail on July 8, 1888. This was an opportune time to arrive in British Columbia; the province was experiencing

an economic boom, and the west was ripe for architects. After two weeks in Vancouver, Tiarks left for Victoria, arriving on July 25, 1888. In 1889 and 1890, Tiarks wrote several letters, called *Notes from the Far West*, to his home town newspaper in England, sharing his judgmental comments about his adopted city:

Architecturally the condition of the city is pitiable indeed, but in this respect there are manifest signs of improvement, and the buildings erected in the last six months (a very large number) are wonderfully ahead, both in external appearance and design and interior arrangement, to anything that has been done here in former years. On the Gorge-road there is now being erected a very English-looking and effectively designed house in the Elizabethan style [Ashnola, 1888] and we may hope that the owners of the lands around this most lonely spot (the Gorge) will, ere long, build their houses of a good description also. There are a great number of churches and chapels in the city. Christ Church Cathedral (Church of England) [**by H.O. Tiedemann, 1871-72**], *is situate on an eminence, and the effect of its tower when seen at a distance (especially when entering the little harbour) is not bad, but unfortunately here "'tis distance lends enchantment to the view," for this would-be-perpendicular tower is found to be the most atrocious architectural abortion.*

Weston-super-Mare *Mercury*, January 19, 1889

(Madge Hamilton Collection)

Carter Residence, Victoria

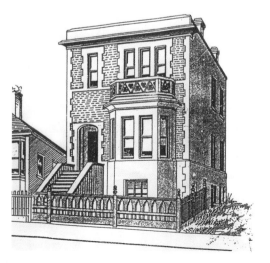

Leishman Residence, Victoria

The Bungalows; the Tupper and Peters Residences, Oak Bay

Tiarks landed on his feet, for within a year, he was working, had bought property (with L.B. Trimen), and was boarding with architect, Thomas Sorby. By 1891 he was boarding at a house with, amongst others, **Samuel Maclure's** brothers. Tiarks quickly became a force in Victoria architectural circles. Only eighteen months after his arrival in the city, and having done a short stint as a draftsman with Trimen, Tiarks could claim a major, though regrettably still unidentified, residential commission worth $5,000, about five times the cost of a usual home.

He had started his own practice by 1890. Tiarks had particularly admired the design of *Ashnola*, the Snowden (Dunsmuir family) home on the Gorge, while it was under construction, and in 1893 built his own home *Kelston Wood*, a large shingled structure, next door. He returned to England in February 1895 to marry Ada Constance Helen Harington in Weston-Super-Mare in a ceremony performed by the groom's father and the bride's uncle. The couple, with the bride's mother, Mrs. Harington, promptly returned to Victoria so Tiarks could attend to his now-thriving architectural practice. In December 1896, a son John Gerhard Edward ('Jack') Tiarks was born at *Kelston Wood*. Tiarks also served as an alderman on Victoria City Council in 1896.

Tiarks's ambitions were exemplified by his double competition entries for the new Parliament Buildings in 1892: one, by his own hand, was sent in under the *nom-de-plume* "Floreat Victoria. Convenience with Economy;" and the second entry was in association with fellow architect, H.W. Wills, and was titled "Justice (No. 2)." Tiarks served as an officer on the British Columbia Institute of Architects in 1894. One of his house designs – that of *Dalzellowlie*, the Bryden

(Dunsmuir family) Residence – was published in the *Canadian Architect & Builder*, April 1899.

Tiarks primarily designed residences, many for socially well-connected clients, and his residential commissions varied dramatically in design. He could deftly handle large Tudor Revival residences with the panache of Maclure, or he could turn his hand to more innovative homes with his trademark exterior siding design, which involved laying a Tudor-like pattern of boards over walls of wooden drop siding, as in the Leishman Residence, 1896. Tiarks was known for his Colonial Bungalow designs, although he also designed homes in the Gothic Revival and other picturesque styles. Some of his houses were planned with the kitchens facing the street so the spectacular water views at the rear of the house were available to the main reception rooms – a concept common today, but unusual in Victorian house design. His homes rarely had the usual Late Victorian fussiness. Bold exterior detailing, with his favourite shallow Tudor-arch motif and broad verandahs, was a hallmark of his style. His interior details often included cedar panelling, more Tudor arches and whimsical details like seashell designs on fireplace tiles for his seaside cottages. One of his major architectural commissions was a massive home called *Clovelly*, for A. Weaver Bridgman. Built in 1894. this Tudor Revival waterfront mansion stood on the border

Kelston Wood, Victoria; Jack Tiarks on front steps.

between Victoria and Esquimalt, and featured cedar panelling, twenty-four light stained glass windows, and an octagonal smoking room. Further residential commissions included a conservatory for *Cragdarroch*, Mrs. Dunsmuir's home, in 1892 (not built); a medieval-style Great Hall for Andrew Keating's house at Koksilah in 1894; and a brick terrace house for Thomas Watson Carter on Herald Street in 1891, which was latterly used as a brothel by the notorious madam Stella Carroll.

In 1898, Tiarks went into business partnership with **F.M. Rattenbury**. They were both aged thirty-one, ambitious, and driven. They jointly purchased about fifteen acres of waterfront property in what would become part of Oak Bay. Rattenbury built his own home on the prime site looking over the sea, and over the next few years, the partners began a tasteful development. Tiarks designed three houses on the property, and two identical large residences, called in the press "Beautiful Bungalows:" *Annandale*, for Sir Charles Hibbert Tupper; and *Garrison House*, for the Hon. F. Peters. Each of these homes encompassed over 7,000 square feet, larger than most city lots, and were lined with cedar panelling and fitted with electric lighting.

Tiarks also designed at least twelve commercial buildings, all now altered or demolished. In the rush to rebuild Columbia Street after the disastrous New Westminster fire of 1898, Rattenbury and Tiarks were jointly credited with the design of several sophisticated structures including the Bank of Montreal, the Bank of B.C. and the Hamley Block. Tiarks also designed an unbuilt project for the Kamloops Hotel Company in 1899.

On April 21, 1901, at the early age of thirty-four, Tiarks died from a "fall from his wheel" (bicycle), ending a potentially spectacular architectural career. He was buried in Ross Bay Cemetery, and his pall bearers included **W. Ridgway-Wilson** and A.W. Bridgman. Now widowed, Mrs. Tiarks took her son and returned to England. She could not claim the money she had left in Canada, and found life somewhat difficult financially. Tiarks's son, Jack, married Evelyn Florence Cripps in 1922 and they had a daughter Anne in 1926. She in turn married Peter Phillips and they had a son and a daughter. The son, born in 1948, was Mark Antony Peter Phillips, who married Princess Anne, bringing the Royal connection in the Tiarks family full circle. With his tragically early death, we can only guess at what influence John Gerhard Tiarks would have had on the architectural scene of the new century, when both Rattenbury and Maclure reached the peak of their careers.

Hamley Block, New Westminster

THOMAS ENNOR JULIAN
1843–1921

DAVID MONTEYNE AND
DONALD LUXTON

Born in Wales, Thomas Ennor Julian worked in London for fourteen years, where he specialized in school, church and hospital architecture. By the late 1880s he was based in Calgary, where he advertised himself as an "architect and civil, sanitary and mining engineer." During his time in Calgary he was responsible for at least one Italianate commercial project, a two-storey brick store on Stephen Avenue, demolished about 1929. Julian first came to British Columbia by February 1889 and "got his shingle hung out in Vancouver as an architect and surveyor." He worked as a moderately successful architect based in New Westminster and Vancouver, and was briefly in partnership with **George W. Grant**, 1893-94. Julian was active in New Westminster for a number of years, and was especially busy immediately after the 1898 fire, undertaking a two-storey brick block for Kwong On Wo & Co. on Front Street; a station and a freight shed on Columbia Street for the B.C. Electric Railway; residences on Carnarvon Street for Dr. Drew and B.W. Shiles; a house on Agnes Street for Dr. Boggs; the St. Patrick's and Young Mens' Institute Hall; an addition to the Electric Light Powerhouse, Tenth Street; and the Queen's Avenue Methodist Church, all designed and built 1898-99 and all now demolished. In Vancouver, Julian worked mostly on the design of houses, small apartment buildings, and businesses, including the extant Wing Sang Building on Pender Street, 1901. Julian is best known, though, for his design of downtown Vancouver's monumental Holy Rosary Cathedral, 1899-1900, a beautifully decorated Gothic Revival building with sumptuous materials, gilding, and stained glass. Julian died in Vancouver on September 10, 1921, survived by two sisters in Wales.

Holy Rosary Cathedral, Vancouver

WILLIAM
TINNISWOOD
DALTON

1854–1931

W. T. Dalton.

MAURICE GUIBORD AND
DONALD LUXTON

The Vancouver partnership of Dalton & Eveleigh was for several decades one of the city's pre-eminent firms, and was highly regarded for the high quality of its commercial and institutional buildings. Their 1903 Royal Bank on Hastings Street (now part of the Vancouver Film School) was the first Temple Bank in the city, and probably the first local building to abandon Victorian eclecticism and embrace the classicism of the Edwardian era. Furthermore, its 1905-06 design for the Davis Chambers established the Edwardian commercial style for tall office buildings in Vancouver, in which the facade is divided into three sections similar to a classical column, with a base, shaft, and capital. This classically-inspired style became the *de facto* idiom for commercial buildings before the First World War.

William T. Dalton was born in Nenthead, Cumberland, England, Nov. 21, 1854, the son of William and Frances Millican Dalton. He was educated at Nenthead Grammar School, Belvedere Academy, and Bishop Auckland School. He was articled from 1871-75 to James Cubitt, a prominent church architect in London, and several years later, he became an assistant and draftsman in the offices of H.J. Paull, a noted London and Manchester architect. In 1880, Dalton sailed to Canada and, after a brief period in the east, made his home in Winnipeg, where he was employed by **C.O. Wickenden**, a prime exponent of the Richardsonian Romanesque style.

DALTON & EVELEIGH
PARTNERSHIP 1902-C.1920

Dalton returned to England in 1881 to marry Frances Mary Walton, of Donck's Villa, Nenthead. They came back to Winnipeg where their two children were born, son Arthur Tinniswood Dalton in 1883 and daughter Joy in 1885. The family moved to Vancouver in 1889, where Dalton opened a branch of the Wickenden office before starting his own practice in 1893.

During the 1890s Dalton's designs including a number of sophisticated essays in the Richardsonian Romanesque style, such as the Martin & Robertson Company warehouse, 1898 on Gastown's Water Street; and the MacKinnon Block at the corner of Granville and Hastings Street, 1897-98. When it was built, the MacKinnon Block, clad with rough-dressed stonework, was considered the city's finest office building. In this period, Dalton was also the supervising architect for a number of Vancouver buildings including the second CPR Station by Montreal architect, Edward Maxwell, 1897-99. In 1900, he

Charter members of the Burrard Literary Society, c.1890-91

was in charge of the additions to the Hudson's Bay Company department store originally designed by Wickenden nine years before. That winter Dalton spent three months abroad, visiting England, New York, and Boston, no doubt learning about the latest building methods and trends. When he returned he continued to design numerous warehouses and residences in Vancouver. One of Dalton's projects outside of Vancouver was the Queen Victoria Cottage Hospital in Revelstoke, 1901-02; this connection, and a lack of local architects, led Dalton & Eveleigh to establish an office in that city.

Dalton had been born in the shadow of the Pennine Hills in the Lake District, and throughout his life was an enthusiastic alpinist, and in 1894, accompanied by George Edwards and Roger J. Casement, he made the initial ascents of many of the mountains north of Burrard Inlet. He was a member of his son's party which was the first to scale Mount Garibaldi in 1907. Dalton bought twenty acres of land near the head of

SYDNEY MORGAN EVELEIGH

1870–1947

Indian Arm opposite Granite Falls, where he built a log cabin, *Deerwylde*, which became a weekend gathering place for his family and friends, and in retirement he spent much time there. In 1930, a mountain east of the Alfred, Alexander and Albert group of mountains at the head of Jervis Inlet was named "Mount Tinniswood" by Dalton's son in honour of his father, Tinniswood being an old family name that continues today in the present generation. Dalton was also artistic, and painted landscape scenes of Burrard Inlet and of the Aboriginal village located near *Deerwylde*.

In 1902, Dalton went into partnership with the younger architect, Sydney Morgan Eveleigh, and for almost two decades they were jointly responsible for the design, planning and supervision of numerous Vancouver buildings. Eveleigh was born in St. Peters, Bedford, England, in 1870, the eldest of four children of Robert Sim Eveleigh and his wife, Jane. He studied and travelled in England and continental Europe for three years prior to moving to Vancouver in 1888, at the age of eighteen. Eveleigh designed a ceremonial entry arch to Stanley Park beside Lost Lagoon for the 1889 visit of Lord Stanley, and the same year began work as an assistant under **N.S. Hoffar**. This was followed by several years of study and travel, and after his return, during the mid- to late-1890s Eveleigh mainly was kept busy with a steady stream of projects for English entrepreneur Harvey Hadden, who had invested heavily in Vancouver real estate, and wanted to protect the steadily-declining value of his bare lots by putting buildings on them. Still young, Eveleigh worked on these projects while under the employ of other architects. While he was in the

Sidney Eveleigh sitting L at table.

MacKinnon Block, Vancouver

office of C.O. Wickenden, The Arcade, a one-storey commercial structure at the corner of West Hastings and Cambie Streets, was designed for Hadden, 1894-95. In the doldrums that followed the arrival of the railway, there were those who said about The Arcade that "the enterprise betokened temerity, for what prospect was there for Vancouver? What was there to lead one to suppose that this far city of the west would ever develop into anything worthwhile?" Twenty years after its construction, The Arcade was demolished to be replaced by the Dominion Trust Building, the tallest in the British Empire, and "the shrewd and cautious ones from the east have had to confess that they were mistaken" about the future of Vancouver. Eveleigh then worked again briefly for Hoffar, during the time he was working on the additions to the Vancouver Court House. In 1895, Eveleigh joined W.T. Dalton as a draftsman, and Hadden commissioned Dalton's office to design the Pender Chambers, between Richards and Seymour Streets, c.1898; and the Hadden Block on his lot at the northeast corner of Granville and Hastings Streets, 1901, the main floor of which was occupied for years by Trorey's Jewellers. However, Hadden commissioned **J.E. Parr** to design the Harvey's Chambers at the northeast corner of West Hastings and Homer Streets, 1896-97; Eveleigh appears to have worked in Parr's office during the course of this project. Hadden's real estate holdings became so extensive that he decided to spend part of each year as a resident, acquired 160 acres of property on the North Shore, and in 1903 had Eveleigh design a grand house, called Hadden Hall, known for its spectacular gardens filled with 500 rose bushes imported from France.

For many years, Eveleigh lived in Vancouver's West End. He was married to Florence Mary Southcott, born in London, Ontario, daughter of Mr. and Mrs. J.J. Southcott, pioneer residents of Vancouver. The couple had one son, two daughters and five grandchildren. Strongly artistic, Eveleigh retained an interest in culture his whole life. An avid photographer,

watercolourist and etcher, he appreciated the culture of the Aboriginal peoples of British Columbia at a time when they were generally derided as savages, and travelled up the coast to study and draw remaining native villages. The Eveleighs were well-connected to the cultural elite of the city, and in 1909, when Pauline Johnson's touring partner Jackson Walter McRaye married Lucy Webling, their daughter Evelyn was the flower girl; Johnson had herself just recently moved to Vancouver. Eveleigh was a charter member and the first "Clerk of the House" (Secretary) of the Burrard Literary Society, and also a member of the original Vancouver Library Board. Eveleigh was instrumental in obtaining a $50,000 grant from Andrew Carnegie for the construction of the new library at Main and Hastings, corresponding directly with Carnegie. The cheques for the library, issued in the sum of ten thousand dollars each, were personally made out to Eveleigh.

During his time in Dalton's office, Eveleigh was given increasing responsibility, and acted as Dalton's chief assistant. By March, 1902, they were in partnership. Dalton & Eveleigh's prominent early buildings included: the rusticated stone Buntzen Power House #1, 1903; City of Vancouver Police Court and Jail, 1903; West Fairview School in Vancouver, 1904-05; St. Alban's Anglican church in Burnaby, 1907-09; and the downtown B.C. Telephone Exchange, 1906-07. Located on Indian Arm, the Buntzen Power House was a utilitarian structure designed for the B.C. Electric Railway Co., as part of a hydroelectric project built to supplied electricity to Vancouver, a function it still serves. The Telephone Exchange was notable for its advanced use of fireproof construction methods, reinforced concrete, and complicated technical planning for the functioning of the switchboards. Between 1907-11, Dalton & Eveleigh also had their hands full as the supervising architects for the new Vancouver Court House designed by Victoria architect, **F.M. Rattenbury**. As supervisors, they had charge of the entire construction process,

Sydney, Evelyn, Isabel and Florence Eveleigh, c. 1907

including ornamentation and even furnishing of the building. Eveleigh wanted the massive stone lions flanking the entry to resemble as much as possible the profile of the twin peaks on the North Shore known as The Lions, so he carved small models for the sculptor out of Ivory soap bars to show his idea of how their noses should be flattened.

The boom period before the First World War saw the partners doing work for many important Vancouver companies and organizations including the Masons, the YWCA, B.C. Electric Railway, Pilkington Brothers, F.T. Cope & Son and Vancouver Breweries. One of their largest warehouses from this period is the Leckie building at Cambie and Water Streets, a beautifully restored Gastown landmark. The Alcazar Hotel was a prominent downtown hotel, built in 1912, that was demolished in the 1980s. They completed a number of projects through their Revelstoke office, including the Imperial Bank, opened on March 24, 1904, and a building for Lawrence Hardware, built in 1905 at a cost of $25,000. Other projects outside of Vancouver included the Russell Hotel in New Westminster, 1908, and a prominent two-storey block for the Hudson's Bay Company in downtown Vernon, 1911-12.

One of their largest projects, located in the interior of the province, was the Sanatorium at Tranquille, west of Kamloops. In the nineteenth century, tuberculosis, or "consumption," was one of the leading causes of death, and had been linked to the foul, damp air of urban environments. The sanatorium movement evolved to provide clinics located in rural or mountain settings; the discovery in 1882 that the disease was caused by bacteria jolted the medical community into promoting even greater isolation for those infected. The British Columbia Anti-Tuberculosis Society had been founded in 1904, and three years later they purchased the Fortune Ranch on Kamloops Lake as the location for their sanatorium, the seventh that would be built in Canada, and the first west of Ontario. Dalton & Eveleigh were chosen as the architects for the new facility, and in 1908 the Society sent Dalton to eastern Canada and New England to study existing sanatoriums. As the Society was a charitable organization, Dalton waived the firm's $3,500 fees, which was greatly appreciated, and acknowledged at the building's opening ceremonies. The exterior of the Main Building was completed in 1910, but the Society's chronic financial problems prevented the interior from being fully completed for several years. Dalton & Eveleigh continued to be involved with the development of the growing Tranquille complex, renamed the King Edward Sanatorium, until 1914.

One of their grandest projects was never built. About 1913 they were engaged to design an extension to the Vancouver Court House. In 1910 **Thomas Hooper** had designed an addition to Rattenbury's building before it was even finished. This west wing faces Robson Street, with its long side along Hornby Street. Dalton & Eveleigh were hired to complete the ensemble by designing a matching building along Howe

W.T. Dalton, c.1895

Buntzen Power House #1, Indian Arm

Street, to house the land registry offices and court of appeal. Although a close match to the west wing, there were subtle differences, and the interior, with a grand central staircase and central skylit dome, would have been magnificent. Unfortunately the project was never tendered due to the collapsed economy, leaving the court house complex forever lop-sided.

Dalton's son Arthur was also briefly involved in the firm. He attended McGill University in Montreal for two years, taking engineering and architecture but his father withdrew him so that he could return to Vancouver and work in his increasingly busy architectural firm. This allowed Arthur to design his own home in Kerrisdale in 1912. He joined the Army during the First World War and after he was discharged in 1918 there was little call for architects. He took a job labouring for the Municipality of Point Grey but his training soon led to his appointment as building inspector; he worked for Point Grey and subsequently the City of Vancouver, although he designed a number of houses "on the side" in the Kerrisdale area, including a bungalow for Laurence Hanbury, Manager of Hanbury Sawmills, on Macdonald Street in 1921. Arthur never

registered as an architect; he died in Oakland, California in July, 1962.

Eveleigh was not accepted for military service, but he worked in New York as a purchasing agent in charge of trans-Pacific shipments for eighteen months. The Dalton & Eveleigh partnership seems to have tapered off about this time, although they received several warehouse commissions between 1917 and 1920. Dalton and his wife were briefly in San Francisco when she died in 1920. Returning to Vancouver in 1921, Dalton registered with the AIBC, but there was virtually no work available, so he retired, spending much of his time at *Deerwylde*. Dalton died May 26, 1931, at his son's residence in Vancouver, and was buried at Ocean View Burial Park, Burnaby. Symbolic of the high regard in which he was held by the profession, his honourary pallbearers included **C.O. Wickenden**, **C.E. Hope**, and **E.G. Baynes**, and his active pallbearers were **Andrew Mercer**, **John Honeyman**, **A.A. Cox**, **G.L.T. Sharp**, **Fred Townley** and his son A.T. Dalton.

Eveleigh went on to serve as President of the AIBC from 1922-24. He retired from the profession, working only occasionally. One later project he took on, likely because of

Alcazar Hotel, Vancouver

his long-term interest in Aboriginal culture, was St. Bartholomew's Hospital in Lytton for the Department of Indian Affairs, designed 1931, but not completed until about 1936. Eveleigh continued living quietly at home – effectively bedridden – until his death in Vancouver on November 29, 1947; he had been predeceased by his wife in 1939. They were both buried in the Eveleigh family plot in Vancouver's Mountain View Cemetery.

Tuberculosis Sanatorium, Tranquille

ALEXANDER
MAXWELL
MUIR
1860-1922

PAMELA MADOFF

The story of A. Maxwell Muir follows the familiar path of a young man in pursuit of a bright future. An accomplished architect and a meticulous businessman, he designed more than fifty buildings in B.C. during an active career that spanned only twenty years and was compromised by poor health. Born in Glasgow, Scotland on February 19, 1860, he was the son of Alexander Muir and Mary Margaret Maxwell, and great grandson of Sir William and Lady Maxwell. He graduated from Glasgow University with separate diplomas as a civil engineer and architect. Some of his perspective plans on the Clyde were exhibited in the Intercolonial Exhibition at Edinburgh, Scotland. He immigrated to the U.S. and worked his way from coast to coast. After his arrival in the United States, Muir settled in Troy, New York for two and a half years. He then moved on to

Nairne Residence, Victoria

a position with William Parson & Sons of Topeka, Kansas, who were engaged in the construction of many public schools and civic buildings throughout the state.

Design work on the Hotel del Coronado in San Diego and employment with the Southern Pacific Railway brought Muir to the west coast and to what would become his final professional destination, Victoria, in 1889. Upon his arrival Muir took up residence at the YMCA and was soon employed by **John Teague**, one of Victoria's most successful architects. While in Teague's employ Muir drew plans for the Victoria City Market building on Cormorant Street, and likely worked on the Royal Jubilee Hospital, additions to City Hall, and extensions to First Presbyterian Church. Teague's practice was flourishing, and by 1892 Muir had established his own office, likely to take advantage of the large amount of work available.

Despite the general economic malaise, Muir remained busy with commercial and residential projects. He soon won a number of major commissions, including the Board of Trade Building in Victoria and the first court houses in Vernon, 1892-93, and Nelson, 1893. He also entered, unsuccessfully, the 1892 competition for the new Parliament Buildings; all entries were required to use a *nom-de-plume* and Muir's was "Patience." His elegant Vernon Public School, 1893, is likely the oldest surviving brick school in the province. In 1897 Muir designed the Kamloops Jail and in 1898 was involved in the development scheme for the Hotel Texada, later known as the Marble Bay Hotel, on Texada Island. The twenty-six room hotel was set on an acre of land on a bluff overlooking the water, surrounded by building lots. The first three hundred purchasers were eligible to win the hotel in a raffle draw. The hotel was completed but few lots were sold and the raffle was never held.

In 1899, now with a reasonably successful architectural practice, Muir married Minnie Hartley Swanwick, a member of Metchosin's pioneering Weir family. She had been married previously and divorced; her one child died as a result of a reaction to a vaccination. In 1901 they built a house, *Bremhill*, in Victoria's Jubilee neighbourhood and two years later they built a modest house, *Hartley Hall*, on land in Metchosin that Minnie had received from her mother. Their daughter, Robina, was born in 1904, followed by a son, William, in 1907.

Precisely at the time that Muir's family responsibilities were growing, his practice was struggling to survive. Muir continued

Court House, Vernon

to design modest commercial buildings including the Chemainus Hospital, 1903 and the Burnside Fire Hall, 1908, but more significant commissions eluded him. Muir assigned the blame for his lack of work specifically on the success enjoyed by **F.M. Rattenbury**, declaring that he "had done more local work in this city during the last ten years than any other man." Although he continued to participate in architectural competitions he saw little success. In 1901, in a letter to the local newspaper, he publicly attacked the awarding of a commission to Rattenbury to design a new high school. "I think," he wrote, "that my plans should have placed first." In 1903 he again lost out to Rattenbury for the commission to design the Strathcona Addition and Isolation Ward for the Royal Jubilee Hospital. In the same year a bitter battle erupted over the hiring of an architect to design the new Carnegie Library. A group of architects, which included Muir (but not Rattenbury) petitioned City Council requesting that one of their group be chosen for the commission. In a letter to City Council Muir suggested that Rattenbury had made enough money, by virtue of circumstance rather than talent, over the years and should retire and leave the field to the less fortunate.

During this same period, a board of arbitration was appointed to look into cost overruns on Government House, another of Rattenbury's projects. The board included Muir, whom Rattenbury described as both a personal and professional opponent. Struggling to support his family at a time when his commissions were at an all-time low, he felt unbounded bitterness towards Rattenbury. Muir's feelings against Rattenbury may also have been coloured by his own scrupulous attention to financial matters. He was once the president of a company involved in oil explorations in Alberta. It was not a limited company and some of his investors suggested that he water down the dividends that were issued to shareholders. He

refused. Coincidentally, accidents began to occur at the site. Muir, as president, was held financially responsible and his insistence on paying these debts contributed to his financial downfall.

A staunch Presbyterian, Muir sometimes acted as a lay minister and, in 1892, donated plans for the East Fernwood Mission Sunday School for the Christian Endeavour Society of St. Andrew's Presbyterian Church, now converted to a residence which still stands on Redfern Street in Victoria. He was also a member of the Vancouver and Quadra No. 2 Chapter of the Masonic Temple where he functioned as secretary and was responsible for the founding of many of the lodge's charitable activities, including the Widows' and Orphans' Fund.

With little work coming his way the Muirs moved back and forth between Victoria and Vancouver. In 1917 the Muirs were back in Victoria. Mrs. Muir was the proprietor of the Minerva Confectionery which was known for its fruit-shaped *fondant* candies. Muir was listed in the directory as a candymaker. Muir also suffered increasing health problems, described as "creeping paralysis," undoubtedly neurological degeneration caused by ALS, later known as Lou Gehrig's Disease. He died in Vancouver August 1, 1922, aged sixty-two. His widow survived him by twenty years, modestly supporting herself as a stenographer.

Hospital, Chemainus

THOMAS BURROUGHES NORGATE

BORN C.1865

MARY E. DOODY JONES

T. Burroughes Norgate resided briefly in Victoria, and during his short local career designed an interesting mix of buildings. He was born in Bristol, England, the son of Frank Burroughes Norgate, a well-off banker, and Anna M. Norgate. After receiving his schooling, Thomas emigrated to the Colonies, settling in Victoria, B.C. where he was listed in city directories in 1889 as a draftsman, and in 1891 as an "architect, engineer and patent solicitor" with an office on 76 Yates Street in Victoria, and residence at 87 Henry Street in Esquimalt. In July 1890 his office was in Moody's Block on Yates Street. The 1891 census lists him as an engineer and an Anglican Englishman, twenty-six years old, single, and boarding.

Only a few of his architectural commissions are known. He called for tenders in November 1889 for a frame dwelling on Chatham Street in Fernwood, and at the time was advertising himself as an architect and mechanical engineer. In April-May 1890, he advertised a tender call for a two-storey, wooden residence for Thomas S. Futcher, a recent English immigrant and a merchant of Japanese goods. This large and well-built Italianate house, with a conservatory at the back, was built at a cost of $5,000, and was described in the *Colonist* as a "pretty cottage home in the new *Gothique á la Japanaise style*." Indeed, a photograph of the balcony shows many curious decorations. According to neighbours, until the 1960s an "old-fashioned garden" remained. The bay window and upper balcony looked out over these gardens rather than to the front. The house is still standing, but has been altered several times. After the turn of the century, the porch and balcony gained heavier Edwardian elements, now replaced, and the roofline was changed due to a fire in the 1920s.

Another commission was a contrast to this opulent house. In July of 1890, Norgate advertised the tender for large barns for the trolley cars of the National Electric Tramway and Lighting Company. At the formal opening of the extended generating plant, on January 17, 1891, many notables came to the car barn for a special lunch and a long series of toasts.

In November of 1890 his plans for St. Saviour's church were accepted by its Anglican congregation, and the corner stone was laid the following April. This church, located in Victoria West, still stands today. After this no more is heard about Norgate as an architect. He next turned up as part of the first Province Exploring Expedition, led by the Rev. William Washington Bolton, which explored Vancouver Island from Cape Commerell to Woss Lake in the summer of 1894. Norgate's photographs and watercolours form part of the permanent record of this pioneering expedition, but he seems to have left the province soon after its return to Victoria.

Fort Rupert Indians in sun dance costumes. This is a staged photograph taken by Norgate, July 1894.

St. Saviour's Anglican Church, Victoria

CORNELIUS JOHN SOULE
1851–1939

RONALD HAROLD SOULE

Cornelius Soule was both adventurous and versatile. He left his London, England home at about twenty years of age to find his own way in life. In addition to architecture he was talented in other fields. Alluding to what he termed "graft," which he felt was rampant in the architectural community, he turned from design to farming, and his wife's teaching salary, to sustain him in his later years.

Soule was born in Paddington, London, England, on April 14, 1851, the only son of Cornelius and Mary (Cole) Soule. His paternal grandfather, also Cornelius, was a surveyor and possibly had some influence over his education. Young Cornelius trained as an architect at the prestigious School of Science and Art at South Kensington, where he won a Queen's Prize for design, and prizes and certificates for other subjects. He studied his profession in the offices of a leading London architect. Soon after completing his architectural training, he travelled to America, where he was engaged by architects in Boston and Cleveland. In 1872, while living in the United States, Soule received a commission for a high school in Campbellford, Ontario. He moved to Canada and settled in Port Hope, as the town was in need of a resident architect. There he met Anna Rubidge, the daughter of a prominent Port Hope lawyer. They were married on October 5, 1875. Children soon followed, starting with their daughter, May. In December of 1876 Soule opened an office in the town of Guelph, Ontario, and only a few weeks later petitioned the council for the position of town architect. Soule also opened a branch office in Galt. During the period 1876 to 1881 he worked on a number of large and prominent residential commissions in Ontario.

Despite his success, in 1881 Soule left Guelph intending to go to Denver, Colorado, where his wife had relatives. However the next record of him is in Portage La Prairie, Manitoba, where he designed the Methodist Church in April, 1882, and where, in the same year, his son Norman was born. From 1882-86 he moved around, and combined professional photography with architecture. He built the camera that he used to take pictures along the Canadian Pacific Railway and to record other events in early western Canada. One theory is that he did this to travel for free on the train to the next boomtown, where he might find an architectural commission. His photographs captured an important period in Canadian history, the coming of the railway, and events, people, and places related to First Nations unrest and the Riel Rebellion. During the spring and summer of 1883 he advertised his services as an architect in Brandon, but by the late summer had moved on to Calgary, where he advertised as an architect and a photographer. The fall of 1885 found him in Regina. In his travels it seems likely that he came as far west as Vancouver and Victoria.

Soule and his family moved back to Guelph around 1886 where he resumed his architectural practice. His son, David, was born there. Finally, in February of 1890 he arrived in Victoria and opened an office. His first known commission was a home for Frederick James Claxton, a realtor. He also designed homes for William Dalby, Claxton's partner, in a similar style to Claxton's, and Joseph Clearihue, both 1890. In 1891, he designed St. Paul's Presbyterian Church in Victoria West and his most notable commission in Victoria, the Willows

Clearihue Residence, Victoria

Left: Willows Agricultural Exhibit
Hall, Oak Bay

Right: North Ward School, Victoria

Agricultural Exhibit Hall. It was a fantastic wood and glass structure sporting towers, bridges and an ornate fountain. Hailed as a significant landmark in the history of exhibition architecture in Canada, this exuberant structure was destroyed by fire in 1907. Also in 1891, he designed the three-storey brick Rock Bay Hotel, and additions for Major Dupont's home *Stadacona*.

In September 1891, Soule took as a partner Robert Scott Day. Born in the city of Cork, Ireland in 1858, Day graduated with a Bachelor of Civil Engineering degree, and then articled in architecture in the office of Thomas Drew, Dublin, as well as the offices of various London architects. Prior to coming to Canada, he practised for five years in the South African diamond fields where his commissions included the Kimberley Stock Exchange and the head office of DeBeers Consolidated Mines. He met and married his wife, Lilla Swanson, in Kimberley, South Africa in 1888, and they had six children. In 1891 Day arrived in Victoria, attracted by his family's considerable property holdings in the province. The work of Soule & Day included the Point Comfort Hotel on Mayne Island, 1892-93, a popular holiday resort for many years. It was reported in the *Daily Colonist* on January 1, 1893: "It is not designed to take the name of "Point Comfort" in vain, but by managing the establishment along the lines of an old English inn, to give all the "comforts" which the name suggests... In this mild and balmy atmosphere those in search of health can regain their shattered strength and take on a new lease of life. On the other hand the well and vigorous in search of recreation will here find themselves in a veritable sportsman's paradise. The fishing along the beach is noted as the finest in British Columbia. The members of the finny tribe swarm in profusion and range in variety from the herring to the salmon."

Soule & Day also won the commission for Victoria's North Ward School, 1893-94, in a competition which included other such notable architects as **T.C. Sorby**, **Thomas Hooper**, and **W. Ridgway-Wilson**, whose second place offering was built as South Park School. The Soule & Day partnership was dissolved early in 1894. In 1895 Robert Day was advertising his services as an architect, but by 1897 he had taken up a career as a land, mining and insurance agent. Day's home, *Dereen*, had a prestigious address on Rockland, and still stands on Dereen Place. Day died December 6, 1920, after succumbing to shock from injuries sustained in a fall on the night of November 26. He had dropped his wife and daughter off at the Empress Hotel to attend the Jubilee Hospital annual ball, and had gone to park the car. Getting out of the car in the dark he fell off a parapet, a sheer drop of several feet, and lay unconscious for almost forty minutes in the cold and rain before being discovered and taken to the hospital.

In June of 1892 the British Columbia Institute of Architects was officially registered, and Soule became its second Vice-President, and in 1894 its Vice-President. He also competed, along with many other architects, for the design of the British Columbia Parliament Buildings in 1892. In 1898 Soule opened an office in Vancouver in partnership with **Samuel Maclure**, which according to directories lasted until the following year but informally may have lasted longer. A mansion built in 1899 for Sir Charles Hibbert Tupper, named *Parkside*, could have been a product of this partnership; however, the Vancouver *World* newspaper of the day gave sole credit to Soule as architect. The mansion stood on the brow of a hill at the corner of Barclay and Chilco overlooking the Stanley Park Zoo. In 1899 Soule's eldest daughter, May, married Henry Woodward, a Port Alberni rancher. Another local architect, **A. Maxwell Muir**, was best man.

In 1901 he competed in the design for the Lieutenant Governor's residence, coming in second to Byrnes & **Sait**. Mysteriously, **Rattenbury** and Maclure, who were not entered

The Soule family, Victoria, 1895

in the competition, jointly ended up with the commission. By November 1903, Soule had an office in Edmonton. He had just called for tenders for the erection of a brick and stone building for the Bank of Commerce when he was abruptly called home to Victoria, owing to the serious illness of his wife, who died November 21 of pneumonia. After his wife's death, Soule gave up his practice of architecture, moved to Fulford Harbour on Salt Spring Island, and took up farming. He occasionally worked for other architects such as **Russell & Babcock**, in Tacoma, Washington in 1906 and **J.C.M. Keith** in 1908. In 1908 Soule was married for a second time, to Mary Emma Schultz, a teacher from Brantford, Ontario, and in the following year their only son, Rupert Frederick was born. Victoria endured a record snowfall in February, 1916, and the following year the family moved to Los Angeles. In 1918 they returned to British Columbia, saying that the California weather was too hot, and that they had to put damp sheets up to the open windows to keep the house cooler and to control the dust.

Over the next few years Soule divided his time between Coldstream, near Vernon, and Milne's Landing, near Sooke, where he farmed his property on Soule Road. Mary taught school at Coldstream. In 1921 she and Rupert moved to Milne's Landing where Soule had completed the building of their small farmhouse. Mary taught school at the William Head Quarantine Station during the week and spent her weekends at home. In 1939, Cornelius Soule died at the age of eighty-eight, and was buried at the Saseenos cemetery near Milne's Landing.

Top right: *Parkside*, Vancouver

Bottom right: Office of Russell & Babcock, Tacoma, Washington, March 18, 1906; C.J. Soule third from left

Point Comfort Hotel, Mayne Island

RICHARD
PRIOR
SHARP

BORN C. 1859

JIM WOLF

R.P. Sharp's career in British Columbia was marked by his talented British Arts and Crafts designs and his brief but influential partnership with **Samuel Maclure**. Born in Sleaford, Lincolnshire, England, Sharp came to the study of architecture early in life and was articled in Peterborough, Northhamptonshire. Following this introduction, he practised his talent "in the largest English Cities" for eight years. In 1888, before immigrating to Canada, he became a Member of the Society of Architects in London.

After arriving on the Pacific coast in 1889, Sharp took up residence in New Westminster. In May, 1890, he opened an office in "Room E" of the Bank of B.C. Building, which also housed the offices of the architectural practice of **Charles Clow** and Samuel Maclure in "Room F." He advertised in the local newspapers and received a number of notable commissions. These included the Anglican Parish Rooms for the Bishop of New Westminster, a brick office block for the legal firm of Corbould, McColl & Jenns on Lorne Street in the Royal City and a new wing to the Mission School in Yale. These projects, combined with a number of residential commissions for prominent New Westminster families, quickly earned him a reputation as an architect of "marked ability, being widely known and esteemed."

On March 4, 1891, Clow & Maclure announced the amicable end of their five-year partnership and Maclure set up a new office alone in "Room G." However, on March 14 the partnership of Sharp & Maclure was announced with another notice in *The Morning Ledger*. The new partnership wasted no time in securing a large number of significant commissions, including New Westminster residences, a church in Nanaimo

and a commercial block in Vancouver in the fifteen months they were together. Of their residences, the Thomas Cunningham home in New Westminster is unusual. It is a direct copy from a pattern book, *Modern Architectural Designs and Details*, which showed a House at Fairmont, New Jersey, by architects Rossiter & Wright, completed in 1880, but pattern copying appears to have been an exception in this busy office.

The majority of Sharp & Maclure's residences display a design aesthetic notable for its sophisticated British Arts and Crafts styling. The mansion *Rosslynn*, at Third Avenue and Seventh Street, designed in 1892 for Isaac B. Fisher, the manager of the Bank of B.C., received praise for "its many new and original ideas in modern architecture and design." It incorporated artistic interior decoration using native woods, in designs never before seen in the province. One of Sharp & Maclure's largest homes was the M.M. English house, which still stands on Royal Avenue. It was described in *The Daily Columbian* as a home with "an exterior design remarkably pleasant to the eye, in good taste, and without elaborate display," and included finely crafted interior features, a central hall and fireplace inglenook. The 1891 Church of St. Alban the Martyr in Nanaimo received favorable press notice for the architects due to the design of a unique altar crafted in native woods by New Westminster's Wintemute Furniture Company and a "lady carver," Miss Ede of Vancouver. *Norland*, for the Misses Schou at Burnaby Lake in 1891, was the first example of a modest home design that would later be repeated in Maclure's Victoria office. In 1892, Maclure's sister, Sarah McLagan, a newspaper publisher, provided a significant commission to design the Vancouver World's new block on Homer Street, described by a rival newspaper as being "plain and business-like architecture." The building owners praised the "artistic skill and ability of the architects" and the completion in record time without "a hitch or a jar." Although heavily altered, the Romanesque Revival-styled building is still extant.

Maclure had made the decision to move with his family to Victoria, and on June 30, 1892 *The Daily Columbian* printed a notice announcing the end of the partnership. Sharp kept busy with a number of commissions for residences and working on an unsuccessful submission for the B.C. Parliament Buildings competition. Sharp was a founding director in 1891

Norland, Burnaby

All Saints' Anglican Church, Agassiz

of the B.C. Institute of Architects, serving as second Vice-President and later as Secretary. Despite the economic recession of the mid-1890s, Sharp did manage to win a number of commissions for cannery buildings on the Fraser River. He also completed two beautiful church buildings, evocative of English parish churches, that still survive in the Fraser Valley. All Saints' Anglican Church at Agassiz, designed in 1894 and completed two years later, is a small church that incorporates unusual Arts and Crafts styling. The scissor-beam roof trusses were originally continued as a series of exterior flying buttresses, and shed wall dormers allow natural light to illuminate the roof structure and fir and cedar woodwork. St. Thomas Anglican Church, built in Chilliwack in 1895, is an excellent example of Sharp's ability to translate his English design training to British Columbia by using local materials. The interior features red cedar panelling and decorative beams.

The economic situation worsened and, despite these few commissions, Sharp was reduced to designing and supervising construction of new privies for the New Westminster Central School and working as the Tax Assessor and Collector for the Municipality of Burnaby in 1896. A notice that year in *Canadian Architect & Builder* reported that he was "about to take up his residence in England." Richard Sharp left British Columbia a legacy of beautifully designed buildings and the experience and knowledge that he shared with native son Samuel Maclure.

West Elevation

CHARLES ELWOOD WATKINS
1875–1942

JENNIFER NELL BARR AND
DONALD LUXTON

Although he spent the first half of his career in the shadow of his more famous partner, native-born C. Elwood Watkins was a prolific and talented designer whose work deserves wider recognition. He was born on October 3, 1875 in Victoria, B.C., the eldest son of Charles Richard Watkins, of Abergavenny, Wales, and Mary Hannah McMillan, of Bowmanville, Ontario. In 1862 both his parents' families moved to Victoria, where Charles and Mary were married on December 12, 1874. Elwood's father died of typhoid in November 1884 at the age of forty-two. Mary and her five younger children went to live with her father, and Elwood was sent back to Ontario to attend high school. Before the age of fifteen he was back in Victoria and began his architectural apprenticeship in the office of **Thomas Hooper**. This was a busy and prolific time, and as Hooper travelled a great deal, it can be imagined that young Elwood was the backbone of the practice, handling many of the practical affairs. The office developed a steadily increasing reputation among numerous clients for solid, competent work. In recognition of his contributions, in 1902 he was made a full partner. Their output was prodigious: within a few short years they designed many of the buildings that still define the character of Victoria's Old Town. The firm also produced a large volume of residential work, and a number of landmark projects around the province.

Their success enabled Watkins to design and build his own home on prestigious Rockland Avenue, 1904-05. On April 19, 1905 he married Lillian Matilda 'Lill' Nisbet, the daughter of Philip and Catharine Nisbet. Elwood and Lill had two children, a daughter, Gwendolyn, and a son, Thomas Elwood, named after Hooper. After an acrimonious split with Hooper in 1909,

Watkins opened his own office in the Green Block on Broad Street.

From 1908 to 1913 the population boom in Victoria, with the influx of new residents particularly from Britain, led to a major expansion programme for local schools. Watkins was one of the group of younger architects who developed more modern school designs, including advanced technology and the use of a wider range of building materials. In his austere design for George Jay School, started in 1908 while he was still in partnership with Hooper, he introduced the "Kahn System" of reinforced concrete construction, patented in the United States by the engineer brother of Detroit architect Albert Kahn. By 1912 Watkins had been appointed official architect of the Victoria School Board, and after **H.J. Rous Cullin** left for overseas service, he also became the architect for the Saanich School Board. His most imposing and lavish school design was the new Victoria High School, the highlight of his career. This glorious essay in *Beaux-Arts* Classicism is richly encrusted with terra cotta. Watkins had been selected as architect for the new building in 1910, and worked closely with Principal Samuel J. Willis, also his brother-in-law, in studying the latest elements of school design. Tenders closed in March 1912, but the school was not opened until April 20, 1914. The final cost of $460,000 made it the most expensive school building in the province.

The years of the First World War were very slow for local architects. Watkins did some school work and private residences, but went one year without making any money at all. Apparently, Watkins and the Victoria Building Inspector, Herbert Shade, played cards together to pass the time. Watkins

P.A. Babbington Residence, Victoria, 1911

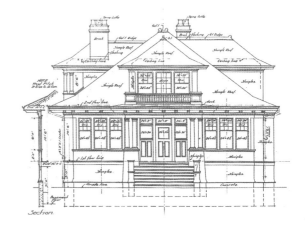

Lee Block, Victoria

did secure the commissions for two large lavish Tudor Revival homes for the Luney Brothers, Walter and William, prominent local contractors. The brothers had won the contract for Provincial Normal School, which allowed them the funds to build their own homes in the middle of the war, at a time when few people could afford to build anything.

After the war, Watkins became very busy again, with a varied practice that included residential, commercial and institutional work. Following the trend towards period revival styles, he designed several Colonial Revival residences, a Spanish Colonial Revival funeral parlour, and an Art Deco crematorium chapel. He provided designs for a number of buildings at Victoria's two major hospitals, and also donated a design for the Saanich Pioneer Society's museum in Central Saanich, 1932-33. During the 1930s Watkins sometimes worked in informal association with other architects, includ-

ing **J. Graham Johnson**. Watkins was a favourite architect of the local Chinese community, and provided designs for Hook Sin Tong, Lee's Benevolent Association, the Lee Block, and several buildings on Fan Tan Alley.

Along with a number of other prominent families, the Watkinses owned one of the first summer homes on the cliff-top lots on Mileva Crescent in north Gordon Head, Saanich, which was developed in 1912. Neighbouring property-owners, the five Parfitt Brothers, were also business associates; as local contractors they constructed many of Watkins's buildings. The families organized numerous tennis and lawn bowling parties. Musical events were often hosted by the Parfitts, who had a twelve-piece family orchestra, and built a concert hall on their property.

Watkins was known for his civic contributions, including membership on the Plumbing Board of Examiners, and the Building Board of Appeal for the City of Victoria. As a prominent member of the Kiwanis Club, he was chairman of the tuberculosis rehabilitation committee and organized the TB Seal Drive at Christmas. For many years he was on the Board of Stewards and Trustees of the Metropolitan Methodist, one of the first buildings on which he had worked in Hooper's office.

Active in the creation of the AIBC and first Vice-President of the organization, at the time of his death Watkins was the chair of the Victoria Chapter. Elwood died on August 14, 1942 at the age of sixty-six, and was buried in Royal Oak Burial Park in Saanich. He had worked at his profession until two days before his death. His wife, Lillian, died on November 26, 1959.

Victoria High School, Victoria

JOHN EDMESTON PARR
1856–1923

J Edmeston Parr

DONALD LUXTON

PARR & FEE
PARTNERSHIP 1899-1912

& Parr, where he remained until he left for North America about 1888. He went first to Los Angeles, and also worked in Seattle and Winnipeg. By 1895 he was in practice in Victoria, but moved the next year to Vancouver, where he opened his own office, working on several impressive commercial buildings, including: the Sullivan Block, 1896, the Harvey's Chambers, 1896-97 in Vancouver; and the Green Building, 1896, in Nanaimo. In 1897 he formed a brief partnership with Victoria-based **Samuel Maclure**.

Thomas Arthur Fee's family had originally emigrated from Ireland to the United States, but 'skedaddled' to Canada to avoid fighting in the Revolutionary War. He was born in Drummond County, Quebec, on May 18, 1860. Fee came west on the Canadian Pacific Railway, arriving in Port Moody without a dime, and walked the last few miles to Vancouver; he likely came in on the first train to arrive after Vancouver's Great Fire. He arrived right after the Great Fire, and worked in real estate and construction. In 1889 he travelled to Minneapolis to study architecture in the office of Harry W. Jones (1859-1935),

John Parr and Thomas Fee had both arrived and worked in British Columbia before forming their partnership in 1899. Together they were successful and prolific, and had a profound effect on the look of Edwardian Vancouver, acting both as architects and speculative developers. They were the ideal team for the times, hard-nosed and competitive, with Parr handling the majority of design work while Fee ran the business aspects. Fee, who was more entrepreneurial than Parr, built the Fee Block on Granville Street in 1903, which became the base of operations both for the architectural firm and for his personal development offices. They took a straight-forward approach to providing buildings appropriate for the unbounded yet sophisticated aspirations of their clients, people with money to spend and a desire to build. Small wonder they claimed *Utilitas* as their motto.

John Edmeston Parr was born May 7, 1856 in Islington, London, England, the son of architect Samuel Parr and Sarahjane Hannah Parr. Samuel Parr worked in partnership with Alfred Pope Strong from 1867-88. Young John was educated at Preparatory School, Gravesend, and then starting in 1872 articled for three years to Parr & Strong. He also attended classes at the Architectural Association and evening classes at University College. By 1883 he was a partner in Parr, Strong

Harvey's Chambers, Vancouver; entry to Parr & Fee's office at columned doorway. Parr & Fee also designed the adjacent Thomson Block

who had worked under Henry Hobson Richardson before establishing his own office in 1885. After a year in Minneapolis, Fee returned to British Columbia. In the late 1880s, Fee married Frances Maud Paton, with whom he had three children.

Parr and Fee entered into partnership by the summer of 1898, by which time they had twenty-eight residences underway in different parts of the city. In rapid succession they provided designs for the Thomson Block on Hastings Street, 1898; a commercial block on Hastings Street for William Ralph, prominent Vancouver merchant and bridge builder, 1899; and the McDowell, Atkins & Watson Building at the corner of Cordova and Cambie Streets, 1899; and a Chinese Methodist Mission on Carrall Street, 1899.

Throughout the Edwardian boom years they were immensely successful, and their output was prodigious. Fully aware of technological developments in construction, they introduced one of the earliest equivalents of the curtain wall in the front facade of a building designed for Buscombe & Co., 1906. The following year they provided the designs for the first half of the

THOMAS A. FEE
1860–1929

Malkin Company's third warehouse on Water Street; when the building was doubled in size four years later the contractor, J.M. McLuckie, essentially copied their plans to produce the expanded structure. In 1907 they designed the Manhattan Apartments, at the corner of Robson and Thurlow Streets, one of the city's earliest large apartment blocks. The Hotel Europe, designed in 1908, was a beautiful response to a triangular site, clearly inspired by Daniel Burnham's 1901-03 design for the Flatiron Building, New York, but also noteworthy for its use of an innovative reinforced concrete structure, built by the Ferro-Concrete Construction Company of Cincinnati, Ohio. The Dunsmuir Hotel, a landmark brick block with deep airshafts, was designed for David Gibb & Sons, proprietors, in 1908. For John J. Banfield, one of the busiest land promoters in Strathcona and also prominent in real estate in Grand Forks, they provided the designs for the gracious and finely-detailed Stadacona Apartments, 1909. The same year, they designed the Mount Pleasant Presbyterian Church on Quebec Street, now converted for use as condominiums. In 1910, they designed the Dufferin Hotel at the corner of Smithe and Seymour Streets. They also designed, and Fee owned, many of the hotels that still line downtown Granville Street, faced with distinctive white glazed bricks and capped with grandiose projecting cornices.

In addition to commercial buildings, the firm designed many residential projects, ranging from palatial to modest. An early commission was a large farm house for Henry Mole and his

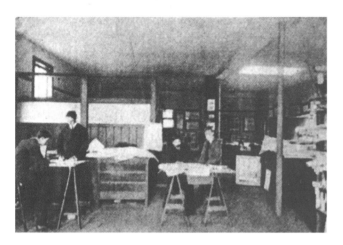

Offices of Parr & Fee in the Fee Block, c.1908

Morin, featuring one of their trademark round turrets, capped with a bellcast dome roof. Among their larger projects was *Glen Brae*, 1910, an enormous home in Shaughnessy for W.L. Tait, expansive enough to warrant a flanking pair of their bulbous turrets.

Parr was more comfortable acting as a designer than a businessman, but although he was the quieter of the two partners, was fiercely protective, and had a reputation for devastating anyone standing in the way of his firm's progress. Conservative in his politics and an Anglican, he was also athletic and counted fencing among his pursuits. He remained single until 1911, when he married Leila Imogene Stuart, daughter of Charles Stuart of West Hampstead, London. Parr's physical appearance was later recalled by Ross Lort, who wrote "In at least one office an architect managed to achieve a resemblance to himself in his buildings. Here and there in Vancouver there are one or two rather over-embellished houses of average looks for their time, but each house has on one corner a rather chunky circular tower topped off with a circular shaped roof that bears some resemblance to a bowler hat or a bald head; and when this particular architect walked along the street, either with his bowler hat or his very bald head rising above a long white beard which in turn rose above his very large circumference it was for all the world as if one of his towers had decided to go for a walk."

Methodist, but not prudish, Fee was outgoing, social and

family on Marine Drive at Blenheim, 1901. They also provided plans for many speculative houses, such as one for Stanley Judson Steeves on Comox Street in 1904; Steves just copied the plans to build a similar house next door, getting two house plans for the price of one. Fee built himself a turreted house on Broughton Street in the West End in 1903-04, but with the firm's increasing prosperity soon started construction on a far grander home, again with one of the firm's signature turrets, on Gilford Street close to Stanley Park, built by Scottish stone masons, 1906-07. In 1909 they designed a house at the corner of Yukon Street and West 12th Avenue for Narcisse

Fee Residence, Vancouver, c.1918

Glen Brae, Vancouver

fond of the good life. He was also self-disciplined, and punctual to a fault, and people commented that they could set their watches by him as he passed by their shops. Stricken with polio at a young age, Fee had to wear braces on both legs, and he installed a hand-operated elevator in his Gilford Street home to reach the second floor more easily. Fee was fond of big cigars, and loved cars and horses. He owned a Detroit Electric automobile, the first in the city. This car often ran out of juice, but fortunately the Fee home was at the bottom of a long hill. He later owned two Packards, the first one of which arrived without wheels, as Fee did not know that they had to be ordered separately. Throughout this time Fee retained a chauffeur, and also kept horses.

By 1910 planning was underway for the grandest of their skyscrapers. Dominic Burns, wealthy land owner and brother of meat-packing magnate, Patrick Burns, chose Parr & Fee to design his fifteen-storey Vancouver Block on Granville Street; included at the top of the building was a grand penthouse for Burns. This prominent structure, which slightly predated the adjacent Birks Building by **Somervell & Putnam**, helped establish Georgia and Granville as the commercial core of early Vancouver. The Vancouver Block, still a landmark on the skyline, is clad both on the main facade and on the alley side with pure white terra cotta. This confection of a structure is capped by an illuminated clock tower, topped on each side by ornate datestones; Burns had his own penthouse apartment in the top of the tower. Six caryatids support a heavy projecting cornice.

The terra cotta was supplied by Gladding, McBean & Co., and was shipped from their California plant between June 1 and August 1, 1911.

In the middle of their greatest successes the partnership split up. Parr formed a new architectural partnership with John Mackenzie and **John Charles Day**, which among other projects was awarded the design for a city hall for the newly incorporated City of Port Coquitlam. This partnership continued until Day withdrew in 1918. Parr's last known project was an apartment block on Beach Avenue, 1923. He passed away at his South Vancouver home on September 15, 1923, and was buried in the Masonic Cemetery.

Fee temporarily retired from architecture in 1912 to pursue his development interests, and went into business with his son, Thomas Arthur Blakely Fee. Now wealthy from his many business pursuits, Fee became publicly outspoken in his beliefs, and was expelled from the Vancouver Board of Trade on September 30, 1914 for opposing Canada's participation in the war effort, and for advocating British Columbia's annexation by the United States. Another of his unpatriotic suggestions was that German national, Alvo von Alvensleben, should be allowed to return from exile in Seattle. During the war, the army wanted to take Fee's horses, but he refused, even though this led to his patriotism being questioned in public. Although he spent most of 1920-25 in Seattle, he also designed a number of commercial projects in Vancouver, and a house for his daughter, Olga's, family on Beverley Crescent in Shaughnessy, 1920-21. On his 1921 application to the AIBC, instead of naming his significant projects, Fee boasted "The list would be too long to fill in here. I can say that I have had in charge the erection or alteration of a greater number of buildings than any other architect in B.C." Thomas Fee was still working as late as 1928, and died on December 21, 1929.

Dunsmuir Hotel, Vancouver

Competition drawing for the extension of the Hotel Vancouver, 1902

Messrs. Parr & Fee have built up their connection upon a strictly commercial basis, and while they welcome any incident that gives expression or beauty to their work their chief endeavor is the production of buildings that will pay. "Utilitas" is their motto and revenue their aim: a larger number of buildings has been erected from their designs than from the designs of any other single firm of architects in the Province... Among the clients of this firm, beside men of business in the city, are a number of wealthy men both in England and the United States, and any one coming to Vancouver with larger sums to invest could not do better than to consult these thoughtful, practical and experienced men.

Greater Vancouver - Illustrated, c.1907, p. 196.

Vancouver Block, Vancouver

PARR & FEE
Architects

Original scheme for the Hotel Europe

ARLEN H. TOWLE

JIM WOLF

Arlen H. Towle was another talented architect who designed landmark buildings in early British Columbia but whose name in the historic record has been lost for decades. What little is known of Towle's life is limited to his work in two cities on the west coast of the United States. He arrived in San Diego, California, sometime between 1885 and 1886 and is listed in local directories as an architect and carpenter. He designed residences, cottages and at least one imposing office building, the John Young Block, in that city prior to 1888. He moved to Seattle in 1889 and established a partnership with Frank N. Wilcox, a trained civil engineer. Towle recognized the opportunities for working in the burgeoning economy of British Columbia, and the firm of Towle & Wilcox placed an advertisement for their services in New Westminster's journal *The Ledger* in April, 1890. The following month they opened an office in the Royal City. However, their partnership ended in 1891 with Wilcox returning to Seattle to practice until 1894.

The confidence shown in Towle by New Westminster's business community in 1891 was a remarkable achievement for a newcomer to the city, and it may indicate that his superior skills and experience inspired the trust of land owners and investors. Towle managed to garner some substantial commissions in 1891 which amounted to over $140,000 in construction value. These buildings included the Duncan-Batchelor Block, Curtis-Burns Block, Odd Fellows Block and the Hotel Guichon, all located on Columbia Street. Terra cotta for the first two projects was ordered from Gladding, McBean & Company in California.

It was noted in *The Daily Columbian* in January 1892 that "Mr. and Mrs. A.H. Towle have returned to the city from Seattle and will make their home here in the future." Towle had so much work on hand in his new office in the Powell Block that he placed a "Wanted" advertisement in *The Daily Columbian* looking for a young man over seventeen years of age, with a good education, to learn to be an architect.

Towle's preferred style was the American Romanesque Revival, as can be seen in surviving photographs of his commissions. The Hotel Guichon, completed in 1892, was a three-storey brick and sandstone structure with special decorative features described as "Grecian," including terra cotta decoration and "rubbed sandstone" with oak store fronts, the first in the city. Described by the local newspaper: "It has an especially fine, massive appearance, and public opinion has it, that it is the finest hotel entrance in the Province." The interior of native woods included a maple staircase, panelled ceiling, and Moorish screen work. This work, completed by Royal City

Duncan-Batchelor Block, New Westminster

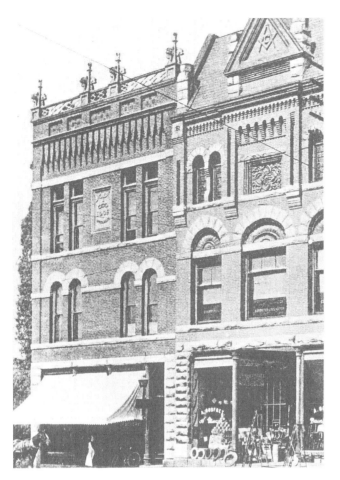

Odd Fellows Hall, New Westminste

Planing Mills of New Westminster, had been placed on exhibit at the Provincial Exhibition in Queen's Park and received numerous press compliments for both Towle and the craftsmen.

The Odd Fellows Block, 1891-92, was described by one reporter when viewing the plans "Mr. Towle has created an idea which suggests a harmony of an English and American modernization of the old school of architecture." It was built in conjunction with the Masonic Block next door designed by George Grant whose design in contrast to Towle's work was described as being derived from "the Gothic and Flemish styles." However, it was the opinion of the reporter that the two blocks "side by side will effect a combination harmonious and pleasing." Certainly it was the interior decoration of the Odd Fellows temple with its generous dimensions of thirty-one by sixty-six feet with a ceiling twenty feet high which received much favorable attention as "the finest in the Province." It was elaborately decorated with pressed steel ornamental panels and ventilators, and lighted with stained glass windows.

In April, 1892, Towle's design was selected from among those submitted by a large number of competing architects for the First Presbyterian Church in Vancouver on East Hastings Street at Gore Avenue. One reporter described its plans as "imposing and handsome in appearance in the modern style of church architecture" and stated that the design "speaks highly for Mr. Towle's skill as an architect." The church, completed in 1893, was certainly an imposing landmark, unique among Vancouver places of worship and was derived from the American Romanesque style, though its exterior was completely finished with wood. The body of the church was octagonal in form with seating for 1,100 in the round and included additional spaces for a ladies' parlour, gallery, four class rooms and a kitchen.

Unfortunately the buildings designed by Towle were completed and celebrated in the local press just as the recession began. His name disappeared from local directories by 1894 and it is not known where he relocated his family and practice, although a return to the United States seems most likely. All four of Towle's New Westminster blocks were destroyed in the Great Fire of 1898 and the First Presbyterian Church in Vancouver was demolished in 1963. The only surviving local buildings known to be designed by Towle are a pair of elegant brick duplexes built in 1892 on Third Avenue in New Westminster.

Brick Duplex, New Westminster

First Presbyterian Church, Vancouver

Festively yours:

James Bloomfield
for self & brother

JAMES ALFRED BLOOMFIELD
1860–1951

JIM WOLF

James Bloomfield was one of British Columbia's most notable early artists and designers. Although he advertised at various times as an architect, he worked mainly in the design and production of Arts and Crafts-styled architectural art glass and interior decorations. He was born in Ipswich, England. His father, Henry Bloomfield, moved his family to Maidenhead where he was a lead worker by trade, worked as a plumber, and manufactured and repaired leaded glass windows. James worked as a junior draftsman in an architect's office and took classes in drawing and design at the local Mechanic's Institute. When the family immigrated to Canada in 1887 and settled in Calgary, James met architect **T.E. Julian**, with whom he continued to study architecture. The Bloomfields moved to New Westminster in 1889, and the following year established "Henry Bloomfield & Sons," the first art glass studio in western Canada. The oldest surviving and documented Bloomfield glass remains in the Charles Murray residence in New Westminster, designed by **Clow & Maclure** in 1890. James became a close friend of Samuel Maclure, they were the same age and shared a love of watercolour painting and design.

When the economic recession began in 1893, James was desperate for work and moved to Victoria and advertised as an architect. With time on his hands, Bloomfield formed Victoria's first art society with Maclure and other prominent artists and architects. Bloomfield also submitted art glass designs to **F.M. Rattenbury**, which were crafted by the family firm for the Parliament Buildings. James returned to New Westminster in 1894 and kept busy with two passions, heraldry and the art of British Columbia's native peoples. He produced two illuminated scrolls for presentation to Canada's Governor General Lord Aberdeen on a visit to the city in 1894. After the presentation, Lord Aberdeen asked him where he had learned his craft. James replied: "I haven't learned anywhere. I just did it." Lord Aberdeen declared: "your talent should not be wasted – you should have training." After learning that James had an offer to work as a junior designer in Chicago, Lord Aberdeen made out a cheque and said: "Pack your bag and catch the next train." Bloomfield left for Chicago in 1895, and was employed as a junior designer in a large art glass firm. In 1898 he received news of New Westminster's Great Fire. The Bloomfield's home and studio was destroyed, and James, out of a sense of duty, returned to British Columbia.

In 1900, Bloomfield designed and crafted the art glass for B.T. Rogers's Maclure-designed mansion *Gabriola*. This included the magnificent stair window of the "three graces," which incorporated local flora such as skunk cabbage and dogwood flowers. The success of this commission led to another, for the new Lieutenant Governor's residence in Victoria. In addition to providing stained glass, Bloomfield completed handsome mural decorations in the ballroom with "totem designs" provided by a Haida draftsman, one of the first collaborations of Aboriginal and European artists in the province. He designed the Vancouver civic coat of arms, still in use today, and the Queen Victoria Memorial Fountain in Stanley Park, 1906. In 1903, Bloomfield won a "remarkable" victory by winning the competition to design the grand marble staircase for the St. Louis Exposition State Pavilion. He began to use the surname Blomfield, apparently as a reference to a distant arm of the family in England that included Sir Arthur Blomfield. Even before the family firm was closed in 1906, James had struck out on his own. However, he soon realized that "it was a case of politely starving to death, or getting the hell out" of Vancouver. He worked out of Spokane, Washington for a brief time, and then returned to Chicago from 1907-16. After the end of the First World War he travelled the United States, working as a writer and illustrator for the Christian Science Monitor. He returned to Canada to reside near Toronto in 1920, and continued to work as a glass artist and painter. He died in 1951 after being hit by an automobile while walking near his home.

EDWARD
COLONNA
1862–1948

DONALD LUXTON

Edward Colonna is better remembered for his international artistic reputation as one of the foremost practitioners of the *Art Nouveau* style than for his Canadian architectural career. A mysterious figure, he obscured many aspects of his life, changing his name from Edouard Klönne when he moved to North America, either to hide his germanic origins or to adopt a more romantic personality, and many people assumed that he was related to the patrician Colonna family of Rome. For the rest of his life he conveniently passed as either French or Italian.

He was born in the town of Wesel, Germany on May 27, 1862, and the following year his family moved to Cologne. In 1877, Edouard left for Brussels to study architecture. Four years later he set sail for New York City, and briefly landed a position with famed designer Louis Comfort Tiffany. In 1884-85 he worked in the office of the fashionable architect **Bruce Price**, who had been providing designs for the Barney & Smith Manufacturing Co. of Dayton, Ohio, which specialized in the production of custom passenger rail cars. Colonna was hired away from Price's office by Barney & Smith, where he worked for the next three years. Colonna promoted his artistic aspirations through the self-publication of two small books. These highly imaginative works pointed a new direction that Colonna was destined to follow. In 1888, he married Louise McLaughlin, the daughter of Cincinnati's most prominent architect. Louise's

Parliament Buildings competition logo

aunt, Marie Louise McLaughlin, was one of the leaders of the American Arts and Crafts movement, and undoubtedly influenced Colonna's artistic development. M.L. McLaughlin was an innovative and accomplished ceramicist and author, who discovered the process for "Cincinnati Limoges," a process of underglaze decoration with colored slips that imitated the process invented in Limoges, France. In 1879, she founded the Cincinnati Women's Pottery Club, an outlet for young women interested in the therapeutic, and commercial, value of handcrafting items.

Colonna moved to Montreal in 1888. The CPR was a good client of Barney & Smith's, and was pursuing an aggressive policy of expansion throughout Canada. Price was awarded a number of important CPR commissions, and Colonna was engaged to work on the interiors of some of the larger commissions such as the Windsor Stration, Montreal, and the Château Frontenac, Quebec City. Colonna also designed a number of CPR rail stations, for Sherbrooke, Banff, Calgary, Regina, Brandon, Portage la Prairie, and Fort William (now Thunder Bay). The Calgary station, 1891, was built in two section, and when a new, larger station was built, the two halves were dismantled and re-erected in other communities; one half survives today in the Town of Claresholm, Alberta and is used as the local museum.

For the new terminal at Vancouver, he provided his grandest architectural design, an imposing structure of which only the foundations had been started when the local economy collapsed. Colonna also planned renovations to the existing Hotel Vancouver. In 1892, Colonna submitted an entry for the competition for the new British Columbia Parliament Buildings. By 1893, Colonna had been sent to Glasgow to oversee the interior decoration of the CPR's steamship *Prince Rupert*. While overseas, he seized the opportunity to establish his residency in Paris, and within a few years he was associated with Siegfried Bing and his celebrated store *L'Art Nouveau*. Bing came from a German mercantile family that had imported French porcelain and glass for many years, and he joined the Paris branch of the business. His store's name became synonymous with the sinuous curves and sensuous forms that were considered the height of fashionable design. Colonna was one of Bing's main designers during his period of greatest success, and he designed jewellry – some of which was acquired by Sarah Bernhardt – as well as furniture and a wide variety of precious *objets de vertu*. Colonna developed an international reputation, but when Bing's enterprises collapsed in 1903, Colonna returned briefly to Canada, then travelled widely and worked intermittently, and in 1923 retired to the south of France. He settled in Nice in 1925, and continued to produce decorative objects. Bedridden, he survived the tough wartime years, and died in Nice on October 14, 1948, his architectural career in the far flung west of Canada long since forgotten.

JOHN CHARLES MALCOLM KEITH
1858–1940

ROBIN WARD AND
DONALD LUXTON

J.C.M. Keith had a surprisingly prolific career over a span of half a century. He was born at Huntley Hall, Nairn, near Inverness, Scotland, on December 19, 1858, the son of Rev. Charles McGhee Keith, and Elizabeth Madeline Christie. Educated in England at Lincoln and Wallasey, Cheshire, he returned to Scotland in the mid-1870s to study under architect Alexander Ross (1834-1925) of Inverness. Ross was a noted ecclesiastical architect who designed St. Andrew's Episcopal Cathedral, Inverness, 1866-69, Inverness Market and Arcade, 1870, and over a dozen parish churches, mostly Episcopalian, in Scotland between 1866 and 1912. Keith's feeling for religious architecture, already well-developed given his family background, was nurtured by Ross's professionalism and numerous church commissions. In 1883 Keith left Scotland for London where he continued his studies.

Keith immigrated to California in 1887. He attempted to practice in San Francisco and briefly opened an office in San Diego in 1888, but in 1889 moved to Seattle where the commercial district had just been destroyed by fire. Rebuilding work was plentiful, but Keith's personality left him ill-equipped to deal with the hurly-burly of American life. He was also out of step with the popularity of the newly-fashionable Richardsonian Romanesque style. In 1891, he relocated to Victoria, B.C. in anticipation of an international competition soon to be held for the new Christ Church Cathedral. Once there, Keith truly found a home away from home - a colonial society run by pragmatic Scots and would-be English gentry - and a clientele for whom his training and temperament were perfectly tailored.

He entered into partnership with Cecil Evers, a Seattle-based architect, and they submitted a design under the pseudonym

Fides, based on thirteenth century medieval French and English Gothic cathedrals to the Christ Church competition, which closed on December 31, 1891. The competitors were half Canadian and half English (including A.R. Scott, Paisley and Henry Wilson, London), and the entries were adjudicated by prominent London-based architect, Sir Arthur Blomfield. He awarded first prize to Evers & Keith; English architects placed second and third. Their triumph was tempered when they found that the church couldn't afford to start construction; as the *Canadian Architect & Builder* later noted "the limit of cost was fixed at $150,000, a sum very inadequate for the purpose." Despite the delay with the church, they remained busy designing several grand residences in Victoria's Rockland neighbourhood, including *Hochelaga* for A.J.C. Galletly, Manager of the Bank of Montreal, 1892, and *Highlands* for William J. Macauley, 1893. **Francis Rattenbury** rented *Hochelaga* in 1898 while he decided where to build his own house, and a comparison of the two indicates that he may have been inspired by the details of their design. Nearby the cathedral site, Evers & Keith designed two modest houses for the Anglican Synod, 1893; the western one, 943 Meares Street, is still known today as the Bell Ringer's House. Their partnership dissolved before the end of 1893, and Evers played no further role in the development of the Christ Church commission. He later moved to New York where he became a "businessman."

Keith remained in Victoria, and was kept busy with many diverse commissions, including a house for J.N. Hibben in the James Bay neighbourhood, 1893, and a power station for the Victoria Electric Railway & Lighting Company, 1894-95. In 1908, he designed a rambling Shingle-style Nurses' Residence at Royal Jubilee Hospital, Victoria, 1908, since demolished. On May 30, 1908, Keith, who had remained unmarried until late in life, was wed in Vancouver to Louisa Esther Shrapnel Barter, daughter of William Barter.

Keith's relationship with the Anglican Church, into which he had been baptized, brought many commissions for parish churches throughout the province. His steady output of churches included: St. Mary's Anglican Church, Mayne Island, 1897-1898; St. John the Baptist Anglican, Duncan, 1905; the New English Evangelical Grace Lutheran Church, Victoria, 1910; and the beautifully detailed First Presbyterian on Quadra

Competition drawing for Christ Church Cathedral, 1891

CHRIST CHURCH CATHEDRAL · VICTORIA, B.C. under construction Jan. 1929

Hesket, Victoria

Street in Victoria, 1912-15. Keith's Arts and Crafts design for the second All Saints' Anglican Church in Vernon, 1907, replaced a modest wooden church built in 1893. He also provided the designs for the Cathedral Church of the Redeemer (Anglican), a sandstone church that still stands today in immaculate condition in downtown Calgary, and is provincially designated. His most pleasing smaller work is also at Royal Jubilee, the Pemberton Memorial Chapel, built in 1909. The chapel was donated by Theresa Jane Pemberton, widow of Joseph Despard Pemberton, the illustrious colonial surveyor and engineer.

Keith was triumphant in another open competition, called in 1908 by the provincial government for a new asylum for 1,800 patients on a thousand-acre farm site, to be known as the 'Hospital for the Mind at Mount Coquitlam.' Henry Esson Young, the Provincial Secretary and Minister of Education, was the driving force behind the establishment of this progressive institution. Franklin B. Ware, State Architect of New York, was appointed adjudicator, and his selection committee chose Keith's plan, which also received the highest commendation from the New York State Lunacy Commission; the plans of **E.G.W. Sait** placed second. The buildings were in the 'corridor-pavilion style,' with a central administration building with twin domed towers that reflected the symmetrical division of the site into male and female halves arranged around a surrounding horseshoe. Little of this grand plan was destined to be fulfilled, and Keith did not remain involved during construction. For unknown reasons, but likely due to the size and experience of his offices in Vancouver and Victoria, **H.S. Griffith** was retained to prepare the working drawings and specifications for the first building, the massive Male Chronic Wing. When the cornerstone was laid in 1911, Griffith's name was carved in as the architect; Keith was not acknowledged as

the original designer. Construction of the concrete frame, brick-clad hospital structure took two years, during which time Griffith was busy designing the next building for the complex, the Female Chronic Wing. By the time the Male Wing was complete, the worsening economy precluded any further construction at the site, later known as Essondale. After the First World War ended, all the design work at the site was taken over by **Henry Whittaker** and his Department of Public Works staff, and they freely adapted Keith's formal plan to suit changing mental health requirements.

During his long career Keith also designed many fine homes, generally in the Tudor Revival style, including *Hesket*, the Joseph Eilbeck Wilson residence on St. Charles Street, 1905; a fine shingle bungalow for Mrs. Louise M.B. Dodds in Oak Bay, 1912; a large house for the Ryan family in James Bay, 1912-13; the Max Enke residence in Oak Bay, 1912-13, demolished; and the extravagant *Dunmora* in Central Saanich, 1922-23. He also designed: Sir James Douglas School, built in 1909 and

Sir James Douglas School, Victoria

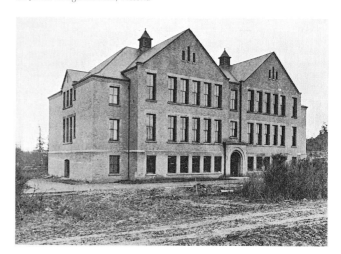

only recently demolished; Beacon Hill School, 1914, since converted to condominiums; and various commercial buildings in Victoria. He expanded his stylistic range in 1914 with the handsome City of Victoria Police Station, a four-storey Florentine *palazzo* dressed in English Edwardian Neoclassical manner with a triple-arched rusticated ground floor, Georgian quoins and an Italianate cornice, only the facade of which has been preserved.

Keith's magnum opus, Christ Church Cathedral, was the commission of a lifetime and it took more than a lifetime to complete. He had to wait for many years for the start of construction, and was frequently asked for revisions by the constantly-changing building committee. Keith, with "infinite patience," resolved the many ongoing problems. He adjusted his plans to recognize the realities of construction and financing, and the structure was redesigned with stone-clad reinforced concrete, rather than load-bearing masonry. The first stone was finally laid on Church Hill in 1926 and the building went up in fits and starts when funds were available. The first service took place in the nave in 1929. The northwest tower was topped out in 1936, the southwest one in 1954, and a truncated apse was finished in 1994. Christ Church Cathedral is, nevertheless, a striking building. The apparent solidity of the stonework, the inscriptions around the walls (in the typographic style of medieval illuminated manuscripts), the flying buttresses, and the Gothic Revival interior finally gave the Anglicans the imperial symbol of power they had desired since 1892.

The stained glass was designed and fabricated in London and Edinburgh. Vignettes above both aisles illustrate secular life and work; those on the north aisle illuminate secular life in nineteenth century Victoria with images of the fur trade, exploration and other topics, including architecture, which shows Keith at his drawing board with the finished building in the background. The more traditional south panels show literature, medicine, music, and other arts. A famous hand laid a stone in 1929 when, as the *Daily Colonist* reported, "the Rt. Hon Winston Churchill and his party visited Christ Church. The superintendent of the work suggested to the British ex-Chancellor that, since he held a union card, the masons would be very pleased if he would lay a stone in the north-west tower. Mr. Churchill's answer was immediately to shin up the ladder and get to work." For his outstanding work on the design of the Cathedral, Keith was awarded an unexpected honour, a fellowship in the Royal Institute of British Architects.

Keith's architectural output remained steady, including the monumental stone-clad Christ Church Cathedral Memorial Hall, 1923-24, positioned to be attached to the east end of the never fully-completed structure; the open space between the apse and the Hall indicates the scale of Keith's original plans. He also designed the third St. Paul's Anglican Church in Nanaimo, 1931, built to replace the second St. Paul's which had been destroyed by fire the previous year. The walls are solid concrete, with precast quoins, providing a modern interpretation of a traditional parish church. The following year a third All Saints' Anglican in Vernon replaced the 1907 church designed earlier by Keith; the local architect in charge of construction was Richard Curtis. Although larger in scale, it is almost identical in detailing to the Nanaimo church, undoubtedly indicating Keith's satisfaction with this new look he had developed, expressive of current technology and construction techniques.

Keith was a reliable, church-going citizen and Rotarian. He was also a popular amateur singer, founding member of the Arion Male Voice choir, 1893-1914, Vice-President of the Victoria Musical Society, 1906-07, and Vice-President of the Victoria Music Festival, 1926-28. Keith, considered the "Dean" of Victoria architects, was still working until just a few weeks before his death, on his eighty-second birthday in 1940, and was survived by his wife and a brother living in San Francisco.

Third All Saints' Anglican Church, Vernon

JOHN
JAMES
HONEYMAN
1864-1934

PAUL BENNETT

Both John Honeyman and George Curtis practised architecture in British Columbia for some years before entering into business together, but it was in partnership that they were most successful. Once established in their Vancouver practice, they were responsible for an increasingly prolific range of work, including many prominent churches, public buildings, private residences, apartment buildings, industrial structures and banks. Individually and collectively they left a rich legacy of sophisticated architecture now recognized in many heritage inventories around the province.

George D. Curtis was born in Ireland on August 1, 1868; his family had been officers in the Royal Navy for generations. Curtis studied at London's Finsbury Technical College from 1884-85, and for the next three years he articled with a London firm. His brother, James, had arrived in Port Moody in July 1886 on the first transcontinental passenger train. George, who was studying at King's Lynn, Norfolk, in 1889 was offered a year's holiday in Canada by his father to check up on James. George decided to stay in Canada, taking up survey work in the 1890s. The Canadian Pacific Railway had built a branch line to Nelson, which had become an important West Kootenay mining supply centre, and by 1897 George Curtis opened an architectural practice there. He undertook various commercial, religious, residential and public commissions in Nelson, Rossland, and Greenwood. His Nelson projects included Reisterer's Brewery, 1897, St. Joseph's Catholic School, 1901, at least half a dozen private residences, and supervision of the construction of the Hume Hotel, designed by **A.C. Ewart**. His St. Saviour's Anglican Church, 1898-1900, is a good example of a Gothic English perpendicular parish church, while his

Cathedral of Mary Immaculate, 1898-99, is a mature example of Roman Classicism, favoured by the Catholic Church in Canada at the time. Modeled on *La Madeleine* in Paris, the exterior features an imposing portico and correct classical detailing while the interior includes a Neo-Baroque tunnel vault supported by composite columns. Although Mary Immaculate appears to be built of solid masonry finished with marble, it is actually made of *faux*-painted wood. In Greenwood, Curtis designed a court house and public school. On December 17, 1900, he married Agnes Bertha Crickmay, a former nurse at Vancouver's City Hospital who with her sister operated Nelson's first hospital.

Born in Glasgow on April 9, 1864, J.J. Honeyman was the son of Helen Orr and Patrick Smith Honeyman, a solicitor. After architectural studies at Heidelberg University, Germany, he returned to Glasgow in 1883 to article with Hugh & David Barclay. No professional connection has yet been found between J.J. Honeyman and his uncle, John Honeyman (1831-1914), one of the most distinguished Scottish architects of the Victorian era. John Honeyman, who had an abiding interest in medieval structures, had a long and varied career in Glasgow, and in 1888 went into partnership with John Keppie (1862-1945). One of the draftsmen in their office was Charles Rennie Mackintosh (1868-1928), and when Honeyman retired in 1904 Mackintosh, an architect of supreme brilliance, went into partnership with Keppie. The 1880s seems to have been a particularly rough period for John Honeyman, as his eyesight was failing and his work was perceived as being old-fashioned; the partnership with the much younger Keppie apparently saved his business. For reasons unknown, John Honeyman never

GEORGE DILLON CURTIS

1868–1940

George Curtis with "Buzzie," c.1900

involved his nephew with the firm, but in 1884, accepted **Robert Claud Kerr** as an apprentice.

J.J. Honeyman left for Canada, and crossed the continent on the CPR in 1889. Upon his arrival he ranched with John Baird from 1889-92 on Ployart's Swamp, near Black Creek in the Comox Valley on Vancouver Island. About 1891 Honeyman established his architectural practice in Nanaimo, first for a year in partnership with F.T. Gregg, and then afterwards on his own. On January 12, 1892, in Nanaimo, Honeyman married Mabel Dempster, also a Scottish immigrant. They settled on a ranch called *Tarara*; their family eventually numbered four daughters and one son. Honeyman enjoyed rugby football and

considered himself both a Conservative and a Presbyterian. He was a modest man; when asked if he could provide examples of his professional competence, he replied "I really don't know. You might perhaps ask one of my clients." Honeyman's commissions at this time included the A.R. Johnstone Block in Nanaimo, 1893, a school in Cumberland, 1895, and Nanaimo Central School, 1895-96.

Honeyman moved to Rossland in 1897, which is likely where he met George Curtis. Honeyman's largest and best known individual project was the Rossland Court House, which is visually prominent from many points both in downtown Rossland and from access routes into the city. It was designed in 1898 but not completed until 1901 as a result of the first contractor's inability to carry out the task. By the time of completion the building's cost rose from $38,500 to $58,122, proving that public works cost overruns are by no means new in British Columbia. The edifice featured a symmetrical front facade, corner towers with steep bell-cast roofs, and an arched entry and window openings. Pinkish-tan brick cladding was used above a base of dark local granite, and the floor plan and interior layout reflect the standardized approach to turn of the century court house planning. The main court room features an open timber roof, detailed cedar panelling, and stained glass windows by Henry Bloomfield & Sons. During his time in Rossland, Honeyman was also busy with residential projects. The exterior of his 1902 cottage for William Wadds featured a gambrel roof and an imposing entrance with a large verandah and columns, fronted by a circular driveway. Honeyman also designed a home in Rossland, *Warriston*, c.1908, for his wife's brother, Charles Dempster.

Curtis family at home, North Vancouver

Cathedral of Mary Immaculate, Nelson

Court House, Kamloops

Hotel Vancouver Annex, Vancouver

Anticipating greater opportunity on the coast, Honeyman and Curtis both moved to Vancouver and established their architectural partnership in 1902. An important commission was the Kamloops Court House, built 1907-09 and still an important downtown landmark. They also provided the design for the Fernie Court House in 1907. Featuring ornamental gables, elaborate front and rear entrances and a beautiful west window, it was completed in the spring of 1908, but was destroyed just a few short months later in the huge fire that devastated most of Fernie on the first day of August. Another of Honeyman & Curtis's landmark projects was the Vancouver Fire Hall No. 6, 1907-09, located in the West End. At the time of its construction it was the "only fire hall in the world completely equipped with Auto Engines." This brick and stone building has a metal tile roof and strong horizontal emphasis, contrasted with a vertical hose tower. The partnership also received a number of church commissions. St. John's Presbyterian, 1909, in the West End, was an impressive stone Gothic Revival structure with a tall corner turret. The First Church of Christ, Scientist, 1925, in North Vancouver is a sophisticated structure consistent with Christian Science's preference for classically inspired forms. Shaughnessy Heights United Church, built 1928-30, is a stone-faced structure reminiscent of a traditional English parish church.

Honeyman & Curtis undertook a number of prominent projects for the CPR. Curtis took over the supervision of the original portion of the Empress Hotel in Victoria when **Francis Rattenbury** resigned late in 1906, and continued to act in a supervisory capacity through the ongoing expansion programme, 1909-1914, that included two new wings and the Crystal Ballroom, all designed by W.S. Painter. Honeyman & Curtis also designed an addition to the Hotel Vancouver for the CPR in 1911. Major industrial projects in Vancouver included an Imperial Rice Milling Company warehouse on Railway Street, 1911, and an office and warehouse for Canadian General Electric, 1913. Corporate clients included the Bank of Montreal, for whom they designed a stone-clad Temple Bank

at Main and Hastings, built 1929-30, that marked the very end of the local use of classicism. Its columned entrance, pedimented doorway and sculpted heraldry were intended to invoke confidence and a timeless sense of stability.

Most of their initial residential commissions were in Vancouver's West End. From 1912 until 1929 their domestic work was located increasingly in Shaughnessy Heights, Point Grey and North Vancouver. For Matthew Sergius Logan, lumberman and Parks Commissioner and advocate of the Stanley Park sea wall, they designed a grand Craftsman-style home on Point Grey Road, 1909-10. The Shaughnessy home of industrial supplier, Bryce W. Fleck, 1929, in the Tudor Revival style, includes a *porte-cochère*, bay windows, stained glass and curved gable above the entrance.

The firm's prosperity allowed the partners to build substantial homes and establish vacation properties for their families. About 1908, Curtis cleared land outside Comox, and in 1912 built a small cottage; this property is still owned by the Curtis family. In 1913, Honeyman built his own home in Kerrisdale, which he called *Kildavaig* after a Scottish home in which he had once lived. By this time, Kerrisdale had become a desirable location, "just far enough from the noise and bustle of the city for peace and contentment." In 1929, he also built a cottage at Hood Point on Bowen Island, used by succeeding generations of his family.

An unusual home designed by Honeyman outside the Lower Mainland was *Fintry Proper*, the main house for a large estate on the west side of Okanagan Lake. This sprawling, Tudor Revival house was built for Honeyman's former Glasgow-era schoolmate, Captain J.C. Dun-Waters, who arrived in the area in 1909 and recognized the possibilities for growing fruit and hunting game – in England, Dun-Waters had been a Master of fox hounds. Honeyman was engaged in 1919 to build a new house for the estate; this first house burned down during renovations in 1924, and he designed a second house to replace it, with rich materials and spaces, including gracious verandahs. Of particular interest was Dun-Waters's trophy room, decorated to resemble a mountain cavern, complete with moss-covered boulders; trophy heads hung on the walls, while the centre-piece was a grizzly bear mounted in a life-like pose.

Their partnership was devastated by the Great Depression, and they had both retired by 1931. Honeyman died at home in Vancouver on February 18, 1934. Curtis, in ill health, retired to Comox in 1931, and died there on September 8, 1940.

St. John's Presbyterian Church, Vancouver

ALEXANDER CHARLES EWART
1854–1916

CAREY PALLISTER AND DOROTHY MINDENHALL

A first generation Canadian of Scottish descent, Alexander Charles Ewart was born in Holland Township, Grey County, Ontario on October 3, 1854 to Andrew Johnston Ewart, a farmer, and Mary Russell. By the late 1870s he had made his way to Oregon, where he settled in Corvallis. There, on February 2, 1881, he married Annette "Nettie" Evelyn Stout (1859-1928) of Montezuma, Iowa, with whom he would have seven children, five of whom lived to adulthood.

Soon after the birth of their fifth child in 1891 the Ewart family moved to Victoria where Alexander found employment in the offices of well-known local architect, **John Teague**. Ewart's first project in 1892 was building his family a superb Queen Anne-style home that still stands on Begbie Street. The design incorporates an asymmetrical roofline and a combination of board-and-batten, patterned shingle work, and other decorative elements of the style. The charming sunburst design popular with the English aesthetic movement, which appears on the porch gable and on the facade, was a motif used by Ewart on many other buildings throughout his career.

Also working in the office of John Teague in 1893 was a young architect named Julius C. Schroeder, previously a partner of **W.T. Whiteway**. Ewart and Schroeder collaborated on two small projects that year but soon parted ways. Ewart, now on his own, began a modest but productive career. He was a talented architect, skilled in incorporating many of the popular architectural elements of the day into his designs. Some of his commissions included the brick and stone Pemberton Gymnasium for the Central School, 1894, the Odd Fellows Lodge in Duncan, 1894, and a three-storey brick and stone building for the well-known wholesale liquor merchant, Simon Leiser. Built in 1896, the Leiser building still stands at the corner of Yates Street and Waddington Alley.

In 1895 William J. Pendray, a successful soap producer, hired Ewart to design a large home on Belleville Street overlooking the harbour, close to the future site of his paint factory. This massive Queen Anne Free Classic-style home boasts a prominent corner tower, three kinds of patterned shingles and recessed balconies. Still standing, it is currently a restaurant and bed & breakfast. Four years later Pendray again called upon Ewart's talents, this time to design the British America Paint Company factory on Laurel Point, 1899. A beautifully preserved Queen Anne house designed by Ewart for Anton Henderson, 1897, still stands on Quadra Street.

During the spring of 1897 Ewart moved his family and practice to Nelson, B.C. arriving just two months after the incorporation of the City. In the late 1890s this town, on the bank of the west arm of Kootenay Lake, was burgeoning, with mining and lumbering as the economic mainstays. During the next seven months he received eight commissions, including the McKillop Block, 1897, Judge John Forin's House, 1897, and the Hume Hotel, 1897. Designed in the Queen Anne style, the Hume had a characteristic corner tower, oriel windows and recessed balconies as well as an ornate interior with all the "modern" amenities such as electricity and steam radiators. In the 1920s it was stripped of all its exterior architectural embellishments and stuccoed in an attempt to "modernize" its appearance.

Nettie Ewart

Pendray Residence, Victoria

In 1898 Ewart took on **Alexander Carrie** as a partner. Carrie was born November 14, 1863 in Toronto, Ontario to Gideon Carrie and Helen Reid. He arrived in Winnipeg in 1892 where he studied for one year under architect, **H.S. Griffith**, and two years with Hugh McCowan, also of Winnipeg. On March 26, 1894 Carrie married Lizzie Elliot in Donald, B.C., and the following year moved to Nelson. One of Ewart & Carrie's first projects together was a hardware store for James Lawrence, 1898. The imposing row of three arched windows on the third storey curving from two-storey-high pilasters, the decorative brickwork and fine row of corbelling on this building are outstanding examples of Ewart's talents. The same year plans were prepared for a competition for the City Hall in Kaslo. Ewart & Carrie's design was one of three submitted to Kaslo City Council on June 3, 1898 for approval. The design proposals were put to a vote. Their design received three of the six votes, the Mayor thought the count too close so a second vote was

taken, and their design was chosen by four votes. Built in the Free Classic style, this handsome two-storey frame building is surmounted by a square bell tower. An unusual two-storey pedimented portico and a double curved staircase dominate the entry. Although the plans came from the office of Ewart & Carrie, it appears that Carrie was the partner who was most involved with the project.

Other commissions the partners received included the Nelson Baptist Church (now unrecognizably altered), 1898, the Tremont Block, 1899, the Congregationalist Church (later St. Paul's), 1900, and the Provincial Land Registry Office, 1899-1900. The decorative brickwork at the entry to the Land Registry is again a key feature, and the dentilated pediment surrounding a semi-circular window gives an elegant look to these well fortified premises. They also designed the city's largest commercial building of the era, the K.W.C. Block, built for three businessmen, Kirkpatrick, Wilson and Clements,

1900-01. Its distinctive corner turret remains a landmark in downtown Nelson.

In 1901 Ewart and Carrie dissolved their partnership and in July, 1902 the Ewart family departed Nelson and returned to Corvallis, where Alexander Ewart continued a successful architectural practice resulting in a number of buildings which survive and are on the United States National Register of Historic Places. Alexander Ewart died in Portland on January 8, 1916. Carrie continued a highly productive practice in Nelson that lasted another forty-six years. Some of his commissions included the residence for the local superintendent of the Canadian Pacific Railway, 1908, the YMCA Building, 1909, and the Kerr Apartments, 1911. This unusual apartment block, constructed entirely of granite quarried from the building site, lacks Ewart's elegant refinement. Instead, the influence of the popular Richardsonian Romanesque can be seen in the rusticated stonework, arched entrance and unpretentious design. Carrie also received contracts to design several schools including the Nelson High School, 1901-02, the Nelson Public School, 1908, and schools in Trail and Grand Forks. In addition to his architectural career, Carrie served nineteen years in the Militia 102nd Regiment (Rocky Mountain Rangers), attained the rank of Captain and became an expert marksman. Alexander Carrie died in Nelson, B.C. on July 29, 1947.

Hume Hotel, Nelson

K.W.C. Block, Nelson

City Hall, Kaslo

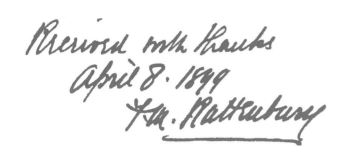

FRANCIS MAWSON
RATTENBURY

1867–1935

PERSONAL BIOGRAPHY BY TERRY REKSTEN

Francis Rattenbury ranked as British Columbia's most prominent early architect, but today he is remembered as much for the sensational nature of his demise as for his distinguished architectural career. Born in Leeds, Yorkshire in 1867, his paternal grandfather was a Methodist minister, famous for the intensity of his religious fervour; his father was a would-be painter and something of a dreamer. And so it fell to his mother's family to nurture his interest in architecture. After spending a few terms at Yorkshire College, he joined his uncles, William and Richard Mawson, in their successful architectural practice in Bradford.

He was only twenty-five when he arrived in British Columbia in 1892 but within months he pulled off an astounding architectural coup, defeating over sixty other architects to win the design competition for the new Parliament Buildings. An opinionated man, Rattenbury later became involved in local politics. In 1906, he was a member of the first council of the Municipality of Oak Bay, for which he designed the original municipal crest. Six years later he allowed his name to stand for Reeve, his successful campaign based on the preservation of the natural environment and on the insistence that quality and beauty should be hallmarks of the built environment.

By the early 1920s, Rattenbury had sunk into a debilitating depression. The Grand Trunk Pacific Railway (GTP), for which he had served as western division architect, had been bankrupted by the Great War. All the structures he had designed – everything from simple country railway stations to the grand scheme for Prince Rupert which included a luxury hotel and transportation complex – would never be built. In addition, the thousands of acres he had purchased along the GTP railway route had become worrying liabilities rather than lucrative investments.

Adding to his mood of despondency was his failing marriage. In June 1898, Rattenbury had married Florence Eleanor Nunn, the adopted daughter of a Victoria boarding house keeper. Florrie had seemed an odd choice for an ambitious young man, for she brought her husband neither position nor property, and she was rather plain with a jutting chin and bulging eyes. But during the early years of their marriage, they seem to have been happy enough. Their first child, Francis Burgoyne, was born in January 1899, and five years later Florrie gave birth to their second child, a daughter, christened Mary after Rattenbury's mother. They settled into a cottage on Oak Bay's waterfront, and Florrie devoted herself to developing the garden, soon acknowledged as one of the finest in Victoria. But over the years, the differences between them grew, and by the early 1920s, while they continued to live in the same house, they no longer spoke to one another, depending on their daughter Mary to carry messages between them.

It was then, when his spirit was at its lowest ebb, that Rattenbury met Alma Clarke Dolling Pakenham. She was beautiful, thirty years his junior, a twice-married woman whose first husband had been killed in the war and who had divorced her second. Alma and Rattenbury fell in love; their affair soon became public. Eventually, Florrie was persuaded to grant him a divorce. However, even after Rattenbury and Alma were married, and Alma gave birth to a son, they continued to be shunned by Victorians who had been scandalized by Rattenbury's conduct. By 1929, recognizing that Victoria would never accept them as a couple, Rattenbury and Alma had decided to relocate to England. They settled in Bournemouth, a city distinctly similar to Victoria. In 1934, with Rattenbury feeling his years and becoming despondent over lack of work, they hired a chauffeur/handyman. George Percy Stoner was only seventeen when he went to work for the Rattenburys, but within a few months of his employment, Alma seduced him.

In March 1935, Stoner, convinced that Rattenbury had discovered their affair, bludgeoned his employer to death. Arrested for the crime, Alma and Stoner were tried for Rattenbury's murder in one of the most sensational trials conducted in London's Old Bailey in the twentieth century. Stoner was convicted and sentenced to hang. Alma was found not guilty but committed suicide a few days after her release. The Rattenbury trial is seldom overlooked in anthologies of famous British trials, and also formed the basis for Terence Rattigan's play *Cause Célèbre*. Francis Mawson Rattenbury is buried in Bournemouth's Wimbourne Road Cemetery. To foil the curiosity-seekers who are attracted by the continuing interest in his murder, his grave remains unmarked.

Iechinihl, Rattenbury Residence, Oak Bay

*Amongst his intimates he is voted a jolly good fellow –
and Victoria and British Columbia are proud to number
him amongst their most progressive citizens.*

Howay & Schofield, *British Columbia Biographical*, Vol. III, p.707

Dining Room, *Iechinihl*

FRANCIS
MAWSON
RATTENBURY
1867–1935

PROFESSIONAL BIOGRAPHY BY RHODRI WINDSOR LISCOMBE

Francis Rattenbury dominated the architectural profession in British Columbia by virtue of his practical expertise and effective manipulation of Imperial symbolism. He was adept at the rich rendering idiom favoured in this period – he won a national competition when articling – and astute in the deployment of a broad vocabulary of historical styles. Those talents enabled Rattenbury quickly to supplant the previous generation of immigrant architects to the coast, most notably **John Teague** and **Thomas Sorby**, whose patronage from the Canadian Pacific Railway (CPR) he would soon seize. For Rattenbury appreciated the tenor of late Imperial culture, especially resonant in the still barely developed colony: a mixture of crude expansionism, evident in the dismissive attitude to indigenous architecture he shared with most of his contemporaries, and a desire to monumentalize those more idealistic societal aspirations then encapsulated in the term "civilization." Rattenbury had the professional knowledge and technical confidence to realize the grander scale and stylistic allusion that could fabricate metropolitan civic scenery.

That potential for opportunity, in contradistinction to increased competition for diminishing commissions in Britain, decided Rattenbury to immigrate to Vancouver in 1892. His initiative, not unlike the flamboyance of his architecture, derived from careful calculation. Through personal acquaintance and reading about Canada, he recognized the potential for development ensured by the transcontinental railway and immigration. He journeyed westward along the "thin Red Line" acting as the agent of Yorkshire entrepreneurs for whom he had designed buildings and who were attracted by the rising real estate market of Vancouver. Initially obtaining little work, Rattenbury entered the international competition for a new provincial legislature at Victoria. His winning scheme

combined an intelligent cross-axial plan with an impressive facade that scenically blended the latest phase of transatlantic eclecticism. The Free Classic style recalled both the medieval association of parliamentary democracy and recent institutional design in Britain (exemplified by Alfred Waterhouse's Natural History Museum, London, 1876-84) while also alluding to the Richardsonian Romanesque popularly regarded as the idiom of progressive North America. Inevitably, construction of such unprecedented size inflated costs and exposed deficiencies in the local building industry heightened by Rattenbury's commendable insistence on the use of local stone and on high quality craftsmanship. Rattenbury compounded the situation by his somewhat arrogant assertion of superior competence, but succeeded in creating an edifice worthy of the province's future promise.

Moreover, Rattenbury retained the confidence of a broad spectrum of legislators, bureaucrats and professionals who controlled architectural patronage. He was engaged to refurbish the Court House in Victoria and to design a new one for Nanaimo, 1895-96, developing a Scots Baronial/Château style he used for his first Bank of Montreal, on Government Street, Victoria in 1897, and the later Court House at Nelson, designed in 1903, built 1906-09. Even his absence from the 1898 opening of the Parliament Buildings was forgiven, doubtless in admiration of his bold and initially profitable participation in the Klondike Gold Rush, shipping in prefabricated steamers that carried prospectors and supplies along the Bennett Lake system. Upon this scheme's collapse, Rattenbury revived his finances by completing four handsome branches for the Bank of Montreal in New Westminster and the Kootenay mining centres including Nelson. There he also built one of a series of outlets for the "Klondike Cattle King," Patrick Burns, already exporting refrigerated meat to Asia as well as Europe. Burns, like several of Victoria's leading citizens, commissioned Rattenbury to design a grand house. The Burns mansion in Calgary, 1903, reflected Rattenbury's adept historicism, synthesizing Gothic motifs – answering the yearning of wealth for heritage – with Arts and Crafts formal simplification. His more compact Victoria houses carry that latter idiom into adaptations of the Queen Anne mode popularized in Britain by Richard Norman Shaw. Exemplified by the Lyman Duff House, 1900-02, each is distinguished by convenience of plan, sympathetic siting and pleasant ambience.

Rattenbury collaborated with **Samuel Maclure** in 1901-03 on the re-building of the Lieutenant Governor's residence in Victoria. Rattenbury preferred the composition of public to private spaces. His ability to organize diverse accommodation into relatively simple structures, enhanced by convincing proportioning and decoration, kept him and at least two assistants busy up to 1914; he would train several young architects, including **David C. Frame**. His tally of building

Parliament Buildings, Victoria

Empress Hotel, Victoria

Has it ever been your good fortune, gentle reader, to enter the harbour of Victoria, British Columbia, on a summer's afternoon or evening? If you have seen this you must have been impressed, as has everyone else, with what is unanimously declared to be one of the most strikingly beautiful spots to be found in the whole world, and you will be interested, therefore, in learning that the subject of this sketch, Francis Mawson Rattenbury, more than anyone else contributed to such splendid achievement in civic development.

Howay & Schofield, *British Columbia Biographical*, Vol. III, p.705

CPR Steamship Terminal, Victoria
(Rattenbury & James)

Parliamentary Library, Victoria

types soon embraced schools, offices and apartments. But government and judicial architecture remained his strong suit despite failure in the 1906 competition for the Saskatchewan Legislature at Regina. Here he faced the Montreal-based Maxwell brothers, one a graduate of the *École des Beaux-Arts*, and hence better schooled in Academic Classicism. Where they elevated the Orders into sublime simplicity, Rattenbury continued an essentially late nineteenth century compositional and thematic variation. Nevertheless his Palladian concept of stepping up to a central triad of portico, rotunda and dome reappeared in the Vancouver Court House, 1906-11. The scenic rather than scholastic imagery of the Court House – exemplified by the incorrect repetition of differently scaled Ionic order columns – nonetheless raised the legal process to one of civic and societal dignity.

Rattenbury appropriated the constituent features of the Baronial-cum-Château style for the Empress Hotel, Victoria, 1904-08, to enhance the Inner Harbour and the corporate ambition of the Canadian Pacific Railway; its President, Thomas Shaughnessy, had Rattenbury draw schemes for grand tourist hotels in Vancouver and Kitsilano to extract higher subsidies from Victoria City Council. The Empress succeeded a string of commissions for building or extending the CPR mountain hotels, including the Mount Stephen House, Field, 1902-03. These hotels confirmed Rattenbury's touristic vision for Victoria, signified by his activities as garden-suburb developer and Reeve of Oak Bay. His major land acquisitions in the "new" northern British Columbia – financed by such major commissions as the library addition to the Parliament Buildings, 1911-16 – were aimed at agricultural settlement. That vision of an expanding northwestern Canada contributed to his winning the patronage in 1908 of the Grand Trunk Pacific Railway, constructing a transcontinental line from the east coast across the newly settled Prairies to Prince Rupert. There Rattenbury planned lavish but unrealized transportation facilities linked to a magnificent hotel.

The First World War heralded the collapse of the Imperial investment and attitudes upon which Rattenbury's B.C. career had depended. A nostalgic historicism unites the Crystal Gardens, 1921-25, and the second Steamship Terminal of 1924-26, both undertaken in partnership with **P.L. James** for the CPR. The Terminal, from which Rattenbury began his last journey back to Britain, has survived to become, along with the Empress Hotel and the Parliament Buildings, icons of Victoria.

Court House. Vancouver

ROBERT BROWN BELL

1850–1940

DONALD LUXTON

Like many who travelled west seeking their fortunes, R.B. Bell tried his hand at a number of endeavours before settling into a career in architecture. Born in Campbellton, Argyleshire, Scotland on August 6, 1850, he was educated at private and public schools, and although he took drawing lessons at night school, only received two years of formal training in the profession, 1868-70 at the School of Architecture, Helensburgh, Scotland. At the age of twenty-one he left for Canada, settling first in Montreal before moving to Ottawa. While in Ottawa, in 1873, he married Elizabeth Conner, another young Scottish *émigré*. He worked on the construction of the new Parliament Buildings, including the Speaker's Chair in the House of Commons, regrettably destroyed by the devastating fire of 1916.

Joining the crowd moving west, Bell arrived in Manitoba in 1878. He acquired 480 acres of timber and farm land, and as soon as a log house could be prepared, Elizabeth, who had stayed in Ottawa, moved out with their three small children. But Bell found life on the Prairies hard, and after a series of disasters, including hailstorms and fire that destroyed his crops, he realized that he was not cut out to be a farmer and the decision was made to continue moving west. Again leaving Elizabeth and their growing family, now with seven children, in July 1886 he took the train west to Port Moody and made his way to New Westminster. By July of the following year he had managed to build a house, and the family moved out to join him. He was busy making a living as a contractor, working on many projects such as St. Mary's Hospital and **Clow & Maclure's** Murray Residence, both New Westminster, and the new Vancouver Court House.

Bell's health "broke" in the autumn of 1891, and following doctor's orders to move to a drier climate, he decided to try the interior of the province. The growing town of Vernon presented attractive prospects, and he set about establishing himself. The family was permanently reunited in October 1894, and the Bells had three more children. Although starting off as a contractor, by 1893 Bell had assumed the duties of an architect, and produced accomplished designs for many grand buildings. His early clients included Vernon merchant, W.R. Megaw, for whom he designed a two-storey, turreted house in 1893. Bell also worked for the two largest land holders in the area, Cornelius O'Keefe, whose house he renovated in 1896, and O'Keefe's partner Thomas Greenhow. Now fully established in the community, he received a steady stream of commissions, including one for a new Vernon City Hall, designed in 1897, but not completed until 1903. His 1897 design for the new Vernon News building, undertaken with his son, Hugh, was given a sense of grandeur through the use of cast iron columns, and pressed metal cornices and siding intended to resemble stone. Bell obviously used American pattern books as inspiration for his residential designs, and he displayed a keen facility for assimilating familiar period revival, and later Craftsman, styles. One of his grandest designs was a Colonial Revival mansion built for local entrepreneur, S.C. Smith, which shows how successfully the self-taught Bell was able to fulfil the aspirations of his wealthy clients. As Vernon prospered, Bell's practice grew, and about 1908 he took on a partner, Reginald O. Constant, about whom little is known except that he remained Bell's partner until 1914.

In 1908 Richard Curtis began working in the offices of Bell & Constant. The son of an English father, Harry, and a German

Smith Residence, Vernon

Vernon News Building, Vernon

mother, Elisabeth Ann (Harle), he was born in South Russia on July 22, 1884. Curtis attended Public School in England before moving to Egypt, where he received training in the Cairo office of the Special Buildings Department, before being employed by the Egyptian Government. He stayed with Bell & Constant throughout their most productive period, was Bell's partner in the 1920s, and later worked on his own, designing the Vernon High School in 1937. He died in North Vancouver on June 30, 1975 at the age of ninety.

Vernon's wealth was based on agriculture and land speculation. In 1907, the O'Keefe and Greenhow lands, 17,000 acres in total, were acquired by the Land & Agricultural Company of Canada, a syndicate of Belgian capitalists. The Company encouraged a number of Belgians to settle to the north and east of Vernon, in the B.X. area, named after the horse breeding ranch established by Francis Barnard for his Barnard Express company. As the land was subdivided, Bell & Constant, now the pre-eminent local architects, provided designs for most of the settlers' houses. By 1912 the firm published their own plan book entitled *A Few Okanagan Homes* with text in both English and French, undoubtedly to target more Belgian clients. In addition to many residences, their work included theatres at Kamloops and Vernon, 1912; Central School at Vernon, 1910; schools in Penticton, 1913, and Enderby, 1914; and branches for the Bank of Montreal at Armstrong, 1910, Enderby, 1911, and Penticton, 1912-13. They also designed Vernon's No. 1 Fire Hall in 1911.

The onset of the First World War brought devastating changes. European capital dried up overnight, and speculative development ceased. After the war, Bell resumed his practice, with Richard Curtis as his junior partner, but there were few commissions available. Bell's eyesight began to fail, and he gradually eased into retirement. Elizabeth "Bessie" Bell died in March 1930, and following a long illness, Robert Bell died on September 19, 1940, at the age of ninety, survived by five of his ten children. Shortly before he died he remarked, "perhaps to some people my life has been an uneventful one, but to me it has been an active one which has brought its joys and sorrows, and I would not have wished it otherwise" – a fitting epitaph for a pioneering spirit.

Union Bank of Canada, Vernon, Bell & Constant

J. EUGENE FREEMAN
1865–1956

DONALD LUXTON

"Gene" Freeman, best known for his design of the grand and elegant Dunsmuir House in Oakland, California, also worked briefly in British Columbia through his connection with the Dunsmuirs. He was born into a seafaring New England family. His father, Joshua Freeman, came from a Puritan background, and worked on square-riggers out of Boston. In 1856 Joshua married a twenty-year old Brewster woman, Lucy Anna Lincoln, and the following year they left for an extended trip to China, with the twenty-two year old Freeman serving as Captain of the *Christopher Hall*. From 1858-59 they made a second voyage to San Francisco via Cape Horn, and in 1861 their first child, Lucy Anna, was born. As the Civil War had devastated the shipping industry, Freeman stayed ashore in Boston for the duration, and on May 31, 1865, a month after the war ended, their son, Joshua Eugene Freeman, was born. By 1866 Freeman resumed his travels, and often took his wife and daughter with him. In 1880 the family was shipwrecked in the South China Sea, and on the way back to Boston Freeman decided to retire, at the age of forty-six. Over the next few years he suffered a series of financial reversals, and despite a stroke that paralyzed his right leg, decided to accept a commission as captain of the *Glory of the Seas*.

Captain Freeman left for San Francisco to take up his new command, taking his wife and daughter with him but leaving nineteen year old Eugene behind to finish his schooling at the Massachusetts Institute of Technology. The *Glory of the Seas* was chartered by Robert Dunsmuir & Sons to carry their coal from Vancouver Island to San Francisco. During these trips Freeman's daughter became acquainted with Dunsmuir's mine manager, Frank 'Dibb' Little, and their budding romance won favour from Lucy's parents. In the meantime Eugene had finished his studies, and had moved to San Francisco. In 1887 Eugene accompanied his family on one of their trips north in order to attend his sister's wedding, which was held on June 15 in the parlour of James and Laura Dunsmuir's house in Nanaimo. After their honeymoon, Lucy and Frank settled in the mining community of Wellington, later moving to Cumberland, farther up the Island.

Freeman worked in San Francisco as a draftsman with prominent architect, William F. Smith for two years, and became his partner in 1890. The best known of their many projects is the Ellinwood Residence of 1893-94. Designed for Dr. Charles Ellinwood, this was one of the earliest mansions built on the crest of Pacific Heights, and is a free and flamboyant adaptation of the Colonial Revival style. Now established in business, Freeman was married to Elizabeth Donald Payne in San Francisco on March 14, 1896. Through his Dunsmuir connections, Freeman was commissioned to design Grace Methodist Church in Cumberland, B.C. in 1894. He was also asked to design a grand house that would act as the local headquarters for the Dunsmuir operations, as a residence for Frank Little, and as accommodation for the Dunsmuirs when they visited their holdings. The result was *Beaufort House*, an immense rustic Shingle-style structure with early Arts and Crafts details, built 1895-96. This was the grandest mansion ever built in the Comox Valley.

After the partnership with Smith dissolved in 1897, Freeman went on to design a number of commissions in San Francisco, including many residences and his own home in 1905. The Freeman and Dunsmuir families became close and visited with each other both in B.C. and California. Eugene Freeman's best known building is a grand mansion built by Robert Dunsmuir's son, Alexander, for his long-time *inamorata*. Alexander, the first white child born in Nanaimo, had moved to San Francisco in 1878 to look after the Dunsmuir's coal marketing interests, and shortly after his arrival he met and fell in love with a married woman, Josephine Wallace. The two began a clandestine affair that lasted until the end of his life. They quickly moved in together, but Alex refused to marry her, even after her divorce, because he was afraid of his mother's disapproval and possible disinheritance. They gained custody of her daughter, Edna, but her son stayed with her husband. Their highly unusual living arrangements were kept secret from his family for twenty years, but finally Alex resolved to build Josephine

Grace Methodist Church, Cumberland

a proper house. He acquired a farm near San Leandro, and commissioned Eugene Freeman to design a house, befitting his fortune and reminiscent of the way his father had built *Craigdarroch Castle* for his mother in Victoria.

By 1899 construction had started, and Alex took an active interest in the design. Josephine's daughter, Edna, who had taken to the New York stage and married the famous actor, De Wolfe Hopper, interfered with some aspects of the design, and insisted on reducing the number of columns on the front facade from four to three, over Freeman's objections. As the house was being finished, Alexander and Josephine were finally married, on December 21, 1899, just forty days before he died at age forty-six from the accumulated effects of alcoholism. Josephine, who received the house but none of the Dunsmuir money, lived for another eighteen months. Edna Wallace Hopper took possession, and sued for a share of her step-father's estate. The sensational trial took four years to resolve, and ultimately she lost the case and had to sell the mansion that she could not afford to maintain. Eugene Freeman continued to live and work in Pacific Heights until his retirement. He died in 1956, and is buried in Cypress Lawn Cemetery in Colma, California.

Dunsmuir House, Oakland, California

mining booms spark a

326 THE WESTERN KLONDIKE OUTFITTERS

brief wave of new settlement

4

THE

WILDEST

EXCITEMENTS

Now there is not a boom – it is the natural outcome of a steady and increasing commerce and population, and the consequent demand for additional business and residential buildings... From morning to night the clink of the stone-cutters' and masons' hammers may be heard, accompanied by sounds of the saw and the rat-tat of the carpenter's hammer... Architects are so busy that they can hardly spare a moment to impart a little information about the works they have in hand.

Vancouver *Province*, August 6, 1898, p.2

THE
GREATEST
ACTIVITY
PREVAILS

Donald
Luxton

British Columbia's languishing economy was rescued from the doldrums by a sharp rise in the international price of silver in 1895, rekindling interest in the rich mines of the Kootenays, where a number of claims had been staked, but not exploited, in the 1880s. The steeply rising prices triggered frantic development, unleashing a wave of settlement throughout the area. A new mining boom was on. Our metal strikes were "as famous as the Rand" strikes in South Africa, and Rossland became known as the Johannesburg of British Columbia. Vast quantities of silver, lead, copper and gold were discovered, but they could not be mined without heavy equipment. The necessity for infrastructure led to the establishment of instant urban centres, connected by new railways throughout the eastern part of the province. Before the end of 1897, Nelson, Rossland, Greenwood and Grand Forks had taken advantage of the provisions of the *Speedy Incorporation of Towns Act*, as the provincial government scrambled to establish an administrative network of court houses, schools and other public buildings. In turn, the growing cities received imposing new court houses: Revelstoke in 1897, Rossland in 1898-1901, and Greenwood in 1902-03. Sometimes the initial facilities were crude, such as in Fernie, where the first court house was simply a shack built in 1898; in April, 1899, the courts moved to a "grander" building of 784 square feet, described as "the merest makeshift." This building served Fernie for the next eight years until a proper court house could be constructed.

In June, 1896 a Liberal government was elected to Ottawa, After eighteen years in opposition, the Liberals were hoping to distribute as much political largesse as possible, and moderated the former harsh economic policies at the DPW. Although they strove to keep expenses down, they embarked on an era of expansion, scattering new federal buildings across the country that kept the Chief Architect's Branch humming with activity. Four months after the Liberals took power, Thomas Fuller retired as Chief Architect of the DPW, and his assistant David Ewart (1841-1921) assumed his position. Recently married, Ewart had immigrated to Canada in 1871, just four years after Confederation, and was

Opposite top:

Post Office and Custom House,

Nelson

Main Street, Dawson City, 1898

David Ewart

immediately hired as an architectural assistant by the Chief Architect's
Branch. His arrival occurred at almost the same time as British Columbia's
entry into Confederation, and Ewart would make significant contributions to
the province's architectural maturation. Born at Penicuik, near Edinburgh,
Scotland, and educated at the School of Arts in Edinburgh, "where he
obtained a thorough grounding in architecture" before relocating to Canada,
Ewart was a career civil servant, and had no profile in the profession outside
of the DPW. Under Chief Architect T. Seaton Scott, Ewart, considered "one of
the Nestors of the civil service," was given responsibility for a wide variety of
duties, including the design of the Canadian Agricultural Hall at the Paris
Universal Exhibition of 1878. Known as a tireless worker, Ewart became *de
facto* second-in-command of the Branch. After Scott's retirement, which had
been orchestrated by Langevin, Ewart temporarily held the position of Acting
Chief Architect, but was passed over in favour of Fuller. Ewart, however, continued as Fuller's right-hand man, and was entrusted with the design of the
Canadian Building at the 1893 World's Columbian Exposition in Chicago.
Ewart's assumption of the top post upon Fuller's departure signalled a new era
of consistency, predictability and conservatism.

The federal government clearly understood the importance of what was
happening in the West in the late 1890s. Nelson became a regional supply
and distribution centre for the Kootenays, and was transformed from a small
commercial settlement into the self-styled "Queen City." In recognition of
Nelson's new-found status, the Department of Public Works started on the
plans for a grand Romanesque Revival post office and customs house. All this
frantic activity in the Kootenays was soon eclipsed by the news of spectacular
new gold strikes far to the north, triggering another round of "excitements." In
1896 large quantities of gold were discovered on Bonanza Creek in the

Yukon, and two steamers arrived in Alaska the next summer with tons of Klondike gold. Newspapers around the world, aching for a good story in the middle of the depression, leapt on the news, and it spread like wildfire. The Klondike gold rush was on, fuelled by wildly exaggerated and misleading stories about the fantastic wealth lying on the ground just waiting to be picked up. The truth was much less glamorous, but this did not prevent an estimated 100,000 people from travelling to this remote part of the world, seeking their fortune. Enough new gold was brought into circulation to snap the depression, but little stayed in the hands of the "stampeders" themselves.

Dawson City became an instant boom town, and for a few short years was the largest settlement west of Winnipeg and north of San Francisco. When the potential impact of the Klondike gold rush was realized, the federal government acted quickly to establish order, and also repel any possible American claims to the virtually unpopulated Yukon. Thomas W. Fuller (1865-1951), the son of former Chief Architect Thomas Fuller, was dispatched in 1899 to Dawson City as Resident Architect for the DPW. Located in the middle of nowhere and perched on treacherous permafrost, Dawson had grown up almost overnight. Between 1899 and 1902, Fuller designed an astonishing set of grand structures that symbolized the federal government's presence and interest in this vast and remote area. His post office, administration building and court house showed a perfect understanding of the pretentious aspirations of the new but rich frontier. He also designed a grand Commissioner's residence, a school and a telegraph office before returning to Ottawa. Due to the remote location, the necessity of importing almost all building materials, a lack of skilled labour and an impossibly difficult climate, the results of the tender calls were astronomical compared to the DPW's standards. Appalled at the price but eager to see these buildings finished, the tenders were pproved, but in order to control costs Fuller was even seen swinging a hammer while he was supervising the construction. His architectural legacy in Dawson remains largely intact today.

The Klondike gold rush lasted only a few years, but the effect on British Columbia was immediate and extensive. After the last few years of economic depression, reports of gold lying on the ground in the Yukon were

Post Office, Dawson City, Yukon

Court House, Dawson City, Yukon

Administration Building, Dawson City, Yukon

electrifying. Although it was mostly Americans who joined the rush to the North, the goldfields were on Canadian soil, and Canadian law prevailed. As there was no way to guarantee that provisions could be delivered, each prospector was personally required to bring enough supplies to last one year. Import duties could be avoided if these supplies were bought in Canada, so the port cities of Victoria, Vancouver and New Westminster were suddenly swamped with men eager to buy anything that could get them on their way. Outfitters sold everything, from boots to blankets, to those on their way to the gold fields, and these cities boomed. Flush with confidence, businesses expanded with an explosion of building activity in the rush to supply the gold seekers.

In addition to the thousands now pouring through on their way north, some local businesses closed so that their owners could join the rush to find gold. Some, much shrewder, looked to ways to exploit business opportunities that would support the activities of the gold seekers, and ultimately support northern development. It was expected that the gold rush would usher in a long, steady period of new growth based on mineral extraction. Those who could provide water transportation to the goldfields would make a fortune. **Francis Rattenbury** clearly saw the potential in providing transportation in the Yukon, especially in moving miners and provisions, for a substantial price, from the end of the Chilkoot Pass, across Lake Bennett to the Yukon River and on to Dawson. When the new Parliament Buildings were opened on February 10, 1898 with great pomp and ceremony, the architect was notable by his absence. He was in London seeking financial backing for his Bennett Lake & Klondike Navigation Company (BL&KNC). Under great secrecy three prefabricated boats were ordered and shipped north, where they were assembled, suddenly appearing on Lake Bennett to everyone's great surprise. To counter the gruesome stories of hardship on the Chilkoot Pass, Rattenbury decided to head to the North himself. Married on June 18, 1898, he took his already-pregnant wife Florrie along on what was more of a business trip than a honeymoon.

Rattenbury and his party made it over the Chilkoot during relatively good weather, and he wrote back an account of their travels to the Victoria *Colonist*, comparing it to a brisk walk, and boasting that he had not seen a single mosquito, statements at complete odds with every other account. His BL&KNC had also acquired a charter to build a light railway that would avoid

Columbia Street, New Westminster, 1896

May Day Parade

The aftermath of the Great Fire in New Westminster

(September 10 and 11, 1898) "annihilation by fire."

the dangers of the Miles Canyon rapids, and Rattenbury decided to accompany the surveyors as they laid out the route. After rowing most of the first day, the party stopped to make camp, and Rattenbury, with painful water blisters on his hands, had to drink his tea without milk. Pouring rain that night soaked everybody to the skin, and in the morning when it started to taper off to a drizzle, they were able to get a fire started. Rattenbury was warned to let his clothes dry on his body, but refused to listen and built a small rack, stripped, and hung his clothes near, too near, the fire. Now comfortable, the red-haired and fair-skinned Rattenbury ignored the more experienced men's comments that the mosquitoes would descend as soon as the fog lifted, which it soon did. Suddenly the attention of a swarm of mosquitoes, Rattenbury frantically tried to dress, but his woolen underclothes had shrunk so badly that he couldn't get them over his legs. Hopping and swearing, he struggled to cover his skin, while one of the crew tried to keep the mosquitoes away with willow boughs, beating his back bloody. As he struggled to pull on his shrunken boots, the men covered him with mosquito netting and lit a smudge, the combined effect of which nearly smothered him. Returning to Victoria shortly afterwards, with oil and grease "rubbed into his swollen body to soothe the sores," Rattenbury had developed a new-found appreciation for the hardships faced by the northern prospectors.

Building activity on the coast was frantic that summer, a welcome relief after the last few sluggish years. Even the supply of building materials could not keep pace. The Vancouver *Daily World* reported on August 8, 1898 that "Bricks and ice are about the two most scarce commodities in Vancouver just now. There are so many new buildings going up that there is a famine of bricks and on two buildings, the DeBeck and Skinner blocks, operations have been temporarily suspended... C.P. Shindler, contractor for the DeBeck building on Hastings street, said this morning that he had been procuring his brick from the North Arm yard, but they had run short. The South Vancouver yard had their hands full in supplying the Molson's bank and the Leckie building. He had been thinking of getting some from Victoria, but no tugs were available. On the Thompson block, considerable delay has been caused on account of the difficulty of procuring iron work, the B.C. Iron Works having shut down. There is room for an improvement somewhere." In the middle of this boom, a devastating fire consumed much of New Westminster. The fire broke out at 11 o'clock on the evening of September 10, 1898 and by dawn the following day the city's downtown core had been destroyed. "With true Canadian pluck the citizens set to work to rebuild," and businesses scrambled to set up again so as not to lose out on the gold seekers' business.

Vancouver was now desperate for a new train station that would replace the simple shed structure that had served the city since 1887. By 1891 **Edward Colonna** had provided the designs for a grand structure in the CPR's characteristic Château style. Two towers, one round and one polygonal, flanked the grand arched entrance. The foundations had just been started when the local economy collapsed, and work on the building was halted. Construction on the much-needed station resumed during the mining boom of the late 1890s, by which time Colonna had left for Europe. His design was enlarged and reworked by Montreal architect, Edward Maxwell in 1897, who kept Colonna's original design intention, including the unusual tower arrangement, but Colonna never received public credit for his work on this landmark building. Set on a rusticated stone base, and topped with steep roofs punctuated by dormer windows, the station was an imposing presence. This building was a victim of the CPR's own success. The city grew so rapidly in the next few years that the station became outmoded, and was demolished in 1914, only fifteen years after its completion, replaced by the much larger, adjacent third CPR station.

Edward Maxwell (1867-1923) and his brother William S. Maxwell (1874-1952) were the only native Canadian architects employed regularly by the Canadian Pacific Railway. The Maxwells worked extensively throughout Canada during the early twentieth century, in part due to their deftness at manipulating historical styles, including Richardsonian Romanesque, *Beaux-Arts* Classicism, and the Château style, to appeal to their varying corporate and individual clients. Prior to the Maxwell partnership being formed in 1902, Edward Maxwell had designed a number of projects in B.C. for the CPR, including additions to Glacier House, 1897-99, a hotel and station at Sicamous Junction, 1898, and an elegant one-storey brick station in New Westminster, 1899, which still stands on Columbia Street.

Despite this provincial economic upswing, global turmoil again intruded on the local scene. In 1899 the Boer War broke out in South Africa, kicking off a wave of patriotism that swept the Empire. Many able-bodied men, at loose ends as the Klondike boom tapered off, volunteered to fight overseas. Canada's military infrastructure was inadequate, and the DPW scrambled to provide new facilities across the country. Vancouver finally received a proper drill hall; designed in 1899 and completed in 1901, it has served since its opening as the headquarters of the British Columbia Regiment, Duke of Connaught's Own Rifles. The original contracts, filed in 1899, specified that the building was to be brick walls over a granite foundation, with an iron truss roof. The building was opened with a gala celebration during the 1901 visit of the Duke of Cornwall (later King George V).

The Klondike boom ended as swiftly as it started. Most of those who went north lost everything, as all the best claims had long-since been staked. The more established architects had benefitted from this brief burst of economic activity, but a number of architects drawn by the boom found that it was over almost as soon as they arrived. By the turn of the century most sectors of B.C.'s economy were in free-fall; by 1903 the province was close to bankruptcy, and a general malaise had set in.

Second CPR Station, Vancouver

WILLIAM
HENDERSON
1837–1931

STUART STARK

With his wide-ranging travels, and his contracting and architectural work, particularly for the Dominion Government, William Henderson assisted in the development of architecture in Canada for most of his long life. Born at Wardend, Lonmay, Aberdeenshire on February 26, 1837, he came from a family background steeped in the architectural and building profession in Scotland. By the age of thirteen was employed as a stonecutter and mason. At twenty, he immigrated to Montreal, where he followed the trade of mason until the latter part of 1861, when he chose to return to Scotland. After a dangerous sea journey, during which he almost lost his life in a shipwreck, he re-established himself in a contracting and building business. On July 21, 1862 at Aberdeen, Henderson married Mary Jane Smith, and the couple had three sons and a daughter. By 1872 the family relocated to Canada, where Henderson at once secured work in Ottawa with the rapidly-expanding Federal Department of Public Works. Henderson and his family moved slowly across Canada during the 1870s-80s, living in Battleford, Winnipeg, Regina, Qu'Appelle and Moose Jaw. During the early 1880s Henderson supervised various temporary wooden government buildings, including Government House at Regina. With this experience, he was deemed qualified to oversee construction of the masonry Government House in Regina, 1889.

Henderson settled in Victoria in 1897, and continued to work for the Federal DPW. With any records dealing with government buildings, researchers are faced with information that is often detailed in the extreme, but typically leaves out the attribution of designers of specific buildings. Henderson's responsibilities were mainly to act in a supervisory role. He oversaw the construction, as well as repairs, maintenance or alterations to buildings. The annual reports submitted by Henderson listed in minute detail the repairs and alterations required for the various buildings in his care. Offices were painted, partitioned and furnished, drains cleaned, baths and lavatories added, electric lighting installed, fences built, skylights constructed and flagpoles painted. Other duties included overseeing the decorations and illuminations of government buildings for the 1901 visit of the Duke and Duchess of Cornwall, and the draping in black of the province's major post offices upon Queen Victoria's death.

The plans for larger federal buildings emanated from Ottawa, and were directed through his office, but given the lack of rapid communications, Henderson was undoubtedly involved in on-site design. The actual buildings definitively attributed to Henderson are therefore few in number. Henderson is, however, credited with the design of the handsome two-storey, shingled Union Bay Post Office on Vancouver Island, 1913. Outside his professional duties, he designed and donated the plans for St. Columba Church, Oak Bay in 1914. The rather severe red-brick exterior of the church hides a wonderful Arts and Crafts-inspired interior with a high vaulted tongue-and-groove fir ceiling supported by massive dark fir gothic beams. About 1900, shortly after arriving in Victoria, Henderson moved into *Jolimont*, a large house outside the city designed by architect **S.C. Burris** in 1892. Henderson renamed the house *Craigellachie*, and made extensive cosmetic renovations. In 1904 his wife, Mary Jane, died. Henderson continued to live at *Craigellachie* until 1910, when he built a smaller bungalow on Oak Bay Avenue, named *Inverallochy* after a seaside town near his birthplace. He married a second time in 1917, to Caroline D'Aguilar of Golden, B.C. Henderson was elected as an alderman to the first Oak Bay Council,1906-08, and then served as Reeve, 1909-11. In 1913 he became the Grand Master of the Masonic Lodge, British Columbia, and supported the Masons extensively, often donating plans for lodges.

Four of Henderson's diaries for the years 1916-19 exist, chronicling his busy working life to the age of eighty-three. Besides detailing his working life, the diaries reflect his love of the theatre and picture shows, and his frequent visits with his family and friends. He kept up a rigorous schedule of site visits around the province, usually travelling by CPR steamships and trains. He worked on weekends, even picking up mail at the office on Christmas. During the winter of 1916 – one of the worst on record – when the streetcars had become snowbound, he went to the office in a sleigh. Henderson died at home on September 24, 1931, aged ninety-four.

GEORGE
CHARLES
MESHER

1860–1938

ALLEN SPECHT

George Charles Mesher developed an excellent reputation as a contractor in Victoria. Although not formally trained in architecture, later in his career he designed a number of very prominent buildings. Born in Weybourne, Surrey, England, in 1860, he was the oldest of eight children. In 1886 George Charles and his widowed father, George Mesher Sr. came to Victoria. Mesher Sr. had earned his living in England as a builder and contractor, and his son had worked with him learning the trade. When they set up shop in Victoria in 1887 they continued as partners in their contracting work. The Meshers were fortunate to arrive in Victoria when a building boom was underway. One of their first substantial contracts was a three-storey Queen Anne house in 1888 for Louis G. McQuade, designed by architect **S.C. Burris**. The Meshers also built the parsonage at Christ Church, designed by **T.C. Sorby** in 1888. There was also a contract in 1889 for a Burris-designed house for Thomas Kains, an important B.C. land surveyor, described at the time as being "Norman" in style.

One factor in their success was the abundant energy of G.C. Mesher. His grandson recalled that he only "needed four hours sleep" and "he liked to get up early." Now established, the Mesher family built a large home at 60 Second Street in 1888. The following year they bought three adjacent lots and built two more houses. Their growing reputation soon led to some of the largest contracts of their career, and they were busy constructing mansions in the prestigious Rockland district, designed by notable architects such as **W. Ridgway-Wilson** and **Samuel Maclure**, as well as a number of downtown commercial blocks. Their biggest contract in the 1890s was a four-storey office building, the Five Sisters Block, designed by

Sorby & Wilson. This was followed by the contract to construct Maclure's Temple Building on lower Fort Street.

Despite a busy work life, G.C. Mesher found time in 1892 to go to England and bring back a bride, Janet Elizabeth McDonald. The couple soon had two daughters, Theresa and Violet. A few years later George bought lots on South Turner Street in James Bay and built a large residence, a fine example of Queen Anne style, along with a similar house he built in the Cowichan Valley; for these houses Mesher was probably adapting pattern book plans. He was also hired to build a $25,000 residence for his friend, W.J. Macauley, on a large estate on Dallas Road. No architect has ever been identified for this house, known as *Pinehurst*, and no tenders were called, so Mesher likely had a hand in its design, possibly through the adaptation of a pattern book plan.

Mesher Sr. retired in the mid-1890s, although he kept his hand in the business almost until his death in 1912. Though construction was slow after 1892, Mesher kept busy by developing property in the Rockland, Fairfield, and James Bay neighbourhoods. Around 1900 he entered into an investment partnership with Dr. I.W. Powell, an important figure in B.C.'s early political history. Among their acquisitions was a two-acre parcel fronting on Dallas Road, where Mesher put up several residences. The finest and largest house built on the Dallas parcel was the one he designed for his own family, completed in 1904. Influenced by the Arts and Crafts movement, extensive use was made of local materials. Situated on a slight rise, the front porch overlooked the Strait of Juan de Fuca.

During Victoria's great building boom, 1907-12, Mesher worked increasingly as an architect. Undoubtedly his diverse experience gave him confidence, and he designed almost all the major buildings he constructed during this period, including several Arts and Crafts-style houses in the Rockland and Fairfield districts. Mesher also built many houses in Oak Bay, a suburb that was growing rapidly. His firm was also involved in what has been described as Victoria's best example of the California Arts and Crafts style, the Goulding Wilson house on St. Charles Street, 1912. The design of the house emphasizes low horizontal lines through the use of shallow gables, broad

Mesher Residence, Victoria

Pemberton Building, Victoria

sweeping eaves and projecting roof timbers. According to Wilson's daughter, her parents hired California-based architect, Charles King, to design the house, and then Mesher's firm was retained to provide the working drawings (signed by his manager, **Harold C. Ferree**) and build this unique structure.

To Victoria's burgeoning downtown, Mesher contributed three reinforced concrete structures, six storeys high, with ground floor retail and upper floor offices. Sparsely ornamented and functional, they reveal the influence of the popular Chicago School. The largest belonged to Pemberton & Sons, the city's most successful real estate development firm. The exterior of the Pemberton Building, 1911, was a grid of large window bays separated by clean horizontal and vertical lines and crowned by a wide bracketed cornice. It was one of Mesher's most accomplished buildings and, for a while, the largest office block in the city. The Sayward Block, 1911, on the corner of Douglas and View Streets, resembled the Pemberton Block, and was named after its principle investor, prominent businessman J.A. Sayward. The last of this triumvirate was the Metropolis Building on Yates Street, 1913, similar to the others but with the upper floors used as a hotel.

During the boom period, attractive apartment blocks with all the facilities for independent and respectable living sprang up in Victoria, and Mesher built three of the finest. The first was the result of Bert Todd's love for his soon-to-be wife, Ada Seabrook. Todd owned property on the corner of Fort and Cook Streets and in 1910 decided to build an apartment block to give her as an engagement present. They named it October Mansion after the month in which she accepted his marriage proposal. The Savoy Mansion, 1911, designed for bachelors "desiring a home with the most convenient appliances to make life easy and comfortable," was located on McClure Street. The most prominent was Hampton Court on Cook Street, 1913, a Tudor Revival-style apartment block with a large central lobby. It was built for Dr. Arthur Pallant, a wealthy, semi-retired dentist. Hampton Court was considered the most elegant apartment block in the city and attracted several prominent citizens as tenants. It is now designated as a municipal heritage building.

There was little construction work available after the outbreak of the First World War. Although Mesher was a prolific builder and generated considerable income, he was not a good business manager. According to his grandson he ran into financial difficulties in 1916 and for a time relied upon liquor revenue from a Yates Street hotel in which he had interests, but that was lost when prohibition started in 1919. Mesher retired about 1924 and in 1928 moved to the Alberni Valley where he built a large house with his own hands. He died in Vancouver in 1938.

Hampton Court, Victoria

Savoy Mansion, Victoria

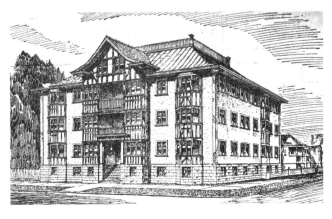

DONALD LUXTON

Like many others, E.G.W. Sait's architectural career in the New World started with great promise, but fizzled with the collapse of the local economy in 1913. Although his most significant project, won in an open competition, was never built, and many of his buildings have been demolished, he certainly achieved a respectable output during his active period. Born in England on January 17, 1867, by 1890 Sait had immigrated to British Columbia. By 1892 he was working in New Westminster as a painter, with rooms on Begbie Street, and the following year married Elizabeth M.W. Morgan. The New Westminster fire of 1898, and the subsequent opportunities for rebuilding, propelled him into the profession of architecture. By the turn of the century he went into partnership with John M. Byrnes, and together they displayed some notable talent. After Cary Castle burned down in 1899, a competition was held to select the plans for a new Government House in Victoria. The judges were **W. Ridgway-Wilson** and **J.C.M. Keith**, who chose the "Colonial" designs of Byrnes & Sait, submitted under the *nom-de-plume* "Volute." The other prize winners were **R.M. Fripp**, **C.J. Soule**, **Parr & Fee**, and **Thomas Hooper**. Detailed plans and specifications were completed

and approved by cabinet in July 1901, but in a surprising turn of events **Samuel Maclure** was appointed architect of the new building, with **Francis Rattenbury** as supervising architect. No official reason was given for the ultimate rejection of Byrnes & Sait's design.

Sait continued working on his own in New Westminster. His most notable design at the time was the Carnegie Library, built 1902-04, but not opened to the public until 1906 due to the lack of a bookfund. Sait then turned up in Vancouver for about two years in partnership with M.S. Williams, 1906-07. He returned to New Westminster, working on his own, and over the next few years his output was steady, including residences for H.T. Kirk, 1908 and Theophilus and Lily Barbaree, 1912, in the Queen's Park neighbourhood, and a renovation of E.J. Fader's house into an apartment block in 1911. Sait designed several large structures at the Provincial Exhibition grounds at Queen's Park. The fisheries exhibition building was built in 1909, and taken over in 1914 by the Federal Government for a hatchery. The building was moved from its original location in the early 1920s because of drainage problems; in 1951 it was handed over to the Vagabond Players and remodelled

Carnegie Library, New Westminster

Fisheries Exhibition Building, Queen's Park, New Westminster

Eldora, H.T. Kirk Residence, New Westminster

for use as a theatre, a use it still serves. Sait also designed a flamboyant "Horse Show Arena" in 1910 that was not completed until 1912. Sports promoter Frank Patrick added an ice plant in 1913, converting the building into a professional hockey arena. It was destroyed by a suspicious fire that swept the Exhibition grounds in 1929.

In 1908, Sait placed second in the open competition for the design of the new provincial asylum in Coquitlam, won by **J.C.M. Keith**. Sait's commercial work in New Westminster included the King Edward Hotel, 1909, and a brick block for Evans B. Dean, 1910, both on Columbia Street, and the Hotel Fraser at Front and Begbie Streets, 1912. For the Royal Columbian Hospital he designed a maternity and nurses'

home, 1907, and three isolation buildings in 1908. Chosen to design the Land Registry Office in 1910, he was replaced by **Frank Gardiner** when the work was deemed to be proceeding too slowly. He was also the architect for the new public hospital in Lillooet, 1910. After submitting an unsuccessful competition design for a new Municipal Hall in Burnaby in 1911, Sait, obviously bitter at having been beaten by **Somervell & Putnam**, sent Burnaby a retroactive invoice for his efforts.

His activities during the war are unknown, but he reappeared in Vancouver in 1923, working from home for a few years until he retired. Sait died in Vancouver April 14, 1949 at the age of eighty-two.

Horse Show Arena, Queen's Park, New Westminster

ALEXANDER ERNEST HENDERSON

1872–1927

DONALD LUXTON

A. Ernest Henderson achieved considerable success, both working on his own and in partnership with George W. Grant. Born July 13, 1872 in Orangeville, Ontario, he was the son of Rev. Canon Alexander and Martha (Taylor) Henderson. Educated at Trinity College in Port Hope, he then spent two years at the School of Practical Science, Toronto University, and studied architecture briefly in Buffalo. He served four years of articles with R.C. Windeyer & Son in Toronto, and then spent time abroad before settling in Montreal working for architectural firms for the next year and a half.

In 1898 Henderson moved to British Columbia, entering the employ of prominent New Westminster architect, G.W. Grant. With fortuitous timing, he opened his own office in 1902, and landed the contract for all the structures for the newly-formed salmon-processing conglomerate, B.C. Packers. In addition to designing a number of new canneries around the province, he renovated the B.C. Packers home port in Steveston as the flagship for their canning operations, including the design of the mammoth New Imperial Cannery, the largest ever built in B.C. He and Grant merged their growing practices in 1903. Together they proved a formidable combination, well-positioned to take advantage of a growing economy, forging ahead with many commercial buildings and large apartment blocks. One of their first projects together was the new Vancouver City Hospital, a landmark institutional structure. Henderson was also in charge of new buildings built at Queen's Park for the Dominion Exhibition in 1905. This success of his career allowed Henderson to start a family, and in October, 1905 he married Mildred Pentreath, with whom he had three daughters.

Grant & Henderson's success continued throughout the boom years, and in 1912 they added W.T. Cook as a third partner. The good times ended in 1913, with a drastic downturn in the local economy, and the firm gradually faded away, closing by 1916. During the war Henderson spent two years with the Imperial Munitions Board inspecting shells and ammunition boxes. By 1918, he re-established his own office, and was able to find enough work to support himself, including designs for the Port Hammond branch of the Bank of Hamilton, 1919, a prominent Masonic Hall, Ashlar Lodge, on Commercial Street in Nanaimo, 1923, and the Sheffield Apartments in Vancouver's West End, 1925. Henderson and his wife, Mildred, had just taken an apartment at Hampton Court on Thurlow Street, one of his own buildings, when he died of heart disease on November 2, 1927.

Recognizing the eternal principle that industry wins, he has made that the foundation upon which he is building his success and well earned reputation.

Howay & Schofield, *British Columbia Biographical*, Vol. IV, p.283

New Imperial Cannery, Steveston

THOMAS DEALTRY SEDGER
1860–1941

JULIA TRACHSEL

Thomas Sedger was a resident of Esquimalt for forty-nine years, and had a productive architectural career. He was born in Kingston, near London, England, May 16, 1860, son of the Rev. Thomas Sedger, then Chaplain of Kingston Jail. His uncle, Bishop Dealtry of Madras, India, was the source of Thomas's unusual middle name. Sedger articled for four years under architect, John Louth Clemence, of the firm Lucas Brothers, Lowestoft, Norfolk. Clemence designed, among other buildings, St. John Church, Lowestoft, one of four great urban churches erected in Suffolk in the nineteenth century. Sedger then worked in offices in London for several years before immigrating to Winnipeg in 1883. During the next nine years he owned a 160-acre farm in Sunnyside, Manitoba, and married Ada Marrion Ground, with whom he had four boys. In 1892 he came to Esquimalt, and by 1899 was advertising as an architect. About 1908 he built a home at Lampson and Lyall Streets, named *Bracondale* after his father's parish in England.

By 1905 Sedger had opened an office in the Five Sisters Block in Victoria. Sedger shared office space with **Guy F. Pownall**, 1906-09, and they designed several residences in Victoria, including those for Arthur Robertson, 1906; Isadore M. Noder, 1907-08; J.T. Redding, 1907-09; and Robert Chadwick, 1908. On his own Sedger designed many structures in and around Victoria, including two residences and a brick building for Arthur Wolfenden, an accountant and later Manager of the B.C. Land & Investment Agency Ltd. Sedger also designed a Masonic Temple in Cranbrook, 1909, and a rectory for St. Saviour's Church on Catherine Street in Victoria West, 1911. For Richard Mason Palmer, Sedger designed a home, known as Cedar Chines, near Cowichan Bay in 1914.

Palmer was Managing Director of B.C. Fruit Lands Ltd. and a previous Deputy Minister of Agriculture. One of Sedger's finest projects is St. John the Baptist Anglican Church in Colwood, known as "The English Church," dedicated on October 26, 1913. Now owned by the City of Colwood, this church has been restored and is used for community functions.

Sedger's design for a grand residence for A.E. Evans on Rockland Avenue was written about in glowing terms in *The Architect, Builder & Engineer* in 1913. It featured a spacious billiard room upstairs, with an adjacent flat deck from which one could enjoy an ocean view. This publication also described his house for H.J. Scott on Craigdarroch Road, 1914: "Sedger, the Victoria Architect, is responsible for the introduction of a novelty in building which is likely to become popular because of its exceedingly pleasing effect... quantities of seashells were put on the walls in stucco fashion and many favourable comments have been made..."

The years preceding the First World War were busy ones for Sedger, as he designed (and redesigned) plans for a Municipal Hall and Fire Station for the newly incorporated Municipality of Esquimalt. Sedger's final version was not destined to be built, and the start of the war killed the project. It was 1929 before a new hall was finally built, designed by **Ralph Berrill**.

The war was not kind to Sedger. One of his three sons who enlisted died of typhoid during an outbreak on the local base, before he could go overseas. Physically ill and emotionally sick with grief, Sedger's wife, Ada, only fifty-five, died five days later. After the war, Sedger built at least six houses in Esquimalt and Victoria under the *Better Housing Act*, and Esquimalt High School, 1926. Sedger died in Victoria on March 29, 1941, aged eighty.

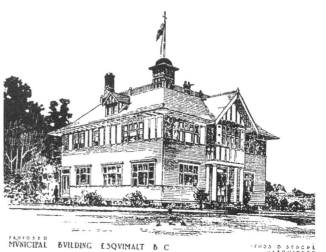

PROPOSED
MVNICIPAL BVILDING ESQVIMALT B C

THOS D SEDGER
ARCHITECT

EMIL
GUENTHER
BORN 1855

DONALD LUXTON AND
DENNIS A. ANDERSEN

Emil Guenther, a man with a very checkered background, travelled extensively throughout western Canada and the United States pursuing his career as an architect. It is difficult to track his movements, as the known references to his name and birthdate are inconsistent. On the frontier, it was difficult to confirm official records, especially for "foreigners," and census information was volunteered, so it was easy to change one's name or age. Legal troubles often provoked such actions. The best evidence is that his birthname was Emil Guenther von Swartzenberg, and that he was born in Germany on May 4, 1855. He received a university education and studied architecture under the "best masters" in Berlin, and for three years after completing his studies remained in Berlin, working for the government, erecting military barracks and other buildings. One account has von Swartzenberg immigrating to the United States in 1880, and on the voyage to New York, he met Albert Berger and his daughter Flora. Upon his arrival, von Swartzenberg set up his practice in New York, and soon afterwards Flora gave birth to her first child. In 1886, von Swartzenberg and Flora moved to San Antonio. One month after the birth of Flora's third child, von Swartzenberg eloped with Mrs. Murphy, a wealthy local widow whose first husband had owned a saloon. In 1887 the new couple arrived in San Diego, about which time von Swartzenberg apparently dropped his last name and continued his practice under the name Emil Guenther. He continued to send money to support his three children; Flora died in 1887 under "mysterious circumstances," and Albert Berger showed up in San Diego with the three children, accusing Guenther of bigamy and desertion. Both Guenther and his wife denied that he ever entered a legal

marriage with Flora Berger but admitted that he had made a "verbal contract." Although he was very busy in San Diego, Guenther moved north about 1888, arrived in Spokane, Washington about the time of the Great Fire of 1889, and established a successful practice in Spokane that lasted for a number of years.

Again using the name Emil Guenther, he appeared in New Westminster right after it was devastated by the Great Fire of 1898. He was briefly in partnership in 1899 with T. Van Aken, with whom he completed the Windsor Hotel on Columbia Street, the Hotel Fraser on Front Street and an Opera House for the Westminster Opera Co. at the corner of Lorne and Victoria Streets. Shortly afterwards Guenther moved his office to Vancouver, and was responsible for the design of the brick and stone Romanesque-style Sherdahl Block, now the Dominion Hotel in Gastown, 1900-01. By 1907 Guenther showed up in San Francisco and seems to have stayed there for the next five years, later claiming that he had been "studying the latest apartments and hotels." In 1912, just after he returned to Vancouver from San Francisco, he designed the Regent Hotel on Hastings Street, Vancouver, 1912, and the prominent Canada Hotel, now the Marble Arch, on Richards Street, 1912-13. Each of the 156 bedrooms of the Canada Hotel was equipped with its own telephone, and the dining room was a replica of that of the Waldorf-Astoria in New York. Both of these hotels were sophisticated essays in the Chicago School idiom, with retrained detailing and simple, classical proportions. Guenther also designed the Vancouver Aerie Lodge No.6 for the Eagles Fraternity on Homer Street in 1913; although there was a permit application the following year, the building never materialized. Guenther's plans for a five-storey brick apartment building near Nelson and Howe Streets were announced in 1913, but the project never went ahead. With his German background and name, he obviously thought it wise to leave Canada after the outbreak of the First World War, and his office closed in 1914 or early the following year. He moved to Seattle, and served in 1922-23 as a Trustee of the Washington State Society of Architects, an alternative architectural association made up of architects who either didn't qualify for the American Institute of Architects or had been expelled from it.

Dominion Hotel, Vancouver

Canada (now Marble Arch) Hotel, Vancouver

JOHN
BAPTIST
HENDERSON
1849–1931

D. BRUCE GRADY

A true pioneer adventurer who changed jobs and homesteads numerous times during his career, J.B. Henderson came from a practical background, and used a wide variety of skills related to carpentry, contracting and design, to survive on the frontier. His architectural career included projects in Grand Forks, Calgary, Revelstoke, Anyox and Vancouver. Born in Rathmullen, County Donegal, Ireland on September 29, 1849, Henderson came from a large family. He was one of four cousins named John Henderson, who were the sons of four brothers. Of the four cousins – John Baptist, John Cottar, John Calvin and John Wesley – the first three became pioneers in the Fraser Valley. John Baptist's father, Isaac Henderson, was lost at sea in 1855, leaving a wife and three sons, who all later left for the New World. Young John received some training in drawing, but was being groomed for the civil service. When he failed to get a position, he immigrated to the United States in 1871, and joined one of his brothers in Little Rock, Arkansas. However it was a "bad time," and he travelled with his younger brother, Archie, to Texas and throughout the mid-west, looking for work. Archie died during the 1873 yellow fever and cholera epidemic. In Baldwin City, Kansas, he met his cousin, Mary C. Henderson, and they became engaged. Henderson then travelled to Denver, which was as far as their money allowed. After some harrowing adventures he reached Los Angeles in February, 1875, and then sailed north from San Francisco on the Pacific. He originally intended to settle in Washington State, but after a chance meeting with John Robson, later Premier of B.C., he decided to seek opportunities in the Fraser

Valley. Henderson moved to Chilliwack to work as a contractor. He travelled back to San Francisco briefly where he and Mary were married on December 22, 1875. In Henderson's words: "And so the knot was tied. I to her and her to me – a dead broke half-baked carpenter. But I had spent a great deal of the night before on my knees, and I believed I should be able to care for her and protect her from all evil."

After their honeymoon they returned to Chilliwack, where they homesteaded. Mary brought with her an organ, reputed to be the first musical instrument in the area. They lost everything in the "High Water" of 1876, and gave up farming to move to rapidly-growing New Westminster, where John could market his skills as a carpenter. He was hired to work on the new hotel being built for P. Arnaud, designed by **James Kennedy**. The hotel had a mansard roof with five round-headed dormer windows; John was able to impress Kennedy with his cleverness, and soon became a favourite on Kennedy's projects.

In the 1880s the biggest game was the construction of the CPR line, and Henderson worked for Andrew Onderdonk in the Fraser Canyon, building several large truss bridges that spanned the river. Granville at the time had been chosen as the new terminus of the CPR line, and John, who didn't like Port Moody, squatted on property on Hastings Street in anticipation of the coming boom. He later received a three-year contract to maintain the Cariboo Road, and started a saw mill business, but through a series of misadventures lost all his investments. He then tried his hand at mining in the Boundary country, but when the bottom dropped out of the market he turned to architecture and contracting. His extensive experience allowed him to complete an abridged course on Architecture through International Correspondence Schools in 1898.

The Hendersons relocated to Grand Forks in 1898, and John opened his architectural practice in June 1899, the only architect then practising there. He ran unsuccessfully for Mayor in 1899, but was elected to both the Hospital Board and the School Board. Henderson did succeed in obtaining work, including the design of the sixty room Province Hotel, 1899, and the construction of the Presbyterian Church, Grand Forks, 1900. His two most accomplished designs were a brick school in Grand Forks, 1901-02, and Central School in Revelstoke, 1902, both impressive structures that were duly noted in local papers. In 1903 the family moved to nearby Trout Lake so that Henderson could superintend the erection of a modern band saw mill, leaving the grand house that they had just built in Grand Forks. Now skilled at industrial projects, he built the greater part of the West Kootenay Power & Light Company's works at Bonnington Falls, but, still unsettled, left about 1910 to work as a draftsman for Union Iron Works in Calgary for several years. In Calgary he was responsible for a number of buildings, the most notable being the Trinity Methodist Church,

School, Grand Forks

the Unitarian Hall, and the Sullivan Block. He then travelled up into Peace River country, homesteading four times. Between 1920 and 1922 he designed and built a power generating station in Anyox, a new mining community near Prince Rupert. In 1923-24 Henderson acted as Clerk of Works during the eighteen months of construction of the Acute Psychopathic Wing at Essondale. He moved to Vancouver in 1925, and maintained his AIBC membership until 1928.

John and Mary Henderson had ten children, four boys and six girls. All four of their sons volunteered during the First World War and were sent overseas; three were killed in action and the other came back partly crippled. John Baptist Henderson passed away on November 19, 1931, predeceased by his wife, leaving four daughters and one son to mourn his passing. He was buried in Mountain View Cemetery in Vancouver.

Central School, Revelstoke

BLACKMORE

1878–1929

*E.E. Blackmore,
Architect
Vancouver B.C.*

DONNA JEAN MacKINNON

Father and son apprenticeships and partnerships were frequent in Britain, where architecture was a family profession, but this was less common in Canada during the pioneer era. Edward "Ted" Blackmore, the son of established architect, William Blackmore, was an exception. Ted was born in Winnipeg, Manitoba, on July 21, 1878, and the family moved to Vancouver when he was about ten years old. The Blackmores lived in the fashionable West End of Vancouver, and Ted trained under his father, later being taken on as a partner. Together between 1901-04 they designed about twenty buildings, many of them frame dwellings, but also a brick and stone store, a warehouse, and a B.C. Electric Railway substation. In 1901 at Anacortes, Washington, Edward Blackmore married Georgia A.M. Billington, with whom he had two sons. Like his father, Ted was an avid cyclist, competing for the Vancouver Bicycle Club, and winning a number of races.

The elder Blackmore passed away in 1904. Between then and 1920 E.E. Blackmore's name appears as architect on more than fifty buildings and structures in Vancouver, including: the YMCA, Cambie Street, 1905; the Princess Theatre, Hastings Street, 1906; Almond's Creamery in Strathcona, 1909-11; and the Rougemont Apartments, Robson Street, 1912. His output was varied, and he also designed a number of Chinese laundries, apartment houses, stores, factories, warehouses, plus a number of frame houses in the West End for prominent individuals including S. Gintzburger, the Consul General for Switzerland, 1913. In 1907 Blackmore won the bid for the design of the English Bay Bathing Pavilion, and two years later for the first Stanley Park Bandstand, which was said to be a "jewel in an emerald setting." A fine Blackmore building in Strathcona is the Jackson Apartments, 1910, a typical west coast walk-up with oriel windows and a broad, bracketed cornice.

Blackmore also designed a "Grand Opera House" on Hastings Street, 1907, that was Alexander Pantages's first theatre in Vancouver, today the oldest surviving purpose-built vaudeville house in Canada, and the oldest surviving Pantages theatre. He also provided the designs for a number of prominent Vancouver schools, including the Model School,

Stanley Park Bandstand

Model School, Vancouver

1905, Lord Nelson School, 1905, and Sir William Dawson School, 1913. In 1914 Blackmore entered into a contract with the Federal Department of Public Works to design the new Vancouver Immigration Hall, built over the next two years and supervised by **William Henderson**, resident DPW architect.

Although he collaborated on projects with **Samuel Buttrey Birds** and with Charles K. Shand, he did not form official partnershipswith them. As the local economy declined, Blackmore's once vital career tapered off. He suffered from cancer and died on February 12, 1929, at the age of fifty.

English Bay Bathing Pavilion, Vancouver

WILLIAM HENRY ARCHER
1855–1922

DONALD LUXTON

Although several of his most prominent buildings have been destroyed, W.H. Archer made a notable contribution to the local architectural profession when he acted as the first B.C. representative to the fledgling national organization that became the Royal Architectural Institute of Canada. "Captain" Archer was also known as a strong advocate of navy affairs before there was even a Canadian navy on the west coast. He

was born in Dublin, Ireland in 1855 to Sarah Wynne and Edward Archer, but nothing is known of his education or early movements. He joined the American Institute of Architects in 1889 when he was living in Freedonia, New York. By 1892 Archer had moved to Buffalo, where he stayed until 1897, becoming a Fellow of the AIA. After this he started his move westward. Archer opened an office in Vancouver, and by 1903 had received the commission to design a grand residence for realtor Thomas H. Calland, called *Edgewood*, which became known as the "Most Beautiful Home West of Granville Street." Built on a tall bluff above the beach at the end of Trafalgar Street, it was the first house in that part of Kitsilano, and for several years had to be reached either by boat or by a long walk from the Granville Bridge. Archer's best known building is a beautiful parish church in the West End, St. Paul's Anglican, built in 1905. The following year he provided the plans for St. Paul's Anglican Church in Nanaimo, consecrated in 1907 but destroyed by fire in 1930. In the remaining years before the First World War Archer received a variety of commissions in Vancouver, including stores, stables, apartments and the city's first Sikh Temple, 1907-08, built in Kitsilano for the Khalsa Diwan Society. In 1910, Archer designed an eclectic Buddhist Temple at Franklin Street and Woodland Drive for the Reverend S. Sasaki.

Archer was a colourful and eccentric character. Vancouver's first archivist, Major. J.S. Matthews, remembered him as "a most agreeable little gentleman," less than five feet tall, who liked to dress in full uniform and march at the rear of the 6th Regiment, even though he wasn't a member, and no one ever determined why he claimed the title of "Captain." When two Japanese warships visited Vancouver following the China-Japan War, there was no naval unit to greet them, so the 6th Regiment, the Duke of Connaught's Own Rifles, decided to pay them an official visit. Being an army unit, they had to rent a boat, and when they finally arrived the officers, including Major Matthews, were shocked to see "Little Archer" and a cadet coming down the gangway. "Mr. Archer in his naval uniform and white cap cover, gilt buttons and sword, was accompanied by an 'officer' equally gaily caparisoned, but in a red coat. What had happened was that both had arrived on the flagship, climbed the gangway, saluted the ship, been received with honours, escorted to the Admiral's cabin, been entertained with wine and refreshment, mutual courtesies exchanged, and then retired. The Japanese had no way of knowing that they were entertaining interlopers."

Archer was actively involved in the move to register architecture as a profession in British Columbia. In April 1907 a letter was sent to 500 architects inviting them to join a proposed Institute of Architects of Canada. An encouraging response led to a convention being held in Montreal, August 19-23, 1907. Archer was the sole representative who attended from British Columbia, and he gained a seat on the Institute's

Edgewood, Vancouver

Provisional Council. This group was officially recognized by the federal government in 1908, and an alliance completed with the Royal Institute of British Architects on May 15 of the following year, allowing this new organization to call itself the RAIC. Archer also continued to work locally for the formation of a professional architect's association.

From 1912-14 Archer was in partnership with **James S. Helyer**, although their output appears to have been very limited. In 1915-16 Archer was listed as sharing an office with his daughter, Lydia H. Archer, the first time that a woman is ever listed in provincial directories as an architect, but the extent of her career is unknown. Archer's career tapered off, and he died at the age of sixty-seven on April 17, 1922.

Sikh Temple, Vancouver

unprecedented western boom,

total collapse and the Great War

5

THE

LAST

BEST WEST

Don't talk of a "Boom." This is a growth, a remarkable growth it is true.

It has its origins in the awakening of the west – The building

railroads, the developing mines, the agricultural lands newly opening,

the forests and coal fields made newly available, the fisheries yearly

increasing in value, the industries only budding, and the Panama Canal

projecting which will materially change the economic location of the

west, and bring it nearer to the great markets of the world.

Modern Architecture, 1911.

Donald
Luxton

A radical change in attitude accompanied the start of the twentieth century, ushering in an economic boom of unprecedented proportions. Queen Victoria's death in 1901 signalled the end of a long, stable and conservative era, and the ongoing Boer War in South Africa disturbed the political *status quo* and challenged Britain's pre-eminence in global affairs. The ongoing construction of the Panama Canal had caused renewed interest in Pacific trade, but its painfully slow progress led many to speculate that this scheme, the largest single construction project ever undertaken, would ultimately fail. This lack of confidence vanished in 1906 when President Teddy Roosevelt travelled to Panama to visit the "Big Ditch." By lending his personal prestige to the Canal, Roosevelt kicked off a whole new era of investor confidence, initiating the last, and greatest, western boom.

In 1903, a powerful symbol of the province's impending prosperity appeared on the local political stage when Richard McBride, "The People's Dick," became British Columbia's first native-born premier, and the youngest in the British Empire to receive such a high position, ushering in a new era of party politics, free-wheeling self-interest and rampantly speculative development. A flood of immigrants started moving west on the railway and streamed in by ship. Vancouver was now firmly established as Canada's premier seaport on the Pacific. The city's growth was explosive, and it was nicknamed "the City which is outgrowing its clothes." The smaller Victorian era buildings were swept aside and replaced with grand Edwardian landmarks "with architectural pretensions" more befitting a world-class city on the "All-Red route" between Britain and the Orient. The Canadian Pacific Railway developed its exclusive Shaughnessy Heights subdivision, a 250-acre suburb south of False Creek, to accommodate the City's affluent who were finding the West End no longer sufficiently haughty. Many other handsome speculative suburbs sprang up throughout the region, such as Ottawa Gardens and Grand Boulevard in North Vancouver, and the Deer Lake subdivisions in Burnaby.

West Hastings Street, Vancouver

In 1903 the Grand Trunk Pacific announced its plans to extend its railway to the west coast and, in a land deal clouded by controversy acquired Kaien Island, about twenty miles south of Port Simpson. Final arrangements were made to allow the development of the new city of Prince Rupert as the terminus, setting off a rush for northern timber licenses.

An economic downturn in 1907 caught everybody by surprise. The situation worsened in late 1907 with the news of a momentous bank panic in New York. With no central bank to provide stability and no guarantee system of deposit insurance to promote investor confidence, the American banking system and the stock market came dangerously close to collapse, and they were rescued only through the personal intervention of J. Pierpont Morgan. Teddy Roosevelt's conservative enemies blamed his continued trust busting, his regulatory measures and his indictments of big business as the primary reason for the financial distress. In British Columbia, unemployment was suddenly rampant, releasing simmering racial tensions against "invading orientalism" exacerbated by the increasing numbers of Chinese, Japanese and East Indian immigrants seeking work in the province. The provincial government tried to pass a *Natal Act* that would have introduced exclusionist policies, but Lieutenant-Governor James Dunsmuir, himself an employer of Asian labourers, would not sign it. Violent anti-Asiatic riots broke out in Vancouver, and many employers vowed to hire only "white" labour. However, the "yellow" labour had been cheaper than "white," and employers scrambled to find ways to replace them without substantially diminishing their profits.

The Fraser River Sawmills in Coquitlam, the largest sawmill in the British Empire and one of the largest in the world, was typical of this struggle. The bustling mill had been taken over in 1907 by an investment syndicate headed by Alexander Duncan McRae of Winnipeg. The syndicate directors, wanting to replace their non-Caucasian employees, decided to return to the traditional source of lumber workers, the villages of Quebec and Ontario. It was hoped that the traditionally home-loving Catholic French-Canadian lumberjacks would generate a permanent, and docile, source of reliable labour. A priest was dispatched to recruit settlers, and the first contingent of French families arrived in September of 1909. A traditional French town, with a central square for a Catholic church, had been laid out for them at the north edge of the existing company town of Fraser Mills. It became known as "Frenchtown," but was officially named Maillardville after the first curé, Father Maillard. Among the terms offered to the French workers was a pledge of free lumber to build their own homes, and wages of twenty-five cents an hour, much more than they could make in Quebec. True to the exact word of their prom-ise, the company provided the settlers with free lumber, but charged them for every incidental expense, including cartage, shingles, nails, glass and any other building materials they required. This occurred at the same time that McRae was building *Hycroft*, the largest and most prominent mansion in exclusive Shaughnessy Heights. The cost of living was also higher in British Columbia than in the East, and although the men worked ten hours a day, six days a week, many slid into long-term debt. "French" labour was not treated much better than "yellow" labour, and relationships between management and the workers deteriorated. The French workers were now anything but docile, and a locally-born second generation refused to remain second-class citizens. Declining wages through the 1920s fuelled talk of unionization, and in 1931 a bitter strike was successful in winning wage

First Post Office, top, and First Custom House,
Prince Rupert, c.1910

West Hastings Street, Vancouver

"MAKE NO LITTLE PLANS..."

DONALD LUXTON

"...They have no magic to stir men's blood." So wrote Daniel H. Burnham about his grand plans for Chicago. The creation of instant towns, based on ideal planning principles, inspired the capitalist visionaries of the boom years. Their bold vision encompassed whole new cities being built in the midst of the province's vast wilderness.

The Grand Trunk Pacific Railway decided to make Prince Rupert the western terminus of their transcontinental railway. Until then the area had been relatively deserted, and the first party of surveyors and engineers landed in May, 1906. Brett & Hall, the landscape architects from Boston who had been chosen to design the new townsite on Kaien Island, visited in January, 1908, and produced a unique and innovative response to the virgin landscape. In George D. Hall's own words "for a city to suddenly spring into being, from what was three years ago a glorious wilderness, is, to say the least, remarkable." Their plan combined elements of formal *Beaux-Arts* planning in grand processional avenues, with a more picturesque and natural approach in the residential areas that took advantage of the island's rocky plateaus. Charles Melville Hays, the visionary President of the Grand Trunk, later chose **Francis Rattenbury** to design several grand hotels along the new line, in direct competition with the rival CPR. Changing economic and political situations slowed the realization of the Grand Trunk's plans, which were dealt a near-fatal blow in 1912 when Hays, their strongest promoter, went down on the *Titanic*. Although the rail line did reach Prince Rupert in 1914, the First World War bankrupted the railway and none of its planned structures were ever built. Brett & Hall's formal road plan was essentially completed as planned, but the city's buildings remained modest, and never fulfilled the grand vision conceived by its promoters. Brett & Hall also provided Hays with a plan for Prince George in 1912, and laid out James Dunsmuir's estate at Hatley Park, outside of Victoria.

A similar grand plan was conceived for a new settlement in the Nechako Valley. Hays persuaded his friend, Herbert Vanderhoof, a Chicago publishing magnate, to found this settlement, and prominent Chicago architects Walter Burley Griffin and Francis Barry Byrne, both trained by Frank Lloyd Wright, were hired to lay out the townsite of Vanderhoof.

Byrne personally visited the site in 1914, and noted in his preliminary report that "the configuration of the ground offers unusual promise both from the commercial point of view as well as from the architect's, and the town's expansion should be rapid and healthy, as I am confident it will be." Griffin had won the international competition to design a new capital city for Australia at Canberra, and the Vanderhoof plan shows the same sensitivity to the rolling landscape and scenic views. Their design was completed in 1915, but wartime constraints intervened, and virtually nothing was ever realized of this ambitious plan.

It was not unusual to import landscape architects from eastern Canada and the United States to design prestigious large scale subdivisions in the larger cities, as there was virtually no local expertise available. The CPR's Shaughnessy Heights subdivision, named after Sir Thomas Shaughnessy, President of the CPR, was laid out in 1907, inspired by the British garden city movement and the work of influential American landscape architect, Frederick Law Olmsted. Frederick Todd, a Montreal landscape architect, provided the plans. In 1908 the Olmsted Brothers of Boston laid out the Uplands subdivision in Oak Bay, Victoria. By 1913, Thomas H. Mawson (1861-1933), an English town planner and landscape architect, had opened an office in Vancouver. "As founder of a business, which aims at the creation of beautiful, healthy and efficient cities, and which now has an important branch in British Columbia, Thomas Hayton Mawson well deserves representation in the history of the northwest." Despite this reputation, almost nothing materialized of his grand plans for Vancouver.

F.L. Townley, Vancouver Civic Centre competition, 1914

concessions. In 1951 a protracted school strike broke out, that brought attention to unresolved issues concerning private Catholic schools. The community of Maillardville fought to retain its unique status as a strong ethnic and cultural enclave within British Columbia.

Only temporarily derailed, by 1908, the local economy was again on the upswing. The Great Northern Railway had reached Vancouver, and in 1909 the province was electrified by the announcement that a third transcontinental railway line, the Canadian Northern Pacific, would be built to the coast. In 1910, the cost of property on Granville Street doubled in eight months. The new B.C. Electric Interurban line was completed, connecting settlements as far away as Chilliwack with the downtown core. The development of municipal infrastructure struggled to keep pace with speculative development. Suburban areas outside Vancouver, now easily reached by ferry or streetcar, one after another received municipal incorporation: the City of North Vancouver, 1907; Point Grey, 1908; South Vancouver, 1911; West Vancouver, 1912; and the City of Port Moody in 1913. Also in 1913, Port Coquitlam and Fraser Mills seceded from Coquitlam to become separate municipalities, but Maillardville's petition to do the same was denied.

Financial investment was now pouring into British Columbia, and some of the largest industrial plants in the world, including sawmills, canneries, and mines, were built in just a few short years to exploit the vast amount of available natural resources. There was a fever pitch of excitement, and intense land speculation quadrupled the value of lots in Vancouver, now touted as the "Metropolis of western Canada." Genuine boosterism gave way to outright hucksterism, and many found themselves swindled when they invested, sight unseen, in speculative schemes that never materialized.

Growth in the Kootenays, if not as spectacular as before, was steady. On August 1, 1908, a huge fire devastated most of Fernie, including the new court house that had been opened that spring. Reconstruction was immediate, with new buildings in the commercial district to be of "fire resistant" materials such as brick and stone. Within two months the provincial government had accepted and approved new court house plans by George Stanley Rees, of Rees, Wilson & Pearse of Calgary, who had just opened an architectural office in Fernie. Built of red pressed bricks, granite cladding at the foundations, and Calgary sandstone trim, the new court house was superbly integrated with the mountain setting through the use of a massive slate roof. The cost was enormous, ending up close to $100,000, showing a confidence in the growth of the region that would prove to be unjustified.

Burgeoning prosperity in the booming west attracted the full attention of the Ottawa establishment. In 1901, DPW Chief Architect David Ewart took a summer tour of Europe, and when in London would undoubtedly have seen the new War Office in Whitehall, then under construction, designed by William Young (1843-1900). This was one of the most significant buildings in the new Edwardian Baroque style, and Ewart's later design for the new Vancouver Post Office bears striking similarities to Young's building, especially in the use of a rusticated base, giant order columns and a domed turret. Ewart, obviously inspired by this new stylistic expression of the power of the Empire, caught its flavour perfectly and planted a little piece of it in far-flung Vancouver. This represented a stylistic shift for the Branch towards the adoption of the Classical Revival idiom, informed by and filtered through the influences of the *École des Beaux-Arts*. Built just a block north of Thomas

War Office, Whitehall, London, 1899-1901

Post Office, Vancouver, 1905-1910

Fuller's now outmoded Post Office, it demonstrated the incredible growth of Vancouver and its new-found prominence within the federal hierarchy. Ewart's design, with its signature corner tower, became the prototype for a number of other post offices designed by the Branch throughout the west.

In 1911 a new Conservative government was elected to Ottawa, and one of its priorities was to cope with the explosive growth of trade throughout the country. Eight large customs examining warehouses were built in important trade centres, including one in Vancouver, 1911-13, designed by Ewart and located diagonally behind his Post Office. In response to the flood of people entering the country, a new Immigration Hall, with separate dining rooms and dormitories for white and Chinese immigrants, was built in Vancouver, 1913-15, designed locally by **E.E. Blackmore**. Many new armouries were also built to accommodate the national need for military training. In 1902 T.W. Fuller was appointed architect in charge of military buildings, a position he held until 1918. The plans for most of the new armouries were provided by Ottawa, such as the North Vancouver Drill Hall, 1913-15, built to Standard Drill Hall Type 'C' plans and supervised by **Henry Blackadder**. A few were designed locally, notably the Victoria Drill Hall, now the Bay Street Armoury, 1913-15 by **W. Ridgway-Wilson**. David Ewart continued to hold the post of Chief Architect throughout the boom years, until his resignation at the age of seventy-three in 1914, after which he became a consulting architect to the DPW until his death in 1921.

The last golden year was 1912. As speculation and investment continued at an ever faster pace, it was announced that another new railway, the Pacific Great Eastern, would be built to connect North Vancouver to the Grand Trunk at Fort George. Throughout the province, unprecedented amounts of new building occurred, and cities swelled in size, straining their roads to capacity. Automobiles were appearing on the streets, allowing unrestricted mobility. It seemed impossible that this boom could end. But end it did. By the end of that year, foreign investment was faltering.

The economy started a precipitous decline halfway into 1913. Sliding debris from the construction of the Canadian National Railway near Hell's Gate clogged the Fraser River, almost destroying the salmon run, a blow from which it never fully recovered. Agriculture and mining were suffering, due to slumping world market conditions and local labour unrest, including the "Big Strike" held by the coal miners on Vancouver Island in 1913. Rumours of an impending war in Europe caused even more anxiety for nervous investors. The Dominion Trust Company collapsed, sending waves of panic throughout the financial community. The National Finance Company and the Bank of Vancouver soon failed. In New Westminster alone, the total value of building permits dropped from a high of over $1,600,000 in 1912 to a low of $85,000 in 1914. Tension mounted as the news from overseas became ever more ominous. The assassination of Archduke Ferdinand, who had once hunted big game in B.C., was received with shock and trepidation. The British declaration of war on Germany set off a wave of patriotic response, and many

who had seen their hopes of financial security evaporate were eager to sign up for overseas duty. Premier McBride hardly left his office during that hot August of 1914, as he was so busy signing recommendations for his friends and admirers applying for army commissions.

The "War to End All Wars" exacted a staggering toll. British Columbia sent almost ten percent of its total population overseas, and about half were killed or wounded. Members of the Canadian Expeditionary Force served in some of the bloodiest battles of the Great War, and they were on the front lines when poison gas was first used as an offensive weapon. Lacking gas masks, they were decimated by the rolling green clouds, and many of the veterans would be plagued for the rest of their lives by a condition known as "gas lung." Many of the survivors were mentally and physically broken, and the province was stripped of a generation of its best and brightest. The world was forever changed by the four years of brutal conflict, and the surviving soldiers returned to a different world, where women were being enfranchised, where traditional social values were breaking down, where Prohibition had been enacted, and all manner of authority was being challenged. The world suffered another tragedy when Spanish Influenza devastated the remaining civilian population in 1918: this pandemic killed more people world-wide than had died during the war. The combined economic impacts were devastating. A number of towns, like Sandon in the Kootenays and Wallachin in the Interior, were simply abandoned. For the next two decades, social and political unrest and upheaval were common, and the seeds were sown for yet another global war.

The local economy was devastated. There was very little work for the returning soldiers, and the building trades languished. Before the end of the war, the federal government stepped in with a series of initiatives to provide hospitals and convalescent homes for returning soldiers who had been wounded in action. The Department of Soldiers' Civil Re-establishment (DSCR), the departmental successor to the Military Hospitals Commission (MHC), was established on February 21, 1918, under the *War Measures Act*. The Federal DPW took over formal responsibility for design but Captain W.L. Symons, who served as Chief Architect of the MHC since 1917, remained in charge of the process. Over 80 military hospital complexes were erected across the country, most to standard plans. The majority were sanatoria for tubercular soldiers or orthopedic hospitals for reconstructive surgery. Shaughnessy Hospital in Vancouver was the department's largest west coast hospital, and the DSCR also provided the design for a large new building at the existing King Edward Sanatorium at Tranquille, just outside Kamloops. The plans for this vast building, which mirrored an earlier structure by **Dalton & Eveleigh**, were sent out from Ottawa in mid-1918, and by September the tender had been awarded to **Dominion Construction**, who completed the three-storey structure the following year. Hospital construction was, however, one of the few bright spots in the construction industry during the first few bleak years that followed the return of peace.

King Edward Sanatorium, Tranquille

THE SCULPTURE BUILDINGS

JOHN ATKIN AND DONALD LUXTON

Terra cotta, literally "baked earth," is one of the world's oldest building materials. Its use has been documented in Egyptian, Greek and Roman civilizations, though after the collapse of the Roman Empire in 409 AD it largely disappeared until a revival occurred in Europe between the 14th and 16th centuries. Terra cotta experienced an even stronger revival in 19th century Britain and Germany, and until the 1870s almost all terra cotta used in North America was imported from Britain. The big push for the North American terra cotta industry came after the disastrous Chicago fire of 1871 where it was found that unprotected cast iron columns – then commonly used as structural elements in the new taller buildings being developed – twisted, burst and collapsed in the heat. Given its lightness and durability, terra cotta was seen as the ideal fireproofing material. Columns were encased in terra cotta panels which were also used to provide fire breaks between floors. As the industry grew and production methods perfected, terra cotta moved from the interior to the exterior where terra cotta ornament began to replace stone decoration because of the savings in cost and weight. Those same advantages made it perfect for the emerging "cloud scrapers" and the new curtain wall construction technology.

Terra cotta is manufactured by pressing prepared clay into plaster moulds, firing the dried clay in a kiln, applying the appropriate glaze and shipping the finished article to the job site. This process meant that ornamentation could be quite elaborate and could be designed and cast specifically for each building. Standard details such as garlands, cornices and column capitals could be ordered from a catalogue and many of these catalogue items can be found on a number of buildings within the shipping range of the factory and even in the same city.

Most terra cotta used in the late 1800s was unglazed, in red or tan colours, and integrated with brickwork as in **Samuel Maclure's** Temple Building in Victoria, 1893. Although the local brickyards in British Columbia produced unfired terra cotta pieces, terra cotta was usually imported as their low-fire kilns rarely produced a satisfactory product. The ornamental

Capital from Royal Bank, Mount Pleasant Branch, Vancouver, 1912, Thomas Hooper, Architect

Winch & Co. Building, Victoria, 1912, Thomas Hooper, Architect

ceramic roof ridges installed on *Craigdarroch Castle* in Victoria were ordered from Gladding, McBean & Company in Lincoln, California, in 1889. The Portland-based architect **Warren H. Williams** was undoubtedly familiar with the company's work, and this was the first known example in British Columbia of imported terra cotta. **Arlen H. Towle**, who had previously worked in San Diego, and **George W. Grant** were ordering terra cotta for their New Westminster projects from Gladding, McBean as early as 1892.

With the adoption of new technology, buildings at the turn of the 19th century were able to break free from the restrictions of load bearing masonry construction and soar above the street and "scrape the clouds." The simultaneous development of the passenger elevator and the skeletal metal frame or cage structure – supporting a building's inside floors and outer walls – enabled buildings to reach new heights. These early tall buildings were distinguished by a careful balance of proportion and scale which resulted in a rectangular massing, flat roof, and a heavy overhanging cornice capping the walls, typically articulated into a base, shaft and capital similar to the proportions of a classical column. The development of cage structures introduced a new concept, the curtain wall, a non load-bearing enclosure for the skeletal frame. This arrangement was perfect for the use of light weight cladding materials such as terra cotta. Glazed cream-white terra cotta became the favoured cladding material, the colour influenced in part by

the Columbian Exposition of 1893, known as the "White City of Chicago." Many architects specified stone for the ground floor and less expensive terra cotta for the rest of the building. In Vancouver there are examples of terra cotta that mimic various granites, limestones, and marbles including the 1912 Sun Tower at the corner of Pender and Beatty Streets which features nine huge caryatids cast to represent carved granite. **H.S. Griffith** designed the Vancouver YMCA, built 1912-13 with products supplied by the Northwestern Terra Cotta Co. of Chicago. The second Hotel Vancouver, designed by **Francis Swales**, was festooned with terra cotta imported from London, England. Eighteen moose and buffalo heads, each eight feet high, were placed at the fourteenth floor.

Vancouver's prosperity during the Edwardian era was indicated by a large number of impressive terra cotta commercial structures. Jonathon Rogers, one of the city's most successful land developers, chose prominent Seattle architects Gould & Champney to design a prestigious skyscraper. Gould & Champney maintained a branch office in Vancouver from 1910-12, and Augustus W. Gould for several years afterwards. The completed Rogers Building, with its glacial white cladding, demonstrates the deft way that the classically-trained architects of the time could manipulate traditional elements in a thoroughly contemporary manner. Terra cotta was sometimes used in conjunction with other masonry, an example being Ferrera Court, a Vancouver landmark since 1912 at the corner

of East Hastings and Jackson Streets. Frank H. Perkins provided the design for this elegant building, the largest that he designed in his short stay in Vancouver in 1911-13. Buff brick was used for the main wall surfaces, highlighted with a profusion of decorative cream-coloured terra cotta.

By far the largest supplier of local architectural terra cotta during the Edwardian boom years was Gladding, McBean & Company, and their corporate records from this time list a number of British Columbia's most prominent buildings. In 1911-12 alone their plant at Lincoln, California manufactured terra cotta for the Vancouver Block, the Vancouver Club, and St. Paul's Hospital in Vancouver, and the Union Club, the Winch Building and the Scott Building in Victoria. One landmark project that used Gladding, McBean terra cotta was the Campbell Building in Victoria, designed by **Thomas Hooper**. One hundred and seventeen tons of terra cotta for the project were shipped from the Gladding, McBean California plant in 1912. Three gigantic moose heads were planned for the cornice, but somehow these were changed during the fabrication process to camel heads, likely as a pun on the owner's name. The camel heads were 'delicate' and Gladding, McBean had an 'accident' with one of them, which had to be remade. Hooper's office was getting anxious about the time frame and any possible further delays, but the three heads, together weighing an additional ton, were finally shipped out on June 19, 1913.

During the mid-1920s the polychromatic possibilities of terra cotta were more fully explored, and the Art Deco style brought bold colours and shapes to contemporary architecture. Given the expanding local use of terra cotta, Gladding, McBean opened a branch plant at Auburn, Washington that supplied a number of projects such as **McCarter & Nairne's** Medical-Dental Building, 1928-29, now demolished. Their

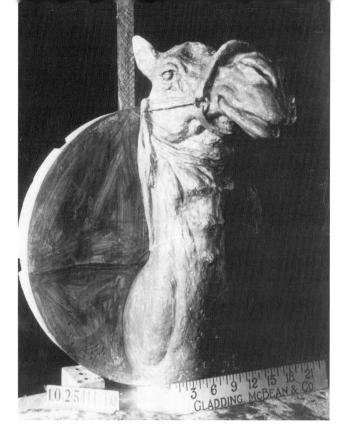

Camel from the Campbell Building, Victoria, Thomas Hooper, Architect

Marine Building, 1928-30, survives, with its extensive ornamentation, huge *verdigris* roof panels and sunburst entry with gilded terra cotta rays.

Terra cotta was used as late as the 1950s; Vancouver's Main Post Office, designed by McCarter & Nairne and not completed until 1958, was one of the last local buildings to make use of terra cotta panels. Shifting styles and building methods meant that this versatile material would soon cease to have a major role in architecture.

Moose head from drawings for the Campell Building, Victoria,

Thomas Hooper, Architect

Left: Vancouver Club, Vancouver, 1912-14,

Sharp & Thompson, Architects

OPERA HOUSES, VAUDEVILLE THEATRES AND MOVIE PALACES

STUART STARK AND DONALD LUXTON

Theatre designers were a breed apart. Hired for their abilities to produce lavish commissions, they could rarely make their specialized livings in just one town, or even one province. As theatre commissions in British Columbia ebbed and flowed with the economy, experts would be brought in to tackle them, or more rarely a local architect would be lucky enough to land one.

On the frontier, an opera house was considered the epitome of sophistication. The Victoria Theatre, the earliest grand theatre in Victoria, designed by **Charles E. Apponyi** and built 1884-85, was able to seat a thousand patrons. Nanaimo's Opera House, designed by **W. Ridgway-Wilson**, opened in 1890. In the instant city of Vancouver, the CPR thought it essential to build such a facility, and hired **J.W. & E.C. Hopkins** of Montreal to design one in 1888. A lavish structure, the Vancouver Opera House was the city's cultural centre, and many travelling performers, notably "The Divine" Sarah Bernhardt, played there. In 1912-13, **James J. Donnellan** was hired to renovate the old Vancouver Opera House into a circuit theatre for the Orpheum vaudeville chain, a purpose it served until the new Orpheum was opened down the block in 1927. Over the years the once proud Opera House slid into decrepitude, ending up as a dank movie theatre, a common fate for older live performance venues.

The phenomenon of the "movies" soon hit the frontier. Commercial spaces were converted into movie theatres by temporarily blacking out the windows, and it was widely assumed that the novelty of this technology would soon wear off. The movies did not go away, but the first purpose-built motion picture theatres in British Columbia were still surprisingly modest. Vancouver's Maple Leaf Theatre, built in 1907, reportedly accommodated 500 people seated on kitchen chairs. The first movie theatre built in Victoria in 1913 by architects **Fleet & Beale** still stands, though it was converted to apartments in 1943. However, it did not take long for the cult of the lavish movie house, the "Palace of Dreams," to take hold of the public's imagination. The movie companies of the day built their own circuits of theatres to control distribution of their "photoplays." The Allen Theatres were one of the prominent theatre chains, and with their more successful competitors, Famous Players, they tried to outdo one another with their spectacular theatre interiors.

In addition to movies, live shows were also an important part of the entertainment business, and the period between the two world wars was the heyday of vaudeville. Several grand theatres were built in Vancouver that were part of the vaudeville circuits. One of the foremost promoters of this form of entertainment was entrepreneur, Alexander Pantages, a former Klondike bar-sweep, said – among other rumours – to have gotten rich by separating the gold dust from the saw dust on the saloon floor. His first theatre in Vancouver, designed by **E.E. Blackmore** in 1907, still stands on East Hastings Street near Main, and its interior remains surprisingly intact. In Victoria, **Jesse M. Warren** designed an eight-storey store and office block for R.T. Elliot, K.C., to be erected on Government Street. Before it was begun, Elliot entered into partnership with realtors and developers McPherson & Fullerton and requested Warren to redesign it as a theatre (now the McPherson Playhouse) for the Pantages chain. In 1913, **Rochfort & Sankey** designed the Royal Victoria Theatre for the Victoria Opera House Company, Ltd., which still stands today as the Royal Theatre. "An Inspiring Sight" and "Local Architects are Congratulated" read the local headlines after the opening in December, 1913. The whole project was a significant undertaking, from the excavation of the site using teams of horses to the detailed plasterwork, decorative brick and terra cotta embellishments. The architects took a year to compile the 805 plans and drawings needed to oversee every aspect of the venture. At the same time Rochfort & Sankey were designing the Kinemacolor Variety Theatre on Government Street, which also opened in 1913. Kinemacolor, a primitive colour film process that was all the rage in Europe at the time, made its North American debut in New York in 1909.

Some of the most spectacular theatres that graced western Canada after the end of the First World War were brought into existence by the hands of three Americans – B. Marcus Priteca of Seattle, C. Howard Crane of Detroit, and Thomas White Lamb of New York. These men brought their experience, and their exposure to the latest theatre designs, to their work in Canada. From 1910 to 1929, "Benny" Priteca (1889-1971) acted as the main architect for the Pantages chain. Born and educated in Scotland, Priteca with his family had settled in Seattle, where he was based for the rest of his life. Pantages had hired J.J. Donnellan in 1914 to prepare plans for a grand new theatre in Vancouver, but the project was delayed due to the downturn in the local economy, and ultimately was never built. Donnellan moved on, and Pantages turned to Priteca to design his new theatre on West Hastings Street when the project finally went ahead in 1916. Lavishly outfitted with a terra cotta facade, this extravagant building was entertainment embodied, with every interior and exterior surface richly embellished, proving that architecture can indeed be "frozen music." This eclectic treasure was demolished in 1967. Priteca later provided the designs for the new Orpheum Theatre, on Granville Street, Vancouver, 1926-27. Frederick J. Peters was the associated architect on the design of the Orpheum; he was living in Seattle at the time, although he had previously

Nanaimo Opera House, Nanaimo

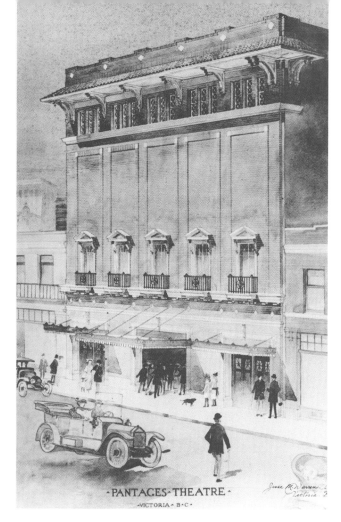

Pantages Theatre, Victoria

Original scheme for the Orpheum Theatre, Vancouver

practised in Vancouver. Peters, Priteca and a vice-president of the Orpheum Chain came to Vancouver on December 3, 1926 to review bids for the project, and as they were much higher than expected, they decided to scale back some of the more elaborate features they had planned for this vaudeville palace. Despite these changes, the Orpheum epitomized the return of prosperity in the 1920s. Later used as a movie theatre, it was allowed to deteriorate, and was threatened with demolition until its last minute rescue. The Orpheum has now been converted back for use as a live performance venue, and is one of Vancouver's preeminent heritage structures.

C. Howard Crane was the architect for nearly every Allen Theatre built in North America. By 1919, there were forty-five Allen Theatres across Canada. Crane's Allen Theatre opened in Vancouver in 1920. It was renamed The Strand in 1923, and was demolished in 1974, along with the Birks Building, to make way for the banal Scotiabank Tower. Crane, acclaimed as the architect of the Music Box and Theatre Guild theatres in New York, also maintained an office in London, and in 1935 was commissioned by the British Pacific Trust to design their enormous Earl's Court Exhibition Building, still the largest covered auditorium in Europe. Through this project Crane became friends with Alfred J.T. Taylor, who was later responsible for the construction of the Lions Gate Bridge in Vancouver.

Thomas W. Lamb (1871-1942) was the premier architect of movie theatres in North America. He was born in Dundee, Scotland and while still young immigrated to New York, where he received his architectural training. He designed a live-performance theatre in New York in 1909, the first in a long and very prolific career. He designed many theatres throughout the United States for the Loews and Fox chains, including some of the largest of their day with up to 5,300 seats. His designs were built in England, Australia, North Africa, India and Egypt. Later in his career he turned to the design of "moving picture houses" at which he was equally successful. His first Canadian theatre was built in Toronto in 1913. Except for the spectacular Wintergarden Theatre in Toronto, Lamb's Canadian theatres were all decorated in variations of the Adam style belying their often-unassuming exteriors. The lavish interiors featured architectural elements such as double oval staircases, and dramatic openings from the lobby areas into the main auditorium. The Adam style was characterised by delicate plaster panels on ceilings and walls, featuring urns, musical instruments and classical faces, all highlighted by rich colours and gilding, making a dramatic setting in which to enjoy the latest movie. In British Columbia, Lamb designed the Capitol Theatres in Victoria and Vancouver, both opened 1921, for their owner, the Famous Players Canadian Corporation. Both have been demolished – Vancouver in 1974 and Victoria in 1980 – and replaced with a new Capitol Six multiplex theatre, signalling a fundamental change in the economics of mass entertainment.

Second Pantages Theatre, Vancouver

"OWN YOUR OWN HOME"

JENNIFER NELL BARR AND
DONALD LUXTON

*No man who has the opportunity should fail to acquire
title to the property in which he is to reside. Until one
owns his own home, his life is not as complete as it
should be. Even if a man must go into debt to secure
his home, it is the thing for him to do... Really the
chances taken are not that formidable. In almost any
city, purchase of real estate at a fair valuation is a good
business investment... there is not even the prospect of a
reversal. If there did not exist the commercial argument
in favour of owning one's own home, there would be
plenty of other reasons for recommending it. Some
one has remarked that it is like reaching the state of
parenthood. When one acquires a home he has
something worth living for – fighting for. It makes him
a better citizen and a better member of society. It gives
him a substantial interest in the great organization
known as government. And while it increases a man's
sense of obligation to society and his country, it gives
him a new sort of freedom... No other possession he
may acquire ever means quite so much to a man as his
first home.*

The Islander [Cumberland], Sept. 26, 1914, p.2.

Home ownership was the dream of working class European immigrants, who poured into Canada from countries where it remained an almost impossible goal. Most arrived with limited financial resources, and struggled to find reasonable housing. Workers were usually forced into rental situations, or if lucky could afford to build a house by themselves. Even during the boom years, job insecurity and high living costs deterred many from home ownership, and high rents, inflation and rampant speculation kept house prices artificially high; in Vancouver in 1911, between one-quarter and one-third of suburban workers were renting accommodation. But with perseverance, many immigrants did indeed achieve their dream.

Land ownership was central to the power structure of the frontier, and private entrepreneurs dictated the terms of financing. Speculative housing schemes could be extremely profitable, and many newly-rich real estate promoters wielded great influence in the ways that settlements around the province were developed. Capital for housing was raised from local and regional sources as well as eastern Canadian and overseas – mainly British – sources, and the local housing market was thus disproportionately affected by international financial conditions. Chartered banks were forbidden by Dominion banking laws to invest in real estate, so mortgage funds were handled through a myriad of private finance and loan companies, private brokers who represented European banks, and individual realtors who sometimes also acted as financial agents. Many trust companies, such as Canada Permanent, lent money that they raised both domestically and abroad, but the greatest amount of mortgage money was made available by Canadian life insurance companies. Mortgages financed through these sources were generally for forty to fifty per cent of the total value of a house, a barrier to most lower income families. This began to change with the prosperity of the great Edwardian boom, as credit became more freely available. **Bungalow and home construction companies**, which sometimes employed their own architects, built houses on a speculative basis that were sold on the instalment plan to the newly developing market of young working-and lower-middle-class families.

This system of private financing effectively collapsed with the economic depression of 1913, and with the subsequent bankruptcy of the financing companies and the retreat of foreign capital, the housing market fell apart. Huge amounts of land that had been surveyed and subdivided for speculative housing – thousands of acres in some municipalities – were forfeited for non-payment of taxes and remained vacant for decades. Many who had taken on the short term mortgages offered by the home construction companies could not meet the payments after the 1913 crash, and had to take in boarders, rent out cottages in the back yard, or keep farm animals for extra income. As the construction of new housing declined dramatically for the next decade, many families were forced to "double up" by splitting their homes.

Although home ownership was praised as the basis for a safe and rational society, for large numbers of families it remained an elusive goal. Paradoxically it has been during times of crisis that Canada made the greatest strides towards national housing policies and initiatives. Progressive funding programs for housing were initiated by the federal government after both world wars, assisting lower income families that did not qualify for private mortgages. Government guarantees for mortgages were gradually phased in, along with central design controls and building codes.

In December 1918, the federal government authorized the *Soldiers' Settlement Act* to provide twenty-five million dollars in loans to the provinces for housing initiatives for returning veterans. As housing was strictly a provincial responsibility at the time, these measures had to be instituted under the *War Measures Act*. Contained within the Act were provisions which allowed for surrendered Aboriginal reserve lands to be purchased for the Soldiers' Settlement Board for Eurocanadian veterans. In the next four years 179 municipalities across the country took advantage of this funding either to finance or construct 6,244 homes, the first significant public sector initiative to promote homebuilding. In March 1919, British Columbia passed the *Better Housing Act* to take advantage of the new federal programmes. Fifty-three homes in Victoria, and 153 in Vancouver, were financed in 1919-22. Some communities, such as Saanich and Cumberland, used the funds to build houses themselves. A number of architects were retained in different communities to design veteran's housing, including **W.A. Owen** in Cumberland, **Swan & Augustine** in Penticton, **Percy Leonard James** in Oak Bay, and **Karl B. Spurgin** and **Ralph Berrill** in Saanich. On behalf of the Provincial Department of Public Works, **Henry Whittaker** developed standard designs for modest bungalows that were built in South Vancouver. One ambitious project was a whole new town for veterans, Merville, built in unclaimed forest north of Courtenay on Vancouver Island. With funds allocated by the federal government, the town was laid out and houses built, which were leased to returned soldiers on a rent-to-own basis. Merville was totally destroyed by a forest fire in 1922.

By most accounts, these housing schemes were relatively ineffective at achieving their primary goal, and became redundant as market conditions revived in the early 1920s. The veterans were finding it hard to get jobs, and could barely afford the subsidized payments. The loans were targeted at the middle classes who likely could have afforded a home on their own, rather than needy veterans or low-income families. Although subsidized, the loans were still at a high rate of interest, and when the housing market went soft during the Great Depression, many mortgage holders quitclaimed or were foreclosed. Municipalities struggled to pay off the debt they had taken on. An example was Cumberland, which as early as 1923 was having trouble securing instalment payments from householders to cover the principal and interest owed to the government and the city, as well as taxes and insurance. It wasn't until December 1949 that the city finally managed to repay the last of their federal loan.

The misery of the Depression sparked another cycle of federal housing initiatives. The provinces were effectively bankrupt, and the federal government assumed responsibility for housing by passing the *Dominion Housing Act (DHA)* in 1935, which clearly set the government on a course of social engineering. The Act provided low-interest loans for the construction of new housing, including single and multiple family units, with financing provided jointly by the government and a private lending institution, a system that prevailed until 1954. Despite government guarantees, financial institutions were reluctant to participate, and after much lobbying the Canada Permanent Mortgage Corporation and Mutual Life of Canada began to accept *DHA* loan applications in April, 1936.

The shortcomings of the Act were recognized quickly, as these initiatives continued to favour middle- rather than lower-income families by promoting standard single family dwellings on suburban lots, doing nothing to improve housing conditions in deteriorating inner city neighbourhoods. The *DHA* was replaced in 1938 by the broader provisions of the *National Housing Act (NHA)*, where loans were given directly to the homeowner, provided certain conditions were met, including approval of the design and location of the house. The applicant had to have a twenty-percent down payment, and the total cost of the house was not expected to exceed two and one-half times their annual salary. Standardized house plans being promoted by the eastern authorities did not reflect the traditional Craftsman styles used on the west coast, nor fit the evolving new modernism that was generally expressed with flat roofs, and struggles over appropriate design contributed to the ongoing nervousness of the lending institutions.

During the Second World War, housing again became a national concern. It was recognised that Canada's housing stock had deteriorated seriously, and wartime shortages of labour and material would make the situation even worse without some assistance. The Wartime Housing Corporation was established; it built 46,000 new homes, mostly for warworkers, and helped repair and modernize thousands of existing units. With central control of housing came a concern for consistent standards of construction, and the first National Building Code was issued in 1941.

In the final years of the war the federal government braced itself to cope with the return of more than a million Canadians from the armed forces to peacetime life, and a revised *NHA* was passed in 1944 that expanded the system of loans and guarantees for homebuilders. The national housing stock was considered a disgrace; only sixty-one percent of Canadian houses had running water, and barely half had an inside flush toilet. The population on the west coast ballooned as veterans were demobilized at coastal ports and many farmers moved off the Prairies. The housing crisis in Vancouver was acute, and after picketing by veterans, the second Hotel Vancouver, which had been used as a military barracks during the war, was opened up to provide emergency housing for 1,200 families, a temporary situation that lasted for two years and delayed the old hotel's demolition. In 1946 the Central Mortgage & Housing Corporation (CMHC) was created, and it rapidly evolved into a key player in the residential housing industry.

In the 1950s a rapidly expanding population and economy, and innovations in building materials and practices, led to the passage of further revisions to the *NHA, in* 1954, the CMHC's mandate was significantly broadened, and the Public Mortgage Loan Insurance Programme was established to replace the CMHC's direct lending plan. Parallel changes to the federal *Bank Act* in 1954 removed the long-standing injunction against bank lending being secured by real estate, and for the first time allowed chartered banks to make chattel mortgages. For prospective homeowners with only a small down payment, the CMHC would now guarantee a "high-ratio" mortgage, allowing many lower income families to buy their own home, a system still in operation today.

McCARTER & NAIRNE

PARTNERSHIP 1921-1982

JOHN
YOUNG
McCARTER

1886-1981

his timing was poor, the economy had begun to sour and the firm broke up before the war. Nairne found a year and a half of work with architect H.H. Johnson in Great Falls, Montana, 1914-15, and prospected for gold in Alaska and the Yukon 1915-17 before returning to Canada to enlist with the Royal Canadian Engineers.

Though also of Scottish background, John McCarter was born in Victoria, B.C. on August 12, 1886, and was raised and educated in that city along with his two brothers. Throughout his life McCarter pursued athletic, cultural, and commercial activities. His youthful prowess in rugby and rowing mellowed over the years into a love of fishing and golf. From childhood, though, it is said that he loved creative tasks such as painting, so much so that his burly, lumberman father smashed John's paint box and began a harangue with the time-honoured admonition: "no son of mine..." Nevertheless, his father saw fit to article John to the successful Victoria architect, Thomas Hooper. Presumably architecture's association with the manly

Spencer's Department Store, Vancouver

DAVID MONTEYNE

McCarter & Nairne was one of the key architectural firms practising in British Columbia for several decades after the First World War. Only two other firms – **Townley & Matheson** and **Sharp & Thompson** – could boast a similar longevity and success. Both John McCarter and George Nairne were active into the 1950s, and the firm continued to do business under their names until it disbanded in 1982.

George Nairne was born in Inverness, Scotland on November 14, 1884, to a family of three boys and three girls; his father, David Nairne, was sub-editor of the *Northern Chronicle*. At the age of twenty-one, George articled to an Inverness architect named John Squair, and concurrently took courses at the technical and art school in that city. After a five year apprenticeship, Nairne left his home town and worked eighteen months as a junior draftsman in Cardiff, Wales, saving up for his eventual passage to North America. Shortly after his arrival in New York in 1906, Nairne began working in the office of another Scottish expatriate architect, Alex Mackintosh. In late 1909, at the height of the western economic boom, Nairne immigrated to Seattle and worked briefly for the architects Blackwell & Baker before moving to **Thomas Hooper's** Vancouver office in 1911. Two years later Nairne entered a brief partnership in Nanaimo with John MacMillan. However,

trade of building and Hooper's reputation for business acumen softened the paternal opposition to artistic pursuits.

After several years of articling, McCarter moved to Hooper's Vancouver office in 1910. Hooper had been commissioned to design an annex to **Rattenbury's** new Court House which, because of Vancouver's exponential growth, was already inadequate for the city. McCarter gained experience working on the annex, as well as on projects such as the Winch Building, and court houses in Vernon and Revelstoke. He studied after hours with a structural engineer, and would later be professionally registered as both architect and engineer. Leaving Hooper's office in mid-1912, McCarter established his own practice designing small homes and businesses in Vancouver, North Vancouver, and Eburne. His first solo buildings included the Patricia Hotel on Hastings Street, 1911-12, and the Alcazar Theatre on Commercial Drive. A contemporary reviewer described the Alcazar as "a very cosy little place in which to enjoy the plays of the winter. It is neat, clean and bright as a new pin, well ventilated and well warmed." This reveals more about the state of architectural criticism in 1913 Vancouver than it does about the theatre itself. McCarter was sent by **Dominion Construction** to Edmonton to open a branch office,

GEORGE COLVILL NAIRNE
1884-1953

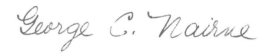

but had just arrived when the local economy collapsed. After his return he had a few other small commissions, including the Morton Residence in North Vancouver, 1914, before leaving Vancouver in 1916 as an officer with the Royal Navy.

Both McCarter and Nairne served overseas during the First World War. Returning to Vancouver with an English wife, Ann Gordon Urie, McCarter designed schools and hospitals for the Federal Department of Soldiers' Civil Re-establishment. Attracted by his short stint in the city, Nairne wanted to re-settle in Vancouver. However, not finding work in the profession, he moved to Seattle and worked for B. Marcus Priteca, famed architect of the Pantages theatre chain. Nairne soon got his opportunity to return to Vancouver. In 1921 he and McCarter, who had known each other from working in Hooper's office, decided to form McCarter & Nairne Architects and Engineers. The two complemented each other well: McCarter's outgoing personality, business sense, and extensive network of local contacts brought the firm a lot of work; the more retiring Nairne possessed broad experience with different firms which allowed him to efficiently manage the many projects soon concurrent in the large drafting room. McCarter expanded his network through service on the boards of local companies, and a multitude of other local and national

organizations. Both architects served as President of the Architectural Institute of B.C., while McCarter (known widely as "J.Y.") was also Vice-President of the Royal Architectural Institute of Canada and the Canadian Chamber of Commerce, as well as President of the Vancouver Board of Trade during the city's 1936 Golden Jubilee celebrations. Once they had become very successful architects, both gentlemen resided in Shaughnessy, and were members of the Golf and Country Club.

Like most architects, McCarter & Nairne commenced their practice with the design of houses and small apartment buildings. An important breakthrough was the commission for the Devonshire Apartments. This large building, designed in the Renaissance Revival style, stood on a prominent Georgia Street site across from the Court House. Other large commissions soon followed, such as the Harrison Hot Springs Hotel and Bath House (with associate architects **Townley & Matheson**), 1925-26, the New Westminster City Market, 1926, the first Richmond High School, 1927, and a prominent department store for David Spencer in Vancouver, 1925-26. McCarter's daughter Joan related how the firm won the contract for Spencer's. The client's original intention was to utilize them as local consultants, while a large Chicago firm would design the store. McCarter and Chris Spencer went to Chicago and were shown three different sets of possible plans. McCarter had brought a set as well which revealed a better design for the proposed store. The Chicago firm then copied McCarter & Nairne's ideas, and reproduced them in a fourth set of plans shown in another meeting that same afternoon. Spencer noticed this deception, paid off the Chicagoans, and engaged the local Vancouver firm as his designers. For their part, McCarter & Nairne strove on all their projects to promote B.C. industries by using local contractors and materials whenever possible.

Spencer's Department Store introduced some of the firm's trademark concepts, such as their advanced use of technology and financially rationalized space planning. The firm's growing reputation led to commissions for their best-known designs, the Medical-Dental Building, 1928-29, and the Marine Building, 1928-30, two of Vancouver's first skyscrapers. They were beautiful examples of the short-lived Art Deco style that was popular in the 1920s-30s. The Medical-Dental Building, the first building in the city erected to San Francisco earthquake standards, was famous for the three large terra cotta nursing sisters that graced the corners where the building stepped back at the tenth floor. The brick facade of the Medical-Dental Building gradually lightened in colour from a dark brown at the base to a lighter tan at the top, achieved by intermingling pallets of different coloured bricks together at the brickyard before delivery to the site. Despite lengthy public protests, this sublime building was imploded in 1989.

The Marine Building is exemplary with its step-backs, verticality, and ornate terra cotta decorative scheme that portrays coastal history and wildlife. The tallest in the British Empire when completed, this landmark is the premier example of the Art Deco style in western Canada. When first conceived, it was described as being in the "perpendicular modified Gothic style," reflecting the influence of Eliel Saarinen's seminal blend of Gothic verticality and modernist detailing in his 1922 Chicago Tribune competition entry. Described by the architects as "some great crag rising from the sea, clinging with sea flora and fauna, tinted in sea-green, touched with gold," the building is encrusted throughout with marine motifs that run riot through the exterior and interior ornamentation. A grand portal symbolizes the city's role as a gateway to the Orient, and the front door frames are encrusted with three-dimensional brass sea creatures. Stained glass panels at each

Marine Building, Vancouver

McLennan, McFeely & Prior Ltd., New Westminster

Proposed Stock Barn, Vancouver Exhibition Association, Vancouver

end of the lobby echo the sunrise and sunset, and subdued indirect lighting shines upward from ship's prows that surge forward from the wall surfaces. The ornamentation and artwork for both the Medical-Dental Building and the Marine Building were executed by **J.F. "Doc" Watson**, Cedric J.M. Young and **John Douglas Hunter**. The terra cotta work was manufactured near Seattle by Gladding, McBean & Company, and the bas relief tiles in the lobby were supplied by the Batchelder Tile Company of Los Angeles. Completed after the onset of the Great Depression, its bankrupt developers offered it to the City of Vancouver for use as City Hall for less than half the price of construction, an offer the City in its wisdom declined.

In later years, McCarter was averse to discussing the different styles used by the firm, insisting instead on the modernist primacy of the rational plan. Indeed, because of the loss of rentable floor space, McCarter argued unsuccessfully with the city against the requested setbacks on the Medical-Dental Building. During this prolific time they were the architects for dozens of residential, commercial and institutional projects across the Lower Mainland of B.C. The firm's emphasis on the science of design, and McCarter's contacts in military and political circles, kept them going through the Depression and war years, with important government commissions like the Seaforth Armoury of 1935-36; the Post Office Extension,

1934-37, commissioned under the Federal Works Programme; and the supervision of federally-funded wartime housing in British Columbia. The latter assignment included the Sea Island community of Burkeville built for workers at Boeing's Vancouver Airport factory; as well as civic centres in Kelowna, Nelson, and Trail. Other major projects of the era included the streamlined Grandview Substation for the B.C. Electric Railway Company, begun 1937, and the YMCA on Burrard Street, 1940, conceived in a stripped-down Art Deco style. The firm produced a steady stream of modernist projects, usually rendered by **Theo Körner**, **"Doc" Watson** or J.D. Hunter. Competitor Ned Pratt, who joined Sharp & Thompson in 1938, jokingly complained that in these years McCarter & Nairne were "as usual hogging all the work." The sleek, Moderne styling of the McLennan McFeely & Prior store in New Westminster foreshadowed the modern functionalism the firm would adopt beginning in the 1940s. The postwar years witnessed another construction boom and McCarter & Nairne continued to flourish, their most important postwar work being the monumental Vancouver General Post Office, built 1953-58. George Nairne retired in 1951, and died on April 23, 1953; J.Y. McCarter retired in 1956 but maintained an active role in public service for many years before his death on May 12, 1981.

Interior (left) and exterior (right), Post Office, Vancouver

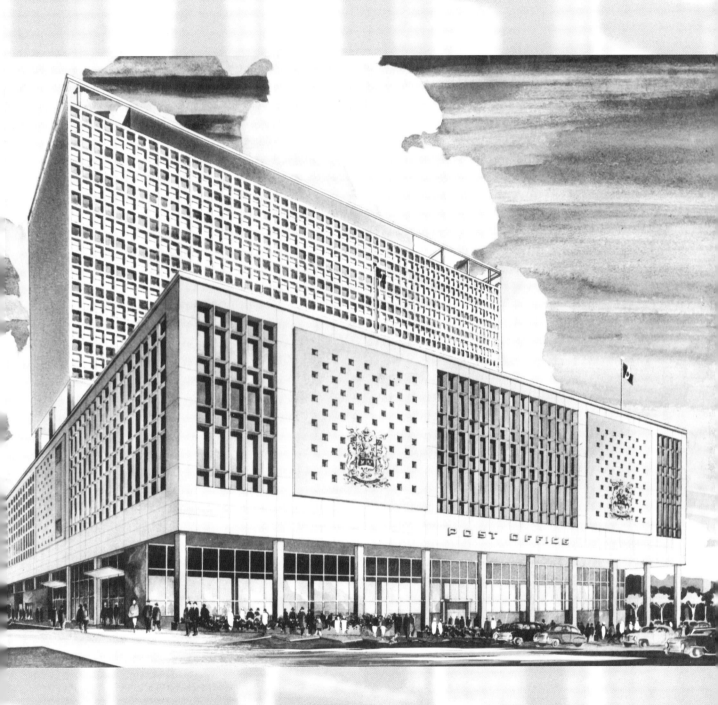

WILLIAM ARTHUR OWEN
1881-1961

JENNIFER NELL BARR

William "Bill" Owen was born in Swansea, Glamorgan, Wales, on August 26, 1881. After articling in Newport, Wales, with architect Benjamin Lawrence, 1899-1902, he worked with E.V. Johnston of Newport, as a draftsman, and then as a partner. Owen developed tubercular trouble and immigrated to Canada in 1904. He went first to Nanaimo, where he met Edith Blanche Horne, daughter of Adam and Emily Horne, and granddaughter of Adam Grant Horne, the first white man to cross Vancouver Island. William and Edith were married April 18, 1906. Owen worked as an architect and engineer for several mining companies, and was City Engineer for Nanaimo for a number of years, including 1914-17. He also maintained a private practice in Nanaimo. His buildings in that city included: the Nanaimo Agricultural Building, which later became the High School, 1912; a 1914 concrete tower addition to the 1894 fire hall; the S&W Apartments, 1910-11; and the Newcastle Hotel, designed in 1913 for Jack W. Black, but not built until after the end of the First World War.

In 1917, Owen was appointed Construction Engineer for Canadian Collieries (Dunsmuir) Ltd. (CCDL) at Cumberland, in the Comox Valley on Vancouver Island. He was responsible for the design of new buildings and alterations to existing structures, including executives' and miners' company housing, offices, and all mine pithead structures. For many years he was also Cumberland's city engineer. In 1918 he oversaw the relocation of forty-three CCDL houses from Bevan townsite, five miles away, to Cumberland. That year he also designed an Arts and Crafts-style home for his family in Cumberland. Other designs in Cumberland included: the parish hall, 1919-20, for Holy Trinity Anglican Church; the Great War Veterans' Memorial Hall and Arch, 1920-22; the Cumberland Literary & Athletic Association Building, 1920; six Soldiers' Settlement houses, 1921; and the Merrifield house, 1936.

Owen retired in the 1950s, but continued to design buildings in the area, such as Courtenay City Hall (a remodelling of Courtenay police premises) and a senior citizens' home, as well as the Park Royal Hotel in West Vancouver, 1955. He was a long-time member of the Masonic Order, an accomplished violinist, pianist and cellist who played both privately and publicly, and a calligrapher. His wife, who left Cumberland in the mid-1920s, died in 1955. In the 1940s, Owen moved to Royston, four miles from Cumberland, on the east coast of Vancouver Island. There he built for himself and his daughter, Olga Blanche, a rustic cottage, with a large, round corner bay, covered in quarter-round, fake-log drop siding. The woodland garden, with a rustic bridge over a stream, lent an enchanted air to the property. Owen died at the age of seventy-nine on June 14, 1961, and was buried in Sandwick Cemetery near Courtenay on Vancouver Island.

Great War Veterans' Memorial Hall, Cumberland

Owen Residence, Royston

Agricultural Hall, Nanaimo

Cumberland Literary & Athletic Association, Cumberland

HAROLD JOSEPH ROUS CULLIN
1875-1935

JENNIFER NELL BARR

H.J. Rous Cullin had a far more distinguished architectural career than has previously been recognized. He was born in Liverpool, England, December 5, 1875, the son of a Canon of the Church of England, Joseph Rous Cullin, and his wife, Ellen. Educated at King's School, Canterbury, where he was an Officer in the school Army Cadet Corps, he distinguished himself in cricket and athletics, and represented his school in gymnastics at Aldershot. He also studied at the Sidney Cooper School of Art in Canterbury 1891-93, and then with architect, W. Stone in London, 1894-95. Cullin was a member of the London Rifle Brigade, 1896-98. In 1899 he became a Lieutenant in the 1st London Royal Engineers and studied at the School of Military Engineering in Chatham. After his studies Cullin obtained, in January 1900, a commission in the 38th Field Company, Royal Engineers, and saw active service in Orange Free State and Cape Colony during the Boer War. A shot through the leg and a serious illness forced his return to England in September 1900. He was made a Captain and Adjutant with the 1st London Royal Engineers, but retired in 1904 and immigrated to Canada.

Cullin first worked in **Samuel Maclure's** office in Victoria, and then opened his own architectural practice in Victoria in May 1905. He was also the bursar of the University School for several years after it was founded in 1906. On August 5, 1908, at the age of thirty-two, he married twenty-year old Frances Elizabeth Olive Bales. The Cullins had two daughters, Alice Evelyn and Doris Olive, and a son, Francis Rowland. In 1912 Cullin was in partnership with architect John W.D. York, as Cullin & York; Cullin designed two houses side by side on lower Cook Street for York's relative, real estate agent, Louis

S.V. York. By January 1913, Cullin was again practising on his own. He retained his interest in the military, and on September 8, 1912, joined the newly-formed 88th Regiment, Victoria Fusiliers as senior Captain. He held a command in the civil aid force throughout the coal miners' "Big Strike" on Vancouver Island in 1913, and was stationed in Nanaimo for the first two months of the strike. At the same time, he was also a member of the Island Arts and Crafts Club, conductor of the Saanich Choral Society, and choirmaster of St. Luke's Anglican Church. Cullin was prominent in the British Columbia Society of Architects, and served on both the Provincial Council and Victoria Chapter Executive Council until 1914.

As architect by appointment to the Saanich School Board for several years, Cullin designed at least seven schools, including Cedar Hill School, 1912, and its Manual Training Hall, 1913. His largest school, designed in *Beaux-Arts* style, is the eleven-room Tolmie School, 1913. Cullin designed a number of residences in the Victoria area, including those of: Thomas Shaw, *Hume Cottage*, 1907; Dr. Valentine de Saumarez and Mary Duke, 1912; music teacher, Algernon R. Dobson; wholesale and retail butcher, Lawrence R. Goodacre, 1912; and real estate agent, J.A. Dewar, 1913. The designs for Saumarez-Duke and Dewar are essays in the Tudor Revival style; *Hume Cottage* and the Goodacre Residence are Chalet-style Arts and Crafts, clad with a combination of shingles and Tudor-style half-timbering. An article in the January 18, 1913 edition of *The Week* stated "These residences are typical of his ability as an architect; they each represent a different style of architecture, and the interior arrangements have been carried out with the idea of combining architectural beauty and convenience, as his plans always keep in view the use of every available inch of space without loss of the artistic." Cullin also designed several commercial blocks and apartments, including Park Mansions at North Park and Quadra Streets, 1913, a four-storey block with ground-level storefronts and elegant, high-ceiling apartments with inset bay windows.

At the beginning of the First World War Cullin retired from his architectural practice. As Commanding Officer of the 88th Victoria Fusiliers, he was promoted to the rank of Major, and then to Lieutenant-Colonel. In October 1915, Ottawa authorized Cullin to recruit the battalion to its full war strength of 1,050 men, and to mobilize it for overseas; he issued a strongly-worded, jingoistic appeal for Victoria's unmarried men to join the regiment. They finally shipped out in May 1916, first by train across Canada and then on a troop ship from Halifax to Europe. Cullin wrote a letter to the Victoria *Daily Colonist* on June 29, 1916, describing, in militaristic brevity but with a jaunty, infectious enthusiasm their progress across Canada: "Arrived Halifax on Wednesday, May 29, at 11 a.m… Men all intact. Wonderful behavior. No sickness in 88th. No deserters. No defaulters. Spirits simply wonderful. Message from Victoria Fusiliers to Victoria: 'Keep on recruiting. The war is only just starting. It will go another two years. Fill up the 88th again. It has only sent a brigade so far. Make it a division before the war is over. Wake up, Victoria, and organize both soldiering and business. Never mind the dollars – get the Hun! We shall want every man.'" Cullin was invalided out of war service in 1917; in army records he was listed as "surplus" on September 6, 1917.

Cullin resumed his architectural practice in Victoria in June 1918, and designed a residence in Oak Bay for Sir F. Ashley Sparks, Principal of St. Aidan's School. But Cullin's health was broken and his doctor advised him to leave the coast. He moved to Kelowna, where, in July 1919, he obtained a temporary appointment in the Provincial Department of Public Works, and worked on ongoing projects at Essondale in Coquitlam. Cullin applied for AIBC membership in March 1922, and several letters in his file tell something of the hardship experienced by many of the returning wounded following the First World War: "my finances were in such a state of ruin, following on the war, my long illness, and the general depression in the building trade, that at times I even had to borrow to live." In 1922 Cullin designed a Georgian Revival residence in Kelowna for William E. and Gertrude E.C. Adams; William Adams was a prominent community leader, associated with land development and the fruit industry. Cullin's last known project was a brick fire hall in Kelowna, built in 1924. He suffered a paralytic stroke in late 1925 or early 1926, and, unable to find work and in failing heath, he returned with his family to Victoria. By 1933, Cullin was a resident in the Old Men's Home. At the time of his death on August 12, 1935, he, Frances, and one daughter were living at the Menzies Nursing and Convalescent Home. A life-long member of the Masonic Order, he was given a Masonic funeral and burial service at Royal Oak Burial Park in Saanich.

Fire Hall, Kelowna

DAVID
COWPER
FRAME
1882-1960

JEAN SPARKS

A talented and versatile architect, D.C. Frame produced work that covered half a century and spanned the decline of traditional architecture and the rise of Modernism. Though his career was sporadic, Frame was able, through his talent and imagination, to adapt to changing tastes and to create buildings of great character and originality. If circumstances had allowed, it is possible his achievements would have rivalled some of his better-known contemporaries. Complicating an assessment of his career is a lack of documentation, as his papers were burned after his death. Frame was born in Larkhall, Scotland on December 2, 1882, to a family of prosperous Lanark wool merchants. He attended Dollar Boys' School before commencing studies at the Glasgow School of Art at age sixteen. In apprenticeship, Frame spent one year with prestigious Glasgow architect, James Miller, who was just completing the plans for the 1901 Glasgow International Exhibition, and then three years with William Ferguson, 1902-05. Frame went on a trip to Jamaica with his friend Jock Findlay, and was a foreman on a relation's banana plantation until falling ill with malaria. He and Jock moved on to Canada, travelling by train to Vancouver, and then on to Victoria. Frame went to New Zealand to check out conditions, but soon travelled back to Victoria, washing dishes for his return passage. He gained employment as an architect's apprentice under **F.M. Rattenbury** for three years, from 1905-08.

Soon known for his sociability and musical ability, young Frame was welcomed into Victoria society. He was a frequent guest of the Rattenburys, and enjoyed fishing and golfing as well as the arts. With his social connections secured, Frame was in a position to receive commissions from his often over-worked colleagues, and in 1908 he established his own firm. An early project, the Chinese Public School for the Chinese Consolidated Benevolent Association, was won in open competition, and displays an eclectic blend of eastern and western influences, including Moorish windows, Gothic trefoils, Italianate eave-brackets, and a pan-tiled pagoda roof. The Alexandra Club, the feminine equivalent of the Union Club, allowed the women of Victoria society a place to gather for cultural events outside their homes. This thirty room, three-storey Edwardian palazzo, with dining facilities and grand ballroom, cost $51,200 in 1910. An imposing school house, the Bank Street School, for the Victoria School Board soon followed. Symmetrical in its massing, it is imposing both for its use of materials, and in its sophisticated handling of details. The walls are thickly articulated brick, relieved by banks of large windows, which are unique in having a stringcourse band that runs in front of the sash. The oversize dentil blocks at the cornice emphasize the monumental scale of the building.

At the same time Frame was establishing himself as a domestic architect of some skill, starting in 1909 with his own home *Larkhall*, a gift to his bride, Evelyn Annie Dickinson. This was followed by *Sheilin* for Mrs. Catherine Wilson, and the James S. Clarke House. Frame established himself as a master in the Arts and Crafts genre. His commission for *Kingsmont*, a massive stone home on the crest of Gonzales Hill is still one of

Chinese Public School, Victoria

Victoria's most impressive architectural landmarks. One distinguished project was a large, steepled Methodist church in Victoria West, 1912, now used by the Salvation Army.

The outbreak of the First World War brought an end to these prosperous times. Frame volunteered for overseas service but was rejected for bad eyesight, and worked from 1916 until the end of the war as a draftsman for Canadian Explosives. In 1919 he moved back to Scotland with his wife and children, to work in the family business, but returned to Victoria in 1921. Frame, an artistic man not much interested in business, suffered from poor health, and had a large family to support. He resumed his career in the offices of former associates – **Hubert Savage**, **C. Elwood Watkins**, **J. Graham Johnson** and **S. Patrick Birley** – not as an architect but as a draftsman. In the 1920s, Frame purchased land in Esquimalt at Fleming Beach. There he built *Solway*, the modest seaside cottage whose design reflects his Scottish roots.

The Depression brought further change. In 1930 Frame built a home on five acres on Shelbourne Street near Mount Douglas, where he farmed loganberries and vegetables for five years. The property also had an orchard, and pasture for a horse and cow. Frame established a tennis lawn, and almost no one could beat him at the game. For financial reasons it became necessary to rent *Solway* out, although the family returned about 1937, and stayed for four years before it had to be rented again. After the family finally returned to *Solway*, Frame lived there until his death on April 12, 1960.

Only a member of the Architectural Institute of B.C. from 1923-25, Frame reapplied in 1940 and set up his own practice again. The apartment buildings he designed between 1944 and 1953 illustrate the change in public taste from Art Deco to the International Style. The Art Deco Park Towers Apartments on Vancouver Street, for George and M.M. Salter, 1945, is one of his more pleasing apartment designs. Frame was also engaged in designing commercial projects and apartment buildings, often in association with other Victoria architects: the Bartle & Gibson Building, 1941, with S. Patrick Birley; the Canadian Imperial Bank of Commerce with Douglas James; and the Memorial Arena, 1947, with Hubert Savage and **Douglas James**.

Top: Alexandra Club, Victoria

Bottom: Methodist Church, Victoria

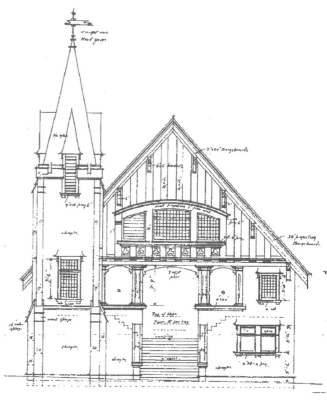

W.H.
CHOW

JANET COLLINS

W.H. Chow was one of the earliest Chinese-Canadian architects working in the province. Somehow he managed to overcome both the legal and the social hurdles that prevented most of Vancouver's early Chinese immigrants from entering professions. Despite that noteworthy fact, little is known about him other than that he referred to himself as a contractor, builder, and timber dealer.

Chow was working at a time when racial tensions were high. Vancouver's Chinatown dates from the 1880s, when more than 10,000 Chinese came to B.C. to work on the Canadian Pacific Railway line. Others worked in goldfields, coal mines, sawmills and canneries. Many only lived in Vancouver between jobs, but others stayed on and established businesses. As the city grew between the affluent years of 1897 and 1913, so did Chinatown, as Chinese merchants invested in new properties. Often, in references to Chinatown in city directories, the occupant's name is left blank or replaced by the disparaging "Oriental" or "Chinese." The translation of Chinese names into English was erratic, and the occupations of those listed are frequently missing. This makes it difficult to determine when an individual first moved to Vancouver, where they lived, and how they made their living.

The limited information available about W.H. Chow indicates that he worked primarily in the Chinatown area. With the exception of his own house on Lorne Street, built 1904, Chow did most of his work between 1912-14, with a few other projects undertaken in the early 1920s. Chow's output was varied. In addition to frame dwellings, he designed and built offices, stores and apartments/rooms. The apartments were likely accommodations for Chinatown's large bachelor population. The Yue Shan Society Headquarters and Ming's, both built in 1920, are examples of his work that can still be seen today; the latter has been extensively altered over the years. Another extant building is the present Ming Wo store on East Pender Street, 1914.

Chow's search for professional qualifications was elusive. He was involved with the British Columbia Society of Architects, and was listed as an architect and patron in their 1913 Year Book; interestingly he did not show up in the list of members. In the early 1920s Chow worked jointly with **W.T. Whiteway** on several buildings in the Chinatown area. On June 7, 1921, Chow was refused admission to the newly-incorporated Architectural Institute of B.C. Concerns were expressed about his joint role as contractor and architect, and ultimately, "Council [was] of the opinion that [the] applicant has not had sufficient technical training and must sit for examination." Given the discrimination against Orientals, it strains credibility to imagine how anyone not from the United Kingdom, the United States, or Eastern Canada could ever have been accepted as an architect at the time.

Henderson's *Vancouver Directory*, 1908

CLAUDE PERCY JONES

BORN 1879

DONALD LUXTON

Claude Jones was born in Kensington, London, England in 1879, the son of William John and Eliza Jones. Educated at North London College, he commenced his career as a civil engineer in his father's office, later taking up architecture. By 1906 he had immigrated to Canada, and by 1908 was established in Vernon. A surviving commission from this period for W. Scott-Allan, at Hughes Road, Vernon, 1908, is a shingle-clad ranch house designed with a deep encircling verandah that responds to the local climate. By 1909 Jones was located in Vancouver, where his career had some import. The brick-faced Pendrell Apartments in the West End is a lovely surviving example of his work. One prominent project was the Stock Judging Pavilion at Hastings Park, built in 1911. Large and utilitarian, the Pavilion was dressed with *Beaux-Arts* elements, including an imposing portico with paired columns, originally designed to hold a grand quadriga, which was never constructed. This wooden structure was demolished to make way for the much larger concrete and steel Livestock Building designed by **McCarter & Nairne**, 1939.

Jones was briefly associated with **W.C.F. Gillam** in 1911, and then went into partnership with J. Drummond Beatson from 1912-15. In 1913 they prepared plans for the competition for a new school and were awarded first prize. Its first official name was Point Grey High School, and was briefly re-named King George V School, but was always known as Magee due to its proximity to Magee station on the Interurban Line, and was officially re-named again in 1926-27. Magee School, with its imposing Classical Revival facade, was their largest commission; it was demolished in the late 1990s by the Vancouver School Board and replaced with a bland new building. In early 1914, Jones & Beatson prepared the plans for a new St. Barnabas church in Victoria, which was never built. As work dwindled with the outbreak of war, Jones left the city after 1915, and Beatson disappeared after 1918.

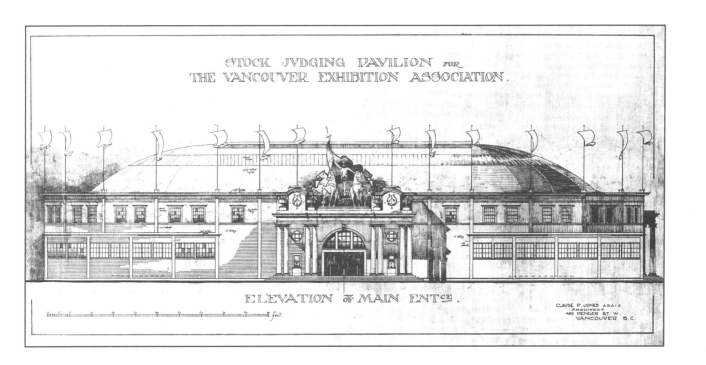

NORMAN
AUSTIN
LEECH
BORN 1880

DONALD LUXTON

Like a number of others who roved the Colonies looking for opportunities, Leech settled briefly in British Columbia during the boom years. He was born in Winburg, Orange Free State Colony, South Africa on April 18, 1880, the son of John Richard and Julia Emma Leech. Young Norman was educated in England, first at St. Leo's College, Clocolan, and then King's College, University of London, where he was awarded the gold medal for Architecture in his final year. He briefly lectured on architecture and building construction at the Technical Institute in Norwich before relocating to Johannesburg, where he practised 1902-06. In 1906 he uprooted again and moved to Vancouver. He worked for several years in the large and busy office of **Thomas Hooper**, and in 1909 was successful in attaining the position of consulting architect to the Vancouver School Board. In the following years Leech was a very active man. In addition to his position with the School Board, he took on private projects, and served as Vancouver's Commissioner for Building Bylaws. For recreation, he enjoyed reading, walking and motoring.

His connection with the School Board proved fortuitous. Vancouver's population growth during the boom years was explosive, and the School Board was trying to catch up to the demand for new facilities. During his three years with the Board, Leech was called upon to design and supervise nine large brick schools and a number of smaller ancillary buildings. He met this challenge by developing a standardized plan for the larger buildings, with optional projecting end wings that could be added when extra classrooms were needed. These buildings reflected the rationalist tendencies of *Beaux-Arts* planning, including a symmetrical and harmonious facade

expression. Typical of these were General Gordon School in Kitsilano, 1911-12, a utilitarian red and yellow brick structure with banked windows and minimal detailing, and the original portion of Hastings School, 1912, an eight room school in a T-shaped plan on Franklin Street near Hastings Park.

Leech also played a key role in the professional organization of the province's architects. The establishment of the Royal Architectural Institute of Canada revived the moribund idea of a local organization in British Columbia. On January 29, 1909 a small group of architects, calling themselves the British Columbia Association of Architects, met to look into the formation of a provincial association of architects, and **Francis Rattenbury** was elected as their President. An entertainment committee was appointed, including Leech, **W.H. Archer**, and **T. Ennor Julian**, to set up a 'smoker' early in February to bring potential members together. By October 1911, the B.C. Society of Architects had been firmly established, with separate chapters in Vancouver and Victoria. Leech served as President of the Vancouver group, and was the first President when the two chapters amalgamated in early 1912. At their first convention held in Victoria in June 1912, **Hoult Horton** was elected President, and Norman Leech Vice-President.

The local economy was buoyant in 1912, and Leech landed the commission for a seven storey hotel proposed for the corner of Burrard and Dunsmuir Streets in downtown Vancouver. Leech left his position with the School Board, and opened his own office on Pender Street. Although construction started on the mammoth hotel, the economy collapsed and it was never completed. It was then announced that Leech was preparing plans for a large shipyard for an English syndicate on the North Arm of the Fraser River, but after the outbreak of the First World War, Leech disappeared from the local scene, and appears to have ended up in Los Angeles.

Hastings School, Vancouver

HENRY SANDHAM **GRIFFITH**

1865-1943

DONALD LUXTON

After his arrival in Canada, H.S. Griffith opened architectural offices successively in Winnipeg and Saskatoon before moving to British Columbia. During the boom years he maintained large and successful offices in both Victoria and Vancouver, and trained many young architects who were just arriving in Canada. Griffith's approach was flexible and diverse, and although he was accomplished in the traditional styles of architecture, by the end of his career he was flirting with the new modernist styles then in vogue.

Born in Aston Vicarage, Oxford, England on June 5, 1865, he was the son of Julia Robberds and Rev. George Sandham

Griffith. Young Henry attended Roysse's School, Abingdon, Berkshire, and Christ Church College, Oxford, and was articled to Webb & Tubb, Reading, Berkshire, from 1882-85. In 1886 he was articled as a draftsman to T.H. Watson, District Surveyor, London. In the spring of 1887, at the age of twenty-one, he moved to Winnipeg, where he worked in the Northern Pacific Railway engineers' office, and later in the Provincial Land Titles office. In 1890 he married Marie Jane Hall, originally from Yorkshire but then living in Kenora, Ontario. He officially began his practice as an architect in 1893. The Griffiths had four children, Eva, George, Alice and Jack, born between 1900 and 1908. Although successful in Winnipeg, like many others he felt the lure of the West, moving first to Saskatoon in 1906, where he designed Alexandra School and the Butler Block, and then on to Victoria in 1907. He bought a grand house in 1909, the first in the new Reservoir Hill subdivision in Victoria, and was soon working on the commission for the Times Building on Fort Street.

By 1910 Griffith had opened a second office in Vancouver. For the remainder of the boom era he maintained a successful practice in both cities, undertaking all types of commissions, from skyscrapers to palatial residences for his wealthy clients. Griffith was retained by the provincial government to prepare the working drawings and specifications for the Male Chronic Wing at the new provincial asylum in Coquitlam, based on the winning competition entry of **J.C.M. Keith**. This enormous building was under construction from 1911-13, during which time Griffith was also designing the matching Female Chronic Wing, destined never to be built. Henry Esson Young, Provincial Secretary and Minister of Education, was respon-

Times Building, Victoria

Landsberg Residence, Victoria

YMCA, Victoria

sible for the asylum, and, obviously impressed with Griffith's work, retained him to design his own home in Victoria in 1911.

Griffith was now riding the crest of the greatest economic boom yet seen in western Canada. One of his most prominent buildings was the Board of Trade Building in Vancouver, 1912. Nine storeys high, clad in brick and terra cotta, this graceful structure epitomizes the restrained and sophisticated Edwardian response to the Classical Revival styles. Typical of the buildings influenced by the Chicago School, it is articulated into three horizontal sections. Anchored with a stone base, the brick-clad shaft soars to a two-storey cap of terra cotta and an overarching cornice. In 1912, his office submitted an entry to the competition for the new University

YMCA, Vancouver

of British Columbia, but was rejected by the assessors on the basis that the design was "pseudo-Gothic of an essentially American type" and therefore unsuitable.

Griffith's prominent clients included Dominion Trust, for whom he designed a waterfront project in Victoria that was never realized. In New Westminster, one of his projects was the landmark Cliff Block, 1910-11. He designed grand new YMCA buildings in both Vancouver and Victoria, both now demolished. Other commercial commissions in Victoria included a charming structure for the Sweeney & McConnell printing company, 1910, with piers decorated with terra cotta lions' heads, the six-storey Empress Building, 1911, faced with cream coloured terra cotta, and the Fairfield Hotel, 1912. For Mr. Stobart, a British investor, and A.J Pease, proprietor of the Hamsterly Farm Jam Company and Tea Room, Griffith designed the Stobart-Pease Building, a five-storey structure on Yates Street clad with terra cotta from Gladding, McBean & Company in Lincoln, California. At the height of his practice in 1913, Griffith could count up $3,000,000 worth of buildings underway at one time, with up to twelve people working in his Victoria office, and seven in Vancouver.

In 1912, Griffith, now established as one of the fashionable architects, could afford to build his own grand home in Victoria. The site he chose was a rocky outcrop with a panoramic view of the city. Known for his use of stone in other houses, here Griffith went wild, building himself a miniature castle, complete with a square castellated turret. Known as *Fort Garry*, the house and associated gardens took two years to complete. Griffith meticulously planned every inch of the house and grounds, including designs for the layout of the planting beds and window boxes. Forced by the wartime recession to close his Victoria office, Griffith was unable to hold onto the property. "I think that when he had to sell *Fort Garry*, part of him died, because that was his life's dream," recalled his daughter Alice. The estate was sold in 1918 to David Spencer Jr., whose family lived there for fifty years. It survives today and is popularly known as *Spencer's Castle*.

The collapse of the Western boom effectively ended Griffith's career as a major architect. Although he remained active, larger commissions eluded him. Until retirement he maintained a modest output of smaller but sophisticated structures, such as the T. Edwards Undertaking Parlour, 1928, on Vancouver's Granville Street, and Fumerton's Department Store, Kelowna, 1933. His work represented a flexible approach to the issue of style. For Mrs. B.A.A. Furber, he designed a traditional English manor house in West Vancouver in 1940. Two commissions were for apartment blocks in Vancouver's West End, 1941, the Chatsworth and the Barrymore, impressive examples of modernism, rendered simply but effectively, given the constraints of the wartime economy. Griffith died on October 18, 1943, survived by his wife and three children.

Project for the Dominion Trust Building, Victoria

Project for the St. Regis Hotel, Victoria

DANIEL BOWDEN EGDELL

1883-1967

DONALD LUXTON

D.B. Egdell was one of those involved in the building trades who occupied the middle ground between architect and builder, when such distinctions were more blurred than they are today. Born in Jesmond, Newcastle-on-Tyne on August 20, 1883, he immigrated to Canada on April 20, 1904, accompanied by his cousin Charles Gordon Bowden. Both young men had served their full time as apprentices in the building trades, Egdell with Elliot Brothers in Jesmond – where there would "always be a job waiting" if he ever returned – and Bowden with Lowry of Gateshead. In a letter to his mother, Egdell wrote that on his twenty-first birthday he was working with Bowden on a farm in Ontario "spreading muck." From there they made

Young Daniel Egdell

their way west, at one time finding work escorting Chinese labourers across Canada to work on railway construction.

They settled in Vancouver, and Egdell began work as a contractor. Egdell travelled to Nanaimo to supervise several building projects. His first trip there was on November 15, 1911, and on this trip he met Agnes Bradshaw Glaholm, a talented amateur singer, and daughter of the first white girl born in Nanaimo; the Glaholm family were successful and well-connected local merchants. Daniel and Agnes were married on July 30, 1912. His wife's sister, Florrie, married William Sloan, a prominent merchant who left Nanaimo for the Klondike, where he made the second largest fortune of the Gold Rush on Eldorado Creek. Sloan later became the provincial Minister of Mines, and son Gordon Sloan later served as Attorney-General.

By this time Vancouver's economy was booming, and Egdell had entered into a partnership with Robert Dixon. Their contracting business was extremely successful; they were responsible for many prominent buildings including Delta Municipal Hall in Ladner, 1912, designed by **Archibald Campbell Hope**. Their Vancouver buildings included a number of Shaughnessy mansions designed by **Maclure & Fox**. During the war, poor economic conditions caused upheavals in the partnership; as a result of financial mismanagement Dixon fled the city. Egdell was left to deal with the bankruptcy, and the payment of creditors. He kept a diary during this time which he called his "Black Book," but later destroyed it because he didn't want to remember such troubled times. Egdell moved back to Nanaimo, and reestablished himself both as a designer and builder. He was responsible for the design of the Parkin Block on Commercial Street, 1922. In 1932 he renovated a small residence into a charming Classical Revival Christian Science Building. Throughout this time Egdell signed his plans as an architect, although he never registered with the AIBC, and was technically in violation of their statutes. His practice, essentially a design-build operation, was prominent, but seems to have escaped the Institute's notice.

In 1927 Egdell made contact with the infamous cult leader Brother XII, who was moving from England to Nanaimo to establish the headquarters of his Aquarian Foundation. As Brother XII and his entourage descended the gangplank of the *Princess Louise*, they were noticed by Egdell, who struck up a conversation with what he assumed to be a group of lost English travellers. He helped them find a hotel for the night, and when he found out that Brother XII needed a place to stay, he arranged for him to rent a small house in nearby Northfield. In short order 126 acres of land were acquired for the Aquarian Foundation at Cedar-by-the-Sea, now known as Yellow Point, nine miles south of Nanaimo. Egdell was hired as the designer and contractor for the structures on the site, including the Centre Building and Brother XII's secluded House of Mystery,

Daniel Egdell on left, with Clare and Charles Bowden
on their honeymoon trip to Vernon, 1907

where he retreated to communicate with the "Masters of Wisdom." The ill-fated spiritual colony was mired in allegations of sexual misconduct and black magic, and Brother XII narrowly avoided legal investigation by fleeing to Europe in 1932, reportedly with half a ton of gold coins.

Egdell designed and built a fanciful storybook cottage in Nanaimo for his only son, Jack, and daughter-in-law, Dolly, after their marriage in October 1939. The following year Daniel and Agnes moved into the house when Jack and Dolly moved to Atlin. He enlarged the house, making a small suite

out of a garage, and continued to live there for many years. He occasionally worked as a draftsman in **Thomas B. McArravy's** office when there was enough work, but gave this up due to the strain on his eyesight. Agnes died on July 30, 1959 on their forty-seventh wedding anniversary. Egdell later suffered from cancer and moved to Vancouver to be near his son's family. He was acquainted with the Bentall family, and was a friend of archivist, Major J.S. Matthews. Daniel Egdell died in Vancouver, June 12, 1967, at the age of eighty-three, and his ashes were interred beside his wife in Nanaimo Cemetery.

Horne Residence, Nanaimo

FRANK WILLIAM MACEY
1863-1935

JIM WOLF

Very little is known of the early life of this talented architect and author, who was born in London, England in 1863. Frank W. Macey's fame in England stemmed from his authorship of two standard texts for the architectural profession. Spon & Chamberlain published Macey's first book, *Specifications in Detail*, in 1898 in London. Macey compiled this book "in the hope that it may be found useful as a reference book for Architects." It set out a standard language for architects to describe architectural specifications suitable for building tenders. Macey followed this book with another reference text, *Conditions of Contract*, published in 1902 by Sweet & Maxwell of London. It also provided architects with a standard language for contracts and legal agreements relating to the architectural profession. These reference works were found in most architects' libraries in England for decades after their first appearance. It is likely that Macey derived more income from his book royalties than from his architectural practice in London.

Macey met Anna Constance Fulner about 1900 while she was in London studying at a finishing school. She had been educated in Switzerland and could speak seven languages. Anna was born in Sweden, but had been raised by an aunt in Finland, then under rule by the Russian Czar. Macey, determined to marry this talented and beautiful woman, had to seek permission from the Russian government, which was finally granted in 1906. With little work in hand, the young couple decided to immigrate to Australia and travelled there via Canada. They arrived in Vancouver to visit with the Peers family, old friends and recent immigrants to B.C., who had set up a new home near Burnaby Lake. The Maceys were so impressed with the surrounding countryside that they immediately abandoned plans to travel further and bought acreage nearby.

In 1907, Macey opened an architectural office in Vancouver and instantly received national press attention for his unique style. The *Canadian Architect & Builder* reported that Macey had "introduced a style of exterior house finish and decoration that is new in Vancouver." The residence for Mr. J.R. Waghorn and Macey's own house, both in the West End, were finished in "English half-timber work, the lower part being roughcast stucco… with overhanging gables the verandahs being kept under the main roof." Although half-timbered houses were not new to British Columbia, Macey's employment of roughcast stucco as an exterior finish was unique for the time.

Macey became the first resident architect of Burnaby, and also located in the neighbourhood that became known as "Burnaby's Shaughnessy." Several prominent commissions from his friends and neighbours at Burnaby Lake soon resulted. His first major client was the New Westminster-based realtor F. J. Hart, who contracted Macey to design his splendid mansion *Avalon* on the north shore of Deer Lake. This home, designed in the Tudor style, sported a tower and mock battlements, and is now open to the public as the Hart House restaurant. Nearby, Hart was developing the Deer Lake Crescent subdivision. When he sold two properties to friends, he also introduced them to the talents of Frank Macey. The William J. Mathers home *Altnadene*, like Hart's mansion, featured a tower with battlements and an exterior treatment of roughcast stucco. The house next door, built for Robert F.

Anderson Residence, Burnaby

Altnadene, Burnaby

Anderson, featured a more refined exterior of wood siding with half-timbered gables.

Macey's talent was noticed by another Burnaby resident, Walter J. Walker, a wealthy philanthropist. In 1911, Walker chose to assist the New Westminster Diocese of the Anglican Church in establishing a presence in the growing suburban residential area of Surrey. Macey was commissioned to design St. Oswald's in Port Kells, and St. Helen's, built on a spectacular site on Yale Road overlooking the Fraser Delta. This commission was the pinnacle of Macey's career and a monument to his tremendous talent. The exterior employs his signature roughcast stucco in elaborate design on the towers and gable decoration. Macey's unmistakable British Arts and Crafts design sensibility is seen in the interior woodwork and furnishing, which combine to produce an awe-inspiring space for worship.

Macey was dealt a significant financial blow when his newly completed house on Douglas Road was destroyed by fire in 1913, just as the local depression hit. Destitute, and without an income, he was forced to sell the property at a considerable financial loss. In order that Macey and his family – which by this time included sons, Rolf and Norman – could stay in the community, his neighbours, the Sprotts and the Schous, deeded him a parcel of land. The Maceys survived the depression and the despair of the First World War, with Anna using her linguistic talents as an interpreter with Canada's War Department. Frank Macey applied to the Architectural Institute of B.C. for registration in 1920. From the complete absence of any known commissions at the time, it appears that he was not able to practice architecture with the success he had previously enjoyed. He died in his summer home at Deep Cove at the age of seventy-two in 1935, and Anna died in 1949. The Municipality of Burnaby purchased the Macey's Burnaby property in 1971 and demolished their cottage. In 1993 the City renamed the property Macey Park in their honour.

St. Helen's Anglican Church, Surrey

HENRY BARTON WATSON

1869-1946

DAVID MONTEYNE

Although H.B. Watson was only active in the Lower Mainland for a brief period, he left a distinguished architectural mark. Born in England on August 9, 1869, he was articled to Austin, Johnson & Hicks in London, and opened his own office in Newcastle-on-Tyne from 1902 until 1907, during which time his younger brother, **Joseph F. Watson**, apprenticed with him. He immigrated to B.C. in 1907, and his brother followed two years later. Henry began his local career with the design of several large apartment buildings, including an extant gem in downtown Vancouver known as the Florence Court (now Banff) Apartments, 1909, originally designed with bulbous onion-domed turrets. He followed this with a string of building commissions won in competition, including Queen Alexandra School, 1908; a fire hall in Grandview; and the Industrial Building, 1909-10, at Hastings Park for the newly-formed Vancouver Exhibition Association. This large exhibition and display hall, at the centre of which stood a "fairy fountain" created with water jets and lighting, was overlooked by a broad, interior balcony or mezzanine. Inspired by World's Fair architecture with its eclectic array of four towers, steel and glass *cul-de-fours*, and exotic ornamentation, the Industrial Building became the fair's iconic building. Unfortunately, the Association built it quickly and cheaply, and the building had to be torn down in the 1930s. Twin towers in a Renaissance Revival style framed the facade of Watson's 1909 St. Patrick's Roman Catholic Church at 12th Avenue and Main Street. His Kitsilano Presbyterian Church, 1910, featured sandstone detailing and a entry colon-nade with giant order columns. In 1909-10, Watson worked in the offices of the B.C. Electric Railway, and designed five mas-sive concrete substations for them located in Cloverdale, Langley, Clayburn, Sumas and Chilliwack along the Fraser Valley line. With circular feature windows in the top storeys, balustrades, small pediments, and the massing of Renaissance *palazzi*, Watson gave these buildings a sense of grandeur and made them landmarks in their communities. In late 1923 he moved to Los Angeles, and continued to prac-vtice until retirement in 1935. He died in Los Angeles on February 4, 1946.

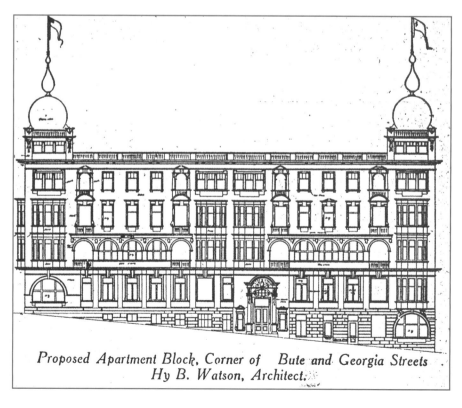

Proposed Apartment Block, Corner of Bute and Georgia Streets Hy B. Watson, Architect.

BCER Substation, Chilliwack

St. Patrick's Roman Catholic Church, Vancouver

RICHARD THOMAS PERRY
B.1884

FIONA AVAKUMOVIC

Richard Thomas Perry, a native of Cardiff, Wales, came to Canada in 1907. He gave his new country several lasting landmarks and a legacy of military leadership. Born on November 28, 1884, Perry left school at fifteen to train in architects' offices. He also spent two years sketching in France, Germany and Italy. After a brief practice in Cardiff, he immigrated to Vancouver with his wife, Dora Olive Scaldwell. During this period, Perry was involved in two partnerships, first with Raphael A. Nicolais, 1911-12, with whom he designed the Sam Kee Hotel, 1911. The second partnership was with **C.B. Fowler**, with whom Perry designed the City of Vancouver's Old People's Home, 1914 and a log and stone Arts and Crafts mansion in Point Grey for James Cashman, 1914.

During the First World War Perry served in the artillery and then, after being poisoned in a gas attack, in England under the Director of Fortifications and Works as the resident engineer for aerodrome construction. In 1919, Captain Perry, freshly returned from war duties, was one of the organizers of the militia artillery in Vancouver, and was asked to design an ideal drill hall. The design went through numerous permutations and the location was changed several times, culminating in 1928 with plans for a grand structure in the heart of Kerrisdale, but it proved too costly, and the plans were scaled back for a concrete structure in Kitsilano, started in 1932. Called the Bessborough Armoury, it was officially opened in 1934, giving a modernistic look to the home of the British Columbia Hussars and the 15th Field Brigade Canadian Artillery, which Perry by this time commanded as he devoted more of his energy to the military.

Other projects epitomize Perry's engaging strength in combining nostalgic British influences with more modern forms. He designed an Arts & Crafts-influenced hall for the Dunbar Heights United Church, 1926, that now serves as its Christian Education Centre. A hospital pavilion for tuberculosis patients at Shaughnessy Hospital, c.1926, was a rambling structure that was more domestic than institutional in scale. The townhouse complex of Tatlow Court, 1927-28, combined the popular California Bungalow with the romantic image of a Tudor village, complete with an Arts and Crafts-style lych gate leading to a communal lawn. The first scheme for the project had been designed by **Frank Mountain** in a purely Spanish style in 1926. When the project passed to him, Perry retained the courtyard apartment form, but reverted to a purely Tudor Revival idiom. Perry worked on several projects in the late 1920s in association with Scottish-born **Robert Claud Kerr**, including two well-preserved religious buildings, the Second Church of Christ Scientist in Vancouver, 1926, in that faith's preferred Classical Revival idiom, and Ryerson United Church, 1927-28, in a slightly modernized version of the traditional Gothic Revival style. In 1929 Perry designed the brick and terra cotta Randall Building, a restored downtown Vancouver landmark on Georgia Street. Perry also designed a number of large apartment blocks in Vancouver during the late 1920s.

Though he resigned his membership in the AIBC in 1930, no doubt for financial reasons, Perry maintained his identity as an architect. In the Vancouver *Province* in 1935, he denounced the proposal by his former employer, **Fred Townley**, for Vancouver City Hall, saying it resembled "a few packing cases of assorted sizes stacked together – certainly not a work of art and obviously not something that has been designed." Perry, in line with the opinion of the AIBC, advocated a competition to give the many out-of-work B.C. architects the chance to land the commission, and he worried that the nation-wide publication of the City Hall design would result in a flood of migrant architects wanting to fill the void of talent in Vancouver. Shortly after, Perry left Vancouver for Great Britain, and never returned.

Bessborough Armoury, Vancouver

CHARLES ARCHIBALD BRODERICK

1885-1953

JENNY COWELL

The legacy of an architect born in South Africa, educated in England, professionally trained and employed in England and in Canada, continues to be very much a part of everyday Trail life in the twenty-first century. Charles Archibald "Archie" Broderick was born December 18, 1885 in Kimberley, South Africa, to English parents. He received his architectural and civil engineering education during the years 1899-1903 at the Brighton Technical College and the Brighton College of Art at Sussex, England. Broderick then articled from 1903-07 to John Blackman, an Architect and Civil Engineer in Brighton, and became Blackman's chief assistant. During this time he designed many private residences and stores, and also assisted with the design and supervision of a theatre and hotel, all on the south coast of England.

In 1907, Broderick immigrated to Canada and likely through a Blackman family connection settled in Trail, B.C. There, in August, he commenced practising as an architect. From 1908-12 Broderick was articled to Surveyor John Drummond Anderson. While with Anderson, Broderick had charge of designing a new city water works system; the design and construction of an irrigation system for the Birchbrook Orchards, owned by the Consolidated Mining & Smelting Company (Cominco); and the location and surveying of wagon roads for the provincial government. During 1911-12 he was assistant resident engineer supervising construction of the Columbia River bridge at Trail. Broderick received his commission as a B.C. Land Surveyor in 1917, and in 1920 applied for registration with the Architectural Institute of B.C.

Broderick designed many commercial and industrial buildings in Trail, almost exclusively of brick, replacing false-front wooden buildings dating from the turn of the nineteenth century. Broderick's designs were straight-forward and boxy, usually with shallow pilasters, simple cornices, and peaked parapets. He was retained as an architect by the Municipality of Trail, the Trail District School Board, the Fruitvale District School Board and Cominco. His most prominent buildings in Trail were Memorial Hall [Legion], 1919; Knights of Pythias, 1922; Trail Tadanac High School, 1922; Fire Hall, 1923; Trail Tadanac Hospital, 1926; Cristoforo Columbo Lodge, 1927; Trail City Hall, 1928; and the Union Hotel of 1939. Except for the hospital and the Memorial Hall, these, as well as many of his private residences, stores, warehouses and garages, still stand. For Cominco, Broderick designed several industrial structures, including a wartime munitions plant in Tadanac, 1915; bath house, change building, and drying building in Kimberley, 1918; additions in brick, concrete and steel to the copper refinery in Trail, 1918; and machine and electrical buildings in Tadanac, 1919. He was also engaged by the Company on the design of a steel and concrete building for a proposed ore concentrating mill at Tadanac.

In 1914 Archie Broderick married Margery, John Blackman's daughter, in Rossland. They had no children, but Margery ran a kindergarten, and also taught art and drawing. Broderick was reported to have been a keen rifleman, and was noted for his watercolour paintings. He was forced to retire from architecture in 1940 due to arthritis, and he died in February 15, 1953, aged sixty-seven. He was buried in Trail's Mountain View Cemetery, which he also designed.

Knights of Pythias Hall, Trail

ROSS ANTHONY LORT

1889-1968

CATHERINE BARFORD

Ross Lort began work in the thriving architectural practice of **Samuel Maclure** on May 11, 1907. He and his father had arrived in Victoria from England on the S.S. *Charmer* via Vancouver just two days before and the young Lort had been hired by Maclure the day after they landed. However, when the newly arrived seventeen-year old arrived for work that morning, he soon learned, much to his chagrin, that he would be by himself because all the rest of the staff had contracted the measles! Those first days were very difficult as he tried on his own to assuage demanding owners and contractors alike. After this rough start, Maclure took a parental interest in the young draftsman, and Lort would go on to a sixty-year career in architecture, designing some of British Columbia's most familiar houses, apartments, institutions and places of worship, as well as playing a significant role in the arts in B.C.

Lort was born October 4, 1889 in Birmingham, England. He attended King Edward VI Grammar School, Birmingham from 1899-1903 and Bishop Vesey's Grammar School, Sutton Coldfield from 1903-06, where he was awarded the prize for drawing. After a year at Vickers Maxim (Engineering) in Birmingham, Ross Lort and his father, John Anthony Lort, a skilled cabinetmaker, came to Victoria in advance of Ross's mother and sisters. They chose Victoria because it was more or less midway on the Pacific Coast between San Francisco, which was rebuilding after the 1906 earthquake, and Prince Rupert, which had been inspected by surveyors and engineers in May 1906 in anticipation of becoming the western terminus of the Grand Trunk Pacific Railway.

Given that Maclure, **Rattenbury** and **Hooper** all had offices in the Five Sisters Block, it is not impossible that matters might have turned out quite differently for the young Lort had he been hired by one of these other architects on that day. That

Lort Residence, Oak Bay

A Cottage at OAK BAY VICTORIA B.C. ROSS. A. LORT des. et del.

said, the remarkable environment of Maclure's office was a providential choice. Maclure surrounded himself with capable people, read widely and remained on good terms with his professional colleagues. Clients with means were drawn to him, and the fortunate students in his office received excellent experience in how to maintain an architectural practice.

Among the many talented, young designers who were attracted to Maclure's office was Cecil Croker Fox, who had worked for the noted exponent of the Arts and Crafts movement, C.F.A. Voysey. It was decided to establish a Vancouver office of Maclure & Fox, with Fox in charge. By 1910, Lort was assisting in the Vancouver office. Later, he would speak of taking the Kitsilano streetcar to its terminus "at the west end of the playground" and then walking along Point Grey Road, 4th Avenue, 2nd Avenue and Trimble to inspect the grand mansion built for J.S. Rear, known today as *Aberthau*.

On July 22, 1913, Ross Lort married Cecilia Marion Frances Rolston, daughter of Williams G. Michell Rolston and Marion Dixon Rolston. Lort designed a Chalet-style cottage in Oak Bay, Victoria, with a stucco finish reminiscent of the British Arts & Craft movement, as their first family home. In August, 1916, Ross Lort enlisted with the Canadian Army Service Corps and the following year transferred to the 8th Battalion, Canadian Railway Troops, serving in France and Belgium. He returned to architectural practice in June 1919.

On Lort's 1920 AIBC membership application, he stated that, "The ability to make my office pay during the past eighteen months" was, apart from professional education, evidence of being competent to practice as an architect. Despite substantial projects like the Gibson House in Oak Bay, it was clear that there was insufficient work for both Maclure and Lort in Victoria and it was decided that Lort would return to Vancouver. The practice would mostly handle residential architecture. Lort also established a brief partnership with **William F. Jones**, 1924-25. With the death of Samuel Maclure in 1929, Wallace Deffett returned from New York to assume his Victoria practice and Ross Lort assumed the Vancouver practice in his own name.

Woodcuts from *All Creatures Great and Small*, 1931

The renown for Maclure's, and later Lort's, superior residential design, evolved into a similar recognition for apartment design which, from the early 1930s on, would become an increasingly valuable part of the practice. The earlier examples were of brick in the Art Deco style, which gave a sense of modernity, quality and security, and displayed Lort's strong sense of appropriate design. Detailing was consistent throughout and the lobbies, stairways, halls and suites were welcoming and generous. Significant examples from this period include two apartments in the West End, the Queen Anne Garden Apartments on Nelson Street, 1930, and the Park Lane Apartments on Chilco, 1931.

As the practice expanded, Ross Lort continued to design distinctive houses. In 1932, he displayed his stylistic versatility with a Spanish Colonial Revival design for *Casa Mia*, a grand mansion for George C. Reifel. In 1936, Lort designed 3846 West 10th Avenue for H.G. and Elza Barber. Cathy Maclure commented that her father had hoped to work with concrete and it must have been particularly interesting for Lort to work with H.G. Barber on this project. A civil engineer, Barber had begun working for the CPR in 1900 and in 1910 was appointed Assistant Chief Engineer, Western Construction. The Barber residence remains one of the most striking houses in the city. It is an excellent example of the Streamline Moderne style, a two-storey poured concrete cube with square-notched corners, rounded balcony edges and a corrugated panel above the front door. Another unusual project was a beauty school in the West End, 1938, for Madame Maxine, designed in the Spanish Colonial Revival style. In 1952, Lort renovated the family home, originally designed by **Fred Townley** in 1912, and the results, which showed the quality of design, practicality and livability which his clients sought, were published in *Western Homes & Living* as "Old House – New Look." During the Second World War, Ross Lort was asked to design a military hospital in Terrace, in preparation for casualties from an expected confrontation in the Northern Pacific. The experience prepared him to design other hospitals, such as the first Western Society Physical Rehabilitation Centre, 1948. Innovative at the time, it is better known today as the substantially larger G.F. Strong Rehabilitation Centre.

Like other architects of his day, Lort was very active in the local arts scene. In 1923, he joined the Vancouver Little Theatre, which had been founded in 1921. Although he did appear on stage, he is best remembered as the long-time scenic director, collaborating on many occasions with fellow architect, **H.H. Simmonds**. Lort was an honorary governor of the Dominion Drama Festival and received the Canadian Drama Award for his outstanding contribution to Canadian Drama. Continuing to sketch, paint, and make woodcuts and linocuts, he participated in sketching parties beginning in the late 1920s with Group of Seven members Jock MacDonald, Fred Varley, and others into areas like the Black Tusk Meadows. He explored and painted Lulu Island and the B.C. Interior and took the urban city for his subject as well. Lort was elected to the B.C. Society of Fine Arts in 1931, served on its Executive from 1933-37 and was President from 1945-48, later being elected Life Member. Some of his work, like the enchanting abecedarian *All Creatures Great and Small*, self-published in 1931, reveals quite another side of his talents. Much later, in 1946, Lort was elected to the Founding Board of the Community Arts Council of Vancouver which was established to "increase and broaden opportunities for Vancouver citizens to enjoy and participate in cultural activities." Among the artists and supporters elected to the Board were Lawren Harris, Patrick Keatley, Dr. Norman Mackenzie, H.R. MacMillan, Frank Ross, Jean Russell, Charles Scott and Albert Steinberg.

In 1932, Ross Lort was elected to the Council of the recently-opened Vancouver Art Gallery (VAG). **G.L. Thornton Sharp**, the Gallery's architect, was already a member and would remain so until 1940. From time to time Lort chaired the Educational and House and Library Committees. In 1945, VAG Council members Lort, W.H. Malkin, and Lawren Harris were appointed to a "New Building Committee" to explore expanding the Gallery to accommodate the late Emily Carr's bequest of her work. In 1950 Lort designed the major additions that completely erased the facade of the original Art Deco structure, and despite changes necessitated by a tight budget, the result was a highly successful resolution of a difficult programme, presenting clean and logical forms that became the new face of the Gallery on prominent West Georgia Street. This modernist landmark became redundant when the VAG moved to **Rattenbury's** Court House in 1983, and has sadly been demolished.

Ross Lort's practice expanded to include churches. After **K.B. Spurgin's** untimely death in 1936, Lort was hired to design several buildings at the Prince of Wales Fairbridge Farm School near Duncan, and in 1939 provided the designs for the school's chapel. Lort's original design was altered when submitted by the Fairbridge Society to renowned English architect, Sir Herbert Baker (1862-1946), who had designed the first Fairbridge Chapel at Pinjarra, Western Australia; during his illustrious career Baker designed the Union Buildings and Government House in Pretoria, South Africa, at the instigation of Cecil Rhodes, and with Sir Edwin Lutyens designed a number of the government buildings in New Delhi, India. Baker suggested the addition of the apsidal sanctuary to give the Chapel "a sense of spaciousness, dignity and beauty, with the five coloured windows to be a 'crowning light' above the alter and the clerestory windows to reveal the beauty of the timber construction of the nave roof, and the heightening and stepping back of the tower." The redesigned chapel was dedicated on April 20, 1940, and still stands today. Among many other churches, Lort was responsible in Vancouver for Augustana Lutheran Church, 1947; Ebenezer Baptist Church, 1954; additions to the Schara Tzedeck Synagogue, 1955 (originally designed by John Harvey, 1947); and St. Matthias Anglican, 1959. In 1958, to celebrate the Centennial of British Columbia, the Royal Architectural Institute of Canada produced a special edition of the *Journal* to which Ross Lort was asked to contribute a feature article about Samuel Maclure. In 1959, Lort's entered into partnership with his youngest son, Williams ("Bill"), a graduate of the Universities of British Columbia and Manitoba. The senior Lort continued to practice architecture until about a year before his death on May 16, 1968. He is commemorated by an oak plaque in St. Paul's Anglican Church in Vancouver's West End.

I think that I have only entered into a signed agreement with a client four times in my forty years of practice. I have always held to the fact that as a member of a learned profession there is a code that is respected on both sides. I don't ask my lawyer or my doctor how much he is going to charge me... even today, with several of my clients, it is customary when the terms are stated to look each other in the face, shake hands and that is all the contract necessary.

Letter to the AIBC, March 17, 1960.

Vancouver Art Gallery, Vancouver

DOUGLAS JAMES
1888-1962

Douglas James (signature)

ROSEMARY JAMES CROSS

Douglas James was one of two English-born and trained brothers who had a substantial impact on British Columbia architecture. Born in London, England, March 17, 1888, from 1902-05 he articled to L.E. Godfrey Page, London, and then became assistant to architect John Slater, Vice-President of the Royal Institute of British Architects. James was a student of the Royal Academy, and in 1904 obtained a First Class Certificate for Architectural Design from the South Kensington Board of Education. During this period he also attended evening classes at Regent Street Polytechnic.

In 1907 James left England for Victoria, where his first job in his new city was with **Samuel Maclure** as draftsman and assistant on *Hatley Park*. Between 1907-09, he completed 248 working drawings for the castle, and also undertook several site inspections per week. As a student in England, Douglas James had measured up the famous country house, *Compton Wynyates*, and the knowledge he gained about such construction was of much use in the building of *Hatley Park*.

After the completion of this large work, he joined his brother, **P. Leonard James**, in the James & James partnership formed in 1910. The family lived in Oak Bay and the brothers received several commissions from the municipality, some of which were early wooden school buildings, now demolished. The chief of these commissions was the Oak Bay Municipal Hall, 1912, which stood at the corner of Hampshire and Oak Bay Avenue, also now demolished. The brothers designed the first St. Mary's Church on Elgin Street, 1911, and added side aisles to accommodate the increasing attendance soon after its completion; it was demolished when the new church was built. They also designed the Oak Bay Grocery, 1912, and the Haynes Building, 1911, in Victoria. Residential work and schools kept them busy until the depressed days of 1914.

During the First World War Douglas James joined the Canadian Army and trained as an officer. His unit was sent up to Duncan and billeted in the Agricultural Hall during the 1916 blizzard. He rescued Florence G.M. "Johnnie" Johnson, a young widow, from the drifts, some of which were eight and ten feet deep; they married just before he went off to Europe for duty at the front. James served in France with the 16th Battalion Canadian (Scots) but suffered shell shock and was discharged in 1917 with the rank of Lieutenant. He returned to Duncan and opened his own architectural office there. A fine craftsman, James fashioned numerous original details and furniture in at least two of the houses he built for his own occupancy, including his first home at Maple Bay, 1922. His interest in boats included collecting books on old sailing vessels, and he and his wife were active boaters at Maple Bay. He built *Radiant*, a two-masted sailing yawl with engine, in the 1920s, and *Tang-O'Sea*, a forty-foot cruiser launched in 1940.

His practice in Duncan consisted of both commercial and residential work. James made a major contribution to the development of the city, completing over forty-five buildings.

His largest house was *Stonehaven*, built in 1926 for Carlton Stone who owned Hillcrest Lumber. Other work includes the 1925 wooden school on Cairnsmore, the Knights of Pythias Hall, 1930, the Bazett Block, 1924, and St. Edward's Roman Catholic Church, 1926-27. Queen Margaret's Anglican Church, 1934, is a lovely rustic building with rough wood siding, a nostalgic throwback to frontier days. He also designed the 1917 and 1938 portions of the King's Daughters Hospital. A 1924 building he designed for Nanaimo Motors on the waterfront in Nanaimo still stands, but in altered condition.

James was also responsible for the design of a traditional campus for a private boys' school at Shawnigan Lake. The school had been founded in 1913, but the original buildings burned down in December of 1926. Starting with the construction of the new Main Building in early 1927, James provided the designs for a number of structures, based on traditional English models. These buildings still form the core of the current Shawnigan Lake School.

In 1938 James moved back to Victoria and established his own office. In collaboration with **Hubert Savage** and **D.C. Frame**, he designed and completed the working drawings for the Memorial Arena in Victoria. His design used a wooden truss construction with clear views for every seat, but at the last minute an engineer from Vancouver persuaded City Council to use a patented concrete arch construction which left a number of seats with poor views of the arena. The City found the upkeep of the patented roof unexpectedly expensive; this arena was demolished in 2003. A final business association was formed in 1946 with his brother to assist with the drawings for the new Federal Building at the southwest corner of Yates and Government Streets. At that time Douglas also undertook the design of the Imperial Bank on the diagonally opposite corner. For this bank he chose Haddington Island stone to complement the Federal Building. Douglas James retired in 1948, and died September 30, 1962.

Images from Shawnigan Lake School, Shawnigan Lake

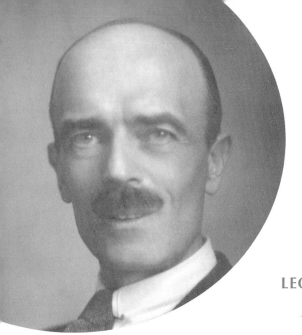

PERCY LEONARD JAMES
1878-1970

ROSEMARY JAMES CROSS

Regrettably somewhat overshadowed since his brief association with **F.M. Rattenbury**, P. Leonard James had a long and prolific career that demonstrated a brilliant and versatile talent for design. His remarkable body of work brought a very English sophistication to his adopted home, that perfectly suited the moods and ambitions of his clients. P. Leonard James, born in London on December 7, 1878, was the eldest son of English architect, Samuel James. His siblings consisted of a sister, Mabel Groos, and two brothers, Harold who went to sea and drowned off Beecher Bay in 1911, and **Douglas James**, who also trained as an architect in England and came to B.C. to practice. Despite having an architect father, in 1893 P. Leonard James articled with John Elford, Borough Architect and Engineer for the City of Poole, England. Between 1899-1906, he worked as a junior architect with A.W. Saxon Snell & Son, rising to the senior assistant's position; Snell (1860-1949)

mainly worked on hospitals and Poor Law Institutions. In 1906 James came to Canada. He won a prize in the Strathcona and Royal Alexander Hospital competitions in Edmonton, and formed a partnership with H.A. Magoon and **E.C. Hopkins**, 1906-08. After his arrival in Victoria in 1908 he received several significant commissions including the extant homes *Stonehenge Park*, built in Esquimalt about 1909 for John Lysle, and *Bannavern*, 1910-11, on Victoria's prestigious St. Charles Street for the Hon. Justice William Galliher. In 1910, P.L. James established a partnership with his brother Douglas, and together they designed many grand houses for the wealthy of Victoria. The Jameses' family home, *Durlston*, was built in Oak Bay in 1910.

In 1914, James returned to London and assisted his former employer, Saxon Snell, in the preparation of plans for East Sussex Hospital at Hastings. While there, James met and married Rose Jesurun Johnston. He joined the Artists' Rifles in 1915, and served in France and Belgium with the 12th London Regiment. In 1917 he was transferred to the Royal Engineers. He succumbed to rheumatic fever, and was invalided from the service with honour. After the war, James returned to Victoria and established his own office. His practice consisted to a large extent of residential work, while partnerships were arranged for specific larger jobs. In 1921-25, James had full responsibility for the design of the east wing of the Royal Jubilee Hospital, and took Major **K.B. Spurgin** as his associate architect.

During the same period, the Rattenbury & James partnership was formed to carry out several projects for the Canadian

Morris Residence, Oak Bay,
James & James Architects, 1913

Pacific Railway Company. Rattenbury was not yet a member of the Architectural Institute of B.C. – he applied in 1923 – and did not have an office. James, with his established office, became the active partner for the Crystal Gardens Swimming Pool and Amusement Centre, and had to produce two complete downsizings of Rattenbury's original grandiose concept. It was James's concept to float the whole building on a structural concrete raft. In their collaboration on the CPR Ticket Office and Terminal on the Inner Harbour, it was James's idea to use cast-stone in place of real stone, which afforded a considerable saving for the CPR. In 1925, after an unpleasant confrontation over the partners' poorly-worded fee agreement, the Rattenbury and James association split up; James was subsequently retained by the CPR as sole architect for the Château Lake Louise swimming pool in Alberta.

Another commission in the early 1920s was the clubhouse for the Royal Colwood Golf Club. Church work included the first St. Mary's Church and Hall in Oak Bay; St. John's Anglican, Cobble Hill; St. Peter's, Comox; the Cathedral Sunday School in James Bay; and the commemorative Chapel of the Peace of God in Victoria, built in memory of John Yarrow, who died while studying at Cambridge, England in 1938.

James already shared an office with **Hubert Savage**, but with an increasing work load, they formed a successful partnership in the summer of 1928 that lasted for five years. After the Royal Colwood clubhouse burned down in 1929, James & Savage were commissioned to design its much larger replacement. After years of being busy, James took a sabbatical year in England in 1934, where he was exposed to, and embraced, the new European Modernism. In the 1940s, he joined with Murray Polson and Robert Siddall to design a number of schools and other projects. He was also associated on the Birks project in Victoria with Percy Erskine Nobbs (1875-1964) of Montreal, to whom he was related by marriage. His last major building, the Federal Building in Victoria, was produced in partnership with his brother, Douglas James. In 1948, two years into the project, Douglas retired, leaving Percy Leonard James with sole responsibility for the Federal Building, which was completed by 1952. James retired in 1955, and died January 3, 1970. His many interests included gardening, tennis, watercolour painting, picnics at the beach, stamp collecting and the study of lepidoptera. He wrote pantomimes for family and friends to perform.

In 1996 his last and largest commission, the Federal Building and Post Office at the corner of Government and Yates Streets, was renamed "P.L. James Place." This was the last of several honours conferred on James: he was a charter member of the AIBC, and the first B.C. architect elected to the College of Fellows of the Royal Architectural Institute of Canada. The two organizations also made James an Honorary Life Member, the AIBC in 1956, and the RAIC in 1967. Architect John Wade later recalled that "James was the gentleman of the profession, always courteous and helpful to young people who came to him."

He is devoted to his profession and familiarizes himself with the latest ideas pertaining thereto. His thorough knowledge and originality entitle him to recognition as one of the leading architects of Victoria.

Howay & Schofield, *British Columbia Biographical*, Vol. IV, pp. 585-586.

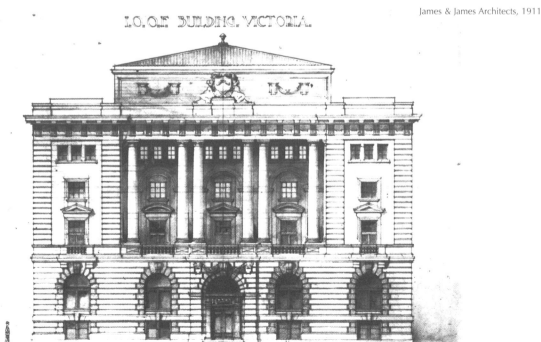

Unbuilt project for IOOF Building, Victoria,

James & James Architects, 1911

WILLIAM FREDERICK GARDINER

1884-1951

DONALD LUXTON

W.F. Gardiner left England as a young man, looking for opportunities in the New World. He chose to settle in far-distant Vancouver, a career decision that ultimately paid off handsomely. Born May 24, 1884 in Bath, he was the son of architect and surveyor, Frederick William Gardiner and Emma Elizabeth Brown. After education at Kingsholme College, Weston-Super-Mare, he entered a three-year course in architecture, and then articled in his father's office in Bath from 1901-07. On October 24, 1907, William left England to start a new life in far-distant Vancouver. His optimism, tinged with fear, was recorded in a diary that he kept during his journey from Liverpool to Montreal. His elder brother, **Frank Gardiner**, who had also articled with their father, travelled with him to Liverpool, and William recorded in his diary:

The time came when Frank & I had to part as I was to be on board at 3 o'clock. It was a very sad sight on the dock when the Victorian was landing nearly everyone was crying & saying Good Bye... Though I was on board at 3 o'clock we never started till close on six o'clock... I waved my hat, hand & handkerchief to Frank who was getting smaller & less distinct as we moved towards sea & when I saw no more I assure you I first realized that I was starting a new life. All that day I lay very ill on deck having nothing to eat all day, in fact the majority of the passengers were considerably worse than I. I shall never forget the awful sight that I witnessed that day in the Steerage it was too awful for words. They were lying like dead dogs on the floor, men, women & children... we were hit by a wave which nearly turned every one grey,

we were thrown from our seats & those who realized it was only a wave rushed to the port holes. Water rushed in the doors of the Saloon & Port Hole where I was sitting & the passengers were thrown off their seats... When we got in the Straights of Belle Isle the sea was lovely but the cold was intense. When I went on the deck in the morning snow & sleet was covered all over the decks & it was awfully cold. Just before lunch we passed a big ice-burge a sight worth seeing. It was like an enormous island covered with snow & the sun was shining on it which made it very effective & beautiful. Them ice-burges are very dangerous, if we should happen to strike one it would mean a hopeless case for everyone. When we arrived [in Montreal] all the Steerage Passengers were landed & we (2nd class) all had to go in front of the Excise Office & Medical & be examined. This I thought was nothing more than red tape.

Gardiner then started on an adventurous train journey across the vast new country, and he described with awe many wondrous sights, including buffalo, glaciers and Native camps.

The "Prairies" as it is called is absolutely flat ground & you can see for miles & miles of pasture ground, no trees of any sort to be seen. It is on the Prairies that most of the immigrants go to farm on. (From each side of the railway on the Prairies the CPR own 20 miles each side of the rail, & the free grant land as you hear of in England is beyond that so that you can imagine what a lot of use this land is & account for them giving it away to immigrants.

William Shannon Residence, Vancouver

After one particularly rough part of the journey,

One of the men in my section who was travelling with his wife & family went up to the brakeman & used all the language imaginable to him. He said he had travelled on this line scores of times but never experienced anything like this. He said he would report the train at Vancouver as he was confident it was due to carelessness & instead of treating us all as human passengers we were being treated like cattle. Instead of the brakeman taking to him kindly & apologizing for all the discomfort & bumping we were put to, he replied he was not in England & what he had paid for in Canada, he would have to get what he could for & be satisfied with that, & if he had any more to say he would throw him off the train. You can imagine what this remark led up to each were going to kill one another & at first I thought it was coming to blows but the brakeman knew he had one too many for him & went to the next car threatening to do I do not know what. At midnight we ran into three deers killing two outright & wounding the third. We pulled up & at the time we were looking over the edge of a Mountain 200 ft high. The Guards of the train got off & after a great deal of difficulty managed to pull the big deer from the edge of the rocks & put it in the train which the guard afterwards claimed.

After this astonishing journey, William Gardiner arrived in Vancouver, ready to start his new life. His family relates that after he set himself up at a boarding house, he started looking for work by knocking on doors in the West End and introducing himself to whoever answered. At one house a young girl's birthday party was underway, and Gardiner, who was proficient at magic tricks and an enthusiastic singer and piano player, ended up entertaining the children. The girl's father, a doctor, was impressed, and hired Gardiner for his first Canadian commission. After four months in Vancouver he submitted the successful plans to the B.C. Permanent Loan Company for the Victoria Block on Pender Street, a substantial project that was completed in just five months. Prospects looked good for the young architect, and by the end of 1908 he entered into a short-lived partnership in New Westminster with Thomas Douglas Sherriff. Born in Scotland in 1884, Sherriff had been indentured to an architect and civil engineer, but was more interested in commercial pursuits and left before he completed his articles, immigrating to British Columbia in 1908.

When William's brother, Frank Gardiner, arrived on the coast, the firm of Gardiner & Sherriff was dissolved by mutual consent, and the two brothers entered into partnership in 1909. They added **Andrew Mercer** to the partnership, but the association was tenuous at best. William also maintained a busy office in Vancouver, and by 1912 he had broken completely free of his brother's practice.

Gardiner's first big break had come in 1910, with the job as supervising architect for the Provincial Normal School in Vancouver, designed by **Pearce & Hope** two years earlier. Typical of his ongoing commercial and institutional work is the Central City Mission on Abbott Street, 1911. He also acted as supervising architect for two Canadian Bank of Commerce projects designed by Toronto architect V.D. Horsburgh, the imposing branch office at Main and Pender Streets, 1914-15, and the Vault Building on East 1st Avenue, 1915. Gardiner enlisted for the First World War on February 1, 1917, and was

Crippled Children's Hospital, Vancouver

The "Victoria Block"
Pender St.
Vancouver, B.C.
Wm. Fred. Gardiner, Architect.

sent overseas with the Canadian Expeditionary Force. He was commissioned to the Duke of Connaught's Regiment, and was transferred on arrival in England to the 2nd Canadian Mounted Rifles. Ranked as Captain, he spent a long time in the trenches in France, and the constant dampness ruined the circulation in his feet. William was in the thick of fighting, which he described in a letter to Frank:

Later we tied our horses to the fence behind the hospital and were billeted in a farm house close by. We hadn't been there ten minutes when we heard a faint whistle which suddenly developed into a hideous scream. What actually happened I don't know, but I found myself later

flat on the ground holding my horse, with huge cakes of mud falling on top of me like hailstones. It was our first experience with a 'Jack Johnson' shell.

He suffered severe shrapnel wounds in his left leg at Cambrai just weeks before the Armistice, was discharged as medically unfit in the summer of 1919, and returned to Vancouver aboard the hospital ship *Essequibo*. Gardiner & Mercer had relocated to Vancouver in 1916, and William Gardiner left them in charge of his practice while he was overseas. While still at the CEF Camp at Vernon in early 1917, William had sent Frank a friendly post card with the note: "Hope everything is going well in the office." When he returned, relations with

Provincial Normal School, Vancouver;
original design by Pearce & Hope

Frank soured beyond redemption, as William felt that Frank had used the public confusion over their names to steal his clients. William moved to an office in the Vancouver Block, and the Gardiner brothers were never again on speaking terms.

On April 6, 1921 William married Amy Doris Lindsay of Vancouver, and over the next few years they had two daughters and a son. They bought a modest house in Vancouver's West End, and Gardiner was content to live in a house that he had not designed. Gardiner continued to work on his own, and established a sound corporate clientele. His main source of work was in bank commissions, and in the growing automobile service industry, which allowed him to ride out the Depression when the careers of many other architects faltered. He served as architect for Austin C. Taylor's Home Oil Distributors Ltd., and starting in the late 1920s, designed over one hundred service stations around the province for the rapidly growing company; a surviving example is the Oak Tree Auto Sales building on Nanaimo's Front Street. Taylor became a personal friend, and when he acquired a large farm in Langley where he could breed horses, Gardiner designed a grand estate house for the property, which still stands today. When Taylor bought the B.T. Rogers mansion, *Shannon*, in 1936, Gardiner provided the plans for the renovations.

In addition to his ongoing work for Taylor, Gardiner continued to serve as the local architect for the Canadian Bank of Commerce and the Sun Life Assurance Company of Canada. He flirted with modernism in the 1930s with buildings like the streamlined Cathay Apartment Hotel in Victoria, but never ventured far from a conservative, main-stream approach, providing solid and consistent design work for his many corporate clients.

In addition to his commercial work Gardiner designed a number of grand, traditional, country estates throughout the 1920s and 1930s. This was a time when the monied classes could afford to build, and Gardiner was one of their favoured architects. In Qualicum Beach he designed a summer lodge for Major James R. Lowery, 1929-30. This enormous structure, with wooded grounds and commanding views, was built entirely from peeled cedar logs, and took the local use of rustic vernacular to its highest level. He designed a large log summer house in Chilliwack for Mr. and Mrs. Fred Haas of Washington, D.C. For Charles Gordon Elverson, a retired Englishman, he designed a landmark Tudor Revival house in the mid 1930s, prominently located on a thirty-five-acre site on Galiano Island, at the entrance to Active Pass.

"Bill" Gardiner was one of the charter members of the AIBC and served as President from 1937-39. During the Second World War his career, like that of many others, languished, but after 1945 his corporate work resumed, one example of which is the Bank of Toronto in Victoria. Through his involvement

Cartoon of W.F. Gardiner by Le Messurier

Bank of Toronto, Vancouver

with the RAIC he maintained many national contacts, and in 1950, he made a trip to *Taliesin*, Frank Lloyd Wright's home and studio in Wisconsin. On March 8, 1951 W.F. Gardiner suffered a stroke at his office, and died shortly afterwards at home.

FRANCIS GEORGE GARDINER

1878-1966

GARDINER & MERCER

PARTNERSHIP 1912-1940

Gardiner, who had immigrated two years earlier. One of their first commissions was the landmark three-storey Hart Building, at Five Corners in the core of Chilliwack, built in 1909 of concrete blocks. Within a year and a half their practice had flourished. In 1911 they went into partnership with Andrew Mercer, designing the landmark Trapp Block on Columbia Street; William also kept a separate office in Vancouver, and by 1912 struck out in a solo practice. Frank returned to England for a holiday, and on the ship back met Kathleen Buckley, an Irish Catholic, and they married shortly afterwards. Frank converted to her religion, and during the course of his career undertook many projects for the Roman Catholic church, including the Sisters of Saint Paul School, North Vancouver, 1932. During the war Gardiner was an Examiner for the Imperial Government Munitions, but he never enlisted, and continued his architectural practice.

Eastman Residence, New Westminster

DONALD LUXTON

The architectural partnership of Gardiner & Mercer in the early half of this century was one of the more enduring and prolific in the province. Andrew Mercer, more outgoing and gregarious, was mainly responsible for the structural aspect of their projects, while Frank Gardiner handled the design end. Friends as well as business partners, their separate firms were competitive after the partnership split, but the two men remained personally friendly, and continued to meet each other regularly at the Vancouver Club.

Typical of many of the young British architects who immigrated to Canada, Frank Gardiner came from a family involved in the profession. He was born in Bristol on September 29, 1878. After attending Bath High School he articled with his father, Frederick W. Gardiner, who was an architect and surveyor in Bath. Looking for greater opportunity, Frank left for South Africa, which was booming from the discovery of gold. He served as Assistant to Macintosh & Moffat, Architects, Pretoria and Johannesburg, 1903-04, after which he was in private practice in Pretoria for two years. He then served as a staff architect with the Public Works Department, but in 1907 he returned to England and entered into a partnership with his father. In 1909 he left for Canada, and arrived in New Westminster that summer with five pounds in his pocket. He established a partnership with his younger brother, **William F.**

Andrew Mercer was born into a very strict Presbyterian family in Ayr, Scotland on July 4, 1878, the son of John Mercer and his first wife, Jane Buist. John Mercer was the son of an engine driver, and trained as an engineer in the offices of the Glasgow & South Western Railway. John set up as an engineer and architect in Ayr about 1872, and served from 1879-89 as Burgh Surveyor. Andrew was orphaned at an early age; his mother died in 1885, and his father in 1893. He completed his education at the Ayr Academy and was articled to William Kerr, Architect, Ayr, from 1894 to 1898. He practised in Carlisle and Glasgow for the following two years, and then moved to Dublin, where he was managing assistant to C.N. Ashworth from 1900-04; he also took a two-year structural engineering course at Dublin Technical College. Andrew married Susan McFeat of Ayr in 1900, and they had three children, Jack, Susan and Betty. He returned to Ayr in 1904, working mostly on modest domestic projects. In August 1905 he acquired the "business and goodwill" of the late William Kerr, which included the completion of additions to the Kyle Poorhouse, to Kerr's plans. For a while Mercer was associated with Ayr architect, James Archibald Morris, a talented and

ANDREW LAMB MERCER
1878-1959

accomplished designer, whose work was firmly rooted in the Arts and Crafts movement. Morris had worked in London for ten years, starting in 1886, and was well acquainted with the work of leading architects such as Richard Norman Shaw and Charles Rennie Mackintosh.

Red-haired and known for his quick temper, Mercer could not wait to get away from Scotland and what he considered his repressive background. Despite his growing family and career, he decided to move to the new world, and by 1911 had settled in British Columbia. Once he left, he never returned, and did not maintain close ties with his remaining Scottish family. New Westminster was booming in the period just prior to the First World War, in anticipation of the opening of the Panama Canal, and the Gardiner & Mercer partnership was soon established as the leading local architectural firm. Mercer detested the Royal City, with all its "bloody hills," and within a year he moved his family to Vancouver. Gardiner & Mercer designed most of the new buildings along Columbia Street, including the city's tallest, the Westminster Trust Building, 1911-12. Their institutional buildings included several New Westminster schools, notably the Duke of Connaught High School and Richard McBride School, and Coquitlam Municipal Hall. In addition to their many commercial buildings they handled a large number of residential commissions, designed in an

Westminster Trust Building, New Westminster

adapted Arts and Crafts style, the largest being the Nels Nelson House in Queen's Park, 1913.

The downturn of the economy in 1913 was especially hard on New Westminster, and the firm was left with little to do. By 1916 they had relocated their offices to the Birks Building in Vancouver, and they received commissions for many of the buildings in the new industrial enclave being created by the federal government on Granville Island. The firm advertised itself as Architects, Steel & Concrete Engineers. Following the end of the war, their buildings were plain and utilitarian, reflecting the grim economic circumstances, and included structures such as the Schara Tzedeck Synagogue on East Pender Street, Vancouver, 1920 and the Franklyn Street Gymnasium, Nanaimo, 1922. This steady stream of work allowed Mercer to build a new family home on West 33rd Avenue in 1921. With the return of prosperity in the mid-1920s their work returned to its old gracefulness, such as the Wellington (now Trafalgar) Apartments in Kitsilano, 1925. Their domestic work at this time was distinctive, using an adapted British Arts and Crafts vernacular, with stucco cladding and hints of period revival details. Surviving examples in Shaughnessy include a grand home for retired piano dealer, William W. Montelius, 1924-25, and the West Residence, 1930. Typical of their solid and conservative institutional work was the Jewish Community Centre, 1928. Not known for stylistic innovations, the firm flirted with modernism starting in the mid-1930s with the Pacific Athletic Club, designed in a Stripped Classicism that was a forerunner of the simple mod-

ernist approach later used in their institutional designs. The firm shifted from the pursuit of general architectural work to a specialization in brewery work and hospital design, including the landmark additions to St. Paul's Hospital, 1931-36, and the design of St. Vincent's Hospital, 1939, both in Vancouver.

Instrumental in the formation of the AIBC, Andrew Mercer filled out Application #1 for membership and served as its first President from 1920-22, and again from 1929-31. He was socially conscious, and supported a number of charities, including the Salvation Army and the Red Cross, by donating his design services. Mercer was politically connected to the Liberal Party, and was personally acquainted both with the local party members, including Gerald McGeer, and those in Ottawa, including Mackenzie King. He was an extremely hard worker, and very rarely took holidays. He golfed for recreation, and was the founder of Shaughnessy Golf Course. Mercer's wife, Susan, died in 1929, and he remarried in 1932, to Margaret Chapman. They had one son, Andrew.

In 1940 Mercer ended the partnership with Frank Gardiner so that he could go into business with his eldest son, John "Jack" Mercer, of whom he was very proud. Jack had apprenticed with Gardiner from 1926-31, and had continued working at the firm, but Gardiner opposed making him a partner. The split was amicable, although the two firms continued to compete for the same hospital commissions.

Gardiner went into partnership with Peter Muschamp Thornton (1916-1996), who had been working in the office, an arrangement which lasted until the end of Gardiner's career.

Thornton, born in Edmonton, had been educated at the Architectural Association in London, England, and moved to Vancouver after he graduated in 1939. Gardiner & Thornton undertook a number of church and hospital commissions, including Guardian Angels Roman Catholic Church, 1948-49, Langley Memorial Hospital, 1947-48, and the new Vernon Hospital, 1949. The firm prospered, adding Norwegian-born Asbjørn Rasmus Gathe (1921-1994) as a partner in 1955; Gathe was responsible for the design of the landmark Westminster Abbey in Mission, a project of over thirty years in duration that started in the early 1950s. Frank Gardiner retired in 1959, and died in Vancouver on November 21, 1966. He was buried in Forest Lawn Memorial Park in Burnaby.

The first large contract for the Mercer & Mercer partnership was Shaughnessy Hospital in 1940, a "million-dollar contract," a very large project at that time. Another large project was a veteran's hospital built at Royal Jubilee in Victoria, 1945-46, now known as the Memorial Building. The firm had a contract for years with the Royal Bank to build branch banks throughout the province. They also built breweries throughout the province, as well as many of the United Distillers liquor outlets. They continued to design hospitals, often adding on to large medical complexes, such as their continuing commissions at Shaughnessy Hospital. A notable modernist project was the Salvation Army Temple on Hastings Street, 1949-50. One of their more successful projects was the Academy of Medicine, 1950-51, which featured a large sculptural relief by Beatrice Lennie, who had previously provided panels for the

Montelius Residence, Vancouver

entrance of Shaughnessy Hospital. Mercer & Mercer also designed several community centres in Vancouver: Marpole, 1949 (and 1952 additions); Dunbar, 1957-58; and South Vancouver (now Killarney), 1961-63. The South Vancouver Community Centre showed the strong influence of a young designer in the office, Henry Yorke Mann. Andrew Mercer was never interested in designing houses, and would only do so for friends, even then under protest. He was a good friend of Robert Mills, for whom he designed the quirky Polynesian-style Waldorf Hotel, and Mills was able to persuade him to design his house as well. Another unusual project was a miniature replica of the Parthenon, built as part of an extensive residence for Nick Kogos on the West Vancouver waterfront over a ten-year period starting in 1946.

Andrew Mercer was involved in the office until his death, on February 28, 1959 at the age of eighty. He was considered the "last of the old gentlemen," and was highly regarded by the contractors with whom he worked. He always had time to talk to the workmen on his projects; so many took unpaid time off work to attend his funeral that it was filled to overflowing, and the service had to be broadcast to those standing outside. Jack Mercer was a shy man, and worked somewhat in the shadow of his father. Although he kept the office open after the elder Mercer's death he only maintained existing clients and did not pursue new opportunities until "it faded away;" he sold the practice and retired in 1970. Jack Mercer died January 21, 1998.

TWIZELL & TWIZELL

PARTNERSHIP 1908-1954

Canadian Memorial United Church, Vancouver

ROBERT PERCIVAL STERLING TWIZELL

1875-1964

WARREN F. SOMMER

The firm of Twizell & Twizell practised in Vancouver for close to half a century. Throughout that time its name was synonymous with quality institutional and residential design. Established in 1908, the firm brought high standards of professionalism to a field that for decades had been heavily infiltrated by practitioners with lesser training. The firm's principals were Robert P.S. Twizell and his younger brother, George Twizell. Both were born in Newcastle-on-Tyne, in the northern English county of Northumberland, Robert in June, 1875, and George on December 24, 1885. Their parents were Robert and Mary Twizell. The brothers were both educated at Rutherford College and Durham University. Both articled with the Newcastle firm of Hicks & Charlewood, a firm responsible for the design of dozens of Gothic Revival churches in England, Scotland, and Ireland. W.S. Hicks and H.C. Charlewood were part of an architectural dynasty. Hicks was the great nephew of Sir Charles Barry, designer of London's Parliament Buildings. He and Charlewood were brothers-in-law, and their sons succeeded them in their firm.

R.P.S. Twizell acquired probationer status with the Royal Institute of British Architects in 1897, and qualified in 1900 when he was elected an associate of RIBA. His examination standing was the highest in England. After qualifying, the elder Twizell worked for Newcastle architect Stephen Piper for a short time. He then returned to Hicks & Charlewood, but soon moved on to work for W.H. Knowles, also of Newcastle. Knowles was a Freemason, and it may have been under his aegis that Twizell joined the Ridley Lodge branch, Newcastle, in the early 1900s. R.P.S. Twizell spent his final years in

GEORGE STERLING TWIZELL

1885-1957

England working as a lecturer in architecture at Durham University and Newcastle's College of Science.

George Twizell's education and career is less well documented than his brother's. Indeed, throughout his life, George Twizell seems to have spent much of his time in his brother's shadow. George served his articles with Hicks & Charlewood several years after his brother (c.1901). He subsequently became an assistant in the firm before moving to Montreal early in the new century. He found work as an assistant with the prestigious firm of Edward and William S. Maxwell, a partnership that had distinguished itself not only for residential construction, but also for public and commercial buildings as well, being responsible for numerous CPR stations and hotels.

The Twizell brothers had relocated to Vancouver by late 1907 or early 1908. George found work as an assistant to the noted architect **C.O. Wickenden**, but soon left to join his brother as a partner. The brothers initially took up housekeeping together, living first in a Cambie Street rooming house, and then moved in 1911 to a house on Pacific Street, where they were joined by their sister, Winifred. By 1913 they had moved to Kitsilano, where they designed a duplex for the family. Their widowed mother joined them at this time. Records of Twizell & Twizell's earliest work have been largely lost. Surviving information suggests that their initial commissions were a miscellany of repairs, additions, small houses, and a few modest churches. The firm's earliest church seems to have been St. George's Anglican, built in Vancouver in 1911. The Anglican Church of St. John the Divine in Quesnel followed in 1912.

Most of the firm's work in the following decade was confined to the growing Municipality of Point Grey. Twizell & Twizell were responsible for a number of major houses in Shaughnessy Heights, including the J.W. Kerr, Walter Walsh, W.L. Coulthard, and M.P. Morris houses, all built in a Neo-Georgian or Arts and Crafts style. Their commission for a lake-side Arts and Crafts-style country residence in Burnaby for Vancouver businessman H.T. Ceperley, *Fairacres* (now the home of the Gallery at Ceperley House), and a home for Dr. A.L. Johnson in Kitsilano, were no less important.

Twizell & Twizell also acquired a reputation as competent designers of schools, designing more buildings for educational purposes than any of their contemporaries in the city. Notable examples include Queen Mary Elementary, a "Jacobethan" structure built on the west side in 1914, and Shaughnessy School (now Emily Carr Elementary) in 1917.

By the early 1920s the firm was well established. R.P.S. Twizell married Mabel Ackroyd Denness in 1919, and the couple had two daughters. Both R.P.S. and George Twizell took an active interest in the affairs of their profession, and both were charter members of the AIBC. R.P.S. Twizell served on its Council in 1926-27. As President of the Art, Historical, and Scientific Association of Vancouver from 1918-22, he was largely responsible for the acquisition of the famed Stanley Park totem poles.

Twizell & Twizell maintained their involvement in school design throughout the 1920s. The firm undertook major repairs and additions to Magee Secondary School (then known as King George V School) in 1919 and 1921, and built Edith Cavell Elementary in 1919. Prince of Wales High School (now Shaughnessy Elementary) and David Lloyd George Elementary followed in 1920, while Kerrisdale Elementary was built in 1921. The firm worked on Lord Kitchener Elementary and designed an addition to Kerrisdale Elementary in 1924. All these schools were institutional in flavour, with Gothic,

Proposed Residence: Kitsilano. for Dr A L Johnson.

Jacobean, or Renaissance detailing. Probably because of the sheer volume of work on their table at this time they brought **Samuel Buttrey Birds** into the partnership during the years 1920-23. The firm also built more modest schools outside the city. Langley's one room Willoughby Elementary School dates from 1931, the Richmond High School addition (now Cambie Junior Secondary), from 1937. The firm's reputation as institutional designers attracted the attention of the Roman Catholic Church. Twizell & Twizell received major commissions in 1924, 1925, and 1927 to design and then add to the Church's high school, Vancouver College. The Church also called upon the firm in 1927 when it required a design for St. Joseph's Oriental Hospital.

But Twizell & Twizell are best remembered for their churches. Both had been trained in the traditions of the Gothic Revival, and in the second half of their careers they were given many opportunities to utilize their knowledge and experience. Their first great ecclesiastical commission was for Canadian Memorial United Church, which was awarded following a country-wide competition. Interestingly, George Twizell submitted an entry of his own, finishing second behind the firm's joint entry. Built as a national war memorial in 1927, Canadian Memorial is a substantial reinforced concrete structure cleverly disguised by granite and plaster facings. The firm's successful completion of Canadian Memorial showed the church community just what Twizell & Twizell were capable of producing. A similarly sized project, this time in brick, followed a few years later, when the Catholic Church called on the firm to design St. Augustine's in Kitsilano. Twizell & Twizell were asked to design what is generally regarded as their greatest work, St. Andrew's-Wesley United Church. Built in 1931-33, this project, along with St. Augustine's and St. Saviour's Anglican (Episcopal) in Kelowna, 1929-30, saw the firm through the worst years of the Depression.

Dozens of church commissions followed, many of them in Vancouver: chancels for St. Mary's Anglican Church and for Christ Church Cathedral; churches for the Anglican congregations of St. Phillip and St. Michael, churches for the Fathers of

St. Peter's Roman Catholic Church, New Westminster

the Blessed Sacrament, St. Peter's Roman Catholic Church, New Westminster, and the East Vancouver Christian Science Church. The firm was particularly popular with the United Church of Canada, designing structures in Vancouver for the Knox, West Point Grey, St. Giles, Dunbar Heights, and Windsor congregations. Twizell & Twizell were also responsible for United Churches in Chilliwack, Willingdon Heights, West Burnaby, Burnaby Lake, Kimberley, and Vernon. Most of these churches were built in the 1940s and early 1950s.

George Twizell retired in 1950 and moved to Esquimalt. R.P.S. Twizell continued to practice until 1954. He became an outspoken critic of the architectural trends of the mid-twentieth century, writing: "Can any stretch of the imagination create the belief that it is possible in modern architecture, which is the embodiment of the spirit of commercialism, to design buildings which will equal the aesthetic beauty of the Parthenon or the awe-inspiring beauty and dignity of mediaeval cathedrals?" He noted of recent construction: "These new buildings, you can't see what's holding them together. You can't see how they are carried."

R.P.S. Twizell's wife, Mabel, died in 1957, and he moved to Vancouver Island to live with his brother, who died later that same year. During his latter years R.P.S. Twizell was lavished with recognition from his peers. He received the Northern Architectural Association's Glover Medal and became a RIBA Fellow in 1951. He was also made an Honorary Fellow of the Royal Society of Fine Arts and a Fellow of the Royal Society for the Encouragement of Arts, Manufactures, and Commerce. His Canadian colleagues made him the first Honorary Member of both the AIBC and the RAIC. In 1957, R.P.S. Twizell married Mary France, former nanny to Dola, the youngest child of James and Laura Dunsmuir, and lived with her until his death in Victoria in 1964.

Fairacres, Ceperley Residence, Burnaby

SAMUEL BUTTREY BIRDS

1871-1960

WARREN F. SOMMER

S.B. Birds practised architecture in British Columbia from 1908 until 1923. He was responsible for a number of major buildings throughout the province, in styles ranging from Gothic to Classical to the purely utilitarian. Several of his more important buildings survive today. Born on April 23, 1871 in Morley, Yorkshire, he was educated at Leeds University and York College. He began his career at the age of fourteen by articling with T. A. Buttrey, likely his uncle, who maintained offices in both Leeds and Morley. After completing his articles, Birds moved to Philadelphia for two years, where he worked for the distinguished firm of Cope & Stevenson, as well as for J.T. Windrim and George Bowman. Cope & Stevenson have been described as "one of Philadelphia's most important and prestigious firms at the turn of the century." The firm was then highly regarded as one of North America's most accomplished exponents of the Collegiate Gothic style, and was responsible for the design of numerous college, university, and school buildings. John T. Windrim, on the other hand, was a noted designer of hospitals, and, though prolific, much of his work seems to have lacked an individual cachet, being described as "utilitarian in nature and relatively anonymous."

Birds returned to England in 1895. He spent the years 1895-1907 in partnership with T.A. Buttrey, designing a number of hospitals, schools, libraries, churches, swimming pools, and club buildings. The pair entered a number of major competitions, including those for Cartright Hall in Bradford in 1899, and for the Conservative Club in Hindley, 1896. Birds married Louisa Lambert of Leeds in 1895, and the couple had one son and one daughter.

Birds moved to Toronto in 1907. He settled in Vancouver later the next year where he initially worked in association

with **E.E. Blackmore**, describing himself as a structural engineer. One of Birds's known works during this period was the Hampton Brothers Bakery on West Seventh Avenue. Birds's career in British Columbia was characterised by a diverse range of commissions: tenements, small houses, commercial buildings, churches, halls, hospitals, and schools, but he seems to have had few opportunities to produce the grand designs for which his English and American training had prepared him.

Most of his work was in the Vancouver area. It included a Gothic Revival church building for Fairview's Sixth Avenue Methodist congregation in 1909; a school room for the Fairview Baptist Church, 1909; a frame tenement house on Pender Street, 1910; a substantial brick commercial block on Richards Street for Captain H. Pybus in 1911; houses for R. W. Suter, Archibald Wright, and General Victor Odlum, 1912-13; two commercial/residential buildings in Chinatown, 1912; stores, offices, and apartments on Granville, Robson and Venables Streets, 1911-14; and a Chinese club on Carrall Street, 1914. Much of this work was built with modest budgets, and was not always distinguished.

Birds's most prominent Vancouver project, which he won in an open competition, was Chalmers' Presbyterian Church. Built in 1911-12, the building was made necessary by the rapid growth of the city's Fairview and Shaughnessy districts. Built of brick with stone and concrete detailing, the structure is Neoclassical in style, with a lofty dome and a prominent Corinthian portico. Its adjacent community centre featured a gymnasium and one of the city's first indoor pools.

Demands for his services were such that he was able to open an office in Victoria in 1912. Most of Birds's larger and more distinguished works were built outside Vancouver. These include a multi-winged four-storey building for New Westminster's Royal Columbian Hospital in 1912, a building for the Kamloops Royal Inland Hospital, as well as smaller hospital buildings for Ladysmith and Merritt. A large Fair building was designed and built for the Cowichan Agricultural Association in 1913-14, and featured a symmetrical plan with modest Palladian detailing. A major design commissioned by the Kootenay Lake General Hospital in Nelson, 1912, was never built. Birds's connections with the Chinese community resulted in his being given a commission to build a large, Neoclassical house for Victoria businessman, Lim Bang, in 1912 in the predominantly white North Park neighbourhood.

Birds's life took a dramatic turn with the outbreak of the First World War. He enlisted with the rank of captain in Vancouver's

Seaforth Regiment of Canada (the 72nd Battalion) sometime in 1915. He appeared to have had an interest in weaponry, if not the military, prior to the war, being a prominent member of the Vancouver Rifle Association for a number of years. Birds was at the front in France by mid-August, 1916. He arrived in time to participate in several of the war's most memorable and bloody battles: the Somme, Vimy Ridge, and Passchendaele. His military career was noteworthy. Not only was he mentioned in dispatches, but his conduct at Vimy Ridge earned him the Military Cross. Birds was awarded the even more prestigious Distinguished Service Order as a result of his actions at Passchendaele. As a chronicler of the regiment noted: "No one who was there can forget... the wonderful work of Capt. S.B. Birds, who, with that uncanny coolness which was a source of wonder to all ranks, led his own Company at the start, and later directed affairs on the spot with a disregard of danger that seemed almost fatalistic." Birds was subsequently promoted to the rank of Major.

Birds returned to Vancouver and civilian life in 1919. In 1920 he entered into a partnership with **R.P.S. Twizell** and his brother, **George S. Twizell**. The Twizell brothers had come to Vancouver at about the same time as Birds, and like Birds, they too were from the north of England. It is tempting to suggest that they knew each other prior to coming to Canada, but what is certain is that they were well acquainted with each other's work prior to the outbreak of the war. Their work together included David Lloyd George and Kerrisdale Schools, both in a vaguely Collegiate Gothic style; extensive repairs and renovations to Magee Secondary School; and houses for William More and Mrs. W.E. Blair. Birds's partnership with the Twizell brothers ended in 1923, and Birds left Vancouver for Los Angeles where he practised for the next six years. He ceased to be listed with California's Board of Architectural Examiners in 1929. Birds died in Los Angeles on January 23, 1960.

In following his profession he has been very successful in open architectural competitions and has developed a specialty in the design and building of public hospitals.

Howay & Schofield, *British Columbia Biographical*, Vol. III, p. 552.

Royal Columbian Hospital, New Westminster

TOWNLEY & MATHESON
PARTNERSHIP 1919-1974

Between the two World Wars the partnership of Fred Townley and Robert Matheson rivalled the success of **McCarter & Nairne** and **Sharp & Thompson**. They left a rich legacy of sophisticated work, including schools, commercial structures, many fine residences, and the landmark Vancouver City Hall. The firm flourished during the 1920s as one of the leaders in the use of traditional period revival styles; however, it was also as adventurous in the early exploration of modernism as any other firm in western Canada. Townley & Matheson's later work was mostly institutional, and the firm specialized in hospital design after the end of the Second World War. Through a stroke of good fortune, the firm's extensive collection of original plans has been preserved, and in 2002 was donated to the City of Vancouver Archives.

Fred L. Townley was born in Winnipeg in 1887, the son of Thomas O. Townley. The family moved west to Vancouver when Fred was just nine months old. T.O. Townley was a lawyer, and served as Mayor of Vancouver in 1901, which, later on, may have been a factor in his son being chosen to design City Hall. In 1908 Townley began a brief apprenticeship under **Sholto Smith**, where he was apparently responsible for one of the designs for the Wigwam Inn. He then worked for **Dalton & Eveleigh**, who were acting as supervising architects on the Vancouver Court House at the time, and also worked for several firms in Seattle before he left to go to university. Impressed

FRED LAUGHTON TOWNLEY
1887-1966

DONALD LUXTON

Townley's entry, Vancouver Civic Centre competition, 1914

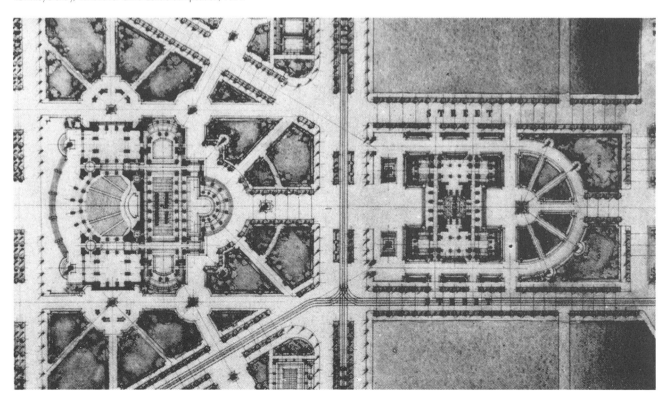

with the reputation of its Dean, Townley decided to attend the University of Pennsylvania, returning home during the summers to work. After graduation in 1911 he established his own firm in Vancouver, although he was briefly associated with Kennerley Bryan in 1912; Bryan & Townley placed third in the competition for the new Vancouver Club, 1912. Townley married Susan Rosamonde Chambers on September 10, 1913. That year he also designed an impressive home for his parents, *Deerholme* on Deer Lake in Burnaby, which demonstrated his deft understanding of the Colonial Revival, a residential style he favoured for many years. The following year he won the competition to design Union Station, the terminus for the Great Northern Railway in Vancouver, but construction on the project was delayed until 1916. This elegant structure, made redundant by the decline in railway travel after the Second World War, was offered to the City of Vancouver for use as a museum and library, but the City fathers declined, and the station was demolished. Townley was accepted for overseas service during the First World War, but not called for duty.

Robert M. Matheson was born in Prince Edward Island on February 21, 1887. His father, John Phillip Matheson, moved the family to Vancouver, and worked as a developer, builder and designer. Robert started his career as a carpenter and general "building artisan" from 1904-08, followed by two years as a general contractor. Matheson even worked as a jeweller at Trorey's in 1907. Like Townley, he travelled from Vancouver to the United States for his education, and graduated from the University of Pennsylvania in 1911; it is likely

ROBERT MICHAEL MATHESON
1887-1935

the two young men knew each other before they left for the United States. After Matheson's return, he went into business with his father as J.P. Matheson & Son; they were responsible for the design of the North-West Trust (now the Lumberman's) Building, 1911-12, and the Caroline Court Apartments, 1912. At about this time, Robert Matheson established his own firm, and in 1913 married Violet Blanche Todhunter. After the war

Deerholme, Townley Residence, Burnaby

Fred Townley in 1907

Fred L. Townley
Aug. 18th 1907.

Townley Residence, Vancouver

he was briefly in partnership with Frederic Claude De Guerre, and together they designed The First Church of Christ Scientist on West Georgia Street in 1918. De Guerre, a civil engineer from Ontario, had been in Vancouver since 1912; he died on October 13, 1918, at the age of thirty, during the height of the Spanish Influenza pandemic.

Townley and Matheson had known each other for years, and formed their architectural partnership in 1919. Both were talented, well connected, and highly regarded. Robert Matheson was an outgoing man, a natural salesman, and was responsible for securing work through his many business and social contacts, and club memberships. Townley was quiet and taciturn, never gregarious even with his family; he stayed mostly in the office, handling the design end of the business. This proved to be a winning combination, and the firm rapidly became one of the most successful in the province.

During the 1920s the firm's work covered a broad range of period revival styles. Different styles were considered appropriate for different uses, but there had to be a style, and it had to be identifiable. Elements of the Gothic Revival were used for the Dick Building and the Stock Exchange, both 1928, although the latter's vertical expression owes a debt to Eliel Saarinen's 1922 second-place entry in the Chicago Tribune Tower competition. Tudor Manor Apartments, 1927-28, was a creative blend of Tudor Revival elements applied to castellated walls. The design for Point Grey Secondary School, 1928-29, followed the traditional Collegiate Gothic idiom in its use of quatrefoils, blind lancet arches and heraldic imagery.

Townley & Matheson were also adventurous in tackling some rather exotic projects. They acted as supervising architects for the Capitol Theatre in Vancouver, for which Thomas W. Lamb had provided the design. On their own they designed the Columbia Theatre in New Westminster, 1927; with its Moorish elements, interior streetscapes and night-time painted ceiling, it was one of the only "atmospheric" theatres ever built locally, and is now being restored as the Burr Theatre. They

went on to act as the local architects for Famous Players. A fanciful Mediterranean influence showed up again in a downtown Vancouver commercial building for R.M. McLuckie in 1931-32, and the Canadian Linen Company building, 1932, displays elements of the late Art Deco style. The Grouse Mountain Chalet, 1926, a rustic lodge built of massive logs was a very unusual project. Matheson, who loved the outdoors, appointed himself as construction supervisor, and once a week made the long and strenuous hike to the site from the north end of Lonsdale Avenue. Swedish and Finnish master craftsmen were employed to build the structure from yellow cedar logs, and in their leisure time carved unbroken chains from single pieces of cedar, that were used to hold back the drapes in the lobby. This unique structure burned to the ground in a spectacular blaze in June, 1962.

The firm was responsible for many of the prominent residences in Shaughnessy, including the Frederick M. Kelly Residence on The Crescent, 1921. Other examples of their residential work were the 1924 Hugh MacLean Residence, the 1926 Buckerfield Residence on South West Marine Drive, and the 1924 W.A. Akhurst Residence, the latter showing the distinctive symmetrical hip roof with extending wings that was a Townley & Matheson trademark. Fred Townley built his own home on Avondale in 1926; it was the first house on the block, and the family moved in when the street was still unpaved. Townley subsequently designed a number of substantial period revival homes in the immediate area, including those for the Whitcrofts, the McCleerys, the Westons, and J.A. Collins (a Colonial Revival home that Townley thought was too big for the lot). In 1929 Matheson built his own home nearby on Connaught, faced with unpainted tan brick. Although many of these houses turned to British models for inspiration, Townley's American education continued to show up in pure white, textbook reproductions of the Colonial Revival style, for which there were no local precedents. Townley was chosen as the first secretary of the AIBC when it was incorporated in 1920, and was given the rather thankless task of notifying

Grouse Mountain Chalet, North Vancouver; interior on following pages

Point Grey Secondary School, Vancouver

those engaged in the profession of architecture of the necessity to apply for registration. Matheson's cousin, Professor E.G. Matheson, a professional engineer, was also appointed to the first AIBC council.

During the 1920s and 1930s, Townley was a good friend of **Charles Marega**, Vancouver's first professional sculptor, and employed him on a number of commissions, including the interior and exterior ornamentation of Point Grey School. Marega also produced the statue of Captain George Vancouver at City Hall. When Marega was unable to make a living at his art, Townley worked hard to help secure commissions for him from other architects, and sent his own daughter for weekly art lessons. At Marega's death in 1939, he left two of his sculptures to Townley as a remembrance.

The Depression signalled the beginning of a drastic change in the firm's designs. Their 1929 design for MacKenzie School abandoned all pretense of revivalism, and helped introduce to Vancouver a new form of modernism based on the reality of the economic situation. MacKenzie School was a truly innovative structure, and was the only school in the city designed in the pure Art Deco style. The firm also designed several innovative Art Deco facades, rendered in multi-coloured terra cotta, for the Canadian Bank of Commerce, 1929, and B.C. Leaseholders, 1930, both on Granville Street. During the early 1930s the firm received few commissions, although some small scale industrial and commercial work trickled in, such as designing service stations for Imperial Oil.

Winning the commission for Vancouver City Hall was the pivotal point in their career, and was crucial in keeping their faltering practice open. In a highly controversial move, Townley & Matheson were unilaterally appointed by Mayor Gerald McGeer in 1935. Matheson had been a friend of McGeer's since they had both attended the old Central School, coincidentally the site originally proposed for the new City Hall; they had continued their friendship through numerous hunting and fishing trips over the intervening years. Townley was also a long-time friend of McGeer, who valued his talents and abilities, and it did not hurt that Townley's father had once been Mayor. McGeer justified their selection by stating that Townley was the most qualified, as he had won second place in the 1914 competition to design a new civic centre on the site of the old Court House on Hastings Street. Despite the firm's credibility and qualifications, the AIBC publicly denounced McGeer for not holding a competition – many architects were desperate at the time for the commission – and many segments of the public were horrified at the remoteness of the site finally chosen at 12th Avenue and Cambie Street. McGeer was ruthless in seeing the project completed according to his, and the architects', vision, which "was evolved from none of the orthodox styles of architecture, but rather, avoids them in its expression of the spirit of modern life." Matheson fell ill, and was in the hospital by the time the commission for City Hall was awarded in 1935. He died on June 30 of that year, at the age of forty-eight. This was devastating to the introverted Townley, who now had to learn how to "hustle" work for the office. Despite Matheson's death, the firm continued to build on its successes, but retained his name for decades as a key part of its identity.

One commission that eluded Townley was the design for the new St. James Anglican Church. His parents had been pillars in this parish, and he had sung in the choir as a child. Despite Townley's offer to provide his services for free, the church chose English architect Adrian Gilbert Scott, a distant relative of the Rector, Reverend Canon Wilberforce Cooper. Townley, mortally offended by their subsequent request that he provide construction supervision *gratis*, never attended church again. After the end of the Second World War he undertook the design for St. John's (Shaughnessy) Anglican Church, but fell out with the building committee (consisting of thirty-five individuals) when they refused his recommendation for a *porte-cochère*. Driven to distraction, Townley resigned the commission, and recommended his friend **G.L. Thornton Sharp**, retired and living in Crofton at the time, to finish the project.

One of Townley & Matheson's technical contributions was the pioneering use of cast-in-place concrete as both a structural and facing material. Point Grey Secondary School and MacKenzie School were early examples where concrete was frankly expressed, rather than being hidden behind a more conventional cladding. Subsequent designs for the Causeway Tower and St. Louis College, both built in Victoria in 1931, continued this exploration. The use of poured concrete for the Educational Building (now the Garden Auditorium) at Hastings Park in 1939-40 demonstrated the sinuous potential of the material, and it remains one of the province's most sophisticated essays in the Streamline Moderne.

From 1937 onwards Townley was the architect for the buildings constructed at the Vancouver General Hospital (VGH). The hospital's expansion programme responded to the city's growing population, but was also spurred on by fears of a wartime Japanese invasion. Townley parlayed his experience at VGH into a number of subsequent hospital commissions, which kept the firm very active through the 1950s and 1960s. The expansion of the firm necessitated the acceptance of new partners, including Allan Cameron Kelly (1908-2001), who had been with the firm since 1928; the firm was named Townley, Matheson, Kelly, Humphrey & Ritchie from 1964-67. After a long and prolific career, Fred Townley died on October 15, 1966. His obituary credited him as the designer of over a thousand buildings. The firm, which continued to use Townley's and Matheson's names until 1974, had been a driving force in B.C.'s architecture since 1919.

Preliminary schemes and completed building (opposite), City Hall, Vancouver

Alfred Arthur Cox

ALFRED ARTHUR
COX
1860-1944

MARCO D'AGOSTINI

A. Arthur Cox brought a refined aesthetic to a series of landmark structures built in Vancouver and Victoria before the outbreak of the First World War, several of which are recognized today for their heritage value. Like many others in the architectural profession, his career was devastated by the collapse of the local economy, and his later projects rarely achieved an equivalent level of grandeur. Cox began his architectural training in 1881 when he articled for William H. Syme of Watford, Hertfordshire for three years, followed by another year as an assistant. In 1885 he passed his qualifying exam and was elected an Associate of the Royal Institute of British Architects. From 1885-89 he was an assistant in the office of Professor Roger T. Smith in London, while attending lectures at University College and completing a three-year term in the Architectural School at the Royal Academy of Arts. Cox was awarded the Grissell Gold Medal in 1886 and in 1890 received

a Godwin Bursary Scholarship that allowed him to travel for twelve months in the United States and parts of Canada before returning to England. He was smitten by Canada and in 1892 moved to Montreal where he commenced a successful and prolific partnership with Louis Auguste Amos (1869-1948) which lasted until 1910. The firm undertook a wide range of projects including many commercial buildings, private residences and churches. On his own, Cox submitted an entry for the 1892 competition for the new B.C. Parliament Buildings under the patriotic *nom-de-plume* "Beaver." He became a member of the RIBA in 1900.

Following the opportunities offered by the western boom, Cox moved to Vancouver in 1908 and established an office. His first Vancouver commission had been obtained before he left Montreal, a seven-storey Classical Revival structure at West Hastings and Cambie Streets, built to house the *News-Advertiser* newspaper for well-connected publisher, Francis Carter-Cotton, MLA from 1890-1900, Minister of Finance 1898-1900 and Chief Commissioner of Lands and Works 1899-1900. Cox signed the drawings for this project under the name of the partnership, and did not officially dissolve his partnership with Amos until 1910.

Carter-Cotton Building, Vancouver

Bowser Residence, Victoria

Cox met with considerable success in the next few years, and secured a number of commissions from business and political leaders. In 1911 he was retained by local merchant, Henry Edgett, to prepare a scheme for the site adjacent to the Carter-Cotton building. He provided Classical Revival designs for the Union Bank and British American Trust Co. Ltd. Building, both in Victoria, 1912. The same year Cox designed residences for William F. Salsbury, an official with the CPR who settled in Shaughnessy Heights, and for the Hon. William John Bowser on Terrace Avenue in Victoria; Bowser was a Progressive Conservative MLA 1903-24, appointed Attorney General in 1907 and later served as premier, 1915-16. Cox's contacts with civic leaders allowed him to become a member of the Vancouver Club in 1913. Another notable commission, the Provincial Industrial Home for Girls, 1912-14, was a reformatory school designed in the Spanish Colonial revival style and located at the easternmost periphery of the city limits in Hastings Townsite. By 1914 Cox had provided the designs for a new court house in Prince Rupert. Tenders closed the following year, but the project was never started due to the outbreak of war. The structure finally built in the 1920s was designed by **Henry Whittaker** of the Provincial Department of Public Works.

Cox also designed a number of bank buildings, smaller commercial buildings, residences, and a number of buildings at Vancouver General Hospital. His hospital experience lead to his appointment as advisory architect to J Unit of the Military Hospitals Commission and Superintendent of Military Hospitals in B.C. during the First World War. After the war he resumed his practice at a modest scale, designing structures such as the Bank of Nova Scotia in Victoria, 1923, and the Vancouver Womens' Building, 1926. By 1934 he had retired to England but remained a member of the AIBC. Cox died after a short illness in November 1944, at his sister's home, the "Laurels," Souldern, Bichester, Oxon, where he had lived for the previous four years.

Mr. Cox has a large and varied practice and this ability places him in the highest rank of the architectural profession on this continent.

[RIBA Application]

Union Bank, Victoria

BRITISH ARTS AND CRAFTS

JENNIFER NELL BARR AND
RICK GOODACRE

By the end of the nineteenth century, residential architecture in British Columbia had begun to come under the thrall of the Arts and Crafts movement. The brainchild of a handful of fervent reformers, it swept first through Britain, and then on to North America. Here, taking on renewed vigour and new forms, it rapidly conquered the continent.

The Arts and Crafts influence occurred just in time for one of B.C.'s great economic booms, and many of the houses built before the First World War express some version of the Arts and Crafts style, especially the quintessential American variant, the ubiquitous bungalow. What is less commonly recognized, however, is that a distinctly British version of Arts and Crafts enjoyed an almost equal preponderance to its American counterpart. The reason was simple. In the boom years leading up to the First World War, British architects were attracted to opportunities in British Columbia. Many of these hopefuls wound up in Victoria, which had yet to capitulate to Vancouver as the province's economic giant. The very British influence of the Arts and Crafts movement was particularly strong in the genteel atmosphere of Victoria, which was more proud of its connections to the Mother Country. The city was described in 1887 as a "transplanted section of Old England, climate, people and all, more vigorous, perhaps, because of the transplanting." The crop of architects newly arrived from Britain who found their way to Victoria in the years before the war were well positioned to fill the growing need for new homes. And Victorians, being Victorians, wanted British architects to build them British houses, which is just what they got.

These British architects brought with them training acquired in firms where Arts and Crafts principles had been forged into architectural ideas. The British Arts and Crafts movement took as its basic lawgivers the architect and theorist, Augustus Welby Northmore Pugin (1812-1852), and the writer, John Ruskin (1819-1900). Pugin was the father of the true Gothic Revival movement in Britain, a prolific designer of churches and all their fittings, who studied Britain's native Gothic styles in detail. Ruskin was an Oxford-trained writer and the first art historian, whose heartfelt and brilliant essays won many to the Ecclesiological movement – the true British Gothic – and instilled in some a hatred of the industrial revolution and its dehumanizing ways. Ruskin was a great influence on the young artists of the Pre-Raphaelite Fellowship, and he championed their work to the public.

Ruskin and the Pre-Raphaelites were in turn a great influence on the man who is considered the Father of the Arts and Crafts movement, William Morris. Morris had abandoned architecture to follow the polymath career of a true renaissance man, translating revolutionary social values and aesthetic dictums into designs for furniture, wallpaper, carpets, and textiles. He and his associates were zealots and reformers. Among other things, they rejected the empty formalism of two and a half centuries of imported architectural revivals – classical, renaissance, baroque – in favour of a return to an honest, essentially British manner of building, in forms that combined function with beauty, and in a way that made beauty accessible to the common man and woman.

When Morris married Jane Burden in 1858, he asked his friend, the architect Philip Webb, to design them a house in Bexleyheath, Kent. In the design and decoration of *Red House* lay many of the basic elements of the Arts and Crafts movement. The Morrises' friends, including the Pre-Raphaelites, took the train out from London on weekends, and everyone, male and female together, helped decorate the house and create beautiful and useful furniture and objects. Thus was

F.J. Marshall Residence, Oak Bay,
A.R. Hennell, Architect, 1913-14

born the idea of the communal workshop, with its Guild and Medieval connotations, and equality of the sexes. Out of these weekends came "the firm," Morris, Marshall, Faulkner & Co, which in 1875 became Morris & Company, a revolutionary and profoundly influential company in interior design and decoration. In 1877 Morris and Webb and their friends became the fathers of the modern heritage restoration movement, when they founded the Society for the Protection of Ancient Buildings, nicknamed "Anti-Scrape."

As a reform movement, Arts and Crafts looked both forward – to a new and better social order – and back – to values rooted in British soil. Some of the best practitioners developed these precepts into a new and distinctive style of their own. They used various vernacular or indigenous materials such as white or cream roughcast stucco, mellow Cotswold stone, sandstone or flint, tiled roofs and tilehung walls, weathered boards, red or brown brick, and half-timbering, with deep roofs and tall chimneys. Charles F.A. Voysey created an instantly recognizable style of his own, incorporating battered, roughcast stucco walls, deep rooflines with overhanging eaves, mediaeval wrought-iron hardware on plank doors, and banks of casement windows.

These were some of the influences from the Mother Country that had such a profound effect on architecture in British Columbia. Important B.C. architects who worked in the British Arts and Crafts tradition included native-born **Samuel Maclure** and his English trained partners and associates, including **Richard P. Sharp**, **Douglas James**, Cecil Crocker Fox (who had trained directly under Voysey) and **Ross Lort**, all of whom profoundly influenced Maclure's work. Maclure in turn, with successful residential practices in both Victoria and Vancouver, influenced many others. Steeped in the British traditions and apprenticed in British architectural offices, others developed their own brand of the style, including **Percy Leonard James** (the brother of Douglas James), and many of his circle – among

others, **Hubert Savage** and **Lord Wilfrid Hargreaves**. **K.B. Spurgin** and **H.J. Rous Cullin** were also highly accomplished designers who provided their own interpretations of the style. **Francis Rattenbury** exploited his deep understanding of Arts and Crafts in his search for a suitable expression of imperial power in this far-flung piece of the British Empire. Another leading and very vocal proponent was **R. Mackay Fripp**, who travelled restlessly back and forth through the colonies, leaving a legacy of drawings and writings that reveal his deep-seated belief in the appropriateness of the Arts and Crafts style to the climate and culture of British Columbia.

In other parts of the province, architects like **O.B. Hatchard** and **R.B. Bell**, based in Vernon, worked in their own, sophisticated version of the style, producing both high-style versions for their wealthy clients, and vernacular adaptations for more modest commissions. In the best Arts and Crafts tradition, designers like **James Bloomfield** began to tentatively explore the native traditions of the province, and incorporate them in his work. Many other British-trained architects practised briefly in British Columbia during the boom years. Too numerous to mention individually, they all contributed to a sense of connection with British traditions, made manifest in the urban fabric being developed to support the growing province.

The building boom ended abruptly in 1913, and it was not until the 1920s that construction picked up again, by which time many of the British architects of the prewar years were gone: possibly casualties of the conflict, or the Spanish Influenza pandemic of 1919, or relocated in search of new opportunities. The British and the American Arts and Crafts traditions became intermingled and institutionalized, resulting in a watered-down Craftsman style that was simple, effective and cheap to build, but only an echo of the previously strong allusions to a romantic and utopian British lifestyle.

Hall Residence, Victoria,

Samuel Maclure, Architect, 1912

"READY-CUT" HOUSES

DONALD LUXTON

Given the difficulty of construction in a frontier environment, including a scarcity of skilled labour, it was often easier to ship ready-made buildings into remote locations and assemble them on site. At a time when much of the cost of the building was invested in hand labour, there were a number of innovative schemes developed to market structures constructed from precut lumber. Many companies such as The Canadian Aladdin Company, Gordon-Van Tine, and The T. Eaton Company Ltd. offered "ready-cut" buildings in a prefabricated package. Once an order was placed, all the loose components of a building, whether a house, bank, barn, church or garage, would be delivered to your building site, and would include all the lumber cut to size, mouldings, glass, staircases, plaster and lath, hardware, and even nails, paint and varnish. The Aladdin Company of Bay City, Michigan, which began operations in 1906, noted in their 1917 pattern book that "complete houses [are] shipped direct from our mills in Michigan, Louisiana, Oregon, Florida, USA and Toronto, Ottawa and Vancouver, Canada." Between 1908 and 1940, Sears, Roebuck & Co. sold 100,000 prefabricated order, shipped out by rail across America. Their success was due to their reputation for good value, but also to the attractive financing options that were available from the company, which in addition to the materials could also include the costs of land and labour; down payments could be as low as one-quarter of the total cost of the house. Following this example, between 1910 and 1933 the T. Eaton Co. sold numerous catalogue houses throughout Canada, mainly on the Prairies, shipped by rail from lumber yards in British Columbia; they also offered barns and schools, other essential components of an agricultural community. Unlike Sears, Roebuck, Eaton's believed in "cash on the barrelhead" and did not offer any financing for their prefabricated houses.

Although these pre-made homes were mainly intended for farmers on the Prairies, they were suitable for many different uses, including remote industrial operations that needed to provide housing for their workers. The Britannia Mining & Smelting Co. at Britannia Beach, the "largest copper mine in the British Empire," ordered twelve ready-cut homes from the Home Builders Lumber Company Ltd. in Vancouver, and provided a testimonial of their satisfaction for the company's next catalogue. These houses tended to follow, rather than lead, architectural fashion, and provided a conservative and economical alternative to custom-built or architect-designed structures. As they have no external distinguishing features, they are difficult to identify except by comparison with plan books. The market for these ready-cut houses continued right up to the time of the Depression.

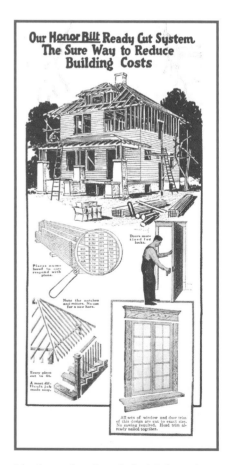

Advertisement from Sears, Roebuck & Co. catalogue

B.C. MILLS, TIMBER & TRADING COMPANY PREFABRICATED BUILDINGS

DONALD LUXTON

In addition to the ready-cut buildings being offered for sale, some companies went so far as to develop prefabricated modular systems that were partially assembled in factories and bolted together on site. The most successful local scheme was marketed by the Vancouver-based B.C. Mills, Timber & Trading Company (BCMT&T) between 1904 and 1910. The western provinces were experiencing unprecedented population growth, and in response Edwin C. Mahoney, manager of the Royal City Mills branch of the BCMT&T, patented a sectional system in 1904 that could be adapted to provide everything from modest one room cottages to churches, schools and banks. Mahoney had the brilliant idea of assembling the short mill ends of lumber and siding, until then just waste material that piled up in the millyard, into three or four foot wide wall panels that could be bolted together. The vertical joints between the panels were covered by narrow battens, which gave these buildings their characteristic appearance. As Mahoney stated: "My invention relates to the construction of knockdown houses especially designed for the use of settlers in a comparatively new or undeveloped country, and is intended to meet the requirements of such a class by providing a framed house the erection of which does not require the services of skilled carpenters or tradespeople." Wall panels were assembled at the mill, prepainted, and packaged with the other components and the instructions necessary to assemble the building. The disassembled building was then shipped by rail to the waiting customer. Until he established his own practice in 1908, **Joseph H. Bowman** was employed by the BCMT&T as their architectural designer, and his inventive elaborations of this simple system – including Mahoney's own West End home and the company's head office – demonstrated its versatility and wide applicability.

Although a number of other companies, including the Colonial Portable House Company Ltd. in Vancouver, offered sectional building systems after 1905, none seriously challenged the preeminence of the BCMT&T system; they were so successful that the company did not have to offer financing on their products. They targetted the export market, especially the rapidly growing prairie communities, but these prefabricated structures found a much wider audience, and a number of them were shipped to San Francisco after the devastating 1906 earthquake.

Institutional clients often found this system a convenient way to establish themselves in the rapidly-sprouting new western settlements. The first two provincial government buildings in Prince Rupert were B.C. Mills prefabricated structures. The unassembled buildings were bought for $5,284.80; labour was an additional $3,236.75, and with all other costs including hardware, plastering, plumbing and wiring, the net cost was $13,429.63, a relative bargain given the remoteness of the location and the shortage of available labour.

The Canadian Bank of Commerce also used the BCMT&T system for many of its western branches. Banking was extremely competitive during the western boom years. Although there was no guarantee which of the new settlements along the railway would survive and prosper, establishing the first bank in a booming town presented a tremendous business advantage. Speed of construction was therefore essential. Each pre-fabricated bank fit conveniently into railway boxcars, which were dropped off at the chosen settlement to await the construction crews that assembled them. The Bank of Commerce retained Toronto architects, **Darling & Pearson**, to adapt the BCMT&T system to a suitably appropriate classical idiom.

As the western settlements became established, labour and materials were more freely available and local construction companies could be more competitive in their costs. Profits from prefabricated systems started to decline. In 1910 the BCMT&T agreed to lease the rights for their system to Prudential Builders, with Mahoney assuming the post as their General Manager. Unlike B.C. Mills, Prudential offered "easy terms" of financing by marketing their houses through a subsidiary, the National Finance Company. Prudential attempted to build an entire prefabricated subdivision, Talton Place, on the outskirts of Vancouver's Shaughnessy Heights, but it was soon found that the use of the panels inflated the cost of construction and the company reverted to standard methods to complete the project. Mahoney subsequently moved to England where his attempts to market the idea of prefabricated bungalows in the 1920s met with some success.

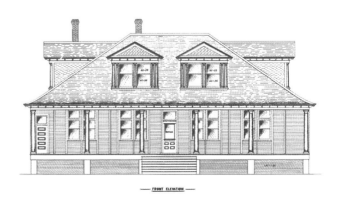

BCMT&T Co. Head Office, Vancouver, Joseph H. Bowman, Architect, 1905-06

BUNGALOW PATTERN BOOKS

STUART STARK

By the time of the building boom of the early 1900s, the pattern book phenomena truly hit its stride. Architectural development always progresses in tandem with economic prosperity, and the boom years from 1908 to 1912 saw huge tracts of homes built from pattern books. As an example, the relatively small community of Oak Bay saw over 1,100 homes constructed each year from 1910 to 1912 – about three per day – and the majority of these were pattern book homes.

It was the age of first home ownership for many working-class people, the majority having been renters through the Victorian period. The developing cult of the suburban home ensured the popularity of pattern books as dream factories. Pattern books were being printed by specialized companies in Seattle, Los Angeles, Chicago and other centres, as well as by individual architects, and were widely distributed by mail. Architects, such as **E. Stanley Mitton** and **Jud Yoho**, saw them as a way of promoting themselves as well as providing an additional source of income. Advertisements in publications such as *Bungalow Magazine* or *National Builder*, which them-selves included "house plans of the month," invited readers to send for plan books. The "Bungalow lifestyle" was exemplified by a philosophy for living that was a reaction against Victorian values. A closeness to nature, the use of natural materials in construction and decorating, and a simpler overall lifestyle that was "cozy" and "artistic" were the goals that homeowners were encouraged to strive for. By reading pattern books, prospective bungalow owners were informed as to appropri-ate architectural design, furnishings and landscaping, in a manner sympathetic with bungalow ideals, in preparation for this new mode of living.

After the economic downturn of 1913, and during the First World War, construction came to a standstill. But early in the 1920s, with a revived economy, pattern books dating from the pre-war boom years were once again used to build homes, and many slightly old-fashioned dwellings were built during that decade. By now, the "Bungalow lifestyle" was forgotten, and the associated philosophy subverted for what had become just another architectural style. For some architects, pattern book designs remained an expedient way to satisfy clients. During the agricultural expansion of the interwar years, promotional house plan books were widely distributed by organizations such as the Western Retail Lumbermen's Association and United Grain Growers Ltd.

Today, the role of pattern books has mostly been taken over by plans featured in the "Homes" section of our daily news-papers, as editorial filler for the advertisements. Modern house plan books are widely available, and are a staple of the lower end of the house design industry.

BUNGAL-ODE
Burgess Johnson

There's a jingle in the jungle,
*   'Neath the juniper and pine,*
They are mangling in the tangle
*   Of the underbrush and vine,*
And my blood is all a-tingle
*   At the sound of blow on blow,*
As I count each single shingle
*   On my bosky bungalow.*

There's a jingle in the jungle,
*   I am counting every nail,*
And my mind is bungaloaded,
*   Bungaloping down a trail;*
And I dream of every ingle
*   Where I angle at my ease,*
Naught to set my nerves a-jingle,
*   I may bungle all I please.*

For I oft get bungalonely
*   In the mingled human drove,*
And I long for bungaloafing
*   In some bungalotus grove,*
In a cooling bung'location
*   Where no troubling trails intrude,*
'Neath some bungalowly rooftree
*   In east bungalongitude.*

Oh, I think with bungaloathing
*   Of the strangling social swim,*
Where they wrangle after bangles
*   Or for some new-fangled whim;*
And I know by bungalogic
*   That is all my bungalown*
That a little bungalotion
*   Mendeth every mortal moan!*

Oh, a man that's bungalonging
*   For the dingle and the loam*
Is a very bungalobster
*   If he dangles on at home.*
Catch the bungalocomotive;
*   If you cannot face the fee,*
Why, a bungaloan 'll do it–
*   You can borrow it of me!*

First printed in *Good Housekeeping Magazine*, 1909

The Rochester $1,387.00

Price, $1,460.00
Cash discount, 5%
Net price, $1,387.00

THE Rochester is of the strong, substantial American type. Square lines give the advantage of utilizing every inch of space to good advantage, while this particular house incorporates some features distinctive to itself. Note the vestibule, large living room with cosy bedroom having projecting bay window; group window in dining room; large pantry attached to kitchen and rear exit grade cellar entrance. Three bedrooms, sewing room, bath and closets complete the second story. Most of the windows are grouped in pairs. Scrolled rafter ends embellish the eaves. Taken altogether, the Rochester is a most satisfying home. On a one-thousand-dollar lot the Rochester would normally sell for at least $5,500. You can easily comprehend the profit available to the owner should conditions arise that he would want to sell it. Owners of Aladdin houses find that the high quality of finish, material, both inside and outside helps make quick sales when a sale is desired.

The Rochester was first built up in Northern Minnesota and the owner is high in his praise of the warmth of Aladdin construction.

See Terms on page 2 and General Specifications on pages 12 and 13.

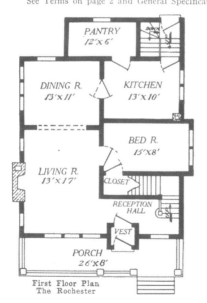

First Floor Plan
The Rochester

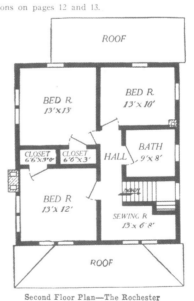

Second Floor Plan—The Rochester

39

Aladdin Company Pattern Book Catalogue, 1917

EDWARD STANLEY MITTON
B.1880

JANA TYNER

E. Stanley Mitton's most significant contribution to early B.C. architecture was his effort to promote the image of the architect, and the architect's importance in home design, to a broader public through his role as architect-businessman. Traditionally, most homes were either designed by the individual builder or developer, or built from purchased mail-order plans. Beginning in 1910, Mitton joined with the Society of the Master Builders to publish the *Mitton Home Builder*. The journal, modeled loosely on Gustav Stickley's *The Craftsman* magazine and Henry Wilson's *Bungalow* magazine, contained articles on planning a bungalow, advertisements for Vancouver craftsmen and designers, and house plans for purchase. Articles emphasized the beauty of homes built of natural materials like wood and stone, quoting John Ruskin as further

endorsement of the Arts and Crafts aesthetic. In the tradition of Stickley's maxims endorsing a simple way of life that were included on the verso of each issue of *The Craftsman*, Mitton inscribed similar pronouncements: "I believe in the religion of the family. I believe that the rooftree is sacred, from the smallest fibre held in the soft, moist clutch of earth, to the smallest blossom on the topmost bough that gives its fragrance to the happy air. The family where virtue dwells with love is like a lily with a heart of fire – the faintest flower in all the world."

Mitton was born in Birmingham, England on August 6, 1880, a son of Edward Moss Mitton, who had a family connection to Jack Mitton, "noted in English history as a celebrated hunter." Young Edward was articled to architects, Ingall & Son, Birmingham for five years, and then moved to London to work for Herbert Bolton. After two years he moved to Loughborough, where he was employed as a specialist in school work. He then briefly opened his own office in Birmingham before joining with his old employers as Ingall, Son & Mitton for two years. In Birmingham on December 28, 1907, he married Edith Thomas, and the couple later had one child, Mary. The marriage occurred about the same time that Mitton moved to Toronto to act as special designer for F.S. Baker, but within two months he met with an unspecified accident, and was sent to Vancouver to recover his health.

In 1908, he opened his own office in Vancouver, which he maintained until he returned to Toronto in 1914. During this period, Mitton designed over sixty buildings, primarily residences for a middle to upper class clientele. In Vancouver, most of these homes were located on the city's west side, and in the newly developed Shaughnessy district. Mitton opened an office in Victoria in 1911 in association with **H.T. Whitehead**. It was boasted in the press that "there are many, many people in Victoria who take a lively interest in building, interior design and architecture. These will receive the news that Mr. E. Stanley Mitton is opening studios here with a great deal of pleasure... No firm in Canada is so fully qualified to deal with high-class residence work, office blocks, apartment houses, hotels, etc., and this fact is so well known that any further comment is unnecessary." Examples of Mitton's work in Victoria include the Heisterman Residence on Shasta Place, and the landmark Lineham Residence at the south foot of Cook Street, jointly designed with Whitehead. These houses were generally in the British Arts and Crafts style prevalent at the

Modern Homes for Modern People

time, characterised by half-timbering, heavy stone or brick foundations, roughcast stucco, gabled roofs, and expansive verandahs.

Mitton further promoted his skills through advertisements in the Vancouver *Province* and Henderson's *Vancouver Directory*. Significantly, Mitton's ad in the directory emphasized the economical aspects of employing an architect: "Completely drawn plans will enable you to take competitive bids on the work, thereby saving on the cost... it will pay you to employ me as an architect." Seeking to find work further afield, Mitton was the only architect who advertised in 1910-11 in the *Portland Canal Miner*, a small newspaper that served the northern town of Stewart, B.C. About 1914 he published a large catalogue, *Modern Homes for Modern People*, with an extensive set of plans that could be ordered by mail. At the time he had formed a partnership with **H.H. Gillingham**, whose name also appeared on the publication.

E. Stanley Mitton recognized that, as today, the architect's role in residential design was jeopardized by the production of cheap, pre-drawn house plans. While the majority of Mitton's designs were for relatively elaborate homes, it is clear from these advertisements and from his writings in the *Mitton Home Builder* that he recognized the potential market for lower priced, modest bungalows that flourished in Vancouver and Victoria during the period.

> *Although he is not a politician he is a public-spirited and progressive citizen, interested in everything pertaining to civic improvement.*
>
> Howay & Schofield, *British Columbia Biographical*, Vol. III, p. 619

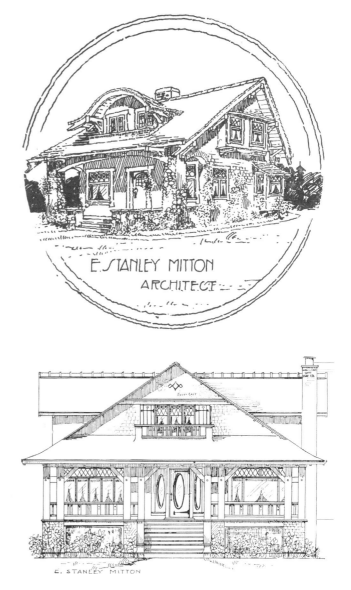

Images from *Modern Homes for Modern People*, c.1914

JUD
YOHO

1882-1968

JENNIFER NELL BARR

Jud Yoho never opened an office in British Columbia. His influence came from his publications and plan books, and a number of buildings in the province are known to have been built to his plans. He was born in Ohio on October 1, 1882 and moved to Seattle in 1897. About 1911 Yoho formed The Craftsman Bungalow Company, which eventually had at least three components: a building company for prefabricated homes (the Take Down Manufacturing Company which produced Craftsman Master Built Homes); the *Bungalow Magazine*, a monthly publication (not associated with the Los Angeles publication of the same name) which was published from August 1912 to about March 1918 and at its peak ran to 40,000 subscriptions; and house plan catalogues, which were published from 1913 to 1921. To keep up with the fashion of the times, these plan books sometimes espoused other architectural styles, such as in *Colonial Homes featuring The New Colonial Bungalow*, which went to a second edition in 1921. *Bungalow Magazine* was subtitled "An Illustrated Monthly Magazine Devoted Exclusively to Artistic Bungalow Homes" and the Manager's Page at the beginning of the first edition promised:

> For the first time the whole subject of bungalows will be set before you in this magazine – the latest achievement in the building field. It will tell you the kind of a house to build, how to build it right, what to plan for and how to enjoy the greatest comfort in your home. There will be articles dealing authoritatively as to the treatment of the home, including suggestions for all manner of interior arrangements, breakfast rooms, sleeping verandas, and living rooms that embody all that the

word implies. Arrangement and preparation of the ground surrounding your house will be thoroughly treated by experts in that line.

To date, nine houses built from Yoho's Craftsman Bungalow plans have been identified, four in Victoria, two in Oak Bay and one in Vancouver. W. Bownass built two houses to Yoho's plans in Victoria, 1911-12; one at 24 Douglas Street and another directly behind it at 27 Olympia Avenue. Yoho also designed two simple bungalows for Seabourne and Company Limited in Oak Bay, and a bungalow for Harold Strange in Vancouver. For the last few years before he left Seattle in 1919, Yoho had a partner, Edward L. Merritt, who continued to publish catalogues of house plans. Little is known about Yoho's subsequent activities after he left the west coast, although once back east he abandoned architectural work and followed other business interests. Yoho died in November, 1968 at Youngstown, Mahoning County, Ohio.

24 Douglas Street, Victoria; Plan 327 from *Craftsman Bungalow*

ELMER ELLSWORTH
GREEN
1861-1928

COLIN BARR

On January 8, 1861 in Janesville, Waseca County, Minnesota, E.E. Green was born into the farming family of Sarah J. and Matthew S. Green. Elmer first came to Canada in 1895, followed two years later by his wife Julia and their family. For eight years Green was superintendent of the Giant Powder Works at Telegraph Bay near Victoria. He returned to the United States in 1903, settled in Seattle and set up business as a draftsman and carpenter/builder. His first known building was constructed in 1904. By 1907, Green was working in Seattle as an architect and constructing engineer. In 1908-09 he joined in partnership with William C. Aiken in Seattle, and in 1909 Green won first prize for best bungalow in a competition sponsored by the Lewis Publishing Co. of St. Louis, Missouri. Green worked primarily in the bungalow style for the middle and working class homeowner, but also designed a variety of other buildings including: a bank in Burlington; mansions in the Mount Baker district of Seattle; and the five-storey Ben Lomond Apartments, a landmark red brick building along the Interstate Highway just north of downtown Seattle. Over one hundred of his buildings have been identified in Seattle, most of them still standing.

Green started making trips to Victoria in 1911 and by 1912 had opened an office in #616, the Sayward Building, a room he shared with several other Seattle architects. In 1912 he published *The Practical Planbook* with sixty-eight plans. In the foreword he stated:

The designing of an artistic and practical Bungalow or residence of any kind requires much skill and education, together with practical knowledge of building construction. When I started to fit myself for the Architectural profession I firmly believed that a man had no moral right to call himself an Architect until he was thoroughly familiar with all kinds of building construction... Before taking up the study of drawing I spent several years with the best and most experienced builders I could find, and learned thoroughly the mechanical end of building construction. After becoming an expert in that line I took up the study of drawing and design, and now with twenty-five years experience on high-class work, I believe that I am in a position to give the very best service that money can buy.

Green's Canadian work was primarily conducted in Victoria, although a bungalow in Chemainus was built about 1912 and two 1911 houses have been identified in Vancouver. In Victoria, most of his work was on private residences, but he also designed a two-storey brick office block for the Canadian Puget Sound Lumber Company at Store and Discovery Streets, 1912. His largest residential commission, for Guy S. Brown, secretary-treasurer of the **Ward Investment Company**, 1913, was later the home of B.C. Premier John Hart. His smallest was a five-room cottage built in 1914. E.E. Green was one of several architects and designers, including **Ralph Berrill**, **Milo S. Farwell** and J. Lennox Wilson, who designed small California Bungalow-style houses for the **Bungalow Construction Company Limited**. At least eleven houses have been identified which the company built to Green's plans.

Many of his homes have distinctively-notched bargeboards with heavy support brackets ending in pyramids on top of the bargeboards. These pyramids are also a frequent interior detail, at the upper corners of door and window casings. Typically, his houses were side-gabled, with large gable- or shed-roofed dormers on the front and back roof slopes. They had deep front verandahs, and cedar shingles, bevelled siding, or stucco and half-timbering used as contrasting wall cladding. Examples of E.E. Green's other Victoria-area buildings include the J. McKay residence on Oscar Street, 1912 (with William C. Aiken), a 1912 house for his brother, contractor Royal H. Green, who worked out of the same office, and a large house for William Scowcroft on Southgate Street, 1913. Elmer Green closed his Victoria office in 1915, and by 1917 had left Seattle. He died in Eureka, California on February 18, 1928, and was buried at Santa Clara.

George and Mary Ann Leach Residence, Victoria,

E.E. Green, Architect, 1913-1914

BUNGALOW AND HOME CONSTRUCTION COMPANIES

1908-1915

JENNIFER NELL BARR

Bungalow to the average person means a cosy comfortable abode not too large and yet not too small, it demands to be heavy and massive in appearance, and built low down to the ground. This in turn, demands low ceilings and heavy trim... Ordinarily, the bungalow cottages type is unsuitable for the narrow lot of the crowded city streets. The type almost essentially requires them to be situated on spacious grounds. Their popularity in the suburbs, however, has developed the storey and a half cottage, combining some of the advantages of both the urban and suburban home.

The Building and Contractor, Vol. 1, No. 6, Toronto, July 15, 1911, pp.253-7.

There were a number of companies, mainly based in Victoria, that built houses on a speculative basis during the building boom before the First World War. They were sold on the instalment plan to the newly developing market of young working class and lower-middle-class families who, a generation earlier, would not have been able to afford their own homes. The potentially lucrative integration of house building and home financing under one company had been pioneered in California by the Los Angeles Investment Company, which had been extremely successful in the competitive Los Angeles real estate market. Many of the home construction companies that sprang up in British Columbia in the years before the First World War were based overtly on this model.

Many prospective home buyers between 1908-14 chose modest California and Craftsman Bungalows, as these "artistic" styles, developed as the American version of the Arts and Crafts movement, were both compact and convenient; plans were available either through architects engaged by the company or from readily available pattern books. Because of the prevalence of British designers and homeowners in Victoria, some of these companies specialized in British Arts and Crafts styles, and sometimes in the more traditional English styles such as Georgian. Most of these companies also had the financial resources to provide mortgages, which at the time was one of the ways in which prospective homeowners could get loans for housing.

British Canadian Home Builders, Limited (BCHB) was formed October, 1911 with an authorized capital of $500,000 issued in $1 shares to the public. Houses were designed in the British Arts and Crafts style, including several by noted English-born architect, **H. Bryant Newbold**. The President of the company was John Armstrong, and the Managing Director was Ernest Kennedy, who in 1913 commissioned a handsome British Arts and Crafts-style house for himself to be built in the new Alta Dena subdivision on Wilkinson Road in Saanich. By August, 1913, BCHB had a subscribed capital of only $125,000; the following year they ran into legal and financial difficulties which forced them into liquidation by October 1914.

However tyrannical their sway, however autocratic their rule in other countries, the landlords in British Columbia have little terror for the majority of residents in that Province. There nearly every house-holder is his own landlord – a state of affairs rendered possible by the system of deferred payments, which is the basis on which the Bungalow Construction Company, Ltd., are operating.

Henry J. Boam, British Columbia, p.78

The **Bungalow Construction Company, Limited** (BCC) was one of the most prominent of the companies working in the speculative field, and certainly the one that built the most distinctive California Bungalows. It began life as the Victoria Bungalow Construction Company, but at the end of 1911 the owners and managers, F.S. Bonnell and C.G. Walsh, parted company with their main designer, J. Lennox Wilson and on January 1, 1912 became the BCC. Wilson had previously been involved in the development of speculative housing in Vancouver; he was listed as a contractor in Victoria in 1912, and an architect in 1913, but left the city the following year. His California Bungalows are notable for their short, chunky verandah columns with wide bases. He also made use of heavy timbers in verandah gables, as exemplified by the 1912 LeRoy Burgess house in Oak Bay. Wilson's houses are prevalent on Linden and Moss Streets and Clover Avenue, and in the area of Cowichan and Quamichan Streets. For the next several years, the BCC used the services of several other architects, including American **Milo S. Farwell** and Englishman **Ralph Berrill**. However, the greatest majority of their houses for which an architect has been identified were designed by Seattle architect, **E.E. Green**. The BCC was recognized twice with articles in **Jud Yoho's** Bungalow Magazine from

BRITISH CANADIAN HOME BUILDERS
LIMITED
312 - 315 SAYWARD BLDG
& Trounce Alley
C H
PHONES 1030 - 3231
Authorized Capital $500,000
Subscribed Capital $125,000

Seattle, the first in January 1913: "From the beginning, the new company specialized in five and six room bungalows, designed with the idea of minimizing the labor of housekeeping and following in a general way the California idea, with adaptations to meet the slightly different climatic requirements." The firm's most impressive line of California Bungalows are those on the east side of Durban Street in Victoria's Fairfield neighbourhood, where they built seven on one block. In 1914 the BCC advertised as dealing in real estate, as home builders and mortgage brokers, but by 1915 was out of business.

William Dunford & Son began constructing houses in

Victoria in 1908, after the Dunfords moved from Winnipeg where they had been in the lumber business. William Dunford was born in Wiltshire, England, and immigrated to Canada in 1858. His son, John Orville Dunford (c.1883-1961), was born in Ontario. From 1910 on they averaged "one bungalow every nine days, and the firm states that each one of these has been sold before the date of its completion... Mr. Dunford, senior, makes annual trips to California and various sections of the United States to gather new ideas for the design and construction of Dunford Bungalows." In January, 1911 Charles H. Walker, formerly of the architectural firm Hooper & Walker of

Dunford Bungalow

Bungalow Construction Company Bungalow

Winnipeg, came to Victoria to run the business end of Dunford & Son. In 1912 the company was incorporated with a capital of $50,000. An article in Henry J. Boam's 1912 book on British Columbia stated that the construction of these houses cost $4,000 to $10,000. "Although all the bungalows which they build are of their own design, Messrs. Dunford employing the exclusive services of a fully qualified English architect, they are always willing to incorporate their clients' ideas. The Californian style of architecture is mostly favoured, but in some of the more expensive of the 150 dwellings which they have built the English style has been frequently introduced." The English architect mentioned was either George V. Bishop or E.W. Arnold B. Stoton, both of whom worked for the Dunfords. Bishop's preferred style was generally Arts and Crafts. He designed a number of houses between 1909-12, and was still active as late as 1947. Stoton came to Victoria in 1912; two projects that year were the Dobbie Residence, 1912, built by William Dunford & Son, and a house for A.C. Jones with unusual Oriental-style bracketing on the verandah. The March 10, 1913 edition of *Architect, Builder & Engineer* published an article by Stoton entitled *The "A" of Architecture*. In it he exhorts those of the architectural and building professions to build a West that all citizens will be proud of: "There are great difficulties in the way, few have the time to devote to research work; but by fostering every tittle of knowledge, or gleaning the fields of our locality for suggestions, we may be able to produce a virile culture characteristic of the best in our people. Advancing step by step, pressing on, refusing to yield to self-satisfaction, with our senses dulled by the fateful voice of self-praise, we may win for the West a world-wide acknowledge-

ment." By 1914 Stoton had left the city, and in 1927 was working as an architect in San Diego. J.O. Dunford worked as a real estate broker, not a builder, after his father's death in 1915.

Modern Homes Limited was active in Victoria during the year 1913, when they built both large homes in the exclusive Uplands neighbourhood of Oak Bay and much smaller houses on Amphion and Wildwood Streets in the Gonzales area of Victoria. W.M. Lucas was managing director of the company, and the architects for the Uplands residences were S.A. Jennings and P.J. Boulanger. The houses in the Uplands included a Georgian-style residence on Cadboro Bay Road, and a double-gabled British Arts and Crafts-style dwelling on Ripon Road. Jennings & Boulanger were responsible for designing the two entrances to the Uplands Estate, with bronze grillwork gates opening between stone pillars. In March 1913 it was announced that Jennings & Boulanger were to design a $300,000 six-storey reinforced concrete apartment block for a syndicate headed by C.C. Pemberton; it was optimistically announced that in January 1914 the project "will be delayed until the financial situation clears up." By early 1914 the local economy was in tatters, the architects were no longer in partnership, and Modern Homes Limited had folded.

The Ward Investment Company (WIC) was formed in 1911 in Victoria, with John H. Moore as president and Guy S. Brown as secretary-treasurer. Moore was manager of Michigan Pacific Lumber Company, which developed three logging camps at Jordan River. In June 1911 that company amalgamated with Jordan River Lumber Company and Michigan Puget Sound Mill to become Canadian Puget Sound Lumber Company, Limited

Henderson's *Victoria Directory*, 1914

(CPSLC). CPSLC shared management with WIC, and Moore acted as president and Brown as secretary-treasurer of both companies. In 1912, Moore and his partners commissioned **H. Elmer Nelson** for plans for a hotel in Sooke. Known as the Sooke Harbour Hotel and later the Belvedere Hotel, this rustic hunting lodge was a grand, three-storey, brown-shingled Craftsman structure with huge rubble stone piers at the entry. Sooke's only resort hotel at the time, it was destroyed by fire in 1934. Both WIC and CPSLC were still advertising as late as 1915. The architects used by WIC were thought to be all Americans. The first known bungalows constructed by WIC were on Linden Avenue and Cambridge Street designed by **Bresemann & Durfee**. Alexander G.L. Lindsay, who designed another on Linden in 1912, was a draftsman with the British Columbia Provincial Lands Department and resided at the YMCA. Two much larger two-storey Craftsman Bungalows were designed by **August B. Schallerer** in 1913. **E.E. Green** designed the 1913 home at 1961 Fairfield Place built by WIC for Guy Brown, who was by then president of the company. WIC used an illustration of a California Bungalow from Green's *The Practical Plan Book* in their 1914 and 1915 advertisements.

Other Victoria area bungalow companies included the Island Investment Co. Ltd. and the Island Construction & Development Co. Ltd., which had interlocking boards of directors, and for which the architects are unknown. They designed and built 1265 and 1275 Roslyn Road and 902 Foul Bay Road, all handsome British Arts and Crafts homes with fine detailing built in 1911, and all extant.

Although not as popular as in Victoria, there were a number of bungalow firms in Vancouver between 1911-14 that offered design-build services, usually based on plan book designs, including the California Bungalow Construction Co., the Craftsman Bungalow Co., and the Western Bungalow Co. One of the more active companies was the Bungalow Construction Association, established by Frank W. Killam in September, 1910 with cash capital of $1,000. Killam built a number of one-storey bungalows in rapid succession, using the money from sales to build even more speculative houses, and by the end of 1911 entered into a contract for the erection of 184 houses, which were completed at the rate of one per day. They were sold at a rate of ten per cent down, with the balance payable over seven years in monthly sums. Killam also opened a real estate department, and by 1912 the company had been reincorporated as the Bungalow Building & Finance Co.

Although none of the bungalow construction companies survived the downturn in the economy and the onset of the First World War, they were very influential in establishing the Arts and Crafts look in many new subdivisions, and allowed many people to own their own home for the first time.

Modern Architecture, 1911

ARTHUR
JULIUS
BIRD
1875-1967

JOHN ATKIN

Hailed in publications as the "Land of Opportunity" and blessed with a great natural harbour and the terminus for the national railways, Vancouver was a booming and rapidly expanding city and fast becoming a major centre on the Pacific coast, with regular steamship services between Seattle, San Francisco and Los Angeles. It was in the middle of this period of prosperity that A.J. Bird, a young, newly-married architect, arrived in late 1907 with his wife, Alice.

Bird was born in the northern industrial town of Bradford, England on July 25, 1875. He was sent south to Rochester, Kent, the ancient English town next to the Royal Dockyards of Chatham, where he was enrolled in the Sir Joseph Williamson Mathematical School. At the age of seventeen he began his long association with London architect Edward Burgess with whom he articled for four years and then spent a further seven years as assistant. During this time Bird was able to take the occasional private commission. Leaving Burgess in 1903, Bird worked in Cheltenham before returning to London and joining the practice of Gotch & Saunders. The firm's principal, John Alfred Gotch (1852-1942), was a collector of globes and an author of a number of books on architecture including *Early Renaissance Architecture in England*, first published in 1894. Gotch had opened his own practice in Kettering in 1879, and established a partnership with C.H. Saunders in 1887. Gotch & Saunders opened additional offices in London in 1903, and Bird was hired an Assistant, a position he held until 1905. Bird married in 1906, and started his own partnership, Boucher & Bird, back in Rochester. The partnership's only building seems to have been the Seaman's House in Rochester. Lasting just under a year the partnership was dissolved in July of

1907. Bird and his wife left for Canada and Vancouver shortly thereafter.

In 1908, Bird set up practice in the new Winch Building on Hastings Street, and from this office he designed an array of residential buildings and commercial structures for clients. His first year was busy. There were five apartment buildings on the drawing board along with a number of houses and one store. He designed two houses on the city's east side for builder A. Mitchell in 1909, and undertook a renovation on Comox Street for the Olmstead family. In 1913, he would design their new North Vancouver home on Keith Road East.

The following years proved to be very productive with a similar range of projects. He found the time to design and build his own house in 1910. Bird continued to design West End apartment buildings such as the Capitola Apartments on Thurlow Street, 1909; Trafalgar Mansions on Nelson Street, 1910-11; Washington Court on Thurlow Street, 1910; and Blenheim Court on Jervis Street, 1910-11. Other projects during this time were the Lotus Hotel on Pender at Abbott, 1912, the Belvedere Court Apartments on Main Street, 1912, and several apartment buildings on the east side. The apartment buildings were typical Edwardian affairs organized like a small house. Each apartment managed to include a sitting room or parlour, dining room, kitchen with pantry, bedroom(s) and bath. Bird's buildings were solid, well designed, pleasant looking compositions which did not call attention to themselves. One of the few designs where he seemed to have some fun is a small three-storey building built in 1912, unremarkable except for an oversize cornice and twin pediments over the top windows. Today it is home to the Afton Hotel and Ovaltine Cafe. Surprisingly, most of Bird's work from this period continues to survive and his apartment buildings, apart from one in the 900 block of Jackson Avenue that has been badly renovated, are still sought after places to live.

By 1913 a severe economic slump brought new construction to a standstill, and the only work Bird had on hand were several repair jobs. In 1914 Bird enlisted with the 47th Battalion of the Canadian Expeditionary Force and was sent overseas. He was not to return to the city until 1919. Once back from the war, he took a job with Vancouver as City Architect. In this role Bird designed a diverse range of projects including additions to Fire Hall No. 6 in the West End, 1929, and alterations to the Holden Building on Hastings Street to make it suitable as the temporary City Hall. There were two airplane hangars, completed in 1931, for the City's airport on

Sea Island, and he even designed three underground public toilets, two of which – at Main and Hastings and Victory Square – still exist, although they were later modernized. Probably the best known building of his career as City Architect was the charming Neo-Georgian Coroner's Court on Cordova Street, 1932, now used as the Vancouver Police Museum.

As the City's architect and chief building inspector, Bird was keen on and advocated for an extensive building programme for public housing. He saw creeping slum conditions as a threat to Vancouver's residential neighbourhoods and sought to halt the invasion with a clearance and rebuilding programme that would create streets of terrace houses based on the English version of the Garden City, as defined by planned communities such as Port Sunlight on the banks of the Mersey River, started 1888-89 on a 135-acre site by the paternalistic and reform minded capitalist William Hesketh Lever to house his Sunlight Soap factory workforce. Bird's plan went nowhere and relations with his employer were strained. In 1933 the Building Department was reorganized amid allegations of unspecified wrong-doing – later withdrawn – by a fellow staff member. The entire staff, including Bird, was let go, though he was later invited by City Council to reapply for his former job. Bird refused and instead decided to leave Canada and return to London where he worked for the London County Council. Later, during and after the Second World War, he worked for the War Damage Commission advising on the demolition of buildings. After the war he spent his retirement in England until 1959 when he decided to return to Canada and take up residence in Victoria. It was here that he died in 1967 at the grand old age of ninety-two.

ARTHUR J. BIRD
Architect
Vancouver

At all times prompted by a laudable ambition, he has so developed his native powers and talents through continuous study and experience that he is now occupying an enviable position among the architects of Vancouver.

Howay & Schofield, *British Columbia Biographical*, Vol. IV, p. 365

Airplane Hangar at Vancouver City Airport, Sea Island, Richmond, 1931

VANCOUVER B C AIRPORT

... Front Elevation ...

SHARP & THOMPSON
PARTNERSHIP 1908-1990

GEORGE LISTER THORNTON SHARP

1880-1974

[signature]

DAVID MONTEYNE

The longest surviving architectural firm in the history of Vancouver was founded by George Sharp and Charles J. Thompson in 1908. Both men were born, educated, and articled in London, England, but arrived on the west coast by different means. They established themselves in Vancouver at the start of a five-year boom, and achieved almost instant success, being one of the few B.C. firms to survive the bust of 1913.

Little has been found regarding the childhoods of Sharp or Thompson, but both attended classes at the Architectural Association in the late 1890s. They may have first met there, although Thompson was a few years older. They also had different interests: Sharp took supplemental classes in painting at the Royal Academy, while the more scientific Thompson studied at the Polytechnic Institute. Thompson articled for the architect, J.A. Thompson (it is not known if this was a relation), and was accredited by RIBA in 1905 before immigrating to Canada. Sharp served his apprenticeship with famed English architect, Thomas Edward Collcutt (1840-1924), travelled in continental Europe as a student, was accredited in 1904, and then took a job with the Public Works Department in Pretoria, South Africa, which was rebuilding after the Boer War.

Sharp married in Pretoria, but soon after was out of a job

when a recession hit. He and his wife returned to England, where the government offered him another job in Ceylon (now Sri Lanka). They turned it down because Sharp heard that the island had a "very unhealthy climate," and the couple had decided that they both wanted to go farming; or, as Sharp later said, "we were fond of animals. So Canada was the sort of place we looked at." Like many prospective immigrants they looked in at the Canadian Pacific Railway offices in London; while there they met someone who gave Sharp an introduction to the Montreal architectural firm of Saxe and Archibald, with whom Sharp found employment. So much for farm animals.

By this time, Charles Thompson had become the CPR's Assistant Chief Architect, based in Montreal, so the two would have likely met at this time. After a brief stint in Montreal in 1906-07, Sharp moved on, working briefly in Calgary for a plasterer who falsely claimed to be an architect. Sharp visited Spokane, Seattle, and Victoria before settling on Vancouver in January 1908. The city was booming and Sharp immediately received some house commissions, and won the competition for a school in New Westminster. Meanwhile, Thompson had progressed west, supervising construction on the CPR's Château-style hotels in Ottawa, Lake Louise, and Banff, before arriving in Vancouver in June of 1908 and forming a partner-

Gilford Court Apartments, Vancouver

ship with Sharp. Sharp, who self-admittedly was weak in mathematics and did not know materials or other technical details of the profession, said that he was very glad for a partner like Thompson who was proficient in all those matters.

As two of the few accredited architects in a growing city, commercial and residential work came their way immediately. Between 1908-12 Sharp & Thompson designed a number of houses including large Tudor Revival mansions for Albert Desbrisay and R.S. Lennie in Shaughnessy Heights; other projects included a large warehouse and a number of brick commercial blocks, the Gilford Court Apartments, and the First Congregational Church in the West End. By 1910, they had made enough money that Thompson could finally send for his English fiancée; they were married that year, and had one son and two daughters. However, 1912 was the firm's breakthrough year as they won two competitions, one for the new Vancouver Club, and, most importantly, for the plan and design of the University of British Columbia.

In the University competition, Sharp & Thompson defeated more established architects, and the university administration was distrustful of their relative youth. Additional experts were called in from eastern universities who upheld the decision and commended the winning design. The plan was based on a major axis which terminated with a viewpoint where Point Grey sloped steeply to the ocean; the buildings were to be styled in the collegiate Gothic popular on campuses at the time. Construction progressed only as far as the erection of the

CHARLES JOSEPH THOMPSON
1878-1961

Charles J. Thompson standing

Science Building's steel frame before the First World War intervened. According to Sharp, the university's funding was redirected into the purchase of a couple of American destroyers to patrol the Pacific coast, and he went off to Europe to defend the firm's right to design the campus. Sharp served as a Captain with the New Westminster Regiment, and was decorated with the Military Cross and Bar.

After the war, the B.C. government stalled on the project until 1923 when, prompted by student protests, completion of the Science Building and construction of the Library and Powerhouse were undertaken by Sharp & Thompson. Despite the 1912 competition, the firm needed to defend its right to design these buildings, as the province attempted to push them aside in favour of its own Department of Public Works. In the 1920s, Sharp & Thompson designed the three permanent, showcase buildings noted above, while the Department erected nine 'temporary' buildings for other faculties and services (many of which still stand). In 1927, they also designed the Anglican Theological College (with **Max B. Downing**, associated architect), and the stone-faced landmark Union Hall on the north edge of the site. The position of Sharp & Thompson as university architects solidified, and the firm would be responsible for everything built through to the early 1970s. Until the 1950s, the partner in charge for the campus commission was Thompson, and it was said by later partner Bob Berwick that "The University was his child – I mean every time the old presidents needed a new porch, you know, they

couldn't get any money out of the government, so they'd repair porches and things like that and 'what would you do, Mr. Thompson so to make it last a little?' Thompson sort of husbanded this thing."

Meanwhile, Sharp was doing so much residential work that he would often go into the firm's offices, say that the design of a certain house was nice, and get the response that "it ought to be, you did it." An example was the English cottage-style Wyman Residence of 1928, a house that – as Sharp would have argued – reflected the architect's experience in South Africa in its plain white stucco facade and its tall windows. Back before the First World War Sharp had settled in the relatively remote village of Kerrisdale, building a house for his family, which included one daughter and a son, who would join the firm in 1950. St. Mary's Anglican parish had a site across the street from the Sharp home. As the only architect in the congregation, in 1913 he designed a homey Arts and Crafts-style English village church with beautiful woodwork and stained glass.

Sharp & Thompson always kept abreast of industry developments. The St. James Clergy House, 1927, was one of their earliest structures to use exposed concrete finishes, a technique rarely used before the First World War but becoming more widely popular in the late 1920s. The use of moulded concrete is also evident on the landmark Burrard Street Bridge: Sharp's applied decoration – Art Deco massing and spirit, with Spanish tilework and west coast themes – was added to mask the engineer's utilitarian design.

Sharp & Thompson were expert in all the traditional styles, and could apply them to technologically advanced structures. Their proficiency in these matters contributed to their great success, as did their profiles within the community. The two moved in a society largely formed of English immigrants and

St. Mary's Church, Kerrisdale, Vancouver

UBC Library, Point Grey, Vancouver, 1923-1925

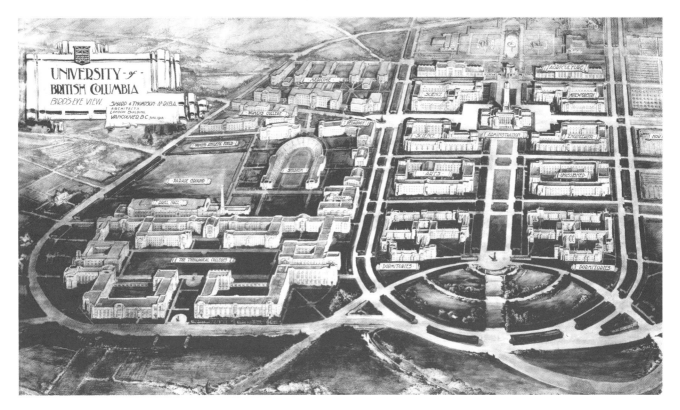

UBC Campus Plan, Point Grey, Vancouver, 1914

their associated pastimes and institutions. Thompson's Point Grey crowd, for instance, enjoyed tennis, lawn-bowling, and yachting, and he was an avid gardener who imported his greenhouse from England. Sharp was also well-known as a watercolourist, was a founding faculty member of the Vancouver School of Art in 1925, and often exhibited his paintings at the new, poured-concrete, Art Deco style Vancouver Art Gallery, which Sharp & Thompson designed in 1931. Both men were charter members of the AIBC, with Sharp serving as President, 1924-26. A wide variety of other professional activities included Thompson's service on the Vancouver Civic Centre Plans Committee in 1914, and Sharp's long-term role as a founding member of the Town Planning Commission that commissioned the Bartholomew Plan (1926-29; partially implemented).

Sharp participated less and less in architectural activities in the late 1930s, until by 1940 he had retired to Vancouver Island to paint full-time, and to fish and golf. From here, though, he worked at his leisure on his most original design, the Anglican church, St. John's Shaughnessy, for which he was recommended by his friend **Fred Townley**. The church hud-dles under parabolic concrete arches which resemble flying buttresses where they meet the ground; applied red brick panels and a Beatrice Lennie frieze enliven the concrete walls. This was Sharp's last architectural project of any size. He continued to live on the Island and paint until his death on July 2, 1974.

Thompson, on the other hand, remained in the office until the age of eighty, although after years of working in eclectic styles he had some trouble adapting to the modernist aesthetic that his firm – particularly Berwick and Ned Pratt, both of whom became partners in 1945 – championed in the postwar period. Indeed, when the UBC administration, wanting an image of progress, insisted that Pratt be the chief designer of the 1951 War Memorial Gymnasium, Berwick recalled that Thompson cried at the loss of control over his pet project. This type of dedication was rewarded, however, when Thompson received an honorary doctorate in 1959 from the University he had done so much to shape. He passed away August 1, 1961, but his name was retained by the firm until 1990, when it was renamed Hemingway Nelson Architects.

Chown Memorial Church, Vancouver

Vancouver Art Gallery, Vancouver

SHOLTO
SMITH
1881-1936

GORDON W. FULTON

Sholto Smith, whose unusual first name is Gaelic, was one of a large number of architects who jumped into Vancouver's roaring building market during the pre-First World War boom years. The tall, athletic Smith toiled with moderate success before making his way to New Zealand, where he became a successful and popular architect. He was born in Nice, France, at midnight on January 25, 1881, the second son of Joseph Burley Smith and Isabella Holmes Hurle. Joseph Smith was an English civil and mining engineer who was in France to supervise construction of a seawall and promenade he had designed. When Sholto was ten, the family immigrated to Canada, settling near Buckingham, Quebec, where his father had business interests. Sholto Smith likely learned his trade in Montreal. In 1902, he worked his way to England on a cattle boat in order to further his architectural studies. By 1906 he was a member of the Province of Quebec Association of Architects sketching club.

Smith reportedly worked for the Bank of Montreal's architects for some time before 1907. It may have been through this job that he met William A. Elliott, a Brandon, Manitoba, architect who was responsible for supervising the construction of a new Bank of Montreal in Brandon in 1905. Elliott offered Smith a position as manager of his new branch office in Moose Jaw, Saskatchewan, where Elliott was involved in a number of projects. Thus, the twenty-six year old Sholto Smith found himself in Moose Jaw on a cold day in January, 1907, in a province where architects were still a novelty: "What the hell is that?" was the mayor of Moose Jaw's response to another architect who told him that he was going to set up an architectural office. The novelty was to be short-lived, however, as archi-

tects flocked to Saskatchewan to ride the boom following provincehood. Smith wasted no time landing a commission for Elliott, winning a competition in 1907 for a new fire hall. Before this building and a school he designed in nearby Caron could be completed, however, Smith packed his bags and left Moose Jaw for Vancouver, arriving some time before mid-June, 1908.

Smith waded into the Vancouver building boom, establishing a short-lived partnership with **William Alexander Doctor** in 1908. Smith subsequently relocated his office to the newly completed Winch Building. The office of architect **Samuel Maclure** was on the fourth floor, while Smith was in the basement. He undertook a number of houses in Vancouver's growing Kitsilano neighbourhood, and a large brick apartment building on West Pender Street. On April 7, 1909, he married Cora Lilley "Peg" Woodward, the youngest daughter of retail magnate Charles W. Woodward. Smith designed a house for them on West 14th Avenue, some way out of town at that time.

In the spring of 1910, Smith formed a partnership with William Douglas Bamford Goodfellow, the son of William Goodfellow, Sr., an architect of some reputation in New Westminster. Smith & Goodfellow landed two commissions from Smith's pugnacious father-in-law: an addition to the main store in 1910, and a warehouse and stable on Hamilton Street in 1911. However, other work of this type was not forthcoming perhaps because Charles Woodward's son, William "Billy" Woodward, the heir apparent in the Woodward clan, was not fond of Smith, and had opposed his sister's marriage to him.

Smith's most notable commission may well have been the Wigwam Inn lodge on Indian Arm north of Vancouver, completed in 1910 for two Vancouver developers, Benjamin Dickens and Alvo von Alvensleben. Von Alvensleben allegedly received financial backing for the venture from several prominent Germans, including Emma Mumm, the champagne heiress. Kaiser Wilhelm's name was also linked to the lodge: in addition to providing funding for it, the Kaiser was rumoured to have had plans to use the Wigwam Inn as a retreat. The Inn was seized by the Custodian of Enemy Property in 1914 due to von Alvensleben's German connections. Dickens claimed that he got **Fred Townley**, who was then apprenticed to Smith, to improve on a sketch he had made, "and the Wigwam Inn resulted." While it is possible that the young Townley designed the Inn, descendants of Smith in New Zealand recalled that he was the architect of a hunting lodge at Indian Arm for the Kaiser. The only building fitting that description on the Lower

Mainland is the Wigwam Inn. The Wigwam Inn also exhibits many of Smith's mature design signatures: a prominent steeply-gabled roof with every fourth course of shingles doubled for emphasis; overscaled gabled dormers; the lower portion of the roof extended to shelter a porch and then returned on the gable ends; overscaled braces; and an Arts and Crafts sensibility about natural materials.

Though commissions of this scale were few, not all was bleak for Smith. His first child, Phyllis Geraldine, was born in Vancouver on November 6, 1910, and he matured architecturally during his stay in Vancouver. Nevertheless, the first taste of what the Vancouver Board of Trade euphemistically called "a pause" in the economy, which would, by 1913, become a dead halt, was in the wind. On the Prairies, though, the boom was running stronger than ever. Early in 1912 Smith decided to pack up his practice and head east with his family to re-establish his Moose Jaw connections. Once again busy, on April 12, 1913, Smith and his wife, Peg, left on a holiday trip to the west coast. Peg at this time was expecting their second child. One suspects a rift in their marriage, for in September, a little more than a month after their first son was born in Vancouver, Sholto and Peg separated. Encouraged by her brother, Billy, she stayed in Vancouver with her father and sister. By September 1913 Smith was back in Moose Jaw, but the building boom collapsed in mid-1914 with the prospect of war. Smith stayed for a while, but on September 23, 1914, he enlisted with the 11th Battalion, CEF, and was sent overseas for five years, attained the rank of Lieutenant, and finally returned to Moose Jaw in 1919. He intended to reopen his Moose Jaw practice after spending a few weeks in Vancouver; instead, he decided to stay on the west coast. He formed a short-lived partnership in 1920 with Edmund Y. Grasset, who seems to have been a dabbler in construction and real estate. The firm Grasset & Smith may have been a marriage of convenience, with Smith supplying architectural expertise and Grasset the real estate moxie. In their only known project, Grasset & Smith undertook renovations to the Elysium Hotel on West Pender Street, which Smith had designed in 1909 as an apartment building.

Smith was clearly unsettled: he had reversed his decision to stay in Moose Jaw after travelling to Vancouver, and if he was looking for reconciliation with his estranged wife and family, this was not forthcoming. He decided to move on, sailed for New Zealand, and arrived in Auckland on March 17, 1920. The choice of New Zealand may have had something to do with his future second wife, Phyllis Mary Hams, whom he had met during the war while on leave in Colwyn Bay, North Wales. She and her family immigrated to New Zealand in 1921. Smith and Hams were married on March 3, 1925, and moved into *Colwyn*, the large house Smith had designed for them in Auckland. Smith's career blossomed during the sixteen years he spent in New Zealand, with more than one hundred buildings to his credit. He died in Auckland on July 8, 1936, at age fifty-five, due to complications from gas poisoning during the war.

Wigwam Inn, Indian Arm

WILLIAM D'OYLY HAMILTON ROCHFORT

1884-1943

CAREY PALLISTER

Many of William D'Oyly Rochfort's buildings still stand in Victoria today, the legacy of a clever and gifted man who contributed to our architectural heritage and fought gallantly for this country. Born in Southsea, England in 1884, William D'Oyly Rochfort was one of seven children born to Captain Thomas D'Oyly Rochfort and Constance Cayley. In the 1890s, the family left England and immigrated to the United States,

settling in San Francisco. By the turn of the century "Bill" Rochfort was working as a sketch artist and reporter for American newspapers and magazines. From an early age he exhibited an incredible ability to draw and a natural theatrical flare. This talent would not only assist him in his pursuit of an architectural career but also later in life when he turned to the stage to support himself.

When Captain Thomas D'Oyly Rochfort died in San Francisco in 1903, his widow and seven children, William, Henry, John, Arthur, D'Oyly, Charity (Cherry) and Winnifred moved to Victoria. In 1904, the Rochfort brothers joined the army. William Rochfort trained with the 5th Regiment as well as pursuing a career in architectural drafting. As far as can be determined, he never received any formal architectural training but his natural artistic ability served him well in this career choice. Soon after arriving in Victoria, he was hired as an apprentice by **Samuel Maclure**. Rochfort remained in his employ for three years before opening his own office. His first commission was the club house for the Victoria Yacht Club, of which he was an active member. Built in 1908, it was located at the foot of Kingston Street. It was a small, practical two-storey Arts and Crafts-style building built on pilings.

Following the completion of the Yacht Club, he received additional commissions including the Dr. Sigfried M. Hartman home on Cook Street. This Tudor Revival house with its massive rock support pillars and fence is an excellent example of his early style. Around the same time, he also designed three speculative houses on Davie Street. Built by the Bevan Brothers, they are similar foursquare Tudor Revival with

Royal Victoria Yacht Club, Oak Bay

W.D'O.Rochfort. Des.
Rochfort a Son
Associate Archt.
1912

Unbuilt project for the Savoy Hotel, Victoria

shingle-clad lower floor and half-timbered upper floor, corbelled masonry chimneys and multi-paned windows. For a while, Rochfort worked exclusively on residential projects, and his style – heavily influenced by Maclure – remained rather static. One departure from his usual residential projects was the three-storey brick clad Mount Edwards Apartments, 1910. In 1910-11 Rochfort designed a home at 1528 Cold Harbour Road for absentee owner H.M. Billings. In the Arts and Crafts tradition but with elements of Gothic Revival style, this home has quoined rubble stonework, shingle cladding, half-timbering and prominent granite porch supports. In 1911, Rochfort displayed a change in style with a home for J. Andrew and Rachel Bechtel on Rockland Avenue, which contained elements of both Tudor and Georgian Revival.

In addition to his design work, Rochfort became involved in the Stewart Land Company, acting as secretary. This real estate company promoted and sold lots in the townsite of Stewart, B.C., located on the Portland Canal on the B.C.-Alaska border. Gold had been discovered there in 1898, but it was not until 1905 that the area attracted attention. The Land Company was founded in 1907 and promoted Stewart as a prosperous place to live, attracting businessmen and investors as well as merchants and miners. Rochfort paid a visit to Stewart, which could be reached by boat from Prince Rupert, in July 1910. A reporter from the Portland Canal Miner wrote that Rochfort "was agreeably surprised at the growth of Stewart and commented favourably on the substantial character of several of the business blocks and hotels."

Rochfort was also quoted as saying that he "would do everything in his power to secure the starting of the International Power Boat Association's long distance race from this port (Stewart)."

On April 20, 1910 Rochfort married Ieglenna "Glen" Switzer, daughter of John William Switzer and Katherine Wilson. Glen was a local actress of some note who had marginal success on the stage in the United States and in England. Her father was a well-known local businessman who had founded the Belmont tannery. The Rochforts had one son, Patrick who was born in 1912.

In 1912, American architect Eben W. Sankey, who had been working in Seattle on both residential and theatre projects, moved briefly to Victoria and formed a partnership with Rochfort. Originally from St. Louis, Missouri, Sankey moved to Seattle in the early part of the twentieth century. In 1907, he had formed a partnership with the successful New York architect G.A. Edelsvald. Sankey was an experienced theatre architect, and was involved with building theatres in the Pacific Northwest including the new K&E Theatre, the Metropolitan Opera House, Seattle, the Portland Theatre and the American Music Hall at Spokane. Sankey was also involved in residential architecture in the new Interlaken Park subdivision on the north slope of Capitol Hill, Seattle. Sankey also designed several homes in the new residential Interlaken Park subdivision on the north slope of Capitol Hill in Seattle, and his Boyer Lambert house is now a Seattle Landmark.

The partnership of Rochfort & Sankey lasted for three years. They designed a number of homes, including *Purcell*, a large Tudor Revival residence for James Oscar and Beatrix Cameron in the Rockland area, and in 1913 they won the competition for the McBride Theatre, the name of which was subsequently changed to the Royal Theatre. Their other buildings of note included: the new Royal Victoria Yacht Club on Cadboro Bay; the Kinemacolor Variety Theatre, Government Street; and a striking Spanish Colonial Revival house for Arthur Levy on Empire Street, 1913. They also submitted an unsuccessful entry to the competition for the new University of British Columbia in 1912.

The outbreak of war ended this prolific partnership. By the time that he was sent overseas as part of the 47th Battalion in the spring of 1915, Lt. William Rochfort had designed more than fifty buildings in Victoria. Eben Sankey left Victoria in April 1915 and returned to Seattle. During the war Rochfort saw action in France and Belgium and was severely injured by an enemy bullet while constructing a trench in No Man's Land. The shell tore a gash in his left arm from shoulder to wrist. After recovering from his injury, he was sent back to the front. In November 1916, during the Battle of the Somme, his nerves were affected by a gas attack. He spent several months in an English hospital before being deemed unfit to return to active service and sent back to Victoria, arriving in August 1917. All the Rochfort sons and their sister, Cherry, served in the Great War.

Rochfort's only known postwar projects are the St. John's Church Memorial Altar, 1919, and two houses on St. Patrick Street, Oak Bay, both 1922. In the early 1920s, suffering from nerve damage from the gas, Rochfort gave up his architectural career, abandoned his wife and son, and went back to the United States to pursue a career in the theatre. He developed a vaudeville act that was reasonably successful, a unique performance where, according to his sister-in-law, he would simultaneously draw three different pictures using both hands and one foot. He divorced his wife, Glen, in England on July 26, 1927, and after that his movements become obscure. He returned to the United States, married twice more, and eventually ended up in Louisiana where he died in New Orleans in 1943.

Mount Edwards Apartments, Victoria, 1910

JOHN R. WILSON

BORN 1884

JENNIFER NELL BARR

Many people may likely have had bad experiences with architects, but few have ever documented them in well-known books. John Wilson's tangle with a famous client has been so immortalized.

Born in 1884 at Sunderland in County Durham, England, John Wilson was the son of a timber importer, Samuel Wilson. Young John trained at Bilton Grange College, Harrogate, Yorkshire. While attending the Technical College & School of Art at Sunderland, he apprenticed from 1900-06 in the offices of Henderson & Hall, and then studied one year with R.H. Briggs, later becoming a member of the Royal Institute of British Architects. On November 5, 1907 he left England to explore business possibilities in Canada, coming first to Victoria and shortly afterward moving to Field, B.C. However, by 1908 he returned to Victoria. In 1910 he formed a partnership with **Warren H. Milner** of Seattle, who had previously designed the Horse Show Building in Vancouver, 1908-09. As Wilson & Milner Ltd., the partners specialized in mercantile buildings, hotels and apartment houses, theatres and schools, as well as residences. They also had a large patronage in Vancouver. Wilson's Arts and Crafts style houses in the Victoria area included those of Mrs. L.A. Heisterman on Elford Street in 1910 and Maurice Cane at Oak Bay Junction in 1911. He also

designed the 1911 "Harvey House," the east dormitory of St. Michael's University School in Saanich. In November 1910, Wilson travelled back to Sunderland to marry Minnie Osborne Lang, and in 1911 he designed their family residence at 136 St. Andrews Street in James Bay, Victoria. Wilson was elected, in 1912, as the first secretary of the B.C. Society of Architects, and later sat on the council of that body. His other interests were in the Masonic Lodge, the Conservative Party, yeomanry, outdoor sports and photography.

In 1913 he was retained by artist Emily Carr, for whom he designed the "House of All Sorts." Carr was not kind about her experiences with Wilson, which she described in her book of the same name. In a chapter called "Friction," she describes how she wanted both a home and studio, and a boarding house to earn money to support herself. Her family had recommended Wilson, and "like a fool I trusted and did not investigate for myself... Always impatient, as soon as I decided to build I wanted the house immediately." Carr went to him with a sketch plan of what she wanted, and in a few days "he returned my drawing so violently elaborated that I did not recognize it... I would have to pay him two hundred dollars whether I accepted his plans or not... I was too inexperienced to fight." She called Wilson "a querulous, dictatorial man who antagonized his every workman... The man hated Canada and all her living. He was going to show her how to build houses the English way. He would not comply with Canadian by-laws; I had endless trouble, endless expense through his ignorance and obstinacy." During the course of construction Wilson contracted measles and abandoned the job for six weeks, even though he lived just around the corner. Despite these problems, the house survives today and is a valued landmark in Victoria.

The Wilson & Milner partnership dissolved about 1915, and Wilson's later whereabouts are unknown.

Douglas Hallam Residence, Victoria, 1909

Heisterman Residence, Victoria

ARCHIBALD CAMPBELL
HOPE
1870-1942

JANET COLLINS

A. Campbell Hope.

The story of Archibald Hope is not unlike that of most young men of his time. He learned his profession at the feet of his father, and brought it with him when he came to North America. His father, Thomas Campbell Hope (1834-1916) was an architect of some prominence in Bradford, England, where he practised from 1850 until his death; two of his sons became architects and later practised in British Columbia. As principal of the firm T.C. Hope & Son, the elder Hope was largely responsible for the layout of Manningham as a residential suburb, and for Bradford Technical College, the Nutter Orphanage, and an extension of the Bradford Markets. He held the office of President of the British Society of Architects & Surveyors, forerunner of the RIBA, in 1889. Archibald's older brother, **Charles Edward Hope**, also an architect, settled in Vancouver in 1889.

Archibald Campbell Hope was born in Bradford on November 28, 1870, and was educated at Bradford Grammar School and Bradford Technical College. He started his apprenticeship with his father in 1888, and entered into partnership with him 1900-01. On September 19, 1901, he married Mary Helena Jane Robson of Chevin End Farm, Ottley, at the Wesleyan Methodist Chapel. They had one daughter. In 1906, an earthquake and subsequent fire destroyed much of San Francisco. Architects and craftsmen from many nations answered the call to assist in the rebuilding, and Hope was among them. He obtained his certification as an architect in California, and established an office in San Francisco, but only stayed two years before moving to Vancouver. He set up an office with **John S. Pearce**, and the firm specialized in designs for steel frame and reinforced concrete buildings; Hope promoted himself as the concrete engineer of the firm. Their major projects included the Provincial Normal School, 1908, and Simon Fraser School, 1908-09, both in Vancouver, but their association was short-lived.

Hope continued to design schools, and was the first architect to be hired as consulting architect by the Vancouver School Board. In 1910, in partnership with H.M. Barker, he designed Lonsdale School in North Vancouver. Himself a Mason, Hope was called upon to design the Spanish Mission-style North Vancouver Masonic Temple on Lonsdale Avenue in 1911. He also undertook civic commissions, such as the Delta Municipal Hall, 1912-13. In 1913 he designed a grand Tudor Revival home for Francis John and Ada Mavis Gavin in Burnaby, demolished in the 1950s. Hope is best known for his design of one of Vancouver's best examples of *Beaux-Arts* Classicism, Postal Station C, at Main Street and 15th Avenue, 1914-15, now known as Heritage Hall.

Hope took on "war work" during the First World War. From 1915-18 he lived in Toronto and was employed by the Government of Canada's Department of Munitions. He then returned to Vancouver, and in the early 1920s, in addition to his continuing architectural practice, he was the building inspector for the Kerrisdale area of Vancouver. The Fort Langley Community Hall, 1930-31, was a commission that he likely received through the auspices of his brother, C.E. Hope, by that time a long-term Langley resident. A.C. Hope died on November 4, 1942 in North Vancouver. His remains were committed to an unmarked grave in the Masonic section of North Vancouver Cemetery.

Competition design, Hampton Court Apartments

Apartment house sketch

Gavin Residence, Burnaby

Postal Station C (now Heritage Hall), Vancouver

Roxborough Apartments, Vancouver

TOWNSEND & TOWNSEND

PARTNERSHIP 1909-1913

DONALD LUXTON

Virtually nothing is known about these idiosyncratic brothers, Alfred and Joseph Townsend, who were in Vancouver for only a few short years, but left an astonishing legacy of highly exuberant buildings. Their lives are a complete mystery. No biographical information has turned up to reveal where the brothers came from, where they were trained, or where they went after they left. It is most likely that they were English. A clue exists in the 1881 British Census, where mason William Townsend of Witney, Oxfordshire, is listed as having two sons: Joseph, age twenty-one, also a mason, and Alfred, age nineteen, a carpenter, but it is unknown if these are indeed the elusive Townsends. However, after travelling through the United States they arrived in British Columbia in 1909, and their first known commission was a hotel for Mrs. P. Thompson on Columbia Street in New Westminster. After this their work was concentrated almost exclusively in Vancouver, until their disappearance in 1913.

The years that the Townsends were in Vancouver corresponded almost exactly with the city's greatest building boom. Their output during this short period of time was truly prodigious, especially as they arrived with no family or social connections. It was the time of the hustler and the entrepreneur, and their over-the-top exuberance suited the mood of the times. What they did was exaggerate, in a way that would horrify academic architects, but delight the average Edwardian businessman. **Ross Lort** later commented on the Townsends:

There was virtually no protection for recognized architects or their potential clients in those days. As an instance, two men of the same name, presumably brothers, arrived from the States and set up an office on the second floor of a building down Hastings Street. They hung blankets across the back of the office and lived and slept there.

While they put up many buildings, they only came up with one elevation; you see it today all over town and recognize it at once. It consists of buff bricks with zig-zag lines of red bricks down every corner. The buildings on the north-east corner of Davie and Denman and north-east corner of Granville and 15th are typical, but I figure there are at least twenty of them, scattered through town. I never met the men nor heard what became of them, nor do I know in how long or short a time they achieved so much monotony to impose on a young city.

Although the Townsends undertook a number of residential commissions, most notably the James Goldie Mutch Residence on Yukon Street, their commercial buildings were the most energetic. Despite Lort's disparaging remarks, these buildings displayed surprising inventiveness in their use of materials, and their decoration was deliberately overscaled for dramatic effect. Their elaborate sheet metal cornices were truly astonishing confections that resembled the icing on a wedding cake. In at least three of their buildings, the entry consisted of an overscaled pediment, supported by bare-breasted maidens sailing out of the walls like ship's figureheads; the one such entry that survives is on the Mount Stephen Block, now called Quebec Manor. They also employed giant order columns, most notably on the Tamura Building on Powell Street, where fluted sheet metal columns run a full three storeys in height at the corners, and the surfaces are encrusted with other metal geegaws; the building also had gigantic urns and other ornamentation now lost. Their trademark zig-zag brickwork reads like a big Argyle pattern, blown up to gigantic scale for maximum visual impact. These buildings were not academically correct architecture, but rather massive stage sets for the excesses of the Edwardian era.

Ross Lort saw fit to criticize the Townsends because they were playing a much different architectural tune, perhaps Tschaikovsky to Lort's Mahler. If their prolific output is any indication, their clients happily embraced the bombast and overstatement that the Townsends offered.

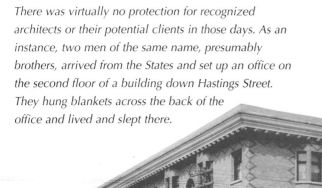

JOHN SMITH DAVIDSON TAYLOR

1885-1952

DONALD LUXTON

J.S.D. Taylor was another restless Scot whose promising young career never really took root in our western soil. He was born at Cloprickford, Savoch, New Deer, Aberdeenshire on July 25, 1885, the son of George Taylor, farmer, and Alice Ironside, married four years previously. In 1900 young John started a five-year apprenticeship in the office of the City Architect, Aberdeen. After this he moved to Canada, and worked from 1905-07 in the architectural department of the CPR. By 1909 he had opened his own office in Vancouver, and one of his earliest projects, designed for A.J. Woodward, was the superb Beaconsfield Apartments in Vancouver's West End, 1909-10, one of the most sophisticated and urbane of the city's apartment blocks. The same year Taylor also designed a brick hall for Woodward on Seymour Street, later used as the Seymour Street Gospel Hall and the Arts Club Theatre, since demolished.

Taylor's career flourished briefly, and he married Lillian Iris Emmeline Collins on January 4, 1911. His next major commission was the Richards Street headquarters for the Canada Permanent Mortgage Corporation, 1911-12. Solid and monumental, this granite-faced two-storey structure is reminiscent of the work of Glasgow architect, Alexander "Greek" Thomson (1817-1875), with which Taylor must have been familiar. Bucking the current trend towards the Gothic Revival, Thomson favoured the example of Ancient Greece as his model: the architecture of podium, column, lintel, wall and roof, controlled by a rigid system of geometry. Canada Permanent's tapered door surround, unique in this province, is a direct quote from Thomson's work. For James Rae, "The Shoeman," Taylor designed a mammoth granite-faced Shaughnessy home in 1912, which still stands on Cedar Crescent.

Taylor's career languished until the return of prosperity in the mid-1920s, when he was again briefly prolific in the years just before the Great Crash of 1929. His work at that time included factories, warehouses, and three adjacent apartment buildings on West 16th Avenue for C.A. Copp: Willingdon Lodge, 1927; Gloucester Court; and York Manor, 1928. One project, a modest thirteen-suite Mission Revival-style apartment block in the West End, Regal Court, was completed in 1930. During the Depression Taylor cancelled his AIBC membership, but reregistered in 1937 with the return of building activity.

Claude Pineo, a New Westminster resident, won the Irish Sweepstakes in 1937, and was looking to build an impressive new residence. He approached contractor S.J. Hopper, who designed the house, and then asked Taylor to stamp the drawings with his architectural seal. Taylor was brought up before AIBC Council for misuse of his seal, and was suspended in 1939. The issue was somewhat moot as work dried up again during the war years. He was reinstated in 1945, and continued to work sporadically, designing several Evangelical churches in 1946. His last known project was a small house on the University Endowment Lands for J.L. Hindin, built in 1952. Taylor died on November 1, 1952, survived by his wife and his daughter. A resident of Burnaby, he was interred at Ocean View Burial Park.

Rae Residence, Vancouver

WESLEY A. PETERS

DONALD LUXTON

Although briefly prominent as an architect in Kelowna, Wesley A. Peters's origins and ultimate fate are obscure. He moved to Kelowna from Winnipeg, and his first large commission was a Presbyterian Church on Bernard Avenue, now First United Church, consecrated in 1909. In the same year he was asked to design a new Anglican church, St. Andrew's, in the Okanagan Mission area. The first set of plans showed a rustic log building which proved too expensive for the parish. The second design was Tudor Revival, with seating for only seventy-five, and was accepted in April 1910. The first service in the new building was held on Sexuagesima Sunday, February 19, 1911, and it remains the oldest surviving Anglican church in the Kelowna district. Peters also submitted the chosen design when the Anglicans decided to replace their first church in Kelowna. Their intentions were clearly stated: "The pioneers of the church were mainly from England. They could not imagine a town or a village without its Parish Church – nor a Parish Church that was not built of stone – nor a stone church not built in the Gothic style, so they built St. Michael's & All Angels." This new structure was built on land they acquired just outside downtown on Richter Street. Impressive in scale and built of stone from the local Wallston Quarry, it was conceived as a landmark building, with a projected cost of $20,000. The cornerstone was laid on July 30, 1911, consecration took place on June 13, 1913, and in 1987 it was dedicated as a cathedral. The three churches Peters designed in Kelowna all remain in active use. Despite his success in the Interior of the province, Peters had moved to New Westminster by 1913 and designed St. Stephen's Anglican Church in Burnaby. He then disappeared from the architectural scene in B.C.

Handsome New Stone Edifice Will Replace Old Church
The new church is to be a handsome structure of which the people of Kelowna will have every reason to be justly proud. A glance at the plans prepared by the architect Mr. W.A. Peters of Kelowna, shows a good Gothic design, but strictly ecclesiastical in style, which when completed will present a most imposing appearance.

(*Orchard City Record*, Thursday, August 3, 1911)

St. Michael's & All Angels, Kelowna

LORD WILFRID HARGREAVES

1880-1966

ROSEMARY JAMES CROSS

L.W. Hargreaves was responsible for many government buildings around the province during his more than two decades with the Provincial Department of Public Works. He was remembered by P. Leonard James as "a good man with concrete." John DiCastri recalled him as "very competent in structural engineering, but short-tempered and demanding." Born in Manchester, England in 1880, he was the son of James Henry and Alice (Lord) Hargreaves. The family immigrated to Canada, where the elder Hargreaves worked as a civil engineer and was elected to the first Edmonton City Council in 1904; he later became the Commissioner of Public Works in that city. L.W. Hargreaves served a three-year apprenticeship with architect George Browne of Winnipeg between 1900-03, and then gained further work experience with J.C. Dow in Spokane, and **W.M. Dodd** in Calgary. In 1908, Hargreaves was the onsite superintendent for Dow & Hubble of Spokane when Bryan Hall, College Hall and Van Doren Hall were under construction at the University of Washington's Pullman campus. It was here that he met Florence Lilian Brutton. At the time she was touring America with her governess. A willowy pale redhead with markedly white eyebrows and lashes, she came from an aristocratic family in England. "Lil" and Wilfrid eloped and married without her parents' permission. By 1908 the Hargreaves were still living in Pullman, where their only daughter, Lilian, was born. Lil's father came to Canada to meet this Lord Wilfrid Hargreaves after they moved to a home in Victoria in 1909. Mr. Brutton stayed at the Empress Hotel. He was shocked at the rough little colonial town of Victoria and would not visit the Hargreaves's new home. Annoyed that his daughter had not married a person with a real title rather than just a lordly name – he considered a mere architect an unsuitable match for his highborn daughter – he disinherited her and went back to England.

Wilfrid Hargreaves was a small, taciturn man, with a nice smile and quiet sense of humour. His wife was a sprightly lady, a great chatterbox. The Hargreaves enjoyed musical life in Victoria. He played the flute and she, the cello and they also both performed on piano and violin. They took an active part in Sunday musicals with the Goward family, and were also part of the group that attended tennis parties held by Alys and **Hubert Savage**. The Hargreaves gardened and kept a palm tree in their house that nearly filled the living room. On visits, one had to peer through the palm fronds.

In 1909 L.W. Hargreaves established himself as an architect in Victoria, and many large buildings are attributed to him in the next few years. In 1910-11 he designed the Prince George Hotel for Lim Bang, a local Chinese businessman. Major commercial projects of 1912 included the Leland Apartments, the Scott Building, and the Yen Wo Society Building in Chinatown. In 1913, Hargreaves also built his own residence on Pacific Avenue, and would design a number of houses in the 1920s such as the Pineo Residence in Oak Bay, 1924.

Hargreaves served overseas with the 88th Battalion, CEF, from 1916-19. In the 1920s, he joined the Provincial DPW staff on a temporary basis. This would parlay into his 1930 appointment as Assistant Chief Architect of the Department. Oral history attributes some of the University of British Columbia "temporary" buildings to him, as well as the Douglas Building in Victoria. It is known that he drew the plans for the Printing Bureau in Victoria, 1926-27, now the Queen's Printers Building. He also designed a standardized plan for government liquor stores, surviving examples of which include those in Nanaimo and Prince George, both 1949. Hargreaves died on August 13, 1966 in Victoria.

Prince George

(now Douglas) Hotel, Victoria

WOODRUFF MARBURY SOMERVELL
1872-1939

DONALD LUXTON

Little is known about these designers, but their buildings speak for themselves. In just a few short years, at the height of the Edwardian boom, Somervell & Putnam designed some of Vancouver's most sublime structures. They attracted the attention of prominent commercial clients with both money and taste, but their instant success faded just as quickly when the boom ended. Although the two men disappeared into obscurity, they left an impressive legacy for such a brief appearance on the local scene.

W. Marbury Somervell was born in Washington, D.C., and studied architecture at Cornell University. He was working for the New York firm of Heins & LaFarge when he was sent to Seattle to supervise the construction of St. James Catholic Cathedral; Joseph S. Coté was sent along as his assistant. Sensing opportunity in the rapidly-growing West, Somervell and Coté stayed in Seattle, and formed a partnership that lasted from 1906 until 1910, becoming one of Seattle's most prominent firms. When this partnership dissolved, Somervell opened his own office in Seattle, but his restless nature caused him to seek other opportunities.

Vancouver developer and realtor, William A. Bauer, had announced his intention to build a hotel on West Hastings Street. **Parr & Fee** prepared the plans in 1909, and the foundations had already been laid, when Bauer changed his mind, and decided to build an eight-storey office block instead. In early 1910 he also changed architects, and the new plans were prepared by Somervell, his first work in Vancouver. The tripartite exterior of the building, clad with yellow brick and cream-coloured terra cotta, is an elegant synthesis of classical elements.

SOMERVELL & PUTNAM
PARTNERSHIP 1911-1929

Somervell opened an office in Vancouver, with John L. Putnam of New York as his office manager. As the two men were not locally connected, their overnight success is hard to explain. At this time Vancouver was growing explosively, and there were many established architects available to the city's elite. Somervell's work was recognizably superior, but he must also have possessed the instincts and persuasiveness of a natural salesmen. Putnam, a graduate of Armour Technical School, Chicago, who had worked in New York, Chicago, Tennessee, Georgia, and Alabama before his arrival in Vancouver, shared Somervell's refined sensibilities, and seems to have been the solid and competent presence that allowed the firm to undertake these large projects. They soon landed the coveted commission for the B.C. Electric Railway Company's headquarters and depot on West Hastings Street at Carrall. Vast in scale, it was the hub for the Company's streetcar system, with the tram depot located at ground floor level.

This project firmly established their reputation, and by 1911, Putnam was a full partner. One of the first projects to bear their names jointly was a new municipal hall for the rapidly expand-

BCER Offices & Depot, Vancouver

ing suburb of Burnaby. Although small in size, the hall's stature was increased by overemphasizing the scale of individual elements, including the windows, base, and entry. Somervell & Putnam had won the competition for this building over **Claude P. Jones**, and a 'late Victorian Gothic' design submitted by **Edwin G.W. Sait**. Incensed that he hadn't won the commission, and that his plans weren't returned, Sait sent the City a blistering letter, noting that the finished building resembled his, and enclosed a hefty invoice. He claimed that the tower was lifted straight from his plans, which accounted for "the present dinky abortion of a Tower you have." One wonders how much of this criticism was jealousy of the obvious talents of this younger, upstart firm. Also in 1911 Somervell & Putnam designed the landmark Bank of Ottawa Building at the corner of Hastings and Seymour Streets in downtown Vancouver.

The following year brought a bumper crop of high-profile commissions. Somervell & Putnam had been hired to design the new building for the Henry Birks Company, and the resulting ten-storey structure was their most distinguished Vancouver project. Prominently located at the city's most important inter-

JOHN L. PUTNAM

section, the gracefully articulated Birks Building knit together the grouping of terra cotta buildings that defined Edwardian Vancouver, including the Hudson's Bay store, the Vancouver Block and the second Hotel Vancouver. Serenely beautiful terra cotta cladding, with its blush of polychrome, blended gently with the city's grey skies. Detailed throughout with the finest materials, it displayed to perfection the confidence and wealth of the time. In a regrettable act of corporate vandalism, the Birks Building was demolished in 1974. Amid the usual promises of 'progress,' one of the city's best buildings was replaced with one of its worst, the banal and inert Scotiabank Tower, and the loss of the Birks Building is still lamented.

Other landmark projects followed in rapid succession. The ten-storey Yorkshire Building on Seymour Street has a richly-modelled terra cotta facade in the Gothic Revival style, fashionable at the time as New York's Woolworth Building, the world's tallest, was then nearing completion. An exquisite Neoclassical structure was designed for the Merchants' Bank in 1912. The triangular site was a leftover parcel adjacent to the CPR right-of-way at Hastings and Carrall Streets. Somervell & Putnam responded by bending the facade in a gentle curve, subtly manipulating the traditional elements to suit the awkward site. Although only the bottom three floors of the projected seven-storey building were ever constructed, the result is one of Vancouver's most elegant buildings. A residential commission was provided by W.A. Bauer, for a grand mansion in Shaughnessy Heights, 1912. The London Building on West Pender Street, with its stone facade carved in shallow relief, was completed in 1913. The firm moved their office to the top floor, and this handsome building has remained a favoured location for many architectural offices over the years.

Somervell espoused the City Beautiful movement, and saw

Municipal Hall, Burnaby

the potential to make Vancouver into a grand city, the "Liverpool of the Pacific." One of his speculative projects exhibited at the first, and only, exhibition of the B.C. Society of Architects in 1913 was a visionary plan for a large urban park in the centre of the city. Its location, and its double row of street trees, anticipated by sixty years the development of Robson Square, except that it ran for two blocks north, rather than south, of the Court House. Competitive designs for the Vancouver Club and a railway hotel show how the city could have developed if its growth had not been devastated by the economic crash of 1913 and the subsequent World War.

After 1914 the firm's output was severely curtailed, although two major projects were completed during the war years. A small but elegant structure at the corner of Granville and Pender Streets was started in 1915 for Merchant's Bank. Although it was designed in 1913, their grandest residential project, a palatial home for sugar magnate Benjamin Tingley Rogers, was not started until 1915. Somervell was delighted to receive this commission; he assured Rogers that "with the general stagnation of business in British Columbia and here, we would be in the position to give your house our entire attention, and I would thus be able to retain on my force for this purpose men whom I must shortly let go unless business picks up." Called *Shannon*, it was built far from the city's centre on a remote ten-acre site at Granville Street and 57th Avenue. This ambitious forty room mansion was the largest residence west of Toronto. The outbreak of war, and Rogers's death in 1918, delayed completion until 1925.

By 1917 Somervell went overseas with the Corps of Engineers, and later served with the Chemical Warfare Service in France. He remained in Europe after the war to assist in the restoration of damaged cultural monuments. The office in Vancouver remained open, and Putnam continued to work on minor projects. When Somervell returned, they received one last grand commission, for the Union Bank at the corner of Hastings and Seymour Streets. This imposing structure is one of the most impressive of the 'temple banks;' its monumental solidity and classical detailing supplied an image that fostered

investor confidence. Stone cladding was used on the bottom two floors, with low-relief terra cotta on the upper storey. Now adapted for use as the Wosk Centre for Dialogue, this structure remains a landmark presence.

Almost nothing is known of how the Somervell & Putnam office operated. During the boom years it must have been a busy place. **Max B. Downing** worked in the office when he first arrived, and after three years overseas with the British Navy, returned to it briefly. **Harry G. Johnson**, who worked in the United States during the war, also worked there briefly after the war. They both likely worked directly under Putnam, who appears to have been responsible for the day-to-day operations. It is unknown how much time Somervell actually spent in Vancouver, as this seemed to have been a branch office of his Seattle operations.

About 1920 Somervell and Putnam left Vancouver, and moved their practice to Los Angeles, where they worked together until 1929. Somervell retired in 1935, and moved to France to pursue his lifelong interest in etching. He died in Cannes on April 2, 1939. Putnam's fate is unknown.

Bank of Ottawa, Vancouver

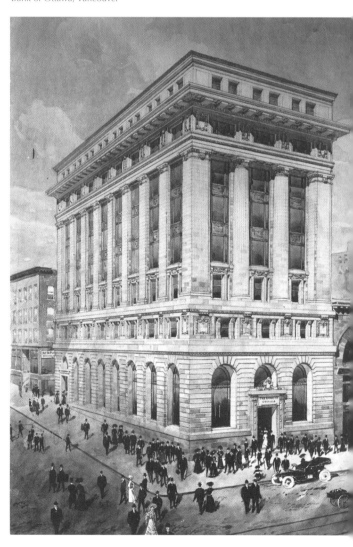

Yorkshire Building, Vancouver

I have been consecrated to a great profession, and am willing to contribute what I know to the world in return for what recompense it will allow me.

W. Marbury Somervell, *The Architect*, 1913.

Unbuilt project for a Railway Hotel

Birks Building, Vancouver

JAMES ANDERSON BENZIE

1881-1930

DONALD LUXTON

Known for his flamboyant personality, Benzie is best remembered for the work undertaken while in partnership with fellow Scot **William Bow**. Born in Glasgow on February 19, 1881, James Benzie was the fourth child, and the first son, of William Benzie (c.1846-1926), master builder, and his first wife, Catherine Auld (died 1888). James received his education at the Glasgow Academy, the Glasgow School of Art, and at Anderson's Technical College. Although it is not known when he left Scotland, by 1910 he was working for **A.A. Cox** in Vancouver, where he remained until 1915. On May 20, 1911 he married Ethel Holt Woodburn in Revelstoke. While in Cox's office, he also worked independently designing at least one house, for Daniel Drysdale, in 1914. In 1915 he served locally in the Canadian Expeditionary Force inspecting munitions, and in 1916 established his own practice. Benzie's projects during the war included work at the Vancouver General Hospital, and after the war he designed the Rotary Clinic on Pender Street, a substantial brick structure used for the treatment of chest diseases. Major J.S. Matthews noted that "successful at first, changing conditions diminished its usefulness, and after occupancy for various social services, was demolished when still in perfect structural condition." Benzie also designed the evocative Japanese-Canadian War Memorial in Stanley Park, dedicated in 1920. One of his trademarks on residential projects was known as the "Benzie roof," with cedar shingles overlapped in undulating courses to resemble traditional thatch.

Benzie entered into the partnership with Bow in 1923. Benzie was well-off, well-connected, and more outgoing than the soft-spoken Bow. A member of the best clubs, including Terminal City, Canadian and Rotary, Benzie was also a Mason and belonged to Shaughnessy Golf Club. Not afraid to be ostentatious, he also drove a flashy and expensive Cord automobile, one of the few in the city. With Benzie and Bow's combined connections, the partnership was an instant success. They embarked upon a series of prominent homes, designed for wealthy clients, including the grand Tudor Revival *Wilmar* for Willard Kitchen, 1925, with sophisticated period details such as brick nogging that infills the half-timbered gables. Other commissions included the British Arts and Crafts J. Lyman residence in Shaughnessy, 1927, and three homes on Grand Boulevard in North Vancouver, for Herbert Taylor, 1925, and Ernest Young and Marcus McDowell, both in 1927. Benzie also designed a residence for A.W. Whitmore in 1924, noted for having a "variegated red roof" obtained by mixing several shades of red coloured shingles together in batches. Benzie & Bow also received commissions for public buildings, including North Vancouver High School, 1923; additions to Ridgeway School in 1926; and the new North Vancouver Hospital in 1929.

From 1926-27 Benzie served as the President of the AIBC. After a brief illness, he died at home on February 6, 1930. After his death his wife, and their daughter, Jean, moved to England, and never returned.

House with a "Benzie Roof"

Japanese Memorial, Stanley Park, Vancouver

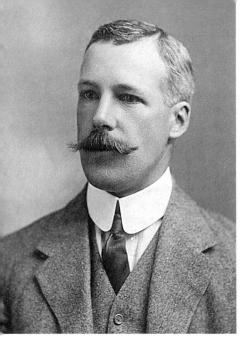

HUGH ASTLEY HODGSON

1880-1965

JOEL LAWSON

Hugh Hodgson had a long and interesting career ranging from West Vancouver (as a pioneer and architect in the early days of the district) to Buckingham Palace. Along the way, he had a thriving practice in downtown Vancouver, and designed numerous buildings that helped to form the fabric of the city. Hodgson was born in Brisbane, Australia on April 2, 1880. His family moved to their estate on the Isle of Man when he was only six years old. He graduated from King William College, Castletown, and apprenticed for a number of years with a local architect. He eventually moved to the "mainland" to further his studies at the Liverpool Art School. Despite the requests of his two brothers to join them in South Africa, Hodgson left Liverpool in 1907 before completing his degree and moved to San Francisco, because he had heard that there would be plenty of work for architects following the 1906 earthquake. He did not like living in the United States, however, and by 1910 had moved to Vancouver, living briefly in a West End rooming house. For a time, he worked for **A.J. Bird**, an association that would be repeated later in life and an ocean away. In 1911, he opened his own office in the Carter-Cotton Building on West Hastings Street, then the heart of Vancouver's business district. The city was growing rapidly and Hodgson was kept busy designing a variety of buildings, including small hotels, office/retail buildings, warehouses, apartment buildings, and houses.

Unfortunately, few of his early buildings remain. Extant examples in Vancouver include a two-storey brick billiard parlour, 1911, now home to the renowned Only Seafood Restaurant; the Brandiz Hotel, 1913, a plain, six-storey brick building; and the Church of St. Peter and St. Paul, 1923, a small, simple Catholic Church. A grand gambrel-roofed mansion he designed in 1912 for Edward H. Moore, Manager of the Prince Rupert Timber & Lumber Co. Ltd., still stands on Laurier Avenue in Shaughnessy Heights. In 1911, Hodgson started the designs for the now-demolished Oakalla Prison in

Inglewood High School, West Vancouver

Hodgson Residence, West Vancouver

Burnaby; construction began in 1912 and continued with a series of additions for many years.

Shortly after moving to British Columbia, Hodgson purchased a large tract of land on Marine Drive in Hollyburn, soon to become part of the newly incorporated District of West Vancouver. He designed a simple, Craftsman-style house with an attractive front porch facing south towards the water and Vancouver. In 1913, he married Gertrude Southorn, whom he had met while at the Liverpool Art School. They had one daughter, Beatrice, who lived in the house until her death in 2004. At the time, services were minimal: water service was not installed until 1916, before which the family depended on a well and a 500 gallon water tank which required, according to Hodgson, "780 vigorous strokes at the hand pump every day to fill." With no connecting bridge, Hodgson could not drive to his office in Vancouver. His commute included a walk to the Ambleside Ferry (past John Lawson's herd of Black Angus cattle); a crossing of Burrard Inlet by ferry boat; and then a short walk from the ferry terminal located close to the foot of Main Street to the Carter-Cotton Building.

Toward the end of the First World War, Hodgson also worked for a short while in Washington State, where his output included design work at Fort Lewis Army Base, north of Olympia. About 1920, **H.H. Simmonds** – who had worked for Hodgson before the war – started working out of his office as a draftsman, and then as a junior partner. The two shared a close personal and business relationship, working in affiliation from 1924 to about 1933. Many Vancouver buildings are credited to them jointly, although both continued to work independently. Their most important remaining building, the British Columbia Electric Railway Co. Showroom, 1927-28, is an impressive three-storey stone-faced building at the corner of Dunsmuir and Granville Streets.

Hodgson also maintained a healthy practice in West Vancouver, which probably limited his need to commute on a daily basis. He served on the West Vancouver School Board in 1915-16, and was later the architect for the school district,

designing Pauline Johnson School, 1922, and Inglewood School, 1927, a large Tudor-style structure that was the first high school in West Vancouver. He also designed additions to the original Municipal Hall and a number of private residences, including the Harrison Residence, 1923, a fine Craftsman-style home still in existence.

In 1932, his daughter received a scholarship to study at the Royal College of Music in London, England, and she and her mother moved there. Economic growth and the construction industry had been severely curtailed by the Depression, and so in 1936, Hodgson closed his practice, and moved to London to join his family. He retained and rented out his house in West Vancouver, and Simmonds continued to work out of the office they had shared. Hodgson eventually withdrew his membership in the AIBC in 1940. In London, Hodgson once again met up with A. J. Bird, who had moved there some years earlier. Bird introduced him to the London County Council. During the Second World War, he worked as a supervising architectural inspector with the Heavy Rescue Squad, assessing the safety of buildings damaged by bombing – which ones were structurally sound enough to be repaired, and which ones had to be demolished. Following the war, he was employed with the Ministry of Works; according to his daughter his projects included the repair of many war-damaged sites including Buckingham Palace and the repaving of Pall Mall. He was not, however, a member of the Royal Institute of British Architects.

In 1953, the family returned to Canada and their house in West Vancouver. For a time, Hodgson worked out of the office of **Ross Lort** although they never formed a partnership. There he accepted small design commissions. His co-workers particularly remembered that Hodgson had an aversion to the telephone, with a distinct dislike for either taking or initiating telephone calls. He died on March 28, 1965 at the age of eighty-four, less than three months after the death of his wife of fifty-two years. Hodgson's funeral service took place in the original St. Stephen's Anglican Church in West Vancouver, which he designed in 1925, and he was buried at Capilano View Cemetery in West Vancouver.

Pauline Johnson School, West Vancouver

"DOC"
WATSON
1885-1967

DONALD LUXTON

Joseph Francis Watson, known to all as "Doc," was an accomplished sculptor as well as an architect. In addition to his work as one of the designers of the ornamentation of the Marine Building in Vancouver, he was responsible for the three gigantic nursing sisters that graced the now-demolished Medical-Dental Building. Born in 1885 in Haltwhistle, Northumberland, England, he was educated in the grade schools of Middleborough. He received first honours in sculpture and modelling from the board of education of South Kensington, London. Determined to make architecture his profession, he started his four-year apprenticeship in 1902 with his much older brother, architect **Henry B. Watson**. Concurrent with his articles, he studied for four years at Rutherford College, Newcastle-on-Tyne.

Watson came to Canada in 1909. The following year he married Sarah Anne "Nance" Lyman, and they had a family of two children. His brother Henry had immigrated to Vancouver in 1907, but they did not seem to have ever worked together in this country. Joseph's first job in Canada landed him in charge of the New Westminster office of **C.H. Clow** in 1910, where he worked on the YMCA Building, New Westminster, and the new Surrey Municipal Hall in Cloverdale. As of 1912 Watson had opened his own office in New Westminster, where he designed the Kwong On Wo Stores and Apartments, 1913. He enlisted on March 15, 1915, and was sent to France where he served for two years with the 29th Canadian Infantry Battalion. He was then transferred to the Canadian Corps Survey Section for two years, and was Sergeant in charge of draftsmen in the Topographic Section. Short and slight in stature, he nevertheless proved his worth and was awarded a War

Service Badge Class A. Discharged on April 26, 1919, he took a job with the municipality of South Vancouver until he resumed his practice in New Westminster. He was briefly employed as a designer and assistant with Hill & Mock, Tacoma, in 1925. Returning to Vancouver, he was hired in January, 1926 by the firm of **McCarter & Nairne**, and worked there for six of their most successful and creative years. For the Medical-Dental Building, the American firm of Gladding, McBean & Co. manufactured the terra cotta. Their modeller was German, and the trio of eleven foot-high nurses that he designed for the building, symbolizing tenderness and devotion, were considered "too Germanic." Doc, whose hobby was sculpture, was given the task of designing more Anglo-Saxon-looking nurses. The construction workers on the project nicknamed them the "Rhea Sisters:" Pia, Dia and Gonna.

In 1932 he again set up his own practice, although he continued to produce renderings for McCarter & Nairne. One of his sculptural commissions was for a brick and limestone memorial to William Shakespeare, unveiled November 25, 1935, which still stands in the Shakespeare Garden in Stanley Park. In addition to a number of residences in New Westminster, Watson designed the streamlined Elks Hall on Columbia Street, which featured colourful tile mosaics of elks above the entrances at each end of the building. In 1937, he formed a partnership with **Henry Blackadder**, which lasted for four years. One of their projects was the still extant Tudor Inn, 1938, located in South Surrey on the Pacific Highway adjacent to the Cloverdale border crossing. Although it was optimistically described as "a happy combination of old English architecture with the modernistic trend," the building shows no trace of traditional design, and is a straight-forward application of the Streamline Moderne style. Another joint project was a building for Empire Stevedoring on Railway Street in Vancouver, 1940-41, an even more striking example of modernism. During the Second World War Watson achieved the rank of Flight-Lieutenant, and afterwards, from 1944-46, he served as President of the AIBC. In 1946 he hired Harold N. Semmens to work in his office, and the two were briefly in partnership in 1947. Watson then went into partnership with James Baxter in 1948. A modernist project undertaken by Watson & Baxter was the glass and stainless steel Collier's Limited automobile showroom, 1948, the furthest east of the dealerships that once made West Georgia Street the most fashionable place to buy a car. One of Watson's last projects was St. Alban's Anglican Church in Richmond, started early in 1949 with Easter services held in the completed shell the following year. "Doc" Watson retired in 1950; he died at Shaughnessy Hospital September 13, 1967, at the age of eighty-two.

Good architecture is not achieved by copying motifs which were designed primarily for religious and court life, but rather by designing for every day use in the function of the state. In this age of steel, concrete and glass, we have the possibility of creating buildings which will give us new values in architecture – increased comfort, utility and aesthetic expression.

Vancouver *News-Herald*, Architectural & Building
Edition, February 27, 1939, p.10.

(below) Original "Germanic" Nurse from Gladding, McBean & Co.

Nurse for the Medical-Dental Building, Vancouver

JOHN McINTYRE
1879-1957

DONALD LUXTON

Powell River has a rich legacy of historic buildings, and the Townsite is now recognized as a National Historic Site. Originally a company town spawned by the lumber industry, during the 1920s there was a flurry of construction and expansion as new paper machines were added to the mill site. For many years the resident architect, John McIntyre, was employed by the Powell River Company in various capacities, and he designed the majority of the town's public buildings and residences. Born January 31, 1879 in Stranraer, Wigtonshire, Scotland, McIntyre commenced his articles in 1895 with A.

Hunter Crawford in Edinburgh. He attended the Edinburgh College of Applied Art and Heriot-Watt College, after which he worked as an architect in Edinburgh, and for five years was in charge of the architectural department of the Scottish District War Office. McIntyre moved to British Columbia in 1910, establishing an office in Vancouver in the Dominion Building, and was briefly associated with Gordon L. Wright in 1911. He worked on a number of residential projects, and when the economy collapsed, he took charge of the design and construction departments for both Point Grey and Burnaby. In 1915 he joined the Powell River Company, and from 1919-35 was Townsite Manager, later handling the Public Relations Division.

During the prosperous 1920s McIntyre provided designs for new houses, including those on "Boss's Row," and for a large new school built in 1926, named for Dwight F. Brooks, one of the founders of the mill. In 1927, McIntyre designed a lavish new ballroom and community facility, Dwight Hall, which featured a large sprung dance floor, meeting rooms and the Townsite's library. Tough times arrived during the Depression, and when the local Bank of Commerce turned down the Company's request for a loan to complete several projects, the Bank of Montreal was lured to town with the promise of a new building, designed in the Tudor Revival style by McIntyre, in 1931.

Outgoing and personable, his "popularity with the fair sex is something that most of the male population prefer to overlook – because they, too, can't resist John." McIntyre was known as "Mr. Powell River" and was elected its first Good Citizen in 1944. He retired from the Company in 1952, suffered ill health through 1956, and died June 21, 1957 in his adopted home of Powell River.

Interior of Dwight Hall, Powell River

OTTO BEESTON HATCHARD
1879-1945

DONALD LUXTON

O. Beeston Hatchard enjoyed an active career that spanned three continents, starting in England, and then working in Africa and Canada before spending his final years in California. Born in London on April 1, 1879, he served three years as an articled pupil to Herbert M. Cally, Architect, in Tunbridge Wells, Kent, from 1896-99, and then worked as an architectural assistant in the office of the Borough Engineer to the Metropolitan Borough of Stepney, London, 1900-05. He also attended Tunbridge Wells Technical College and the London Polytechnic School of Arts and Crafts. In 1905 he was appointed Chief Architect to the Sudan Government, and designed all the buildings constructed by the Sudanese Government at Port Sudan, including the government offices, hospital, custom house, schools, prison, officer's quarters and the harbour works, to a total value of five million dollars. From 1906-09 he served as the Town Architect of Khartoum, Sudan, and designed the new law courts, civil hospital, power station, and many other buildings throughout the country. The reasons Hatchard left Africa are unknown, but he next turned up in Vernon, B.C., where he established his practice in June, 1910. He introduced the latest Craftsman style to the area through a series of Arts and Crafts bungalows in and around Vernon, including residences for D.W. Spice, 1911; Mackenzie Urquhart, 1913; Patricia Ranch, Coldstream, 1914; Charles T. Kinloch, 1919 (extant), and Hatchard's own house, 1912. He also designed a set of iron gates in Polson Park for the vice-regal visit of the Duke of Connaught in 1912. On November 12, 1913 he married Edith Edna Hennell. Hatchard was on overseas duty from June, 1916 to February, 1919, holding a commission as Lieutenant in the Royal Navy. He returned to Vernon after the war, but left for California in 1922 "for his health." Hatchard died in 1945, of the illness he contracted while on active service during the Great War.

Mr. Hatchard's professional ability combined with a pleasant personality augur well for his success as an architect in the Okanagan Valley.

Vernon *News*, Special Holiday Number, 1912, p.77

Summer Cottage for Lord De Vesci, Okanagan Lake

Okanagan Steam Laundry, Vernon

HARRY WALTER POSTLE
1877-1955

DONALD LUXTON

Known for his many school designs, Harry Postle displayed great professional competence and surprising stylistic versatility. He was born in Norwich, England on May 4, 1877. Starting in 1892 he articled for five years to Mr. A.C. Havers, and then worked in various offices until setting up his own practice. Moving to Vancouver in 1910, he was employed by various firms, working exclusively on residences, but while in the office of **W.M. Dodd**, he worked on the design and working drawings for the Douglas Lodge apartments. He acted as a draftsman for other firms, including **Gardiner & Mercer**, **S.M. Eveleigh**, John Graham of Seattle and **McCarter & Nairne**, until his 1928 appointment as the architect for the Vancouver School Board. Among his projects in this position were Vancouver Technical School, the first technical school in Vancouver and the largest in western Canada, 1928; an addition to Lord Byng School, 1938; and Queen Elizabeth Elementary and Southlands No. Two, both 1939. The design for Queen Elizabeth was an unusual variation on British Arts and Crafts, with cross-paned windows, and a mixture of stucco, brick and board-and-batten cladding that gave a somewhat residential feel to the complex.

Postle retired from the School Board in 1942, but there were so many requests for him to design schools that he set up an office at home, and went back into business. His later projects included schools in Kamloops and Osoyoos. After the war he entered into a partnership with **Theo Körner**. The two had likely met through their earlier association with McCarter & Nairne, and had remained personal friends for years. Postle recognized the brilliance of the younger man, and thought that his talents had never been fully appreciated. In April, 1945 Körner provided the rendering for Postle's design for a large new high school in Oliver. The final design, produced in 1946 after they had gone into partnership, shows Körner's strong influence, and was a startling essay in poured concrete, its horizontal massing beautifully balanced by strong corner elements. Körner's influence on the final design was obvious. Covering one and one-half acres, with over two acres in floor space, the construction of this massive building required twenty-five carloads of cement and 900 tons of steel. The Minster and Deputy Minister of Education were at the opening ceremonies on January 28, 1949, and the building was lauded as "the finest in the province, and was likely to remain so for years to come." The baffled community considered it far too modern and extravagant, and nicknamed it the "Taj Mahal."

Their promising partnership ended suddenly when Körner died of a heart attack in 1946. Postle went on to design a church in a more traditional idiom that sits in stark contrast across the street from the Oliver High School. Harry Postle died in West Vancouver on August 7, 1955.

The Church of St. Edward the Confessor Anglican, Oliver

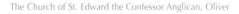

Queen Elizabeth Elementary School, Vancouver

Vancouver Technical School, Vancouver

BERTRAM DUDLEY
STUART
1885-1977

DONALD LUXTON

B. Dudley Stuart moved to Vancouver during the boom years, and left for Seattle after the crash, but during this short time period designed several striking buildings, all of which displayed Classical Revival elements. Stuart was born in London, England in 1877, and subsequently practised in Edmonton before moving to Vancouver. He designed the Palace of Horticulture for the Vancouver Exhibition Association in 1911. By 1912 he was in partnership with Howard E. White. Their most distinctive structure was the B.C. Wood Products Building for the Vancouver Exhibition Association. Commonly known as the Forestry Building, it was built in time for the 1913 fair. It was a showcase for local wood products, built in an overt Classical Revival style, with unpeeled logs used as Doric columns. This was an interesting twist on the origins of classicism, as the familiar stone Greek temples that were the model for the revival styles were actually mimetic adaptations of even earlier timber structures. This distinctively British Columbian building succumbed to dry rot, and was demolished in the 1930s.

Later in 1913 the Stuart & White partnership ended. On his own Stuart designed Campbell Court, 1914, a sophisticated brick apartment with a Classical entry gate that screens its entry court. Stuart stayed on in Vancouver until the end of 1915, when he moved to Seattle, and began a long and productive career that lasted until his death in 1977. White remained in local directories until 1917, after which he disappeared.

Forestry Building, Hastings Park

GAMBLE & KNAPP

JIM WOLF AND DONALD LUXTON

Gamble & Knapp were active briefly in Vancouver, from 1910-12. Jacob H. Knapp came from Seattle, where he was in partnership with Thomas L. West from 1904-09. West & Knapp undertook mostly residential work, including many middle-class bungalows and Craftsman-style homes. A regular contributor to local magazine, *The Coast*, West was pretentiously described as "one of the most successful architects of the Northwest." Knapp moved north to Vancouver, B.C., where he formed a partnership with John T. Gamble. Starting early in 1910 they produced a large number of high quality residential designs, producing such gems as a superb bungalow in the West End for Alfred C. Hirshfield, 1910, a house for John Purse in North Vancouver, 1911; and a large Arts & Crafts residence

for C.H. Macauley on Hudson Street in the heart of Shaughnessy Heights, 1912. In 1910 they provided the plans for a forty-room "Swiss Chalet" for Arthur Neville Smith, at Vedder Creek, near Chilliwack, but the ambitious plans for this resort hotel were never realized. Gamble & Knapp's grandest commission was a home on The Crescent for George E. MacDonald, known as *The Hollies*. Construction started in 1912 on this massive Colonial Revival residence, distinguished by its entrance portico with four giant order columns. Knapp disappeared from the city by 1913, and Gamble by the following year. Gamble reappeared briefly in Vancouver from 1921-22, but his fate is unknown.

The Hollies, G.E. MacDonald Residence, Vancouver

FRANCIS S. SWALES
1878-1962

DONALD LUXTON

Young and talented Francis Swales appeared for a few years in Vancouver, and was responsible for what was possibly the city's most opulent building. Born in Oshawa, Ontario on June 14, 1878, he received his professional training at the *Atélier Masqueray* in New York, at Washington University, St. Louis Missouri, and at the *École des Beaux-Arts* and the *Atélier Pascal* in Paris. In his early career he travelled through the United States, working from 1901-02 with chief designer E.L. Masqueray on buildings at the Louisiana Purchase Exposition, held 1904 in St. Louis, Missouri; later he won the competition for the San Francisco Customs House, 1903, and collaborated with Edwin Otto Sachs (1870-1919) on the design of the Cairo Opera House. In 1903, he married Maude Hartford of Detroit, Michigan, with whom he had three daughters. Swales left America in 1903 to study at the *École*, and stayed in Europe until 1911. While travelling he met Wisconsin-born entrepreneur, Gordon Selfridge, who was planning to build a modern, American-style department store in London. Swales provided the design for the grand facades of the new store, to be built at the corner of Oxford and Duke Streets. Selfridge carried Swales's sketch with him and it was "fingered so frequently that it had become dog-eared" in his pocket. Chicago architect, Daniel H. Burnham (1846-1912), was also consulted on the project, and the final plans were prepared by English architect R. Frank Atkinson (1871-1923). The first section of Selfridges opened in 1909, and embodied the complementary strengths of American enterprise and French academic rigour. Swales received acclaim for the conception of this great structure. Skilled in self-promotion, his lecture to the RIBA in 1909 on the Franco-American connection prompted the

chairman, Ernest George, to conclude that the United States was "preeminently a practical nation, dealing with vast commercial interests and building huge monuments, not as monuments, but as works for which they had a practical necessity. They grafted the tradition, and training, and exact knowledge, and delicate feeling for Classic beauty which they obtained from France upon their own gigantic needs, and produced colossal works."

Swales relocated to Montreal in 1911, where he went into partnership with Walter Scott Painter (1877-1957), an American who had trained in Pennsylvania and Michigan and was appointed the CPR's first chief architect in 1905. When Painter returned to private practice in 1911, he retained his connections with the CPR, and in addition to contributions to Windsor Station, the Château Frontenac, and the Banff Springs Hotel, was responsible for the extensions to the Empress Hotel in Victoria, 1909-14. In 1911, when the CPR decided to demolish the original Hotel Vancouver and replace it on a much grander scale, Painter was chosen for the project.

Painter & Swales were promised all of the CPR's architectural work in western Canada. Painter was temporarily located in Vancouver and took care of the "executive work" of the firm, while Swales remained in Montreal. By 1913 the partnership had dissolved and Swales was in total charge of the Hotel Vancouver project, and he was solely responsible for the evolving final design. The monumental reinforced concrete building was an opulent expression of the Edwardian era's boisterous elaboration, but with its brick walls and relatively flat, stepped tile roofs retained few allusions to the CPR's typical Château style. The roof was devoted to a trellised outdoor garden café, famous for its panoramic views. Construction dragged on through the depression and the start of war, and the hotel finally opened in 1916. It only operated until 1939, when the third Hotel Vancouver was finished. The CPR stipulated that this grand structure could not be used again as a hotel, and it was scheduled for demolition, but limped on for a number of years as an army barracks and hostel. The site was purchased by Eaton's in 1948 for a proposed new department store. The hotel was demolished in 1949, but the site sat empty for years, and the store was not completed until 1972.

HENRY HERBERT
GILLINGHAM
1874-1930

DAVID MONTEYNE AND DONALD LUXTON

Henry Herbert Gillingham was a rather prolific designer of predominantly domestic architecture in British Columbia, but little is known of his life. As his modest application to the AIBC indicates, Gillingham was likely a man of few words. Born in London, England, on November 25, 1874, Gillingham entered his father's London architectural practice at age seventeen, and then later worked with his brothers' firm in Claxton. He arrived in Vancouver during the boom in 1911, and undertook a large amount of residential work in and around Vancouver and Victoria. Gillingham's house designs show a distinctive British Arts and Crafts sensibility. One of his clients was Herbert Burbidge, a breeder of outstanding Jersey cattle and son of a long-time managing director of Harrod's department store in London, who had come to Canada to oversee the construction of the Hudson Bay Company's department western stores. Burbidge commissioned **Burke, Horwood & White** to design the stores, but chose Gillingham as the architect for his own home, a cross-gabled Tudor Revival structure reminiscent of an English farm estate house. Located at Cordova Bay, it was called *Babbacombe Farm*, and was constructed during the middle of the First World War.

Gillingham was involved in two short-lived partnerships, one with **E. Stanley Mitton** in 1914, and another with **Theo Körner** in 1919-20. Although work was scarce in Vancouver right after the First World War, Gillingham designed the Victory Flour Mills, 1919, and a grand home in Shaughnessy for Mrs. Lester Brooks on Connaught Drive, 1921. The Brooks residence was one of the largest houses built in Vancouver between the wars, and similar to the Burbidge house has a strict linear contrast between the main and upper floor. The brick cladding, with half-timbering above, and the rolled-eave roof covered with steam-bent shingles to resemble thatch, are elegant references to a rustic English cottage vernacular, here expanded to gigantic size.

Displaying stylistic versatility in the last two years of his life, Gillingham designed the impressive Spanish Colonial-style Besner Block in Prince Rupert, 1928, built for sometime boot-legger, Olier Besner, with retail space on the ground floor and gracious court apartments above. The Samuel Apartments in Vancouver, 1929, is a simpler block with Arts and Crafts elements such as multi-paned casement windows. In 1930, at the age of fifty-five, Gillingham suffered a cerebral hemorrhage on a Vancouver street car and died, leaving his wife and two sons. At the time of his death, he was working on his best known building, the Commodore Ballroom in downtown Vancouver, a premier example of the local use of the Art Deco style.

Besner Block, Prince Rupert

Brooks Residence, Vancouver

ROBERT LYON
1879-1963

DONALD LUXTON

Robert Lyon was one of the most brilliant of British Columbia's early architects, but his accomplishments remain little-known. A combination of circumstances, including bad eyesight, precluded him from pursuing architecture full time, but his buildings demonstrated an innovative approach to style and structure that was rarely equalled. He is better remembered as the City of Penticton's first Mayor.

Lyon was born at Orwell Terrace, Edinburgh, on November 8, 1879. His parents were John Lyon, master grocer, and Rebecca Stewart, married four years earlier in Clumie, Perthshire. As a young boy Robert had contracted measles, and by not staying in the dark while he was afflicted he developed a corneal ulcer, which left him effectively blind in one eye. This did not prevent him from wanting to study architecture, so his father arranged a five year apprenticeship as a carpenter, 1896-1901. Following this he served two years as an Architect's Pupil with Lessels & Taylor, Edinburgh, a firm of some minor importance. From 1896-1903 he also attended Heriot-Watt Technical College, studying building construction and architecture. After his apprenticeship ended in 1903 he acted as Architect's Assistant and Inspector of Construction with various firms in Scotland until about 1908, and then worked for about a year in New York in 1909. Not liking it there, he returned to Scotland, but now restless, he decided to leave, and asked the ticket agent to "sell me a ticket for as far as I can go." He ended up in Victoria, B.C.

Soon after, he relocated to Vancouver and gained employment as an "architectural engineer" with the B.C. Electric Railway Company (BCER) in 1911. During this time Lyon worked on a range of projects including appraisal and valuation of all the company's main buildings, and superintendence of the construction of the Quebec Street Car Barns in Vancouver in 1913-14, valued at $300,000. Lyon designed and supervised many of the most prominent industrial structures for the BCER, which was expanding to suit the area's rapidly growing population. These structures were significant for their early large-scale use of reinforced concrete as both a structural and a finishing material. The largest was Buntzen Power House #2, located on Indian Arm, completed in 1914 at a cost of $300,000 to generate power from Buntzen Reservoir; architects Somervell & Putnam also claimed the design of Buntzen, and may have been responsible for its original conception. Substations that Lyon designed in a similar vocabulary included the Earles Street Substation, Vancouver, 1912; the Point Grey Substation (known as Sperling Annex), 1914; the Horne-Payne Substation, Burnaby, 1916; and the Brentwood Bay Steam Plant on Vancouver Island. These enormous structures were intended as functional shells for generating equipment, but attained a sense of ecclesiastical

Buntzen Power House #2, Indian Arm

monumentality through the consistent use of alternating pilasters and shallow arches framing large window openings. Loosely inspired by Gothic Revival, the stepped massing and angular corner articulation of these structures also foreshadowed the Art Deco style that was to develop after the First World War.

Lyon also designed a range of other buildings for the BCER, including a unique surviving Men's Quarters at the corner of Main and Prior Streets in Vancouver in 1913. Tall and narrow, this landmark brick-faced building was located across the street from the company's car barns, and provided dormitory accommodation for unmarried streetcar motormen and conductors; it was considered expedient to house them nearby, so that they would be more likely to show up for work on a regular basis. Lyon's stylistic versatility was demonstrated by his Tudor Revival design for the Granville Bridge BCER Station, 1913, by his other interurban stations on the Fraser Valley line, and also the ornamental stone gates that form the entry to Central Park in Burnaby, 1913-14. He also designed a rustic Arts and Crafts hotel and tearoom on the waterfront at Deep Bay (now Deep Cove), at the northern terminus of the Saanich line on Vancouver Island. In this period, Lyon also designed various private dwellings in Vancouver valued from $4,000 to $10,000. While he was in Vancouver he took the "darkness

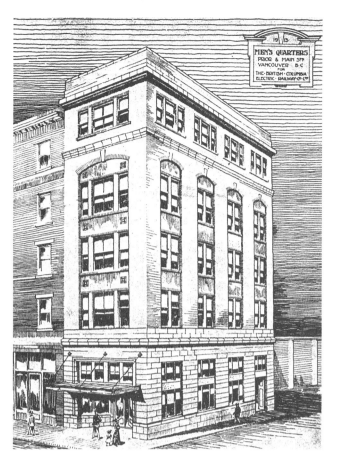

BCER Men's Quarters, Vancouver

cure" at least once at St. Paul's Hospital, which involved staying in a completely blackened room for at least thirty days, after which the room was illuminated by lighting one candle at a time. Despite his poor vision he was an avid sportsman, enjoying tennis and hiking, and was a member of a mountaineering club that camped out on the far side of Grouse Mountain.

Lyon spent most of the war years working for the BCER, as his poor vision prevented enlistment. On April 18, 1918, he married Sarah Evelyn O. Coleman in the First Presbyterian Church in Victoria. They left immediately on the afternoon boat for a honeymoon trip to Seattle, Portland and California. The August 1918 edition of *The B.C. Electric Employee's Magazine* reported that "**R. Lyons Steps Out:** Club and social circles of the company are going to miss the energetic Scottish figure of Mr. Lyon, architectural engineer, who, after eight years of service, has gone forth to enter the lumber business as a shareholder and secretary-treasurer of the Anthony Rerrie Lumber Company, of Warwhoop [near Stave Falls] on the Fraser Valley line. He will look after the business end of the concern while his partner will be the mechanical brains. The head office staff parts with Mr. Lyon with regrets, and wishes him the best of luck in his venture. It is to be hoped that he – and his bride – will not forget entirely the social affairs of the company."

His involvement with the lumber industry did not last. In

G.D. Loane Residence, Kelowna, 1937 designed by Robert Lyon

Unknown residence designed by Robert Lyon

1920, Lyon registered with the AIBC. He and Evelyn had one son, Stewart, born in 1920. Two years later Lyon moved to Penticton to establish his practice, and the family moved up the following year. Lyon occupied an office upstairs in the Boyle Block, and had little professional competition. He designed the Penticton Cooperative Growers' Packing House on the lakeshore, at the time the largest such structure in the British Empire, and all of the other large packing houses built at the time throughout the Okanagan and the Kootenays, including those at Creston and Salmon Arm. These imposing, utilitarian structures were built with walls two feet thick, filled with wood shavings for insulation.

Major residential commissions included a huge stone house for Hugh Charles Musgrove Leir, 1927-29 and a waterfront home for Judge L. McLeod Colquhoun, 1939, both in Penticton, and a modernist house on the Kelowna waterfront, 1939 for William B. Hughes-Games (Mayor of Kelowna 1947-51), all still extant. In Penticton he designed several local schools, as well as the Three Gables Hotel, 1931, and the brick-faced Penticton Post Office, which opened on March 28, 1937. Penticton Municipal Hall, 1940, was a beautifully-designed example of the Streamline Moderne style, demolished when the new city hall was built. A modernistic building for the Penticton *Herald*, similar to city hall, survives but has been badly defaced by alterations.

Lyon's most interesting building from this time was the Kelowna Post Office, 1937, designed in a flamboyant interpretation of the Art Deco style. Plans for a new brick and stone-clad post office and public building had been prepared by **Townley & Matheson** in 1935, which was more in keeping with the restrained style then favoured by the Federal Department of Public Works. Their scheme was not built, possibly due to cost, and when Lyon later received the commission, he was determined to make it "look different" from the Penticton Post Office, and designed the exterior in reinforced concrete, as he had with his earlier industrial buildings. The result was a truly striking building, but regrettably, it has

been replaced by a banal modern structure.

Because of the strain on his eye, Lyon had tried switching professions, but even during the Depression design work was available, and he continued his architectural practice. He was also a successful businessman, and in addition to owning orchards, he was one of the first to recognize the potential of car-based entertainment, and became one of the first partners in the Pines Drive-In on Main Street. He was generous to a fault with his clients, and always cut his fees in half for other orchardists. When he designed the Pyramid Packing House, the fee should have been $6,600. He cut it in half and rounded it off to $3,000, at which his wife protested to leave the extra $300 on as she had never had a fur coat. He sent it on at the lower figure, but even at that price the co-op manager complained, not realizing the bargain he had been given.

Lyon was known as an accomplished musician, and was actively involved in community life, including the Men's Choir and the Dramatic Society; he always wore a mustache until he shaved it off for an amateur theatrical production in the mid-1930s, and never grew it back. Lyon and two others put up $500 each to build a badminton hall in Penticton; Lyon also designed badminton halls at Kelowna, Summerland and at the

Post Office, Penticton

Vernon Preparatory School in Coldstream. Active politically, he served as a Penticton Councillor from 1929-32 and again 1943-44. After his election as Reeve in 1946-47, he was instrumental in the incorporation of Penticton as a city, and on May 10, 1948 Viscount Alexander, Governor-General of Canada, presented the city's charter. Lyon thus became Penticton's first Mayor, a post he held until 1949. Another proud moment was the first Peach Festival, held in August of 1948, when Penticton-born Hollywood star, Alexis Smith, arrived to crown the first Peach Queen.

Throughout this time Lyon maintained his architectural connections, including friendships with **Ross Lort** and **Henry Simmonds**. He retired from the profession in 1958 at the age of seventy-eight 'with an arthritic knee,' and was elected an Honorary Member of the AIBC the following year. Lyon died on October 13, 1963 at the age of eighty-three, after living in Penticton for forty-one years. Evelyn died in 1980.

News of your election to the high office of Chief Magistrate of the City of Penticton is received with great pleasure and pride... It is conceded that you are the first Architect to be so signally honoured.

Letter from the AIBC, June 4, 1948.

Post Office, Kelowna

WILLIAM CHARLES FREDERICK GILLAM
1867-1962

DONALD LUXTON

W.C.F. Gillam was a well-known architect in Vancouver before moving to California to pursue a career as an artist. He was born October 14, 1867 in Brighton, England, the son of Richard Gillam, a fish merchant. He became an articled pupil of Arthur Lewis, Sussex, starting in 1882, and then spent three years as an improver, followed by eleven years as assistant to Arthur Simpson, father of J.W. Simpson, the President of the RIBA. For the next twelve years Gillam practised on his own in London and Brighton, becoming a Member of the Society of Architects in 1896. In 1911 he immigrated to Vancouver, where he entered into a brief association with **Claude P. Jones.** Gillam was known as an expert in the field of school planning, and with Jones landed the contract for Ridgeway School, North Vancouver, 1911-12. On his own Gillam designed Queen Mary High School, North Vancouver, 1914-15, and won the open competition for the Provincial Normal School, Victoria, 1912-14. The Normal School was a plum job, considered the most noteworthy example of school construction in the province. In addition to its handsome ninety-five foot high central tower, it boasted a gymnasium, and a large auditorium with a gallery. Gillam had offices in both Vancouver and Victoria in 1913.

Between 1913 and 1919 Gillam was also in a loose partnership with Kennerley Bryan, who had arrived on the local scene in 1910. On his own Bryan had been busy designing houses, apartments, and a series of structures for the B.C. Sugar Refining Co. on Powell Street. Bryan was also briefly associated in an informal partnership with **Fred Townley** in 1912. Together, Bryan & Gillam designed a number of commercial projects, including what is now known as the world's thinnest commercial building, built for Cantonese businessman, Chang Toy, the owner of the Sam Kee Co., on Pender Street after a portion of his property was expropriated for road widening. Incensed that the city left him only a narrow strip of land, he was determined to build on the remnant portion, resulting in an oddball structure that tapers to just several feet in width at one end. Late in 1912, Bryan & Gillam prepared the designs for a dramatic Greek Orthodox Church in the "Byzantine" style of architecture; however by that time economic conditions had deteriorated, and the project was never started.

During the First World War, Gillam served as a munitions inspector under the Imperial Munitions Board. Bryan disappeared in 1919, and Gillam entered into a brief partnership with **Frank Mountain** in 1920-21. Gillam's last known local project was three-room MacLean High School in Port Haney, designed in 1922 and opened the following year. Architectural work was scarce, however, and Gillam left B.C. for northern California. After settling in Burlingame, he was active as an artist in the San Francisco Bay area. He was a member of the California Society of Etchers, the Palo Alto Art Club, and the Berkeley League of Fine Arts, and exhibited at the Oakland Art Gallery, 1928, the California State Fair, 1930 (where he won a prize), and the California State Library, 1951. Gillam died in Sonoma County, California on February 10, 1962. Examples of his artwork are held at the De Young Museum, San Francisco; St. Paul's Episcopal Church, Burlingame; Church of Latter Day Saints, Oakland; the California State Library, Sacramento; and St. David's Episcopal Church, Pittsburgh, California.

Ridgeway School, North Vancouver

Proposed Greek Orthodox Church, Vancouver

Queen Mary School, North Vancouver

Provincial Normal School, Victoria

Sam Kee Building, Vancouver

MacLean High School, Port Haney, Maple Ridge

Architect,

WILLIAM MARSHALL DODD
1872-1948

DONALD LUXTON

W.M. Dodd had a long, distinguished and prolific architectural career that ranged across much of Canada, but his contributions to the development of many western cities are virtually forgotten, and he died in obscurity in North Vancouver. Born in Almonte, Ontario on January 29, 1872, after finishing high school at the age of fifteen he served three years with his father Thomas at plastering, bricklaying and stone cutting. He then worked for five years as a journeyman during which time he studied architecture for two years with Henry Pope in Bracebridge, Ontario. Afterwards he took a one year course with J.B. Cassells in Gravenhurst, and then worked for three years in offices in Toronto.

Dodd got caught up in the great westward migration. Moving to Winnipeg by 1896, he spent three years in the office of **H.S. Griffith**, and then a year supervising projects for George Browne. In June, 1900 he set up his own office in Calgary, which grew into one of the largest in western Canada. Although many architects were moving in at the time, Dodd arrived at the start of this pack; he managed to establish a firm foothold in Calgary and remain one of its main architects for about a decade. He designed a large number of buildings in the city and in other parts of south and central Alberta, in B.C., and southern Saskatchewan. One B.C. project was the C.B. Hume Block in Revelstoke, 1902, for a time the largest department store in the Interior. Dodd was credited with introducing the Classical Revival style to commercial buildings in Calgary. Practical in his application of building techniques, he was the inventor of Dodd's Interlocking Brick, for which he held patents in five countries. On June 15, 1904 the now-successful architect married Evva May Powell, and they honeymooned on the west coast.

Dodd's clients included some of Calgary's wealthiest men, such as Senator James A. Lougheed, and ranching barons Patrick Burns and William Roper Hull. The prairie region was being rapidly developed with the construction of railway branch lines, which opened new lands for homesteading. Dodd established branch offices in Fernie, Lethbridge, and Edmonton. He had a number of contracts in the "Eastern Territories," an area which became southern Saskatchewan, and in 1905 opened a Regina branch office. He won two important competitions there, for Knox Presbyterian Church and the new city hall, both now demolished. Regina City Hall, considered Saskatchewan's most impressive example of the Romanesque style, was Dodd's single most important building. The success of this design likely led him to receive the top prize for Calgary's 1907 city hall competition which was only open to Canadian architects. During 1908 over a dozen employees worked in his Calgary office alone. Dodd was active in the development of his profession in Alberta, and in 1908 became a charter member of the Alberta Association of Architects.

Owing to ill health, Dodd moved to Vancouver, where he commenced practice on June 1, 1911. His output included many apartment blocks, most notably Douglas Lodge at Granville Street and Twelfth Avenue, 1911-12, numerous commercial projects, and houses, such as the H.L. Jenkins Residence on Point Grey Road, 1912-13. Dodd was just getting established on the coast when the economy went sour. He was rejected as medically unfit during the First World War.

His largest single undertaking in British Columbia was the design of the plant and townsite at Ocean Falls for Pacific Mills Ltd. Shares in the plant were being sold by 1914, and construction proceeded despite the onset of war. Dodd designed the buildings for this remote and rainy company town, including over fifty residences, eleven bunkhouses, offices, a bank, court house, post office and an Opera House. "Many houses had small lawns and flower gardens maintained at Company expense. The streets were all exactly four inches thick, being made of two by four lumber. The hills, cleated for rainy days, were named for what they were close to – the Store Hill, the Dam Hill, the School Hill."

After the war Dodd relocated to the farming community of Aldergrove, where he remained until the 1940s. He continued in active practice, an example of his work being a grand Spanish Colonial Revival mansion for W.E. Anderson, president of the Hayes-Anderson Motor Company, that stands at the corner of Granville Street and Angus Drive in Shaughnessy

Heights, 1921. By 1944 Dodd had moved to Deep Cove on Vancouver's North Shore, where he died on October 11, 1948, survived by his wife, two sisters and a brother. He was active as an architect right up to his death, with several buildings, including the Olympic Steam Baths on Hastings Street, being completed posthumously. During his long career Dodd claimed to have designed five city halls, designed and supervised seventy-five schools, twenty-seven theatres, thirty apartments, twenty-two hospitals and numerous residences.

One thing is certain, that all work entrusted to him has in every instance given the greatest satisfaction, and of him it might be aptly quoted: "Si monumentum requiris circumspice" (If thou seekest his monument, look around).

Manitoba *Free Press* (Winnipeg), 30 April 1904; p 32.

ELEVATION ON McKENZIE AVENUE.

C.B. Hume Block, Revelstoke

Anderson Residence, Vancouver

KARL BRANWHITE SPURGIN
1877-1936

JENNIFER NELL BARR

K.B. Spurgin produced a large and important body of work, but died relatively young, and his name was unfortunately rather forgotten in the latter half of the twentieth century. He was born in Maryport, Cumberland, England, April 17, 1877, son of Dr. W. Henry and Emma Steward Spurgin. Young Karl trained as an architect for five years with J.W. Taylor, FRIBA, in Newcastle-on-Tyne, and then for nine months with Civil Engineer L.H. Armour in Gateshead-on-Tyne. He served in the Boer War with the Northumberland Yeomanry for a year and a half, and published a book, *The South African War*, on his return to England. He then returned to Armour's office for another year before setting up his own architectural practice in Newcastle in 1903.

In 1911, Spurgin immigrated to Canada, where he worked first as a draftsman and outside superintendent for **Henry S. Griffith** in Victoria. In 1912 he became partners with Edmund O. Wilkins, whom he likely met through Griffith's office. Their first major commissions together were Margaret Jenkins School on Fairfield Road in Victoria, the Qualicum Beach Power Plant, and the Qualicum Beach Hotel for the Merchants Trust and Trading Company Limited, whose shareholders were mostly in Newcastle-on-Tyne in England. In May 1913 Spurgin was elected to the executive of the British Columbia Society of Architects, Victoria Chapter. The partnership lasted until Spurgin left for the Western Front in November 1915; Wilkins continued practice on his own until he left Victoria in about 1920.

Spurgin joined the Canadian Expeditionary Force as second-in-command of the 103rd Battalion (Timber Wolves). He served in France, Belgium and Germany, and then was seconded to the British Imperial forces from July 1917 to

February 1919. At the end of the First World War, he spent a short time with the army of occupation before being discharged on May 3, 1919 in Seaford, England. Upon returning to Victoria, Major Spurgin was appointed superintendent of the Soldiers' Housing Scheme in Saanich, and designed and supervised construction of the first fourteen houses (the last five were designed in 1921 by **Ralph Berrill**). Spurgin was also associate architect to **Percy Leonard James** on the 1921-25 four-storey East Wing of Royal Jubilee Hospital. With Richard G. Rice, Spurgin designed the Saanich War Memorial Health Centre, 1920. A symmetrical building combining elements of both British and American Arts and Crafts styles, it is built of hollow tiles on a concrete foundation and clad in roughcast and dark-stained clapboard. Rice was a draftsman for the Esquimalt & Nanaimo Railway and later with the B.C. Department of Public Works; he also designed the extant 1914 stone and brick Arts and Crafts house at 3149 Cook Street in Victoria. On his own, Spurgin designed a small hip-roofed, stuccoed, British Arts and Crafts-style bungalow in 1920 for Saanich municipal clerk Hector Cowper, and an American Arts and Crafts-style bungalow in Oak Bay for plumber Robert Smith. He also did work for the Sidney Roofing and Paper Company, including the Saturator House and Motor House, 1921, on the Songhees Reserve in Victoria West. In 1926 he designed the Arts and Crafts half-timbered and brick Fairfield United Church for the newly formed congregation.

In 1927 Spurgin and **J. Graham Johnson** designed a row of five storybook houses, the two end ones each with round towers with conical caps, on Patio Court in Oak Bay. Spurgin on his own designed an Arts and Crafts house on Dallas Road in Victoria for Hunter & Halkett in 1929; the design included Arts and Crafts front and back fences, garage and doghouse. Spurgin and Johnson together in 1932 designed the Mount Baker Block of four apartments and five shops, for **S. Patrick Birley**, who was at that time working in their office, and may himself have been the chief designer. Spurgin designed many houses in and around Victoria, including *The Bourne*, 1927, for Colonel G.A. Phillips, and a "semi-bungalow," at 1590 Despard Avenue, 1927. He also designed numerous bunga-

Qualicum Beach Hotel, Qualicum Beach

lows up-island and in the Kelowna area.

In association with **William J. Semeyn**, Spurgin worked on the design of Oak Bay Secondary School, 1929. In 1936, Spurgin collaborated with **Hubert Savage** on the design of a drill hall in HCMS *Naden* in Esquimalt. Two of Spurgin's most prestigious projects, the Prince of Wales Fairbridge Farm School complex south of Duncan and Qualicum College, Qualicum Beach, for Robert and Ivan Knight, both begun in 1935, were unfinished at the time of his death. Spurgin designed all the early Fairbridge Farm buildings, including the principal's house, and travelled there several times a month to supervise construction. **Douglas James**, who lived in Duncan, took over construction supervision after Spurgin's death. Several years later **Ross Lort** was hired to design other buildings at the site, including the distinctive chapel, 1939-40.

Spurgin's first wife, Janet Coote, was born in Newcastle-on-Tyne, England; she came to Victoria in 1912, but spent the war years back in England. Spurgin designed their home at Oak Bay in 1912 as a one-storey, hip-roofed bungalow, and in 1919 he added a gable-fronted second storey. They had a son, Eric, and a daughter, Joan. Janet died March 1, 1927 at the age of forty-six. In 1928 Spurgin designed a new family home, a cross-gabled British Arts and Crafts-style house in Saanich. Called a Sussex Bungalow, it has an asymmetrical plan with half-timbering and facade cartouches. In December 1928 he married widow Ann Isobel (Buss) Paterson, whose first husband, Lieutenant William Paterson, had died of Spanish Influenza in 1919 on his way home from the First World War. Ann Paterson was headmistress of St. Margaret's School for girls from 1928-34, and Spurgin had twice designed buildings for St. Margaret's School, the first in 1911, and the second in 1926. Karl and Ann had one son, Robin Hugh.

Spurgin was a prominent Victoria member of the British-founded Oxford Group movement, which contributed significantly to the Christian basis of Alcoholics Anonymous, and he took a trip to western Ontario in 1936 for the cause. He was active in St. Matthias Anglican Church, a member of the United Services Institution of Vancouver Island and President of the 103rd Battalion Association. An expert horseman, he was associated with the Victoria Riding Academy. Karl Branwhite Spurgin practised his craft as an architect until a week before his sudden death, at the age of fifty-nine on November 27, 1936, of pneumonia aggravated by malaria which he had contracted during the Boer War. He was buried at Royal Oak Burial Park; S. Patrick Birley and Ian Phillips represented the AIBC as pallbearers, while Major Brian H. Tyrwhitt Drake, Captain F.G. Dexter and Lieutenant Charles Milligan represented the military.

Margaret Jenkins School, Victoria

Second Spurgin Residence, Saanich

Qualicum College School, Qualicum Beach

HENRY
BLACKADDER
1882-1968

NANCY BYRTUS

Henry Blackadder was born in Dundee, Scotland on September 11, 1882. His architectural career spanned four decades in British Columbia, but began at his birthplace with a four-year apprenticeship to the trade. Blackadder first entered the architectural profession in 1899 by joining the office of T.M. Cappon in Dundee. Upon completion of his four-year apprenticeship, he accepted work as an assistant to one of the most talented Edwardian architects in London, Sir Ernest George (1839-1922). The designs created by George, and his partner Alfred Yeates, made an indelible impression on Blackadder. During the eight years he worked with them, George & Yeates completed several large commissions, one of which was the design for the British Pavilion at the World's Fair of 1904.

In 1911, Blackadder moved to British Columbia and spent a short time as a draftsman with the firm of **Dalton & Eveleigh**. In the same year he secured his first independent commission, for the Garner residence in Vancouver. He also served as the architect for the huge and imposing Tudor Revival Thomas Nye residence in North Lonsdale, 1912. Blackadder jointly designed one project in North Vancouver with **Reyburn Jameson**, a Boarding and Day School announced in January 1912, but shortly afterwards he entered into partnership with the British architect Alexander Sinclair Wemyss MacKay (born 1878); their practice thrived in the booming prewar economy. MacKay had taken classes at the Architectural Association in London before arriving in Canada. He designed a few buildings in Nelson, B.C., moved to North Vancouver in 1911, and served overseas as a Lieutenant during the First World War. Their partnership was to be Blackadder's longest, lasting approximately fifteen years. Together, Blackadder & MacKay furnished North

Vancouver with a surprising number of residences in the Tudor Revival and Craftsman Bungalow styles. Ten of their houses in North Vancouver featured unusually narrow staircases, a design idiosyncrasy attributed to Blackadder's belief that wide staircases are for those "too weighty in... body and head." The Larson residence, built in 1921, illustrates the firm's use of the Craftsman style. Its asymmetrical plan, heavy porch columns, and half-timbered details are comparable to the designs published in the builder's catalogues of the day. In 1920 they provided the plans for eighty-four bungalows for the Employees Housing Company in Ioco, the company town adjacent to Imperial Oil's Port Moody refinery.

Blackadder spent his early years in the province living in the board-and-batten house he designed on Carisbrooke Road in North Vancouver. He and his wife Maud were well known within the predominantly English and Scottish community of Lonsdale. It was in this community that Blackadder cultivated fruit trees, vegetables and flowers on his property and became an accomplished self-taught pianist. During the first years of the First World War he supervised the construction of the North Vancouver Drill Hall, built according to Standard Drill Hall Type 'C' plans prepared by the Department of Militia & Defence, and then in 1917 enlisted for overseas service as a Lieutenant with the Fourth Divisional Engineers in Germany, England and France. Later he supported the Second World War efforts through his work in the drafting rooms of the Burrard Dry Docks in North Vancouver.

Like most firms, Blackadder & MacKay did not restrict their commissions to residential design. Other works included the Cenotaph in Victoria Park, 1923, and the Dundarave Block in Lonsdale, a large commercial building featuring square pro-

Blackadder with the Fourth Divisional Engineers in Germany, c.1918

jecting bays and an angled corner entrance built in 1912. Their sophisticated design for the brick and precast concrete Lynn Valley Elementary School suggests the influence of Blackadder's former employer, George & Yeates. Competed in 1920, the school is noted for its bull's-eye windows and bold decorative horizontal facade banding. After the completion of an impressive residence named *Stanmore* in 1927, MacKay moved to Auckland, New Zealand, ending the firm's collaborations. Blackadder resumed work independently and undertook small additions, structural repairs and the design of several warehouses on Granville Island. As with other firms the Depression slowed his practice. From 1937-41, he formed a partnership with **Joseph F. Watson**, and their buildings conformed to the preferred modernist aesthetic of the time. In 1941, Blackadder channelled his expertise into wartime demands.

Wallace Shipyards Drafting Room, September 1943, Blackadder standing on left

Blackadder's dedication to the architectural profession extended beyond his practice. In 1929 he became a member of the RAIC, and was elected Vice-President, 1940, and President, 1941-43, of the AIBC. Before he died on April 11, 1968, the AIBC declared him an Honorary Member in recognition of his contribution to the field in B.C. Continuing to work well into old age, Blackadder completed an apartment building in 1954 on Lonsdale at the age of seventy-one. A number of the structures he designed are recognized today in heritage inventories in Vancouver, Port Moody and North Vancouver. Except during wartime, his business was constant and productive. His labours helped to shape the residential character of Ioco and North Vancouver.

Nye Residence, North Vancouver

Bessborough Apartments, Victoria

PERCY
FOX
1877-1939

JENNIFER NELL BARR AND
MARY E. DOODY JONES

Percy Fox was born on January 4, 1877 in Bradford, Yorkshire, son of Andrew Chadwick Fox. He articled in the Bradford office of B.W. and J.B. Bailey, Architects, 1893-98, and worked as an assistant in the same office until 1900. He established his own office in Bradford in December 1900, and designed numerous houses and business premises, including Bradford Old Bank in Leeds. In February 1911, Fox and his wife, Edith, immigrated to Canada, and he worked as office manager in **Thomas Hooper's** Victoria office until December 1911. He then went into private practice, during which time he undertook alterations and additions to a number of Victoria buildings. In 1913 Fox entered into a partnership with **Ralph Berrill**. Their styles tended toward the utilitarian for commercial buildings and an eclectic mix for residential. The "1914 Outlook" of *The Week*, January 24, 1914, declared that "they have studied the different schools of architecture, and have the faculty of adapting the various styles to modern requirements, while carrying out the ideas of the old masters of the art." Their projects included a rooming house for Kong Sin Wing in Victoria's Chinatown, 1913, and a residence in Oak Bay for Dr. Herbert Brown and real estate agent Austin Brown, 1913.

Berrill served in Europe during the First World War. After his return, he and Fox shared an office until about 1921, and then separated. Fox alone signed the plans for rebuilding three stores on Douglas Street in 1920, and for a many-gabled California Bungalow on Faithful Street for dentist, Samuel G. Clemence, in 1921. However, in 1921 Fox and Berrill together designed a side-gabled Craftsman house for George F. Carey. Fox's commercial structures included a business block on Douglas Street for Otto Weiler, 1920; alterations and additions to the Glenshiel Inn in 1925; a woollen mill for The British Columbia Worsted Mill Limited in 1928; an apartment block on Yates, 1929, for F.G. Purser, built by the Victoria Realty and Building Company; the Bessborough Apartments on McClure Street, 1930, now Abigail's Bed & Breakfast; and several apartment blocks for building contractor John Moxam, including the Harrogate Apartments on Beach Drive in Oak Bay, 1929-30, a symmetrical Tudor Revival composition with half-timbering and facade cartouches. He also designed small structures such as the conjoint summer cottages in the seaside resort of Cordova Bay, just north of Victoria, 1931, for C.C. Johns, owner of the local general store. House designs included one for A.C. Pike, 1925; a small but notable one in English Cottage style for H.G. Graham, 1927; and one on Upper Terrace Road in Uplands, 1929, for H.B. Darnell. Percy Fox served as President of the AIBC 1927-29, and during that time frequently aired his views on the profession in the Victoria *Daily Colonist*.

Fox was a devotee of thoroughbred horse racing, and for a time was managing director of the Colwood and Willows Park race tracks. In the 1930s he became involved in the gold mining boom on the west coast of Vancouver Island, including the Privateer Mine and the settlement of Zeballos, and lived at the Windermere Hotel when he returned to Victoria. In his last year he directed the affairs of Kennedy Lake Gold Mines Limited, spending much of his time there. Percy Fox died on November 30, 1939 and was buried in Royal Oak Burial Park.

Weiler Block, Victoria

Geo E Hutchinson

GEORGE EDGAR HUTCHINSON
1862-1942

BRUCE M. FORSTER

George E. Hutchinson was born in Berwick, Kings County, Nova Scotia, on January 11, 1862, the only son of Elizabeth van Buskark and Enoch Hutchinson, a Morristown farmer. "At the age of fourteen he commenced work in his uncle's wood-working mill, where he developed a fondness for mechanics... and at the age of seventeen started for Boston." When he didn't find work, he was hired as an assistant of the bicycle school at the Pope Manufacturing Co. "During the following three years he visited most of the cities of Canada and the United States and was generally acknowledged as the champion trick rider and fancy bicyclist of the world having competed in a score of contests with the greatest performers of the day to prove his claim to the title."

Expanding his horizons, he took a job in a woodworking factory, and enrolled in freehand and architectural drawing classes at the Boston Industrial School for Art. After three years he was foreman at the factory, and had graduated at the head of his night class. Pursuing his interest in architecture, he landed a position at the firm of Gould Brothers in Boston, where he rose to the position of chief designer. Ever the entre-preneur, in 1894 he built, owned and managed a "large and handsome lunch waggon... will accommodate 15... light lunches, oysters, etc., can be procured at all hours." Returning to Canada, he opened an architectural office in Middleton, Nova Scotia in 1898. Seeing greater potential in the booming town of Sydney, he relocated in 1900, and obtained a position with Chappell Brothers & Co., woodworkers and builders. Late in 1903 he resigned to open his own firm, where he designed several residences, a tenement block and an addition to a branch store. After a short stint in St. John's, Newfoundland,

he moved west with his family to Regina by April, 1905. In 1906 he became Saskatchewan's Provincial Architect, but was dismissed the following year over a disagreement on design and construction costs of the proposed new Regina Land Titles Building. He entered private practice, partnered first with George E. Nobles, and then Ernest McGlashen. Hutchinson became a Fellow of the RAIC in 1908, and designed a number of prominent structures including schools, churches and other public buildings.

Drawn by the western boom, Hutchinson relocated to Victoria in 1911. His architectural output appears to have been minimal. He was briefly in a partnership with **Guy Singleton Ford**, and they worked on an industrial plant for the Victoria Steam Laundry Company with **J.C.M. Keith** in 1912. Hutchinson claimed to have designed the Duchess Street Fire Hall, 1913. He went overseas as a munitions worker in the summer of 1915, and was involved in mechanical and aircraft work in Great Britain until 1920, when he returned to Victoria. Finding little work, Hutchinson joined a toy company, Hiker Manufacturing, where he was a worker and director. Hutchinson was also remembered as the "lamplighter," as one of his side jobs was to ride around on his bicycle and light the local gas street lights.

In 1929 he was offered the opportunity to design a new garrison church, the Queen of Peace in Esquimalt, in memory of the overseas dead. In anticipation of this commission, he made application to join the AIBC, but his membership was not immediately granted. Letters of support were sent on his behalf by Pastor Rev. A.B.W. Wood, Captain and Chaplain, and R.H. Pooley, Attorney-General, and he was finally granted registration in 1931. Given the constraints of the Depression, Hutchinson's original plans for a brick Romanesque-style basilica had to be scaled back to a second plan in sandstone, with the final church built in wood frame. Hutchinson died in Victoria on August 15, 1942, and was interred in Colwood Burial Park.

MacDonald Block, North Sydney, Nova Scotia, 1900

JESSE MILTON WARREN
C.1889-1953

JENNIFER NELL BARR

Jesse M. Warren was born in San Francisco about 1889 and began studying to be an architect in 1907. He then moved to New York to complete his training. He travelled for some time through Eastern Canada and the United States, and arrived in Seattle by 1909 at about the age of twenty. The *Pacific Builder & Engineer* of October 23, 1909 listed him as the architect of a $40,000, three-storey brick store building at 1400-10 Third Avenue for the Liberty Building Company. After working with several Seattle architectural firms, including Beezer Brothers and Thompson & Thompson, Warren entered into partnership with **William P. White**, the firm known as White & Warren, with a suite of offices at #926-7-8 Northern Bank Building.

Warren moved to Victoria in 1911. Two of his first buildings were the B.C. Hardware Company building on Fort Street, east of Blanshard, and the landmark Central Building at View and Broad Streets, a handsome brick-faced office block with Classical Revival detailing delineated by cream-yellow glazed terra cotta columns, stringcourses, capitals and cornice. In April 1915, Warren designed a large addition to an old house at Quadra and Cormorant Streets for Sands Funeral Furnishing Company. During his time in Victoria, he designed a number of residences ranging in size from small Craftsman Bungalows on Stanley and Chamberlain Streets; to substantial homes for the wealthy, including one on Dallas Road for A.A. Belbeck, 1912; and a number of apartment, office and store blocks, including the 1913 Station Hotel at Store Street and Pandora Avenue for the Victoria Phoenix Brewing Company. Although an American, he was hired to design the Eastern-Canadian-style Hudson's Bay Block House for the Victoria-Vancouver Island Exhibit in 1913. One of his grandest designs, for which he won a public competition in 1912, was the First Baptist

Church, which was never built at the proposed Fisgard and Vancouver Street site. The First Baptist congregation later took over the Congregational Church by architects **Bresemann & Durfee** at 1600 Quadra Street.

Jesse's older brother, George Irving Warren, known as "Mr. Victoria," helped found the Victoria and Island Publicity Bureau in 1921 and was its Commissioner for forty years; he was also managing secretary of the Victoria Chamber of Commerce for many years. Both Warren brothers were prominent members of the Victoria Rotary Club, of which Jesse was a founding member in 1914. Jesse addressed the group on at least two occasions, in February 1914 and May 1915. In 1914, he spoke on "Why Victoria is destined to be the New York of the Pacific," linking the construction of the Panama Canal with the need for Victoria to work to secure industries and hasten development:

Perhaps too much time and money had been spent in making the city known to outsiders as an ideal place to live in and too little done to attract attention from the standpoint of industrial possibility…In the construction of the few buildings of which he, as an architect, had charge in the three years of his residence, he had sent away for approximately $1,000,000 worth of material.

Victoria *Daily Colonist*, February 13, 1914, p.5.

Warren moved to Seattle about 1916 and continued to work as an architect. In 1952 he retired with his family to Santa Barbara, California, where he died in September 1953 at the age of sixty-four.

Hudson's Bay Block House, Victoria

Sands Funeral Furnishing Company, Victoria

Unbuilt project for the Elliot Building, Victoria

HOULT
HORTON

Duncan Gillman McBeath Residence, Victoria, 1911

JENNIFER NELL BARR AND DONALD LUXTON

Hoult Horton, who served as the first President of the B.C. Society of Architects in 1912-13, worked in Victoria from 1911 until 1915, sometimes alone and sometimes in partnership. He was partnered with **Paul Phipps**, with whom he had offices in Vancouver and Victoria 1912-13, and they were responsible for one of the landmarks on Victoria's Inner harbour, the Belmont House. Originally conceived as an eight-storey hotel, a decision was made, before construction was complete, to change the use to offices. Cream coloured matte-glazed terra cotta, relieved with moulded decoration, was used as cladding on all three main facades. The austere and restrained Classical Revival style popular for commercial buildings of the Edwardian era was used to good advantage, and some *Art Nouveau* motifs

are also evident, especially in the main lobby woodwork and newel posts. Also structurally innovative, this was one of the first large-scale reinforced concrete buildings in Victoria. Horton & Phipps also designed several residences in Victoria, including those for C.B. Schreiber; the Misses Emily Alice, Florence Lella and Harriet O'Brien; and J.R. Matterson; all designed in 1912 and all currently extant. They also designed a commercial block on Powell Street, Vancouver for Mrs. E.T. Tuthill; work commenced late in 1912, but the project was stalled due to the deteriorating economic conditions and was never completed.

Hoult Horton moved his office into the Belmont Building after it was finished, and was responsible for several handsome British Arts and Crafts-style residences in the Victoria area, such as those of D.G. McBeath and John D. Hallam. Horton went into partnership with Robert J. Horton, possibly his brother, and they left Victoria by 1915, their fate unknown.

Belmont House, Victoria

PAUL
PHIPPS
1880-1953

STUART STARK

Paul Phipps was originally American, but trained and worked mainly in England. He is best remembered as the father of famed British actress, singer and comedienne, Joyce Grenfell, popular in the 1950s and 1960s. Born in 1880 at No 1 Fifth Avenue in New York City, to an American father and an English mother, Phipps's family travelled between the United States and England. He was schooled at Eton and Balliol, and later educated at Oxford. From as early as 1902, he was one of those articled with Sir Edwin Lutyens (1869-1944) in his offices in Bloomsbury Square, working for two pounds a week, in what was remembered as "a happy office," though Lutyens wrote to his wife in 1906: "Two new pupils this morning. They terrify me." As a "penniless young architect" in 1909 in London, Phipps married Nora, one of the famous Langhorne sisters of Virginia; one sister, Nancy, married Waldorf Astor; and the other, Irene, married artist Charles Dana Gibson. Phipps was tall, stylish and liked to wear bow-ties with his stiff collars. He and Waldorf Astor were credited with introducing the daring "reverse" into the ballrooms of London, allowing waltzers relief from the continuous room-spinning previously in fashion.

The Phipps's first child, Joyce, was born in England in 1910. The family lived in Winnipeg and in Vancouver around 1912 and 1913. He must have done well, as he was driving an open Hupmobile automobile during his time on the west coast and worked as a partner with **Hoult Horton**, designing buildings in both Vancouver and Victoria. Phipps on his own is known to have designed at least one grand mansion in Vancouver's exclusive Shaughnessy Heights, on Angus Drive, for J.B. Johnson in 1912. Shortly before the First World War, the family was living in America, but Phipps left at once for Canada and joined the first regiment going overseas, The Princess Patricia's Light Infantry. He transferred to the Sherwood Foresters in England and went to France as a commander in 1915.

As a young girl, Joyce Grenfell made a spring visit to Hampton Court with her father. She later wrote: "I fetched up beside my father who was looking at the long wall behind the herbaceous border in the palace garden. "Look at the colours in those bricks" "It's red," I said, seeing it that way. "Have another look," said my father, pushing his hat further back on his head. As I looked again the solid red dissolved and now the bricks were many different colours; some were almost blue, or grey, or mauve, or pink, or sandy-yellow. Only a few were brick-red. Revelation! The colours came out at me, subtle in their differences, exciting in their unfamiliarity. From that moment I saw more than primary colours. The discovery was that the colours had been there to be found all the time." Phipps shared his interests with his daughter on other trips in London: "I learned to recognize Grinling Gibbons and developed a feeling for Christopher Wren. We wandered in the week-end empty streets, looking for special treasures, a moulding round a door, a fine fanlight, or the lettering on a tomb that he had earmarked for me to see."

Phipps continued his work as an architect in England. He worked on a widely-published country house called *Quietways* in Kent in 1923 with Oswald P. Milne, one of the other architects who had also articled with Lutyens at the same time as Phipps. He also had a hand in garden design at Monteviot House in the Scottish Borders. During the Second World War, Phipps served as one of the team of architects detailed to fire-watch St. Paul's Cathedral, a building he particularly loved. Joyce Grenfell recalled: "We would go and stand under the great dome. He pointed out the harmonious disposition of the tall windows that he found so successful, and I felt the power of St. Paul's that makes it so satisfying... He enjoyed exploring the building, climbing up the inner stairways to the leads, standing in the dark with London all round him and the skies raked by searchlights." Paul Phipps died in England in 1953.

Joyce Grenfell and Paul Phipps at Cliveden, Buckinghamshire, England, 1936

E.J. Bresemann

EMANUEL JOSEPH BRESEMANN

1881-1971

MORIEN EUGENE DURFEE

1885-1941

JENNIFER NELL

BARR

Unlike many others about whose experiences we can only guess, Emanuel Bresemann wrote an autobiographical essay in 1966 when he was eighty-six that tells in his own voice his stories of a busy and prolific career. Born to German immigrant parents near Tacoma, Washington on March 5, 1881, by 1903 he had moved to Everett where he worked as a woodworker, and began his architectural studies through correspondence school and classes conducted by architect **A.J. Russell**. The following year he relocated to San Francisco, and studied architecture by night. Bresemann became friends and then roommates with a young draftsman, Morien Eugene "Gene" Durfee, born December 31, 1885 in Chippewa Falls, Wisconsin. They were in San Francisco during the earthquake and fire of 1906, and Bresemann related: "Several incidents occurred during the period of adjustment....at the time of the second quake. At that time I had gone down town to the Flood building, a large steel frame building with basement containing safe deposit vaults, of which I had a box containing a few gold pieces. I was unable to get in as the wide stairway was packed solid, extending from the basement to the Market street level. Then came the second shock and humanity rushed out and up into the street, giving me free access to my box and I hurried down, got what money I wanted, and let the crowd go by. It was truly a case of the first shall be last, and the last shall be first."

Late in 1908, Bresemann returned north, and with Durfee, opened an architectural office in Seattle. In 1909, Bresemann married Anna B. Crofts; he was twenty-eight and she was sixteen, and the couple had five children. As Bresemann related:

BRESEMANN & DURFEE
PARTNERSHIP 1911-1913

"After some four years in Seattle business became slack and Morien and I decided to investigate the possibilities of opening an office in Canada. This was particularly inviting as the C.P.R. was offering special rates to prospective home seekers. After going as far as Calgary and Edmonton with a friend, I returned and suggested to Morien that we open an office in Victoria. Morien thought otherwise so we decided to try both Victoria and Vancouver. Victoria went along in fine shape, but not so Vancouver. Morien took over the Victoria office and I the one in Vancouver where things were not good. It was suggested to me that I should investigate Nanaimo, which I did and after a few months in Vancouver we moved to Nanaimo, some seventy miles north of Victoria, and where we remained for four years... However after about two years in Victoria, Morien and I dissolved our partnership, and he moved to California with considerable success." The team's first known building in Victoria was an undertaking parlour for Charles Hayward and the B.C. Funeral Furnishing Company. Their masterpiece in Victoria was the First Congregational Church on Quadra Street, designed in early 1912. The handsome Classical Revival structure with four Ionic columns was designed with a cupola, and had a cornice and balustraded parapet on either side of the pediment. Bresemann & Durfee also designed a Classical Revival Knights of Pythias Hall, with a five-bay terra cotta facade. Their largest local project was the St. James Hotel on Johnson Street, 1912. Clad with tan brick and cream glazed terra cotta ornamentation, the original structure consisted of nine bays, but was extensively added to in 1981. They also designed a Methodist church in Esquimalt in 1913, paid for by crew members of Canada's first warship, the HMCS *Rainbow*, and a number of houses in the Victoria area between 1911-13: several houses from late 1911 and early 1912 were designed for the **Ward Investment Company**.

The firm designed an addition for the Commercial Hotel, Nanaimo, and hotels for Peter Swanson in Nanaimo and Princeton, B.C. By September 1913, the partners were acting independently on commissions, and in December they announced the dissolution of their partnership. Bresemann's last known building in B.C. was a grocery store in Nanaimo, 1916. He returned to Tacoma and opened an office in 1916, and was successful in a career that lasted until 1961, when he closed his office and went into semi-retirement. He died in Tacoma on May 5, 1971 at the age of ninety. Durfee initially relocated to Los Angeles in 1914, and then to Anaheim and finally Long Beach, California. He also spent some time in Tucson, Arizona in the early 1920s and designed Tucson's 1929 Fox Theatre. He was for a short period associated with architect, Theodore C. Kistner (1874-1973) of San Diego, with whom he designed the Anaheim City Hall, 1921. He died in Long Beach on December 26, 1941.

H. LINDSAY SWAN

1890-1938

DONALD LUXTON

Although primarily a civil engineer, Hamilton Lindsay Swan also practised architecture at a time when there was a greater porosity between the professions. Born in Gilford, County Down, Ireland on August 29, 1890, he studied the short course at the Crystal Palace School of Practical Engineering, Norwood, London, following which he served a three-year apprenticeship in Manchester. In 1910 he had decided to move to Penticton, B.C., and by the following December he was appointed Chief Draftsman to the Kettle Valley Railway Company. He was in charge of all architectural work for the company, including fruit warehouses, station buildings, ice houses, and round houses, including a reinforced concrete Engine House in Penticton, 1912. In 1916 he joined the Canadian Engineers and was sent overseas in March, 1917, serving in England, France and Belgium. After the war he returned to Penticton and started his own practice, his major buildings at this time including the B.C. Growers Warehouse and the Penticton Municipal Power House, both 1919.

In December 1919 he entered into partnership with Alpheus Price Augustine. Born March 23, 1886 in Middlesex County, Ontario, Augustine was a graduate in Civil Engineering from the University of Toronto, and worked in private practice 1909-14 in Vancouver. He enlisted with the Canadian Engineers in 1916, and was transferred to the Royal Engineers the following year. After being gassed at Armentières in 1918, he was sent to Northern Russia, where he constructed military buildings at Kolmagorskaya and Archangel. Augustine returned to Canada, and settled in Penticton, likely because of the dry climate. Swan & Augustine won the competition for the local Soldiers' Housing Scheme in 1920, and also designed the Maternity

Hospital in Penticton, 1920-21, and an addition to Central School in Cranbrook, 1922. The poor market for architecture led to Price Augustine's decision to moved to New Westminster, where he started the Augustine Coal Company. He died prematurely on September 11, 1928 at the age of forty-two.

In 1924 Swan moved his wife, Valerie, daughter, Valerie Ethel, and son, Denis to Vancouver, and within a few months was hired by the Provincial Department of Public Works as Resident Engineer supervising the construction of the Alexandra Suspension Bridge over the Fraser River at Spuzzum, 1925-26. After a brief assignment in Victoria, Swan was appointed Assistant District Engineer for New Westminster, 1926-27, Merritt, 1927-28 and Cranbrook, 1928-29. He was then promoted to District Engineer for Vancouver Island and the Mainland Coast from Powell River north. Swan designed their family home in Oak Bay, a charming British Arts and Crafts cottage on McNeil Avenue. Talented in handicrafts, one of his projects was to make his own Monopoly set, complete with local hotels like the Empress and transportation companies like the Esquimalt & Nanaimo Railway. Just months before his untimely death of pneumonia at the age of forty-seven on August 23, 1938, he was made first Administrator for the Highway Transportation Branch in Vancouver.

Swan Residence, Oak Bay

GORDON
BERNIE
KAUFMANN
1888-1949

DONALD LUXTON

Famous for his later accomplishments as an architect in the United States and as the designer of one of the world's greatest dams, Gordon B. Kaufmann established offices briefly in Vancouver and Kamloops before moving to California. Born in Lewisham, South London, on March 19, 1888, he was the elder son of Gustav Kaufmann, a merchant. He was educated at the Hausa school in Bergedorf, Germany, and in 1899-1904 at the Whitgift School, Croyden, England. From 1908-10 Kaufmann served an architectural apprenticeship with Alfred William Stephens Cross (1858-1932) in London, and passed the first two examinations of the Royal Institute of British Architects. Relocating briefly to Germany, he moved to Canada in 1910, working briefly in Montreal and Winnipeg. He married Elsie Bryant in 1911.

By late 1911, Kaufmann had arrived in Vancouver, and was soon busy designing houses and apartment blocks. In Vancouver he designed homes for real estate developer C. Nelson Ecclestone, 1912-13; lawyer Cecil Killam, 1913; and a grand Shaughnessy Heights mansion for Herbert Bingham, the Manager of Railway Townsites Ltd., 1913-14, that cost $35,000 to build. Kaufmann had also designed two speculative Kitsilano duplexes for Ecclestone in 1911. His commercial projects included stores and apartments for Le Patourel & McRae, Druggists in Kitsilano, 1912; a shingled apartment block, Iona Court, for D.H. Mott, 1912; and a large Craftsman-style apartment block for E.E. Crandall, 1912. Kaufmann's designs for the Hanscome residence were featured in the October, 1912 issue of *Bungalow Magazine*, published in Seattle. In 1912 he was chosen as the architect for the Acadia Block, a substantial brick structure in Kamloops, and opened an office in that city. The

following January, E. Phillips, an architect in Vancouver, relocated to Kamloops as Kaufmann's partner; George Sohannessen, who had been in charge of Kaufmann's Kamloops office for the last six months, then returned to Vancouver. Surviving houses in Kamloops by the Kaufmann & Phillips partnership include those for E.H. Grubbe, 1912; W.J.C. Hibbert, 1913; and E.F. Busteed, 1913. Work tapered off drastically during the 1913 downturn, and Canada joined the war against Germany the following year. In 1914 Kaufmann moved to Los Angeles, ostensibly in the hope of improving his wife's health, but at this time in Canada his Germanic name would have been a major liability.

He worked at odd jobs for several years until he was licensed as an architect in California in 1920. Kaufmann also maintained his office in Vancouver until 1920, although it appears to have generated little work. In the polyglot milieu of the Roaring Twenties in California, the "rugged, lantern-jawed" Kaufmann was soon recognized as a pragmatic and talented architect, and his personal charm, combined with an "air of mystery" established a solid reputation with the wealthy elite of Los Angeles. His facile use of period revival elements reflected Hollywood's current vogue for historical fantasies, and provided the architectural equivalent of giant stage sets for his clients. In 1925 he designed an enormous medieval-inspired mansion in Beverly Hills for oil magnate, Edward L. Doheny. In 1926, Kaufmann was chosen to design Scripps College, and created a Mediterranean-style campus with arcades and intimate courtyards. These led to commissions for the new California Institute of Technology, Pasadena, 1928, and the first buildings on the Westwood Village campus of the University of California, Los Angeles. These buildings helped create a distinctive southern California style characterised by terra cotta tiled roofs and white stucco walls, which became popularly known as "Californian."

His best-known achievement came about almost by accident. After the onset of the Great Depression in 1929, the American government responded with massive public works programs, a key element of which was the development of power generating facilities and flood control projects. The single largest proposed project was the construction of a massive dam on the Colorado River, straddling the borders of Nevada and Arizona. Kaufmann was hired in 1931 by the U.S. Bureau of Reclamation as consulting architect for the administration building in Boulder City, where the dam workers would be housed. When asked, Kaufmann proposed that he design the dam itself. With no background in industrial design, he was awarded "the single greatest industrial project in the history of the United States." Hoover Dam is recognized as a definitive masterpiece of the Art Deco era, and it has been suggested that it was strongly influenced by Kaufmann's enthusiasm for movies, especially Fritz Lang's futuristic German film *Metropolis* of 1927. Kaufmann abandoned the use of historical motifs and created an heroic image of modernism. Lightened in colour from bottom to top through the use of a complicated patterning of water pipes that allowed differential cooling of the concrete, the dam soars in a simple and unbroken arc. Its sheer monumentality reflects the massive centralization of federal power that was occurring in America in the 1930s.

Kaufmann went on to design several other dams, and was also a supervising architect for Works Progress Administration buildings in the Los Angeles area. As the economy improved in the mid-1930s, he assumed a preeminent position among California architects, and produced a steady stream of projects including the first high-rise residential tower in Los Angeles, the grandstand and clubhouse at Santa Anita racetrack in Arcadia, and the modernistic Hollywood Palladium. Among the architectural honors garnered by Kaufmann during his career were the Home Beautiful award, 1931; the United States Legion of Merit, 1937; and a fellowship in the American Institute of Architects. His Los Angeles Times Building, 1934-35, won the gold medal in commercial and industrial design at the Paris International Exposition in 1937. During the Second World War, the Kaufmanns moved to Washington, D.C., where Kaufmann was commissioned as a colonel in the U.S. Army's Chemical Warfare Service, serving until November 1945. After the war he returned to Pasadena, and his long and successful architectural career ended with his death on March 1, 1949 in Los Angeles.

Boulder (now Hoover) Dam, USA

HENRY HOLDSBY SIMMONDS

1883-1954

DONALD LUXTON

H.H. Simmonds's architectural career was unusual in that it did not follow the common centrifugal pattern that spiralled outwards from the Mother Country. A child of the colonies, he left his family roots to follow opportunity in another colony. Born August 17, 1883, in Moyhu, Victoria, Australia, he was the seventh of nine children of Catherine (Holdsby) and George Thomas Simmonds. In 1893 Henry and four of his siblings were in attendance at remote State School No. 2676 at Boggy Creek, about a mile away from the property where their father grew grapes, and some twenty miles from Wangaratta. His architectural education commenced about 1904 when he was a pupil in the Sydney office of James Nangle. He later graduated from the Sydney Technical College, and passed his examination as an Associate of the Institute of Architects of New South Wales.

We can only guess what restless motivation caused him to leave Australia, and his early movements are unclear. He travelled to San Francisco, and worked there briefly, and is known to have visited the Alaska Yukon Pacific Exposition in Seattle in May, 1909. By 1911 he was in Vancouver, likely drawn by the booming economy in western Canada. However, Simmonds arrived in Vancouver at the tail end of the boom era, and his career had barely started before local work dried up. His first known project in Vancouver was a house for W.H. Murphy on Powell Street in 1912. He started working for **Hugh A. Hodgson**, who was English-trained but Australian by birth. Hodgson had opened an office in 1911 in the Carter-Cotton Building, and was busy designing a variety of projects, including Oakalla, the Provincial Jail in Burnaby. Simmonds and Hodgson had many things in common: they were close to the

same age, born in the same country, and had both worked briefly in San Francisco. They developed a close personal and professional relationship that would last until Simmonds's death.

In a letter written to his youngest brother, dated June 7, 1913, and sent from Hodgson's office, he referred to how things would have been different "if that confounded thing I was after in London had eventuated this year." The economy did not improve, and in a letter to his mother dated April 21, 1914, Simmonds explained his situation:

Things are so dead quiet... They had a boom here and now they are having the re-action just like they had in Victoria [Australia] about '94. Hodgson is a white man & I am still in his office but most of the time I am doing nothing. I would upstakes & back to Australia only for that London scheme, it is still in abeyance, perhaps until the end of the year, but its really worth waiting for, and the co. have two English actors in Canada now playing to very successful houses so that things look quite good and I must just sit down & wait... My old boss in 'Frisco has been writing me about a theatre for down there & if he gets it lined up I may go down for a month or so, at his expense.

With the outbreak of the First World War, Simmonds enlisted on November 3, 1914 and went to Montreal with the 23rd Canadian Infantry Battalion. He trained in Montreal and Quebec until February 1915, and then shipped out to England. He was promoted to Corporal, and was stationed at Shorncliffe Camp until he was sent to France at the end of April as part of the 3rd Infantry Battalion, First Canadian Division of the British Expeditionary Force. He was promoted to Sergeant, and on May 26, 1915, at La Basse (Rouen) suffered a gunshot wound to the right shoulder. He was returned to his unit by July, where he stayed until the end of 1916. Suffering from rheumatoid arthritis in both hands, he was invalided to London, and spent 1917 and part of 1918 in casualty and training units. In the latter year he was transferred to the Canadian Engineers. He received his commission as a Lieutenant on January 20, 1919, just six days before he was discharged in Vancouver.

By July, 1919, he had re-established his practice in Vancouver, working out of Hodgson's office. Throughout his life, Simmonds preferred to work alone, but teamed up with other people when required. Hodgson and Simmonds formed a loose partnership from 1924 to about 1933, working together on some projects, and singly on others. Simmonds later had a similar relationship with **Ross Lort**, where they shared office space, and some business dealings, but never formally organized a partnership. "Simmonds was more of an engineer than a designer, and my father was more a designer than an engineer, and they worked well together," recalls Lort's son. **McCarter &**

Nairne also acted as consulting architects on some of Simmonds's larger projects, notably the British Columbia Electric Railway Co. Showroom and the Automotive and Ice Rink Building.

Throughout the 1920s he worked steadily at a number of projects, and even after the Crash of 1929 his output was prolific. In the 1920s the City of Vancouver had embarked on a programme to replace the aging wooden pavilions at the Pacific National Exhibition with fireproof, concrete structures. This coincided with the onset of the Great Depression, and over the next few years Simmonds, who had previously provided the plans for a number of other structures at the site, designed a consistent grouping of Art Deco buildings. Severe economic constraints dictated the cheapest construction methods, and cast-in-place concrete walls were used for both structure and finish. Often assembled by unskilled labour, the formwork was made of rough boards resulting in a low quality of exterior finish. Faced with these constraints, Simmonds skillfully relieved the sheer massiveness of these structures with a rhythmic articulation of the surfaces, and a judicious application of inset Art Deco detailing. This grouping included the Livestock Building, 1929; the Pure Foods Building, 1931; the Women and Fine Arts Building, 1931; and the Automotive and Ice Rink Building, 1933. At the time of construction, the Ice Rink was the world's largest sheet of artificial ice; unfortunately, its under-designed wooden truss roof collapsed under an exceptionally heavy snow load and had to be replaced by a steel structure. Despite budgetary limitations, the scale of these buildings was impressive, and they worked well together as an ensemble.

These large, clear-span structures, with concrete walls and steel truss roofs, were similar to the neighbourhood movie theatres that Simmonds was also designing throughout the city. Many of these have been demolished or seriously altered, but the Stanley Theatre, 1930, one of his most accomplished designs, has been restored as a venue for live theatre. Other commissions included an unbuilt project for a new City Market, 1936, private homes such as the mansard-roofed Con Jones Residence in Shaughnessy, 1924, commercial buildings, and apartment blocks, most notably the Stanley Park Manor Apartments, 1929. He was also adept at industrial work, and in 1932 was appointed as architect for the B.C. Electric railway gas plant project. That year, Simmons sailed in the 1932 Los Angeles Olympic Games, finishing fourth in the "Star Class".

"Simmie" was described by friends as a "self-contained" man and "a real bachelor." He built himself a house in Kerrisdale in 1931-32, with a double-height living room and minstrel's balcony, where he lived alone. He was an active sportsman and an enthusiastic yachtsman, and a devoted volunteer and stage manager, along with his friend Ross Lort, with the Vancouver Little Theatre Association. This amateur troupe had been founded in 1921, but like other such groups across the country, blossomed during the Depression and with the advent of the "talkies."

Despite his advancing age, Simmonds tried to get back into the army during the Second World War. During wartime he was appointed resident engineer for the HMCS *Discovery* headquarters in Stanley Park. After the war's end, he acted as the local architect for the Odeon Theatre chain, and designed a number of movie theatres, exuberant in their streamline details and use of neon. These included the Studio Theatre and the Fraser Theatre, both in Vancouver, 1948, and Victoria's 1500 seat Odeon Theatre, 1947-49. Simmonds was well regarded by members of the profession, and served as President of the AIBC from 1948-50, and as Vice-President of the RAIC, to which he was elected a Fellow in 1952.

In 1951 he was asked to head a team of technical personnel in Ottawa, and spent two years there working for the RCAF. Shortly after his return he began to suffer the effects of lung cancer, and his health deteriorated rapidly. Felix A. "Dil" Jones, an Australian bachelor and close friend of Simmonds, took care of him at this time, and then made arrangements for him to go into a private hospital, Chatham House, where he died on August 1, 1954. He was buried in the Field of Honour in Mountain View Cemetery. His pallbearers included Hugh Hodgson and Ross Lort.

Patricia Theatre, Powell River

Odeon Theatre, Victoria

Project for Collingwood United Church, Vancouver

BCER Showroom Building, Vancouver

ODEON
J. ARTHUR RANK PRESENTS
MARGARET LOCKWOOD IN THE WHITE UNICORN
ALSO ROYAL WEDDING PRESENTS IN TECHNICOLOR
CAFE
CLEANERS

E. EVANS & SON
PARTNERSHIP 1912-1962

ENOCH EVANS
1862-1939

DONALD LUXTON

The partnership of Enoch Evans and his son, George, was an enduring and prolific one. Enoch was born in Walsall, Staffordshire, England on November 12, 1862, the son of Enoch Evans, a silver plater. At an early age young Enoch apprenticed to George Davis, Architect, Westbourne Street, Walsall, where he stayed for a number of years. From 1884 to 1909 he worked as an architect, designing mostly industrial buildings, but also thirty-one houses for W.M. Lester in Walsall, 1894. By this time Enoch had married and started a family. His son, George Norris Evans, with whom he would later go into partnership, was born on June 9, 1887. Like many other sons of English architects, George entered his father's office in 1906 to start his apprenticeship.

In search of greater opportunities, the family immigrated to the colonies, arriving in Vancouver by 1910. Enoch established his office in March, 1912, in partnership with his son. George, very short and slight in stature, and genial in nature, was drafted under the Military Service Act of 1917, served with the

Grace Hospital, Vancouver

Loyal Protestant Home for Orphaned Children, New Westminster

Canadian Expeditionary Engineers, and was discharged on November 30, 1918. After George's return, their practice resumed, and in 1921 George married Gladys Mary Radcliffe. The Evanses undertook a variety of projects until the time of Enoch's death. *Elworth*, in Burnaby, was designed for retired CPR executive, Edwin Bateman, in 1922, and is now part of the Burnaby Village Museum. The Loyal Protestant Home for Orphaned Children, a British Arts and Crafts complex, was built in 1925. Grace Hospital, a maternity hospital for the Salvation Army in Vancouver, was designed in 1926 and opened the following year. In 1927 they designed a large service station for J.A. Irvine, 10 Commercial Street, Nanaimo, 1927. One of their Depression era projects was Westerham Court in Vancouver's West End, 1936, a streamlined design that showed George's facility with modernist styles.

Enoch Evans died on October 23, 1939, and was buried at the Masonic Cemetery in Burnaby. George continued his practice during the Second World War, and retained the firm's original name, E. Evans & Son until 1962. He served as President of the AIBC from 1943-44, and was briefly in partnership with William Bow in 1945. In the postwar years Evans worked on several major school commissions in New Westminster, starting with the New Westminster Junior High School (later Vincent Massey Junior High), 1949, with **William Bow** as associated architect. Evans was later responsible for the

GEORGE NORRIS EVANS
1887-1964

additions to the school that created the sprawling complex that exists today as Lester Pearson High School in New Westminster. George Evans died on January 19, 1964 at the age of seventy-six, survived by his wife, two sons, five grandchildren and his brother, William, and was also buried at the Masonic Cemetery.

New Westminster Junior High School, New Westminster

RUSSELL, BABCOCK & RICE

DONALD LUXTON

Russell, Babcock & Rice were an American firm who maintained an office in Vancouver about 1912-14. These partners had a varied history as they opened offices in Tacoma, Seattle and Vancouver during the boom years. Ambrose J. Russell had attended the *École des Beaux-Arts* in Paris and had worked briefly in Kansas City, Missouri, prior to locating in Tacoma during the early 1890s. He met Bernard Maybeck while at the *École* and again while working in Kansas City, although nothing of substance developed from this acquaintance except possibly Russell's decision to locate on the west coast. He entered into a number of short-lived partnerships in Tacoma before forming a more lasting association with Everett P. Babcock about 1905. Babcock first appeared in Tacoma as an assistant superintending architect for the City of Tacoma during the construction of its downtown Carnegie Public Library. Russell & Babcock produced a significant number of commercial, religious and residential projects in Tacoma, including an enormous residence for W. R. Rust, 1905, and the Governor's Mansion in Olympia, 1908. **Cornelius Soule** worked briefly in their busy Tacoma office in 1906. Russell also formed a partnership with Walter E. Rice in Seattle, but most of their work was undertaken in association with Harlan Thomas, and the firm was far less prominent than the Russell & Babcock firm in Tacoma.

Russell & Babcock closed their Tacoma office, and presumably the Seattle office of Russell & Rice, shortly after opening an office in Vancouver in 1912, possibly in hope of matching the local success of **Somervell & Putnam**. In what must have been a great disappointment, they placed second in the 1912 competition for the Vancouver Club, won by **Sharp & Thompson**. Their most prominent Vancouver commission was the Weart Building, 1912-14, at the time of construction the second highest tower in Vancouver, and one of the last major commercial buildings to be completed during the local depression. The top storey was fitted out as a spectacular penthouse residence. Buff-coloured terra cotta was used to both anchor and cap the tan brick shaft of this structure, and modified Gothic Revival detailing reflected the influence of New York's Woolworth Building, then the world's tallest structure. When significant other work failed to materialize, the firm started to disintegrate. Russell returned to Tacoma in 1915. Babcock & Rice still maintained a Vancouver office, but the following year Babcock relocated to Portland, and Walter Rice disappeared.

Sketch by Walter E. Rice

Weart (now Standard) Building, Vancouver

Unbuilt project for the Grossman Building, Vancouver

HUBERT SAVAGE
1884-1955

ROSEMARY JAMES CROSS

During his long career, Hubert Savage worked in many different circumstances, but his designs always reflected a profound attachment to his English roots. Born in London on July 1, 1884, he was educated at Hilmartin College, St. Albans. From about 1900-03 he articled to E. Harding Payne in London, and he attended Regent Street Polytechnic for about five years. From 1903-11 Savage was assistant to several London architects, including five years with Slater & Keith. He became Clerk of Works on the Carnegie Library in Wales, and on the Council Office in Aldershot. In 1907 he was a prize winner in a London Society of Architects design competition, and about this time became accredited with the RIBA.

Savage met his wife, Alys Peake, while working in Wales, and they married in 1910. The Savages left England in 1912, planning to immigrate to New Zealand. They travelled via Victoria where they had been invited to stay with the James family. Savage and **Douglas James** had worked in the same office in London, and attended Regent Street Polytechnic together. James persuaded Savage to stay, and he worked briefly in the James & James office. For a short while Savage worked for the Canadian National Railway on Vancouver Island. His job took him out checking the roadbed on a speeder. In later years, he used to amuse his daughter telling of the near misses when unexpected trains appeared on the same track and he had to quickly manhandle the speeder out of the way. By November 1912 he had set up his own office. Projects from this period include the Harvey House on Knapp Island, opposite the Swartz Bay ferry terminal, and his family residence on Grange Road in Saanich, both 1913.

During the First World War he was declared medically unfit for service. Savage became engaged in the manufacture of shells at the Victoria Machinery Depot, and also worked at James Island Powder Plant for several months during the war. He joined the AIBC in 1921, but always retained his membership in the RIBA. Naval buildings at Naden, and many schools in Victoria and up Vancouver Island were designed by Savage. In 1923 he designed the War Memorial for Esquimalt for which he was paid $150. The Memorial was finally dedicated by Lt. Gov. Robert Bruce on September 8, 1927. In the later 1920s, Savage worked as an associate with **Samuel Maclure** on the Solarium at Mill Bay, and on the Cridge Memorial Hall beside the Church of Our Lord in Victoria.

From 1928-33, Savage worked in partnership with **P. Leonard James**. Savage was responsible for the design of the *Queenswood* estate in Saanich for Col. F. Sharland, c.1928; although the main house burnt down, the Gamekeeper's Cottage survives. Savage's work reflects all the best attributes of the late British Arts and Crafts style in both large residences and cottages. The butterfly plan residence for Col. H. W. Laws in Saanich, 1930, is perhaps his masterpiece. Many Uplands residences survive and there are records for the partnership having designed over sixty houses. Savage worked in association with **K.B. Spurgin** in 1935 on the design of a drill hall and administration building in Esquimalt.

The Royal Oak Inn, 1939, later the Maltwood Museum, was a particularly interesting commission for Savage. Designed in imitation of a half-timbered English medieval cottage, its double-height great hall has exposed roof beams, and its jerkin-headed roofs have rolled edges that are covered in steam-bent shingles resembling traditional thatch.

A keen tennis player, Hubert Savage built a fine grass court behind his Grange Road house. It became a centre for neighbours and members of the architectural fraternity. These same friends enjoyed New Year's Eve parties in the Savages's comfortable home, Alys always being the warm, welcoming, totally unflappable hostess. Hubert had a great reserve of nervous energy and was quick in his movements. He loved people, laughter, witticisms and repartee. He retired in 1954 due to ill health, and died on May 3 the following year.

A.C. Johnston Residence, Duncan

HARRY
BRYANT
NEWBOLD
1883-1952

JENNIFER NELL BARR

H. Bryant Newbold began his career in London, worked throughout the United States, and then returned to London for three years until he responded to the lure of the Pacific and chose Victoria as his home. Only in Canada for a few years, once he returned to England he became a well-known author on architectural issues. His publications included *House and Cottage Construction* and *The Modern Carpenter and Joiner*, both in three volumes; *Woodwork in Building*; and *The Ideal House*, 1928, in which several drawings of Victoria projects appear. Possibly more influential than his books were the four professional journals which he founded and edited in England: *The National Builder* in 1921, *Practical Building* in 1925, *Builder's Manual* in 1931 and *Official Architect* in 1937. He was editor of the latter for ten years, and continued as a consultant until 1950; it is still published today as *Built Environment*. As well as his monthly editorials, Newbold wrote many entertaining and thought-provoking articles containing his observations and ruminations on architecture and buildings and their place in history, under the *nom-de-plume* of "Journeyman Architect."

Born in East Retford, Nottinghamshire in 1883, Newbold matriculated in London in 1900, and the same year became an articled pupil to Henry W. Burrows, and later Charles Henry Bourne Quennell (1872-1935), a prominent London architect who had worked in the offices of John Dando Sedding (1838-1891) and Henry Wilson (1864-1934), both of whom were important to the British Arts and Crafts movement. Quennell designed a number of buildings for Hampstead Garden Suburb, one of the prime monuments of the Arts and Crafts. In 1903 Newbold became Quennell's assistant, and also began to carry out work on his own. In 1905 he moved to the United States, where he worked as an assistant to Cram, Goodhue & Ferguson in New York, and then Maginnis & Walsh in Boston, and later, several architects in San Francisco. By 1912 Newbold was in Victoria, where he advertised himself in the *Victoria Daily Colonist* as "The Specialist in Residence Designs." This audacious style of self-promotion, combined with an unusual style of sketching and his highly-personal interpretation of the British Arts and Crafts style, was quickly noticed in Victoria building circles. Newbold designed houses for the **British Canadian Home Builders, Limited**, such as the Denny Residence on Avebury Avenue, 1912. Two Oak Bay examples of his work in 1913 included the Payn Le Sueur Residence on

Beach Drive, and a British Arts and Crafts house for the Alford Family, later owned by the Redpath family, on King George Terrace, now relocated to Saturna Island.

Leaving Victoria for active service during the First World War, Newbold returned to Britain and opened an office in London. In 1925 he was accepted as a Fellow of the RIBA, proposed by fellow architectural journalist, Herbert W. Wills and C.H.B. Quennell. Newbold died in 1952 at the age of sixty-nine, in a road accident a few days before Christmas. John Gloag wrote an appreciation that appeared in the March 1953 edition of *Official Architect*: "My admiration for his robust, outspoken courage was unqualified. Between the wars, when everyone was being as tactful as possible... it was refreshing and inspiring to hear a voice that told the truth, and to meet a personality diversified by the most engaging prejudices and enriched by original ideas. Meeting, arguing, disagreeing, or agreeing, with Bryant Newbold was always a stimulating experience. He will long be remembered by everybody who met him; and his work, dedicated as it was to the improvement of architectural practice and design, still endures and exerts a far-reaching influence upon a great profession."

Payn Le Sueur Residence, Oak Bay

THEODOR FREDERICK KÖRNER

1885-1946

DONALD LUXTON

A brilliant designer who was little recognized for his abilities, Theo Körner lived and worked in British Columbia for many years. Born in London, England to parents with a German background, he worked in Seattle before coming to Canada in 1912. He was hired as a draftsman in the Vancouver office of T.H. Mawson, and on June 25, 1914 he married Dorothy May Harman in Vancouver. In 1914 he and co-worker, Robert H. Mattocks, entered the open competition for a new Vancouver Civic Centre, and to everyone's surprise, the two unknown draftsmen won first prize, beating out many established archi-

tects and also entries from eastern Canada and the United States. Unfortunately their grand design was never realized, as the outbreak of the First World War put the plans on hold. When the new Vancouver City Hall was finally built at a different location in 1935-36, the second place winner, **Fred L. Townley**, was given the commission.

Körner had moved to West Vancouver by 1917, and lived there the rest of his life. After the war, he was briefly in partnership with **H.H. Gillingham**, and about 1921 he became associated with **J.C. Day**. Following some difficulty in the payment of their AIBC fees, a notice was published in the *British Columbia Record* that they were "no longer entitled to practise as members of the Architectural Institute." Day and Körner, claiming that this implied they were guilty of misconduct, unwisely sued the AIBC for $20,000 in damages. The action was soundly criticized by Mr. Justice Morrison, who stated "Personally, I do not think it is a case that should have been launched at all. These men did not pay their fees, they should have paid them, and one would be somewhat puzzled to know what they meant or how they thought they were going to carry on. Thank you, gentlemen, this action is dismissed." This aborted lawsuit damaged their careers, and poisoned their personal relationship. In a 1927 letter to the AIBC, written on **R.T. Garrow's** letterhead, Körner stated "I have not been in partnership with Mr. J.C. Day for some years now and have no intention of reopening with him."

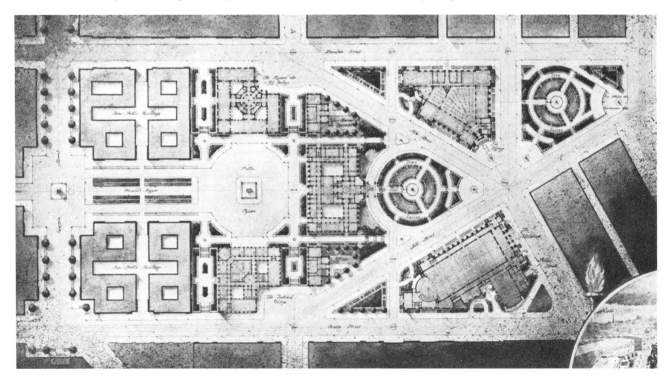

Körner designed a First World War memorial stone arch in West Vancouver in 1925. By 1927, he was working in the Construction Department of the B.C. Electric Railway Company, and the following year he produced his single most striking design, the Bay Street Sub Station in Victoria, that combines elements of the new Art Deco style with overt Egyptian references, popularized by the media attention given the discovery of King Tutankhamen's tomb in 1922. Körner also designed B.C. Electric's large concrete power plant at Ruskin, which opened in 1930. During the Depression Körner struggled to find work, and the AIBC continued an ongoing correspondence about his non-payment of fees. As the economy improved later in the 1930s, he designed a number of prominent houses, notably one on the West Vancouver waterfront for Martha and Frank Wiley, 1937, and a charming octagonal summer house for Miss Andrée Finqueneisel near Gleneagles, 1938. Accomplished in his rendering, he was retained to do presentation drawings for other architects, including a number of striking images of modernist buildings for **McCarter & Nairne**. Körner was briefly in partnership with **H.W. Postle**, who considered Körner a "brilliant man" but thought he lacked the "spark" to succeed on his own. Their association showed great promise, demonstrated by their design for Oliver High School, but was cut short when Körner died of a heart attack at the age of sixty-one, on October 19, 1946.

Left: Körner & Mattocks entry for the Vancouver Civic Centre Competition, 1914

Top right: Bay Street Sub Station, Victoria

Centre right and below: Oliver High School, Oliver

SISTER MARY OSITHE

1867-1941

SISTER MARGARET CANTWELL

Sister Mary Osithe was born Elizabeth Labossiere, on May 23, 1867 in Sorel, Quebec and entered the Sisters of Saint Ann (Lachine) at age twenty-seven. She had a natural artistic propensity and became an accomplished artist in a variety of media. In 1897 she was assigned to St. Ann's Academy in Victoria as an art teacher. She was able equally well to create beauty with pencil, chalk, watercolour, oil, and other media. Her eye for line, as well as her interior "vision" of what *could be*, encouraged people to seek her advice in the laying out of rooms and the efficient arrangement of structures. and her architectural accomplishments were a complement to her ability as an accomplished artist.

Although her drawing of plans started as early as 1912, one of the first large structures she designed was a two-storey wooden gymnasium at St. Ann's Academy, 1922. A statement of cost duly records Sister Mary Osithe as the architect, and Morry & Chamberlain as the contractors. With the growing interest in modernist or in commercial art, the number of pupils in her Art Studio decreased as time went on and Sister Mary Osithe, relieved from continuous teaching, was free to devote more time to personal pieces and to the making of building plans required from time to time by the Order. During the 1920s-30s she was involved as an architect on several institutional projects in Nanaimo, Vancouver, Victoria, and Kamloops. One work of importance was Little Flower Academy in Shaughnessy Heights, Vancouver. Surviving elevations and floor plans for Sister Mary Osithe's projects attest to her artistic and architectural skill, as well as her detailed meticulousness. In 1932-33, Sister Mary Osithe supervised the construction of the Bulkley Valley District Hospital in Smithers. With regard to this hospital, a newsletter recording the opening events reads: "The plans were sketched by Sister Mary Osithe, but drafted gratuitously by the Provincial Architect, Mr. **H. Whittaker**, and his assistant, Mr. **Hargreaves**." Throughout the construction, Sister Mary Osithe supervised the carrying out of the plans.

Sister Osithe died on Feb. 3, 1941 in Victoria, and is buried in Ross Bay Cemetery. Although first recognition should be given to her as artist, she also merits recognition as a British Columbia architect.

Foundress Hall, Little Flower Academy, Vancouver

BERNARD CUDDON PALMER

1875-1936

DONALD LUXTON

Well-connected to the cream of Vancouver society, Bernard C. Palmer provided grand residential designs for wealthy clients even during the Depression. Born in Southampton on December 2, 1875, the son of Alfred J. Palmer, a brewer's agent, he served his articles with local architect, Stanfield C. Greenwood. Young Bernard also studied architecture, building construction, and other subjects at Hartley Institute, Southampton, and later worked as an Improver and Junior Assistant with M. Hobbis, architect, in Southend, England. He relocated to London, where he worked as an assistant to Messrs. Ernest Augustus Runtz (1859-1913) & George McLean Ford (died 1921) Architects, later serving as manager of the firm's Sussex branch office for seven years. From 1910-11 Palmer practised on his own in Lewes, Sussex, but he saw opportunity for advancement in Canada, and by 1912 had moved to the booming city of Vancouver.

The increasingly successful, Victoria-based architect, **Samuel Maclure**, had gone into partnership with Cecil Croker Fox in order to open a Vancouver office, and Palmer was hired to assist on the numerous mansions they designed in the boom years before the First World War. The Vancouver office closed in 1915 when Fox enlisted, and Palmer opened his own office in April 1916. During his time with Maclure & Fox he had developed a facility for the use of different historical styles, and his exposure to prominent clients gave him solid connections with local society. After the war he designed a number of prominent mansions, including the Tudor Revival *Knoll* for Blythe Rogers, 1918-19, and the Spanish Colonial Revival *Rio Vista* for Harry F. Reifel, 1929-30, both still standing on Vancouver's fashionable South West Marine Drive. For the Rogers family he also designed a large rustic log lodge on Bowen Island, *Fairweather*, built in 1930. An English Catholic, he also designed a number of commissions for the Roman Catholic Church, including St. Joseph's Convent, 1927, noted at the time as one of the few examples in western Canada of the pure English Georgian style.

In November, 1928 Palmer published an article in the RAIC *Journal* on the "Development of Domestic Architecture in British Columbia," in which he described the history of housing in the province, but also espoused his personal philosophies. His outlook was clearly traditional, even slightly snobbish. He mostly dismissed the Arts and Crafts movement, decried the use of bungalow pattern books, and advocated the use of architects whenever possible, writing: "It is the custom to refer to most buildings as of some particular architectural style, such as Colonial, Tudor, Spanish, Italian, etc., but although there are probably few, at any rate in British Columbia, that can be accurately designated in that way, there should be no serious objection taken provided there is no gross mixture of styles and a harmonious whole is maintained. This is in reference to domestic work only. Purity of style is presumably far more important in public or large commercial buildings than private residences."

In 1930, after the death of **James A. Benzie**, **William Bow** was seeking a new partner to handle business matters, and he was drawn to the outgoing Palmer, who was well-connected, and eminently suited to the role of business promoter and "front man." Among their large commissions was *Minnekhada Lodge*, a lavish Scottish Baronial hunting lodge built in Coquitlam for Mr. and Mrs. Eric Hamber, 1934, that shows strong evidence of Palmer's influence on the partnership's designs. Palmer & Bow were also the favoured architects of entrepreneur, A.J.T. Taylor, and designed and supervised a number of his commissions. On May 24, 1936, Palmer died suddenly, survived by his wife, son, and daughter, and was buried in the family plot in Mountain View Cemetery. After Palmer's death, William Bow retained the name of the partnership for a number of years.

Minnekhada Lodge, Coquitlam

RALPH
BERRILL
1880-1955

JENNIFER NELL BARR AND
MARY E. DOODY JONES

Ralph Berrill is remembered for his architectural practice on the west coast, but also for his service as one of the first bureaucrats to work in the new federal housing programs that started in the 1930s. By the end of his career he was considered one of Canada's top authorities on housing and loans. Born in Birmingham, England on November 4, 1880, by September 1896 he was articled to Alfred Reading, ARIBA, for four years. He then spent one year with architects, Henman & Cooper of Birmingham, two years with Rolfe, Matthews & Loman, and a final year with Elwood & Loman. Concurrently he studied at the Birmingham School of Art, 1896-1900. He passed the RIBA final exam in June 1902, and John Belcher was one of his proponents for membership. He practised in Birmingham 1904-08, and then immigrated to Canada and practised in Montreal for four years. He came to Victoria in 1912 with his wife, Ethel Fredericka "Freda" Wheeler from Montreal. Their son, Ronald, died at birth in 1913; they adopted a daughter, Gwendoline Muriel.

Berrill worked both by himself and for the **Bungalow Construction Company** of Victoria, designing small residences in the California Bungalow style. A striking example is the house at 435 Kipling Street, 1912, listed as Design No. 20 on its plans, with cedar-shingle siding (doubled-coursed or two-to-the-weather), stucco and half-timbering in the front gable, heavy verandah beams, and clinker-brick piers, chimney and fireplace. In 1913 Berrill formed an architectural partnership with **Percy Fox**. They designed a number of commercial buildings and several residences, but the First World War interrupted their partnership. Berrill returned to England in November 1914 and joined the Second King Edward Horse; he later

became a commissioned officer with the Worcestershire Regiment. In 1917 in France he was promoted to Captain.

When Berrill returned to Victoria in July 1919, he again shared an office and a partnership of convenience with Fox. He designed utilitarian commercial buildings such as a 1921 two-storey structure for the Victoria Baggage Company, 1921, and the 1925 Carlton Court apartment block in New Westminster. He also designed the last five of the nineteen houses commissioned by Saanich under the Soldiers' Settlement Scheme; the first fourteen had been designed by **K.B. Spurgin**. They were small, stripped-down British Arts and Crafts-style bungalows, some with half-timbered detailing.

Berrill designed a number of residences for wealthy clients, including a Colonial Revival-style residence with Georgian detailing for William L. McIntosh, 1924; a house for Harold M. McGiverin, 1926, an articled clerk in Berrill's office who did much of the design work himself; and the Tudor Revival-style house for insurance agent, Gilbert G. Fraser, 1928. Possibly the best known of Berrill's houses is the Kathleen and Seldon Humphries Residence, designed in a California Spanish style, 1929. Kathleen was one of the daughters of James Dunsmuir, former Premier and Lieutenant-Governor of B.C.

Berrill designed Spanish Colonial Revival-style showrooms and garages for Begg Motor Company, 1926, and for National Motors Company, 1927. Berrill designed Esquimalt Municipal Hall, in a spare version of an Italian Renaissance palazzo with Classical details, 1929. For Sidney Roofing and Paper Company he designed a warehouse building of hollow tile with Art Deco parapets, 1931.

Berrill and his family lived in a house he designed in 1929 on Mount Joy Avenue in Oak Bay. In 1931 he resigned from the AIBC due to lack of work and an inability to pay the fees. When he lost his money in the Depression, he sold the Mount Joy house, separated from his wife, and went to live in rooms on Yates Street.

On January 18, 1937, Berrill started work for the Federal Department of Finance in the new Dominion Housing Act Administration in Ottawa. This later became the Housing Branch under the revised National Housing Act of 1938, and he worked under contract with them until 1946. The office was responsible for administering federal housing legislation and preparing plans for affordable housing across the country. There were as many as seven assistant architects in the office; his annual salary of $2,200 for most of this period didn't place him anywhere near the top, though he seems to have been one of the first hired. In 1946 the staff was transferred to the newly-formed Central Mortgage & Housing Corporation (CMHC). Berrill retired as chief appraiser of the loans division of CMHC in July 1951. At the time of his retirement, he had the longest service record with the corporation. He died on March 21, 1955, and was buried in Ottawa's Pinecrest Cemetery.

WILLIAM JACOBUS SEMEYN
1890-1952

JENNIFER NELL BARR

W.J. Semeyn was a rarity in British Columbia, an architect who did not emigrate from the British Isles or the United States. Born in Grouw, The Netherlands, on June 4, 1890, he was of noble birth, and later in life inherited the family title, bestowed on his ancestor by Prince William of Orange, and became Baron William Jacobus Semeyn van Einkhausen. However, he never used this title in his professional life. Semeyn trained in architecture at the Technical School in Amsterdam 1904-07. After graduation, he worked with leading Amsterdam architects for five years before immigrating to Canada.

Semeyn worked in the Victoria office of **Samuel Maclure** before he set up his own practice in August 1912. One of his most notable designs was also one of his first, the 1912-13 Tudor Revival residence with heavy Dutch massing for John and Catherine Brown in Saanich. During the First World War he worked in the United States Shipping Board's Drafting Department. After the war, his residential designs included those for: carpenter, John Main, who built his own house to Semeyn's design, 1922; Grace Lutheran Church parsonage, which he designed with architect **Elliott Totty**, 1922; and a two-storey Arts and Crafts house with Tudor Revival details for builder and contractor, Herman R. Brown, 1927. Semeyn produced, but never submitted, an entry for the international competition in 1922 for a new home for the Chicago Tribune. This large watercolour sketch hung on his office wall until the end of his career.

In 1928 Semeyn designed the ornately-tiled, Moorish-style Jameson Motors building. Although the building is now demolished, the wall fountains still exist, one in its original location and one in Bastion Square. In 1929 he entered into partnership with **Karl Branwhite Spurgin**. They designed Oak Bay Secondary School, 1929, and residences, including in 1930 for Mrs. W. Howell and for Mrs. M.E. Bowden (the latter designed by Semeyn). In 1936, on his own again, Semeyn designed the striking Streamline Moderne-style Tweedsmuir Mansions, the "last word in apartment house design" and the first building in Victoria to have a penthouse. Bordering Beacon Hill Park, this landmark structure has an asymmetrical butterfly plan, and is recognized as one of the seminal modernist buildings in Canada. Eleven years later, Semeyn designed the Rainbow Mansion apartments on the north side of Beacon Hill Park, in a more muted version of the Moderne style.

In the late 1930s Semeyn married Yvette Germaine Cross, and they had one son, William Alexander. Yvette was born in Vevey, Switzerland, in 1907, of Scottish and Swiss parents. Her father, William Heber Cross, was the son of William Alexander Cross, who owned much of Mount Royal in Montreal. W.H. Cross moved west to Calgary, Alberta, and established himself as a rancher and owner of the Calgary Brewing Company. Cross was a member of the French Syndicate which first organized the Uplands residential development in Oak Bay. He retired to Victoria in 1915, and built a house, *Valrose*, for his family at 3125 Uplands Road. It was in this house that Semeyn lived with his wife and son until the end of his life.

Semeyn worked at Victoria Machinery Depot during the Second World War, and afterwards he again practised as an architect until his retirement in 1950. His projects included a "movable" school building, used as an elementary and high school for Alert Bay, B.C. in 1948. On May 23, 1952 at the age of sixty-one, Semeyn accidentally fell from a motorboat and drowned in Maple Bay, near Duncan. He was buried at Mount View Cemetery, Somenos, in North Cowichan. Yvette died on June 22, 1968.

Tweedsmuir Mansions, Victoria

WILLIAM BOW
1882-1956

DONALD LUXTON

William Bow, soft-spoken and over six feet tall, was a gentlemanly architect of the old school. Scottish-born and trained, he produced a steady output of sophisticated work over the course of a long career in British Columbia. More interested in design than business, Bow was content to remain in the background and "run the office," and let his partners take care of promotion. Born to a middle-class background in Glasgow on January 4, 1882, he was the son of John William Bow, a drapery warehouseman, and Margaret Roger Bow. On September 3, 1898, William began a five-year apprenticeship to John Burnet & Son, Scotland's leading architectural firm. John James Burnet (1857-1938), the son of John Burnet, had been educated at the École des Beaux-Arts in Paris, went into partnership with his father in 1882, later developed a considerable practice in London and was knighted in 1914. J.J. Burnet has

been described as "a Frenchified Scotsman, extraordinarily nice, with a tremendous love of order and system. He used to say that nothing ought to be done without a decision behind it. He had no interest in style as such. He really was a great man."

After Bow finished his articles, J.J. Burnet kept him on as Junior, Senior, and later, Chief Draftsman. Bow also continued his education by attending Glasgow School of Art and Glasgow Technical College. Burnet's office was busy with major projects and continued to grow, but Bow grew dissatisfied with his slow advancement, even though Burnet had dangled a promise of eventual promotion to partner.

One of William's brothers immigrated to Australia; the other, Douglas Scott Bow, moved to Vancouver, and in 1912 sent William information on the competition for the new University of British Columbia campus. William entered the competition under Douglas's name, and placed a surprising second, winning a $3,000 prize. The design was commended by the assessors as thoughtful and practical, and given the withering criticism they poured on the other entries, this was high praise indeed. William decided to emigrate, left Burnet's office in January, 1913, and set up an office in Vancouver with Douglas the following month. William had been married in Scotland to Jean Creber, and they had four children; two born there, and two born after they arrived in Canada. When the First World War broke out he decided not to enlist, as he had his wife and four children dependent on him. He worked during the war years in the District of North Vancouver Municipal Hall.

By 1920 Bow had entered into a partnership with **James C. Mackenzie**, which was not particularly prolific as the economy was torpid in the postwar years. By 1923, Bow formed a partnership with **James A. Benzie**, and as conditions improved they developed a successful institutional and residential practice. Benzie was more flamboyant than Bow, and tended to bring in the business, while Bow undertook more of the design work. Their projects included the design for the North Vancouver High School, 1923, a handsome building with grey

North Vancouver High School, North Vancouver

Bow Residence, North Vancouver

stucco cladding with black trim and a black roof; the North Vancouver Hospital, 1929; and several prominent houses in Vancouver and on Grand Boulevard in North Vancouver.

Benzie died in 1930, and Bow, seeking a new partner, was naturally drawn to the outgoing **Bernard C. Palmer**. Together they proved a formidable team. Among their large commissions was an interpretation of a Scottish-inspired hunting retreat in Coquitlam, *Minnekhada Lodge*, 1934, for Eric W. Hamber. Although the firm remained relatively busy during the Depression, Bow found the time to serve as President of the AIBC from 1933-35. Palmer & Bow were also the favourite local architects of entrepreneur, A.J.T. Taylor. Their projects for Taylor included the first building in the British Properties, the Company Cottage, and the Toll Booth Plaza at the north end of the Lions Gate Bridge. Although Taylor, with his international connections, sometimes used architects from outside the province, he used Palmer & Bow as his local supervising architects. They acted in that capacity on the lavish penthouse that Taylor installed on the top floor of the Marine Building in 1936, and for the Capilano Golf & Country Club.

On May 24, 1936, Bernard Palmer died unexpectedly at the age of sixty, but Bow retained the name of the partnership and continued his ongoing commissions for Taylor. When Taylor was ready to build his own home, *Kew House*, on an expansive waterfront site at then remote Kew Beach in West Vancouver, he had plans prepared by five different architects before settling on the elegant Mediterranean villa conceived by Bow. Taylor even insisted on a blush of pink in the wall colour, and shopped in Italy for items for the house, which he shipped back as construction proceeded.

After the outbreak of the Second World War, Bow worked for Pacific Salvage as a designer. He was briefly partners with **George Evans**, but retired in 1946, shortly after he built himself a new home in West Vancouver. He continued to be associated with Evans, notably on the New Westminster Junior High School, 1949. William Bow later moved to Gower Point, Gibsons, and died on August 10, 1956.

Wilmar, Kitchen Residence, Vancouver,
Benzie & Bow, Architects, 1925

CHARLES BUSTEED FOWLER
1849-1941

DONALD LUXTON

Major C.B. Fowler, "Vancouver's grand old Irishman," had an eccentric and varied colonial career, of which architecture was only a small part. He gained a solid reputation for the design and restoration of churches, but also claimed his occupations as soldier, railway engineer, author, antiquarian, archaeologist, watercolour painter, marathon walker and runner, marksman, and musketry instructor. Born in Cork, Ireland, on April 28, 1849, he was the second son of Richard Tarrant Fowler, surgeon. From 1862-68 he studied at the Cork School of Art, and starting in 1865, he was articled for six years to architect, William Atkins, a former pupil of Augustus Welby Pugin. While he was with Atkins, Fowler worked on a wide range of projects including the City Lunatic Asylum, the restoration of Blarney Castle, and a number of churches. Charles had vivid memories from early childhood of watching soldiers marching off to the Crimean War, and he began his own part-time military career in 1867 when he joined the 4th Dragoons at Ballingcollig, Ireland, later serving in the First Egyptian War and the Boer War. When he retired from the 3rd Welsh Rifles with the rank of Major, he was given leave to wear his uniform for the rest of his life.

Fowler was a restless type and relocated a number of times, continuing his involvement with the military wherever he went. After completing his articles in 1871 he moved to Nottingham, where he worked as a railway and bridge engineer, and also joined the Robin Hood Rifles. By 1887 he had been invited to Llandaff, South Wales by the executors of the estate of the late architect John Pritchard, and he took charge of Pritchard's unfinished works, including a number of church restoration projects. While there, he worked in partnership with Frederick Robertson Kempson, Diocesan architect of Llandaff. Fowler moved his practice to Cardiff, became a Fellow of the RIBA in 1895, member of the RIBA Council and Gold Medal Committee in 1898, and was President of the Cardiff, South Wales & Monmouthshire Society of Architects.

Like many others, Fowler saw opportunity in the New World, and wrote that "Having received an invitation from New York's great architect Mr. [Charles] McKim to practice in that city with promises of his support I crossed the Great Atlantic in 1907." He worked on a number of projects around New York, including additions to the New Amsterdam Theater, a new church at Bangor, Maine, and a Christian Science Church in Brooklyn.

In 1913 Fowler moved to Vancouver, and practised briefly before his retirement. He was in partnership with **R.T. Perry** in 1914. Their largest project was the City of Vancouver's Old People's Home, 1914. Fowler continued his involvement with the military, and was in command of Vancouver's Home Guard, 2,600 strong, during the Great War, but being too elderly was not allowed to go overseas. Fowler designed an Odd Fellows Hall in Vancouver, 1922, which was his last known commission.

Two months before the 1939 Royal Visit to Vancouver, Fowler wrote to Lord Tweedsmuir asking to meet the King and Queen, citing his war experience and his previous introductions to royalty. During his lifetime he claimed to have met Napoleon III, the Kaiser, Queen Victoria, King Edward VII, and many other crowned heads and famous people. However, his request, along with thousands of others, was turned down, as the Royals could not possibly accommodate all these requests during their short stay. This did not dim Fowler's love of Empire, and on the Sunday before his death he marched in his red tunic in a mammoth military parade. "Upright, tall, distinguished looking and always nattily dressed, he strode along at a gait which would put to shame many a younger person."

Although he never registered with the AIBC, in 1939 he was given an honorary life membership in the Institute. He was highly regarded within the profession, and attended the Vancouver Chapter meetings until the end of his life, including one just hours before he died. He died at home, one month short of his ninety-second birthday, on March 29, 1941, survived by his wife, Lilly and their five children. Burial was in the Returned Soldiers' Plot at Mountain View Cemetery. As reported at the time:

Unbuilt project for St. Catherine's Church, Coquitlam, 1915

Death had no morbid aspect for the late Major C.B. Fowler, Vancouver's 'young' nonagenarian. He talked about it and he went about making his preparations for it as cheerfully as he took his walks around Stanley Park. To him the box in which his body was to be laid away was a symbol, and he believed it should be carefully prepared as one. So today he went to his last rest in the box of unfinished pine, designed by himself. It was painted green and adorned with a large golden cross and raised shamrocks. The old soldier's sword and military cap reposed on the top, which was later draped with a flag and banked in flowers. The date of the major's birth is painted on the lid.

Vancouver *Daily Province*, April 1, 1941, p.9.

For his last journey a small toy doll was placed in one arm and a box of shamrocks in the other hand. A firing party from the First Battalion, Irish Fusiliers, fired a volley over the grave, and a bugler from the same regiment played "The Last Post." **George Nairne**, President of the AIBC, was a pallbearer, and **W.F. Gardiner**, representing the RAIC, was an honorary pallbearer. As Nairne was quoted at the time: "Major Fowler was held in high regard by the architectural profession of British Columbia. As an indication of the warmth of feeling by his fellow members in the profession, he was given an honorary life membership in the British Columbia Institute. As he, himself, often remarked, he has had a full life, and was a keen participant in all architectural matters right to the last. His genial manner and ready wit will be missed by his *confrères* at future gatherings."

A·R·HENNELL·F·R·I·B·A
ARCHITECT
419 PEMBERTON·BCK
VICTORIA B·C

ALEXANDER
ROBERT
HENNELL
1872-1961

JENNIFER NELL BARR

A.R. Hennell, steeped in the traditions of the Arts and Crafts movement in England, was briefly in Victoria before he moved on to a long career in New York. In addition to his career in architecture, he was a talented watercolourist and coppersmith. He was born on March 14, 1872 at Oakwood, Mayow Park, London, England, the son of Laura Hart and architect Alexander Gordon Hennell (1838-1914), who had an office in

London as early as 1868. A.R. Hennell's uncles, Robert and James Barclay Hennell, were the last active silversmiths in the House of Hennell, a well-known English silversmith firm established in 1736 by David Hennell. Young Alexander Hennell was articled to prominent British architect, John Belcher, from 1889-94; in 1894 he won the Tite Prize, travelled to Italy and passed his qualifying exam to become an architect. In 1895, Hennell became an Associate of the Royal Institute of British Architects, and later entered a partnership with his father and brother, Frank, as A.G. Hennell & Sons, London. In 1905, A.R. Hennell married Edith Rose Besson, and in 1906 he was made a Fellow of the RIBA. Because he was the second son, Alexander "went to the colonies," travelling to Victoria to "look around." By 1913, he had entered practice in Victoria. A beautifully detailed example of his work is the F.J. Marshall residence in the Uplands in Oak Bay.

One of his first local commissions was a seven-room residence for newly-weds, Nora and Hew Paterson, on Victoria Avenue in Oak Bay. It is an overtly British Arts and Crafts design, with quirky details on all four elevations. In 1914, Edith followed him out to Victoria with their four children; their last son, Paul, was born there in 1917. Alice Carr, the sister of artist Emily Carr, became the family nanny, and kept up a lifelong relationship with the Hennells. Following the outbreak of the First World War, **Col. William Ridgway-Wilson** arranged a partnership with Hennell, who carried on the architectural business while Wilson went into the army full-time.

Right after the war, Hennell was working as an assistant engineer with the Municipality of Oak Bay. In 1922, the Hennell family moved to New York, where Hennell went on to design houses, churches and libraries, many of which are located in New Jersey. Hennell never embraced the modernism that swept through the profession starting in the 1930s, and maintained his attachment to the Arts and Crafts movement and the use of traditional materials and expressions. In 1946, Hennell designed a lectern and font, which were carved by A.H.H. Benson of North Vancouver and donated in 1948 to the newly formed congregation of St. David By The Sea Anglican Church at Cordova Bay, north of Victoria; they are British Arts and Crafts in style, with leaves, birds and animals, rather in the manner of the great Victorian British architect, William Burges. In 1952, the year before she died, Alice Carr had enough money saved up to build a bridge in Beacon Hill Park in honour of her sister. Alice asked A.R. Hennell to design the bridge, which was dedicated February 10, 1953. Hennell's third son, Valentine, attended the dedication with Alice Carr. Alexander Robert Hennell died in New York City on February 19, 1961.

New Library,
Forest Hill, England,
1899

Interior and exterior of the Marshall Residence, Oak Bay

HENRY WHITTAKER
1886-1971

DONALD LUXTON

During his many years as the province's Chief Architect, Henry Whittaker had a significant impact throughout British Columbia, and many of his landmark institutional buildings remain in active use. The Provincial Department of Public Works had been established in 1908 when the Department of Lands and Works was split to form the Department of Lands and the Department of Public Works (DPW). The DPW was responsible for the construction and maintenance of government buildings, roads and bridges and other infrastructure. When it was formed the DPW had no architects on staff, and private sector architects were hired on a project-by-project basis. In the system that evolved under Whittaker after the end of the First World War, in-house architects took over the design of government buildings, providing many specialized plans but also standardized plans that could be repeated in different communities. Whittaker's name was synonymous with the DPW until he retired in 1949. The in-house design system continued for a number of years, until the DPW was replaced by British Columbia Buildings Corporation, a Crown Corporation formed in 1977.

Whittaker had a varied colonial background before settling in Victoria by the time he was thirty. Born to English parents in Rio de Janeiro, Brazil on May 15, 1886, he relocated to England, and in September, 1900, commenced his articles with J. Perry, Architect, Dudley, England. After two and one-half years, he became an assistant with Haywood & Harrison, Architects, in Accrington. After this he spent a year in London, employed as an architectural assistant at Waring & Gillow, an early department store known for specializing in furnishings. Restless, he relocated to the Sudan, where he worked as an architect and engineer for Public Works Department of the Sudanese Government, travelling throughout the country for the next five years. Whittaker returned to England for two years, and then moved to Canada. By 1913 he had arrived in Victoria, armed with a suitcase full of personal letters of reference.

His timing was the worst possible. The local economy had hit bottom, and construction was at a standstill. In May, 1913 he was lucky enough to land a job as a draftsman with the Provincial Department of Public Works. An early example of the type of project he was involved in was his design for the new Point Grey School, 1914, a handsome four-room school with elaborate articulated wooden detailing, and a high hip roof. During the war years Whittaker was "honourably exempt" from overseas service, but served with the 88th Regiment Canadian Active Militia. In 1916 he was appointed Acting Supervising Architect of the DPW, and in 1919 he became Supervising Architect. Whittaker was promoted to Chief Architect in 1934, a position he held until 1949. Following the end of the First World War, Whittaker launched into the design of a series of standardized plans for modest bungalows for the Soldiers' Housing Scheme in South Vancouver. In the increasingly prosperous 1920s, Whittaker was remarkably prolific, working on numerous projects throughout the province, including hospitals, schools and the prominent Classical Revival-style Prince Rupert Court House, 1921-23. A typical example of his repetitive school designs was a four-room school for Ocean Falls, 1918.

At the same time the capacity of the provincial asylum at Essondale in Coquitlam was being rapidly expanded. In 1904, when the asylum at Woodlands was filled beyond capacity, the province purchased one thousand acres to establish the "Hospital for the Mind at Mount Coquitlam." **J.C.M. Keith** had won the competition in 1908 to design a campus of buildings for the facility, but only the first structure of his plan, the Male Chronic Wing, was completed. After the end of the First World War numerous structures were built on the site, and Whittaker and his staff handled the design work. Over time they designed the Acute Psychopathic Wing, 1922-24, the Female Chronic Wing, 1928-30, and the Veterans' Unit, 1929-34 (later converted to the Crease Clinic of Psychological Medicine in 1949), all massive brick-clad structures that define the campus-like environment of the site now known as Riverview. The DPW designed numerous other structures at the site, including the Boys' Industrial Training School, 1920-22, training facilities for psychiatric nurses, and many residences for staff.

Whittaker's work was solid, monumental and competent, suiting exactly the tenor of the times and the needs of government. During his tenure at the DPW, literally hundreds of buildings, large and small, bore his imprint, including the Provincial Buildings at Salmon Arm, 1929-30, and Powell

Court House, Prince Rupert

Provincial Building and Court House, Powell River

River, 1938-39. Under Whittaker, the DPW also provided numerous designs for the tuberculosis sanatorium at Tranquille, a rambling complex of medical buildings, residences and agricultural structures that formed its own self-sustaining community. The sanatorium had been founded by the Anti-Tuberculosis Society, but the provincial government took over its operation in 1921. The DPW continued to provide designs for the structures at the sanatorium from the 1920s until its closure in 1958.

In Victoria alone Whittaker's DPW projects included the B.C. Power Commission Building, 1939-40; Mount St. Mary's Hospital, 1940, an addition to the Nurses' Home, 1942, the Maternity Pavilion at the Royal Jubilee Hospital, 1944-46, and the Douglas Building, 1949-51. Although some of these proj-ects hinted at modernism, they never strayed far from a conservative mainstream approach. Whittaker remained professionally active, and served as President of the AIBC in 1935-37.

He retired from his government position in 1949, and established a private practice with Donald Wagg from 1949-57; their firm specialized in the design of hospitals. One of their prominent projects was the boxy modernist Federal Building and Customs House, Victoria, 1956, which replaced **Thomas Fuller's** old Post Office on Government Street. Whittaker retired in 1957, and died in Victoria on August 18, 1971, at the age of eighty-five. In his obituary, it was noted that his hobbies had included photography and philately, and that his collection of Sudanese stamps was world famous

Female Chronic Wing, Essondale, Coquitlam

View towards Boys' Industrial Training
School, Essondale, Coquitlam

JOHN GRAHAM JOHNSON
1882-1945

JENNIFER NELL BARR

J. Graham Johnson was born in London, England, on January 26, 1882. He obtained his architectural training in London in the 1890s, first as an articled pupil for three years to Charles Forster Hayward, and then as improver for two years and assistant for two more years to J.E.K. & J.P. Cutts, and finally as assistant for one year to Col. Hopkins. He first entered private practice as Johnson & Boddy for four years, with offices in the Strand, Gerrards Cross, and Beaconsfield, Buckinghamshire. That firm later became Johnson, Boddy & Green, with offices as above and in Ruislip, Buckinghamshire.

Johnson worked briefly in Victoria in 1914, and after overseas service during the First World War he returned to Canada, first to Kentville, Nova Scotia where he was in private practice for five years. For health reasons Johnson returned to the west coast. He became Resident Architect for the Canadian Pacific Railway and supervised construction of the north and south wings of the Banff Springs Hotel, as well as the north wing, power house, and laundry of Victoria's Empress Hotel. At the end of 1930 he resigned to establish his private practice in Victoria, although the CPR continued to hire him for work in Victoria until his death in 1945.

For a number of years Johnson was associated with **Karl Branwhite Spurgin**, with whom he designed the five fantasy cottages in Patio Court in Oak Bay, 1927, built for C. Walden for a total cost of $22,000. Spurgin & Johnson designed the prestigious Moderne-style storefront for Gibson's Ladies' Wear in 1931. They also designed the Mount Baker Block, 1932. Johnson sometimes worked in informal association with **C. Elwood Watkins**.

Following the disastrous 1933 fire in Cumberland on Vancouver Island, Johnson designed two of the rebuilt hotels: the Cumberland, in British Arts and Crafts style with a hipped and half-hipped roofline and half-timbering; and the King George, in minimalist Georgian style fronted by a one-storey commercial facade. During the 1930s and 1940s, he designed many houses in the Victoria area, particularly in Oak Bay, in a number of styles. His essays in British Arts and Crafts include two 1935 bungalows, the first with heavy hipped roofs for W.H. Norton-Taylor, later owned by Sir Ernest W. Petter, and a house with Tudor half-timbering for Carl and Leona Pfender. In 1936 Johnson designed his own house, on Rockland Place. Two charming stuccoed British Arts and Crafts, mirror-image bungalows on Selkirk Avenue, backing onto the Gorge Waterway in Victoria West, were designed in 1938 for former

Victoria Mayor Robert Cross's grandparents, and are still owned by the family. In the Moderne style, Johnson designed the Clark & Cordick building, 1939, and two townhouse buildings for T.C. Rogers in that same year.

From 1940 until his death, Johnson was in partnership with architect C. Dexter Stockdill (1915-1994). Their work included three Moderne designs for Safeway Stores Ltd. on Esquimalt Road, Douglas Street and Fairfield Road, 1941. Johnson & Stockdill also continued to work in traditional modes when requested. Warren Hastings, a retired naval architect from Sussex, and his wife, Barbara, retired to Ganges on Salt Spring Island in 1940. They shipped their collection of antique furniture by sea, and as the Second World War had already been declared, they vowed that if it reached the island, they would build a house similar to the 11th century manor they left behind. The furniture arrived safely, and they commissioned Johnson & Stockdill to turn their dream of an authentic Tudor-style manor house into reality. It has been beautifully preserved on its waterfront lot as the Hastings House Country House Hotel. Johnson & Stockdill's eight-suite Wavell Apartments won a glowing report in the Victoria *Daily Times* in 1941: "From the simple exterior, designed with restraint and dignity, to the automatic laundry, it is an example of the best in modern architecture." However, the Sandholme Apartments of the same year was perhaps a more successful essay in the style. A small house designed in 1945 by Johnson for Mr. and Mrs. A. Dods on Cadboro Bay Road appeared in the national *Small House Annual* published in 1947 by *Home Builder* magazine.

On July 27, 1945, at the age of sixty-three, J. Graham Johnson died of bronchial asthma in an ambulance on the way to hospital. He was survived by his wife, Hilda Constance (Old) Johnson; they had no children. He had worked in the profession thirty-four years, and was still working the day of his death.

Wavell Apartments, Victoria

staggering recovery, another collapse

CITY HALL

1939

and the threat of another war

6

ON THE

VERGE OF

MODERNISM

Out of the flux of period styles emerged the "MODERN," which was

introduced to, and which the public accepted with misgivings, as a

"Style." This was unfortunate. Actually its development was inevitable.

W.F. Williams

**Donald
Luxton**

Despite the overwhelming economic difficulties that followed the end of the First World
War, British Columbia still had vast natural resources. With peace restored, and the Panama
Canal now open, British Columbia's resources were more readily available to European and
eastern United States markets. By the mid-1920s, general conditions were improving: pulp
mills were expanding, and mines were busy again. Grain shipments through Vancouver
were increasing, and new steamship lines were established. The CPR opened up southern
extensions to its original Shaughnessy Heights subdivision; the lots proved very popular
with Vancouver's elite and sold out quickly. After years of delay, construction finally began
in earnest at the Point Grey campus of the University of British Columbia, and a low-level
bridge connected the north and south sides of Burrard Inlet for the first time in 1925. The
next few years were prosperous, especially in Vancouver where industrial development was
intense. New skyscrapers, rivalling and surpassing those of the Edwardian era, appeared on
the skyline, some in the daring new Art Deco style. A new residential boom started in
Vancouver, as rows of bungalows began to stretch towards the growing university.
Amalgamation of Vancouver with neighbouring Point Grey and South Vancouver on January
1, 1929 created an urban power base that would dominate the rest of the province.

Once again, the boom ended quickly. The crash of the stock market in October, 1929
had a devastating effect on the local economy. The next few years were unimaginably
difficult, and a grim reality set in. With its benign climate and easy access, Vancouver
became the end of the line for a huge army of unemployed. Hoboes "rode the rods" to the
Coast, and then squatted in "jungles" on the False Creek flats and near the Georgia Viaduct

Proposed Aero Club Headquarters,
Vancouver Airport, Percy C. Underwood,
Architect, 1938

while they looked for work. The summer of 1931 was the first of a series of exceptionally hot and dry seasons that exhausted the water supply in the Okanagan Valley. Some federal relief trickled in during 1931, allowing for the construction of new roads and even some airports, but British Columbia was mostly left on its own to deal with its problems. The next few years were, by all accounts, the most difficult of the Great Depression.

Not all suffered equally. After the Crash, corporate and institutional commissions for architects virtually disappeared, but capital was still concentrated in the hands of wealthy individuals, who used the downturn in the economy, and the subsequent deflation in labour and material costs, to build lavish estate homes. Most architects closed their practices, and resigned from the AIBC. A few architects, with the right connections, remained very busy. **William Gardiner**, **Palmer & Bow** and **Ross Lort**, among others, designed a number of grand homes during the Depression. An example was the house Lort designed in 1932 for wealthy liquor merchant, George Reifel, *Casa Mia*. This lavish home was one of the largest ever built in Vancouver, and Reifel paid for everything in cash. Lort supervised the construction, and one Friday, Reifel, who hadn't paid the architect for a while, peeled a $1,000 banknote off a huge roll of bills and handed it to Lort, who took it home, and hid it under the bedroom carpet under one leg of the bed. He and his wife took turns sitting on the bed until Monday when he could take it to the bank. No one at the bank had ever seen one before.

As economic conditions tentatively improved in the mid-1930s, there was

Federal Building, Powell River, Charles F. Dawson, Architect, 1938-1939

cautious optimism. A few large scale institutional projects were finally underway in Vancouver, with a new city hall as the symbolic flagship. In the second largest land deal ever signed in Vancouver, a tremendous suspension bridge was built by private English capital to span the First Narrows and gain access to over 4,000 acres of undeveloped North Shore lands. Confidence was just starting to revive, when new rumours of conflict in Europe were heard. In September, 1939 the rumours became all too real, culminating in the declaration of war.

In the meantime a whole new design sensibility was starting to emerge, one not based on traditional precedents. After the devastation of the First World War, European architecture had reinvented itself as a truly modernist expression. Many notable European designers, including Walter Gropius and Mies van der Rohe, fled Nazi oppression in the 1930s, and brought to North America a new and influential style of teaching and building. Their message was warmly received at a time when local designers were struggling with the costs associated with traditional building styles, and a lack of skilled labour. This modernist approach perfectly suited the grim realities of a new social and economic order. Inexorably, the traditional, male and British hold on British Columbia's architecture began to crumble and a new generation of architects evolved in a direction far different from the pioneers of the profession.

Powell River Company Store, Powell River, C.B.K. Van Norman, Architect, 1940-1941

HAROLD
CULLERNE
1890-1976

Harold Cullerne.

DONALD LUXTON

Right after he returned from overseas service during the First World War, Harold Cullerne joined **J.H. Bowman** in a partnership that would last from 1919 until 1934, then continued to practise on his own until his retirement about 1967. Cullerne was born at the Lewisham Hotel in Slaithwaite, Yorkshire, England on May 24, 1890, and was educated at Longwood Grammar School. His mother died when he was eleven, after which his father and his two younger brothers moved to Monmouthshire. Harold was sent to room and board five days a week, and articled to architect Ernest G. Davies from 1906-09. He then moved to London and worked in the offices of both R. Langton Cole and W. Ernest Huzell until his departure for Vancouver, where he arrived in April, 1912. Over the next few years, he found employment with **H.S. Griffith**, **Hugh A. Hodgson**, and Bowman. From late 1913 to 1915 he also was engaged by the Office of the Chief Engineer, Pacific Great

Eastern Railway, and his work there included the design of the PGE Station at the south foot of Lonsdale Avenue, North Vancouver.

Although a very slight man at 5 foot four inches and 130 pounds, in February 1916, Cullerne enlisted in the 143rd Battalion, and served overseas as a Lieutenant in the Artillery. The nephew of Haydn Wood (the famed composer of "Roses of Picardy"), he was also a talented musician and played flute and piccolo in the Battalion's band both in British Columbia and England. After his return he played flute for several seasons for the Vancouver Symphony Orchestra, and in 1921 entertained the first annual Architectural Institute of B.C. banquet with a flute solo. Right after his discharge in 1919, the partnership with Bowman was formed, and Bowman & Cullerne were kept busy with many commissions for school buildings, residences, and institutional buildings such as the Metropolitan Tabernacle in Vancouver's Mount Pleasant neighbourhood, 1931. Cullerne also spent a great deal of time thinking about the provision of low-cost housing in the 1930s, asking rhetorically "is there any reason why every workingman in this country should not occupy a decent, comfortable, aesthetically-pleasing home instead of the dismal, gerry-built hovels in which so many of them are forced to live?" Cullerne produced numerous standard plans for modest houses, and authored several residential plan books. One of his modest designs, called *The Ideal Bungalow*, was built as the first Exhibition Prize Home for the Pacific National Exhibition and raffled off at the end of the fair.

After Bowman retired in 1934, Cullerne practised on his

Pacific Great Eastern Railway Station, North Vancouver

The Ideal Bungalow (PNE Prize Home, 1934)

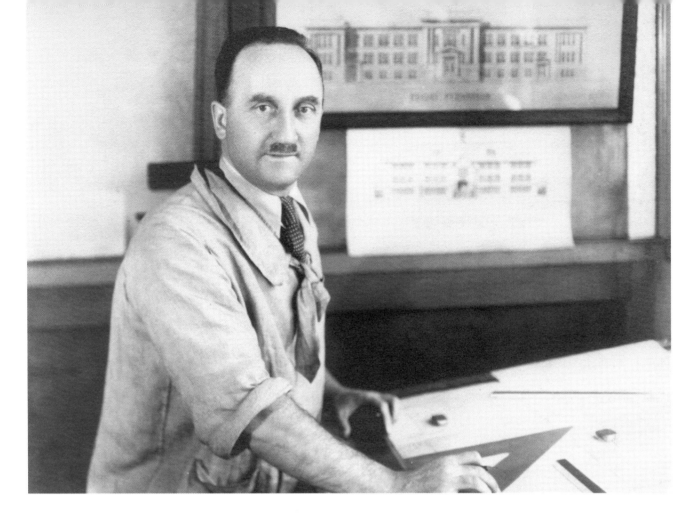

own, continuing to work on schools and institutional buildings, including a number of churches in the Vancouver area and the Fraser Valley. Prominent surviving designs by Cullerne include: a modernist Legion Hall in downtown Mission, 1936; the exuberant Art Deco Hollywood Theatre on Broadway in Vancouver, 1935-36, still owned and operated by the same family; and St. Francis of Assisi Church and Franciscan Friary in East Vancouver, 1938. Cullerne also designed a Moravian Evangelical Church in South Vancouver, 1936. In 1938, Cullerne was one of ten architects awarded a prize in the competition for designs for minimum cost houses to be built under the *Dominion Housing Act.* Cullerne's entry was one of three hundred submitted, and his was the only design chosen from outside Ontario and Quebec. In 1944, Cullerne designed a community hall for Capitol Hill in North Burnaby; the scheme was delayed, and redesigned, before it was finally built in 1946. When building activities resumed after the end of the Second World War, Cullerne was asked to design Dunbar Heights United Church, but his scheme was never realized, and Twizell & Twizell were hired to in 1950 to undertake the project. In 1949, Cullerne acted as associated architect with **George Norris Evans** on the modernistic Edmonds Junior High School in Burnaby.

Cullerne married late in life. He had boarded for about thirty years with the Sutcliffe family, who were family friends of Cullerne's parents from England. Annie Sutcliffe, who had married Perry H.F. Dawson in 1915, was widowed in 1950, and she and Cullerne married five years later. After they married, Cullerne designed a new home in north Burnaby. He also had a small cottage on North Pender Island, which they expanded, and where they spent some time. Cullerne, who is remembered as lively, kind and opinionated, but modest and gentlemanly in demeanor, died on March 8, 1976.

Legion Hall, Mission

MAX
BREEZE
DOWNING
1892-1976

Max B Downing [signature]

DONALD LUXTON

Max Downing was born in Kingston, Ontario on July 9, 1892. From 1910, he worked for a series of Vancouver architects, starting with **Sharp & Thompson**, **G.P. Bowie**, and briefly with **Somervell & Putnam** before the First World War. He served for just over three years with the Royal British Navy in the North Sea, off the Belgian Coast and in the English Channel. After he was demobilized he returned to Somervell & Putnam's office before establishing his own practice in October, 1919. A year later Downing formed a partnership with **Swinburne A. Kayll**, that lasted until 1924. In the mid-1920s Downing worked on projects as an associated architect with Sharp & Thompson, including the English Arts and Crafts-style Anglican Theological College at the University of British Columbia, 1927. Typical of Downing's small projects of this time is a commercial building on Seymour Street, 1933, with cast concrete and terra cotta Art Deco detailing, built for the Hudson's Bay Company and occupied later in the 1930s by the Deutschland Café. Downing was clearly a talented designer, and also proficient at the technical aspects of the profession.

Following a pattern of delay seen with many public buildings, the federal government had proposed an office building for Prince Rupert in 1908. Plans were prepared by the Department of Public Works by 1913 and excavations started. War broke out, and then a long period of postwar restraint and depression further delayed construction. In 1936 the project was revived. In a memo to the Deputy Minister from the Secretary to the Minister of Public Works, a common practice at the time, "the name of Max B. Downing, 55 Howe Street of Vancouver has been suggested for employment." He was contacted by the Chief Architect and terms of the contract were laid out. Correspondence with the Department continued until 1938 discussing the details of the design. Downing advocated the use of monolithic concrete rather than brick because of the low cost of construction and maintenance. The use of concrete as a cladding material was now fairly common, especially in California where it was recognized for its seismic performance, and it also suited the tastes of the era for crisp, clean, integral detailing. The resulting building, completed in 1938, was startling not only for its uncompromising modernism but also for its use of cast-in-place native motifs, sculpted by William Jeffries, as the primary decorative element.

Downing was also retained as the local supervising architect for the federal building at Powell River, 1938-39, designed by Federal Architect **C.F. Dawson**. During this time Downing hired Harry Barratt (1898-1964), a Gibraltar-born graduate of the University of Manitoba who had previously worked for **Townley & Matheson**, to assist with the preparation of working drawings for the two federal projects. In 1939 Downing also designed the Hanson Block in Prince Rupert. Max B. Downing died at Shaughnessy Hospital in Vancouver on April 23, 1976 at the age of eighty-three.

Federal Building, Prince Rupert

SYLVIA GRACE HOLLAND
1900-1974

JULIA TRACHSEL

In 1933, Sylvia Holland became the first registered female architect in British Columbia, overcoming obstacles that would have discouraged a less indomitable person. Despite this distinction, her career was fraught with difficulties, and when architecture could not support her, she pursued art and design, and finally worked as a freelance illustrator and cat breeder. Holland's chief claim to fame was as one of the Disney Studio's first women story artists. She was born on July 20, 1900, in Ampfield, England, daughter of the conductor of England's first women's string orchestra. Early in her life she displayed a flair

for the artistic, particularly in drawing and design, filling sketchbooks with flora and fauna that she encountered in walks near her home. At age nineteen, Sylvia was accepted into the Architectural Association School in London, and in 1924 received her diploma. Howard Robertson, principal of the school and partner in the firm Easton & Robertson, hired Holland as an assistant and she registered as a member of the Royal Institute of British Architects. Easton & Robertson were considered leaders of modernism in British architecture at the time, and among the first projects Holland worked on were the British Pavilion for the *Exposition Internationale des Arts Decoratifs et Industriels Modernes* in Paris, 1925, the Royal Horticultural Hall in London, 1925, and the new Billingham offices and laboratories for the Imperial Chemical Industries Ltd. and Synthetic Ammonia and Nitrates Ltd., 1926.

In July 1926, Sylvia Moberly married Francis "Frank" Cuyler Holland, a former classmate at the Architectural Association. Sylvia and Frank immigrated almost immediately to Victoria, B.C., Frank's home town. They collaborated on the design of their own home, an Arts and Crafts cottage, featuring a steeply pitched roof, half-timbered cross gables and rough-cut stone exterior. Unfortunately, antibiotics had yet to be discovered, and Frank died suddenly on December 28, 1928, of complications from severe mastoiditis. Sylvia was left to raise their daughter, Theodora "Theo," and son, Boris, born a month after

British Pavilion, *Exposition des Arts Decoratifs*, Paris, 1925

Wedding of Sylvia and Frank Holland, Compton, Winchester, England

Holland Residence, Saanich

his father's death. Frank's parents offered her their rural farm retreat at Rocky Point, Metchosin. Architectural work was scarce after the stock market crash, but she collaborated with Frank's one-time friend, **H. Daborn Day**, on house design projects, an example of which is an undated, but jointly signed plan for a two-storey house on Arbutus Road, for John Eden Tysoe.

Boris was plagued with a predisposition for ear infections that would precipitate the family's move from B.C. to the deserts of southern California. Holland applied to the American Institute of Architects, but was refused membership when they wouldn't recognize her academic and professional credentials. She ordered a new car, picked it up in Los Angeles upon arrival there by train, and drove east into the desert, needing a place for her son to recover and a school for both children. She came to a sign indicating "The Desert Sun (Boarding) School," which specialized in the education, care and healing of children. Theo and Boris were to live there for six years. Confident that her children were well-cared for, she headed to Hollywood and the next phase of her career.

Seeing *Snow White* was Sylvia's first encounter with anima-tion, and she wanted to be a part of a "treatment that was so startlingly new." She set her sights on the Disney Studios, and was eventually hired there in 1938. Holland's credits as story artist and director for Disney include *Fantasia*, 1940 (Pastoral Symphony, Waltz of the Flowers, Snow Fairies and Autumn Leaves sequences), *Bambi*, 1942 (The Storm Sequence), de Verersky's *Victory Through Air Power*, 1943, *Make Mine Music*, 1946, and *Melody Time*, released 1948 (Bumble Boogie). Holland left Disney in 1947, and opened a studio for herself on Ventura Boulevard, from which she conducted her freelance work.

Sylvia also purchased a block of land, part of a 540-acre country estate, *Tarzana*, located in the San Fernando Valley in the foothills of the Santa Monica Mountains. She subdivided her property, and on the piece she retained, she designed and built two long low bungalows. Holland's Farm Cattery was designed to blend with its environment, fitting neatly into the context of the hill located directly behind it. Always an animal lover, Sylvia had tried breeding cats at Rocky Point, her goal being to develop a lemon yellow variety with sapphire blue eyes. Her California house was the perfect place to indulge her love of cats. She first bred Siamese, and in 1958, acquired her first Balinese, a new breed of longhaired Siamese. She is renowned as the person most instrumental in advancing the Balinese breed, by setting up a collaborative network that allowed new genes to be introduced through the exchange of cats, kittens and sharing of stud services. As a result, she was eventually able, in 1970, to realize her goal of having the Balinese recognized as an official breed in the Cat Fanciers Association. Almost all current Balinese can be traced to the Holland Farm line. Sylvia Holland died on April 14, 1974, just one year before the first Balinese grand champion was chosen at the prestigious Santa Monica show, culminating over twenty years of tireless work on her part.

Sylvia Holland (kneeling) and Ethel Kulsar at the Disney Studios working on storyboards for *Fantasia*.

Drawing by Sylvia Holland

ERIC
CHARLESWORTH
CLARKSON
1895-1977

DONALD LUXTON

Eric C. Clarkson had a varied and prolific career before settling in Victoria, where his work straddled the gap between traditional and modernist polarities. He was born in Esholt, Yorkshire, England in 1895, the son of architect, John C. Clarkson. Educated at Ripon School, 1909-11, and Bradford Technical College and Art School, 1911-13, he was employed as a draftsman with his father's firm, Empsall & Clarkson, Architects & Surveyors, Bradford, from 1911 until April 1915. When he left his father's office he enlisted for service in the First World War, and after taking courses in drafting and surveying he was accepted as an official Indian Army Architect in 1917, and that year designed the Bombay Military Isolation Hospital. While in the army he designed numerous buildings in Iraq, and was attached to the Field Headquarters of the Mesopotamia Expeditionary Force. After the war he returned to Bradford, England, where he designed the Pilkington Glass Warehouse, 1919 and the Rees & Co. Woollen Warehouse, 1920. He was accepted as a junior partner with Empsall & Clarkson in 1920, and worked on residences, schools and churches until 1923, when he came to Toronto to study Canadian architecture.

From 1924-27 he was located in Santa Barbara, California, where he designed and superintended between ninety and one hundred residences and apartment buildings. Relocating to Victoria, by 1928 he was employed by **Samuel Maclure** as an assistant, but was in practice on his own by the following year, producing designs for large, traditional houses such as the Tudor Revival Howard Residence in the Uplands subdivision, 1929, for which the plans are signed "Maclure & Clarkson." Throughout the 1930s he continued to produce solid, conservative residential work, such as the Kipling Residence, Victoria, 1938, but his commercial and institutional work varied in style from Tudor Revival, such as Mount View High School, Saanich, 1931, and the Oak Bay Cinema, 1936, to modernist, including the Atlas Theatre, Victoria, 1936, and Red Cross House, Victoria, 1945-46. From 1932-38 he also designed many residences in Victoria and Oak Bay that were built by contractor Robert Noble. About 1938 he was briefly in partnership with **Douglas James**, but there is no record of any of their commissions. Clarkson worked with the B.C. Department of Public Works for many years, retiring from architecture on January 1, 1964. The Clarksons did not have children. His wife, Beatrice, died in 1976, and Eric died in Victoria on February 23, 1977.

Atlas Theatre, Victoria

NORTHWOOD & CHIVERS

DONALD LUXTON

George W. Northwood (1878-1959) was born in Ottawa, and was educated at McGill University. He commenced his career as an architect with K. Arnoldt in Ottawa in 1900, and moved to Winnipeg in 1905, where he acted as the architect for the Northern Crown Bank and the Dominion Bank of Canada.

C.W.U. Chivers (1879-1969) was born in Avebury, Wiltshire, England, and grew up in Chislehurst, Kent. He spent one year at London Polytechnic Institute, in 1897, studying architectural drawing and moved to Winnipeg the next year, where he worked for two or three different architects, and then landed a job as a draftsman with the CPR at one dollar a day, considered a great salary at the time. By 1907 he had become chief draftsman. He began practising architecture in 1910 in Manitoba.

Both men went overseas during the First World War. Northwood was captured and spent three years in prison camps, before being returned to Canada at the end of the war. Chivers began with the 1st Canadian Mounted Rifles, and was later transferred to the Engineers. He was awarded the George Medal, among other decorations.

They established the firm Northwood & Chivers, Architects, in Winnipeg about 1924, but were interested in expanding during the increasingly prosperous 1920s. The west coast looked promising, and both Northwood and Chivers applied for membership with the AIBC on July 19, 1929. Their only commission in B.C. was the Hall Building on Howe Street in Vancouver, for which **McCarter & Nairne** were associated architects. Chivers described himself as a "Superintendent" to McCarter & Nairne at the time. This ten-storey Tyndall stone-faced office block is a sophisticated essay in restrained modernism. Verticality is emphasized by continuous piers that step back as they rise. Abstracted Gothic Revival ornamentation reflects both the historical roots of the skyscraper style, and the Stock Exchange Building across the street. Lightly incised panels display an early use of Art Deco motifs. The refined confidence demonstrated by this project was soon brought to a halt by the Great Crash of 1929.

In 1930, both Northwood and Chivers removed their names from membership in the AIBC, continuing their relationship in Winnipeg until the 1950s. Northwood died in 1959. Chivers retired in 1958, and his son John, who had been with the firm since about 1947, continued practising under his own name until he retired in 1979.

Hall Building, Vancouver

HANNS
CARL
BERCHTENBREITER
1891-1957

DONALD LUXTON

Despite his arrival in Vancouver at the onset of the Great Depression, H.C. Berchtenbreiter had a productive ten-year career as a designer and contractor. Born in Munich, Germany to a middle-class family, Berchtenbreiter went to art school in Dresden, then received formal training in architecture, and was later awarded a Doctorate at the Faculty of Architecture, University of Munich. His thesis, *Bürgerliche Wohnhausbauten der Barockzeit in Unterfranken* (*Civilian Apartment Complexes of the Baroque period in Unterfranken*) was published in 1925. He was married in Germany to a woman

Unidentified house (likely Germany)

from a prominent family; they had two sons, and until 1929 he practiced architecture successfully in Germany, Holland, and Belgium. One of his largest projects was a grand home he designed for the wealthy Gildemeister family, built at Vina del Mar, Chile in 1924. Berchtenbreiter was under pressure to succeed professionally and financially, but he wanted more time to "be free" and enjoy outdoor activities, which led to family friction. He decided to move to Canada, but his wife refused, and he left to start a life in the New World.

On July 5, 1930, Berchtenbreiter, aged thirty-nine, arrived by steamship in Halifax. He moved to Vancouver, B.C., but there was precious little architectural work available, especially for a recently-arrived foreigner. Berchtenbreiter began working as a general contractor, designing and building houses, using unemployed European craftsmen and builders. During the mid-1930s he was usually listed in directories as an architect, but never registered with the AIBC. Although he was known as "Hanns," this was likely a shortened version of Johannes. His unusual last name translates as 'farm (or ranch) of the Goddess Bertha," and properly it was spelled as one word, but once he moved to Canada he hyphenated it to make it easier to pronounce. An active outdoorsman, Berchtenbreiter enjoyed skiing and hiking, and often went up Hollyburn Mountain to enjoy winter sports. Impressed with the openness of the province, he corresponded with the German government about the possibility of having them buy the Pacific Great Eastern Railway and shipping German emigrants into the Interior.

In addition to a number of houses, he also acted as a designer for several theatre remodellings, as an interior designer for Woodward's Department Store, and also designed the Deutschland Café on Seymour Street, 1936. Until the mid-1930s his style was generally traditional in flavour, using period revival elements in convincing pastiches, pleasing in their proportions and masterfully executed by his European workmen. His most accomplished design of this period was a residence for Vito and Sybil Cianci, both graduates of the Vancouver School of Art. Built in West Vancouver in 1933, the direct inspiration for the house remains unknown, but it is a miniature version of a rustic hunting lodge, evocative of the National Parks Service vernacular architecture popular at the time. Soaring above a rocky site, and anchored with a rubble stone base, the Cianci residence is finished inside and out with high-quality woodwork. The living room, a two-storey high vaulted space with roof trusses, has a stone fireplace, a mezzanine and panoramic views on three sides.

In the later 1930s, Berchtenbreiter shifted away from these

period elements towards a more severe modernism. The Bennett Residence, West Vancouver, 1937, is an excellent example of the Streamline Moderne style. Typical of his smaller modern houses from this time period was one for H.C. Ramsden, a CPR employee, in Vancouver, 1939. Several of his houses were quite radical, including: a large residence for Mrs. Wharton Shaw on Belmont Avenue in Vancouver, 1937; the startling and cubistic "House with the Two Blue Lions," for A.C. Langley in West Vancouver in 1938; and two modern houses on Denison Road in Oak Bay, built 1938 and 1939. These projects demonstrate what he may have accomplished if his career had not been cut short by difficult circumstances.

To drum up business, Berchtenbreiter set up a booth at the Pacific National Exhibition, where he displayed his designs and drawings. One young visitor to his booth was very impressed, and brought a friend of hers, Irene Lewis, to see him. Berchtenbreiter and Irene started dating, even though he was twenty-four years her senior. They were married in 1939, lived briefly in an apartment in the West End, and then bought acreage in Haney, but the Second World War soon broke out, and Canada declared war on Germany. It was a terrible time for the Berchtenbreiters, as his Germanic name and background led to suspicion that he was a spy. Irene had relatives in the United States, and they were able to obtain visitors' permits and travel to California, where they decided to stay and "make the best of it." Berchtenbreiter received a few commissions for interiors, and did occasional work for other architectural firms. Irene was a talented artist and ceramicist, and helped him in his endeavors. Together they developed a low cost alternative to brick facings, a prefabricated system of thin brick veneer, attached to sheets of plywood and mortared; they applied for a patent for this system, and used it for a number of projects. After the end of the War, Irene bought a small

Unidentified house, 1935

property in Thousand Oaks, Ventura County, where they opened a shop for "Unusual Gifts" and sold Irene's artwork. The Berchtenbreiters also maintained a display room near the Farmer's Market in Los Angeles. On June 13, 1957, H.C. Berchtenbreiter died suddenly of a heart attack, survived by Irene and his two sons, both of whom were in Germany where one was a doctor and the other a lawyer. His funeral was held at the Church of our Lady of Guadaloupe in Los Angeles. Irene Berchtenbreiter remained in California for another decade before returning to British Columbia, where she still lives.

Irene and Hanns Berchtenbreiter, Thousand Oaks, California

WILLIAM FREDERICK WILLIAMS
1904-1947

ELSPETH COWELL AND
DONALD LUXTON

W.F. "Bill" Williams practised in Nelson from 1935 until his premature death. Born in Melbourne, Australia, Williams studied architecture at Swinburne Technical College, and then received *Beaux-Arts* training at the Melbourne University Architectural Atelier, where he graduated with Honours in 1926. He moved to the United States in 1927, where he worked for a year in Chicago, and then a year for Bertram G. Goodhue Associates in New York. While in New York in 1928 he married Ilsa Julie Clara Baker (1904-1984); Baker had also trained as an architect in Melbourne and they had worked in the same office there after graduation. The following year the Williamses relocated to Montreal, where he worked for J. Cecil McDougall (1886-1959). In 1930 they went to London,

England for a year, also touring continental Europe, after which Williams returned to McDougall's office. McDougall was commissioned by Selwyn Gwillym Blaylock to design a grand Tudor Revival house just outside Nelson, B.C. After he graduated from McGill University in 1899, Blaylock was hired to work in the assay office of the Canada Smelting Works, later the Consolidated Mining & Smelting Company (Cominco), in Trail, B.C.. Williams was asked if he would travel west to supervise construction of this large project. He agreed, fell in love with the Kootenays, and in 1935 moved Ilsa and their infant daughter across the country by train to settle in Nelson. Blaylock Manor was a grand affair, with a richly articulated half-timbered exterior and an ornate panelled interior, decorated with hand-carved wooden ornamentation. Completed by 1936, this fifteen thousand square foot residence stands today, and is used as a resort centre.

Williams was now established in Nelson, and in his own practice demonstrated a deft facility for modernism that was in stark contrast to the period revivalism of the Blaylock house. In the small mining town of Trail he designed a Stripped-Classical Masonic Temple, 1937-38. He designed a number of structures for Consolidated Mining & Smelting, including Tadanac Hall, 1938, the Cafeteria, 1940-41, and a development of 150 low-cost houses at Warfield for company employees, 1938-39. For Palm Dairies, he designed a series of modernist buildings in Trail, Nelson and Victoria; the Victoria project was a 1937 renovation of an existing structure. Williams was a fervent convert to modernism, and to the great surprise of more established architects, Williams won several important prizes in national competitions. In the T. Eaton competition for an Ideal Ontario home in 1930, Williams placed seventh. In 1936 he entered the Dominion Housing Act Small House Competition, winning third prize and an honourable mention. Also in 1936 he entered the T. Eaton Architectural Competition for House Design and won an honourable mention in the small house category, and the grand prize and first prize in

"International Modern,"

T. Eaton Architectural Competition, 1936

Palm Dairies, Victoria

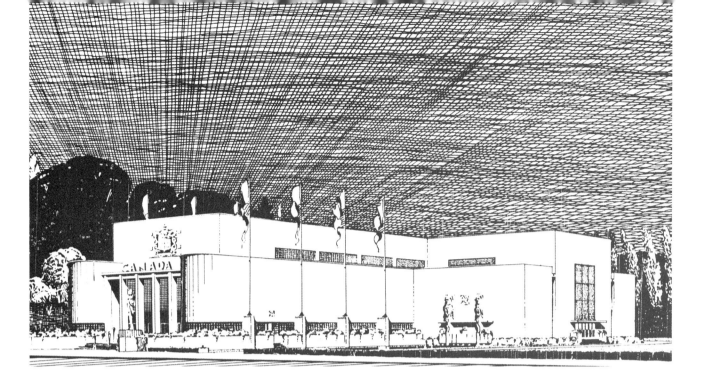

Canadian Pavillion, New York World's Fair, 1939-1940

medium house category. Two years later he won the competition for the design of the Canadian Pavilion for the 1939 New York World's Fair. Williams's striking modernistic design was chosen from 155 entries; **Ernest I. Barott** placed second, and Ross & Macdonald placed third. Williams served during the Second World War with the Royal Canadian Engineers, and was discharged in January, 1946 with the rank of Major. He died on December 22, 1947 at the age of forty-three, and his Australian obituary lauded him as "a prodigious worker, an exceptionally fine draftsman, and a master of detail – undoubtedly one of the ablest architects Australia has yet produced." Williams's Nelson office was very busy at the time of his death, and among his many commissions was the large Mt. St. Francis Home for the Aged for the Catholic Church. With two architects already working there and two draftsmen due to arrive the following week, Ilsa Williams had no choice but to step in and take over the office. She continued to practice as an architect, and designed many schools, hospitals and residences in and around Nelson, until her retirement in 1958.

Unbuilt project for the Nelson Aquatic Centre, Nelson, 1947

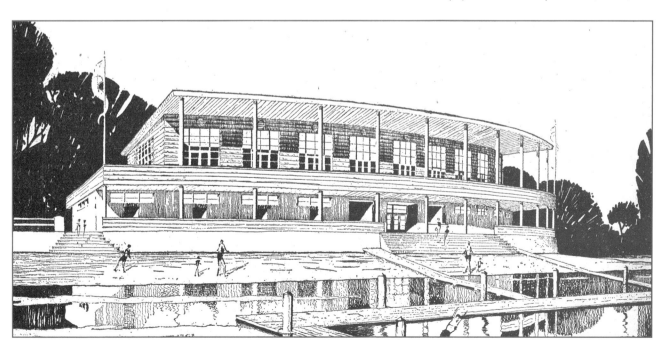

ADDITIONAL

SIGNIFICANT

ARCHITECTS

ALEXANDER, J. Thomas
1875-1945

DAVID MONTEYNE

J. Thomas Alexander had a lengthy but sporadic career in architecture, interrupted by war, illness and attempts at other vocations. Born in Tynemouth, England, he was one of five children raised by his widowed mother, Mary. He began his architectural training at age seventeen under G.A.T. Middleton in London, later serving a five-year apprenticeship with Henry Gibson, and practicing architecture on his own for five years before immigrating to Canada. Alexander arrived in Vancouver in 1908 during that city's great boom period, and found work with both **W.T. Whiteway** and **J.H. Bowman**. In the latter's office, Alexander worked on the design for a number of public schools in South Vancouver, as well as the design for St. Peter's Anglican Church, 1908, for which he seems to have been solely responsible. Alexander formed a partnership with Percival H. Brown that lasted from 1912-14. They designed the shingle-clad Gothic Revival St. Andrew's Presbyterian Church in North Vancouver, 1912-13, and the impressive Tudor Revival Brydone-Jack residence in Shaughnessy Heights, 1912-13. Nothing further is known of the partner Brown, who only lived in Vancouver from 1909-14. Alexander spent most of the First World War in Kamloops tending to his ailing wife, Sylvia. After the war his own health was failing and he moved from job to job. He suffered from an ulcer of the eye; was run over by an automobile, and later suffered a hemorrhage of the lungs. In this period, he worked as a draftsman or architect for the Cut-To-Fit Buildings Co., and for the firms of **H.H. Gillingham**, **A.E. Henderson**, and **Bowman & Cullerne**. During this time he was not able to register as an architect due to these injuries and his doctor's bills; his inability to obtain steady employment led him to try a different field, and he worked for a time as a confectioner. From 1926 until 1940 when he retired, Alexander worked again as an architect. His only known designs from these later years are an unbuilt project for an extension to Glacier House in the Rocky Mountains, 1926, and the Alma Court apartments on Alma Street, 1931, one of Vancouver's finest surviving examples of the Spanish Colonial Revival. Alexander died on June 4, 1945, at the age of seventy-one.

ARCHIBALD, John Smith
1872-1934

DONALD LUXTON

Born in Inverness, Scotland on December 14, 1872, J.S. Archibald was apprenticed to Inverness architect William MacIntosh from 1887-93. He immigrated to Canada at the end of his articles, and settled in Montreal, where he joined the office of Edward Maxwell as a draftsman and assistant. He had a busy and productive career, first in partnership with Charles Jewett Saxe (1870-1943) from 1897 until 1915, and then afterwards on his own. In the 1920s, the Canadian National Railways commissioned him to design a chain of grand hotels, including the third Hotel Vancouver, designed in 1928 but not completed until 1939; a hotel in Halifax, 1928; the Bessborough Hotel in Saskatoon, 1931; and a major extension to the Château Laurier in Ottawa, 1928. Archibald was assisted on the Hotel Vancouver project by associated architect John Schofield (1883-1971), also based in Montreal. After he arrived in Canada, the English-born and trained Schofield specialized in railway work, and later worked for the CNR, for whom he designed the Jasper Park Lodge, built 1922-23. The landmark Hotel Vancouver, with its imposing Château-style copper roof, was not completed by the time of the 1929 Crash, and sat as a rusting steel skeleton until rushed to completion in time for the Royal Visit of 1939. It remains one of the city's most distinctive landmarks Archibald died on March 2, 1934 in Montreal.

AUGUSTINE, Alpheus Price
1885-1928

DONALD LUXTON

Born March 23, 1885 in Middlesex County, Ontario, Augustine was a graduate in Civil Engineering from the University of Toronto, and worked in private practice 1909-14 in Vancouver. He enlisted with the Canadian Engineers in September, 1916, and was transferred to the Royal Engineers the following year. After being gassed at Armentières in 1918, he was sent to Northern Russia, where he constructed military buildings at Kolmagorskaya and Archangel, and was promoted to the rank of Captain. Augustine returned to Canada, and settled in Penticton,

likely because of the dry climate. In December 1919, he entered into partnership with **H. Lindsay Swan**. The lack of architectural work led to Price Augustine's decision to relocate to New Westminster, where he started the Augustine Coal Company. He died prematurely on September 11, 1928 at the age of forty-two.

BADGLEY, Charles G.

DONALD LUXTON

Charles G. Badgley was an architect based in Seattle from 1908-13, undertaking mainly residential commissions. In 1911 he became the latest of a series of Seattle architects to "invade the British Columbia territory," and opened an office in Vancouver. His one known local commission was a grand one, for the Convent of the Sacred Heart in Point Grey, 1911-12. This landmark Gothic Revival structure, with a 300 foot long granite facade, was used as a convent until 1979, and is now operated by St. George's School as their Junior School. Badgley was only active in Vancouver from 1911-12. From 1913 until 1918 he was resident in Seattle, but did not maintain a professional listing, and disappeared from directories after 1918, likely to work in the Eastern United States.

BALE, David Herbert
1866-1945

JENNIFER NELL BARR AND CAREY PALLISTER

D.H. Bale was a versatile and shrewd businessman who targeted the middle-class housing market. Although he began primarily as a builder, he later broadened his line of business to include design. Born on May 6, 1866 in Bristol, England, his family immigrated to Canada when he was eighteen years old. He furthered his education in Woodstock, Ontario, and began working in the building and contracting business in the late 1880s, moving to B.C. in 1890, and to Victoria in 1898. He seems to have started designing his own projects about 1905. On January 12, 1900 Bale married Emily Frances Haslam of Woodbridge, Ontario. In 1906 his designed his own house at 1510 Elford Street. The house was featured in a full-page article in a special 1906 Christmas issue of the Victoria *Daily Times*, which noted its unusual treatment of B.C. woods used in the interior decoration. A year later he built himself another home, *Argos*, at 1402 Stadacona Avenue, 1908, where he lived until his death on March 15, 1945. Bale built hundreds of affordable houses in Victoria, and advertised himself as Architect, Builder and Contractor and offered "houses built on instalment plan – no money required." He was certainly influenced by the English and American Arts and Crafts movements, evident in the design of his own homes as well as 566 Gorge Road, 1920, and 1017 Catherine Street, 1913. He also ventured into the late Queen Anne style which can be seen in his designs of 1406 Elford Street, 1905, and 1125 Fort Street, c.1907. The house at 2895 Colquitz Avenue, 1911, was an essay in the Craftsman Bungalow style, and 1606 Wilmot Place, 1911, is in the Colonial Bungalow style. His house designs are quite recognizable and many examples are still standing. Apparently at the height of the prewar building boom he had over a hundred projects going on at one time, and was finishing two houses a week. Perhaps his finest surviving house is the one he designed and built for William Henry Lettice on Faithful Street, 1911-12. Although he had the opportunity, Bale never joined the AIBC when it was formed in 1920. He was often opposed to their proposals and, in 1928, he conducted a heated debate in the Victoria *Daily Colonist* with **Percy Fox**, President of the Institute. The AIBC had requested the provincial government amend the *Architects Act* to "prohibit all building or additions or alterations in remodelling of buildings (except those to be personally occupied by the person having this work done) unless designed and supervised through members of the AIBC." Bale took umbrage at this proposal because, as a architect outside the organization, he and others like him would be greatly affected by this change. He was active as a builder and designer until about 1940.

BAMFORTH, T.H.

DONALD LUXTON

By 1911, T.H. Bamforth was working as an architect in Vancouver. He designed several houses for Vancouver Free Homes Ltd. in late 1911-12. In 1913 his plans for the six-room Central School in Port Coquitlam were accepted. Each classroom was twenty-three by thirty-two feet, and provision was made for future additions. Bamforth's last known large project was a large heavy timber warehouse for Columbia Block & Tool in the South False Creek industrial area, 1918, built by **Dominion Construction**, and later occupied by Opsal Steel. His career tapered off in the lean postwar years, and he continued to work as a builder and draftsman until about 1930.

BARNET, James
1865-1932

DONALD LUXTON

James Barnet followed the reverse of the usual colonial pattern, moving from one British colony to another. He was born in Sydney, New South Wales, Australia on February 13, 1865. Starting in 1882 he trained under his father, James Barnet (1827-1904), a Scottish emigrant who was Colonial Architect of New South Wales from 1861-90. Young James also worked under W.S. Kemp, architect for Public Schools. Despite an apparently successful career in Australia, for reasons unknown he moved in his middle years to the Okanagan, settling first in Short''s Point. With his background in designing hospitals in Australia, he landed the commission for the new Jubilee Hospital in Vernon, 1908-09. His plans were accepted in January, 1908. Construction started that spring, and the hospital was officially opened on September 27, 1909. An unusual, rambling structure with a glass-roofed operating room located above the main entry, it was a design suited for a warmer climate, and its long extended wings would have been difficult to heat in Canadian winters. In addition to some Vernon residences, Barnet also designed the landmark St. James Catholic Church, built from concrete blocks that imitate convincingly the appearance of stone. With the downturn of the local economy, he left to work in Spokane, Washington, but returned in 1914 to work as an assistant engineer on the improvement of the Narrows at Burton City, Arrow Lakes. He enlisted in the 54th Battalion in 1915 and served two months in the Vernon Camp. Owing to ill health he retired and joined the Consolidated Mining & Smelting Co. of Canada at Trail, where he designed a reinforced concrete office, a house for the Managing Director, and many smaller residences. He also designed a school building for Tadanac, two additions to the Trail School, and a Roman Catholic Church at Trail. His career in architecture appeared to have ended by 1922. He died in Vancouver on December 8, 1932, and was interred at Ocean View Burial Park in Burnaby.

BAROTT, BLACKADER & WEBSTER

JANA TYNER AND DONALD LUXTON

While the Canadian Pacific Railway's luxury hotels were built typically in the Château style, their architects often adopted *Beaux-Arts* Classicism for their railway stations to symbolize corporate pride and a dignified past. Characterised by broad facades with colonnades and central rotundas, this monumental style came to Canada from the United States where it was particularly popular for public and corporate structures during the early twentieth century. Barott, Blackader & Webster of Montreal were responsible for Vancouver's third CPR Station, located on Cordova Street just to the east of the second station at the foot of Granville Street. Ernest Isbell Barott (1884-1966) was born in Canastota, New York, and studied architecture from 1902-05 at Syracuse University, then apprenticed in the New York office of McKim, Mead & White. Gordon Home Blackader (1885-1916) was born in Montreal and studied both at McGill University and at the *Atélier Laloux* in Paris, which was affiliated with the *École des Beaux-Arts*. In 1908 he worked at the offices of McKim, Mead & White. In 1912 Blackader formed a partnership with Barott and Daniel T. Webster. The third Vancouver CPR station is an excellent example of *Beaux-Arts* classical architecture. Behind the expansive Ionic-columnar facade, the pilastered central hall is decorated with scenes of the Rocky Mountains celebrating the picturesque landscape of the railway. Barott, Blackader & Webster also designed the Credit Foncier office building on Hastings Street in Vancouver, 1913-14, a ten-storey structure of reinforced concrete; **H.L. Stevens & Co.** was responsible for the working drawings and construction. Built at the end of the boom years, the monochrome treatment of this impressive structure is relieved only by its copper cornice. Grey terra cotta block cladding has been used above the granite-faced ground floors. Clearly articulated into a base, shaft, and capital, it is an excellent example of the classically-inspired commercial structures typical of the Edwardian era. Blackader died in action overseas during the First World War; the Blackader-Lauterman Library of McGill University was set up as his memorial. Barott continued to use his name when he resumed practice after the end of the war. The Montreal-based firm continued its work with the CPR with the addition of a wing on the Château Lake Louise, 1924-25.

BARRS, Frank Arthur Ambrose
1871-1963

DONALD LUXTON

F.A.A. Barrs was born in Repton, Derbyshire, England, the son of Eliza Ann Grace Davey and Henry Barrs, "Farmer of 206 acres employing three men." Young Frank was a pupil to Thomas Gibbs, Barteby, Burton on Trent, in the year 1888, and then a designing draftsman with Tomlinson & Co. Architects & Engineers, Derby. He arrived in Vancouver in 1907, and established an office on Commercial Drive for about one year. He then worked for three years for the Vancouver Exhibition Association during the time of the construction of the buildings and laying out of the grounds at Hastings Park. Barrs won the competition for the Machinery Building, and also designed the Second Unit to the Grandstand and the Fisheries Building, all now demolished. After finishing with the Association, Barrs opened an office on Powell Street for three years, during which time he designed St. Nicholas Anglican Church in Vancouver Heights, Burnaby, 1912, and became a member of the British Columbia Society of Architects. He was briefly in partnership in 1912-13 with Samuel Bernard Dean Shewbrooks (1877-1957), but the economy failed just as they were setting up an office. Shewbrooks, born in Chesterfield, England, was the son of architect Charles Shewbrooks, and had immigrated to Vancouver in 1912; after 1920 he also entered into the real estate business and was later active in Burnaby politics. Barrs did not enlist during the First World War, being "too old and medically unfit," but took a position

with the Vancouver School Board, where he designed a number of schools including the four-roomed Laura Secord School on Lakewood Drive, 1913 and the eight-roomed Kitsilano High School, 1917. His most elegant school design was for the Senior Building at Strathcona School, facing Jackson Street at Pender, 1915, a reinforced concrete structure clad in red pressed brick and Haddington Island stone, with a Portmadoc slate roof. Active as an architect until about 1933, Frank Barrs died on December 16, 1963.

BAUER, Frederick J.
DIED 1909

DONALD LUXTON

Frederick Bauer was drawn to New Westminster after the 1898 fire. Between 1898 and 1899 he designed the Blackie Block, the Central Hotel, and the Occidental Hotel, all on Columbia Street, several residences on Carnarvon Street, and the Shaake Machine Shops on Front Street. In November, 1900, his plans for a new City Hall were selected, and the building was completed by the following year. The Holmes Block on Columbia Sreet followed in 1901. Bauer was active as an architect until about 1904, and died in 1909.

BAYNE, Richard Roskell
1837-1901

MARTIN SEGGER

R.R. Bayne's Canadian legacy remains his personal papers, mainly sketchbooks and measured drawings that document his travels throughout Europe, the Middle East, and India. Born in Balsall Temple, Warwickshire, England, July 7, 1837, he received his first training in architecture from his father. In 1858 Bayne worked in the office of the famous British architect, Sir Charles Barry (1795-1860, a leader in the revival of the Renaissance styles of architecture, and co-designer of the English Houses of Parliament), while attending classes at University College in London. By 1859, Bayne was studying at the South Kensington School of Design in London, and was awarded the Queen's Prize by that institution in 1860. After completing a year of travel in Europe, he returned to London where he worked in the office of

architect, Sir Matthew Digby Wyatt (1820-1877). In 1864, he was awarded the Royal Institute of British Architects Soane Medal, a prize which enabled him to make an extensive sketching tour in Europe during 1864-65. In 1866 he passed his examinations and became a member of the RIBA. Bayne entered the service of the East India Railway Company on March 20, 1866, and moved to Calcutta. By the time he retired from the Company in 1890, he had earned the title Assistant to the Chief Engineer. Numerous structures in India are attributed to Bayne: the East India Railway offices; the Huseinabad Clock Tower at Lucknow; Mayo Memorial Hall; and the Thornhill and Mayne Memorial Library, both at Allahabad; Public Markets in Calcutta and Madras; as well as hospitals, halls, hotels, houses, a theatre and a synagogue. After his retirement, Bayne and his second wife, Florence (b.1867) moved to Victoria in 1890, possibly to join relatives living there and in the Alberni Valley. He opened an architectural office in May, 1891, and was briefly busy before the local recession set in. He called for tenders for a two-storey house on Battery Street, and designed a building at the corner of Quadra and Chatham Streets, both 1891, and was preparing plans for his own home in Oak Bay the following year. Despite the slowdown in his career he was active in professional circles. From its inception he was involved with the British Columbia Institute of Architects, and delivered an address, highly critical of the design capabilities of Victoria's architects, to its third annual meeting in 1893. Bayne died in New Westminster on December 4, 1901, and was buried in Ross Bay Cemetery.

BAYNES & HORIE

DONALD LUXTON

Baynes & Horie were mainly a contracting firm, but designed many larger projects in-house. The firm was very successful, and prospered as the Lower Mainland developed in the boom years prior to the First World War. Edgar George Baynes (1870-1956) was born at Braintree, Essex, England. He started his apprenticeship as a carpenter with his uncle, Joseph Franklyn, "Coffin Maker & Cabinet Work." When Franklyn and his family immigrated to Canada, Baynes came with them, arriving in Vancouver in May, 1889. The day after he arrived Baynes was at work helping clear the site for **N.S. Hoffar's** Dunn-Miller Block. He was soon working on the erection of the first animal cages for the new Stanley Park Zoo. He became a charter member of the local Carpenter's Union when it was formed in 1890, and worked on a number of projects with another young carpenter, William McLeod Horie (c.1858-1940) who was born in Quebec and came to Vancouver in 1888. Early projects they worked on with their friend, **Joseph Bowman** included construction of the wooden arch at the entry to Stanley Park in 1889, designed by **S.M. Eveleigh**. The three men also placed the long fir beams during the construction of Vancouver's Christ Church Cathedral. Baynes & Horie established their contracting partnership in 1893, and built many early schools, including the original wooden Fairview School, and a number of warehouse buildings in Gastown. They also built the first office building in Vancouver to be serviced with an elevator, **Dalton & Eveleigh's** Davis Chambers, 1905-06, as well as the exclusive Douglas Lake fishing and hunting resort at Fort St. James. In order to supply bricks for their many projects, in 1907 Baynes, Horie, and Harold Burnet formed the Port Haney Brick Works in Maple Ridge, which operated continuously for the next seventy years, providing drain tile and clay partition blocks as well as their trademark bricks. In 1912-13 the firm designed and built the Grosvenor Hotel; when the economic depression hit that year, Baynes had to take over the hotel, and continued to run it until his death. Horie was remembered by his wife and eight children as a master craftsman and carpenter who spent his leisure time in Stanley Park and on the beaches of English Bay, and could recite with gusto many of the *habitant* poems of his native province. After Horie's death in 1940, the sons of the original partners continued the firm's activities for several years. Baynes, who died at the age of eighty-seven in 1956, also served as a park commissioner for seventeen years, and was a long time member of the Vancouver Town Planning Commission. In 1944 he was awarded the Good Citizenship Medal by the Native Sons of B.C. His son, Ted, wrote of Edgar Baynes: "He loved planning and drafting and building things. His contribution in the proper development of Vancouver in sixty-four years was not exceeded by any man."

BEALE, L. Bernhardt

JENNIFER NELL BARR

L Bernhardt Beale first appeared in Victoria as general manager of the Reliance Investment and Building Company, Limited. *The Week* of January 18, 1913 stated: "the company own the property on which they build and as they will design and build to suit the tastes and ideas of their clients, it will be greatly to the advantage of newcomers and prospective homeowners to consult them." Beale's partner in the design of these houses was Arthur Fleet, under the name of Fleet & Beale. Soon after they designed the Avenue Theatre for The Victoria Motion Picture, Limited, in 1913, the partnership was annulled. Beale went on to design a $20,000, thirteen-room stone and half-timbered residence on St. Charles Street for John Ross in 1914, but had disappeared by 1915.

BIKER, Walter John Ellsworth
1879-1954

JENNY COWELL

Walter Biker was born in Skipton, Yorkshire, England, and was educated there as an architect and civil engineer. He was a pupil for three years, 1895-97, with E. Barton Johnson in Ilkley, Yorkshire, and in 1897 was hired as an architectural assistant to the Borough Engineer and Surveyor of Harrogate; in two years he was promoted to architect. He came to the East Kootenay in 1911, serving as manager and engineer for a group of twenty-five families leasing land near Elko. In 1912 he was working as an engineering assistant in the Water Branch of the Department of Lands, and the following year he moved to Nelson where he became District Water Engineer, 1913-26. He was involved with the building and design of the Cora Linn Dam on the Kootenay River near Nelson, for West Kootenay Power. After 1917, Biker also had a private architectural practice, designing and building houses, including his own home near Nelson. Walter Biker died in Trail in 1954.

BIRLEY, Studley Patrick
1904-1962

DONALD LUXTON

S.P. Birley had a varied background, but became one of the more accomplished modernist architects in the traditional context of Victoria, B.C. Born in Swinton, Lancashire, England on March 17, 1904, he was the son of Edith Gladys Fernandes Lewis and Joseph Harold Birley. He graduated with a B.A. Honours in History from Trinity College, Cambridge in 1927, and an M.A. in Latin, and in 1929 was married to Patience Hilda Lloyd. The Birleys moved to Victoria in 1930, where he was appointed Mathematical Master at Brentwood College. By November 1931, S. Patrick Birley was a pupil under **Spurgin & Johnson**, and then later under J. Graham Johnson alone. Birley established his own practice in Victoria by 1934, and over the next few years designed mainly residences, but also some strikingly modern buildings, including the Sussex Apartment Hotel, 1937-38 - one of the first in Victoria to cater to auto tourism – and the streamlined Athlone Apartments, 1940. After Spurgin's untimely death in 1936, Birley completed his Qualicum Beach College School project. Known as an affable person, Birley had many hobbies including boating, and was an accomplished musician. For the six year duration of the Second World War, he served with the Canadian Navy: until March 1944, he was in charge of planning and maintenance for the West Coast Bases, then was transferred to the Directorate of Planning, Naval Service Headquarters in Ottawa. During the war, Birley continued to design modest projects, several of which were in association with **D.C. Frame**, such as the Bartle & Gibson Building on Yates Street, 1941. On March 1, 1946 Birley formed an architectural partnership with John Howard Wade (1914-1997) and C. Dexter Stockdill. The firm was very successful and prolific, but by 1952 Birley was practising on his own, formed a partnership with Ian Simpson in 1955, and then with Donald Wagg in 1958. Birley remained active in the office until his death, after a short illness, on July 29, 1962, at the age of fifty-eight.

BLAIR, William Wallace
1853-1916

STUART STARK

Irish-born W.W. Blair took his architectural training in Belfast, and later worked in Toronto, Hamilton and Chicago before he settled in Winnipeg for a short time. His projects in Winnipeg included: the Roslyn Apartments, 1908; the Princeton Apartments, 1909; the Warwick Apartments, 1908-09; the Victory Building, 1909 (demolished); and two warehouses. Blair moved to Victoria to retire, and in 1913-14 built himself a grand home called *Anketell Lodge*, that still stands on Beach Drive in Oak Bay. Bearing a strong resemblance to one of his Winnipeg commissions, a large 1911 Tudor Revival home for realtor, Mark Fortune, Blair's own home features a stone first floor with half-timbering above, and an entry flanked by rustic round stone columns. A fine granite wall and gates, as well as a two-car stone garage, add to the architectural composition. Blair died on July 7, 1916, and his widow and son lived in the house until the late 1920s.

BOUGHEN, Edmund John
1874-1967

DONALD LUXTON

E.J. Boughen was born in London, England on November 30, 1874. He came to Canada in 1911, settling in New Westminster. Known mostly for his residential designs, his commissions in New Westminster included a grand Craftsman-style residence for Dr. P. MacSween, 1912; a modest yet sophisticated bungalow for bridge tender, William Furness, 1913; and his own home, *E-Dee-Nie*, built 1912-13. In North Vancouver he designed a home for James H. Keller, the first principal of the local high school, 1912. During the First World War Boughen relocated to Vancouver, and continued in practice until the early 1950s. One of his last known buildings was a Chapel for the Roman Catholic Archbishop of Vancouver, 1951. He died on October 31, 1967, at the age of ninety-two.

BOWIE, George Pigrum
1881-1915

DONALD LUXTON

G.P. Bowie appeared briefly on the Vancouver scene during the boom years. Born in London, England, on March 29, 1881, he arrived in Vancouver by 1911, and was engaged to design some Shaughnessy residences, apartments and commercial buildings, such as the Montgomery Block, 1912. One of Bowie's projects remained unbuilt, a large Tudor Revival mansion in Point Grey for J.R. Seymour, 1913, designed by **Max B. Downing** while he was employed in Bowie's office. Also in 1913, both Bowie and **C.H. Clow** submitted plans for a city hall to the new municipality of Port Coquitlam, but neither one was chosen. The following year **Parr, Mackenzie & Day** were chosen to design the new building, and Bowie's and Clow's plans were returned. Bowie's most striking commission was a commemorative arch for the 1912 vice-regal visit to Vancouver of the Duke of Connaught, the Governor-General of Canada. This arch, built of massive logs in the form of a classical temple, was donated by the Lumberman's & Shingleman's Society, and stood over Pender Street between Hamilton and Cambie Streets. The next year, the arch was dismantled, and the logs floated to Stanley Park, where it was rebuilt at the shore at the termination of an allée of plane trees. Bowie enlisted on August 12, 1914, and was sent overseas with the 5th Battalion, 2nd Infantry. He died of wounds in Belgium on July 7, 1915, survived by his family in England and his fiancée in Vancouver, Alice Margaret Scott. In 1919 the arch in Stanley Park, the first permanent commemorative arch in the province, was renamed "Bowie Arch" in honour of Bowie's war service and sacrifice. A prominent Vancouver landmark, it was demolished in 1947, and replaced by a new Lumberman's Arch in 1952.

BRAUNTON & LEIBERT

DONALD LUXTON

Hugh Braunton was active in Vancouver starting in 1905, and by early 1912 went into partnership with John Grant Leibert, who appears to have been a native of San Francisco. This was the middle of Vancouver's great boom period, and they were very successful in obtaining a number of commercial and industrial commissions, including: the Astoria Hotel, 1912; the City Mission for Messrs. Brown and Howey, 1912; the Irwinton Apartments, 1912-13; the Standard Furniture Co. Building, 1913, and the Allen Building, 1914, all extant. One of their most prominent projects was the landmark Ashnola Apartments on Main Street, 1912-13, where Leibert took up residence as soon as it was completed. Their work was elegant and restrained, generally using tan brick cladding capped with metal cornices, suiting the straight-forward requirements of Edwardian mercantilism. Although their partnership lasted only a few short years, Braunton & Leibert were prolific, and left a notable legacy of commercial blocks and early hotels. By mid-1914 they had left Vancouver, and appear to have relocated to El Paso, Texas. Leibert likely retired to San Francisco; Braunton also likely ended up in California.

BROWN, Ernest T.
1876-1950

DONALD LUXTON

Ernest T. Brown, whose career kept him on the move between the three westernmost provinces, was born in Brighton, England on April 24, 1876 and attended Brighton Technical School 1898-1900. After his arrival in Canada, he trained as an architect in Guelph, and then moved to Regina about 1906, where he registered with the Saskatchewan Association of Architects in 1912. Leaving Saskatchewan in 1914, he lived and worked primarily in Calgary for the next twenty-five years. Looking further afield for work, Brown applied to join the AIBC in 1926. The Kamloops Lodge 44 of the Benevolent & Protective Order of Elks had been formed in 1920 with 170 members. In 1927, Brown was chosen as the architect for their impressive new lodge building, which he designed in the Spanish Colonial Revival style. During the 1920s the local Board of Trade was promoting Kamloops, the "Hub City," as a tourist destination. The Board's president headed up an association of businessmen who raised $90,000 in shares to build a hotel intended to be the finest in the B.C. Interior. Brown was selected as the architect for the new hotel, and again chose the Spanish-inspired style, popularly referred to as "Californian" and symbolizing the freedom offered by the now readily-available automobile. The Plaza Hotel, with its top floor outdoor roof garden, opened in 1928. Brown also received a similar commission in Lethbridge, Alberta, where a group of businessmen, through the Board of Trade, had committed themselves to the building of a $250,000 community hotel. Brown was hired as the architect, and in August, 1927 presented his plans to the directors of Lethbridge Community Hotel Ltd., and they accepted his suggestion for a "pseudo-Spanish" design for the new Marquis Hotel, which was essentially a larger version of the Plaza. Construction began in October, 1927, and was completed the following June. Late in 1927, Brown was also chosen as the architect for the Lethbridge Collegiate Institute, which opened in September, 1928. By mid-1928, Brown was commissioned to design an Elks Lodge in Calgary, and as his future seemed brighter in Alberta, in July, 1928 he moved to Calgary with his wife and two daughters. Although he stated that he intended to return to Kamloops to attend to his business interests, his career in B.C. had effectively ended, and he resigned from the AIBC in 1931. From 1941-45 he was the resident architect for the Federal Department of Public Works in Calgary. Brown's two "Californian" style projects survive in Kamloops, but the Marquis Hotel in Lethbridge was demolished in 1988. Brown died in Calgary on May 1, 1950.

BROWN, John Graham
1860-1937

CAREY PALLISTER

Although relatively unknown, J.G. Brown held the position of Assistant Dominion Government Architect of British Columbia for twenty-four years and attained the senior position from 1925-32. He was born in Glasgow, Scotland on July 17, 1860, and later attended Glasgow Technical School for a two year course in architecture and construction, and Glasgow Athenaeum for a course in architectural drawing. He came to Canada in 1882, first stopping in Winnipeg where he was involved in contracting. Brown arrived in Victoria in 1888 and was again occupied in the construction trades, variously as a bricklayer, contractor and builder. In 1901 he joined the Department of Public Works, working under **William Henderson**.

By his own description, Brown was the supervising architect for all Department of Public Works post offices built in B.C. between 1901 and 1924. Furthermore, he oversaw alterations and repairs to buildings in many small towns in the province. On November 5, 1889, John Graham Brown married Catherine Palmer Teague, daughter of the prominent architect **John Teague**. For twenty-five years Brown served as choirmaster for the First Presbyterian Church. As well, he was involved in the organization of the Victoria Music Festival and had a long association with the Victoria Opera Society. Also a sportsman, he held several positions in the Lawn Tennis Club, Badminton Club and Vancouver Island Football Association. He was also first President of the Burns Club. His wife died in February 1931, and he retired the following month. He returned to Scotland to live for five years, but came back to Victoria in the fall of 1936. Brown died on February 6, 1937, aged seventy-six, and was buried in Ross Bay Cemetery.

BURKE, HORWOOD & WHITE

DAVID MONTEYNE

The successful Toronto architectural firm of Burke, Horwood & White designed four important buildings in British Columbia: the First Baptist Church on Burrard Street, Vancouver, 1910-11; Mount Pleasant Baptist Church, Vancouver, 1909-12; and the monumental Hudson's Bay Company (HBC) department stores in Vancouver, 1913-16 and 1925-26, and Victoria, 1913-21. All four of these buildings remain standing. The elder partner, Edmund Burke (1850-1919), a devout Baptist, had a long list of churches in Eastern Canada to his credit, so the firm was chosen to design the two in Vancouver. One of Burke & Horwood's first commissions together in 1895 had been the Robert Simpson store in Toronto, and they had built a reputation for large commercial structures of all kinds before being chosen as architects of the flagship HBC stores in B.C. and Calgary. Murray White (1869-1935) joined the firm in 1909 and, like Horwood, was registered in B.C. Horwood, however, acted as the project architect for the HBC commissions. J.C.B. Horwood (1864-1938) was born in Newfoundland, but educated in Toronto.

He articled under his future partner at the firm of Langley, Langley & Burke, and then worked in New York during the Classical Revival of the early 1890s, and travelled in Europe. Horwood's times abroad influenced his firm's implementation of the most modern American technology, and their use of ornamental styles, such as the fashionable and bombastic Edwardian Baroque which attracted the HBC. Horwood's emphasis on the art of architecture complemented Burke's interest in functionalism. Both men were influential in the professionalization of architecture in Ontario. Burke played another small part in the history of Vancouver architecture as the judge in the new Vancouver Court House competition won by **F.M. Rattenbury** in 1906.

BUTLER & HARRISON

JENNIFER NELL BARR

Ernest N. Butler and Reginald Harrison were in partnership in Victoria by 1912. In October of that year they designed a half-timbered, "Old English-style" hotel, which was never built, for the Foul Bay area of Victoria. Later that year they considered the possibility of opening an additional office in Vancouver. Butler was a member of the Alberta Association of Architects as well as being a member of the executive council of the B.C. Society of Architects, and the team designed a large warehouse in Edmonton in mid-1913. At the same time, they designed two buildings in the British Arts and Crafts style for the Wilkinson area of Saanich: the Wilkinson Road Methodist Church; and a $7,000 residence for Ernest Kennedy, managing director of **British Canadian Home Builders, Limited**. The Architect, Builder & Engineer notes that Butler & Harrison designed five $3,000 residences in Parksville on Vancouver Island, and they also designed a number of residences in Victoria and Oak Bay, including for Mrs. Lemon on Belmont Avenue, and an alteration and addition to the Rockland Avenue mansion of Frederick W. Jones. By 1914 they had a branch office in Duncan, and designed the Prince George Hotel in Prince George for D.A. Brewster. The final word on Butler & Harrison was that they had designed a $20,000 country residence for H.R. Hammond which was under construction in Metchosin: "The stucco finish, brown stained woodwork, and many gabled architecture give a quaint Old Country effect that is carried out right through the interior where the beam work and high, open fireplaces are all built in Old English style." After this they disappear from the province.

BUTTERFIELD, Ernest

JENNIFER NELL BARR

Butterfield was in Victoria by 1908, earlier than some of the other British Arts and Crafts architects, and generally designed smaller working class houses, some of which were Colonial Bungalows with bellcast hipped roofs. Other houses he designed were the common Arts and Crafts Edwardians: front-gabled, one and one-half storeys high with dormers on each side, and inset corner front porches balanced by shallow, cantilevered bays on the front facade. They generally sported cedar-shingled foundations, bevelled or double-bevelled siding on the main floors, and stucco and half-timbering in the gables. These houses included those for Mrs. Ada Shaper, 1909, H. Harris, 1912 and H. Bickerdike, 1912. One grand commission was a granite-faced house with a slate roof for John Haggerty on Manor Road, 1913. Butterfield was appointed secretary-treasurer of the Victoria Chapter of the B.C. Society of Architects in the summer of 1912, after the resignation of **John Wilson**. In December that year, he made a three-month trip back to England. He disappeared by 1914.

CAMPBELL, Clive Dickens
1911-1975

DONALD LUXTON

Clive Campbell was born in Ramsgate, England in 1911. Once he moved to British Columbia, he began working in the office of **Samuel Maclure** in April, 1928. After a year he became an assistant with the firm of **James & Savage**. In December 1929 he started work at the Department of Public Works under **Henry Whittaker**, and remained there for a large part of his professional career. Typical of his work at the DPW was the Recreational Building at the Tranquille Sanatarium, 1940, for which he was the project architect. Campbell suc-

ceeded **G.S. Ford** as Chief Architect of the DPW in 1949. In 1957 Government House was destroyed in a spectacular fire, and its replacement was a priority, because of the impending British Columbia centenary celebrations the following year, with a projected visit by HRH Princess Margaret. Although the AIBC advocated a design competition, Premier W.A.C. Bennett announced that the DPW would design the new building, modelled as closely as possible on the old building, and Campbell was given orders to proceed forthwith. Campbell worked closely with Lieutenant Governor Frank Ross, and the building was completed early in 1959. While Campbell was Chief Architect, he was also received a concurrent appointment as Deputy Minister of Public Works. He retired from the civil service in 1959 and went into private practice, where he was involved in the redevelopment of Centennial Square in the early 1960s. Among his other duties, Clive Campbell was one of the founding members of the City of Victoria's Design Panel. He also served as President of the AIBC from 1956-58. While on vacation in Spain, Campbell died suddenly on January 11, 1975. He had been a long-time director of the Victoria Senior Citizens Housing Society, and was the architect for several of their housing projects. Three years after his death he was one of the people after whom the Society's Campbell Lodge was named.

CANE, Henry
1860-1935

DONALD LUXTON

Born in Slinfold, Sussex, England on September 30, l860, "Harry" Cane was the son of Henry Cane, Sr., architect to the Maharajah of Coochbehar, India and studied under his father for six or seven years. Harry Cane then moved from India to Oregon, taking up farming, but later moved to Portland to practice architecture. He moved to Nelson, B.C. in 1899, drawn by the mining boom, and by the following year had entered into an architectural partnership with **James A. MacDonald**, which lasted until about 1901. After the partnership ended, Cane was active as an architect and artist in Nelson until he was forced into retirement by failing eyesight in 1907. He died at home on December 28, 1935 at the age of seventy-five, after an illness of six months.

CARTHEW, James Arthur
1865-1936

JENNIFER NELL BARR

James Carthew was born of Cornish stock in Antigonish, Nova Scotia, in 1865. He apprenticed as a carpenter and came to Nanaimo in 1885, where he built many houses. Maggie Milmore was an English nanny who came to Nanaimo with her employers. Jim whistled at the nanny, and in 1890 married her. He first came to Union (now Cumberland) in 1891 with Kenneth "Kenny" Grant, but there was no construction at the time, so they returned to Nanaimo. In 1893 Union's building boom began, and Jim was called to come and work, and once established, sent for his family. Carthew was a prolific carpenter, contractor and architect of many early Cumberland buildings. He constructed the 1898 elementary school designed by **Thomas Hooper**, and Grace Methodist Church and *Beaufort House*, both designed by **Eugene Freeman** of San Francisco. These were three of Cumberland's most distinguished buildings, but unfortunately all have been demolished. Carthew himself designed St. George's Presbyterian Church, and designed and built a number of homes, including those for the Mounces, McKims, and Dentons; bungalows for Harry Hamburger; and cottages for William Matthewson. He also constructed many buildings in Union Bay, Comox and Courtenay. Carthew was an alderman on the first Cumberland City Council in 1898-99, but asked for leave of absence to superintend construction of a large hotel at Fort Wrangel in the Yukon, during the Klondike gold rush. A letter he wrote to Dr. Westwood was published in the newspaper; he gave "advice to any one down below, making ends meet – to stay there!" Carthew was Cumberland's mayor in 1900-01. In 1898, perhaps because Cumberland's initial building boom was over, Carthew opened a livery stable. He sold it in 1903, and the family moved to Comox. There he was secretary of the school board for twenty-four years, and chairman of the hospital board from the time he built the hospital until his death on June 21, 1936.

COATES, H., Crawford, Jr.
1866-1944

JENNIFER NELL BARR AND
CAREY PALLISTER

Although Crawford Coates only worked in British Columbia for seven years, he brought a wealth of experience to the local building scene. Born in Cape Town, South Africa on May 24, 1866, by the age of seventeen he had crossed the Atlantic and enrolled in Architecture at the University of Pennsylvania in 1883. He practised in Philadelphia until 1906, when he started moving westwards, a journey that would take him through Idaho, San Francisco, Seattle, and finally to British Columbia in 1911. Coates had the distinction in 1912 of designing the first mansion in Uplands, a Georgian Revival-style residence (called "Virginia Colonial" at the time) for Alexander McDermott. The *Daily Colonist* for August 20, 1912 reported: "Many advanced ideas have been incorporated in the building... A unique heating system will be installed... Broomell Vapor heating system for perfect regulation and instantaneous action." In June 1913, Coates set up offices with Arthur Fleet, who had terminated his partnership with **L. Bernhardt Beale**. As Coates & Fleet, they designed several commercial buildings, including alterations to the Brown Jug Saloon, and extensive alterations and the addition of gymnasium and dormitory wings to the Collegiate School on Rockland Avenue. In 1914, the partnership designed two unbuilt projects, a rink for the Victoria Curling Club and a Courthouse for the federal government in Duncan. Coates worked on a number of other projects, with and without Fleet. On his own, in September, 1913, Fleet won second place in the competition for the design of Margaret Jenkins School; the local firm of **Spurgin & Wilkins** placed first. By 1915 their joint office was in the house they shared at 637 Avalon Street; by 1917, Fleet had left town. The following year, 1918, Coates left for California. He worked in Los Angeles for the remainder of his career, and died at his home in Manhattan Beach, California, aged seventy-eight, on October 10, 1944.

COCKRILL, Harold Woodruff
1879-1965

DONALD LUXTON

Harold W. Cockrill was an example of how the building trades were often a family pur-

suit in England. Born in Gorleston, Norfolk on November 16, 1879, he was the eldest son of Master Carpenter Joseph Cockrill. He was articled to W.B. Cockrill, Architect, Gorleston, from 1896-1900, and stayed in his office until 1903. During his apprenticeship he also studied at the Great Yarmouth School of Art. From 1905-07 Cockrill worked in South Africa, but returned to Norfolk where from 1907-08 he was in the office of R. Scott Cockrill, Architect and District Surveyor. Drawn to the New World, in 1908 he relocated to Vancouver, where he landed a job as an assistant with **J.S. Helyer**. From 1909-10 he was in practice with Walter M. Thornton, and then from 1910-14 he was Assistant-in-Charge for the Vancouver office of **Maclure & Fox**. During the boom years he also undertook private work on the side, including a number of projects for Chinese clients. From 1914-16 he worked for a private building management firm, and then worked as an Assistant Chief Draftsman for the City Engineer's Office, Vancouver. He also worked in North Vancouver as an architect until 1924. After this, Cockrill's career shifted from architecture to civil engineering, and he worked at that profession until his retirement in 1947. He died in North Vancouver on December 21, 1965, at the age of eighty six.

CORBY, Percy Edmund
1879-1966

DONALD LUXTON

P.E. Corby was born in Stamford, Lincolnshire, England on November 22, 1879, the son of Elizabeth Pollard and architect, Joseph Boothroyd Corby. He articled with Edmund Jeeves, Architect & Surveyor, Melton Mowbray, Leicestershire, from 1895-99. He then became an assistant to his father from 1899-1902, and they went into partnership as J. Boothroyd Corby & Son, with offices in Stamford and Spalding, and Uppingham, Rutland, from 1903-11. His establishment as a full partner allowed him to marry, in 1903, Marion Wright, also from Stamford, and they had two sons, Edmund Boothroyd and Alaric. The Corbys moved to Canada in 1911, first to Penticton from May 1911 until June 1912, and then to Kelowna until March 1915. Two extant examples of Corby's work in Kelowna from 1912 are the British North American Tobacco Co. Ltd. Building on Ellis Street, and an imposing residence built for English civil engineer, Grote Stirling, on Belgo Road.

During the First World War, Corby served with the Royal Canadian Artillery before being transferred to Headquarters, Military District XI. The Corbys moved to Victoria after he was discharged in 1920, and he continued to work as an architect and builder until his retirement in 1943. After a start in banking, their son Edmund joined the military, achieving the rank of Major during the Second World War. Afterwards he took a job with the British War Ministry in London, England, where he married a White Russian Princess in 1958, and died in 1963. P.E. Corby died July 2, 1966, and Marion died two years later. Both were eighty-six when they died.

CRESSWELL, Henry John
1848-1918

GWEN SZYCHTER

H.J. Cresswell was one of the early architects who settled in a smaller community, being part of its growth and content to work on a more modest scale. Born at Louth, Lincolnshire in 1848, the son of Samuel (a school master) and Catherine Cresswell, he immigrated to Canada, probably British Columbia, in 1888. Going into business in Victoria, his advertisement in the *Victoria Colonist* of June 15, 1889, stated that he was an "Architect and Real Estate Agent" located at 6 Bastion Square. In April 1889, soon after his arrival in Victoria, Cresswell entered a competition for a landscape design of Beacon Hill Park. The prize was $200. City Council considered five entries, including one by HO Tiedemann. Cresswell's design was selected and the prize awarded. However, Creswell's involvement seems to have ended there. A month later, the project was taken over by John Blair, whose name is often associated with the park. He married Helen Anne Taylor in Victoria in 1889, and moved to Delta in the 1890s, although he does not appear in the *B.C. Directory* under "Ladner" until 1903. Nothing is known of his work in Victoria, but in the village of Ladner he was responsible for at least five buildings: his family home, 1911; manses for the Presbyterian Church, 1902, and the Anglican Church, 1904; a commercial building that housed J. Reagh's Shoe Store, 1905; and the Odd Fellows Lodge, 1904. Now owned by the Ancient Light Lodge No. 88 of the Masonic order, the Lodge remains a distinctive landmark on one of Ladner's main streets. Cresswell's professional activities seem to have been limited after 1905, although he is known to have laid out a new portion of Boundary Bay Cemetery, Tsawwassen, in 1908, and he did appear in directories as an architect as late as 1913, and that year was also a member of the B.C. Society of Architects. His wife predeceased him in 1912. Henry Cresswell died in March, 1918, and was buried in Boundary Bay Cemetery.

CRICKMAY, William
C.1832-1900

DONALD LUXTON

William Crickmay was born in Oxford, England, and then lived in Caterham, Surrey before immigrating to Canada. He arrived with his extended family in Vancouver on August 5, 1888. Although Crickmay advertised as an architect in Vancouver for several years starting in 1889, he seems to have practiced more as a "practical engineer" and surveyor. When later questioned about his architectural activities, he said "he had not laid himself out for that kind of work: it was scarcely in his line." Crickmay's major business venture was the Imperial Opera House at Pender and Beatty Streets, opened in 1889, and for two years the city's most prominent theatre. He also represented a number of companies, especially the manufacturers of mining machinery. In the late 1880s and early 1890s the Crickmay family were the first summer campers to holiday along the Kitsilano seashore.

CROSS, Frederick William Franklin
1856-1936

DONALD LUXTON

Frederick William Franklin Cross was born in Birmingham, England on November 14, 1856. In 1875 he articled to Thomas Naden FRIBA, and also studied at Queen's College, Birmingham. He was an original member of the London Society of Architects and remained a member until coming to Canada in 1911. Two years later he opened a practice in Vancouver, undertaking mostly residential work. He spent over two years with the Canadian Expeditionary Force during the First World War, and received an Honourable Service medal. One of his surviving postwar projects is the Coniston Lodge Residential Hotel on Bute Street, in Vancouver's West End, 1926. He retired in 1928, and died September 14, 1936.

CUMMINGS & MORCOM

JENNIFER NELL BARR

Vivian John Cummings was born in 1875 in Plymouth, England, then worked in London as managing draftsman in the office of Thomas E. Collcutt, a major English architect who designed the Savoy Hotel. In 1912 he was working as an architect in **F.M. Rattenbury's** Victoria office. Thomas Richard Morcom (1872-1936) was born in North Wales, immigrated to California, and appeared briefly in Vancouver before moving to Victoria. In 1913, Cummings & Morcom opened an office in the Finch Building in Victoria. As well as designing houses, offices and public buildings, in April 1914 they let the contract to **Dunford & Son** to construct a $7,500 "fireproof moving picture theatre building" in Esquimalt for owner J.R. Butler. About the same time, Cummings & Morcom were commissioned to design a two-storey apartment building with five stores in Esquimalt, but it was likely not built, due to the financial situation and the declaration of war in August. By 1916 they had both enlisted. After the war, Morcom moved to North Vancouver, where he built a home in 1923. He was living in the City of North Vancouver when he died in 1936.

DARLING & PEARSON

DONALD LUXTON

The Classical Revival style was ideally suited to the mood of financial institutions during the Edwardian era, who appreciated its allusions to stability and strength. The Temple Bank was a wide-spread phenomenon, and throughout the province, on the main streets of virtually every community, these "temples" were built to honour Mammon, and, especially in smaller centres, were seen as an important symbol of civic pride and progress. From a different perspective, Canada's pre-eminent early humourist, Stephen Leacock, observed in *My Financial Career* that such buildings were both rattling and humbling. Toronto-based architects Darling & Pearson, as the architects for the Canadian Bank of Commerce, provided many sophisticated Classical Revival designs for branch banks built throughout western Canada. The partnership of Frank Darling (1850-1923) and John Andrew Pearson (1867-1940) was a

long and prolific one, including work for various banks including the Bank of Montreal and the Bank of Nova Scotia. Soon after his arrival in Toronto from England in 1888, Pearson joined the staff of Darling & Curry and worked on the plans for the Victoria Hospital for Sick Children. So marked was his talent that three years later the firm took him into partnership along with the equally youthful and able Henry Sproatt. From 1892-95 Pearson spent time in Newfoundland helping to rebuild St. John's after a major fire. From 1908-32 the firm was known as Darling & Pearson, and was a major force in Canadian architecture, climaxing in the federal government's request for Pearson, along with J. Omer Marchand, to provide the design for the rebuilding of the Centre Block of the Canadian Parliament Buildings in Ottawa after it was destroyed by fire in 1916. Darling & Pearson were responsible for close to a thousand bank projects. Their most monumental work in British Columbia is the massive granite Bank of Commerce headquarters in downtown Vancouver, 1906-08; they later provided the plans for the adjacent Canada Life Assurance Building, 1910-11. Other Bank of Commerce branches in British Columbia included an ornate branch in Kamloops on Victoria Street, 1904, and a sophisticated Classical Revival structure on Columbia Street in New Westminster, 1911, with giant order terra cotta columns. Recognizing the frontier nature of many of the settlements where these banks were being built, Darling & Pearson developed standardized designs using the **B.C. Mills, Timber & Trading Company** prefabricated system, although these buildings were sometimes used in more established cities, including one that survives in Victoria. By 1911 the Bank of Commerce's push for westward expansion had tapered off, ending Darling & Pearson's western career.

DAVENPORT, Sumner Godfrey
1877-1956

DONALD LUXTON

American-born and educated, Davenport immigrated to Canada and became a prominent bank architect. Born in Framingham, Massachusetts, in 1877, he graduated from Harvard University and the Massachusetts Institute of Technology. He was hired by the Montreal architectural and engineering firm

Purdy & Henderson, and was sent to the West Indies, where he designed many of the Royal Bank's southern branches. He joined the Royal Bank's staff in Havana, Cuba in 1920, and later moved to the Montreal head office, where he was associated with New York architects York & Sawyer in the design and construction of the bank's head office on St. James Street. Davenport also designed the Royal Bank's London, England headquarters. In 1929, he provided the design for the skyscraper main branch of the Royal Bank in Vancouver, located at Hastings and Granville Streets; only the western half of the building was ever built due to the onset of the Great Depression. Typical of the conservatism of financial institutions, the dynamic Art Deco massing of this landmark building was disguised with historical motifs, to avoid the appearance of excessively daring modernism. Romanesque motifs were used throughout, blended with classical details. The monumental and impressive appearance of both the exterior and the public rooms has been beautifully maintained. Davenport retired in 1942, but continued to consult to the Royal Bank on specific commissions. He died at his home in Georgeville, Quebec in 1956 at the age of eighty.

DAVIDSON, Bedford
1872-1963

DONALD LUXTON

Bedford Davidson was born in Tidnish, New Brunswick on May 16, 1872. He moved to B.C. around the turn of the century, and acted as a general contractor in Vancouver starting about 1911. He provided the designs for some of his projects, including speculative houses. He also advertised his services as an architect from 1913-14. His name is associated with the design and construction of one landmark building, the Dawson (now Ford) Building, 1911-12, for George Dawson, which still stands at the corner of Hastings and Main Streets. Davidson the requirements of professional registration, and in 1928 was cited by the AIBC for calling himself an architect in a newspaper advertisement. He retired from contracting in 1948, and died in North Vancouver on July 4, 1963.

DAWSON, Charles Frederick
BORN 1885

DONALD LUXTON

C.F. Dawson was born in Birmingham, England, and was educated at Birmingham Public School and Grammar School, and then won a scholarship to the Birmingham School of Art. He was articled to Streeton & Sons, Architects & Builders, then immigrated to Canada, arriving in Victoria, B.C. in 1907. He worked as a journeyman for nine months, then worked as a contractor from 1908-15. He was married to Irene Alice Laing in 1911, and they had four children. Involved with the militia from 1908, he was sent overseas in February 1915, was severely wounded on the front line the following year, and was awarded the Distinguished Conduct Medal. After several major operations in England, he was returned to Esquimalt Military Hospital, where during his recovery he was appointed in charge of construction under the Military Hospitals Commission. In 1925 he was hired by the Provincial Department of Public Works as an assistant architect, and in 1931 became District Resident Architect for B.C. and the Yukon for the Department of Public Works of Canada. In this capacity, Dawson designed the Federal Building in Powell River, built at a cost of $50,000. The working drawings and supervision for this two-storey brick structure were by Max B. Downing. Trimmed with stone, it contained the post office, customs facilities, the government telegraph office, and caretaker's quarters. The sloped site allowed level access to both floors. It was completed in April 1939.

DAY, Harry Daborn
1873-1965

HELEN EDWARDS

Harry Daborn Day was born on June 28, 1873 at Leatherhead, Surrey, England. He articled in England for four years with Samuel Wehman from 1890, and then served as an assistant to Saville & Martin, London, W.J.R. Withers, Shrewsbury, and Still & Wheat, London. He designed numerous buildings in England before moving to Victoria, B.C. in 1911. Day worked as an assistant to **F.M. Rattenbury** and **L.W. Hargreaves** in 1911-12, and began his own practice thereafter.

One house he designed on his own was for Messrs. Day & Hallward, on Empress Avenue in Victoria, 1911. Day preferred to work from his residence on commissions for friends, chiefly additions and alterations to existing structures. He returned to England in 1916, but came back to Victoria in 1920 and worked as an assistant to **Percy Fox**. Day was most prolific in the 1930s when he was responsible for several significant commissions scattered throughout Greater Victoria. His designs were based on the British Arts and Crafts style with an emphasis on stucco and multi-pane leaded glass windows. Existing plans are signed "H. Daborn Day" and are generally not dated. Several commissions were completed in Oak Bay about 1931: a home for Mrs. Hilda Unwin, on Beaverbrooke Place; a substantial residence and coach house for Thomas A. and Beatrice Beeching on Upper Terrace; and a waterfront cottage for Miss Ethel Ballard. Day's later buildings were generally smaller in scale with small multi-paned windows in the front gables and an exterior cladding of unadorned stucco, including the Harold Beckwith residence, c.1936 in Oak Bay; and the Vowles residence in Saanich, c.1936. Day lived at 1240 Tattersall Drive in Saanich and in 1936 built two adjacent houses at 1238 and 1244, both extant. Together with **Sylvia Holland**, he designed the Collinson residence on St. Patrick Street in Oak Bay, 1935, and a waterfront home on Arbutus Road for John E. and Fernanda B. Tysoe, c.1936, but it is unknown if this latter project was ever built. During the Depression, Harry Daborn Day also began a new career as the proprietor of the View Royal Auto Camp. He remained active as an architect until about 1943, and died in Victoria on October 14, 1965 at age ninety-three, in virtual obscurity; no mention of his architectural career appeared in his brief obituary. He was survived by his wife, Mary Elizabeth.

DAY, John Charles
1885-1941

DONALD LUXTON

John Charles Day was born in London, England on March 28, 1885. He first came to notice locally in Vancouver in 1912, when **Thomas Fee** retired from his extremely successful partnership with **J.E. Parr**. The firm was reconstituted as Parr, Mackenzie & Day, and this new-found status either enabled or encouraged Day to marry, on July 17, 1912, Miss Evangeline Gordon Cowan. The Parr, Mackenzie & Day partnership continued through the First World War, but never achieved its previous heights, and Day withdrew in 1918. In the latter part of the war he was living in Morrissey, B.C., and he enlisted on June 15, 1918. His active service consisted of being engaged in railway construction with prisoners of war in Alberta, and he achieved the rank of Lieutenant by the time he was discharged in Regina the following April. After he returned to Vancouver he formed a partnership with **Theo Körner**, with ultimately disastrous results. Day continued in private practice, designing mainly comfortable middle-class homes in Vancouver, examples of which include those for W.R. Bonnycastle, 1927 and T.W. Greer, 1928. His best known surviving building is a small, gem-like structure, clad in yellow terra cotta, originally built for the Royal Financial Company on West Hastings Street, Vancouver, 1927. Designed with an eclectic blend of Classical and Gothic ornamentation, it is a noteworthy counterpoint to the adjacent Georgian-style Ceperley-Rounsfell Building, by **Sharp & Thompson**. In 1927 Day was censured, but not expelled, by the AIBC for offering his services at 3.5%, and other cases of underbidding and misconduct. His career faltered, and he died prematurely at home on November 12, 1941, at the age of fifty-five, survived by his wife and their five children.

DE LA PENOTIÈRE, William H.L.
C.1840-C.1893

CAREY PALLISTER AND DONALD LUXTON

In Victoria in 1884, William H.L. de la Penotière and George F. Wake formed a partnership as real estate agents and surveyors. Wake had previously been a bookkeeper with Janion's Commission House, and de la Penotière had recently arrived in the city, likely from Ontario. Although architecture was not their main pursuit, they designed one prominent building, St. James Anglican Church in James Bay, Victoria, 1884-85. The following year de la Penotière formed a brief partnership with **S.C. Burris**, and they are known to have designed a residence on Victoria Crescent and the fittings

for the Victoria Club Rooms. Shortly afterwards, de la Penotière disappeared from the city, and relocated to Ingersoll, Ontario.

DOCTOR, William Alexander

DONALD LUXTON

William A. Doctor arrived in Vancouver about 1908, and was briefly in partnership that year with **Sholto Smith**. He then practised on his own from 1909-10, before entering into partnership as Higman & Doctor, Engineers & Architects, 1910-11. The St. Alice Hotel in North Vancouver was one of their most prominent commissions, but the partners had split before this landmark building was complete and Doctor took sole credit for its design. On his own again, Doctor designed a stone-faced two-storey commercial building on Hastings Street for the Hudson's Bay Insurance Company, 1911-12, of which only the facade has been retained. From 1912-17 he was in partnership as Doctor, Stewart & Davie, and the firm had a few successful years before the local economy collapsed. Their grand *Beaux-Arts* entry in the 1914 competition for a new Vancouver Civic Centre placed in the top three, behind **Körner** & Mattocks and **Fred Townley**. An important commission was a new headquarters for the Vancouver Police on East Cordova Street, 1913-14, a lavishly appointed edifice with an imposing Roman brick and cream-coloured terra cotta facade, now demolished. The firm dissolved by 1917, and Doctor disappeared from Vancouver.

DOMINION CONSTRUCTION COMPANY LIMITED

DONALD LUXTON

Primarily known as one of the largest and most successful construction companies in Western Canada, Dominion Construction also has a long and varied history in the design of buildings through the employment of in-house architectural staff. Charles Bentall (1882-1974) was the mastermind of the business. Born in Essex, England to a tenant farming family, he lost his father when he was seven, leaving his mother to raise five chil-

dren. Charles left school at the age of fourteen to apprentice as a draftsman, and although he never received a formal professional education, by his mid-twenties he was working as an engineer. By 1907 he had saved enough money to buy his mother a house and himself a passage to Canada. The following year he arrived in Vancouver, which was experiencing its greatest ever building boom. Bentall was hired as a draftsman by J. Coughlan & Co., steel engineers and fabricators, and his designs for the frameworks for the new Vancouver Court House dome and for the World Building – at the time the tallest structure in the British Empire – soon won him a promotion to Chief Engineer. Emboldened by his success, Bentall struck out on his own, and soon was hired as an Assistant General Manager by the Dominion Construction Company Ltd., that had been founded in 1911. An astute businessman, Bentall saw an opportunity to provide in-house design expertise to their clients. At this early stage in the company's development **J.Y. McCarter** was sent to Edmonton to open a branch office in 1913, just before the local economy collapsed. Through patience, hard work and the right connections, the strongly religious Bentall kept the company afloat during tough times, and put aside money every month to buy shares in the company, eventually extending himself into "onerous indebtedness" to buy a controlling interest in 1920. Bentall's gamble paid off with the increasing prosperity of the 1920s. In 1927, he landed the contract to both design and build the huge new bus barns for the B.C. Motor Transportation Company on Cambie Street, taking the project away from an architect that the client was not happy with. That year, Bentall had accumulated enough capital to found the New Building Finance Company, which facilitated financing by offering low-interest loans to clients. This enabled a number of projects that might not otherwise have gone ahead, among them the Queen Charlotte Apartments, designed and built by Dominion Construction in Vancouver's West End, 1927-28 at a cost of $170,000. This handsome structure epitomizes the urban ideal of gracious apartment living, with an exterior styled in a conservative period revival appearance, complete with Spanish Colonial parapets and projecting pantiled roofs, that reflects the influence of Californian design. The interior public spaces, however, are more adventurous, and embrace the new, and locally unknown, Art Deco style.

Throughout the 1930s and 1940s, Dominion Construction designed and built numerous high-quality structures in the Streamline Moderne style, including the Bay Theatre on Denman Street in the West End, 1938. With this project the company ran afoul of the AIBC, which brought a successful lawsuit against them for designing buildings without being a registered architectural firm. Dominion Construction was found guilty, but their nominal fine of $25 was a phyrric victory for the AIBC, as the trial's publicity and the glowing testimonials for the contractor's abilities generated a whole new spate of projects for them. Right after the end of the Second World War, the company continued to be highly successful in providing design/build services, maintaining a consistently-high quality output of well-designed structures: some Vancouver examples included the St. Regis Paper Company Building, 1946; the B.C. Motor Transportation (later Greyhound) Bus Terminal, 1946; and the Labour Temple on Broadway, 1948. Another modernist project was the Kelowna Club in downtown Kelowna, 1949. Even more successful in the 1950s and 1960s, Dominion Construction continued to expand its operations. After Charles Bentall retired in 1955, his two younger sons took over. Although the original company has now been split into several diversified components, Dominion Construction remains today under family control and is a powerhouse in the design and delivery of large construction projects.

DONNELLAN, James J.

DONALD LUXTON

James J. Donnellan appeared briefly on the Vancouver scene at the height of the western boom, and specialized in the design of vaudeville theatres. Based in Seattle, he was already recognized for his theatre designs, and was working in Vancouver as early as 1906. Some of his projects involved the remodelling of older theatres into more modern facilities, including his work on the People's Theatre on West Pender Street in 1906, while others were new structures, such as the Lonsdale Theatre in North Vancouver, 1911. Loosely associated with Frank H. Donnellan and J. Clarke Donnellan, he joined in a number of partnerships in rapid succession: Donnellan & **Stroud** and

Donnellan & Donnellan in 1910; Donnellan & **Morcom** and Donnellan & Robertson in 1912, assumed to be associations of convenience. In 1910, Donnellan & Donnellan were hired by the National Amusement Company to design the National Theatre on Hastings Street in downtown Vancouver. Two years later, Donnellan & Robertson were hired by the same company to design a new, larger theatre next door, called the Columbia, "Vancouver's newest, cosiest, most luxurious and up-to-date playhouse," which opened its doors to the "votaries of vaudeville" on December 9, 1912. Donnellan also designed a school and chapel for the Oblates of Mary Immaculate, St. Augustine's Church in Kitsilano, 1911, that was not built. Another grand project, St. Mary's Hall, a school and gymnasium for Holy Rosary Parish proposed for a site on Haro Street, was announced late in 1912 but was never built; a new scheme for St. Mary's Hall was prepared by Tegen & Vezina the following year but also never went ahead. In 1911 the CPR sold off the old Vancouver Opera House, and J.J. Donnellan was hired by the new owners to renovate it into a circuit theatre for the Orpheum vaudeville chain, 1912-13. In 1914, Alexander Pantages hired Donnellan to design his grand new theatre on West Hastings Street in Vancouver, but the project was delayed, and Donnellan moved before the project resumed, cheating him out of the chance to design his largest local project. By 1915 he had left the province, and the following year Pantages hired B. Marcus Priteca to design the theatre. Donnellan likely returned to the United States.

DONOVAN, J.P.
C.1852-1886

DOROTHY MINDENHALL AND
DONALD LUXTON

J.P. Donovan was born in Chicago, Illinois. In 1879, he was located in Portland, Oregon, and became the partner of established architect William W. Piper. Nothing much seems to have resulted from this partnership, as Piper's career was virtually over by this time. Donovan, a Roman Catholic, moved to Victoria, B.C. with his parents about 1884, and quickly developed a reputation as a skilled architect. His projects included the Clarence Hotel at the corner of Yates and Douglas Streets, 1885-86, and several cot-

tages on Fort Street. J.P. Donovan died suddenly on May 20, 1886, aged thirty-four, of "consumption, that fell disease which so far has baffled the skill of the ablest physicians." He was "sincerely mourned by his large circle of friends." For a few years after this, a P.H. Donovan worked in Victoria as an architect, but it is not known if this was J.P. Donovan's father or other relation. Starting in 1890, P.H. Donovan acted as local superintendent for the construction of St. Andrew's Roman Catholic Cathedral, the plans of which had been prepared by Perrault & Messiard of Montreal. After reports of problems at the job site, he was replaced by **John Teague** in 1891, and P.H. Donovan subsequently disappeared from Victoria.

DUNHAM & WALLWORK

DONALD LUXTON

Dunham & Wallwork were architects based in Portland during the early twentieth century. George Foote Dunham (1876-1949) was born in Iowa and trained in Chicago, where he worked until he moved to Portland about 1907. Dunham was known for his design of Christian Science churches, built throughout the west, including Seattle, Spokane and St. Louis. In the 1920s he moved to Orlando, where he lived the rest of his life, and where his most significant work was a Christian Science Church. Carl Harding Wallwork (1879-1946) was a native of the mid-west, and studied in Boston and Kansas City before moving to Seattle in 1909, and then Portland the following year, where he practised for almost forty years. Dunham and Wallwork were only briefly in partnership after the end of the First World War. Their First Church of Christ Scientist in Victoria, 1919, is a pristine example of the classicism that symbolized the churches of this denomination, and is prominently sited at the end of a long vista up Harris Green.

DUNLOP, Alexander Francis
1842-1923

DONALD LUXTON

A.F. Dunlop, born in Montreal, apprenticed there with George and John James Brown. From 1871-74 he worked in Detroit, returning to Montreal to set up a practice in 1874. Dunlop developed an extensive practice, and among the students who worked for his office were Edward Maxwell and **Robert Findlay**. Dunlop was one of the original members of the Royal Canadian Academy in 1880, a member of the organizing committee of the Province of Quebec Association of Architects and a founding member and first president of the Royal Architecture Institute of Canada from 1907-10. Dunlop designed a prominent building for the Molson's Bank in downtown Revelstoke, opened in 1910 and still standing today.

FABIAN, Bruno

WARREN SOMMER AND DONALD LUXTON

Bruno Fabian was an architect living in Langley by 1890, and was resident in Harrison River from 1893-94. One known commission was a house for John Chapman in Chilliwack, 1891, now demolished. With the downturn in the local economy, he left for parts unknown.

FAIRALL, James
1872-1963

JENNIFER NELL BARR

James "Jim" Fairall was born on September 20, 1872 in Ryde, England. His family immigrated to Orillia, Ontario in 1881 and then to Victoria in 1888. His father established the Fairall Brewery in Orillia, and then founded and operated the Esquimalt & Nanaimo Brewing Company in Victoria West in 1888. With his first wife, Lucy Ann Milton, Fairall had five children. He became a prolific building contractor and designer, and was responsible for five of the six houses for Thomas Perkins built in 1911-12 on Alma Place off Michigan Street in James Bay. Fairall built dozens of other houses in the Victoria area, including the British Arts and Crafts bungalow on Niagara Street, 1909 and a number of others for realtor, Thomas McConnell. He designed and built many for himself as speculative houses, including a bungalow on 238 Robert Street in Victoria West, 1946. Jim Fairall was also a brewer and frequently referred to himself as a brewery architect and engineer. In 1895 he built a

two-storey frame brewery on Esquimalt Road, likely for his father, at the corner of Catherine Street, a site later renowned for the Silver Spring Brewery. In 1913-14 Fairall built the Esquimalt Brewing Company on Viewfield Road in Esquimalt. He and partner W.T. Hagen were large ale producers, but in January 1916 the brewery exploded and burned to the ground. His wife, Lucy, died at the age of thirty-one in 1911, and the following year Fairall married Victoria-born, Lillian Anne Brown, and they had another six children. A member of the Gorge Vale Golf Club and an ardent hunter and fisherman, Jim Fairall retired in the late 1940s, and died on June 2, 1963, aged ninety-one.

FARWELL, Milo S.
1890-1966

JENNIFER NELL BARR

Milo S. Farwell was born in Oregon on January 18, 1890, and from 1909-12 was a draftsman in the Portland office of William C. Knighton. By 1912 he was working as an architect in Victoria, B.C. Farwell designed houses in the California Bungalow style, including those in Victoria for Mrs. A.W. Hill, 1912; Frederick R. Wille, 1912; and Edward H. Rider, 1914. The latter was designed for, and built by, the **Bungalow Construction Company**. Commercial designs included a three-storey brick warehouse on Store Street, 1913 for Scott & Peden, alterations to a two-storey storefront immediately to the north, and a two-storey brick store for Hip Yick & Company on Fisgard Street, 1912. In March 1914, Farwell relocated his office to Seattle, Washington, and later returned to Portland where he received his license under the "grandfathers clause" when the licensing of architects commenced in 1919. He died in Sonoma, California on August 27, 1966.

FERREE, Harold C.
1879-1965

JENNIFER NELL BARR

Harold C. "Harry" Ferree was born in Illinois on February 12, 1879, and first appeared in Victoria in 1912 as the manager of the architectural and building firm of **George C. Mesher & Company**. Ferree's name

appeared on the June 1912 plans for the important California Bungalow residence for Goulding Wilson at 610 St. Charles Street. The design of this house was provided by a California architect named Charles King, but George C. Mesher & Company provided the working drawings, which were signed by Ferree. By early 1913 Ferree had left Mesher and set up his own office. He served on the Executive Council of the Victoria Chapter of the British Columbia Society of Architects in 1912-13. In 1913 he designed the Westcott Building which was to have featured *verde* antique marble and copper work but was never built, and a two-storey house for R.H. Green on Joan Crescent. Ferree left Victoria by 1917, and later practised for many years in Berkeley, California. He died in Alameda County, California on November 18, 1965 at the age of eighty-six.

FINDLAY, Robert
1859-1951

DONALD LUXTON

Robert Findlay was born in Inverness, Scotland in 1859. At the age of seventeen, he began a five-year apprenticeship under Inverness architect, John Rhind. Later Findlay worked at the office of John Burnet (1813-1901) in Glasgow. After immigrating to Montreal in 1885, Findlay worked for **A.F. Dunlop**, and later for the Wright brothers. In 1887, Findlay gained prominence by winning a competition for the design of the headquarters of the Sun Life Assurance Co., which established his career and enabled him to develop an extensive practice, largely based on residential projects for affluent Montreal merchants and industrialists. In 1910, Findlay was commissioned to design two adjacent grand houses on Kalamalka Lake near Vernon, for Ronald C. Buchanan, a Montreal businessman and his brother-in-law, Ronald P. McLimont. They were built on five-acre lots that had been subdivided from the Coldstream Ranch for orchard lands. McLimont's house was a grand home with elements of the Shingle and Tudor Revival styles, with a verandah encircled by Classical columns; it was later destroyed by fire and has been replaced by a condominium development. Buchanan's house was tendered by local firm **Bell & Constant**. Designed in an unusual style that combines Arts and Crafts elements with a high Château roof, it was considered one of the finest private homes in the Okanagan. The exterior is clad with stucco and board-and-batten siding, with distinctive bellcast roof edges supported on scrollcut brackets. Interior features include an extensive use of fir panelling, and fireplaces inset with Arts and Crafts tiles. Acquired in 1940 by the Mackie family, it has been willed to a private foundation and preserved as the Mackie Lake House. In 1913, Findlay's son, Francis R. Findlay (1888-1977) joined his father's firm as a partner. The two Findlays practised architecture together until the elder Findlay's retirement in 1941. In 1938, Robert Findlay became the first recipient of the gold medal of merit from the Quebec Association of Architects, for outstanding contribution to architecture.

FORD, Guy Singleton
1885-1963

JENNIFER NELL BARR

G.S. Ford was born September 9, 1885 in Nottingham, England to William Joseph and Frances Emma (Gover) Ford, the second youngest in a family of ten. The family, including Guy's father and several brothers, were in the horse racing business, managing several race courses in England. Guy started his architectural apprenticeship in Melton Mowbray, Leicestershire in 1901-02, and finished in Nottingham in 1902-03. He worked as an assistant in several offices before opening his own practice at Moot Hall Chambers, Nottingham, that ran until 1910. Ford moved to Victoria and opened an architectural office in September 1911, and was briefly in partnership with **George Edgar Hutchinson**. Ford designed a number of residences in Victoria, Saanich and the area, including two for himself on Davie Street. However, much of his time was spent taking care of investment properties for English clients. He closed his practice in January 1915. On May 15, 1915, he married Harriet Muriel Louise Rowley, who was born in Balham, near London, England in 1889. During the First World War, Ford joined the 88th Battalion Canadian Expeditionary Force Victoria Fusiliers, which shipped out in May 1916 under its commanding officer, Lt. Col. **H.J. Rous Cullin**. Muriel went to England for the duration of the war. Because he was a draftsman, Ford was assigned to the planning of railway routes in France, where he spent

twenty months. Following his return to Victoria after the war, Ford found work with the Provincial Department of Public Works in the Architects Branch. He began in 1919, the same year **Henry Whittaker** was appointed supervising architect. Ford worked on plans for the Boys' Industrial School Buildings at Essondale (in Coquitlam), schools at Armstrong and Courtenay, the Court House at Prince Rupert and others. Under Whittaker, Ford was the project architect for a number of the buildings at the Tranquille Sanatarium near Kamloops, including the Farm Boarding House, 1923, and the new Sanatarium (the Greaves Building), 1927-28. Later he worked more on the supervision of construction, including many schools around the province, and on maintenance and modifications of provincial government buildings. When Whittaker retired as Chief Architect of the Branch in 1949, Ford briefly succeeded him, but he retired himself that same year, and **Clive Campbell** took over the top post. Guy and Muriel Ford had two sons, Hugh Singleton in 1920 and John Gordon in 1921. They lived on St. Patrick Street in Oak Bay from about 1921 to 1937, and then moved to Uplands Road where they were living at the time of Ford's death on February 11, 1963. Guy Ford loved gardening, and the family also had a cottage at Saseenos near Sooke on southern Vancouver Island.

FORRESTER, Alexander
1868-1949

DONALD LUXTON

Alexander Forrester straddled the line between architect and contractor, producing serviceable commercial and residential designs when required. Born in Kingskettle, Fifeshire, Scotland in 1868, Forrester came to Nanaimo from Utah in 1891, and quickly became a prominent local contractor and designer. He experienced the life of a "sourdough" in 1898 when he followed the Yukon Trail, travelling two thousand miles up the Yukon River to Dawson. He soon returned, and on April 4, 1900 he married a twenty-two year old native of Nanaimo, Rhoda (known as Rose), the daughter of Sheriff Samuel Drake and a descendant of the pioneer Malpass family. The couple had four children – two sons and two daughters. Other architects passed quickly through

Nanaimo, but Forrester firmly established himself in the community, helped by his marriage into a pioneer family. Claiming to be an architect, he appeared to have been self-taught, and never registered with the AIBC, indeed flouting its regulations by continuing to use the title architect as late as 1926. In 1904 Forrester supervised the construction of additions to the Nanaimo Post Office. His surviving designs include a 1913 addition to the Globe Hotel, and a store for Angell's Trading on Fitzwilliam Street, 1926. In addition to his design and construction work, Forrester also served for nine years as an alderman, six years as a school trustee and many years as director of the Hospital Board. After his retirement, Alexander Forrester was still active, and enjoyed a daily walk along the waterfront. Although he had never taken a drink of liquor, or smoked, in his life, he did not attribute his apparent youthfulness to abstinence. At the age of eighty, he was quoted as stating "liquor never hurts anybody, providing they do not abuse it." After almost fifty years of marriage, the Forresters died in 1949 within three months of each other, Alexander on April 25 at the age of eighty, and Rose on July 24 at the age of seventy.

GARROW, Robert Thompson
1884-1952

DONALD LUXTON

The peripatetic R.T. Garrow could claim a thorough architectural training and a lifetime in the field, but his most highly developed skills lay in structural design and project management. Born in Aberdeen, Scotland on February 26, 1884, he started his apprenticeship in 1903 with James A. Souttar, a distinguished Aberdeen architect. He was also a student for five years in Building Construction and Architecture courses at Robert Gordon's Technical College and Gray's School of Art, Aberdeen, and a member of the Aberdeen Architectural Association. In March 1907, he immigrated to Victoria, and started work with **Hooper & Watkins**; in June he was transferred to their Vancouver office. After Watkins withdrew from the partnership in 1909, Garrow was placed in charge of Hooper's Victoria office, and for the next two years designed and supervised numerous buildings, including George Jay School and the additions to St. Ann's Academy. During this busy time, he was also in the part-time employ of contractors Skene & Christie as an architectural assistant during the erection of additions to the Empress Hotel and the Vancouver Hotel. In 1910 he became the Construction Manager for Skene & Christie, a post he held until 1918. He was also kept busy designing a variety of houses and commercial buildings, including a grand home for Alexander Walter Elliot in Oak Bay, 1912, and the Shaughnessy Heights Golf Club House for the CPR, 1912-14. In 1915, he completed the Dance Hall and Apartments for Maud Lester's Dancing Academy, Vancouver, 1915, a project that had been designed by Hooper's office in 1911, but construction had halted during the 1913 depression; Garrow's final design was a much reduced version of the original. Work was scarce during the war years, although Garrow landed the commission to design the Security State Bank in Chehalis, Washington, in 1916. From 1918-22 he had an architectural office in Vancouver, and then joined the Puget Sound Bridge & Dredging Company, Seattle, as a construction assistant and structural engineer from 1922-26. From 1926-32 he returned to Vancouver and opened his office again, and his Seattle connections landed him his largest single project, the Hotel Georgia in Vancouver, jointly designed with John Graham Sr. of Seattle (1873-1955). Garrow's office produced the drawings and specifications for this elegant and restrained building, which opened in 1927, and has now been restored. In 1932, Garrow returned to Seattle, where he worked until his death in 1952.

GILMORE, James

Donald Luxton

James Gilmore, who appeared for one year in Prince Rupert as an architect, designed the Prince Rupert Exhibition Building, 1914-15. Situated on "Acropolis Hill," it was the city's centre for sports and social activities. Although the proposed dome shown in the original rendering was never built, its prominent location made it a local area landmark. The area was taken over by American troops garrisoned in Prince Rupert during the Second World War, and renamed Roosevelt Park Hill. The Americans built a number of other structures nearby, and used the Exhibition Building as their Post Exchange

Theatre. It was demolished, along with their other installations, after the end of the war.

GIRVAN, John
1876-1957

JIM WOLF

John Girvan, although not an architect, was a talented artist and decorator who can be credited with some of British Columbia's most inspired interior design schemes. Born in Campbelltown, Scotland in 1876, he acquired a "good education and a thorough training in the arts of painting and artistic decorating." After a six year apprenticeship he was a partner in a decorative painting firm with John Lindsay. They specialized in Arts and Crafts inspired designs and won several British Gold Medals for their craft. In 1912 he immigrated to Canada, locating in Edmonton, Alberta where he established Girvan Studios. He also served with the Royal North West Mounted Police and in 1915 joined the Canadian Expeditionary Force as a Sargeant in the First World War. After returning to Canada in 1918 one of his first commissions was the decoration of the Canadian Memorial Hall in Edmonton. In 1924 he moved Girvan Studios to Vancouver and was soon rewarded with many commissions for theatre decoration. In the Columbia Theatre in New Westminster, designed by **Townley & Matheson i**n 1927, he created one of the province's first atmospheric theatres in the style of a Moorish courtyard garden. Girvan displayed considerable stylistic versatility throughout his career from Art Nouveau to Art Moderne in projects that included residences, churches, restaurants, department stores and office buildings. John Girvan was honored as the first Canadian Fellow of the Incorporated Institute of British Decorators. He died in Vancouver at the age of eighty in 1957.

GODDARD, Samuel May
1843-1906

DONALD LUXTON

S.M. Goddard was born in Birmingham, England on May 16, 1843. Although the date of his arrival in North America is unknown, he served his apprenticeship with the eminent Detroit architect, Gordon W. Lloyd, and while in the office, drew plans for twelve of the churches in that city. Goddard later

moved to Winnipeg, where the partnership of Kilpatrick & Goddard was formed in 1884. Following the westward momentum of settlement, Goddard worked in Seattle for several years as a draftsman for William E. Boone, the city's most prominent architect. Goddard did not stay long, and relocated to Victoria in 1890. There he formed a partnership with **Thomas Hooper**, who had just opened an office to handle the commission for the Metropolitan Methodist Church on Quadra Street, while still maintaining his practice in Vancouver. The firm was described in 1890: "What is being Done Under the Direction of One Firm of Victoria Architects: The firm of Hooper & Goddard into whose offices on Government street a *Colonist* man strayed yesterday is composed of Mr. Hooper, well known among other qualifications, as the architect of the new Methodist Church. His partner and associate is appreciated on this coast upon both sides of the line. Coming here from Winnipeg in 1887 he established his family in this city, but, for a long time, took charge of Fisher & Boone's offices, in Seattle." On June 1, 1891 the partnership of Hooper & Goddard was dissolved, and Hooper gave notice that he would settle the accounts and assume outstanding projects. By June 17, the partnership of McCoskrie & Goddard was formed, to no known success, and **Edward McCoskrie** died two years later. Goddard's career languished, although he remained in Victoria until 1904. Moving to Los Angeles with his wife and four of their six children, Goddard met a tragic end on January 20, 1906. Stricken with heart disease while at an office building in Los Angeles, police assumed that the elderly Goddard was intoxicated, and took him to the police station instead of the hospital. "It is said that he had not breathed his last when taken by the police and that he really died in the *tank*."

GRAHAM, Thomas Wilson
DIED C.1899

DAVID MONTEYNE AND DONALD LUXTON

Thomas Wilson Graham made his living as an architect and builder, but typical of the pioneers that came to British Columbia, also experimented with different entrepreneurial pursuits. Over the years, Graham was responsible for a variety of residences and modest frontier-town stores in New Westminster and up the Fraser River. His first known activity in the province consisted of a contract to build the Pitt River trail in 1860. Graham was briefly in partnership in New Westminster with Robert McLeese as a contractor; he also acted as the architect for the Hicks Building and a building for Mr. Smeaton, both on Columbia Street, 1861. Graham withdrew from the partnership in April 1861, and received contracts in New Westminster to build the Attorney General's house, 1861, the Royal Columbian Hospital, 1862-63 (designed by the **Royal Engineers**), and the Captain William Irving House, 1865 (designed by **James Syme**). Graham also co-founded (with fellow carpenter George Scrimgeour), built, and operated Pioneer Mills, the first sawmill on Burrard Inlet in 1863. Unfortunately, the partners could not pay their creditors and, after operating only one season, were forced to sell the mill at auction. It eventually came into the hands of Sewell Moody, and was greatly expanded under his guidance to become the mill and settlement of Moodyville on the north shore across from the future site of Vancouver. Having "lost more money than he had made" in the colony Graham moved to California in 1869, but continued to travel back and forth between California and British Columbia for the next thirty years. In 1878 he designed the Holbrook Arms Hotel, and a house for **Henry Hoy**, both in New Westminster. The following year he brought his wife and four children back to New Westminster, with a "large lot of Italian bees in patent hues" to start a apiary, and at the same time designed several buildings on Front Street. In 1880, he designed a large store and warehouse for Captain John Irving in Chilliwack. Graham died in San Diego about 1899.

GREENE & GREENE

EDWARD R. BOSLEY

Charles Sumner Greene (1868-1957) and Henry Mather Greene (1870-1954) are appreciated today as architects who gave high-art form to the North American Arts and Crafts movement in the early years of the twentieth century. For a fortunate clientele they combined their fraternal talents with formal training into a rare symbiosis that produced houses and complementary furnishings of acclaimed artistic beauty and craftsmanship. Beginning their Pasadena,

California, practice in 1894, the Greenes were soon known for distinctive dwellings that harmonized with the topography and climate of the region. Adhering to a few simple tenets – looking beyond the dictates of history, learning from the best examples of contemporary architecture, and executing work to the highest standards – successfully sustained the Greene & Greene firm for more than twenty years. Ultimately, though, it was the brothers' familial bond that sustained their collaborative genius and made possible the creation of exceptional works of art and craft. Charles was the principal designer and Henry, the younger of the two, ran the office and made sure the draftspeople on staff converted his brother's conceptual sketches into buildable architecture.

Of the more than 200 Greene & Greene houses only one was designed for a site outside California, the exception being the house designed in 1904 for Roger Henry Carlton Green on Robson Street in Vancouver's West End. The two-storey, five-bedroom house was drawn up in elevation and plan by Greene & Greene in Pasadena, with construction probably supervised by a local architect. Eight drawings of the house survive at Columbia University's Greene & Greene collection in the Avery Library. The client had only recently moved from the Southern California town of Sierra Madre. Descendants of the original client recall the solid construction of the house, the extensive use of stain-grade finish panelling, and the occasional sash of hand-crafted leaded art glass. The half-timbered exterior treatment of the Green house recapitulated the architects' earlier James Culbertson house, 1902, in Pasadena, which had been inspired by the publication of an American architect's interpretation of an English country house. The historical reference to, and physical characteristics of, the English house makes far less sense in Pasadena than it does in Vancouver, however, where the inherited culture and a cooler climate are more sympathetic to the style.

The house presented an imposing and balanced mass to the street, with a single-level octagonal glass-roofed conservatory creating visual interest on the east side. The interior plan allowed for a clear line of sight from the reception hall on the south, through the drawing room windows, to the rear verandah that over-looked Coal Harbor and Burrard Inlet. This treatment of the plan was an important pre-

cursor to the close connection between natural views and interior spaces that the Greenes promoted in their later, classic designs such as the Blacker, Gamble, Pratt and Thorsen houses. Also prescient in the design for the Green house was the square-cross plan of the drawing room, which, like the Gamble House, 1907-09, divided the room into functional subsets, with an inglenook set opposite a bay of windows.

Sadly, the Green house in Vancouver was demolished for high-rise construction in 1969, and did not survive into the era of renewed interest in the work of Charles and Henry Greene. If it had, we would still have today a rare insight into the only built work of architecture the Greenes saw fit to export from their adopted Southern California.

GROB, T.

DONALD LUXTON

T. Grob, "recently derived from San Francisco," appeared in Victoria in 1861, advertising himself as an architect and artist "now prepared to fulfil orders in all of the different branches of his profession." One of his first projects was to design a red silk banner, trimmed with gilt fringe, for the Tiger Engine Company for their Fireman's May Day procession. The matter of payment ended up in court, and Grob lost the case. Nothing is known of his architectural activities, and Grob appears to have disappeared soon afterwards, his fate unknown.

HARVIE, Robert
1857-1932

DONALD LUXTON

Robert Harvie was born in the parish of Bottewell, Lanarkshire Scotland, on May 17, 1857. He served an apprenticeship as a junior building contractor for ten years, and studied construction and architecture at the Glasgow Technical College and Glasgow School of Art. Harvie was hired as the Inspector of Works for Bottewell Parish School Board for four years, during which time he erected six schools. For the following six years, he was Inspector of Works for Scotland for Pugin & Pugin of London, and supervised the construction of seven churches and five schools. From 1895-1912 he practised as an architect in Scotland, and then in 1912 moved to Vancouver, B.C. Unfortunately for Harvie, he arrived at the end of the boom years and his career languished, although it picked up again during the mid-1920s. In 1926, Harvie designed two prominent surviving Presbyterian churches, in the Mount Pleasant and Kerrisdale neighbourhoods, and the Metal Crafts Building on Beatty Street; of these three buildings, the church in Mount Pleasant survives. Harvie died at the age of seventy-five on March 10, 1932, survived by his wife and five children.

HAYES, Warren H.
1847-1899

DONALD LUXTON

Warren H. Hayes, an architect from Minneapolis, provided the plans for St. Andrew's Presbyterian Church in Nanaimo, 1892-93. Born in Prattsburg, Steuben County, New York, he studied architecture at Cornell University before settling in Minneapolis in 1881. A specialist in church design, he was credited with developing the diagonal form of auditorium, in which the altar was set in one corner of the square plan to allow a more efficient layout of the mezzanine, of which St. Andrew's is a fine example. Despite his early death, he designed over fifty churches.

HAZELTINE, Louis R.

JENNIFER NELL BARR

From 1908-10 Louis R. Hazeltine had his architectural practice in Salem, Oregon, but by 1912 he was working in Victoria, B.C. It is not known whether he was originally British or American, because his Victoria buildings conform to both the British Arts and Crafts and California Mission styles. Among the former is a house for Messrs. Ford and McIntyre on St. Andrews Street, 1912. The latter includes a residence for P.D. Morrison on Rockland Avenue, 1912, and the spectacular Alkazar Apartments, 1913, for local contractor **Alex McCrimmon**. The latter stood high above Fairfield Road at the corner

of Linden Avenue until its demolition in 1977. Hazeltine also designed two back-to-back Craftsman Bungalows on Empress Avenue and Bay Street for builder, John Robin Clarke, and a vaudeville and moving picture theatre on Fort Street between Blanshard and Douglas Streets. By September, 1913 he was involved in a lawsuit with developers, K.S. Patrick and George Ireland, who had reneged on the payment of the architect's fees. After the preparation of two sets of plans, the proposed structure was not built, because the owners couldn't finance the project. The judge decided for the plaintiff, and Hazeltine was awarded $400 as the fee of 2% of the tendered cost of the building. Architects **J.C.M. Keith** and **Jesse M. Warren** "gave testimony substantially endorsing the plaintiff's statements as to the rates charged by the profession." By August 1914, Hazeltine's office was located in his residence, and by 1915 he had disappeared from the Victoria area, later practising in Portland, Oregon.

HELYER, J.S & Son

DAVID MONTEYNE AND DONALD LUXTON

J.S. Helyer and his son, Maurice, formed a partnership in Vancouver that was responsible for numerous small buildings as well as several large commercial structures. John Shaw Helyer (1857-1919) was born in England. He married Mary Jane Young, and they and their son Maurice (1887-1973) had immigrated to Canada by 1902. Maurice moved to San Francisco in 1904-06 to apprentice with the firm Myers & O'Brien, and then returned to Vancouver to work as a junior partner in his father's office. The firm was immediately successful. The most famous of their designs is the *Beaux-Arts* skyscraper on Victory Square known as the Dominion Trust Building, 1908-10, at the time of its completion the tallest building in the British Empire. The firm also erected the Renaissance-style, ten-storey Metropolitan Building on Hastings Street, 1911-12, and the poured-in-place concrete Board of Trade building at Homer and Cordova, 1909, arguably one of the earliest local uses of concrete as both a structural and a finishing material. Another project was a tall and narrow speculative office block, the Exchange Building on Hastings Street, 1909, for which John S. Helyer was also one of the investors. Maurice

Helyer later joined **McCarter & Nairne** in the capacity of structural engineer, and it was likely his expertise that allowed Helyer & Son to tackle their early skyscrapers; indeed, John McCarter later recalled that John S. Helyer was the artist in the father-son partnership. J.S. Helyer was involved in a short-lived partnership with **W.H. Archer** in 1912-14, but their output appears to have been negligible. In 1915 Helyer suffered a stroke, and was largely bed-ridden until his death on October 29, 1919. Maurice Helyer enlisted in 1916 and became a Lieutenant in the Canadian Railway Troops, winning a Military Cross for conspicuous gallantry and devotion to duty. Although he registered with the AIBC, *Maurice Helyer* seems to have done mainly engineering work in the 1920s. One building where he was responsible for the design was the sophisticated Medical Arts Building on Granville Street, 1922-23. Maurice Helyer remained in practice until 1964. Predeceased by his wife Mabel, he died October 17, 1973.

HODGINS, Arthur Edward
1861-1939

DONALD LUXTON

Although primarily a civil engineer, surveyor and railway builder, Arthur Edward Hodgins rode the crest of Nelson's building boom, and had a brief but active architectural career. Born in Toronto on April 15, 1861, he attended Upper Canada College and the Royal Military College at Kingston. After graduation in 1882 he joined the CPR construction department as a civil engineer. He also acted as the divisional engineer for the construction of the Inter-Oceanic Railway of Mexico, and was in charge of surveys for straightening the Don River through Toronto. By 1890 he had settled in Nelson, and supervised various public projects, including the construction of the government wharf and the grading of city streets. In 1893 he oversaw construction of the first court house, designed by Victoria architect, A. Maxwell Muir. Throughout the 1890s he supervised a number of other buildings in Nelson and, on the basis of his practical experience, was hired to design some on his own, including a commercial block for J.A. Mara and F.S. Barnard on Baker Street, c.1897; the Madden Hotel on Ward Street, c.1898; the London & B.C. Goldfields Block on Baker Street, 1899-

1900; and an imposing residence, Hochelaga, 1899 for A.H. Buchanan, the manager of the Bank of Montreal. Hodgins was agitating for a local militia, and when the Rocky Mountain Rangers were re-established as an active unit in 1897, he became the commanding officer. At six foot four inches, he was noted as being the tallest man in the unit. When the Boer War broke out in 1899, the Rangers joined the Royal Canadian Regiment and went to South Africa. At the time of his departure, Hodgins left a number of his building projects unfinished or not yet started. After action at Paardeburg and Bloemfontein, Hodgins was promoted to the rank of Major. In 1901 he was appointed officer in charge of construction for Imperial military railways in South Africa, and remained there after the end of the war. Returning to Canada in 1904, he became District Engineer in charge of the location and construction of the Grand Trunk Pacific Railway from Winnipeg to Lake Nipegon. In 1907 he visited Victoria with a view to settling there, and in 1909 he and his wife retired to Duncan. Not long idle, Hodgins was appointed assistant public works engineer for Vancouver Island in April 1914, and moved to Victoria in 1915. During the First World War he went overseas but was invalided home after fourteen months. Lieutenant-Colonel Hodgins died December 18, 1939 at the age of seventy-eight, survived by his wife and three children.

HOPE, Charles Edward
1864-1949

JANET COLLINS

Charles Edward Hope played a prominent part in the early development of British Columbia. Like his older brother, Archibald Campbell Hope, he articled with his father's architectural firm in Bradford, Yorkshire. He immigrated to Canada the year after the Dominion was spanned by the Canadian Pacific Railway, finally settling in Vancouver in 1889, and was one of the few trained architects working in the period after the Great Fire. C.E. Hope's work as an architect, civil engineer, and estate and financial agent caused him to travel extensively throughout the province on business. In 1890, Hope arrived in Langley to survey the subdivision of Alexander Mavis's farm; two years later, he married Mavis's daughter, Lily

Dawson. He maintained an office in Vancouver, and until the end of 1893 was busy designing a number of large business blocks and "a goodly number of residences." However the local downturn meant there were few architectural commissions available, and Hope turned primarily to work as a land surveyor. After the floods of 1894 subsided, he walked from Agassiz to Ladner while inspecting damage for British interests. In 1897, he formed a timber agency and surveying partnership with W.E. Gravely, which became known as Hope, Gravely & Co. The partnership was dissolved in 1930. In 1909, the Hope family settled in Fort Langley, and it is here that Charles Hope's finest architectural designs were made. He designed the Coronation Block on Glover Road, 1911, and Illahie, an estate home for his growing family built on five acres of property, 1912. Charles Hope died April 27, 1949 in Fort Langley. As testament to his importance to the community, his funeral was the largest held in the town up until that time. Hope was survived by three sons and two daughters.

HOPKINS, John W. & E.C.

DONALD LUXTON

Based in Montreal, this father and son partnership designed two prominent buildings in early Vancouver, the Vancouver Opera House, 1888-91, and the Lord Elphinstone Block, Granville Street, Vancouver, 1888-89. John Williams Hopkins (1825-1905) was born in Liverpool, England and moved to Montreal in 1852. His son, Edward Colis Hopkins (1857-1941) was born in Montreal and trained with his father. The Hopkinses formed a partnership that lasted until Edward relocated to Edmonton, Alberta where he was appointed first Provincial Architect in 1906. The Lord Elphinstone Block was "much admired, not only for the exceedingly tasteful front on Granville Street, consisting entirely of granite, but for the thorough and perfect manner in which all the details have been carried out." Both of these early Vancouver buildings have been demolished.

HORSBURGH, Victor Daniel
1866-1947

DONALD LUXTON

Horsburgh was a Scottish architect who immigrated to Canada during the Edwardian boom years and became one of the country's leading bank architects. Born in Edinburgh, he was the son of well known artist John Horsburgh. At a young age Victor was apprenticed to Sir Rowand Anderson in Edinburgh, and later worked with other leading Edinburgh and London architects. In 1907 he won the Essay Medal of the Royal Institute of British Architects. While engaged in private practice in Edinburgh in 1910, he was appointed supervisory architect of the Dominion Realty Co. Ltd., the property-holding subsidiary of the Canadian Bank of Commerce based in Toronto, a position he held until his retirement in 1933. He designed many prominent and sophisticated bank buildings throughout the country, including a number in British Columbia. His surviving projects for the Bank of Commerce include a branch in Nanaimo, 1913-14 (now the Great National Land Company Building), and two buildings in Vancouver: the imposing branch office at Main and Pender Streets, 1914-15; and the Vault Building on East 1st Avenue, 1915, now converted to condominiums. **W.F. Gardiner** acted as local supervising architect for the two Vancouver projects. Horsburgh, remembered as a "kindly, courteous and scholarly gentleman," retired to Victoria, B.C., where he lived for the last two years of his life with his niece. He died on September 12, 1947.

HOUGHTON, Edwin Walker
1856-1927

DONALD LUXTON

For a number of years, E.W. Houghton was the leading theatre designer in the Pacific Northwest, and his projects were built through the Western United States and even in Canada. Born in Hampshire, England on August 5, 1856, he was trained in the family profession of architecture and quantity surveying. In the mid-1880s, he immigrated to the area near El Paso, Texas, and for the next four years was unsuccessful in his attempts to farm. He moved west to Pasadena, where he established an architectural practice, and then moved north to take advantage of the opportunities offered by Seattle's Great Fire of 1889. Houghton remained in Seattle for the rest of his life, and established a prolific practice, specializing in theatres, with over seventy to his credit. In 1909 he hired B. Marcus Priteca as a draftsman, who quickly eclipsed Houghton as the leading local theatre designer when he was hired in 1910 as the exclusive architect for the Pantages chain. Houghton, however, continued a steady stream of theatre and other projects. His first known project in British Columbia was a proposed four-storey brick and stone theatre and hotel for Messrs. Dean & Barrett on Columbia Street in New Westminster, 1907, which was never built. From his office in Seattle he sent the plans for a tall, narrow office skyscraper on Granville Street for real estate and mining broker Miss Rosa L. Leigh Spencer, which included her fashionably fitted-out penthouse residence, one of the first in Vancouver; when the building was finished in 1910 Houghton opened his Vancouver office there. Called the Leigh-Spencer Building, this sophisticated brick and terra cotta-clad structure was demolished in the 1990s. By 1912 Houghton was in partnership with his son, Gordon, and E.W. Houghton & Son maintained an office in Vancouver until 1913. For the E.R. Ricketts Amusement Co. they provided the design for the Kinemacolor Theatre, inserted into the old Van Horne Block on Granville Street, 1912-13. Opened on February 24, 1913, this was the first of its type in Canada; Kinemacolor was an early colour film process, but proved to be a short-lived phenomenon, and the following year it was renamed the Colonial Theatre, a name it retained until its final demise in the 1970s. The Houghton office's largest local project was a proposed theatre and apartment building for the Vancouver Opera House Company on West Pender Street, which would have cost $400,000 to build. The plans were finished in early 1913, but construction of this large complex was never completed due to the downturn in the local economy. Houghton died in Seattle on May 16, 1927.

HOY, Henry
1845-1931

DONALD LUXTON

Henry Hoy was primarily a contractor but also participated in the design of buildings.

Born in Fifeshire, Scotland on March 2, 1845, he apprenticed as a carpenter, and immigrated to Toronto in 1869. After four years he moved to Chicago, and then Winnipeg, and settled in New Westminster in 1876. Hoy built his own home in 1878 to plans provided by **T.W. Graham**. Hoy, however, designed the still extant St. Andrew's Presbyterian Church on Glover Road in Fort Langley, 1885. In addition to his contracting business, Hoy served several terms on New Westminster Council and a term as Mayor in 1894. He died in Royal Columbian Hospital on February 9, 1931, after being struck by a car.

HUNTER, John Douglas
1907-1989

DONALD LUXTON

J.D. Hunter worked with only one firm, **McCarter & Nairne**, during his entire career. He was born in Wandsworth, London, England, in 1907. When he was a few years old, his family immigrated to Departure Bay on Vancouver Island, where his sister, Hilda, was born in 1912. The family relocated to Burnaby, where "Doug" attended school before being engaged as a junior draughtsman at McCarter & Nairne in about 1928. It was a busy time at the office, with several of their most prominent projects under development. Hunter was called into J.Y. McCarter's office to take over some design work on the Marine Building from an architect who was proving to be unreliable due to his fondness for women and drink. On the Marine Building and many others, Hunter demonstrated real artistic talent, and over the course of his career produced presentation renderings for many of the firm's projects. Although he never registered with the AIBC, he remained with McCarter & Nairne until his retirement in the 1970s. A long-term resident of West Vancouver, he died in 1989.

IRVING, David W.

JENNIFER NELL BARR

In 1912 David Irving was in Victoria, working as an architect in the office of **J.C.M. Keith**. In July that year he completed plans for a shingled Arts and Crafts church for the St. Paul's Evangelical Lutheran congregation on Princess Avenue. These plans were sub-

mitted under his own name but the office address given was that of Keith's. The same is true of a house for Thomas Sumner designed in January 1913. However, by the next month, when he designed a house on Gladstone Avenue for W.F. Emery, Irving's address was 422 Menzies Street. By 1914 he was no longer in Victoria.

JAMESON, Reyburn

DONALD LUXTON

Reyburn Jameson was active in North Vancouver for just two years, 1911-12, and designed a handful of buildings. His impressive hall for the North Vancouver Knights of Pythias opened on January 4, 1912, and was demolished in 1989. He also undertook one project in North Vancouver, a Boarding and Day School, with **Henry Blackadder** in 1912. Surviving house designs include a beautifully-detailed Craftsman style residence perched on the edge on a ravine on West 15th Street, and a grand home for A.B. Diplock, both in North Vancouver, 1912. Jameson's origins and fate are not known.

JOHNSON, Harry G.
1894-1970

DONALD LUXTON

Professionally restless, Harry G. Johnson worked for some of the more prominent firms in Canada and the United States before ending up in Vancouver. Born in London, England on March 13, 1894, from 1910-12 he was articled to architect D.A. Beveridge of Liverpool, then moved to Montreal, where he worked in office of Ross & MacDonald, and studied in the *Atelier Maxwell*. Johnson then moved to Chicago, where from 1915-18 he was employed by Graham, Burnham & Company, the successor firm to D.H. Burnham & Company. Johnson then worked briefly for Howells & Stokes in Chicago. In these offices he worked under designers "considered among the best... in Eastern Canada or the Eastern States." During the First World War he was rejected for active service, and was engaged by the Industrial Housing Bureau of the American Department of Labor & Transportation in Bremerton, Washington, until April, 1919. He then relocated to Vancouver, B.C., where he worked for the next few months for **Gillingham & Körner**, **Maclure & Lort**, and the 20th Century House Co. From August, 1919 to April 1920, he was employed by **Somervell & Putnam**, and when their office folded, shifted over to the **Dominion Construction Company**. By 1923 he had left Vancouver; he died on September 13, 1970 in San Jose, California, survived by his wife, Alice, their son and daughter, and five grandchildren.

JONES, Morley Oscar
1869-1956

DONALD LUXTON

Morley Jones was born in Cannington, Ontario on November 17, 1869. After completing high school, he spent seven years in a study of construction with his father, an architect and builder who had technical training in these fields. Young Morley spent two years in technical school in Toronto, and then headed west to Winnipeg in search of opportunity. He commenced work for architect, Frank Evans, and during his time in this office worked on the first reinforced concrete office building erected in Winnipeg, for Sir James Akins. Jones was later employed by the Provincial Architect of Manitoba, Samuel Hooper, the brother of **Thomas Hooper**. After completion of the Grey Nuns Convent, Jones opened his own office and erected ten rural schools for the Board of Education before he left Manitoba to move to Vancouver in 1907. Soon after his arrival, he met English-born George Joseph Ketterer Aspell (1884-1974), who was working as a draftsman at the B.C. Drafting & Blue Printing Co., and the two men entered into partnership. They rode the crest of the boom years, working on a variety of different commissions, including St. Edmund's Catholic School and Rectory in North Vancouver, 1911-13. Jones & Aspell specialized in grand Craftsman style-homes for wealthy clients in the Shaughnessy Heights and Mount Pleasant neighbourhoods, including one for Vancouver Mayor Truman S. Baxter that made extensive use of granite and random, oversize clinker bricks, 1913. Jones also designed dozens of smaller buildings, a Catholic School at Cranbrook, and an eight-room public school at Emerson, Manitoba. During the First World War Aspell went overseas on active service, but Jones continued his architectural work,

and was also employed at a local contracting firm. Aspell never resumed an architectural practice, but remained in the building industry until his retirement; he died in White Rock in 1974 at the age of ninety, survived by his wife Caroline, and was interred in the Field of Honour at Sunnyside Lawn. After the First World War ended Jones resumed a solo practice, registering with the Architectural Institute of B.C. in 1922. Jones retired in 1940, and died on April 17, 1956 at the age of eighty-five.

JONES, William Francis
1881-1947

DONALD LUXTON

William F. "Bill" Jones was born in Aberdovey, North Wales on September 24 1881. He articled in architecture and surveying with Frank H. Shayler, Oswestry, Shropshire, starting in 1896, and by 1903 had immigrated to Winnipeg. Four years later he moved to Vancouver, and in 1908 opened his own architectural office. He landed a plum commission, for the design of the new Point Grey Municipal Hall, 1909. That year he married Frances Caroline Foster, with whom he had two children. He was busy designing a variety of commissions, and was listed as an architect in Eburne, obviously retaining an interest in agriculture which later became his primary pursuit. From 1910-13 he was in partnership with Walter M. Thornton, and for the next few years they had a productive output of commercial and apartment blocks, including the Felix Apartments in Vancouver, 1910, and the Arundel Mansions in New Westminster, 1912-13. The Arundel, hailed as the "last word in comfort, convenience and home-like appearance," is beautifully preserved, displays especially fine Arts and Crafts tile and woodwork detailing throughout its interior, and retains its original "Van-E-Mon" elevator, the first in New Westminster to operate without an attendant. Thornton disappeared from the local scene in 1913. After the end of the First World War, Jones was chosen to design the new Richmond Municipal Hall, Richmond, 1919, which like his earlier Point Grey Hall, relied on Tudor Revival elements to unify a large rambling structure. In 1924-25, Jones was briefly in partnership with **Ross Lort**, but gave up architecture at that point. After years of 'hobbying' with cattle, he opened up the

Brooksbank Laboratories Limited "Certified Milk" Farm on No. 3 Road in Richmond, producing "Vitamine D and other special milks for infant and invalid use." By the 1940s he owned about one hundred head of cattle, and conducted "successful investigation into feeding for increased mineral content of milk," but lost the farm during the Second World War when his son "mortgaged the cows." He lived in Marpole at 8390 Heather Street for many years, and died on March 10, 1947 at the age of sixty-five.

JULIEN, Phillip

DONALD LUXTON

Philip Julien's known output was meagre, but two prominent waterfront buildings that he designed still stand. The Kensington Apartments, 1912, is a prominent landmark on English Bay in Vancouver. *Riffington* is a magnificent waterfront home on Beach Drive in the Uplands, Oak Bay, built in 1913 for Andrew Wright, the manager of the Lansdowne Floral Gardens Company. It was later occupied by the U.S. Consul, and then by Hubert Wallace, brother of Lieutenant-Governor Clarence Wallace. Julien also designed a movie theatre for the Rex Amusement Co. Ltd., 1913, announced in the papers as a "Magnificent New Photo-Playhouse." The Rex Theatre was located on West Hastings Street, and has since been demolished.

KAYLL, Swinburne Annandale
1892-1962

DONALD LUXTON

Swinburne Annandale Kayll was born in Middlechurch, Manitoba on June 17, 1892 to Andrew James and Sarah Jane Kayll. Starting in 1909 he worked and studied under **W.F. Gardiner**, and later worked as an assistant to **R. Mackay Fripp**. He continued his studies for two years at the University of Pennsylvania, Philadelphia, before returning to Canada, and served with Royal North West Mounted Police for one year, 1915-16 before going overseas with the Canadian Expeditionary Force. He returned in May 1919, and by October of that year he had opened his own practice in Vancouver. The following year he established a partnership with **Max B. Downing** that lasted for four years. Kayll was noted as playing a banjo solo at the first annual AIBC banquet, held on February 25, 1921. He resigned from the Institute in 1929 when he gave up his practice and went to work for **Townley & Matheson**, but was reinstated in 1938. In the mid-1950s he opened an office in Prince George, with James Hutchinson in charge. One of his last buildings was the Grandview Citadel for the Salvation Army on East 1st Avenue, 1957. Kayll resigned from the AIBC in 1958 due to ill health, and died in 1962.

KEAGEY, James W.

DONALD LUXTON

J.W. Keagey started work in Vancouver about 1910, and through the boom years designed a variety of residences, warehouses and commercial projects. His best known building is a large Tudor Revival structure on the waterfront in Stanley Park designed for the Vancouver Rowing Club, 1911. He also designed two adjacent Arts and Crafts houses in the Kerrisdale neighbourhood in 1913. Keagey was active in Vancouver until about 1920, but his output after 1914 appears to have been minimal.

KELLY, James

DONALD LUXTON

James Kelly was a self-taught designer and builder who made his mark in Nanaimo. In 1889 he was working as a coal miner, and between 1890-92 as a contractor. He began to advertise as an architect, and during the local building boom of 1892-93 he was kept busy designing, and sometimes building, commercial blocks and residences. One of his surviving designs in Nanaimo is the Davidson Block on Victoria Crescent, built in 1892 at a cost of $12,000, and known since 1899 as the Queen's Hotel. This was the time when more permanent brick buildings were replacing pioneer wooden structures, and the Davidson Block helped establish Victoria Crescent as an important business strip. In 1893 Kelly designed and built Nanaimo's grandest Victorian era mansion for prominent busi-

nessman and politician Andrew Haslam, who was Mayor at the time. Designed in high Queen Anne style, *Haslam Hall* was a marvel of carpenter ornamentation, festooned with brackets and scrollwork that reflected Haslam's position as the owner of Nanaimo's largest sawmill. The interior was equally opulent. The large front hall had a twelve-foot-high domed ceiling with bas-relief cherubs against a painted sky, and an elegant curved staircase. Haslam ultimately lost his fortune, and by 1906 the house was sold at auction. It began a long, slow decline which culminated with its destruction by fire on Christmas Eve, 1977, just five days after it received heritage designation. It was commented at the time that the house may have suffered 'financial combustion.' The site remains today as a vacant lot. Kelly designed two small houses for Haslam on Hecate Street, 1893; the Wolfe Block, a two-storey brick and stone structure at the corner of Commercial and Bastion Streets in 1895; and a similar structure in 1901 for the Canadian Bank of Commerce, demolished in 1913 to make way for larger quarters. In 1897, he was preparing plans for the women's ward for the City Hospital. Kelly supervised the relocation of the Abbotsford Hotel from Wellington to Ladysmith in 1900, and the following year designed additions to the Union Brewery in Nanaimo. The following years saw little construction underway in Nanaimo, and Kelly moved to Vancouver, opening a practice there by 1905. That year he called for tenders for a Catholic church in Vancouver. Until he closed the office in 1915 his architectural output appears to have been minimal, and he likely followed pursuits other than architecture.

KENWAY, Balston C.

DONALD LUXTON

The restless Balston C. Kenway passed through Vancouver briefly in 1889, seeking opportunities as he moved throughout the west. During the early 1880s he practised as an architect in Winnipeg, providing designs for the new St. Mary's Church and the Bank of Montreal. From there he moved to Calgary, where he worked for the federal government as Superintendent of Public Works until late 1888. It was reported in the Calgary *Daily Herald* on October 3, 1888 that "Mr. B.C. Kenway intends severing his connection with

the public works department shortly, and will open an office in a few days for the practice of his profession, in which he has had twenty-four years experience." By February of the following year he had left to try his hand in Vancouver, and the Vancouver *Daily World*, May 1, 1889 stated "We call attention to the public to the card of Mr. Balston C. Kenway, architect, who is a late arrival in the city. He is opening an office in the Wilson block." The extent of his practice is unknown, and by 1890 he was back in Winnipeg, where he undertook several commissions for the Hudson's Bay Company.

KERR, Robert Claud
1866-1938

DONALD LUXTON

R.C. Kerr was born in Glasgow, Scotland in 1866. In 1884 he was articled to John Honeyman, Glasgow, the uncle of **J.J. Honeyman** and one of the most distinguished Scottish architects of the Victorian era. During his apprenticeship Kerr also attended evening classes held by the Architect's Association of Glasgow, and Anderson College, Glasgow. By 1898 he was working in Chicago, Illinois, and for the next two years was employed by a number of firms, including J.L. Silsbee, gaining experience on a variety of projects including steel-frame construction. In 1900 he practiced briefly in Webb City, Missouri, but from 1901-11 worked in Seattle, Washington. His projects there included work on the State Armory, Seattle, 1909; three Seattle fire stations, 1906-1907; and numerous residences. In 1912 he relocated to Vancouver, where he designed a number of residences. Kerr was informally in partnership with **Richard T. Perry** from 1926-28, and together they designed the Second Church of Christ Scientist, 1926 and Ryerson United Church, 1927-28, both in Vancouver. On his own, Kerr designed the Third Church of Christ Scientist in Vancouver's West End, 1927, an unusual low-slung shingled hall with stone-clad foundations, since rebuilt as an apartment building. Kerr died in Vancouver on October 22, 1938 at the age of seventy-six, survived by his wife Janet.

KERR, Thomas Logan
1887-1941

DONALD LUXTON

T.L. Kerr was born in Edinburgh, Scotland on November 8, 1887, the son of John Kerr, a labourer, and Georgina Logan, who had emigrated from Ireland. He was a pupil of Sir Rowand Anderson, Fellow of the Royal Institute of British Architects, Edinburgh, and attended a three-year Course at Heriot-Watt College in construction and art, starting in 1903. Following opportunity, Kerr relocated to North America and moved around restlessly to a number of different cities, including Montreal, and Winnipeg, where he worked for five years for **J.H.G. Russell**, and was licensed to practise in 1921. By 1925 he was working in California, and designed a string of projects, including the Municipal Buildings in Alhambra, 1925, a school in Santa Anita, 1927, and churches in Los Angeles, Long Beach and Pasadena. He relocated to Vancouver, and worked for **Townley & Matheson** for three and one-half years, where his office nickname was "Silhouette Tommy." In 1931, Kerr opened his own practice, and designed several prominent theatres in Vancouver, including the Plaza Theatre on Granville Street, 1936, and the Lux Theatre on Hastings Street, 1939. He died in Vancouver on January 13, 1941 at the age of fifty-three, survived by his wife Muriel and two children.

KING, William

DONALD LUXTON

William King was active as an architect in Revelstoke between 1909 and 1912, usually listed in the local newspapers as King & Co. He was responsible for the design of the eight-room brick and concrete Selkirk School, Revelstoke, 1909-10, which remained in active use until it was demolished in 1983. In 1910, King designed an imposing hotel in Revelstoke for the McSorley Brothers, named the King Edward to commemorate the death of King Edward VII; this landmark structure burned down in 1995. One of his notable surviving projects in downtown Revelstoke is a concrete block structure built for R. Howson & Co., 1910-11, now used as a Masonic Hall. King prepared plans in 1911 for a warehouse in Revelstoke for the F.H. Bairne

Company, which was never built. A surviving example of his residential work in Revelstoke is a house designed for E.A. Bradley, carried out in a "bungalow pattern" in 1909. King also provided the plans for the new court house and provincial building at Kaslo; the cornerstone was laid on the date of the coronation of King George V in 1911, and the building was completed in 1912. Two stories high with a full basement, this structure remains in active use. Despite his success in British Columbia, King appears to have left suddenly, and his origins, and his fate, remain unknown.

KING, William R.
BORN 1846

DONALD LUXTON

William R. King was active as an architect in New Westminster from 1888-96, but his local career came to an end with the economic downturn of the mid-1890s. Born in Canterbury, England in July, 1846, he was the son of a railway engineer. When King was a boy, the family moved to Ashford, Kent, where he received his education at public school under a teacher who had spent many years in eastern Canada. Young William was inspired to follow the progress of the Canadian Pacific Railway, which led to an interest in the "promising colony of British Columbia." King was apprenticed to an architect, and at the age of twenty-one commenced his own practice in partnership with his father. Soon after, he married the daughter of John Fowler, one of the leading local builders. "When his boys became old enough to start in life for themselves, the overcrowded condition of the Mother Country caused him to direct his attention to British Columbia." In the spring of 1888, King and his family set sail from England, and arrived in New Westminster a few weeks later. King is known to have prepared plans in 1888 for a residence for James Rousseau on Royal Avenue, and for an elaborate "Italian Renaissance" building on Lytton Square for the New Westminster Southern Railway Company that was never built. The following year in New Westminster he designed a brick residence for T.J. Trapp, a block on Columbia Street for Sheriff Armstrong, and five cottages for Mr. A. McInnes on St. Andrews Street. King also

designed the Anglican Bishop's Palace on Blackwood Street, New Westminster for Dr. Sillitoe in 1889, built at a cost of $15,000, and described at the time as "severe in appearance, and extremely ecclesiastical in design, being ornamented with crosses at its gable ends." Most of King's work in New Westminster was destroyed in the Great Fire of 1898. Another example of his work was the First Baptist Church on Hamilton Street in Vancouver, 1888-89, located on two lots donated by the Canadian Pacific Railway. the exterior was finished to resemble sandstone, and the style was described at the time as "Elizabethan." Typical of the city's first churches, it reflected the lofty ambitions of its congregation, which was determined to establish itself as part of the community. Given the difficulty of travel between Vancouver and New Westminster, construction of the church was supervised by **Thomas Hooper**, who was based in Vancouver at the time. The congregation later moved to a new church on Burrard Street; the old church was demolished in 1941 and its site later became part of the Queen Elizabeth Theatre complex. Despite his initial success, by late 1891 King was admitting financial embarrassment to his creditors. He stayed in business until 1896, after which he left New Westminster, and his subsequent fate is unknown.

KISHIDA, Isaburo

JIM WOLF

One of the most important early influences on British Columbia's distinctive landscape architecture style was the introduction of the Japanese garden, and the pioneer Japanese landscape architect in the province was Isaburo Kishida. He was a formally trained *Ko-en* (park) designer and gardener who had worked extensively in his home city of Yokohama. In 1906 his son, Yoshijiro "Joe" Kishida, who had immigrated to Victoria, began a partnership with Harry Takata to build and operate an authentic Japanese Tea Garden. They selected a location on the Gorge Park that had just been connected to the city by a BCER streetcar line. Isaburo Kishida was brought to B.C. to undertake the design and construction of this ko-en and all of its associated decorative elements and pavilions. The garden opened in 1907 and was a great success. It introduced the people of Victoria as well as tourists to Japanese hospitality and culture until the garden was closed and demolished in the 1940s during the forced displacement and internment of the Takata family. Local architects and home-builders of Victoria were impressed with the tea garden, and Kishida was subsequently asked to undertake a number of prominent commissions. One of the largest of these was at James Dunsmuir's *Hatley Park*, where Kishida worked in concert with the estate's architect, **Samuel Maclure**. The Japanese Garden became a focal point of the estate's 1913 plan, and was enlarged and elaborated with bridges and pavilions that were designed by Boston landscape designers Brett & Hall. This large formal garden still remains today. Maclure provided Kishida with two additional garden commissions. At Jennie Butchart's famous garden at Tod Inlet, Kishida left his mark with a distinguished garden, adapted to the superb local setting. Another garden collaboration by Maclure and Kishida emerged at the now-demolished *Clovelly* in Victoria West, which Maclure remodelled for client Sir Frank Barnard between 1912-28, including the design of a rustic garden pavilion. Although Kishida returned to Japan in 1912, he left the legacy of authentic Japanese architecture and landscape design in some of British Columbia's most visited, admired and photographed gardens. In the process, he influenced and inspired generations of local gardeners and landscape designers.

LAW, Alexander
1874-1956

DONALD LUXTON

Alexander "Alex" Law was one of many drawn briefly to western Canada during the boom years, and who kept moving after "things went bust." He was born in Edinburgh, September 18, 1874, the son of master joiner, Henry Law and Elizabeth Brown Law. The family was not wealthy, and in order to attend school, Alex had to earn scholarships. He studied architecture at Heriot-Watt College, and being athletic, he also played soccer and was well-known as a "heel-and-toe" long-distance walker. In 1902 he married Gwendolyn Millward of Rhyll, Wales, and by 1905 they had two daughters. Law had a good job in Edinburgh but "got the wanderlust," so in 1905 he packed up his family and moved to Canada, first to Toronto

but by 1907 had settled in Vancouver. He built their first home downtown near English Bay, but Law saw opportunity on the booming North Shore of Burrard Inlet, and soon relocated there. Much of what was happening in North Vancouver was speculative, and Law was soon in the thick of it, designing but also building houses. He was an investor and agent for an old friend, P. McOmish Dott of Edinburgh, and was soon so busy that in 1908 he persuaded his older brother, Robert, to move to North Vancouver to be in charge of the construction end of the business. In addition to a number of speculative houses, Law designed and built a prominent apartment building in North Vancouver, the Law Block on East 3rd Street, 1913, for Vancouver Properties Ltd. During the First World War he worked in Victoria for the Foundation Building Company, an American firm with interests in San Pedro, California. Through this contact he ended up in California in 1920; when work dried up during the Depression, the Laws bought an apple orchard in Oak Glen. They lived there until Alex died in 1956, and Gwendolyn in 1961.

LAWRENCE, R. Farror

DONALD LUXTON

R. Farror Lawrence passed through British Columbia just long enough to design one major building. He worked for the Provincial Department of Public Works in 1911, and was given the commission to design the new court house in Grand Forks, then a bustling mining community. This imposing brick and stone structure remains intact today as one of the Boundary County's heritage landmarks.

LEE, Robert Henry
1859-1935

DONALD LUXTON

Although primarily employed as a surveyor during his long career, Lee was a versatile pioneer who worked in a number of capacities, and also provided architectural designs when requested. R.H. Lee was born in Virginia, USA, in 1859, and then at an early age moved with his family to Portsmouth, Ohio and attended public schools there until

the age of sixteen, the year that he was orphaned. He joined a railway survey party, apprenticed as a chainman, and worked his way up to leader of his own survey party. He followed the railroads west to Colorado, settling there briefly before relocating to Washington, where he worked on projects for the Northern Pacific and Union Pacific lines. Seeing opportunity in the impending completion of the CPR line, Lee moved to Kamloops in 1884, and remained there for the rest of his life. He advertised his services as a surveyor and civil engineer, noting that his clients would receive "prompt attention." In addition to his preliminary survey of Kamloops, he laid out many townsites in the Interior, including Nicola, Merritt and Princeton. By May, 1885 his ad had changed to include his services as an Architect, and in addition to being the only local surveyor, he remained the only architect in Kamloops for many years. His busiest year as an architect seems to have been 1887, the climax of the railway's impact on Kamloops. That year alone, he provided designs for a Roman Catholic church, a number of private residences, a branch for the Bank of British Columbia, and the first Presbyterian church, which still stands today, and has been restored by the City of Kamloops. In addition to his busy surveying practice, lee briefly opened an assay office, and was a partner in a grocery and feed store. In 1889, he married Violet J. Tite in Victoria, and they returned to Lee's newly renovated home in Kamloops, which included "complicated plumbing involving hot and cold water" and one of the city's first fitted baths. Lee, now established, became active in civic affairs, and was elected to the first Kamloops Council in 1893. The following year he was elected as the city's second mayor, and was re-elected in 1895 and 1896. From 1897-1912 he spent many of his summers absent on long surveying trips, but also acted as City Engineer until his retirement in 1928. Kamloops had long been a transportation hub in the Interior, and Lee was kept busy after 1912 when the Canadian National Railway established their North Thompson line. He also continued to advertise his architectural services, and an example of his work is the extant Frederick E. Young house, 1910. Lee died in Kamloops on February 8, 1935, at the age of seventy-six, the last surviving member of the first Kamloops City Council.

LESLIE, H.H.

DOROTHY MINDENHALL AND
CAREY PALLISTER

H. H. Leslie left his architecture practice in Portland, Oregon, and travelled to Victoria in company with Mr. Tod, a builder, in April 1884; they had, according to the *Colonist*, "decided to embark on business in this city." The pair probably hoped to take advantage of the city's economy, which, due to railway construction, was not as depressed as elsewhere. Leslie worked in Victoria for about a year, during which time he designed houses in the more fashionable parts of the city, including a residence at the corner of Pakington and Cook Streets for prominent lawyer, William Tyrwhitt Drake, 1884 and a house at the southwest corner of Birdcage Walk and Superior Street (today the site of the Queen's Printers) for Provincial Auditor James McBraire Smith, 1884, both now demolished. The Smith house was of the same size, and probably style, as the Hunter and Robson houses which still stand just to the south. Leslie also designed a seventeen-room mansion for David W. Higgins, proprietor of the *Colonist*. The Higgins house, *Regents Park*, at the corner of Fort and St. Charles Streets, built 1885, still stands as a fine example of the high Victorian Italianate style and is notable for its split cantilevered staircase. This seems to have been Leslie's last work in Victoria.

LIGHTHEART BROTHERS

DONALD LUXTON

Primarily acting as contractors, the Lightheart Brothers established their firm in Vancouver in 1904, "since which time it has been a very real factor in the wood finish trade." Prior to this William Akitt Lightheart (1875-1966) and Joseph Robert Lightheart (1877-1971) had been working individually as builders. In 1904 they built a large factory at the corner of Helmcken and Seymour Streets. The Lighthearts went on to design and built a number of speculative apartment buildings during the pre-First World War boom years, including the grand Lightheart Apartments on the site of their factory, 1910-11, and the Royal Alexandra Apartments in the West End. Their activities as developers

and designers started again with the increasing prosperity of the mid-1920s. Oliver Richard Lightheart (1888-1971) designed a handsome three-storey brick apartment block in the West End, the Marlborough, 1928, built by **Baynes & Horie**. J.R. Lightheart designed the prominent three-storey brick Vallejo Court Apartments on West 10th Avenue at Oak Street, 1929. The Lighthearts made a living by managing the apartments that they built, until their retirement in the 1950s.

McARRAVY, Thomas Black
1900-1979

DONALD LUXTON

T.B. McArravy was Nanaimo's most prominent architect for many years, and was one of the pioneers of the use of modernism on Vancouver Island. Born in Glasgow on June 8, 1900, the son of Margaret Stewart and David Borland McArravy, he received his early education there before moving to Vancouver, where he entered the Model School. After this, he served four years with the Wallace Shipyards Ltd. as loftsman, and by the end of this time was working in the drawing office. Showing his ambition, he was also taking correspondence courses in shipbuilding and architecture. Starting September 1, 1921, he became an indentured pupil in the offices of **Gardiner & Mercer**. After he passed his final AIBC exams in 1927, he moved to Nanaimo, where he remained for most of his career. As the economy began to improve in the late 1930s, McArravy was kept busy with a number of commissions, including a contextual addition to the Globe Hotel, 1936 and a streamlined garage for Tom Brown's Auto Body, 1937. As early as 1940 he was preparing plans for his most significant project, Nanaimo City Hall. His earliest schemes bore a remarkable similarity to the dignified landmark structure that was finally built in 1950-51. Built of cast-in-place concrete, with steel windows imported from England, City Hall has survived in pristine condition, a testament to the skill of its designer. McArravy also undertook a number of residential projects in Nanaimo, and his Wardill Residence, 1945, remains one of the purest examples of the Streamline Moderne style in the province. He later formed a partnership with A.L. Barley, with whom he designed the

Vancouver Island Regional Library in Nanaimo, 1961. McArravy retired from active practice on December 31, 1963, and moved to Wellington, near Nanaimo. He died in Vancouver on September 19, 1979, leaving an impressive legacy of cleanly designed modern structures.

McCRIMMON, Alexander
1876-1958

JENNIFER NELL BARR

Alexander "Alex" McCrimmon, the only son of contractor, Duncan Farquhar McCrimmon and his wife Ellen, was born in Cornwall, Ontario on September 18, 1876. The family moved to Victoria in 1891. Duncan McCrimmon died in 1907 at the age of fifty-seven, and Alex continued in the contracting business. He built at least ten homes on or near Linden Avenue; Numbers 75 and 532 Linden are his most distinctive one-storey design – a bungalow with a chunky hipped roof and front hipped extension sheltering the corner verandah – and this design appears in a number of places in the city. He also designed and built elegant versions of the two-storey Arts and Crafts Edwardian house common in Victoria. His earliest known plans are for a 1908 house on Medana Street in James Bay, and his last known project was an alteration in the Rockland district in 1957. In 1913 he commissioned architect, **Louis R. Hazeltine**, to design the landmark Alkazar Apartments on Fairfield Road. Possibly Victoria's most distinctive early apartment block, it was demolished in 1977. Alex married Edna Heathfield Simons in Victoria in 1909, and the couple had two sons. Alex was a charter and life member of the Benevolent & Protective Order of Elks, Victoria Lodge No.2, and a member of Modern Woodmen of the World. He retired in 1957, died on May 7, 1958, and was buried in the family plot in Ross Bay Cemetery.

MacDONALD, James A.
1859-1926

DONALD LUXTON

James A. MacDonald was born in Exeter, Ontario in 1859, grew up in Winnipeg, and then trained as an architect in Minneapolis.

He arrived in the booming town of Nelson, B.C. and from 1900-01 was in partnership with English-born Henry Cane. They designed a number of residences, the most prominent being a Queen Anne-style home for successful plumber, Harold J. Strachan, and also shared supervisory duties on the Nelson Court House with **William Henderson**. MacDonald practiced on his own in Nelson from 1902-03, during which time he acted as the resident architect for the Federal DPW, and then left for Lethbridge, Alberta, where from 1903 until 1910 he had a busy architectural practice. In its early years, Lethbridge was connected to the CPR's Crowsnest-Medicine Hat railway by a 1.5 mile long spur, but in 1905 it became the CPR's regional divisional point, setting off a building boom that lasted until the outbreak of the First World War. MacDonald designed a number of the city's most prominent commercial and institutional buildings, including the extant Fire Hall #1, 1908. He relocated to Calgary in 1910, where he died in 1926.

MacKAY, Donald
C.1846-C.1887

D.E. MACKAY

The origins and fate of Donald MacKay remain obscure. American census data tells us that in 1880 he was living in Walla Walla, Washington, that he was thirty-four years old, and that he was a native of Scotland. His English wife of less than a year, Margaret, was seventeen. In 1882, in his capacity as architect, MacKay arrived in Seattle to supervise the construction of Providence Hospital, 1882-83. He designed a number of buildings, including both Protestant and Roman Catholic churches, and civic and institutional buildings throughout Washington State, demonstrating his skills and ability in handling different styles and types of structures. MacKay opened an office on Cordova Street in Vancouver in 1887, undoubtedly to take advantage of the rebuilding that followed the Great Fire, but it is uncertain how prolific he was. One project he tendered was a house for L.R. Johnson on Seymour Street, 1887, which featured an "observatory" on the roof. By the following year his wife, Margaret, was living in Portland, and was listed as a widow.

MACKENZIE, James Clark
1877-1941

DONALD LUXTON

James C. Mackenzie was born on November 6, 1877 in West Kilbride, Ayrshire, Scotland. He was educated at Ardrossan Academy, Ayr Academy and Glasgow High School, and in 1897, started a five year apprenticeship in Alexander Nisbet Paterson's office, Glasgow. Paterson, described as a "fastidious, comfortably off, and retiring architect, whose best work is too little known," had studied at the *Atélier Pascal*, and later worked for Aston Webb. After Mackenzie completed his services with Paterson, he went to Italy in 1902 for four months, and then practised in Dumfries for two years. Seeking new opportunities, James followed his older brother, William, to Prince Rupert, where one of their aunts lived. By 1908 he moved to Vancouver, where he entered the office of fellow Scot, **William Bow**. Mackenzie commenced his own practice in 1909, and worked mostly on residential projects in the Shaughnessy Heights subdivision. He also received the commission for the new West Vancouver Municipal Hall. The Vancouver *Daily Province*, June 1, 1912, reported that "the contract was awarded this week for the municipal hall... It has been designed to conform to the general style of suburban architecture. The whole building will be heated by hot air." In 1912 Mackenzie married Amy Crabtree, an English probationary nurse, and the following year he designed an elegant Craftsman-inspired home in the North Lonsdale area of North Vancouver for his new family, which included three children by 1917. From 1913-15 he worked in partnership with A. Scott Ker. Their largest commission was a grand home in Shaughnessy Heights for Frank L. Buckley, *Iowa*, on Osler Avenue, 1913-14. As work dried up during the First World War, Mackenzie moved his office to his home. Although times were lean, he designed at least one large residence, for Robert Gibson in the North Lonsdale area, 1915, and published an extensive catalogue of house plans, of which his own house was No. 514. After the war he was associated with the Architects Small House Service Bureau (B.C.), which offered a large selection of home plans for thirty dollars each. Mackenzie was also known as a designer of teapots depicting Haida designs, which were made in Japan and were very popular there. By 1920

Mackenzie had gone into partnership with William Bow, whose daughter remembers Mackenzie's wife as a large, imposing woman, who would drop their three children off at the office when she wanted to go shopping, creating endless disruption. The partnership terminated in 1923, and Mackenzie again practised on his own. He died on May 21, 1941 at age sixty-three.

McKENZIE, Robert
Alexander McKay
1888-1952

DONALD LUXTON

Robert A.M. McKenzie worked in the building trades for many years, and finally registered as an architect in 1925. Born January 30, 1888 in Uisden, Manitoba, by 1903 he was in Vancouver working in **Dalton & Eveleigh's** office, where he remained for five years. He then worked for a number of years as a building inspector for the City of Vancouver, during which time he also designed the Frontenac, one of the earliest brick apartments in the Mount Pleasant neighbourhood, 1910. McKenzie later worked for over five years in North China for Murphy, McGill & Hamlin, a firm based in New York. His experience apparently strengthened his ties to the local Chinese community in Vancouver, and he was chosen to design a headquarters building for the Chin Wing Chun Society in 1925. This tall and ornate balconied structure still stands on East Pender Street. He later worked as a draftsman for **Dominion Construction** until his retirement in May, 1953. Divorced, and living in a rooming house in the West End, he committed suicide on October 6, 1953 by sealing his room and turning on the gas. McKenzie was buried in the Returned Soldiers' Plot in Mountain View Cemetery.

McLUCKIE, John Macfarlane
1860-1927

Donald Luxton

J.M. McLuckie was born in Scotland in 1860, and came to Vancouver about 1884. Two years later he came to Vancouver and established himself as a contractor, and was extremely busy after the Great Fire levelled the settlement in 1886. He established a solid reputation, especially for Gastown commercial buildings, schools, hotels, and residences such as *Gabriola* for Benjamin Tingley Rogers, designed by **Samuel Maclure**. McLuckie constructed Vancouver's first "skyscraper," the massive nine-storey Kelly, Douglas Building on Water Street, by W.T. Whiteway, 1905. Although primarily a contractor, McLuckie also provided building designs when necessary. For the Malkin Company Warehouse, 55-65 Water Street, **Parr & Fee** designed the original, western half in 1907; McLuckie was hired as designer and contractor to double the size of the structure in 1911-12. McLuckie continued his contracting business until his death in Vancouver in 1927.

MACLEAN, Charles B.

DONALD LUXTON

C.B. Maclean was briefly active in Revelstoke at the turn of the century, undoubtedly drawn to the area by the mining boom. He was active as an architect from 1897-1901. In 1897 he was busy with designs for the Imperial Bank downtown, a "unique and comfortable" home for T. Downs on Mara townsite, and a home for Thomson Edgar Leon Taylor, the President of the Revelstoke Water, Light & Power Company. His most prominent design was for the new court house and jail. The sudden growth during the mining booms of the late 1890s overwhelmed the administrative facilities throughout the Boundary country and the Kootenays, and the authorities were scrambling to build court houses and establish law and order. Maclean prepared the plans and specifications in January, 1897. By May, "hard labour prisoners" were clearing the site. The new court house was opened with due pomp and ceremony on October 6, 1897 by Judge Forin, who "alluded to the charge of severity which had been brought against the administration of justice in the province... but the criminal classes would either have to behave themselves, or be punished, or leave the country." The new court room was impressive, measuring twenty by forty-five feet, with cedar wainscoting. Maclean's design bore more than a passing resemblance to the Nelson court house designed by **A. Maxwell Muir** in 1893, and actually copied the overall form and many of

the details. In about 1901 Maclean left Revelstoke, and his later movements are unknown.

MALLORY, John Wesley

DONALD LUXTON

J.W. Mallory practised briefly in Vancouver during the Klondike era. He was the son of Ontario architect William H. Mallory Sr., and trained under his father in Chatham, Ontario. From 1878-80 he was a member of the firm of W.H. Mallory & Son, then moved to Toronto in 1882. After the death of his father in 1886, John Mallory formed a new office with his brother Frank S. Mallory, called Mallory Brothers, Architects, which was active until 1896. In the June 1898 issue of *Canadian Architect & Builder* it was announced that J.W. Mallory had recently opened an office in Vancouver. Two months later it was noted in a local paper that he was in charge of a "vast amount of building work," although this claim appears to be highly exaggerated. Sometime during 1901, Mallory left Vancouver, likely to return to Ontario.

MAREGA, Charles
1871-1939

DONALD LUXTON

Charles Marega, the first and best known of Vancouver's professional sculptors, left his mark in stone, bronze and concrete. It was said at his funeral that 'there is no need to build him a monument - because of his sculpture he will never be forgotten.' Originally named Carlos, he was born on September 24, 1871 in Lucinico, in the commune of Gorizia near Trieste, then part of the Austro-Hungarian Empire. Marega and his wife Berta were on their way to California in October, 1909 when they passed through Vancouver. Staying at the Hotel Vancouver, when they woke up the next morning, the view north towards the mountains on a fine sunny fall day so reminded Berta of her native Switzerland that they decided to stay. Their timing was excellent. These were Vancouver's boom years, and as the most proficient local architectural sculptor and decorator, Marega soon attracted notice,

and numerous commissions. During the First World War the work dried up, but afterwards Marega was again busy. In 1925 the Vancouver School of Decorative & Applied Arts opened, and Marega was hired to teach sculpture, a part-time position he held until his death. The onset of the Great Depression brought tough times for Marega. He did secure some high profile work, such as many of the motifs for the Marine Building, the statuary for the new Vancouver Art Gallery on Georgia Street in 1931 and the sculptural decoration on the Burrard Bridge, opened in 1932, but these commissions did not appear with the same frequency as before. His beloved wife Berta, whom he referred to as *mama*, died in 1934, a blow from which he never fully recovered. Ironically, this low point in his life was a time of artistic triumph. His good friend, **Fred Townley**, the architect of Vancouver City Hall, ensured that he received the commission for a statue of Captain George Vancouver, which was unveiled by the Lord Mayor of London on August 20, 1936. His last and greatest public work was the monumental Lions, cast in concrete, that grace the southern entry to Vancouver's Lions Gate Bridge. Installed in January, 1939, the artistic success of these beautifully modelled sculptures were a remarkable culmination to Marega's career. Despite his many commissions, he died almost penniless. On March 27, 1939, just months after the Lions were finished, Marega collapsed and died of a heart attack at the Vancouver School of Art.

MELLADO, Bruno
1843-1922

DONALD LUXTON

Bruno Mellado was born in Santiago, Chile on October 19, 1843, and his family subsequently lived in Esquimalt, where he studied drafting and architecture. He moved to Nanaimo after he was hired by Robert Dunsmuir. In 1871 Mellado eloped with fifteen year old Mary Ann Thompson. Newspaper accounts reveal that "On Sunday afternoon – better the day better the deed – a young couple whose hearts had been pierced by Cupid's darts, embarked in a canoe at Nanaimo and were paddled to Victoria with all the speed with which the brawny arms of four Indians could propel the frail bark. They travelled all Sunday and Monday and yesterday in the afternoon a license was procured and the happy pair were made one at Mr. Alex Young's residence." They were married on August 22, 1871, and their wedding license was the first one issued by the new province of British Columbia. Mellado built, and possibly designed, the Identical Hotel on Victoria Crescent, for James McKay Sabiston in 1872; this "first class" hotel had its furniture shipped from England. Mellado built the first publicly-funded school in Nanaimo in 1873, designed by **Edward Mallandaine Sr.** After working in Nanaimo for a few more years he bought a farm in Nanoose sometime after 1881. The family later moved to Cumberland where Mellado again worked for the Dunsmuirs. Bruno and Mary Ann had at least twelve children, but only eight survived to maturity. Several of their children died in a diphtheria epidemic in December of 1892, during which the family was quarantined in their home; Mary Ann had to pass the dead babies through the window to her husband for burial. Despite a dramatic start and many hardships, the marriage was a long and happy one. Bruno died in Yakima, Washington, on August 4, 1922, and Mary Ann died soon afterwards.

MELLISH, Frederick William
1860-1928

DONALD LUXTON

F.W. Mellish was born in Ontario on April 11, 1860. He was active as an architect in Galt, Ontario from 1888 until 1909. Mellish relocated in 1909 to Vancouver and started working as a contractor and an architect. His earliest known project was a brick warehouse for the A.R. Williams Machinery Company, 1909, for which he also designed alterations in 1913. He worked mainly as a designer of houses; during the booming real estate market of 1912-13 he designed a number of speculative houses for Prudential Builders in Vancouver. In 1919 he built a superb Craftsman-style house on East 1st Avenue as a home for himself, his wife, Agnes, and their daughter, Winnifred; the Mellish Residence is in excellent condition and has recently been restored to its original colour scheme. Mellish also designed St. Saviour's Church on Semlin Drive in 1910, including later additions in 1918 and the Parish Hall in 1920. He died at home on April 15, 1928 aged sixty-

eight.

MIDDLETON, William
1864-1951

DONALD LUXTON

English-born William Middleton worked for many years for the Provincial Department of Public Works (DPW). Born in Tavistock, Devonshire, England, Middleton studied science, architecture, construction, drawing and drafting, and worked as a Head Master at various technical schools starting in 1880. About 1885, he was appointed as Head Master at the Tavistock School of Art, where he stayed for twenty-five years, until he and his wife, Louise, left in 1910 for Victoria, B.C. In July, 1911 Middleton began working for the Provincial DPW, and on April 1st, 1914 was officially appointed as a draftsman. He worked on many of the DPW's larger projects, including the Boys Training School, Coquitlam, 1920-22, and the Prince Rupert Court House, 1920-23. Middleton remained with the DPW until his retirement in about 1931. He died on February 12, 1951 at the age of eighty-six, survived by one son, Percy.

MILLS & HUTTON

DONALD LUXTON

Based in Hamilton, Ontario, the architectural partnership of Charles Mills (1860-1934) and his partner Gordon Hutton (1881-1942) designed two adjacent extant buildings, the Bank of Hamilton Chambers and the Aberdeen Block, in the City of North Vancouver. These brick-faced structures, both with sandstone trim and projecting metal cornices, form a substantial grouping on Lonsdale Avenue, and help define the character of North Vancouver's original commercial spine. Mills & Hutton designed most of the Bank of Hamilton branches in Canada between 1905-10.

MILNER, Warren H.

DONALD LUXTON

In 1910, **John R. Wilson**, who was based in Victoria formed a local partnership of

convenience with **Warren H. Milner** of Seattle, that lasted until about 1915. Milner had previously designed the Horse Show Building in Vancouver, 1908-09. Located at the corner of West Georgia and Gilford Streets, Vancouver, by the entry to Stanley Park, at the time of construction it was reportedly second only in size, for a building of its type, to Madison Square Garden in New York. It was temporarily converted into an armoury in 1914, and survived until it burned to the ground in 1960. Wilson & Milner Ltd. specialized in commercial and institutional buildings, apartment houses and residences, both in Victoria and Vancouver.

MITCHELL, Henry

DOROTHY MINDENHALL AND
CAREY PALLISTER

Henry Mitchell, architect and landscape gardener, and his wife Annie, came to Victoria in July 1862. In 1868, Mitchell and Philip Johnston formed a partnership in the seed and flower business and opened a store in the Occidental building, corner of Fort and Government Streets. The partnership lasted six years. Mitchell also undertook design work, the first record of which was the plans and specifications for fencing and road making at Ross Bay Cemetery in September 1872. Mitchell went on to design a number of frame cottages and houses as well as a school house and lecture room in 1882, on the Church Reserve at the corner of Rae and Quadra Streets, for Christ Church Cathedral. Among his houses was a large two-storey frame house on brick foundations for Henry Heisterman, 1875, which had a rustic finish in the "latest fashion," and a two-storey frame house at the head of Yates Street on the south side for Henry Moss, 1882. In 1877 he was operating Mitchell & Co., which offered both landscaping and building design services. The Mitchells left Victoria in May, 1888 to return to London, England due to the declining health of Mrs. Mitchell; in noting their departure the Colonist described Henry Mitchell as "the well known landscape gardener." Emily Carr had known the Mitchells when she was a child. She wrote about them in a chapter called "Loyalty" in *The Book of Small.*

MOBERG, Otto

DAVID MONTEYNE AND DONALD LUXTON

Almost nothing is known about this architect, likely of Scandinavian extraction, who practised in Vancouver for just a few years during the pre-First World War boom. Otto Moberg is known to have designed some large hotels downtown, including an extant six-storey hotel for William Walsh on Pender Street, 1912-13, and a few small apartments and industrial buildings. However, Moberg is best remembered for his work in both Hastings and Stanley Parks. At Stanley Park he designed the charming rough masonry and cedar shingle, chalet-style pavilion now used as the Tea House, 1911. For the fledgling Vancouver Exhibition Association (later the Pacific National Exhibition), he designed the gigantic Manufacturers' Building. In January of 1913, the citizens of Vancouver had passed a by-law to lend the Association $165,000, and several new structures were rushed to completion in time for that year's fair. Moberg's design was a *mélange* of exotic and fanciful elements, with a floor area of 47,000 square feet. It was used for the exhibit of machinery and automobiles. Heavily altered during the course of its life, it has been demolished.

MOORE & HENRY

DONALD LUXTON

John Mackenzie Moore (1857-1930) was a native of London, Ontario and remained there his entire career. In addition to his architectural practice, Moore was actively involved in the city's public life, and served as mayor of London for two terms, 1926-27. For a number of years, Moore was in partnership with Frederick Henry (1865-1929), also from London. In 1886, Moore married Louisa M. McClary, daughter of Oliver McClary. This was a fortuitous match, as Moore & Henry received the contract to design all of the McClary Manufacturing Company's buildings across Canada. One such structure was the McClary Stove Building, on a prominent corner location on Water Street in the heart of Vancouver's Gastown warehouse district. Designed in 1897, the McClary Building demonstrates a sophisticated approach to the stylish new Classical Revival influence that was just coming into favour in eastern Canada and supplanting the now-

outmoded Romanesque Revival. Examples of this new influence were rare in Vancouver at the time. The McClary Building is now a designated heritage structure.

MORRIS & EDWARDS

JENNIFER NELL BARR

William A. Morris and Ieuan C. Edwards were working in Victoria by 1912. Morris was a bookkeeper and Edwards an architect, and both lived on Colville Road. The firm built several houses on Pembroke Road in 1912 and on Bank Street in 1913. Ieuan Edwards designed his own Craftsman Bungalow in the Gonzales area of Victoria in March 1912, with a side-gabled roof, a large, gabled front dormer and a wide, full-length verandah. By 1913 Morris was no longer in Victoria, and the following year Edwards was listed as a builder and living on Blackwood Road in Saanich.

MOUNTAIN, Francis
1882-1943

DAVID MONTEYNE

Francis "Frank" Mountain was a well-established architect in England before he immigrated to Canada during the First World War. He was born in Braunton, Devon, on June 24, 1882, the son of Fanny Pascoe and William Mountain. Frank's background was described in his own words, "1899 to 1914 entirely devoted to the profession: four and a half years articles; seven years assistant; five years in practice in Oxford." In Oxford, Mountain was responsible for a number of large buildings including a church, a corporate headquarters, and upper class residences. Arriving in Vancouver during the First World War, he took a managerial position in munitions at Vancouver Engineering Works. He was briefly in partnership with **W.C.F. Gillam**. In Vancouver his work included the Melton Court Apartments, facing Kitsilano Beach, 1923, and a grand, masonry-faced bungalow for Mrs. Mary Allen on West 10th Avenue, 1922-23. The interior of this unusual house has no plasterwork, and is finished with a combination of wood panelling and ceramic tile work throughout. Mountain was commissioned to carry out the preliminary

scheme for Tatlow Court, 1926, a Spanish Colonial Revival-style bungalow court for Henry Rosenblat, President of Fordyce Motors. Popular in California at the time, courtyard apartments recognized both the mild climate on the west coast and the new importance of the automobile. Mountain's scheme was never built, and a second plan by **Richard T. Perry**, which dressed the scheme in Tudor Revival clothing, was completed two years later. During the 1920s Mountain had a very busy practice, designing a number of homes in the tony Second and Third Shaughnessy subdivisions. Frank Mountain died in Vancouver on December 24, 1943, while working as an architect for the Vancouver Parks Board. He was survived by his wife Rosina, and siblings in Victoria.

NELSON, Horatio Elmer

JENNIFER NELL BARR

H. Elmer Nelson was first listed in Victoria in the 1910-11 city directory as a draftsman in the office of architect, **H.S. Griffith**. Shortly afterwards he was listed on his own as an architect, and designed a house for W.H.P. Sweeney on Linden Avenue, 1911. The plans show superb interior and exterior details, but the house suffered a disastrous later renovation which obliterated the exterior. By 1914 he had joined the office of architect, **L.W. Hargreaves**, and then entered the Federal Department of Public Works; by 1917 he was on active service during the First World War. After the war he remained with the Federal DPW, but by 1922 was working for the Provincial DPW, and that year provided the designs for some of the bungalows at the Tranquille Sanatorium. By 1927 he had left Victoria. His most ambitious known project was a large, Craftsman-style hotel at Sooke for the **Ward Investment Company**, designed in 1912 and destroyed by fire in 1934.

NEWLANDS, William

DONALD LUXTON

Newlands practised briefly in Grand Forks at the turn of the century. In 1899 he designed the Cottage Hospital, since demolished, and the following year an eclectic cottage for Sidney Almond, which still stands on 12th

Street. By 1900 he disappeared from the area.

OKAMURA, Paul Louis (Tsunenojo)
1865-1937

JIM WOLF

Paul Louis (Tsunenojo) Okamura was the first Japanese-Canadian in Canada to advertise as an architect and artist. He was born on April 21, 1865 in Katamonmaemachi, Shibaku, Tokyo, Japan, and demonstrated his artistic ability from an early age. In 1879 he was accepted as a student at the Technical Fine Arts School, part of the Engineering Department of Tokyo Imperial University. Its creation in 1876 was intended to facilitate the use of western artistic techniques for cartography, drafting, and architectural rendering. The government hired three Italian artists for the faculty, including Antonio Fontanesi (1818-1881), an adherent of the Barbizon school of painting. Okamura and his fellow students were so enamored of Fontanesi, that when he left and was replaced by another Italian artist, they felt compelled to leave the school and start their own study group called the "Society of the Eleven." Among this group, the idea of travelling to the western world to pursue their art became a mission. While some artists chose Europe, Okamura immigrated to the United States in the 1880s, where he spent several years before coming to British Columbia in 1891. He is said to have found Vancouver "crass and garish" and could not find work as an artist. By chance, he saw a newspaper advertisement placed by St. Louis College in New Westminster, seeking an art teacher. This was a venerable Roman Catholic school for young men founded by the Oblate Fathers in New Westminster in 1865. In a remarkable decision, College officials hired him, despite the widespread racism that existed against all Asians at the time. Okamura's success in convincing them of his ability is a testament to his superior talent, ambition and personality. During his time there he converted to Catholicism, and acquired his English first name Paul Louis. It appears Okamura was restless to use his artistic skills, and was listed in local directories between 1897-98 as an architect. It was not an opportune time to begin a career in architecture; the construction industry was so stagnant that many of

British Columbia's most prominent architects had few commissions. Okamura may have decided that the poor economy, lack of a larger Japanese community and widespread racism made his pursuit of the profession a futile endeavor. He began working in a New Westminster photography studio as a part-time apprentice in 1893. In 1900, he exhibited "a collection of photography" at the first Arts and Crafts Association exhibition held in Vancouver. His participation in this group remains another indication of his close affinity with local architects, engineers and designers such as **James Bloomfield**. In 1902, he opened his own studio for art and photography, and quickly rose to prominence in New Westminster as an artistic portrait photographer of renown. When he died at the age of seventy-two in 1937, he was recognized as a pioneer and was buried in the city's Fraser Cemetery. Although Okamura's legacy in terms of an architectural contribution to the province may be negligible, his story as the first Japanese-Canadian artist remains one of inspiring success in the face of adversity.

OWEN, Frank Ifor Moran
1878-1955

JENNIFER NELL BARR

Frank I.M. Owen was born in North Wales on May 25, 1878. He spent three years in architectural apprenticeship in North Wales from 1894-97, and then six years as an assistant in the office of Pugin & Pugin in Liverpool, England. In 1908 he immigrated to Canada and set up an architectural practice in Victoria. During this time he appears to have mostly been engaged in government projects, and he provided designs for the Provincial Home for Old Men in Kamloops about 1911, and a temporary building for the provincial government at the corner of Government and Superior Streets in Victoria, 1912. He also designed the cover for the 1911 publication, Victoria Architecturally. The AIBC accepted his application for membership in 1944. That year he designed a small, hip-roofed bungalow with truncated eaves for Martin Payne on Forbes Street in Victoria. He also designed alterations in 1944 under the National Housing Act for $8,000 to convert the 1907 Maclure-designed house at 228 Douglas Street to apartments for owner Colonel A. Kent. He retired in

1949, resigned his membership in the AIBC in 1951, and died on July 16, 1955 in Sidney, B.C.

PARLETT & MACAULAY

DONALD LUXTON

The partnership of John Parlett and William Henry MacAulay was one of the more prolific architectural firms in Kamloops in the first decades of the twentieth century. Parlett, advertising as an Associate of the Royal Institute of British Architects, opened an office in Kamloops in January, 1911. By April his designs for the new Queen's Hotel were announced; later renamed the Hotel Patricia, it proudly advertised "Cuisine unexcelled – all white help. Motor bus meets all trains." Another significant project was the Fremont Block, 1911-12, a two-storey commercial structure that Parlett moved his offices into when it was completed. Busy with a variety of residential and commercial projects, he was considered the city's leading architect, and in 1912 it was stated: "As a London man of extensive experience, his services are in very considerable demand. The English element, so strongly in evidence in the district, require residences of the detached type with modern architectural features... The increased precautions taken against fire in recent years encourage the erection of permanent business structures in the main thoroughfares, and the banks and larger stores are a credit to the town." In 1912 he took on the Scottish-born MacAulay (1874-1953) as his business partner. MacAulay had articled to Latham & Bosworth, Birmingham, and then worked for a number of years in Johannesburg before relocating to Fort William, Ontario and then west to Kamloops. Among Parlett & MacAulay's projects that still stand in Kamloops are grand homes designed for: Frederick J. Fulton, 1912; Thomas D. Costley, Dundurn Place, 1912; and James Gill, 1914. Cattle ranching and the railway contributed to Kamloops' growth prior to the First World War, and the growing population required a new high school. Parlett & MacAulay were chosen as the architects; the large brick and stone school was completed in 1912, and survived until 1990. MacAulay served overseas during the war, and after he returned in 1919 with the rank of Captain, his architectural partnership with Parlett resumed. Both men had been members of the BCSA before the war, and although MacAulay registered with the AIBC after its formation, Parlett never did. The brick Sacred Heart Cathedral, 1921-25, built to replace an earlier Roman Catholic church destroyed by fire in 1919, was their most significant project in the postwar years. Parlett's ultimate fate is unknown; MacAulay retired in 1943 and moved to Saanich, where he died in 1953 at the age of seventy-eight.

PAUW, John Adrian
1891-1931
MARCO D'AGOSTINI

A native of Amsterdam born on April 14,1891, John Adrian Pauw practised in British Columbia for a short period of time from 1927 until his untimely death in 1931. He was educated at the Polytechnical School at Delft, Netherlands from 1909 to 1913 but did not graduate as an architect. He worked in Brussels first in Thomas Jusenki's office for two years followed by a year and a half for Jernan Bodson, also of Brussels. Pauw practised as an architect in Amsterdam from 1915-21 with J.M. van Hardeveld where he was responsible for designing a hotel and theatre, a bank, and a public library building in Heerlen which was the result of a competition. During this time he was also commissioned to complete several residential buildings experimenting with the use of concrete (including concrete block and poured-in-place concrete building systems) to replace traditional brick structures. Pauw moved to Bucharest where he designed an apartment house that was built in 1924 and prepared a scheme for a League of Nations Competition for building in Geneva 1926-27. He arrived in British Columbia on June 30, 1927. During his time in the province he designed several houses in Vancouver, the most notable being the B.T. Lea Residence in Shaughnessy Heights, 1930. Pauw cancelled his registration with the AIBC in March, 1931 and moved to Seattle. He died under tragic circumstances in a car accident in August, 1931 when his car broke through a guard rail on a curve in the road and plunged 200 feet down from the highway to the bottom of the Columbia River Gorge. Despite his short stay in Vancouver Pauw's work was admired by his contemporaries as evidenced by the following excerpt from *Western Homes and Living* in 1958: "John A. Pauw, a Dutch architect who competed for the League of Nations Building in Geneva, designed sev-eral revolutionary houses in Vancouver around 1930. His treatment reminds many of the work of Frank Lloyd Wright."

PEARCE, John S.
DONALD LUXTON

Pearce acted as an assistant to **F.M. Rattenbury** from 1901-05, and then set up offices in Victoria and Vancouver. By mid-1905 he had entered into partnership with Charles K. Shand, formerly of Seattle and Chicago, that lasted less than a year. Pearce designed a building in Revelstoke for the P. Burns & Co. Meat Market, 1906-07, and by 1908 was in partnership with **Archibald Campbell Hope**. They undertook several major projects, notably two schools in Vancouver. After the partnership split in 1909, Pearce designed the Holt Residence, 1909, the Canyon View Hotel in North Vancouver, and in 1912 was the architect for a proposed Lynn Valley Tourist Hotel, a grand facility that was never built due to the sudden downtown in the local economy. Pearce was active as an architect until 1913, when the local economy collapsed completely.

PEARSON, Lawrence Lewis
JENNIFER NELL BARR

L.L. Pearson was born September 4, 1879 in Kidderminster, Worcestershire, England. He apprenticed from 1897-1903 as an articled pupil to the architectural firm of Yates & Payton in Birmingham while studying at the Birmingham School of Art. From 1903-05 he worked as an assistant to R.W.W. Carter, and from 1905-07 to B.L. Pritchard, both in England. He then set up in practice with W. Horwood from 1907 to 1910. In 1910 Pearson immigrated to Canada and became an assistant to **William Wallace Blair** in Winnipeg, Manitoba. Pearson moved to Vancouver in 1911 and entered the office of **Samuel Buttrey Birds**. In August 1912 he relocated to Victoria, where he worked for Birds until 1915. In Birds's office, Pearson worked on projects such as stores and rooming houses in Victoria in 1912, a public school in Ladysmith in 1913 and the Cowichan Agricultural Society Building in Duncan. He was listed as "delineator" on the plans for a two-storey duplex on Queens Avenue, Victoria for Wong Dick Jong and Chu Chew in February 1914, but the plans were signed by Birds as architect. In 1915 Pearson began working for Canadian Explosives Limited on their James Island site off Sidney, and until 1920 designed numerous industrial buildings, residences and boarding houses. He did not join the newly-formed AIBC in 1920, and his later career is unknown.

PELTON, Arthur F.
DONALD LUXTON

Pelton came to Penticton by way of Halifax, Nova Scotia, where he was working as an architect in 1910. His largest known Penticton project was the landmark Incola Hotel on Lakeshore Drive, 1911-12. This rambling structure, dressed in Tudor Revival clothing, was built by the Okanagan Land Company, which had the CPR as its chief stockholder. Set on 1.23 acres of lakeshore frontage, it had sixty-two guest rooms, fourteen of which had private baths. Construction on the hotel began in August 1911, and it was opened August 19, 1912. Although the Incola suffered several renovation indignities over the years, it functioned as a hotel until its demolition in March, 1981. Pelton was briefly based in Kelowna, where in 1913 he designed the still extant Willits-Taylor Building, 1913. His movements after 1915 are unknown.

POTTER, Joseph Walter
1881-1962
DONALD LUXTON

J.W. Potter was Prince Rupert's leading early architect, and went on to establish himself in San Diego. He was born in Worcester, England on October 9, 1881. When he was still young, his family immigrated to Canada, and he was articled for seven years to Joseph Connelly of Toronto, starting on May 1, 1896. He worked briefly for H.P. Smith in Kingston, Ontario, and then moved to New York where he worked for two years in the offices of Carrère & Hastings. Returning to Ontario, he served as principal assistant to the Provincial Architect for several years. He commenced his practice in Prince Rupert on May 1, 1910. Potter provided designs for the first Prince Rupert City Hall and the Fire Hall, both 1912, several apartment blocks in 1914, and St. Joseph's Convent, 1917. In 1920 he designed Booth Memorial School (Hays Cove School). Allegations were made that the school was unsound, and a report on its condition was undertaken by **A.A. Cox** of Vancouver on behalf of the School Board. Cox's report was so derogatory, charging the use of inferior materials and workmanship, and public opinion so divided that A.M. Jeffers, former provincial government architect of Alberta, was brought in to further study the issue. Potter continued to maintain that the school was sound, but Cox estimated that it would need almost $50,000 in repairs. The issue was ultimately debated in the provincial legislature. **Henry Whittaker** examined the building, and found that there were defects, "due primarily through the building being erected during unsuitable weather." Some repairs were undertaken, but Potter obviously felt that his reputation had been tarnished. He was living in Seattle when he requested resignation from the AIBC in 1923, and then moved to Los Angeles where he went back to school at the University of California, and received a degree in architecture. Potter moved to San Diego in 1927, and practised there until his retirement in 1939. His first wife Jean died in 1939, and he remarried three years later. Potter died on March 1, 1962 in San Diego.

POWNALL, Guy Frank
1867-1939

JULIA TRACHSEL

Guy Frank Pownall was born in London, England in 1867, son of George H. Pownall. He immigrated to Canada, and obtained a quarter section under the Canada Dominion Land Grants, in the Fish Creek area southeast of Calgary, Alberta. He married Lily Winterbottom, of Fish Creek in 1892, but she died only four years later. Pownall married a second time in 1899, to Adalene Banister of Davisburg, Alberta, who survived him by fourteen years. In 1898 Pownall was living on Abbott Street in Kamloops, occupation, "gentleman." He later owned a home named *Nuneham* on Dickens Street (now Selkirk Street) in Victoria West, and it was during this time that he worked with **Thomas Dealtry Sedger** on several extant homes in Victoria:

a residence for Arthur Robertson on Rockland Avenue, 1906; a Queen Anne house for Isadore M. Noder on Cook Street, 1907-08; a British Arts and Crafts residence for J.T. Redding on Catherine Street, 1907-09; and an Arts and Crafts-style house for Robert Chadwick at 215-217 Government Street, 1908. When he died, suddenly, on November 13, 1939, he had been living at his home at 1355 Victoria Avenue for four years, having moved there from his farm in North Saanich, exactly where the Victoria Airport is currently situated.

PRATT & ROSS

DONALD LUXTON

Pratt & Ross were a very successful firm based in Winnipeg who specialized in railway work. Ralph Benjamin Pratt (1872-1950) was born in London, England and trained in the South Kensington School of Art before immigrating to Canada in 1891. By 1895 he was working for the CPR in Winnipeg as an architectural and engineering draftsman. In 1901 he joined the fledgling Canadian Northern Railway, designing a variety of structures including stations and roundhouses. He left the Canadian Northern's employ in 1906, and went into partnership with Donald Aynsley Ross (born 1877), a native Winnipeger who had served as a rodman with the CPR in 1897, and was a locating engineer in the West for the CNR from 1900-06. They proved to be a successful combination, and together as Pratt & Ross, Architects, Structural and Civil Engineers, they retained their connections with the railway and were hired by them on an ongoing basis. Pratt acted as the designer in the firm, while Ross provided more of the engineering expertise. During the time of the First World War they were given the commission to design the Canadian Northern's grand terminal in Vancouver, located on the newly filled-in False Creek flats, started in 1916 but not completed until 1919; during this time they maintained an office in Vancouver. The Canadian Northern Station is a symmetrical and imposing Classical Revival presence that contains a complex series of public spaces and private offices. Construction also started in 1916 on the adjacent Great Northern Railway station, designed by Fred L. Townley, but this complementary structure was demolished in the 1960s. The Canadian

Northern Station, now renamed Pacific Central, is still a transportation hub, and remains one of the city's heritage landmarks.

PROCTOR, G.L.

DONALD LUXTON

G.L. Proctor was briefly active in Prince Rupert during the boom years, from 1909-14. He was the architect of a number of buildings in Prince Rupert, including the Roman Catholic Church of the Annunciation, 1909-10, and several houses. He also acted as the local architect for St. Andrew's Anglican Church, which was designed by Gordon & Helliwell of Toronto, started in 1912 but not completed until 1925. By the time the First World War broke out, he had left the province.

REA, Kenneth Guscotte
1878-1941

DONALD LUXTON

As a bank architect based in Montreal, Kenneth Guscotte Rea (1878-1941) claimed to have built major buildings "in almost every city in Canada." He was born in Montreal and studied at McGill University, and received training in architecture as an apprentice with the Montreal architectural firm of **A.F. Dunlop**. In 1900 Rea moved to Boston where he worked at the architectural firm of Shepley, Ruttan and Coolidge; 1902 he worked in New York City for the firm of Cram, Goodhue and Ferguson. Upon Rea's return to Montreal in 1905, he first worked for the Montreal Light, Heat and Power Company and later practised architecture independently. From his office, Rea supplied the plans for a number of branch banks for the Bank of Montreal, including Halifax, Quebec, Grandmère, Vancouver, Victoria, Trail, Calgary and Hamilton, as well as the Montreal Badminton and Squash Club and a number of private residences in Montreal. Projects attributed to Rea are scattered around British Columbia, including a Royal Bank branch office in Kamloops, 1911-13. In 1922, the Merchants' Bank amalgamated with the Bank of Montreal. The Vancouver main branch of the Merchants' Bank, by **Somervell & Putnam**, 1915-16, was more than doubled in size by Rea, 1924-25, to serve as the Bank of Montreal's new divisional headquarters. He duplicated the sophisticated classical detailing, but stretched the building farther along Granville Street, and greatly enlarged the imposing banking hall. The resultant structure remains one of the most imposing local examples of the Temple Bank movement.

RICHARDS, William Austin S.

DONALD LUXTON

W.A.S. Richards was working in Seattle, then practised briefly in British Columbia, starting in Vancouver, where he maintained an office from about 1905-10. One project from his time in Vancouver was a brick commercial block for Mrs. E. Gould on Robson Street, 1910. By 1912 he had relocated to Kamloops, where he established a practise, advertising his office hours as 9 a.m. to 5 p.m. during the week, and Saturday 9 a.m. to noon and 7 p.m. to 8 p.m. In early 1913, he was chosen to design an Exhibition Building for the Kamloops Agricultural Association, a project that failed to materialize. A fractious incident involving Richards was reported in the local newspaper in May, 1913. Richards was sued by Howard Smith over the ownership of a coyote hound. Smith alleged that Richards stole his dog, so he went to Richards's home in Kamloops, retrieved the dog, and took it back to his farm at Tranquille. Richards, who maintained the badly injured animal had shown up at his door, went to Smith's farm with a constable, who could not arrest the dog, so he arrested Smith. At the subsequent civil trial that lasted for two days, the judge awarded custody of the dog to Richards, but ordered him to pay fifty dollars to Smith as compensation for his improper arrest. The judge also expressed regret that the case ever reached court. Richards suffered further misfortune when his office was damaged by fire in October, 1913: "But for the promptness of the Fire Brigade on Wednesday morning, who, in spite of a wildly incoherent call over the telephone as to where the fire really was, made a rapid run, a serious conflagration might have occurred. Through what is believed to have been a defective coal oil stove in the block on Third Avenue in which the offices of W.A.S. Richards, architect, are situated, fire broke out in a room on the ground floor adjacent to the small barber's shop, and spread rapidly. Mrs. Richards was the first to discover the flames, which had got a firm hold and after telephoning for the brigade hastily removed books, papers and other valuables. Prompt and efficient work by the firemen soon had the flames extinguished, but not before considerable damage had been done. It is understood that the premises were not insured." There is no further reference to Richards in Kamloops, and his later whereabouts are unknown.

RIXFORD, Loring Pickering
1870-1946

JENNIFER NELL BARR AND
DONALD LUXTON

The Union Club, a $200,000 *Beaux-Arts* clubhouse for Victoria's most prominent gentlemen, was designed by San Francisco architect Loring P. Rixford, who had been chosen by club members, including **Francis Rattenbury**, through an open competition in 1911. Built between 1911-13, it still serves its original function today. Cream yellow matte-glazed terra cotta was used extensively for the base, cornice, window surrounds, and quoining. Low relief, classically-inspired ornamentation, contrasted with a dark brick background, provided the warm and rich appearance. The cornice blocks were punctured for a dramatic lighting system, with a socket between each elaborate modillion. Rixford, born in California on September 20, 1870, was a graduate of the *École des Beâux Arts* in Paris, and in 1907 began practice in San Francisco, where he was for some time City Architect. He designed the San Francisco City and County General Hospital, and the Bohemian Club, with its famous outdoor redwood grove and stage. Although Rixford maintained an office in Victoria, managed by Alf Kuhn, from the time he won the Union Club competition, there was an objection from the Victoria Builders' Exchange in September 1913 after he also placed first in the competition for the new Royal Provincial Jubilee Hospital. Despite his selection, local builders wanted the architect and contractors to be British subjects. Perhaps due in some part to the ensuing debate, and to the outbreak of the First World War less than a year later, Rixford's plans were never realized. Instead the new Royal Jubilee East Wing was finally built in 1921-25 to plans by local architects **P. Leonard James** and **K.B. Spurgin**. Rixford also submitted an unsuccessful entry to the competition for a new Civic Centre in Vancouver in 1914. By the middle of the First World War, Kuhn was away on active service, and Rixford closed his Victoria office. In 1916 Rixford submitted designs to the competition for the new California State Building. His Sacramento City Library, a three-storey Italian Renaissance-style building, was funded by the Carnegie Foundation and completed in 1918; it was added to the National Register of Historic Places in 1992. Rixford died in Santa Ana, California on September 24, 1946.

RUSSELL, John Hamilton Gordon
1863-1946

DONALD LUXTON

As has always been the case, architectural commissions were generally awarded on the basis of reputation and personal connections. In 1907 the Canadian Western Lumber Company, a huge sawmill operation located in Coquitlam, was taken over by an investment syndicate headed by A.D. McRae of Winnipeg. Prominent Winnipeg architect J.H.G. Russell was chosen to design the company's new head office in 1908, an elegant structure with wood-panelled interiors that featured the company's products. The following year McRae chose local architect **Thomas Hooper** to design his palatial home in Shaughnessy Heights, *Hycroft.*

SANSOM, C. Wyndham H.

DONALD LUXTON

C. Wyndham H. Sansom began practising architecture in Alberta in 1883, advertising his services in both Calgary and Fort McLeod. He appeared in Vancouver right after the Great Fire of 1886, where he went into partnership with **Edward Mallandaine Jr**. They were successful in obtaining a share of the work available in the rapidly growing city, including commercial work and a number of residential commissions. Their association was somewhat fluid, and Mallandaine seems to have spent some of this time in Victoria. From 1889-91 Samson was in partnership with John W. Dawson; in addition to working together they both lived at the Granville Block on Main Street. Their main commission was the first Vancouver City Market building on Main Street. A competition had been held in 1889 for its design, and other plans had been submitted by **T.E. Julian**, **A.E. McCartney**, **C.E. Hope** and **N.S. Hoffar**, but Sansom & Dawson's design, with its impressive rounded corner turrets, was chosen. It was completed in 1890, and the second floor used also as City Hall from 1898-1929. Sansom disappeared from the local scene at the time of the economic downturn in the early-1890s, and then reappeared briefly as an architect in Greenwood, B.C. from 1900-03, after which he again withdrew from the local scene.

SCHALLERER, August B.

JENNIFER NELL BARR

An American of German descent, August B. Schallerer was one of several American architects who shared office #616 in the Sayward Building, 1207 Douglas Street, Victoria. He was listed there in the 1913 city directory, at the same time as Seattle architect **Elmer E. Green**. Plans of houses in Victoria and Oak Bay designed by Schallerer have been found for 1912-14. These include two impressive Craftsman houses in Victoria for the **Ward Investment Company**: 1069 Joan Crescent, 1912-13, a two-storey Craftsman house with an elaborate verandah and gable timberwork; the other is located at 352 Moss Street, 1913. In 1914 he designed a small bungalow, again with elaborate detailing, for H.T. Barnes, on Monteith Street in Oak Bay, 1914. This house was originally designed with a small *porte-cochère* with square columns on double-coursed shingled piers, and latticework over top; instead a matching garage was built at the back of the property. A confusion arises over the unsigned plans for a Craftsman-style house designed for, and built by, the McCarter Brothers at 1015 Joan Crescent. On plans by both Schallerer and E.E. Green, the unusual wavy lines of their printing styles look identical; because they both designed houses in the Craftsman style, the attribution of 1015 Joan Crescent would appear to be, at present, unsolvable.

SCHLOMER, Herman H.

DONALD LUXTON

Briefly active in Vancouver from 1911-12, Herman H. Schlomer's built projects were minimal, but he advertised his services with fanciful drawings that indicated his talents as a designer. His origins and later whereabouts are unknown.

SCOTT, Adrian Gilbert
1883-1963

DONALD LUXTON

When the decision was made by St. James' parish in Vancouver to build a new church, the Rector, Reverend Canon Wilberforce Cooper, asked his distant relative, famed English church architect Sir Giles Gilbert Scott, to provide the design. Pleading that he was too busy, he passed on the commission to his brother Adrian Gilbert Scott, also a distinguished church designer. When the plans arrived in Vancouver, they were not what the parish had anticipated. Scott's daring design was a free adaptation of Fourteenth century Gothic, and bore not even a passing resemblance to his earlier Anglican Cathedral in Cairo. There are touches of exotic, almost Byzantine motifs, but the predominant influence was the stripped-down modernism of the Late Art Deco era. The use of monolithic reinforced concrete was not Scott's first choice; he would have preferred a brick facing. Scott, who was studying recent experiments with concrete finishes in industrial atmospheres, ultimately determined that it would be feasible to leave off the brick. This remarkable structure was completed in 1936, with **Sharp & Thompson** acting as the local supervising architects.

SHARP, Kendrick
1869-1935

JENNIFER NELL BARR

Kendrick Sharp (frequently misspelled as Kenneth Sharpe) was born in Huntingdonshire, England and came to Cumberland in the Comox Valley of Vancouver Island c.1894. He worked in Cumberland and later Victoria as a builder and architect. Sharp was on the building committee of Cumberland's Church of England congregation when he was asked to design Holy Trinity Anglican Church in 1895. He also built many houses in Cumberland, including one for himself and one for school principal J.B. Bennett, both on Penrith Avenue. Sharp was a founding member of the Comox Valley Fire Department and of Cumberland Masonic Lodge No.26. In July 1897 he left for the Klondike gold rush. He remained in the north for about seven years before relocating to Victoria. He acquired extensive property during the boom years before the First World War, and built many houses, particularly in the Fairfield district. In 1904 he constructed the Clay residence at 810 Linden Avenue, and later used the distinctive trefoil device at the top of the bargeboards on his own house on Fort Street. He built two of the British Arts and Crafts houses on Trutch Street, residences for the Gillespies, 1907, and the Bennets, 1909. Ill health forced him to take a trip to Australia and New Zealand for a couple of years, but he then returned to his contracting business in Victoria. In 1917 he was involved in arbitration with the City of Victoria in a claim for compensation because the City had altered grades on upper Pandora Avenue, next to a number of lots that Sharp had purchased near the Dupont Estate (Stadacona Park) in 1912. He was awarded damages and costs of $2,500. Sciatica forced his early retirement in 1923, and he moved into the Ritz Hotel on Fort Street. He was a member of Victoria & Columbia Lodge No.1, AF&AM, and a life member of the Pacific Club; it was at the Club's annual dinner that he was stricken and died on April 11, 1935.

SPROAT, William Edwardes
1878-1953

DONALD LUXTON

W. Edwardes Sproat was born in Glasgow, Scotland on February 18, 1878, the son of Samuel Sproat, master shoemaker, and Christina Livingstone. He was articled to Robert Wilcox in Glasgow from 1894-99, and as an independent architect in England his subsequent work included the Wombwell Library, Yorkshire, 1904, Birkenhead Central Library, 1909, Ellesmere Port Library, 1909, various schools, and additions to the Congregational Church, Liverpool, 1910. Sproat arrived in Vancouver in 1912, where he mainly designed residential buildings.

His activities during the First World War are unknown. One landmark structure that he designed in 1920 survives at the edge of Vancouver's Chinatown, a four-storey political headquarters at the corner of East Pender Street and Gore Avenue for the Kuomintang, the Chinese Nationalist League. This building is a fascinating blend of eastern and western architecture; grafted onto a standard commercial building are arched recessed balconies on the top floor, and a highly ornate entry that recalls traditional Chinese motifs. Sproat disappeared from Vancouver by 1922; he died in Los Angeles on September 2, 1953.

STEVENS, H.L. & CO.

DONALD LUXTON

H.L. Stevens & Co. was an architectural firm based in New York, and by 1911 had opened a branch office in Vancouver. Based on their experience with large construction projects, they acted in a design-build capacity on several significant projects, billing themselves as Architectural Engineers. They were responsible for the design of the Duncan Building for barrister and solicitor, Howard J. Duncan, and the Molson's Bank on Hastings Street, 1912, now the Roosevelt Hotel. Another structure they designed was Shaughnessy Lodge, 1912, a large brick apartment block with refined brickwork details. They prepared the working drawings, and acted as the contractors and local supervisors for the Credit Foncier Building, 1913-14, designed by Montreal architect Ernest I. Barott, of the firm **Barott, Blackader & Webster**. Although the Vancouver branch lasted only a few years, the company persisted into the mid-1930s in New York, and was responsible for a number of landmark buildings in the United States, including the fifteen storey Bankshead Hotel in Birmingham, Alabama, built in 1926.

STONE, Howard Colton
DIED 1918

DONALD LUXTON

H.C. Stone, an architect based in Montreal, designed many elegant banks across Canada between 1900 and 1913. His busy practice included industrial buildings, theatres and private residences, and designs for branches of the Molson's Bank, the Bank of Ottawa, the Royal Bank, the Bank of Toronto, the Dominion Bank, and the Sovereign Bank. His commissions for the Royal Bank stretched from Saint John, New Brunswick to Vancouver. Stone provided the handsome design for the Royal Bank's East End Branch in Vancouver, located at the corner of Main and Hastings Streets, 1910. The principal facades are expressed as an Ionic colonnade, surmounted with an ornate cornice, evocative of Beaux-Arts Classicism. The intersection of Main and Hastings was once the focus of the old city, and each corner still retains a landmark heritage structure, creating a fine urban ensemble, of which this bank is an important component.

STROUD, Allan B.
BORN 1885

DONALD LUXTON

Allan B. Stroud was born in Ontario on May 10, 1885, and educated in Toronto, where he commenced practising as an architect in 1902. Seven years later he relocated to Vancouver, and was briefly in partnership with **James J. Donnellan** in 1910. The following year he was in partnership with A. William Keith as Stroud & Keith, and the firm completed plans for a seven-storey mixed use commercial, office and apartment building at the corner of Main Street and Broadway for H.O. Lee. Stroud on his own supervised the construction of the Lee Building, which is still a landmark presence in the Mount Pleasant neighbourhood. He appears to have left the city after 1912.

TEGEN, Robert F.

DONALD LUXTON

Robert F. Tegen was a German-born architect who immigrated to the United States, and worked in the architectural offices of "the leading members of that profession" in New York and other eastern cities before he ended up in Chicago. From there, he moved to Portland, and by 1909 formed a partnership with prominent Portland architect Francis J. Berndt. Together, they won the competition for St. Joseph's Hospital for the Sisters of Charity of the House of Providence at Vancouver, Washington. In 1912, Tegen opened an office in Vancouver, B.C., and designed several major institutional buildings in the Lower Mainland just prior to the First World War. Although the reason remains unknown, his name was consistently spelt as Tegen in Canada, and Tegan in the United States. For the Sisters of Providence he designed a Renaissance Revival structure for St. Paul's Hospital, on Burrard Street in Vancouver, 1912-13. With a floor plan laid out in the shape of a cross, this landmark was built of red brick, banded at the base, with extensive terra cotta trim and a pantile roof. Terra cotta for this project was ordered from Gladding, McBean & Company in Lincoln, California. Tegen also prepared the plans for a three-storey addition to St. Mary's Hospital in New Westminster, 1912-13. Briefly in partnership with Alfred L. Vezina, 1913-14, they designed a grand school and gymnasium for Vancouver's Holy Rosary Parish, St. Mary's Hall, in 1913. Tenders were called for its construction, but the local recession put the project on hold, ending Tegen's Canadian career. In 1914, he was commissioned to design the Cotillion Hall in Portland, also known as the Crystal Ballroom; it was inaugurated with a formal dress ball, and from all accounts, was a great success from its inception. Apparently Tegen was chosen for this project based on his experience designing ball bearing dance floors in Chicago and Los Angeles. Both Cotillion Hall and his Elks Building in Vancouver, Washington, are listed on the United States National Register of Historic Places. Despite these accomplishments, by 1918 Tegen had left Portland, and his later whereabouts are unknown.

TOTTY, Elliott
1890-1960

JENNIFER NELL BARR

Elliott Totty was born July 19, 1890 in Dawson, Yukon Territory, and began his professional education in 1908, working for architects during his holidays while going to college. He apprenticed in Victoria with **Jesse M. Warren** for five years, and continued to work for him until 1915. With Warren, he worked on the Central Building and the Pantages (now the McPherson) Theatre. In August 1915 Totty left for overseas service with the Canadian Expeditionary Force during the First World War. He later transferred with a commission to the British Artillery, serving in Egypt and Salonika. After demobilization Totty returned to Victoria and lived in the YMCA. He continued his apprenticeship from 1919-22 under **Henry Whittaker** in the Provincial Department of Public Works. Totty was only able to get a small amount of residential work, but did apply to join the new AIBC in 1920. Two years later he designed the parsonage for Grace Lutheran Church in Victoria with **W.J. Semeyn**. His AIBC membership lapsed and was cancelled in 1925, when he gave up architectural work to become the proprietor of the Rock Creek Hotel. Totty was commissioned in 1941 in the Royal Canadian Engineers and was discharged toward the end of 1946 with the rank of Major. He began working again for Whittaker in the DPW and was reinstated with the AIBC in 1949. He continued his career in Victoria, an example of his work being a home for Mr. M. Jones at the corner of St. Charles Street and Bywood Place, 1958. Totty died in Victoria on September 10, 1960 at the age of seventy. He was survived by his wife, Mary (MacKinnon), whom he had married in Victoria in 1924, and his son, Garth.

UNDERWOOD, Percy C.
1894-1978

DONALD LUXTON

Percy Underwood was born in London, England, and moved to Montreal in 1909. After service overseas during the First World War, he moved to Vancouver in 1921. Underwood worked for John Graham in Seattle from 1922-25, and then returned to Vancouver to work with **McCarter & Nairne** during their heyday, until 1930 when he opened his own office. He practised on his own, and then in a series of successive, and successful, partnerships, until his retirement.

VAN NORMAN, Charles
Burwell Kerrens
1906-1975

DONALD LUXTON

C.B.K. Van Norman was born in Meaford, Ontario and studied architecture at the University of Winnipeg. He moved to Vancouver after graduation and worked for **Townley & Matheson** from 1928-30, after which he went into private practice. At six foot four inches in height and 230 pounds, "Charlie" was a presence as immense as his name. Known for his extravagance, he was called "the meanest piano in town." His modernist masterpiece was a new City Hall for Revelstoke, 1939, an uncompromising design that was startling for its time and context. Another project was a new Company Store in Powell River, 1940-41, which was so at odds with the Townsite's traditional architecture that people thought "a spaceship had landed." He went on to a very successful career that helped define modernism in Vancouver. C.B.K. Van Norman died in Vancouver in 1975.

VAN SICLEN,
William Doty
1865-1951

DONALD LUXTON

Van Siclen was born in Hillsdale, Michigan on April 29, 1865, the son of William B. Van Siclen and Amarilla Doty. He ranged around the Pacific coast, starting in San Jose, California, where he practised from about 1895 to 1900. In 1901 he arrived in Seattle, where he was based for a number of years. From 1911-13 he was working in Vancouver, in partnership with Lewis E. Macomber, although the extent of their practice seems to have been minimal; Macomber was based in Portland from 1912-15, and was known for his exceptional drawing skills. For one year, in 1912, Van Siclen also shared an office in the Sayward Building in Victoria with Seattle architects, **E.E. Green**, and Joseph S. Coté, the former partner of **W.M. Somervell**. Somewhat transient, he moved his family to Edmonton from 1912-15, where he designed the still extant Kelly Building. About 1925 he moved to Brownsville, Texas, where he died in 1951.

VERHEYDEN, Charles
DIED 1872

DOROTHY MINDENHALL AND
CAREY PALLISTER

Charles Verheyden, a native of Belgium, was in business in Victoria at least by January 1859 when he advertised in the Victoria *Gazette* as a carpenter, contractor, and builder prepared to contract for or superintend erection of all types of buildings "in the best style and architecture in the cheapest and best workmanlike manner." He claimed to have "long experience in Europe and the United States and a perfect knowledge of his profession..." His first known commission, in December 1859, was for an 800 seat theatre on the east side of Douglas Street between Fort and View, about which the *Colonist* commented "from our knowledge of this gentleman's talents as a builder we are sure no better qualified person could be found." He designed the three-storey New Hotel de France at Government and Broad Streets for Pierre Manciot in 1869. M.C. Humber & Co. were the contractors for this project, which included seventy-two sleeping rooms, a ladies parlour, a restaurant, and private dining rooms. Verheyden also designed various brick and wood houses, stores and barns in Victoria. In 1871 he invited tenders for the construction of the four-storey brick convent for the Sisters of St. Ann to designs of **Father Michaud**, the plans, in the Second Empire/Quebecois style, having been sent from the mother house in Lachine, Quebec. In addition to his building activities Verheyden was Mining Manager for the Royal Columbia Anthracite Coal Co. and in 1870 led an expedition to Queen Charlotte Island to search for coal on the Company's land reserve. Verheyden died in August 1872, "aged about fifty," and was buried in the Quadra Street Burying Ground.

VULLINGHS, Father
Adrian Joseph
1868-1940

MARTIN SEGGER

Born and educated in Holland, Father A.J. Vullinghs was ordained in 1892 and arrived on Vancouver Island in 1893 where he was assigned to Our Lady of the Assumption Church, Saanich. He amazed the local populace by building a small but very impressive parterred garden in the late Victorian style adjacent to the church. In 1911 he provided the plans for the meditative garden and arboretum at St. Ann's Academy, Victoria. While in charge of Our Lady of Lourdes Church in Oak Bay in 1914 he developed a similar, quite remarkable garden. Vullinghs died in Victoria on April 13, 1940.

WENYON, George H.

DONALD LUXTON

George Wenyon appeared for the briefest time in Vancouver, likely arriving in 1912, and landed one major commission, for additions to the Woodward's Department store on Hastings Street, 1913. He was advertised as an architect in both Vancouver and London, and disappeared as soon as the local economy collapsed.

WHITBURN, James Boulton
1882-1931

DONALD LUXTON

James Boulton Whitburn was born at Woking, Surrey, England on December 27, 1882. At the age of sixteen he started his articles with Messrs. Clamp & Drower, Victoria Chambers, Woking, and stayed with them for five years, after which he worked in a builder's office as Clerk of Works for another five years. Joining the westward flood of immigration, his first known commission in B.C. was a design for a welcome arch erected at Edmonds and Kingsway in Burnaby for the 1912 vice-regal visit of the Duke and Duchess of Connaught. In June, 1913, Whitburn opened his own office in the Westminster Trust Building in New Westminster. The economy was slowing down just as he arrived, but he was rejected as medically unfit for overseas service during the First World War, and his career languished until after the armistice. When he applied for AIBC membership in 1921, he stated "My practice has been made up principally of private residences since coming to this country, and owing to the quiet times, nothing very large has been done by me... I have been connected with the building trades all my life, and my family have done nothing else for the last century." Whitburn remained in New Westminster,

and his persistence finally paid off in the late 1920s, when he received some substantial commissions, notably Trapp Technical School (later John Robson School), 1928, and Richard McBride School, 1929, both extant; and the Spanish Colonial Revival Seaman's Institute Building, 1929, now demolished. His output in the 1920s included some very finely executed residential designs which show his affinity and his training in the Arts and Crafts tradition. His success allowed him to build himself a finely crafted English cottage home in New Westminster, 1927, with impressive interior details including beamed and panelled ceilings and a fireplace inglenook. Whitburn, who remained single his whole life, was active in many community causes, including the Kiwanis Club, the Odd Fellows, chairman of the Child Welfare Committee in 1930, and first President of the local Boy Scout Association. He died at home on February 2, 1931, at the age of forty-eight, survived by three sisters in England.

WHITE, William P.

NANCY BYRTUS

In the two years W.P. White spent in British Columbia, he designed one of Vancouver's best-loved landmarks and set the standard in gracious apartment living. Although he was responsible for the design of many notable buildings in Seattle and Vancouver, very little is known about him. The details of his place of birth, death and education remain undiscovered. White's first known project in Seattle, the Jefferson Apartments, 1905, established him as a designer of apartments and hotels. Practising in Seattle until 1922, his work there included the Kinnear Apartments, 1907-08, the Astor Hotel, 1909, and the Calhoun Hotel, 1909-10. White's most prolific period occurred between 1910-12 when he worked both in Seattle (in partnership with **Jesse M. Warren**) and in Vancouver. His Vancouver office was located on Pender Street and was shared with the architecture firm of Randall & Baker. During a two-year period he completed approximately twenty-two apartment buildings and several residences in the Vancouver region. When a massive port was planned for Sturgeon's Bank, White provided the design for a Craftsman-style port manager's house on No. 2 Road in Richmond. Although plans

for the port failed to materialize, the house was built and still stands today. White's apartments are generally clad in brick and feature decorative terra cotta or brick detailing at the cornice. The Engelsea Lodge, completed in the Second Renaissance Revival style, 1911, exemplified the charm of his designs. White's most widely recognized structure is the Sylvia Hotel, 1912, a prominent seaside building that has long been a Vancouver favourite. Today the Sylvia's facade is draped with Virginia creeper and the building is well loved for its "European air." His extant Vancouver structures include the Bonaventure Apartments, 1910, the Allen Building, 1911, the Buchanan Building, 1912, a brick block for J.H. Bayliss in Kitsilano, 1912, the Wenonah Apartments, 1912, and the Del Mar Hotel, 1912.

WHITEHEAD, Edwin A.
BORN 1860

DONALD LUXTON

E.A. Whitehead practised in Vancouver from 1898-1914. Born in Ontario on November 28, 1860, he was active as an architect in Toronto from 1878, then relocated to St. John's, Newfoundland from 1892-95. He arrived in Vancouver about 1898, and then appeared briefly in New Westminster after the Great Fire. His best known surviving building is Seymour School #1 on Keefer Street, a neighbourhood landmark built in 1900 as a response to the rapidly growing population of Strathcona. Seymour is one of the largest remaining early Vancouver schools built of, and clad with, wood; after this time brick became the favoured facade material. Whitehead disappeared from the local scene after 1914.

WHITEHEAD, Herbert Thomas
1882-1936

JENNIFER NELL BARR

H.T. Whitehead was born in Yorkshire, England, on March 5, 1882. It is not known when he immigrated to Canada, but he moved to Victoria during the summer of 1911 and opened an architectural studio with architect **E. Stanley Mitton**. In 1913, Mitton & Whitehead designed a landmark house for Arthur Lineham on the waterfront at the south end of Cook Street. An article in *The Architect, Builder & Engineer*, April 25, 1913, described the features of the house: "The hall is panelled in slashed grain fir, dining room in oak, and the drawing room has richly plastered cornice and ceiling." Among the many luxury features was a "stationary electric vacuum cleaning installation." In 1913 Whitehead designed Victoria residences for jeweller, William H. Wilkerson on Rockland Avenue; a two-storey house with a double-height verandah and Arts and Crafts detailing for R. Alderton on Princess Street, constructed by Matthew Wightman; and Wightman's own house on St. Charles Street. For himself, Whitehead designed a California Bungalow in the Colquitz district of Saanich, c.1913. In 1914 Whitehead again worked with contractor Wightman, this time on a now demolished apartment building at the corner of Cook and Mackenzie Streets in Fairfield for Frederick C. Pink, a printer with the Victoria *Daily Times*, one of a number of apartments Whitehead designed that year. Following the end of the war Whitehead worked as a farmer. By 1935 he was working as a clerk with the provincial government, living with his family in James Bay. When Whitehead died at age fifty-four on March 8, 1936, the fact that he had been an architect was not mentioned in his obituary.

WILLIAMS, Warren Heywood
1844-1888

DREW WAVERYN

Two of Victoria's finest buildings from the 1880s were designed by prominent Portland architect Warren Heywood Williams, who died only months into the construction of his largest residential commission, *Craigdarroch Castle*, in Victoria. The project was completed by his son, David L. Williams, and Arthur L. Smith, who had been a draftsman in Williams's office since 1880. Born in New York City, Warren Williams was the son of an architect and grew up in San Francisco, where he entered his father's office for training in about 1862, and they became partners in 1865. He moved to Portland, Oregon in 1873 after a major fire provided an opportunity to start a practice, and quickly became one of the city's most prominent architects. In Victoria, he was responsible for the Bank of British Columbia, 1885-86, and

Craigdarroch, built 1887-90; Williams perhaps secured the *Craigdarroch* commission while in town supervising the bank construction. The Bank of B.C., described by the *Colonist* as "Ionic" and "the most perfect piece of architecture so far existing in this province," is a signature example of Williams's favourite style, the Italianate he learned from his father, characterised by brackets, classical ornamentation, and a variety of window surrounds. *Craigdarroch* departs from this style, being an eclectic Victorian pile composed with Romanesque arches, Scottish baronial towers, chimneys and gables, and steep Château-style roofs. While returning from a trip to the east coast, Williams caught pneumonia and died in Fresno City, California at the age of forty-four. In addition to the unfinished mansion in Victoria, Williams left a legacy of debt. He was a successful and prolific architect, but he also had a taste for the finer things life had to offer. When travelling he hired private rail cars where he enjoyed champagne and caviar. As a consequence, his widow was forced to move to Seattle to live with her recently married daughter.

WILSON, Henry
1877-1972

DONALD LUXTON

Henry Wilson was born in Liverpool, England on October 16, 1877 at 10 Amberley Street, Toxteth Park, Liverpool, the son of Robert Wilson, master mariner, and Emily Harriet (Brewer) Wilson. Young Henry worked in the drafting department of a contractor's office in 1900, and passed a course in building construction, quantity surveying and sanitary engineering at Liverpool. After his arrival in Vancouver in 1911 he worked on several dwellings in Vancouver, and then set up an architectural office in South Fort George in June 1913. He was rejected from military service during the First World War on account of deafness, and during the war years remained in Prince George, designing the new City Hall, 1917, and the Hospital, 1918. After the war his projects included supervision of the Bank of Montreal (designed by K.G. Rea, 1919-1920), and houses built under the *Soldiers' Housing Act*, 1919. Wilson served as mayor of Prince George in 1921. The local economy remained poor and he hoped to relocate to Vancouver. In 1923

he wrote the AIBC: "things are very dull here and are likely to remain so until some definite decision has been made re. the proposed pulp mill." This was the first of a number of such letters. Wilson stopped remitting his dues to the Institute, stating "I... regret that at the present time that I am unable to remit the dues for 1934. It is now three years since I have had any work, with the exception of a small alteration job." He was living on a small farm in Sidney by 1940, moved to Kelowna about 1950, and died there at the age of ninety-five.

WILSON, Robert
1859-1940

DONALD LUXTON

Robert Wilson was born in Montreal on April 21, 1859. He learned architecture by working in the offices of Hutchinson & Steele, 1875-76, and **A.F. Dunlop**, 1877-78, after which he spent one year with the Board of Arts, Montreal. From 1880 to 1899 he acted as superintendent of construction for his father Daniel Wilson, after which he left for Vancouver. He set up an office in the Fairfield Building in January, 1900. His own practice did not flourish, and the following year he took a job with the Canadian Pacific Railway, Pacific Division, as superintendent of construction on hotel works; this lasted until the completion of the Empress Hotel in Victoria, 1908. He immediately landed a job with the rapidly expanding office of **Thomas Hooper**, and became his right-hand man and office manager in Vancouver. He supervised many of Hooper's buildings during the boom years, and his practical experience was an invaluable asset. In addition to supervising warehouses, residences and commercial buildings in the lower mainland, he also worked on the court houses in Revelstoke and Vernon, City Hall in Chilliwack, and Hooper's competition entry for UBC, 1912. When the economy went sour, Hooper's extensive office structure collapsed, and Wilson opened his own office in January, 1914. During the war he designed a few local residences, and seems to have picked up some of Hooper's old clients, including David Spencer, after Hooper left for New York in 1915. After the war Wilson was busy working on residences in Point Grey, and several commercial buildings, and his output was steady throughout these years. In 1927 he designed the Huntley Lodge Apartments on Oak Street, Vancouver, and the following year formed a brief partnership with Hooper, who had returned to Vancouver after his extended absence, but they only designed one known building together, the Vladimir Apartments, 1928. In 1935, Wilson sent a letter to the AIBC, stating that he was confined to home and unable to work, and that he was compelled to resign from the Institute. He died in Vancouver at the age of eighty-one on July 3, 1940.

WOLFE, James E.
1820-1901

DOROTHY MINDENHALL

James E. Wolfe was an American, drawn north from California as he followed the gold rush. He came to Victoria in 1858 and set up business in Bayley's Hotel as a carpenter, contractor, and builder in partnership with a Mr. King. Born in Baltimore, Maryland in 1820, Wolfe served an architectural apprenticeship in Maryland before heading west to San Francisco in 1851; he brought with him to Victoria plan books and special equipment for lifting and moving buildings. His only known structure in Victoria was a two-storey brick building for liquor seller, J.D. Carroll, on Yates Street, 1860. By June 1861 he had tired of the city, possibly because he had angered other builders by bidding on buildings he had designed, and returned to San Francisco where he opened a practice with his son, George H. Wolfe. The firm designed a three-storey Second Empire house for the noted historian, Hubert Howe Bancroft, and the Sutro House for millionaire Adolph Sutro, 1863. In 1879 Wolfe founded *The Quarterly Architectural Review* which later became *The California Architect & Building News* edited by his son. A member of both the Druids and the *Knights of Pythias*, Wolfe died in 1901 in San Francisco. His obituary stated "Although he was a man of marked abilities, he was of a retiring disposition and little known outside of his profession and the fraternal societies of which he was a member... He succeeded in amassing a large fortune, but invested in stocks and lost a large portion of it."

WRIGHT, RUSHFORTH & CAHILL

DONALD LUXTON

This San Francisco-based firm operated a branch office in Vancouver from 1910-13. Bernard Joseph Stanislaus Cahill (1866-1944), a native of London, England arrived in the United States in 1888 and opened his architectural practice in San Francisco in 1891. He was an early advocate of town planning, and his 1904 design of the San Francisco Civic Center was the basis for the plan adopted by the city in 1912. Also considered a specialist in mortuary buildings, Cahill was responsible for the catacombs and columbarium at Cypress Lawn Cemetery in Colma, California and the Diamond Head Memorial Park at Honolulu. George Rushforth (1861-1943) was known for his design of the Forest Hill Hotel in Pacific Grove, California and the First Methodist Church in Berkeley, California. George A. Wright (1858-1918), was born and educated in Plymouth, England. The three men formed their architectural partnership in San Francisco in 1907. Seeing opportunity north of the border, they opened an office in Vancouver, and installed William T. Sherman Hoyt as the manager. The office produced several warehouses and residences, but their landmark commission was a grand apartment block in the West End, Holly Lodge, 1913, that still stands today. It displays an urban sophistication rarely seen in local buildings, with a generous screened forecourt and banded brickwork. Built to a density that may have prevailed in the West End if the economy had not crashed, it was the largest apartment block in Canada at the time of its construction, and still towers above its immediate surroundings. After the economic bust in 1913 that preceded the first World War, Cahill withdrew, although Wright & Rushforth remained in partnership for a few more years. Cahill later entering into a partnership, Gibson & Cahill, which was responsible for buildings such as the Multnomah Hotel in Portland. In addition to his architectural career, Cahill invented the butterfly map, an octahedral system of projection for meteorology, geography, and geophysics. The map was designed to eliminate exaggeration at the top and bottom and distortion at the edges and sides found in traditional maps. The surface of the globe was represented by eight equilateral triangles. Cahill founded The Cahill World Map Co., which sold shares and promoted the map for educational and other uses.

YELLAND & RILEY

JENNIFER NELL BARR

Yelland & Riley were active in Victoria for two years beginning in 1912. They designed *Tanhaven*, 1913, in the British Arts and Crafts style for William V. Coon. This nine-room house cost about $8,000 and had a concrete basement, roughcast exterior and brick-paved porch. The surviving interior plans give very detailed descriptions, including "Kean's cement wainscot" and a terrazzo floor in the one bathroom. At the same time Yelland & Riley completed plans for a $300,000, eight-storey structure for the German-Canadian Trust Company, for the corner of Douglas and Fort Streets, but due to the worsening financial situation, it was not built. They designed several houses in Fairfield, including a two-storey Arts and Crafts Edwardian house for J.V. Perks, 1913, that is now designated as a municipal heritage site. Yelland & Riley disappeared by 1914.

The faintest ink is more reliable than the strongest memory.

Few of these early architects have ever been written about, and many had been completely forgotten. The best source of information on their lives – and for some the only source – are the membership files of the Architectural Institute of British Columbia. After the Institute was incorporated in 1920, prospective members were required to submit documentation of their qualifications. Applicants were asked at a minimum for their full name; date and place of birth; date of commencing practice in B.C.; a list of their buildings; and activities during the First World War. Some of the information is embellished, and architects are notoriously bad at spelling and dates. The more established practitioners grumbled fiercely – for Principal Buildings, Thomas Fee claimed: "the list would be too long to fill in here. I can say that I have had in charge the erection or alteration of a greater number of buildings than any other architect in B.C." – but what has survived in these files in invaluable. Those for which a membership file exists are shown below with AIBC listed under Sources. A significant amount of historical material relating to the history and development of the Institute itself has survived, but in widely scattered places. A detailed history of the establishment of the AIBC has been published by Donald Luxton, "Taming the West: the Thirty Year Struggle to Regulate the Architectural Profession in British Columbia," *Journal of the Society for the Study of Architecture in Canada,* 22:4 [1998], pp.108-123. As research sources have been extensively referenced in this article, they have not been repeated here.

Primary research, whenever possible, was used to verify the information in this book. Bibliographical references and architectural citations for individual architects are listed below. For sources that refer to more than one architect, the full citation is listed in the Bibliography. Building permits for the cities of North Vancouver and Vancouver have been entered on comprehensive databases, a boon to our research. Other available databases include *An Inventory of Residential Buildings in Oak Bay* by Dr. Len McCann, University of Victoria, and the City of Victoria Archive's collection of demolished building plans. The City of Victoria has an extensive collection of building plans that is currently being catalogued by the Victoria Heritage Foundation. Underway since 1999, this project is headed by Jennifer Nell Barr, under the auspices of the City's Planning & Development Department and Heritage Planner Steve Barber, with funding from the British Columbia Heritage Trust, and many thousands of hours of volunteer labour. These plans have proven to be a remarkable resource, and have allowed the correct attribution of numerous buildings and the identification of many previously unknown architects. Since first publication in 2003, Numerous databases have become available, most notably the references from the *Victoria Daily Columnist* tirelessly assembled by Dorothy Mindenhall and now included on the Victoria's Victoria website (http://web.uvic.ca/vv/).

It should be noted, however, that a number of citations in this book are the result of previous research contained in heritage inventories, local histories, and other secondary sources. Although verified wherever possible, some of these sources have still proven to be of dubious accuracy, including the catalogue of building plans at the City of Vancouver Archives, which is currently being revised. We know that there is far more research material available that we have not yet been able to locate, and welcome any additions or corrections to this information.

There has been no attempt made to assemble definitive project lists for each architect. If we have a reference to a project but cannot determine its exact location or status, we have left that information out rather than guess at it. Only the B.C. projects of each architect are listed, even though buildings in other locations may be mentioned in their entry. Partnerships were sometimes informal and fluid, and it is difficult to determine exact attributions; known projects are listed only under one partner's name. The given dates for each project bracket from the start of design to completion of construction, when known. Dates not known to within one year of accuracy are listed as *circa* [c.].

The Madge Hamilton Collection refers to personal notes kept by Madge Hamilton, one of British Columbia's premier archivists. The daughter of Colonel Richard Wolfenden, one of the original Royal Engineers who came to British Columbia in 1858, Miss Wolfenden joined the British Columbia Provincial Archives in 1914, where she worked for the next thirty-nine years. After her retirement she continued to research and write about British Columbia's history, focusing on the early homes of the province, and their owners and architects. References found while she researched other topics were kept on notes both in card files and on the backs of envelopes. Upon her death in 1992 at the age of ninety-eight, she bequeathed her notes to Stuart Stark who has made them available to many of the researchers writing for this book. Madge Hamilton had an eagle eye for historical mistakes and always corrected printed works. She once famously remarked: "It's really not important, perhaps – a small matter. But after all, a fact is a fact, and there is no getting around it. Laziness is the reason for most of these regrettable mistakes." We all owe Madge Hamilton our grateful thanks.

ABBREVIATIONS

Locations

- City of North Vancouver = North Van. City
- District of North Vancouver = North Van. Dist.
- New Westminster = New West.
- Vancouver = Van.
- Victoria = Vict.
- West Vancouver = West Van.

Status

- Altered = alt.
- Demolished = demo.
- Destroyed = dest.
- Extant = ext.

Type

- Apartment = Apt.
- Building = Bldg.
- Residence = Res.

Sources

- Architect, Builder & Engineer = AB&E
- Canadian Architect & Builder = CA&B [Note: now available online]
- Pacific Builder & Engineer = PB&E
- Vancouver Daily Province = Province
- Vancouver Daily World = VDW
- Vancouver Sun = Sun
- Victoria Daily Colonist [or variation] = VDC or Colonist
- Victoria Daily Times = VDT
- Victoria Times-Colonist = VTC

Archives

- British Columbia Archives: BCA
- Canadian Architectural Archives, University of Calgary: CAA
- Canadian Centre for Architecture, Montreal: CCA
- Canadian Architecture Collection, McGill University, Montreal: CAC
- City of Vancouver Archives: CVA
- North Vancouver Museum & Archives: NVMA
- Victoria City Archives: VCA
- Vancouver Public Library: VPL

Note: B.C. Vital Events refers to both the online records available through the B.C. Archives website, and the microfilmed records available at BCA and several library sources.

ALEXANDER, J. Thomas

AIBC; Point Grey bldg. permits; 1881 British Census; obituary *Sun*, June 6, 1945, p.17; and B.C. Vital Events. The attribution of the Glacier House extension is from a copy of the rendering, VPL #12297. **PROJECTS**: St. Andrew's Presbyterian Church, 1044 St. George's Ave., North Van. City, 1912-13 (ext.); Brydone-Jack Res. (now the Chinese Consulate), 3338 Granville St., Van., 1912-13, (ext.); Alma Court Apts., 2222 Alma St., Van., 1931 (ext.).

APPONYI, Charles E.

Colonist Special Edition, Jan. 1, 1886; James K. Nesbitt, *Colonist,* Jan. 8, 1945; McIntosh, *A Documentary History of Music in Victoria, Vol.I*; tender calls and notes for the Theatre from the *Colonist* compiled by Dorothy Mindenhall, (Oct. 31, 1884; Mar. 4, 1885; Mar. 21, 1885, p.3; Mar. 26, 1885; Mar. 31, p.3; May 12, 1885; May 21, 1885; Oct. 8, 1885; Oct. 16, 1885; Nov. 11, 1885; Nov. 17, 1885); Sehl Mansion, *Colonist*, Sept. 26, 1885; San Francisco *Morning Call* database (http://feefhs.org); *Beyond The Horizons: The Lockheed Story* by Walter J. Boyne (1998); City of Salt Lake City web site (www.ci.slc.ut.us). The 'Macaroni' quote appeared in the *Colonist*, Oct. 14, 1885, p.3. **PROJECTS**: Sehl Mansion, Montreal and Belleville Sts., Vict., 1885 (dest. by fire 1894); Vict. Theatre, Vict., 1884-85 (demo. 1980s).

ARCHER, William Henry

B.C. Vital Events; CVA Plans, directories, and the Nanaimo Community Archives. Information on Archer's American career provided by the American Institute of Architects, Washington, D.C. *Edgewood* is covered in Kluckner, *Vanishing Vancouver*, pp.157-58. Attribution for St. Paul's Anglican Church, Nanaimo, from T.D. Sale, *125th Anniversary: St. Paul's Anglican Church, Nanaimo, B.C. 1861-1986*. The Sikh Temple is mentioned in *Construction*, Nov., 1907, p.72. Major Matthews's recollections from CVA 0054.013.000851. Archer's participation in the formation of the RAIC is covered in *First Congress of Canadian Architects & First Annual Convention of the Institute of Architects of Canada: Programme*, Montreal, Aug. 19-24, 1907, pp.12-13; copy in CVA Add.MSS.326 Vol.1 File 2. **PROJECTS**: *Edgewood*, for T.H. Calland, 2601 Point Grey Rd., Van., 1903-4 (demo. in the 1940s); St. Paul's Anglican Episcopal Church, 1130 Jervis St., Van., 1905 (ext.); Second St. Paul's Anglican Church, Church St., Nanaimo, 1906-07 (dest. by fire 1930); Sikh Temple, 1866 W. 2nd Ave., Van., 1907-08 (demo.); Bhuddist Temple, 1603 Franklin St., Van., 1910-11 (demo.).

ARCHIBALD, John Smith

Irene Puchalski's entry on Archibald in the *Grove Dictionary of Art*, 1996, Vol.2, p.308; and CAC Accession Nos.4 & 4.01, McGill University, Montreal. **PROJECT: John S. Archibald, Architect, and John Schofield, Associate Architect:** Third Hotel Vancouver, 900 W. Georgia St., Van., 1928-39 (ext.)

ASPELL, George Joseph Ketterer

Directories; War Records, National Archives of Canada; B.C. Vital Events and obituaries in the *Sun*, Apr. 23, 1974, p.48, and *Province*, Apr. 23, 1974, p.32.

AUGUSTINE, Alpheus Price

AIBC; Interview with daughter Kay Carter, North Van.; directories; and B.C. Vital Events.

BADGLEY, Charles G.

Local inventories; other references and directory searches by David A. Rash, Seattle. United States National Register of Historic Places website. Notice of Badgley opening his Van. office is from *PB&E*, Aug. 12, 1911, p.51, "Trade Notes, Personal Factors – Seattle." **PROJECT**: Convent of the Sacred Heart, 3851 W. 29th Ave., Van., 1911-12 (ext.).

BALE, David Herbert

B.C. Vital Events; *Who's Who & Why* 1912; *PB&E*; inventories; references in *VDC* and *VDT*; Vict. plumbing permits; directories; and VCA files [including VCA G.I.024.012]. Additional primary research by Julia Trachsel. **PROJECTS**: Res., 1406 Elford St., Vict., 1905 (ext.); Bale Res., 1510 Elford St., Vict., 1906 (demo.); Res., 1125 Fort St., Vict., c.1907 (alt.); *Argos* (Second Bale Res.), 1402 Stadacona Ave., Vict., 1908 (ext.); Newbury Res., *Koble Hurst*, 2895 Colquitz Ave., Saanich, 1911 (ext.); *Thorsecliffe* (Young Res.), 1606 Wilmot Place, Oak Bay, 1911 (ext.); Lettice Res., 1120 Faithful St., Vict., 1911-12 (ext.); Res., Hamilton Res., 1017 Catherine St., Vict., 1913 (ext.); Morrow Res., 566 Gorge Rd., Saanich, 1920 (ext.).

BAMFORTH, T.H.

CVA Plans and directories. Plans for, and description of, Central School Port Coquitlam, from the *Coquitlam Star*, May 7, 1913, p.7; description of the school in the *Herald/Enterprise*, Jan. 31, 1984, p.6B. **PROJECTS**: Central School, 2280 Central Ave., Port Coquitlam, 1913-14 (demo.); Columbia Block & Tool (later Opsal Steel), 97 E. 2nd Ave., Van., 1918 (ext.).

BARNET, James

AIBC; B.C. Vital Events; bldg. references from *Construction*, Feb. 1908, p.73; and the Greater Vernon Museum & Archives, which holds the original plans for the Hospital. Barnet Sr. in Felstead et al, *Directory of British Architects 1834-1900*, p.52. **PROJECTS**: Jubilee Hospital, 2101 32nd St., Vernon, 1908-09 (demo. by 1949); St. James Catholic Church, 2607 27th St., Vernon, 1908-09 (ext.); Cominco Office, Trail, 1916; Cominco Managing Director's House, Trail, 1916; School, Tadanac, c.1916; Additions to Trail School, Trail, 1916; Roman Catholic Church, Trail c.1916.

BAROTT, BLACKADER & WEBSTER

CAC Accession No. 10.01, McGill University, Montreal; and Weir, *The Lost Craft of Ornamented Architecture*, p.40. Credit Fonçier citation in the *Province*, July 12, 1913, p.26. **PROJECTS:** Third CPR Station, 601 W. Cordova St., Van., 1912-14 (ext.); Credit Fonçier Bldg., 850 W. Hastings St., Van., 1913-14 (ext.).

BARRS, Frank Arthur Ambrose

AIBC; 1881 British Census; International Genealogical Index; CVA plans; and B.C. Vital Events. **PROJECTS**: Machinery Bldg., Second Unit to the Grandstand and Fisheries Bldg., Pacific National Exhibition, 2901 E. Hastings St., Van., c.1908-1911 (demo.); St. Nicholas Anglican Church, (now Christ the King & St. Nicholas Anglican), 3883 Triumph St., Burnaby, 1912 (alt.), Laura Secord School, 2500 Lakewood Dr., Van., 1913 (ext.); Kitsilano High School, 2550 W. 10th Ave., Van., 1917 (ext.); Senior Bldg. at Strathcona School, 592 E. Pender St., Van., 1915 (ext.).

BAUER, Frederick J.

The Columbian, Souvenir Exhibition Supplement, Oct. 4, 1899, p.4; *New Westminster Heritage Resource Inventory*; and the *History of the New Westminster Library*, p.15. **PROJECTS**: Blackie Block, Columbia St., New West., 1898-99 (demo.); Central Hotel, Columbia St., New West., 1898-99 (demo.); Occidental Hotel, 716-718 Columbia St., New West., 1898-99 (completely rebuilt); Shaake Machine Shops, E. Front St., New West., 1898-99 (demo.); City Hall, New West., 500-block Columbia St., 1900-01 (demo.); Holmes Block, 635 Columbia St., New West., 1901 (alt.).

BAYNE, Richard Roskell

The Bayne Collection, now housed at UVIC, consists of 733 items and is under active research. See Segger, *The Buildings of Samuel Maclure*; B.C. Vital Events; Bayne's obituary in the *Colonist*; the 1892 Williams *B.C. Directory*, p.1151; Felstead et al, *Directory of British Architects 1834-1900*, p.63; and the 1901 Canadian Census. References from the *Colonist* supplied by Dorothy Mindenhall: two-storey house on Battery St., Apr. 2, 1891, p.1 (tender call); R.R. Bayne's bldg. cor. Quadra and Chatham Sts., May 9, 1891, p.5; and Bayne preparing plans for his own house in Oak Bay, Apr. 23, 1892, p.5. Further information online (www.maltwood.uvic.ca/bayne/).

BAYNES & HORIE

Considerable information on both Baynes and Horie in the Major Matthews collection at the CVA. Specific information on Edgar Baynes is extracted from his entry in Howay & Schofield, *British Columbia: Biographical*, 1914, Vol.IV, pp.317-318; CVA Bu.P.96; and Ben Swankey, *Building British Columbia: A History of Union Carpenters 1883-1978*. Members of the Baynes family are still actively involved with the Maple Ridge Museum, which is housed on the old Haney Brick & Tile site, and have provided further information. **PROJECTS**: Baynes Res., 1200 W. Broadway, Van., 1906 (demo.); Grosvenor Hotel, 836-848 Howe St., Van., 1912-13 (demo.).

BEALE, L. Bernhardt

Directories; Vict. plans, bldg. and plumbing permits; Oak Bay bldg. permits; and inventories. **PROJECTS: L.B. Beale:** Ross Res., 908 St. Charles St., Vict., 1914 (ext.). **Fleet & Beale:** Vict. Motion Picture Ltd., Moving Picture House, 2013 Oak Bay Ave., Oak Bay, 1913 (alt.).

BELL, Robert Brown

AIBC; Article published by his daughter, Flora M. Cooper, in the *15th Annual Report of the Okanagan Historical Society* (p.191-94), *The History of the O'Keefe Ranch* by Stan McLean, and Bell's obituary, published in the Vernon *News*, Sept. 26, 1940. Information on Constant from directories. The collection of the Greater Vernon Museum & Archives contains other references to Bell's work. Attribution from the Vernon *News* for the Vernon News Bldg. (Jan. 6, 1898) and the Central School (Sept. 15, 1910, p.1). **PROJECTS: R.B. Bell:** Megaw Res., 3203 Pleasant Valley Rd., Vernon, 1893 (ext.); Thomas Greenhow Res., O'Keefe Ranch, Spallumcheen, 1894 (dest. by fire 1939); Renovations to the Cornelius O'Keefe Res., O'Keefe Ranch, Spallumcheen, 1896 (ext.); Vernon News Bldg., Vernon, 1897 (demo,); Vernon City Hall, 2925 30th Ave., Vernon, 1897-1903 (demo.); S.C. Smith Res., 1800 32nd Ave., Vernon, 1905-08 (ext.). **Bell & Constant:** Central School, 3302 27th St., Vernon, 1910 (ext.); Bank of Montreal, Armstrong, 1910, No.1 Fire Hall, 3005 30th St., Vernon, 1911 (demo.); Union Bank, 3025 30th Ave., Vernon, 1911 (ext.); Bank of Montreal, Enderby, 1911; Theatre, Kamloops, 1912; Theatre, Vernon, 1912; Bank of Montreal, Penticton, 1912-13; School, Penticton, 1913, School, Enderby, 1914.

BELL-IRVING, Henry Ogle

Raymond Eagle, *In the Service of the Crown: The Story of Budge and Nancy Bell-Irving* (Ottawa: The Golden Dog Press, 1998); Elizabeth O'Keily, *Gentleman Air Ace: The Duncan Bell-Irving Story* (Madeira Park: Harbour Publishing, 1992); Cicely Lyons, *Salmon: Our Heritage* (Richmond: British Columbia Packers Ltd., 1969); *Business Leaders of the Century*, pp.6-7 (*Business in Vancouver* Supplement to Issue 529A, 1999); *VDW*, Dec. 31, 1888, pp.4-5; CVA Duncan Bell-Irving Fonds [Photograph Collection 1158]; *Vancouver Voters 1886*; and the B.C. Land Surveyors Annual Report, 1979, pp.83-90. Tatlow's House can be seen in CVA BU.P.245. Some erroneous information about the Bell-Irving Block appears in the *Province*, Aug. 7, 1932; see Major Matthews corrections on CVA Bu.P.85; see also *Province*, June 29, 1932, p.12. **PROJECTS**: Spinks Res., Hastings St., Van., 1888 (demo.); Tatlow Res., Pender St., Van., 1888 (demo.); Bell-Irving Block, Cordova St. near Richards St., Van., 1888-89 (demo. 1932); *The Strands*, Bell-Irving Res., Harwood St., Van., 1907 (demo.).

BENZIE, James A.

AIBC; B.C. Vital Events; obituary; CVA plans; Point Grey bldg. and plumbing permits; information from Robert Close, Scotland; 1881 British Census; and an interview with William Bow's daughter, Clara S. Coles. Additional information from Janet (Whitmore) Bingham. Citation for the Drysdale house from Van. bldg. permits. Information on the Rotary Clinic from CVA PAM 1918-28 and CVA Photograph Bu.P.423. Extant bldgs. in North Van. are described in the *City of North Vancouver Heritage Inventory, 1994*. **PROJECTS**: Drysdale Res., 1847 Barclay St., Van., 1914 (demo.); Rotary Club T.B. Clinic, 100 W. Pender St., Van., 1918-19 (demo.); Japanese-Canadian War Memorial, Stanley Park, 1920 (ext.).

BERCHTENBREITER, Hanns Carl

Interviews with Irene Berchtenbreiter, Mission; obituary in the *Camarillo News* [California], Thursday June 20, 1957, p.1. National Archives of Canada Immigration Records 1930, Vol.10, p.72 [RG76-Immigrations Series C-1-b]. Inventories; directories; and additional research by John Mawson. **PROJECTS:** Cianci Res., 2607 Nelson Ave., West Van., 1933 (ext.); Interior Design, Deutschland Café, 615-619 Seymour St., Van., 1936 (interior demo.); Mrs. Wharton Shaw Res., 4791 Belmont Ave., Van., 1937 (ext.); Bennett Res., 2909 Mathers Ave., West Van., 1937 (ext.); A.C. Langley Res., 1660 W. 29th St., West Van., 1938 (ext.); Denny Res., 210 Denison Rd., Oak Bay, 1938 (ext.); Harrison Res., 301 Denison Rd., Oak Bay, 1939 (ext.); H.C. Ramsden Res., 3908 W. Broadway, Van., 1939 (ext.).

BERRILL, Ralph

AIBC; Saanich Municipal Archives; Berrill's daughter, Gwendoline Rodger, Sidney, B.C.; RIBA membership file; B.C. and Ontario Vital Events; inventories; *VDC, VDT, VTC* references; Vict. plans, bldg. and plumbing permits; Oak Bay permits and plans; directories; VCA files; Esquimalt Archives files; *AB&E; The Week "1914 Outlook" Edition*; Margaret Browning and Jill Sewell for research on Soldiers' Settlement Act Housing in Saanich; *Ottawa Evening Citizen*; and City of Ottawa assessments. Information on Berrill's Ottawa career from Gordon Fulton. **PROJECTS**: Vict. Baggage Co. Bldg., 510 Fort St., Vict., 1921 (ext.); McIntosh Res., 1509 Shasta Place, Vict., 1924 (ext.); Carlton Court Apts., 317 Third Ave., New West., 1925 (ext.). McGiverin Res., 3615 Cadboro Bay Rd., Oak Bay, 1926 (ext.); Begg Motor Co. Showroom, 865 Yates St./1250 Quadra St., Vict., 1926 (alt.); National Motors Co., 819 Yates St., Vict., 1927 (demo.); Fraser Res., 1520 Despard St., Vict., 1928 (ext.); Humphries Res., 1621 Prospect Place, Oak Bay, 1929 (ext.); Berrill Res., 987 Mount Joy Ave., Oak Bay, 1929 (ext.); Esquimalt Municipal Hall, Esquimalt, 1929 (ext.); Sidney Roofing & Paper Co. Warehouse, Songhees Rd., Vict., 1931 (demo.).

BIKER, Walter John Ellsworth

AIBC; information supplied by his granddaughter, Jane Merry, Trail; and West Kootenay Power Co. Archives.

BIRD, Arthur Julius

AIBC; Howay & Schofield, and *British Columbia: Biographical*, 1914, Vol.IV, p.365. Information on Gotch & Saunders from Gray, *Edwardian Architecture*, pp.196-7, and Roy Hargave, Historian, Gotch, Saunders & Surridge Architects, London. **PROJECTS**: House, 2270 McGill St., Van., 1909 (demo.); House, 2240 Eton St., Van., 1909 (demo.); Capitola Apts., 1209 Thurlow St., Van., 1909 (ext.); Bird Res., 2590 W. 2nd Ave., Van., 1910 (ext.); Trafalgar Mansions, 840 Nelson St., Van., 1910-11 (demo.); Blenheim Court, 1209 Jervis St., Van., 1910-11 (ext.); Washington Court, 998 Thurlow St., Van., 1911 (alt.); Salsbury Court, 1010 Salsbury Dr., Van., 1911-12 (ext.); Lotus Hotel, 455 Abbott St., Van., 1912 (alt.); Belvedere Court Apts., 2545 Main St., Van., 1912 (ext.); Afton Hotel and Ovaltine Cafe, 224 E. Hastings St., Van., 1912 (ext.); Apts., 900-block Jackson Ave., Van., 1912 (alt.); Olmstead Res., 372 Keith Rd. E., North Van. City, 1913 (ext.); Additions to Fire Hall No.6, 1500 Nelson St., Van., 1929 (ext.); Airplane Hangars, South Terminal, Van. Airport, Richmond, 1930-31 (ext.); Coroner's Court, 238-240 Cordova St., Van., 1932 (ext.).

BIRDS, Samuel Buttrey

AIBC; Vict. plans, bldg. and plumbing permits; Sarah Tatman and Roger W. Moss, *Biographical Dictionary of Philadelphia Architects 1700-1930* (Boston: C.K. Hall & Co., 1985), p.165; Withey & Withey, *Biographical Dictionary of American Architects (Deceased)*, p.665; R.H. Harper, *Victorian Architectural Competitions* (London: Maxwell Publishing, 1893), p.198; Henderson's *British Columbia Directory*, 1911; Howay & Schofield, *British Columbia: Biographical*, 1914, Vol.III, pp.552-555; Wrigley's *British Columbia Directory*, 1920-24; *AB&E*, Aug. 15, 1912 and Apr. 25, 1913; Cowichan *Leader*, Apr. 17, 1913; Bernard M. McEvoy and Capt. A.H. Finlay, *72nd Seaforth Highlanders of Canada* (Van.: Cowan & Brookhouse, 1920). Sixth Ave. Methodist from the *Province*, July 3, 1909, p.7, "Opening of New Fairview Church." **PROJECTS**: Sixth Ave. Methodist Church, 1610 W. 6th Ave., Van., 1909 (demo.); Hampton Brothers Bakery (with **E.E. Blackmore**), 1695 W. 7th Ave., Van., 1911 (demo.); Pybus Block, 579 Richards St., Van., 1911 (ext.); Royal Inland Hospital, Kamloops, 1911 (demo.); Chalmers' Presbyterian Church (now Holy Trinity Anglican Church), 1440 W. 12th Ave., Van., 1911-12 (ext.); Royal Columbian Hospital, 330 E. Columbia St., New West., 1912 (demo. 1975); Odlum Res., 2023 Grant St., Van., 1912-13 (ext.); Public School, Ladysmith, 1913 (demo.); Suter Res., 1012 Montcalm St., Van., 1913 (demo.); Cowichan Agricultural Society Bldg., Duncan, 1913-14 (demo. 1968); Lim Bang house, 952

Queens Ave., Vict., 1912 (demo. 1975); Chinese Club, 509-521 Carrall St., Van., 1914 (ext.); Hospital Bldg., Ladysmith, pre-1914; Hospital Bldg., Merritt, pre-1914; Duplex for Dick Jong & Chu Chew, 940 Queens Ave., Vict., 1914 (alt.).

BIRLEY, Studley Patrick

AIBC; B.C. Vital Events; *Who's Who in British Columbia*, 1933-34, p.20; Luxton, *CRD Art Deco and Moderne*; research by Robert Patterson, Victoria; and Pam Birley Wilson and Rob Wilson, Saanich. **PROJECTS:** Sussex Apartment Hotel, 1001 Douglas St., Vict., 1937-38 (only facade retained); Athlone Apartments, 895 Academy Close, Vict., 1940 (ext.).

BLACKADDER, Henry

AIBC; War Records, National Archives of Canada; NVMA collection of photographs and plans. Personal information about the architect from an oral history recorded by Roy J.V. Pallant of Joyce Loutet, Blackadder's neighbour. Pallant's research also forms the basis of the North Van. Planning Department publications, *The Walking Tour of Historic Lynn Valley in North Vancouver*, and *The Walking Tour of Historic North Lonsdale in North Vancouver*. Citations in inventories conducted by F.G. Consultants (*Heritage Inventory: District of North Vancouver* and *Ambitious City: Heritage Inventory*) and Luxton & Assoc. (*City of Port Moody Heritage Inventory*). Blackadder's application for RIBA Assoc. Membership in the Assoc. Papers (V.16 1903-7, p.151) provides valuable information about his education and training. Boarding and Day School citation from *Contract Record*, Jan. 17, 1912, p.72. Other publications of interest include the *Journal* of the Royal Architectural Institute of Canada (1929-68); *Contract Record*, Nov. 24, 1920; the *Wallace Shipbuilder Magazine* (Sept. 1943, pp.2-3); the *Express* newspaper; Chuck Davis, *Reflections: One Hundred Years: A Celebration of the District of North Vancouver's Centennial*, 1990; and *Early Days in Lynn Valley*, 1978 by Walter M. Draycott. **PROJECTS: Henry Blackadder:** Garner Res., 1865 W. 12th Ave., Van., 1911 (ext.); Nye House, 230 E. Carisbrooke Rd., North Van. Dist., 1912 (ext.); Parade and Drill Hall (supervising architect), 1555 Forbes Ave., North Van. City, 1913-15 (ext.). **Henry Blackadder & Reyburn Jameson:** Boarding and Day School (Chesterfield School), 3371 Chesterfield Ave., North Van. Dist., 1912-13 (ext.). **Blackadder & MacKay:** Dundarave Block, 1601-07 Lonsdale Ave., North Van. City, 1912 (demo. 1994); Blackadder House, 172 Carisbrooke Rd., North Van. Dist., 1916 (demo.); Lynn Valley Elementary School, 3250 Mountain Hwy., North Van. Dist., 1920 (ext.); Larson Res., 254 West 6th St., North Van. City, 1921 (ext.); Cenotaph, Victoria Park East, North Van. City, 1923 (ext.); *Stanmore* (H.A. Stevenson Res.), 461 Windsor Rd. E., North Van. Dist., 1927 (ext.).

BLACKMORE, Edward Evans

B.C. Vital Events; CVA Pioneer sheets; CVA plans; Van. bldg. permits; *CA&B*; *Construction*, Nov. 1908, p.65; *Annual Report of the Department of Public Works for the Fiscal Year ending 31 Mar. 1914*; First Pantages Theatre references from the *Province*, Apr. 20, 1907, p.26; and Mills & Sommer, *Vancouver Architecture*, pp.373-382. Drawings for the English Bay Bathing Pavilion at CVA; also *Construction* [Toronto], iii, Nov., 1908, p.65, "First Beach Bath House and Promenade." See Wright, *Crown Assets*; plans for the Immigration Hall held at the National Archives of Canada. **PROJECTS:** Model School, 555 W. 12th Ave., Van., 1905 (only facade retained); YMCA Bldg., 590 Cambie St., Van., 1905 (demo.); Lord Nelson Elementary School, 2235 Kitchener St., Van., 1905 (ext.); Princess Theatre (designed with Charles K. Shand), Hastings St., Van., 1906 (demo.); First Pantages Theatre, 136-150 E. Hastings St., Van., 1907 (ext.); English Bay Bathing Pavilion, Van., 1907-09 (demo. 1939); Almond's Creamery, Pender and Dunlevy Sts., Van., 1909-11 (demo.); Jackson Apts., 600 Jackson Ave., Van., 1910 (ext.); Stanley Park Bandstand, Van., 1911 (replaced in 1934 by the Malkin Bowl); Rougemont Apts., 1689 Robson St., Van. 1912 (ext.); Gintzburger Res., Harwood St., Van., 1913 (demo.); Sir William Dawson School, 901 Burrard St., Van., 1913 (demo. 1978); Van. Immigration Hall, Foot of Thurlow St., Van., 1914-16 (demo. 1976).

BLACKMORE, William

B.C. Vital Events; CVA Pioneer sheets; CVA plans; CVA Add.MSS.54, Vol.13 f.201; Van. bldg. permits; *Vancouver of Today Architecturally*; *CA&B*; references in contemporary newspapers including the *VDW*, Dec. 31, 1888, pp.4-5; *VDW*, June 4, 1889, p.1; and *VDW*, July 13, 1894 supplement p.1. Larrabee School information from Whatcom Museum of History and Art. Congregational Church, cornerstone laid, *VDW*, Mar. 5, 1889, p.4. Manor House from *VDW*, May 9, 1889, p.4. Second St. Andrew's from *VDW*, May 26, 1890, pp.2-3. Flack Block in *VDW*, Jan. 2, 1900, p.8. Wesley Methodist in *VDW*, Dec. 31, 1900, p.8 and Jan., 2, 1901, p.6. **PROJECTS: William Blackmore:** Fire Hall #2, Seymour St., Van., 1888 (demo.); St. Andrew's Presbyterian Church, Melville St., Van., 1888 (demo.); C.D. Rand Res., Georgia and Burrard Sts., Van., 1888-89 (demo.); Manor House (Badminton Hotel), cor. Howe and Dunsmuir Sts., Van., 1889 (demo.); First Congregational Church, 500 W. Georgia St., Van., 1889 (demo.); Vermilyea Block, 925 Granville St., Van., 1889 (ext.); St. Andrew's Presbyterian Church, 686 Richards St., Van., 1890 (demo.); Larrabee School, Bellingham, Washington, 1891 (demo.); East End School addition (now Lord Strathcona School), 592 E. Pender, Van., 1897 (ext.); Fairfield Block, 445 Granville St., Van., 1898 (demo.); Flack Block, 157-199 W. Hastings St., Van., 1899-1900 (ext.); Wesley Methodist Church, 705 Burrard St., Van., 1900-04 (demo.); Hendry Res., Burnaby St., Van., 1901-02 (demo. 1968).

Wm. Blackmore & Son: Sacred Heart Academy addition, Dunsmuir and Homer Sts., Van., 1903 (demo.); BCER office and substation, Main St., Van., 1903 (demo.).

BLAIR, William Wallace

Stark, *More than Just Bricks and Boards*, pp.48-49; and the Manitoba Provincial Archives. **PROJECT:** *Anketell Lodge* (Blair Res.), 1101 Beach Dr., Oak Bay, 1913-14 (ext.).

BLANCHET, Jean-Baptiste

Sisters of Providence Archives, Seattle, Washington, including *Livre-Souvenir de la Famille Blanchet, 1646-1946*, and *Le Petit Journal*, Feb. 1913, pp.245-257; tender call for St. Paul's Hospital, Van., by J.B. Blanchet, in the *Daily Columbian*, May 1, 1894, p.4; and Providence Orphanage in *The Daily Columbian*, Oct. 14th, 1901, pp.1 & 4.

BLOOMFIELD, James Alfred

R.D. Watt, *Rainbows in Our Walls: Art and Stained Glass in Vancouver, 1890-1940* (Van. Museums & Planetarium Association, 1980. p.6-12). VCA Add. Mss. 973 "Bloomfield Family." *CA&B* Apr. 1901, p.80 and Feb. 1906, p.III; *Weekly News-Advertiser* (Van.) Sept. 8, 1903, p.7 "Local Artist's Success;" *The Telegram* (Toronto), Apr. 21, 1923 "Lots of Atmosphere Here;" *Province*, Aug. 4, 1945, p.6 (Magazine Section) "I Live the Life I Love Best."

BOUGHEN, Edmund John

B.C. Vital Events; directories; City of North Van. bldg. permits; CVA plans; and Scott, *Once in the Royal City*. Boughen's own home from the British Columbia *Weekly*, Aug. 5, 1913, p.27. **PROJECTS:** MacSween Res., 433 Eighth Ave., New West., 1912 (ext.); Furness Res., 340 Tenth St., New West., 1913 (ext.). *E-Dee-Nie* (Boughen Res.), 315 Fourth Ave., New West., 1912-13 (ext.); Keller Res., 524 E. 11th St., North Van. City, 1912 (ext.); Chapel for the Roman Catholic Archbishop of Vancouver, 602 W. 33rd Ave., Van., 1951 (demo.).

BOW, William

AIBC; CVA Plans; City and District of North Van. bldg. permits; and the *City of North Vancouver Heritage Inventory, 1994*. Biographical information was obtained from Robert Close, Scotland, and through an interview with Bow's daughter, Mrs. Clara S. Coles, in 1998. Ray Baynes provided the attribution for *Minnekhada Lodge*. UBC Competition placement confirmed in UBC Competition documents held at University Archives, UBC, and *Colonist*, Dec. 11, 1912, pp.1 & 3. Burnet's career is well documented; the quote is by Goodhart-Rendel from *Architectural Review*, Oct. 1965, p.261. **PROJECTS: Benzie & Bow:** North Van. High School, 230 E. 23rd St., North Van. City, 1923 (demo. 1979); Whitmore Res., 1192 W. 32nd Ave., Van., 1924 (demo. 2001); Bow Res., 320 Tempe Cres., North Van. City, 1925 (ext.); *Wilmar* (Kitchen Res.), 2050 S.W. Marine Dr., Van., 1925 (ext.); Taylor Res., 1653 Grand Boulevard, North Van.

City, 1925 (ext.); Ridgeway School additions, 420 E. 8th St., North Van. City, 1926 (ext.); Young Res., 1753 Grand Boulevard, North Van. City, 1927 (ext.); McDowell Res., 1160 Grand Boulevard, North Van. City, 1927 (ext.); Lyman Res., 4641 Connaught Dr., Van., 1927 (ext.); North Van. Hospital, 230 E. 13th St., North Van. City, 1929 (ext.). **Palmer & Bow:** *Minnekhada Lodge,* 4455 Oliver Rd., Coquitlam, 1934 (ext.); *Kew House* (Taylor Res.) 5324 Marine Dr., West Van., 1937 (ext.); British Properties Co. Cottage (relocated to 742 Keith Rd.) West Van., 1938 (ext.). **William Bow:** Bow Res., 846 Anderson Cres., West Van., 1946 (ext.).

BOWIE, George Pigrum

Van. bldg. permits; CVA Plans; directories; and AIBC files. Further information on the "Bowie Arch" comes from the plaque at Lumberman's Arch. The plans for the Seymour Res. are in the collection of Charles A. Osborne, Ottawa. Bowie's war records at the National Archives of Canada, Ottawa and online records of the Commonwealth War Graves Commission. **PROJECTS:** Lumberman's & Shingleman's (later Bowie) Arch, Van., 1912 (demo. 1947); Montgomery Block, 806 Richards St., Van., 1912 (ext.).

BOWMAN, Joseph Henry

AIBC; Entry in Howay & Schofield, *British Columbia: Biographical,* 1914, Vol.III, pp.92-95, and *British Columbia Pictorial & Biographical* (S.J. Clarke Publishing, 1914) provide early biographical detail. His obituary in the *Province,* May 10, 1943 provides details of his later volunteer activities. His early work is documented in Van. bldg. permits; *AB&E;* and local newspaper sources. Many of Bowman's bldgs. have been identified in inventories. **PROJECTS: J.H. Bowman:** St. John the Divine Anglican Church, 3891 Kingsway, Burnaby, 1899 (dest. by fire); St. John the Divine Anglican Church, 3891 Kingsway, Burnaby, 1905 (alt.); BCMT&T Co. Head Offices, 50 Dunlevy St., Van., 1905-06 (ext.); Mahoney Res., Chilco St. at Comox St., Van., 1906 (demo.); St. Peter's Anglican Church, 4580 Waldon St., Van., 1908 (with J.T. Alexander, alt.); Roe Res., 2227 St. Johns St., Port Moody, 1910 (ext.); Selkirk School, 1750 E. 22nd Ave., Van., 1910-12 (ext.); Tecumseh School, 1850 E. 41st Ave., Van., 1910-12 (ext.); Alexander Res., 3698 Cypress St., Van., 1912 (ext.); Port Moody City Hall, 2425 St. Johns St., Port Moody, 1914 (ext.); Gilmore Ave. School (central block), 50 S. Gilmore Ave., Burnaby, 1915-16 (ext.); General Currie School, 8200 General Currie Rd., Richmond, 1919 (ext.). **Bowman & Cullerne:** Robertson Elementary School, 8855 Elm Dr., Chilliwack, 1921 (ext.); Gilmore Ave. School (north wing), 50 S. Gilmore Ave., Burnaby, 1921-22 (ext.); Seaforth School (now relocated to Burnaby Village Museum), 1922 (ext.); Burnaby North High School (now Rosser Elementary), 4375 Pandora Street, Burnaby, 1923 (alt.); Chilliwack Central Elementary School, 9435 Young Rd. N., Chilliwack, 1929 (ext.); Metropolitan Tabernacle, 189 W. 11th Ave., Van., 1931 (ext.).

BRAUNTON & LEIBERT

CVA plans; directories; *Modern Architecture; Province,* June 8, 1912, p.28 and Nov. 30, 1912, p.27; and the United States National Register of Historic Places website. **PROJECTS:** Astoria Hotel, 769 E. Hastings St., Van., 1912 (ext.); City Mission, 150 Alexander St., Van., 1912 (ext.); Irwinton Apts., 777 Burrard St., Van., 1912-13 (ext.); Ashnola Apts., 203 E. 6th Ave., Van., 1912-13 (ext.); Standard Furniture Co. Bldg., 1090 Granville St./649 Helmcken St., Van., 1913 (ext.); Allen Bldg., 814 Granville St., Van., 1914 (alt.).

BRESEMANN & DURFEE

Information on E.J. Bresemann comes from an unpublished autobiographical essay written in 1966, from his granddaughter, Linda Silver, and his daughter-in-law, Myrtle W. Bresemann, in Tacoma, Washington; directories for B.C.; *Seattle Post Intelligencer; AB&E; PB&E; VDC; City of Victoria Downtown Heritage Inventory; Heritage Resources of Nanaimo;* Vict. plans, bldg. and plumbing permits; Website research by Carey Pallister: Tacoma Public Library; Sumner, Washington; Fullerton, California; Anaheim, California; Tucson, Arizona. Further information on M.E. Durfee in California supplied by Jane Newell of Anaheim Public Library, including *Southwest Builder & Contractor, Who's Who in Los Angeles County 1925-26,* and obituary from *Anaheim Bulletin,* 12.27.1941, p.1. **PROJECTS: Bresemann & Durfee:** Residences for **Ward Investment Co.,** 134 and 217 Linden Ave., Vict., 1911 (ext.); B.C. Funeral Furnishing Co. Bldg., Broughton St., Vict., 1911-12 (demo.); Houses for **Ward Investment Co.,** 85 and 156 Cambridge St., Vict., 1911 and 1912 (ext.); Knights of Pythias Hall, 842 North Park St., Vict., 1912, (facade ext.); Hotels for Peter Swanson, Nanaimo and Princeton, 1912 (unknown if built); alterations to Ritz Café, Van., 1912; St. James (now Olympic) Hotel, 642 Johnson St., Vict., 1912 (ext.); First Congregational Church, 1600 Quadra St., Vict., 1912-13 (alt.); Esquimalt Methodist (now United) Church, 500 Admirals Rd., Esquimalt, 1913 (alt.); W.J. Barclay Res., 1063 Bank St., Vict., 1913 (ext.); Commercial Hotel addition, 121 Bastion St., Nanaimo, 1913 (ext.). **E.J. Bresemann:** Rawlinson & Glaholm Grocers, 437 Fitzwilliam St., Nanaimo, 1916 (ext.)

BRETT & HALL

Brett & Hall's town plan for Prince Rupert is covered in Kalman, *The Prince Rupert Heritage Inventory and Conservation Programme.* Their plan, described by George D. Hall, was published in *The Architectural Record,* Vol.26, No.2, Aug. 1909, pp.97-106.

BRITISH CANADIAN HOME BUILDERS, LIMITED

Vict. plans, bldg. and plumbing permits; *AB&E; VDC, VDT;* directories; and inventories. **PROJECT:** Kennedy Res., 4040 Wilkinson Rd., Saanich, 1913 (ext.).

B.C. MILLS, TIMBER & TRADING COMPANY

Extensively covered in Mills & Holdsworth, *The B.C. Mills Prefabricated System.* Additional information from the Company's catalogue CVA Und-507. Prince Rupert Government Buildings covered in *British Columbia Sessional Papers,* Report for 1909 [Public Works: Works & Buildings, Vote No. 123b].

BRODERICK, Charles Archibald

AIBC; B.C. Vital Events; Trail Archives; City Clerk, Trail; Elspeth Cowell, *W.F. Williams (1904-1947): On the Edge of Modernism,* Master's thesis, Carleton University, 1993; and Jenny Cowell, "Charles Archibald 'Archie' Broderick," *Trail Journal of Local History,* Spring 2001, p.35. **PROJECTS:** Cominco Munitions Plant, Tadanac, 1915; Cominco Buildings, Kimberley, 1918; Memorial Hall, Trail, 1919 (demo. 2000); Cominco Machine and Electrical Buildings, Tadanac, 1919; Trail Tadanac High School, Trail, 1922 (ext.); Fire Hall, Trail, 1923 (ext.); Trail Tadanac Hospital, Trail, 1926 (demo.); Cristoforo Columbo Lodge, Trail, 1927 (ext.); City Hall, Trail, 1928 (ext.); Union Hotel, Trail, 1939 (ext.).

BROWN, Ernest T.

AIBC; SAA, *An Interactive History of Architects;* Kamloops Museum & Archives; Kamloops inventories; the Kamloops *Inland Sentinel,* Feb. 4, 1927, p.1; Feb. 21, 1928, p.1; and July 10, 1928, p.1; Lorne Simpson, Calgary; and Dogterom, *Where Was It?* p.43 & 51. **PROJECTS:** Elks Lodge, 409 Seymour St., Kamloops, 1927 (ext.); Plaza Hotel, 405 Victoria St., Kamloops, 1927-28 (ext.).

BROWN, John Graham

AIBC; Death certificate and obituaries (*Times* and *Colonist*); McIntosh, *A Documentary History of Music in Victoria, Vol.I;* city directories; *Who's Who in British Columbia,* 1931; *AB&E* references 1914; Vict. plumbing plans; and biographical information collected in the course of researching his father-in-law, John Teague.

BUNGALOW CONSTRUCTION COMPANY, LIMITED

Jud Yoho, *Bungalow Magazine,* Seattle, 1913; Boam, *British Columbia,* p.78; B.C. Vital Events; Vict. plans, bldg. and plumbing permits; *AB&E; VDC; VDT;* directories; and inventories. **PROJECTS:** Residences, 400 Blk. Durban St., Vict., 1912-13 (ext.).

BUNGALOW CONSTRUCTION ASSOCIATION/ BUNGALOW BUILDING & FINANCE CO.

Boam, *British Columbia,* pp.191-2 & 194; and directories.

BURKE, HORWOOD & WHITE

For detailed information and an extensive bibliography see the monograph by Angela Carr, *Toronto Architect Edmund Burke: Redefining Canadian Architecture* (Montreal & Kingston; McGill-Queen's

University Press, 1995). See also David Monteyne, "Constructing Buildings and Histories: Hudson's Bay Co. Department Stores, 1913-26," SSAC *Bulletin*, 20:4 (Dec. 1995). There are AIBC files on Horwood and White. **PROJECTS**: First Baptist Church, 969 Burrard St., Van., 1910-11 (ext.); Mount Pleasant Baptist Church, 2600 Quebec St., Van., 1909-12 (ext.); Hudson's Bay Co. Department Store, 632-674 Granville St., Van., 1913-16 and 1925-26 (ext.); Hudson's Bay Co. Department Store, 1701 Douglas St., Vict., 1913-21 (ext.).

BURRIS, Samuel Cyrus
Notes by Madge Hamilton in the author's collection formed the foundation for research on S.C. Burris, primarily *VDC* references. Other information was from census records; directories; BCA; and VCA. Reference in *CA&B* to the sale of his practice, July, 1888; Hannington Res. from *VDC,* Jan. 1, 1889, p.2 and *CA&B.* See also Cotton, *Vice-Regal Mansions.* Colonial Hotel from the *British Columbian,* Feb. 27, 1884, p.3. Additional information from Jim Wolf, Carey Pallister and Donald Luxton. **PROJECTS**: Allen Res., Collinson and Rupert Sts., Vict., 1883 (demo.); Conservatory at *Armadale,* 241 Niagara St., Vict., 1883 (demo. 1940s); McLaughlan Res., 1342 Pandora Ave., Vict., 1883 (ext.); Third Colonial Hotel, Columbia St., New West., 1884 (dest. by fire 1898); William Smithe House, 425 Michigan St., Vict., 1886 (demo.); McQuade Res., 900 Blk. Vancouver St., Vict., 1888 (demo.); Conservatory for Cary Castle, Belcher Rd., Vict., 1888 (dest. by fire 1899); Thomas Kains Res., 430 Dallas Rd., Vict., 1889 (demo.); *Aldermere* (Hannington Res.), Millstream, near Langford, 1889; Warehouse, Broughton St., Vict., 1889; *Jolimont* (Bainbridge Res.), 1936 Hampshire Rd., Oak Bay, 1892 (ext.). **Burris & de la Penotière:** Vict. Club Rooms, Vict., 1885 (demo.); Res., Victoria Cres., Vict., 1885 (unidentified).

BUTLER & HARRISON
Vict. plans, bldg. and plumbing permits; *AB&E*; directories; and inventories. **PROJECTS**: Foul Bay Hotel, Vict., 1912 (unbuilt project); Wilkinson Rd. Methodist Church, 4274 Wilkinson Rd., Saanich, 1913 (ext.); Kennedy Res., 4040 Wilkinson Rd., Saanich, c.1912 (ext.); Lemon Res., 1045 Belmont Ave., Vict., 1913 (ext.); Jones Res. additions, 1759 Rockland Ave., Vict., 1914 (ext.); Hammond Res., Metchosin, 1914 (unidentified).

BUTTERFIELD, Ernest
AB&E; Vict. plans, bldg. and plumbing permits; and directories. **PROJECTS**: Shaper Res., 2316 Quadra St., Vict., 1909 (demo.); Harris Res., 1033 Princess Ave., Vict., 1912 (demo.); Bickerdike Res., 1048-50 Queens Ave., Vict., 1912 (ext.); Haggerty Res., 1385 Manor Rd., Vict., 1913 (ext.).

CAMPBELL, Clive Dickens
AIBC; interviews with Campbell's son, Douglas A. Campbell, Vict.; Cotton, *Vice-Regal Mansions*; *VDT,* Jan. 13, 1975, p.22 and Jan. 16, 1975 p.37;

VDC, Mar. 17, 1978, p.21. **PROJECT**: Government House, Rockland Ave., Vict., 1957-59 (ext.).

CANADIAN DEPARTMENT OF JUSTICE
Annual reports of the Department of Justice, 1867-1962. B.C. Penitentiary covered in G. Edward Mills, Federal Heritage Buildings Review Office: *Building Report 83-17*; Jack David Scott, *Four Walls in the West: The Story of the British Columbia Penitentiary* (Retired Federal Prison Officer's Association of British Columbia, 1984); and Dana H. Johnson, SSAC *Bulletin* 19:2 (June 1994), pp.36-7. The plans for the Pen are described in the *VDC,* May 27, 1874. The quote about the Pen's storm windows is from Inspector Moylan's Annual Report to the Minister of Justice. **PROJECT**: **Thomas Painter & James Adams:** British Columbia Penitentiary, 65 Richmond St., New West., 1874-77 (ext.).

CANADIAN DEPARTMENT OF MILITIA & DEFENCE, ENGINEERING BRANCH
Jacqueline Adell, *Architecture of the Drill Hall in Canada*, 1863-1939 (Ottawa: Report prepared for the Historic Sites & Monuments Board of Canada, June 1989). Numerous references in the *Colonist,* including tender calls; information from Dana H. Johnson. **PROJECT**: **Henry James, Designer:** Vict. Drill Hall, 431 Menzies St., Vict., 1891-94 (ext.).

CANE, Henry
B.C. Vital Events; *Nelson: A Proposal for Urban Heritage Conservation*; Nelson Museum; and obituary, Nelson *Daily News*, Dec. 30, l935.

CARRIE, Alexander
AIBC; *Nelson: A Proposal for Urban Heritage Conservation*; Nelson directories; 1871 Ontario Census; B.C. Vital Events; International Genealogy Index; Nelson *Daily News*; City of Nelson web site; research by Henry Stevenson from the Nelson Museum. **PROJECTS**: Nelson High School, Latimer St., Nelson, 1901-02 (dest. by fire 1960s); Nelson Public School, Stanley St., Nelson, 1908 (ext.); CPR Superintendent's Res., 420 Railway St., Nelson, 1908 (ext.); YMCA Bldg. (with Egg & Haldane), 402 Victoria St., Nelson, 1909 (ext.); Kerr Apts., 514 Victoria St., Nelson, 1911 (ext.).

CARTHEW, James Arthur
Local newspapers *The Weekly News, Nanaimo Free Press, Cumberland News, The Enterprise, Islander, The Cumberland Islander, Comox District Free Press*; interviews with descendants; inventories; tax assessments in BCA; Land Titles; B.C. Vital Events. **PROJECTS**: Mounce Res., 2696 Derwent Ave., Cumberland, 1894 (ext.); McKim Res., 2714 Maryport Ave., Cumberland, 1894 (ext.); Denton Res., 2732 Maryport Ave.), Cumberland, 1894 (ext.); Hamburger Houses, 2750 Allen Ave., 2741 and 2745 Derwent Ave., Cumberland, 1894 (ext.); Matthewson Cottages, 2721 Windermere Ave., Cumberland, 1894 (demo.); St. George's Presbyterian Church, 2688 Penrith Ave., Cumberland, 1895 (alt.); Livery Stable, 3274 Third St., Cumberland,

1898 (destroyed by weight of snow 1933).

CHOW, W.H.
Chinatown: A Walking Tour Through History (Van. Planning Department and the Van. Museum, 1987); Kalman, *Exploring Vancouver 2*; Rosemary Neering, *The Vancouver Walking Guides: East Side: Chinatown, Strathcona, the Working Port.* (Van.: Whitecap, 1994). The information about the refusal of Chow's admission to the AIBC is contained in the AIBC Council Minutes, 1920-21, CVA AM.326. **PROJECTS**: Ming Wo Store, 23 E. Pender St., Van., 1914 (ext.); Yue Shan Society Headquarters, 33-37 E. Pender St., Van., 1920 (ext.); Ming's (with **W.T. Whiteway**, unattributed), 141-147 E. Pender St., Van., 1920 (alt.).

CLARKSON, Eric Charlesworth
AIBC; Vict. and Oak Bay plans and permits; and obituaries, *Times,* Feb. 26, 1977, p.59, and *Colonist,* Mar. 1, 1977, p.34. Plans for the Howard Res. are in the possession of the owner, Tim O'Conner. **PROJECTS**: Howard Res., 3420 Beach Dr., Oak Bay, 1929 (ext.); Mount View High School, 3814 Carey Rd., Saanich, 1931 (ext.); Oak Bay Cinema, 2184-2194 Oak Bay Ave., 1936 (interior rebuilt); Atlas Theatre, 834-840 Yates St., Vict., 1936 (facade partially retained); Kipling Res., 707 Moss St., Vict., 1938 (ext.); Red Cross House, 1044-1046 Fort St., Vict., 1945-46 (ext.).

CLOW, Charles Henry
Biographical information on Clow is limited to an 1892 Biography in the Williams British Columbia 1892 directory (p.1154), and his obituary in *The British Columbian,* July 23, 1929. Information on Jessie Clow was found in the marriage notice printed in *The British Columbian,* Sept. 20, 1884, p.3, and her death notice in *The British Columbian,* June 13, 1895, p.4. B.C. Vital Events and *The British Columbian,* June 14, 1918, p.6 "Death of Mrs. Clow" provide details regarding his second marriage. An article published in *The Weekly British Columbian,* May 27, 1929, p.45 provides detailed information about his estate. Information about his New West. commissions has been discovered primarily through tender notices and bldg. descriptions published in local newspapers and New West. bldg. permits 1911-20. Royal Columbian (plans accepted, $10,000) in the *Colonist,* July 3, 1889, p.4. **PROJECTS**: **C.H. Clow:** Odd Fellows Hall, Cloverdale, Surrey, 1904 (alt. and relocated); YMCA, 514 Royal Ave., New West., 1910 (demo. 1964); Surrey Municipal Hall, 17675 - 56th Ave., Surrey, 1912 (ext.). **Clow & Maclure:** Royal Columbian Hospital, 330 E. Columbia St., New West., 1889 (demo.); Clow Res., 507 Fifth St., New West., 1890 (demo.); YMCA Block, Church and Columbia Sts., New West., 1890 (dest. by fire 1898); Murray (later Gilley) Res., 403 St. George St., New West., 1890 (ext.); *Idlewild* (A.J. Hill Res.), Fourth St. near Fifth Ave., New West., 1891 (demo.). **Clow & Welsh:** Reformed Episcopal Church, 628 Royal Ave., New West., 1899 (ext.).

COATES, H. Crawford, Jr.

Philadelphia Architects and Buildings Project website; *Who's Who in American Art* IV-1940-47 (available on the Society of Architectural Historians website); VCA demo. bldg. plans; directories; *AB&E*; *PB&E*; *VDC*; Vict. plans, bldg. and plumbing permits; Oak Bay bldg. permits; inventories; and walking tour brochures. **PROJECTS: C. Coates:** Hunter Res., 1057 Moss St., Vict., 1913 (ext.); McDermott Res., 3655 Beach Dr., Oak Bay, 1912 (ext.); **Coates & Fleet:** Alterations to Brown Jug Saloon, 1017-19 Government St., Vict., 1913 (ext.); Collegiate School wing additions, Rockland Ave., Vict., 1913 (demo.).

COCKRILL, Harold Woodruff

AIBC; 1881 British Census; B.C. Vital Events; directories; and obituary in the *Sun*, Dec. 22, 1965, p.32.

COLONNA, Edward

Dr. Martin Eidelberg, *E. Colonna* (Dayton, Ohio: Dayton Art Institute, 1983). Other references in *VDW*, Oct. 3, 1891, p.2; Harold Kalman, *A History of Canadian Architecture* (Vol.2), p.488; Mary McAlpine, "The Sad Saga of E. Colonna, Architect," The *Sun*, Apr. 12, 1978, p.A6; and the Parliament Bldg. Architect's Competition Submission Documents, BCA C/C/30.7/P23.3. Colonna's plans for the CPR Station and the renovations of the Hotel Vancouver are part of the collection of the CAC, McGill University, Montreal. Information on the significance of Mary Louise McLaughlin from Donald S. Hall, Rochester, New York. **PROJECT:** Second Van. CPR Station, preliminary designs, c.1891-92 (redesigned by Edward Maxwell).

CORBY, Percy Edmund

AIBC; B.C. Vital Events; Kelowna Heritage Register; *Kelowna Heritage Walking Tour*, city directories and Robert G. Hill. The Corbys are mentioned in the *Colonist*, Nov. 28, 1963, p.33; and the *Times*, Aug. 27, 1963, p.13 and Jan. 25, 1968, p.17. **PROJECTS:** British North American Tobacco Co. Ltd. Bldg., 1250-1298 Ellis St., Kelowna, 1912 (ext.); Grote Stirling Res., 1590-1640 Belgo Rd., Kelowna, 1912 (ext.).

COX, Alfred Arthur

AIBC; RIBA membership file; CCA Vertical Files; *CA&B*; *AB&E*; Van. bldg. permits; inventories; Vancouver Club files at CVA; Vict. plans and bldg. permits; and the *Victoria Downtown Heritage Register*. Carter-Cotton Bldg. references from *Construction*, Oct. 1908, p.65 and rendering from the Bentall Archives. Prince Rupert Court House from *Contract Record*, July 8, 1914, and 1915 issues of the *B.C. Building Record*. **PROJECTS: Cox & Amos:** Carter-Cotton (later *Province*) Bldg., 198 West Hastings St., Van., 1908-09. **A.A. Cox:** Bldg. for Henry Edgett (now the Architecture Centre), 440 Cambie St., Van., 1911 (ext.); Union Bank, 1205 Government St./612-618 View St., Vict., 1912 (ext.); British American Trust Co. Ltd. Bldg., 737 Fort St., Vict., 1912 (ext.); W.F. Salsbury Res., 1790 Angus Drive, Van., 1912 (ext.); Bowser Res., 1001

Terrace Ave., Vict., 1912-13 (ext.); Provincial Industrial Home for Girls, 800 Cassiar St., Van., 1912-14 (ext.); Prince Rupert Court House, Prince Rupert, 1914-15 (unbuilt project); Bank of Nova Scotia, 702 Yates St./1301-09 Douglas St., Vict., 1923 (alt. 1963); Van. Womens' Bldg., 752 Thurlow St., Van., 1926 (demo.).

CRANE, C. Howard

D'Acres & Luxton, *Lions Gate*; Russell, *All That Glitters*. **PROJECT:** Allen (later Strand) Theatre, 600-620 West Georgia St., Van., 1919-20 (demo. 1974).

CRESSWELL, Henry John

Gordon D. Taylor, grandson of Mr. Cresswell's brother-in-law; Lincolnshire Archives, Lincoln, England; *Delta News* and the *Delta Times*, 1902 to 1904; the 1901 Census; B.C. Vital Events; and B.C. directories (for Delta) 1890 to 1903. A drawing showing the front elevation of the Reagh Shoe Store, dated May 1905, is located in the holdings of Delta Museum & Archives. Reference to the new portion of Boundary Bay Cemetery is from the *Delta Times*, July 14, 1908, p.1. Information on Beacon Hill Park provided by Carey Pallister (Colonist 10 April 1889 p. 3 ad for competition; Colonist 19 April 1889 p. 4 description of Creswell's plan; 23 April 1889 letter to Cresswell from City Clerk; 29 May 1889 Council minutes). **PROJECTS:** Presbyterian Manse, Ladner, Delta, 1902 (demo.); Anglican Manse, Ladner, Delta, 1904 (demo.); Odd Fellows Lodge, 4873 Delta St., Ladner, Delta, 1904 (ext.); J. Reagh Shoe Store, Ladner, Delta, 1905 (demo.); Cresswell Home, Ladner, Delta, 1911 (demo.).

CRICKMAY, William

Directories; B.C. Vital Events; CVA Major Matthews Topical File AM0054.013.010104; *Vancouver Voters 1886*; *VDW*, Mar. 9, 1889, p.4; *VDW* Souvenir Edition, June, 1896, p.30; *VDW*, March 13, 1897, p.3; and Kluckner & Atkin, *Heritage Walks Around Vancouver*, p.145.

CROSS, Frederick William Franklin

AIBC; CVA Plans; directories; and B.C. Vital Events. **PROJECT:** Coniston Lodge Residential Hotel, 894 Bute St., Van., 1926 (ext.).

CULLERNE, Harold

AIBC; B.C. Vital Events; War Records, National Archives of Canada; CVA Plans; Scott, *Once in the Royal City*; Vancouver *Sun*, Nov. 2, 1938; and the *Colne Valley Guardian*, Feb. 25, 1927 and Jan. 20, 1939. Information from niece, Marjorie Cullerne-Koers, Parksville (including newsclippings and photographs), and step-daughters Jeannette Dawson, Burnaby, and Helen Hurley, Vancouver. PNE Prize Home from *The Ideal Bungalow: Its Description* [BCA NWp 728.37 I19]; David Breen & Kenneth Coates, *The Pacific National Exhibition: An Illustrated History* (Vancouver: UBC Press, 1982); *Sun*, Aug. 21, 1982, p.C1; Van. *Courier*, Sept. 6, 1998, p.12; *Province*, Aug. 22, 1999, p.A22. Hollywood Theatre from Vancouver *News-Herald*, Oct. 22, 1935; Mission

Legion Hall from *The British Columbian*, Jan. 13, 1936, p.3. Dunbar Heights United from United Church Archives, Toronto. Edmonds School in Burnaby *News-Courier*, Oct. 27, 1949, p.7. **PROJECTS: Harold Cullerne:** Pacific Great Eastern Train Station, S. foot of Lonsdale Ave., North Van. City, 1913-14 (ext.); PNE Prize Home (*The Ideal Bungalow*), relocated to 2812 Dundas St., 1934 (alt.); Hollywood Theatre, 3123 W. Broadway, Van., 1935-36 (ext.); Legion Hall, 32900 Blk. 1st Ave., Mission, 1936 (ext.); Moravian Evangelical Church, 626 E. 58th Ave., Van., 1936 (alt.); St. Francis of Assisi Church and Franciscan Friary, 2025 Napier St./1020 Semlin St., Van., 1938 (ext.); Capitol Hill Community Hall, 361 Howard Ave., Burnaby, 1944-46 (alt.); Dunbar Heights United Church, Van., 1946 (unbuilt project). **Harold Cullerne & G.N. Evans Associate Architects:** Edmonds Jr. High School (now Edmonds Community School), 7651 18th Ave., Burnaby, 1949 (ext.).

CULLIN, Harold Joseph Rous

AIBC; B.C. Vital Events; inventories; *VDC* and *VDT* references; Vict. plans, bldg. and plumbing permits; Oak Bay permits and plans; directories; Census; War Records, National Archives of Canada; Madge Hamilton Collection; BCA files; *The Week "1914 Outlook" Edition*; Riverview Heritage Evaluation; Kelowna Centennial Museum; and the Kelowna Heritage Register. **PROJECTS:** Cedar Hill School and Manual Training Hall, 3851-61 Cedar Hill Cross Rd., Saanich, 1912-13 (ext.); Tolmie School, 556 Boleskine Rd., Saanich, 1913 (ext.); Thomas Shaw House, *Hume Cottage*, 806 Linden Ave., Vict., 1907 (ext.); Saumarez-Duke Res., 1140 Tattersall Drive, Saanich, 1912 (ext.); Dobson Res., 1134 Dallas Rd., Vict., 1912 (ext.); Two residences for Louis S.V. York, 17-19 and 25 Cook St., 1912 (ext.); Goodacre Res., 1392 St. David St., Oak Bay, 1912 (ext.); Dewar Res., 2431 Currie Rd., Oak Bay, 1913 (ext.); Park Mansions, 903 North Park St./1725 Quadra St., Vict., 1913 (ext.); Sir F. Ashley Sparks Res., 2320 Windsor Rd., Oak Bay, 1918 (ext.); Cottage 116, Riverview Hospital, 500 Lougheed Hwy., Coquitlam, 1919 (ext.); Adams Res., 1998 Abbott St., Kelowna, 1922 (ext.); Kelowna Fire Hall, 1616 Water St., Kelowna, 1924 (ext.).

CUMMINGS & MORCOM

Directories; B.C. Vital Events; Esquimalt Archives; *AB&E* references, including May 10, 1913; Military Attestation Papers; and *The Week "1914 Outlook" Edition*, Jan. 24, 1914. **PROJECT: Cummings & Morcom:** Moving Picture Theatre Bldg., 941 Esquimalt Rd., Esquimalt, 1914 (alt.). **T. R. Morcom:** Morcom Res., 389 St. James Rd. E., North Van., 1923 (ext.).

CURTIS, Richard

AIBC; and B.C. Vital Events. Plans for the Vernon High School in the CAA, Calgary. **PROJECT:** High School, Hwy. 6, Vernon, 1937 (demo. c.1997).

DALTON & EVELEIGH

AIBC; *Who's Who & Why*, 1913; *Vancouver of Today Architecturally*, c.1900; Scott, *Once in the*

Royal City; Eveleigh's entry in Howay & Schofield, *British Columbia: Biographical*, 1914, Vol.III, pp.908-911; articles in *CA&B;* the *Province;* the *Sun;* CVA Eveleigh dockets [Add.MSS.54]; CVA Major Matthews topical files; CVA plans; Revelstoke Museum & Archives; and interviews with Eveleigh's grandsons, Robert Eveleigh "Buzz" Walker, William R. Walker, and Peter Walker, who have an extensive collection of family papers and photographs, and plans of the proposed east wing of the Van. Court House. Information from Phyllys Dalton Brown, the daughter of A.T. Dalton, who also provided an early project list. Furnishing specifications for the Van. Court House, 1910-11, in BCA GR-0054 Box 36 File 512. The records of the Burrard Literary Society are in the CVA. The Webling/McRaye wedding is described in Betty Keller, *Pauline: A Biography of Pauline Johnson* (Vancouver: Douglas & McIntyre, 1981). Buntzen Power House from Weekly Engineer's Report, May 23, 1903, BCER Collection, Special Collections, UBC and tender call from *Contract Record* [Toronto], xiv, July 1, 1903, p.3. Alcazar Hotel CVA Plans AP-232. Plans for St. Bartholomew's Hospital held by Technical Services, Indian & Northern Affairs Canada, Hull, Quebec. For the Tranquille Sanatorium see Norton, *A Whole Little City by Itself* and *The Contract Record*, Jan. 14, 1914, p.55. Dalton listed as supervising architect for the CPR Station in *Vancouver of Today Architecturally* and the *Province*, Aug. 6, 1898, p.2. Queen Victoria Hospital, Revelstoke from Revelstoke Hospital Society Minutes, Aug. 27, 1901. Dalton's obituary appeared in the *JRAIC*, July 1931, p.286. Dalton information from the Kerrisdale Collection, CVA, courtesy Janet Bingham. **PROJECTS: S.M. Eveleigh:** Lord Stanley Arch, Lost Lagoon, Van., 1889 (demo.); St. Bartholomew's Hospital, Lytton, 1931-36. **W.T. Dalton:** MacKinnon Block (later the Williams Bldg.), 409-425 Granville St. at Hastings, Van., 1897-98 (demo. 1959); Martin & Robertson Co. Warehouse, 313 Water St., Van., 1898 (ext.); DeBeck Block, 300 Blk. W. Hastings St., Van., 1898 (demo.); Skinner Block, Van., 1898; Pender Chambers, between Richards and Seymour Sts., Van., c.1898 (demo.); Hudson's Bay Co. Department Store addition, Granville and Georgia Sts., Van., 1900 (demo. 1926); Hadden Block, northeast cor. Granville and Hastings Sts., Van., 1901 (demo. by 1929); Queen Victoria Cottage Hospital, First St., Revelstoke, 1901-02 (dest. by fire 1960s). **Dalton & Eveleigh:** Royal Bank, 400-404 W. Hastings St., Van., 1903 (ext.); Buntzen Power House #1, Indian Arm, 1903 (alt.); Hadden Hall, West Van. (current location of the Capilano Golf & Country Club), c.1903 (demo.); Police Court and Jail, E. Cordova St., Van., 1903 (demo.); Imperial Bank Bldg., 200 Mackenzie Ave., Revelstoke, 1903-04 (demo); West Fairview School, 2251 W. 4th Ave., Van., 1904-05 (demo. 1946); Lawrence Hardware, 115 Mackenzie Ave., Revelstoke, 1905 (alt.); Davis Chambers, 609-615 W. Hastings St., Van., 1905-06 (demo. 1977); B.C. Telephone Exchange, 555 Seymour St., Van., 1906-07 (demo.); St. Alban's

Anglican Church, 7717 19th Ave., Burnaby, 1907-09 (alt.); Russell Hotel (now College Place), 740 Carnarvon St., New West., 1907-08 (ext.); Leckie Bldg., Cambie and Water Sts., Van., 1908-09 (ext.); Tuberculosis Sanatorium, Tranquille (near Kamloops), Main Bldg., 1908-1910, other bldgs. 1912-14 (Main Bldg. alt.); Pilkington Bldg., 120 Powell St., Van., 1910 (ext.); Hudson's Bay Co. Store, cor. 32nd St. and 30th Ave., Vernon, 1911-12 (demo. 1976); Alcazar Hotel, 337 Dunsmuir St., Van., 1912 (demo. 1980s); East Wing, Van. Court House, 800 Robson St. at Howe St., Van., c.1913 (unbuilt project); Cope & Son Warehouse, 780 Beatty St., Van., 1914 (alt.). **A.T. Dalton:** Dalton Res., 6369 Macdonald St. (originally Kaye Rd.), Van., 1912 (alt.); Hanbury Res., 6061 Macdonald St., Van., 1921 (alt.).

DARLING & PEARSON

Local inventories; Vict. plans, bldg. and plumbing permits; CVA plans; National Film Board, *Stones of History*; and Eric Arthur, Toronto: No Mean City, p.256. (3rd edition, rev. by Stephen A. Otto. Toronto, Buffalo and London: University of Toronto Press, 1986). Biographical information on Darling from William Dendy's entries in the *Grove Dictionary of Art*, 1996, Vol.8, p.528, and the *MacMillan Encyclopedia of Architects*, 1982, Vol.1, pp.502-503. Information on Pearson from Robert G. Hill. **PROJECTS:** Bank of Commerce, 118 Victoria St., Kamloops, 1904 (ext.); Bank of Commerce, 698 W. Hastings St., Van., 1906-08 (ext.); Canada Life Assurance Bldg., 686 W. Hastings St., Van., 1910-11 (demo.); Bank of Commerce, 2420 Douglas St., Vict., 1910 (ext.); Bank of Commerce, 540-544 Columbia St., New West., 1911 (ext.).

DAVENPORT, Sumner Godfrey

Robert G. Hill; obituaries; McDowall, *Quick to the Frontier*; and inventories. **PROJECT:** Royal Bank Bldg., 675-685 W. Hastings St., Van., 1929-31 (ext.).

DAVIDSON, Bedford

Directories; CVA plans; Van. bldg. permits; *Province*, Aug. 26, 1928, p.16; AIBC Council Minutes, 1928 [CVA]; and B.C. Vital Events. **PROJECT:** Dawson (now Ford) Bldg., 189-197 East Hastings St., Van., 1911-12 (ext.).

DAWSON, Charles Frederick

Who's Who in British Columbia (Vict.: S.M. Carter) 1933-34, p.192; Powell River *News*, July 6, 1938; the Powell River *Digester*, Apr., 1939, p.5; and directories. **PROJECT:** Federal Bldg. (now Dr. Dave's SmokeHouse), 5824 Ash St., Powell River, 1938-39 (ext.).

DAY, Harry Daborn

AIBC; BCA; Vict. plans, bldg. and plumbing permits; directories; Chamberlin, *Maltwood Museum Architectural Plans Series*; *Colonist,* Oct. 16, 1965, p.25; Hallmark Society archives; and Surrey tourist

information online (www.surreyheath.gov.uk). **PROJECTS:** House for Day & Hallward, 1144-46 Empress Ave., Vict., 1911 (demo. or unbuilt project); Unwin Res., 3178 Beaverbrooke Pl., Oak Bay, c.1931 (ext.); Beeching Res. and Coach House, 3270 Upper Terrace, Oak Bay, c.1931 (ext.); Ballard Cottage, 309 King George Terrace, Oak Bay, c.1931 (alt.); Beckwith Res., 1149 Oliver St., Oak Bay, c.1936 (ext.); Vowles Res., 1010 Burnside Rd. W., Saanich, c.1936 (ext.); Residences, 1238 and 1244 Tattersall Dr., Saanich, 1936 (ext.).

DAY, John Charles

AIBC; B.C. Vital Events; directories; and his war records in the National Archives of Canada, Ottawa. **PROJECTS:** Bonnycastle Res., 2535 S.W. Marine Dr., Van., 1927 (alt.); Greer Res., 1790 W. 38th Ave., Van., 1928 (ext.); Royal Financial Co. Bldg., 840-844 W. Hastings St., Van., 1927 (ext.).

DAY, Robert Scott

Vict. newspapers; Howay & Schofield, *British Columbia: Biographical*, 1914, Vol.IV, pp.461-462; directories; and *Who's Who & Why, 1913, Vol. 3, p.188.* A short article on R.S. Day appeared in *Victoria Illustrated 1891.* **PROJECT:** *Dereen* (attributed), Pemberton Rd. (later 1606 Rockland Ave., now 806 Dereen Pl.), Vict., c.1892 (ext.).

de la PENOTIÈRE, William H.L.

VDC, Apr. 15, 1884, p.3 on the formation of the partnership, and Sept. 30, 1884, p.1 for St. James Church. Burris & de la Penotière references are from directories; and the *Colonist,* Apr. 16 and July 15, 1885. **PROJECT:** St. James Anglican Church, James Bay, Vict., 1884-85 (demo.).

DEPARTMENT OF SOLDIERS CIVIL RE-ESTABLISHMENT

Norton, *A Whole Little City by Itself*; Wright, *Crown Assets*, pp.142-47; Bentall, *The Charles Bentall Story*; and information from Dana H. Johnson. Specifications in BCA GR-0070 Box 2, File 27. **PROJECT:** King Edward Sanatorium, Tranquille, 1918-19 (demo.).

DOCTOR, William Alexander

Directories; CVA plans; Van. bldg. permits; and inventories. Van. Police Headquarters in *Contract Record*, Oct. 28, 1914, pp.1326-27. **PROJECTS: Higman & Doctor:** St. Alice Hotel, 120 West 2nd St., North Van. City, 1911-12 (demo. 1989). **W.A. Doctor:** Hudson's Bay Insurance Bldg., 900. W. Hastings St., Van., 1911-12 (demo.; facade retained). **Doctor, Stewart & Davie:** Van. Police Headquarters, E. Cordova St. at Gore Ave., Van., 1913-14 (demo.).

DODD, William Marshall

Dodd's AIBC application contains a four page list of projects. Extensive newspaper references and project lists were provided by Barry Elmer; additional references from Robert G. Hill; inventories;

CA&B; Contract Record; Gerry Eckford; and Dodd's RAIC War Service application [CVA]. C.B. Hume Block from the Revelstoke Herald & Railway Men's Journal, August 21, 1902. Anderson Res. from Point Grey bldg. permit #3476. The Ocean Falls quote is from J.D. Bonney, "The Central Coast," as quoted in Ormsby, British Columbia, p.410. **PROJECTS**: C.B. Hume Block, 123 Mackenzie Ave., Revelstoke, 1902 (dest. by fire 1960s); Douglas Lodge, 2799 Granville St./1507-1509 W. 12th Ave., Van., 1911-12 (ext.); Jenkins Res. (later Seagate Manor), 2831 Point Grey Rd., Van., 1912-13 (demo. 1977); Anderson Res., 1499 Angus Dr., Van., 1921 (ext.); Buildings at Ocean Falls for Pacific Mills Ltd., 1916 and following; Olympic Steam Baths, 404-406 E. Hastings St., Van., 1949 (demo.)

DOMINION CONSTRUCTION COMPANY LIMITED

Bentall Archives; Bentall, The Charles Bentall Story; Business Leaders of the Century, pp.38-39 (Business in Vancouver Supplement to Issue 529A, 1999); Sean Rossiter, "The Company That Built Vancouver" (Western Living, June, 1986, pp.32 h-p); CVA Plans; and Van. bldg. permits. **PROJECTS**: B.C. Motor Transportation Co. Garage, Cambie St. at 14th Ave., Van., 1927 (demo. 1980s); Queen Charlotte Apts., 1101-1105 Nicola St., Van., 1927-28 (ext.); Bay Theatre, 935 Denman St., Van., 1938 (only facade retained); St. Regis Paper Company Building (later Twinpak), 2725 Arbutus St., Van., 1946 (demo.); B.C. Motor Transportation (later Greyhound) Bus Terminal, 150 Dunsmuir St., Van., 1946 (demo.); Labour Temple, 307 W. Broadway, Van., 1948 (ext.); Kelowna Club, 442 Leon Ave., Kelowna, 1949 (ext.).

DONNELLAN, James J.

Bldg. permit records at the City of North Van. and the City of Van.; CVA plans; and directories. People's Theatre from Contract Record [Toronto], Vol.16, Jan. 31, 1906, p.6. Columbia Theatre from Province, Nov. 9, 1912, p.31. St. Mary's Hall from Province, Nov. 30, 1912, p.27. Pantages Theatre from The Contract Record, Apr. 8, 1914, p.438. United States National Register of Historic Places website. **PROJECTS**: **Donnellan & Donnellan:** National Theatre, 58 W. Hastings St., Van., 1910 (demo.). **J.J. Donnellan:** Alterations to People's Theatre, 805 W. Pender St., Van., 1906 (demo.); Lonsdale Theatre, 1545 Lonsdale Ave., North Van. City, 1911 (demo.); School and Chapel for the Oblates of Mary Immaculate, St. Augustine's Church, 2016 W. 7th Ave., Van., 1911 (unbuilt project); St. Mary's Hall, Haro St., Van., 1912 (unbuilt project); Renovation to Van. Opera House, 751-775 Granville St., Van., 1912-13 (demo. 1969). **Donnellan & Robertson:** Columbia Theatre, 62 W. Hastings St., Van., 1912 (demo.).

DONOVAN, J.P.

B.C. Vital Events; directories; Ritz, Architects of Oregon; tender calls in the Colonist; and VDC,

May 21, 1886, p.3 and May 23, 1886, p. 3. **PROJECT:** Clarence Hotel, Yates and Douglas Sts., Vict., 1885-86 (demo.).

DOWNING, Max Breeze

AIBC; Wright, Crown Assets; Kalman, The Prince Rupert Heritage Inventory and Conservation Programme; Prince Rupert City & Regional Archives; CVA plans; directories; and B.C. Vital Events. The Prince Rupert Federal Bldg. is documented in the National Archives of Canada, RG 11, Vol.4105, File No.684-1 Part A-E; plans held by the City of Prince Rupert; see also Prince Rupert Daily News, Nov. 12, 1936, Vol.XXV, No.265. p.1 and the Van. News-Herald, Architectural & Building Edition, Feb. 27, 1939, p.16. Information on Harry Barratt from AIBC and CVA Add.MSS.1455 Harry Barratt fonds. **PROJECTS**: Anglican Theological College (now part of Van. School of Theology) (with **Sharp & Thompson**), 6050-6090 Chancellor Blvd., Van., 1927-28 (ext.); Commercial Bldg., 615-19 Seymour St., Van., 1933 (alt.); Prince Rupert Federal Bldg. (now City Hall), 424 3rd Ave. W., Prince Rupert, 1936-38 (ext.); Hanson Block, 526-532 3rd Ave. W., Prince Rupert, 1939 (ext.).

DUNCAN, William

Peter Murray, The Devil and Mr. Duncan: A History of the Two Metlakatlas (Victoria: Sono Nis Press, 1985); Veillette & White, Early Indian Village Churches, pp.57-59; Henry S. Wellcome, The Story of Metlakahtla (London: Saxon & Co., 1887); Kalman, A History of Canadian Architecture; and the Anglican Archives, Diocese of Caledonia. **PROJECT**: St. Paul's Anglican Church, Metlakatla, 1873-74 (dest. by fire 1901).

DUNLOP, Alexander Francis

CAC Accession No. 16, McGill University, Montreal; Construction [Toronto], Vol.v, Feb., 1912, p.89; and Revelstoke Museum & Archives. **PROJECT**: Molson's Bank, 122 Mackenzie Ave., Revelstoke, 1910 (ext.).

DUNFORD, William & Son

Boam, British Columbia; Vict. plans, bldg. and plumbing permits; B.C. Vital Events; AB&E; PB&E; VDC; VDT; directories; and inventories. Walker reference from VDT, Jan. 3, 1991, p.5. Additional information on Stoton from Brandes, San Diego Architects, p.173. Quotes from The Week, Dec. 23, 1911. **PROJECTS**: **George V. Bishop:** Hawkins Res., 821 Princess Ave., Vict., 1911 (ext.); McKay Res., 1604 Stanley Ave., Vict., 1947 (demo.). **E.W. Arnold B. Stoton:** Dobbie Res., 232 St. Andrews St., Vict., 1912 (ext.); Jones Res., 2658 Avebury Ave., Vict., 1912 (ext.).

DUNHAM & WALLWORK

Withey & Withey, Biographical Dictionary of American Architects (Deceased), pp.183-184 & 628; and Ritz, Architects of Oregon. Plans of the Christ Scientist Church in UVIC Special Collections AP-2094. **PROJECT**: First Church of Christ Scientist, 1205 Pandora Ave., Vict., 1919 (ext.).

EGDELL, Daniel Bowden

Interviews with his daughter-in-law Olive 'Dolly' Egdell. Egdell's bldgs. in Nanaimo have been identified though previous inventories, and their attribution confirmed through city bldg. permits and plans, and the holdings of the Nanaimo Community Archives. Information on Dixon & Egdell in Van. was obtained through bldg. permit and directory searches. The connection with Brother XII is briefly covered in John Oliphant, Brother Twelve: The Incredible Story of Canada's False Prophet (Toronto, McClelland & Stewart Inc., 1991); Dolly Egdell has confirmed that Egdell was the contractor for the Cedar colony. **PROJECTS**: Parkin Block, 143-155 Commercial St., Nanaimo, 1922 (ext.); Centre Bldg. and House of Mystery, Aquarian Foundation Colony, Yellow Point, late 1920s; Christian Science Society Bldg. (renovation), 20 Chapel St., Nanaimo, 1932 (ext.); Egdell Res., 725 Terminal Ave. N., Nanaimo, 1939 (ext.).

EVANS, E. & SON

AIBC; 1881 British Census; B.C. Vital Events; obituaries; and George Evans's war records in the National Archives of Canada, Ottawa. Grace Hospital CVA Plans AP-475. Personal interview with William Bow's daughter, Clara S. Coles. Information on the New West. schools from plans and renderings at the School. **PROJECTS**: **E. Evans & Son:** Elworth, 6501 Deer Lake Ave., Burnaby, 1922 (ext.); The Loyal Protestant Home for Orphaned Children (now the Royal City Christian Centre), 601 Eighth Ave., New West., 1925 (ext.); Grace Hospital, 4230 Heather St., Van., 1926-27 (demo.); Service Station for J.A. Irvine, 10 Commercial St., Nanaimo, 1927 (demo.); Westerham Court, 1065-1085 Bute St., Van., 1936 (ext.). **G.N. Evans:** New West. (later Vincent Massey) Junior High School (**William Bow,** Associated Architect), 8th Ave. and 8th St., New West., 1949 (alt.); Lester Pearson High School, 8th Ave. and 8th St., New West., 1955 (alt.).

EVERS, Cecil

Mentioned in Ochsner, Shaping Seattle, pp.28-29 & 157. Further information from Jeffrey Karl Ochsner and Carey Pallister. Evers was likely the same Cecil C. Evers that was the author of The Commercial Problem in Buildings (New York: The Record & Guide Co., 1914).

EWART, Alexander Charles

Information provided by granddaughter, Elizabeth Genné, great-grandson, W. Thomas Genné, and other members of the Genné family, of Corvallis, Oregon. Nelson: A Proposal for Urban Heritage Conservation; Vict. and Nelson directories; tender calls from the Colonist compiled by Dorothy Mindenhall; 1871 Ontario Census; B.C. Vital Events; International Genealogy Index; Shallenbarger Index for the Portland Daily Abstract, University of Oregon; Corvallis Planning Department web site; United States National Register of Historic Places website; Benton County Historical Museum, Philomath, Oregon; Benton

County Genealogical Society; Kootenay Lake Historical Society & Archives; Nelson *Daily News*; Alexander Carrie's AIBC application form; City of Nelson web site; Heritage Inn web site; research by Henry Stevenson from the Nelson Museum and Ritz, *Architects of Oregon*. **PROJECTS: A.C. Ewart:** Ewart Res., 1458 Begbie St., Vict., 1892 (ext.); Pemberton Gymnasium for Central School, School St. (now 1100-block Ormond St.), Vict., 1894 (demo.); Odd Fellows Lodge, Duncan, 1894 (demo.); Pendray Res., 309 Belleville St., Vict., 1895 (ext.); Leiser Bldg., 522-524 Yates St., Vict., 1896 (three eastern bays ext.); Henderson Res., 522 Quadra St., Vict., 1897 (ext.); McKillop Block, 364-370 Baker St., Nelson, 1897-98 (ext.); Judge Forin Res., 519 Cedar St., Nelson, 1897 (ext.); Hume Hotel, 422 Vernon St., Nelson, 1897 (alt.); British America Paint Co. Factory, Laurel Point, Vict., 1899 (demo.). **Ewart & Schroeder:** Central School Toilet Bldg., School St. (now 1100-block Ormond St.), Vict., 1893 (demo.). **Ewart & Carrie:** Lawrence Hardware Store, 446 Baker St., Nelson, 1898 (ext.); Kaslo City Hall, Kaslo, 1898 (ext.); Baptist Church (now Kootenay Christian Fellowship), 812 Stanley St., Nelson, 1898 (alt.); Tremont Block, 652 Baker St., Nelson, 1899 (partially ext.); Provincial Land Registry Office, 403 Vernon St., Nelson, 1899-1900 (ext.); Congregationalist Church, later St. Paul's Presbyterian (then United), 702 Stanley St., Nelson, 1900 (ext.); K.W.C. Block, 488-498 Baker St., Nelson, 1900-01 (ext.).

EWART, David

Archibald, *By Federal Design*; Wright, *Crown Assets*; *Sessional Reports*; CVA plans; Hector Charlesworth, A Cyclopedia of Canadian Biography, p.174 (Toronto: Hunter-Rose, 1919); and further information provided by Gordon Fulton. **PROJECTS:** Van. Drill Hall, 620 Beatty St., Van., 1899-1901 (ext.); Nelson Post Office and Custom House, now Nelson City Hall, 502 Vernon St., Nelson, 1900-02 (ext.); Van. Post Office, 701 W. Hastings St. (now part of Sinclair Centre), Van., 1905-10 (ext.); Custom Examining Warehouse (now part of Sinclair Centre), 324 Howe St., Van., 1911-13 (ext.).

FABIAN, Bruno

Directories; Canadian Inventory of Historic Buildings; and *Architecture of the Fraser Valley*. **PROJECT:** Chapman Res., 10944 Chapman Rd., Chilliwack, 1891 (demo.).

FAIRALL, James

Information from granddaughter, Linda Jury, and other Fairall family members; research by Greg Evans and Julia Trachsel; *VDC*; inventories; Vict. plans, bldg. and plumbing permits. **PROJECTS:** Brewery, Esquimalt Rd., Vict., 1895 (demo.); Bungalow, 646 Niagara St., Vict., 1909 (ext.); Res., 238 Robert St., Vict., 1946 (ext.).

FARWELL, Milo S.

Vict. plans, bldg. and plumbing permits; VCA files and demo. plans; inventories; *AB&E*; Segger & Franklin, *Exploring Victoria's Architecture*; and Ritz, *Architects of Oregon*. **PROJECTS:** Hill Res., 194 Olive St., Vict., 1912 (ext.); Wille Res., 2511 Quadra St., Vict., 1912 (demo.); Hip Yick & Co. Store, 860 Fisgard St., Vict., 1912 (demo.); Scott & Peden Warehouse, 1601 Store St., Vict., 1913 (alt.); Rider Res., 1619 Pinewood Ave., Vict., 1914 (ext.).

FERREE, Harold C.

Vict. plans, bldg. and plumbing permits; directories; *AB&E*; and California Death Index. **PROJECTS:** Westcott Bldg., Vict., 1913 (unbuilt project); R.H. Green Res., 1076 Joan Cres., Vict., 1913 (ext.).

FINDLAY, Robert

Greater Vernon Museum & Archives, including plans for the Mackie Lake House; and CAC Accession No. 3, McGill University, Montreal. **PROJECTS:** Buchanan Res. (now Mackie Lake House), 7804 Kidston Rd., Coldstream, 1910 (ext.); *Orchardleigh* (McLimont Res.), Kidston Rd. Coldstream, 1910 (dest. by fire).

FISHER, Elmer H.

Fisher's career is covered by Jeffrey Karl Ochsner and Dennis A. Andersen in *Shaping Seattle Architecture*, pp.22-27. Further information, including biographical data, has been published by J. Kingston Pierce in "The Elusive Architect," *Seattle* (Mar. 1994); Mr. Pierce also provided further helpful suggestions. Information on Fisher's B.C. practice is derived from information in contemporary newspapers and directories. Tender calls from Dorothy Mindenhall; additional confirmation of ext. bldgs. by Carey Pallister and Christine Meutzner. Notice of Fisher & Wilson partnership in *VDC*, May 5, 1888, p.4. Further information from Ochsner & Andersen, *Distant Corner: Seattle Architects & the Legacy of H.H. Richardson, 1880-1895*. **PROJECTS: Elmer H. Fisher:** Spencer's Arcade, Government and Broad Sts., Vict., 1886 (demo.); Alhambra Hotel (Byrnes Block), 2 Water St., Van., 1886-7 (ext.); Wille's Bakery, 537 Johnson St., Vict., 1887 (ext.); Goldstream Hotel, Goldstream, 1887 (demo.); Bank of B.C., Columbia St., New West., 1887 (dest. by fire 1898); Pimbury Bldg., 27 Commercial St., Nanaimo, 1887 (alt.); Second Court House, Nanaimo, 1887 (demo.); Two houses for A.J. Langley, 1133 and 1141 Fort St., Vict., 1887 (ext.). **Fisher & Wilson:** W.G. Cameron Bldg., 579-581 Johnson St., Vict., 1888 (ext.); White House, Government St., Vict., 1888 (demo.); Craft & Norris Block, 1319-1329 Douglas St., Vict., 1888 (alt.).

FLEET, Arthur

Directories; *AB&E*; *The Week*; *VDC*; Vict. plans, bldg. and plumbing permits; Oak Bay bldg. permits; and inventories.

FORD, Guy Singleton

AIBC; interviews with son J. Gordon Ford; *AB&E*; *VDC*; B.C. Vital Events; and Vict. plans, bldg. and plumbing permits. **PROJECTS:** Houses, 1714 and 1716 Davie St., Vict., 1912-13 (ext.).

FORRESTER. Alexander

B.C. Vital Events; City of Nanaimo plans; personal files held at the Nanaimo Community Archives; Nicholls, *From the Black Country to Nanaimo 1854*, Vol.5. **PROJECTS:** Forrester Res., Wentworth & Prideaux Sts., Nanaimo, c.1900 (demo.); Addition to the Globe Hotel, 25 Front St., Nanaimo, 1913 (ext.); Angell's Trading, 426 Fitzwilliam St., Nanaimo, 1926 (ext.).

FOWLER, Charles Busteed

Fowler was extremely proud of his military career and his meetings with royalty, but recorded little about his architectural career. Entry in Felstead et al, *Directory of British Architects 1834-1900*, p.322. While in Van., Fowler was a good friend of Major J.S. Matthews, and after his death his papers, including autobiographical notes and the plans of his coffin, were deposited with the CVA [Add. MSS.214]. There are additional references to Fowler in CVA Add.MSS 560; plans for the Van. Odd Fellows Hall (CVA AP-439); and correspondence regarding the 1939 Royal Visit [CVA Add. MSS.73-509-g-2-File 1]. Fowler was a well-known local character, and a number of articles about him, and his eccentric burial, appeared in newspapers after his death; see the *Province*, Mar. 29, 1941, p.13 and Apr. 1, 1941, p.9. **PROJECTS:** St. Catherine's Church, Coquitlam, 1915 (unbuilt project); Odd Fellows Hall, 1443 W. 8th Ave., Van., 1922 (alt.).

FOX, Cecil Croker

See Janet Bingham, *Samuel Maclure Architect*, for sources of information.

FOX, Percy

AIBC; VCA files; B.C. Vital Events; inventories; Vict. plans, bldg. and plumbing permits; Oak Bay permits and plans; *AB&E*; Segger & Franklin, *Exploring Victoria's Architecture*; *The Week* "1914 Outlook" Edition, Jan. 24, 1914, p.XVIII; *VDC* and *VDT* references. **PROJECTS: Percy Fox:** Business Block for Otto Weiler, 1000-1012 Douglas St./680-690 Broughton St., Vict., 1920 (ext.); Clemence Bungalow, 1149 Faithful St., Vict., 1921 (ext.); Glenshiel Inn alterations and additions, 606 Douglas St., Vict., 1925 (ext.); A.C. Pike Res., 39 Linden Ave., Vict., 1925 (ext.); H.G. Graham Res., 204 St. Andrew's St., Vict., 1927 (ext.); B.C. Worsted Mill, 25 Montreal St., Vict., 1928 (demo.); Apts., 1189 Yates St., Vict., 1929 (demo.); H.B. Darnell Res., Upper Terrace Rd., Oak Bay, 1929 (ext.); Harrogate Apts., 1203 Beach Drive, Oak Bay, 1929-30 (ext.); Bessborough Apts.(now Abigail's Bed & Breakfast), 906 McClure St., Vict., 1930 (ext.); Summer cottages, 4920-22 Cordova Bay Rd., Saanich, 1931 (ext.). **Fox & Berrill:** Rooming

House, 624 1/2 Fisgard St., Vict., 1913 (ext.); Brown Res., 501 Newport Ave., Oak Bay, 1913 (ext.); Carey Res., 1696 Earle St., Vict., 1921 (demo.).

FRAME, David Cowper

AIBC; VCA; Vict. plans, bldg. and plumbing permits; Esquimalt Archives; Geoffrey Castle; Stuart Stark; personal correspondence from Frame's daughter, Janet, to Madge Hamilton and a personal interview with Mr. Frame's daughter-in-law Elvera Frame. Further information from grandson, Robert Frame. We are indebted for confirmation of facts by Frame's daughter, Peggy Dole. **PROJECTS**: Chinese Public School, 636 Fisgard St., Vict., 1908-09 (ext.); *Larkhall* (Frame Res.), 337 Foul Bay Rd., Vict., 1909 (ext.); Alexandra Club, 714 Courtenay St., Vict., 1909-10 (ext.); *Sheilin* (Mrs. Catherine Wilson Res.), 1535 Prospect Place, Oak Bay, 1909 (ext.); Bank St. School, 1625 Bank St., Vict., 1910 (ext.); *Kingsmont*, (George Ogilvie Leask House), 305 Denison Rd., Oak Bay, 1911 (ext.); James S. Clarke Res., 1086 Louis St., Vict., 1912 (ext.); Methodist Church (now Salvation Army), 949 Fullerton Ave., Vict., 1912 (ext.); *Solway* (Frame Res.), 1143 Munro St., Esquimalt, 1920s (ext.); Bartle & Gibson Bldg. (with **S.P. Birley**), 960 Yates St., Vict., 1941 (alt.); Park Towers Apts., 905-09 Vancouver St., Vict., 1945 (ext.); Canadian Imperial Bank of Commerce (with **Douglas James**), 1301 Government St., Vict., 1946 (ext.).

FREEMAN, J. Eugene

Freeman's life and career have never been fully documented, and some sources of information are contradictory. Freeman is mentioned in Michael Jay Mjelde, *Glory of the Seas* (Middleton, Connecticut: Published for the Marine Historical Association, Incorporated by Wesleyan University Press, 1970) and Barr, *Cumberland Heritage*. Citation for the Methodist Church in Cumberland from Nanaimo *Free Press*, Apr. 20, 1894, p.1. John Bumpus, Vict., provided access to family papers in his possession, including a copy of Freeman's will. Biographical references and photographs are contained in the VCA, Lucy Anna Little Fonds [VCA PR 93]. Photographs and some papers are in the Freeman Family Portrait File, BCA; see also Freeman Family Album [BCA 98208-18]. References may be found in two books by James Audain, *Alex Dunsmuir's Dilemma* (Vict.: Sunnylane Publishing, 1964) and *From Coalmine to Castle: The Story of the Dunsmuirs of Vancouver Island* (New York: Pageant Press, 1955). Some anecdotal research is included in the City of San Francisco Landmarks Preservation Advisory Board, *Final Case Report on the Ellinwood Res.* Edna Wallace Hopper's role in the design of Dunsmuir House is contained in her testimony in the court case against the Dunsmuir estate. **PROJECTS**: Grace Methodist Church, Cumberland, 1894 (demo.); *Beaufort House*, Cumberland, 1895-96 (demo.).

FRIPP, Robert Mackay

Brief biographical sketches appear in two books published during his lifetime, C.W. Parker, ed., *Who's Who & Why*, Vol.2 (Toronto: International Press Ltd., 1912), p.186, and Howay & Schofield, *British Columbia: Biographical*, 1914, Vol.III, pp.291-292. An earlier biographical source is the *VDW Souvenir Edition*, 1891, p.22. RIBA membership file; B.C. Vital Events; the headstones at the Fripp plot, Mountain View Cemetery; his obituary notice which appears in the Jan., 1918 edition of *Construction Magazine*, p.33, and several manuscripts held by the CVA, notably the Minutes and Records of the Van. Arts and Crafts Society [Add. MSS.142]. Information on Fripp & Wills from *The Daily Columbian*, Jan. 21, 1892, p.4. Commissions from Fripp's initial Van. phase (1888-96) appear in issues of various Van. newspapers; Van. permit records dating from 1901 to 1914; *CA&B*; and *AB&E*. The most important source of information on Fripp consists of the various letters and articles he submitted to architectural journals over the course of his career. These include twenty-three contributions to the *CA&B* between 1894 and 1901, and two lengthy articles on the state of the architectural profession that appeared in *The Contract Record* in Mar., 1913 and Oct., 1914. Biographical sketches of Charles Edwin Fripp and Thomas William Fripp can be found in J. Russell Harper, *Early Painters and Engravers in Canada* (Toronto: University of Toronto Press, 1970). The activities of Shaw and Morris in Berkshire during the 1870s are described in Nicholas Pevsner, *Berkshire: Penguin Building of England Series* (London: Penguin, 1966). Citation for the Provincial Home, *VDW*, Dec. 30, 1893, p.8; specifications for the "Old Mens Refuge" in BCA GR-0070 Box 2, File 40, dated Sept. 30, 1894. Henry Ramsay bungalow from *Province*, June 8, 1912, p.28. Greater Vernon Museum & Archives: Jam Factory, Vernon *News*, Oct. 27, 1892 (tender call) and Feb. 2, 1893; Fripp to open office, Vernon *News*, July 6, 1893. Jam Factory, Vernon from *Contract Record* [Toronto], iii, Nov. 26, 1892, p.2. Ongoing research is being conducted by Michael Milojevic, Department of Architecture, University of Auckland, New Zealand, who has provided much useful information. **PROJECTS**: **R. Mackay Fripp & Charles E. Fripp:** Van. Boating Club, Coal Harbour, Van., 1888 (demo.); Ferguson Block, cor. Hastings and Richards Sts., Van., 1888 (demo.); Harry Abbott Block, 500 Granville St., Van., 1889 (demo.). **R. Mackay Fripp:** Fripp Res., Foot of Melville St., Coal Harbour, Van., c.1888 (demo.); A.J. Dana Res., Howe and Georgia St., Van., 1889 (demo.); *The Bungalow* (B.T. Rogers Res.), W. Georgia St., Van., 1890 (demo.); B.C. Land & Investment Agency Bldg. (O'Brien Hall/ Metropolitan Club), Hastings and Homer Sts., Van., 1892 (demo. 1949); Jam Factory for Lord Aberdeen, Vernon, 1892-93 (demolished before 1954); Bank of Montreal, 2908 32nd St., Vernon, 1893 (alt.); The Provincial Home, Columbia St., Kamloops, 1893-5 (demo. 1972); Snider Res., 1106 Maple St.,

Van., 1910 (ext.); Henry Ramsay House, 7864 Stanley St., Burnaby, 1912 (ext.); F.W. Morgan Res., 3538 Osler St., Van., 1912 (ext.); *Oakhurst*, 950 W. 58th Ave., Van., 1912 (alt.); First Unitarian Church, 1550 W. 10th Ave., Van., 1912-13 (demo.); Grace Court Apts., 1601-1607 Comox St., Van., 1912-13 (ext.); Victor Spencer Res., cor. Laurier and Alexandra Aves., Van., 1913 (ext.); Stone Res., 2537 W. 49th Ave., Van., 1913 (ext.); Walkem House, 3990 Marguerite St., Van., 1913-14 (ext.). **Fripp & Wills:** Spinks Res., 2159 36th Ave., Vernon, 1893-94 (alt.).

FULLER, Thomas

Christopher A. Thomas's entry in the *Dictionary of Canadian Biography*, Vol.XII, pp.343-346 (Ramsay Cook, ed., Toronto: University of Toronto Press, 1990). See also Christopher A. Thomas, *Dominion Architecture: Fuller's Canadian Post Offices, 1881-1896* (University of Toronto, MA Thesis, 1978); Archibald, *By Federal Design*; Wright, *Crown Assets*; Janet Wright's entry on Fuller in the *Canadian Encyclopedia*; Withey & Withey, *Biographical Dictionary of American Architects (Deceased)*, p.226; Robert G. Hill; National Film Board, *Stones of History*; and *Sessional Reports*. A bibliography on the Parliament Buildings is provided in Christina Cameron, *Charles Baillairgé: Architect & Engineer*, pp.183-84 (Montreal: McGill-Queen's University Press, 1989). Information on the Van. Post Office from the *Estimates of Canada for the Fiscal Year ending 30 June 1892.*; tender call from the *Colonist*, Sept. 13, 1891, p.1 supplied by Dorothy Mindenhall. Margaret Archibald, *Thomas William Fuller (1865-1951): A Preliminary Report* (Ottawa: Parks Canada Research Bulletin No.105, July 1979). Further information provided by Gordon Fulton. New West. Drill Hall citation from DPW annual report, 1896. Alderman Wilson quoted in the *Colonist*, Dec. 4, 1890, p.8. BCIA quote from *VDC*, Feb. 10, 1894, p.5. **PROJECTS**: Nanaimo Post Office, 54-66 Front St., Nanaimo, 1882-84 (demo. 1954 to make way for new Post Office); Van. Post Office, Granville and Pender Sts., Van., 1889-92 (demo. 1926); Vict. Post Office, 800-block Government St., Vict., 1894-98 (demo. for new Federal Bldg. and Custom House in 1956). **F.C. Gamble, Designer:** Drill Hall, 530 Queen's Ave., New West., 1895 (ext.).

FULLER, Thomas William

Margaret Archibald, *Thomas William Fuller (1865-1951): A Preliminary Report* (Ottawa: Parks Canada Research Bulletin No.105, July 1979); Archibald, *By Federal Design*; Wright, *Crown Assets*; and Les McLaughlin, *Canadians in the Yukon: Thomas Fuller* (Whitehorse *Star*, Apr. 12, 2002, pp.10-11). **PROJECTS**: Buildings In Dawson City, Yukon, 1899-1902: Administration Bldg. (ext.); Court House (ext.); Post Office (ext.); Commissioner's Res. (alt.); School (dest. by fire 1957); Telegraph Office (ext.).

GAMBLE & KNAPP

Van. and City of North Van. bldg. permits; and directories. MacDonald Res. from *Province*, July 6, 1912, p.25. Macauley Res. from *Province*, Nov. 9, 1912, p.31. Vedder Creek Chalet from Chilliwack *Progress*, Aug. 17, 1910, and *Contract Record* [Toronto], xxiv, Sept. 21, 1910, p.26. Additional information from Dennis A. Andersen; Imbi Harding; and Phillip S. Esser's online entry on West & Knapp (www.historylink.org). *Pacific Record*, Dec. 10, 1904, p.6: West & Knapp partnership announced; *PB&E*, Mar. 13, 1909, p.80: West & Knapp partnership dissolved. **PROJECTS:** Hirshfield Res., 1963 Comox St., Van., 1910 (ext.); Chalet at Vedder Creek, Chilliwack, 1910 (unbuilt project); Purse Res., 513 Keith Rd. E., North Van. City, 1911 (ext.); *The Hollies* (G.E. MacDonald Res.), 1350 The Crescent, Van., 1912 (ext.); Macauley Res., 3590 Hudson St., Van., 1912 (ext.).

GARDINER, William Frederick

AIBC; Howay & Schofield, *British Columbia: Biographical*, 1914, Vol.IV, pp.376-379 provides an overview, as do entries in *Who's Who*. Other biographical information and bldg. attributions were assembled from the collection of primary documents held by Gardiner's children, Mrs. Gloria Fleck, Van.; Mrs. Rosemary Hathaway, Qualicum Beach; and Mr. Lindsay W.F. Gardiner, Vict.; who generously allowed access; the collection includes a number of diaries; numerous press clippings; renderings; and photographs. Information on Sherriff has been gleaned from his entry in Howay & Schofield, *British Columbia: Biographical*, 1914, Vol.III, pp.1101-1102, and references in the Gardiner documents. An extensive project list has been developed for Gardiner, of which the following is only a small sample. **PROJECTS:** Victoria Bldg., 334-350 W. Pender St., Van., 1908 (ext.); Central City Mission, 233 Abbott St., 1911 (alt.); Oak Tree Auto Sales, 75 Front St., Nanaimo, 1929 (alt.); Major James R. Lowery Summer Res., 320 E. Cres. Rd., Qualicum Beach, 1929-30 (ext.); Austin Taylor Estate, 22415 72nd Ave., Township of Langley, early 1930s (ext.); Crippled Children's Hospital, 250 W. 59 Ave., Van., 1934 (demo.); Haas Res., Chilliwack (unbuilt project); Elverson Res., Galiano Island, c.1935 (dest. by fire); Cathay Apt. Hotel, 855 Douglas St., Vict., 1936-37 (demo.); Bank of Toronto, 3396 Cambie St., Van., c.1949 (alt.); Bank of Toronto, 630 Yates St., Vict., 1949-50 (ext.).

GARDINER & MERCER

AIBC; inventories, and CVA Plans. Other plans survived in the Gardiner & Thornton collection, CCA, Montreal. Additional projects were identified in *Once in the Royal City*, and in a Gardiner & Mercer monograph published in the 1920s (*Gardiner & Mercer, Architects*, D.A. Clark, Publisher; copy in the collection of the New West. Museum & Archives). Personal information on F.G. Gardiner was derived from entries in *Who's Who*, and from interviews with his niece, Mrs. Gloria

Fleck. Information on Gardiner & Thornton was gleaned from background material from successor firms to the partnership, and interviews with R. Michael Garrett, a later partner. Personal information on Andrew Lamb Mercer was derived from his AIBC application and a 1912 *Who's Who & Why* entry. Biographical data and information on Mercer's Scottish career from Robert Close, Scotland. Andrew H. Mercer provided further background material, photographs and personal insights into his father's personality. Information on Mercer & Mercer practice from Jans Visscher, who worked in the office from 1954-68. Additional project information in CVA Add.MSS.1431 Mercer & Mercer Architects fonds. Further information on John Mercer from his AIBC file. **PROJECTS: Gardiner & Gardiner:** Hart Bldg., 5 Yale Rd. E., Chilliwack, 1909 (demo.). **Gardiner, Mercer & Gardiner:** Trapp Block, 668 Columbia St., New West., 1912 (ext.). **Gardiner & Mercer:** Westminster Trust Bldg., 713 Columbia St., New West., 1911-12 (ext.); Richard McBride School, 331 Richmond St., New West., 1912 (dest. by fire 1929); Eastman Res., 411 Third Ave., New West., 1912-13 (alt.); Nels Nelson House, 127 Queen's Ave., New West., 1913 (ext.); Duke of Connaught High School, New West., Royal Ave. (demo.); Schara Tzedeck Synagogue, 700 E. Pender St., Van., 1920 (alt.); Coquitlam Municipal Hall, Brunette Ave., Coquitlam, 1920 (demo.); Mercer Res., 1475 W. 33rd Ave., Van., 1921 (ext.); Franklyn St. Gymnasium, 421 Franklyn St., Nanaimo, 1922 (ext.); Montelius Res., 1599 King Edward Ave., Van., 1924-25 (ext.); Wellington (now Trafalgar) Apts., 2630 York Ave./1615 Trafalgar St., Van., 1925 (ext.); Jewish Community Centre, 2675 Oak St., Van., 1928 (ext.); West Res., 1504 Balfour Ave., Van., 1930 (ext.); Sisters of Saint Paul School, 524-540 W. 6th St., North Van. City, 1932 (ext.); Additions to St. Paul's Hospital, 1081 Burrard St., Van., 1931-36 (ext.); Pacific Athletic Club, 535 Howe St., Van., 1935-36 (ext.); Woolworth's Store, 475 W. Hastings St., Van., 1938 (ext.); St. Vincent de Paul Hospital, 749 W. 33rd Ave., Van., 1938-39 (ext.). **Gardiner & Thornton:** Langley Memorial Hospital (now Cottage Hospital), 22051 Fraser Hwy., Township of Langley, 1947-48 (ext.); Guardian Angels R.C. Church, 1161 Broughton St., 1948-49 (ext.); Vernon Hospital, 2101 32nd St., Vernon, 1945-49 (ext.); Westminster Abbey, Mission, 1950s-80s (ext.). **Mercer & Mercer:** Shaughnessy Hospital, 4500 Oak St./855 W. 31st Ave./4595 Heather St., Van., ongoing work from 1940-72 (ext.); Veterans' Hospital, 1900 Fort St., Vict., 1945-46 (ext.); Parthenon Pavilion (Nick Kogos Res.), 5538 Parthenon Place, West Van., 1946-56 (demo. 1984); Waldorf Hotel, 1469-1489 E. Hastings St., Van., 1947 and additions 1954-55 (ext.); Marpole Community Centre, 990 W. 59 Ave., Van., 1949 and additions 1952 (alt.); Salvation Army Temple, 301 E. Hastings St., Van., 1949-50 (ext.); Academy of Medicine, 1807 W. 10th Ave., Van., 1950-51 (ext.); Dunbar Community Centre, 4747 Dunbar St., Van., 1957-58 (alt.); South Van. (now Killarney) Community Centre, 6265 Kerr St.

(now 6260 Killarney St.), Van., 1961-63 (ext.).

GARROW, Robert Thompson

AIBC; Van. bldg. permits; *Who's Who in Canada* 1928-1929; and Stark, *More than Just Bricks and Boards*, pp.100. Further research by Catherine Barford. Information on Souttar from Robert Close, Scotland. See Sean Rossiter, *The Hotel Georgia: A Vancouver Tradition* (Van.: Douglas & McIntyre, 1998). Garrow's original middle name was Thomson, but while in North America he usually reverted to the English spelling. **PROJECTS:** Lester Dance Academy, 1014-1018 Davie St., Van., 1911-15 (alt.); Elliot Res., 1255 Victoria Ave., Oak Bay, 1912 (ext.); Shaughnessy Heights Golf Club House, near Oak St. between 33rd and 35th Aves., Van., 1912-14 (demo.); Hotel Georgia (with John Graham, Sr., Seattle), 801 W. Georgia St., Van., 1926-1927 (ext.).

GILLAM, William Charles Frederick

AIBC; directories; bldg. permits; *AB&E*; *The Contract Record*; Felstead et al, *Directory of British Architects 1834-1900*; California Death Index; obituary in the Sonoma *Index Tribune*, Feb. 15, 1962, p.3. Specifications for Provincial Normal School and 1913 tender call in BCA GR-0054 Box 36 File 517. Port Haney Central School specifications in BCA GR-0070 Box 2, File 26. Greek Orthodox Church from the B.C. Society of Architects *Year Book*, 1913 and the *Province*, Nov. 30,1912, p.27. Information on Gillam in California from Edan Hughes, *Artists in California 1786-1940*, 2nd Edition (Hughes Publishing, 2000). There are only scant references to Kennerley Bryan. **PROJECTS: W.C.F. Gillam:** Provincial Normal School, (now Camosun College), 3100 Foul Bay Rd., Vict., 1912-14 (ext.); Queen Mary High School, 230 Keith Rd. W., North Van. City, 1914-15 (ext.); MacLean High School, Dewdney Trunk Rd. near 9th Ave., Maple Ridge, 1922-23 (demo. 1970s). **Jones & Gillam:** Ridgeway School, 420 E. 8th St., North Van. City, 1911-12 (ext.); **Bryan & Gillam:** Greek Orthodox Church, Van., 1912 (unbuilt project); Sam Kee Co. Bldg., 2-14 E. Pender St., Van., 1913 (ext.).

GILLINGHAM, Henry Herbert

AIBC; B.C. Vital Events; obituary, *Province*, Sept. 26, 1930. Prince Rupert, Saanich, and Van. inventories. **PROJECTS:** Burbidge Res. (*Babbacombe Farm*), 6187 Hunt Rd., Saanich, c.1916 (ext.); Brooks (later Hager) Res., 5055 Connaught Dr., Van., 1921 (ext.); Besner Block, 3rd Ave. and 3rd St., Prince Rupert, 1928 (ext.); The Samuel Apts., 1315 W. 16th Ave., Van., 1929 (ext.); Commodore Ballroom, 870 Granville St., Van., 1929-30 (ext.).

GILMORE, James

Prince Rupert City & Regional Archives; Prince Rupert City Directory 1914; and Phylis Bowman, *Land of Liquid Sunshine* (Chilliwack: Sunrise Printing, 1982). **PROJECT:** Prince Rupert Exhibition Bldg., Acropolis Hill (later renamed Roosevelt Park Hill), Prince Rupert, 1914-15 (demo. 1945-46).

GIRVAN, John

The Rotor, Vol. XVII, Aug. 14, 1936 No.7 p.4; *Who's Who*; Girvan Studios Collection courtesy Colleen Mitchell and Anthony Atkins.

GODDARD, Samuel May

Scattered references in contemporary newspapers, mostly relating to the Hooper & Goddard partnership; quote from *VDC*, Nov. 13, 1890, p.5. Herbert A. Layfield, grandson of William T. Whiteway, and Robert G. Hill have generously provided their research. Some biographical information from his obituary in the *VDC*, Jan. 21, 1906, and from the 1901 Canadian Census. **PROJECTS: Hooper & Goddard:** Indian Mission School, Port Simpson, 1891; Wilson & Dalby Block, 1400-1480 Government St., Vict., 1891-92 (alt.).

GORDON, D.W.

Obituary and funeral, *Nanaimo Free Press*, Feb. 20, 1893, p.1 and Feb. 21, 1893, p.4; Colonial Correspondence [BCA GR-1372 B-1331, File 655]; BCA Vertical File 54-1537; *VDC*, Jan. 22, 1956, p.5; *VDC*, June 27, 1976, pp.14-15; *Castle Quarterly*, Vol.44 No.4 Winter 2001, pp.2-3; and information supplied by Bruce Davies, Craigdarroch Castle Historical Museum Society; Peter Scott; and Robert G. Hill. Court House additions from *British Columbia Sessional Papers*, 1884, Public Accounts chapter, p.52. **PROJECTS:** Franklyn House, 400 Blk. Wallace St., Nanaimo, c.1862 (demo. 1951); Van. Coal Co.'s Offices and Mine Manager's House, Haliburton St., Nanaimo, 1860s (dest. by fire 1884); Mechanic's Institute Hall, Bastion St., Nanaimo, 1864-65 (demo. 1972); *Ardoon*, Albert St., Nanaimo, 1876 (demo. c.1912); Additions to first Court House, Nanaimo, 1884 (demo.).

GORE, Thomas Sinclair

Ontario Land Surveyors *Annual Report*, 1922, pp.133-35; references in the *Colonist* (Jan. 1, 1886, "General Progress" reference to Gaol); BCA Vertical Files; BCA GR-0080 69 [18] Public School, James Bay, 1883; and B.C. Vital Events. **PROJECTS:** School, James Bay, Vict., 1883 (demo.); Provincial (Hillside) Gaol, Topaz Ave., Vict., 1885-86 (demo.).

GOULD & CHAMPNEY

Dennis A. Andersen's essays on Gould, pp.108-113, and Champney, pp.132-37, both in Ochsner, *Shaping Seattle Architecture*. Rogers Building in *Province*, June 7, 1913, p.7. **PROJECT:** Rogers Bldg., 450-480 Granville St., Van., 1911-13 (ext.).

GRAHAM, Thomas Wilson

Contemporary newspaper references from A.L. "Dick" Lazenby and Archie Miller. Bee quote from the *Guardian*, Mar. 22, 1879; information on the Front St. bldgs. is from the *Guardian*, Oct. 22, 1879 and Feb. 28, 1880; Irving Store and Warehouse, Chilliwack from the *Guardian*, Dec. 22, 1880. References from Jim Wolf from *The British Columbian*. Feb. 13, 1861, p.2 (Hicks and Smeaton Buildings); Nov. 12, 1861, p.2 (Attorney General's House); June 27, 1861, p.4 (dissolution of partnership); Feb. 18, 1863, p.3 (Royal Columbian Hospital); and July 4, 1863, p.3 and Nov. 28, 1863, p.3 (both Pioneer Mills). Holbrook Arms from the *Mainland Guardian*, Oct. 26, 1878, p.3. References to Graham in James Morton, *The Enterprising Mr. Moody, The Bumptious Captain Stamp: The Lives and Colourful Times of Vancouver's Lumber Pioneers* (North Van.: J.J. Douglas Ltd., 1977). **PROJECTS:** Hicks Bldg., Columbia St., New West., 1861 (demo.); Smeaton Bldg., Columbia St., New West., 1861 (demo.); Holbrook Arms Hotel, New West., 1878 (demo.); Hoy Res., New West., 1878 (demo.); Irving Warehouse, Chilliwack, 1880 (unidentified).

GRANT, George William

Primary sources on Grant's work can be found in *The Daily Columbian* newspaper and its various supplements published in New West.; and *Vancouver of Today Architecturally*. The calculation of Grant's New West. projects 1888-92 is based on published bldg. lists: 1888, eleven projects, $52,000; 1889, fifteen projects, $125,000; 1890 thirty-eight projects $225,000; 1891, thirty-one projects, $378,000; 1892, twenty-two projects $139,000 (117 projects $919,000). Biographical sources include his entry in Howay & Schofield, *British Columbia: Biographical*, 1914, Vol.III, pp.803-804, and *Who's Who & Why* 1911, 1912 and 1913, and an article in the journal *Opportunities*, Mar. 1911, "Vancouver's Architectural Beginnings and Development," by G.W. Grant. Ladner Presbyterian Church citations from *The Daily Columbian*, Aug. 20, 1891, pp.2 & 4. Tender call for additions to Asylum in the *Colonist*, Mar. 3, 1895, p.8. Leckie Block from *Province*, Aug. 6, 1898, p.2 and the *VDW*, Nov. 6, 1898, p.8. Grant's obituary in the Province, Nov. 11, 1925, p.24. Secondary source material is also available in *The New Westminster Courthouse* by Lucy Chambers and an unpublished paper by Garry Colchester. **PROJECTS:** *Hillcroft* (Hendry Res.), 214 Ash St. and 725 Queen's Ave., New West., 1886 with wing added 1888 (alt.); Queen's Hotel, 401-409 Columbia Sts., 1887, New West. (ext.); Masonic Block, Columbia and Lorne Sts., New West., 1887 (dest. by fire 1891; rebuilt 1892 and dest. by fire 1898; rebuilt 1899; the third structure is ext.); Provincial Asylum alterations and additions, 9 E. Columbia St., New West., 1889 and 1895 (alt.); Exhibition Hall, Queen's Park, New West., 1889 (dest. by fire 1929); H.V. Edmonds Res., First St. and Queen's Ave., New West., 1889 (demo. 1930s); A. Ewen Res., Begbie and Carnarvon Sts., New West. (built 1887; Grant designed substantial additions in 1890; dest. by fire 1898); A.E. Rand Res., Queen's Ave. and Third St., New West., 1891 (demo. 1925); Douglas-Elliot Block, Columbia and Sixth Sts., New West., 1891 (dest. by fire 1898); Harris-Dupont Bldg., Columbia and McKenzie Sts., New West., 1891 (dest. by fire 1898); Court House, 653 Clarkson St., New West.,

1891 (partially dest. by fire in 1898 and rebuilt 1899); City Library, Columbia St., New West., 1891 (dest. by fire 1898); St. Andrew's Presbyterian Church (now Ladner United Church), 4962 48 Ave., Ladner, Delta, 1891-93 (ext.); West End (later Dawson) School (renamed King George High School in 1913), 901 Burrard St., Van., first section 1892-93, second section 1896-97 (demo. 1978); T.E. Ladner Res., Trunk Rd., Delta, 1894 (demo. 1973); Phoenix Cannery, 4460 Moncton St., Steveston, 1897 (demo. 2001); Rebuilding of Holy Trinity Church, 514 Carnarvon St., New West., 1898 (1867-68 church rebuilt incorporating the surviving walls; ext.); Leckie Block (Imperial Bank Block), 524 Granville St., Van., 1898-99 (alt.); Walker Block (also known as the Ormidale Block), 151-155 W. Hastings St., Van., 1900 (ext.); Carnegie Public Library (now the Carnegie Centre), 401 Main St., Van., 1900-03 (ext.). **Grant & Henderson:** City Hospital (now the Heather Pavilion), Heather St. and 11th Ave., Van., 1903-06 (alt.); Hampton Court Apts., 1243 Thurlow St., Van., 1911 (ext.).

GREEN, Alfred Harold

Directories; and *Early Land Surveyors of B.C.*, pp.56-59.

GREEN, Elmer Ellsworth

1901 Canada Census; 1910 US Census; inventories; *VDC* and *VDT* references; Vict. plans, bldg. and plumbing permits; directories; VCA files; *AB&E*; *PB&E*; Segger & Franklin, *Exploring Victoria*; BCA files; Minnesota and California vital statistics. **PROJECTS: E.E. Green:** Two houses, 3124 and 3130 W. 2nd Ave., Van., 1911 (ext.); Royal H. Green House, 2580 Bowker St., Oak Bay, 1912 (ext.); Bungalow, Chemainus, 1912 (ext.); Canadian Puget Sound Lumber Co. Offices, Store and Discovery Sts., Vict., 1912 (demo.); G.S. Brown (later Hart) Res., 1961 Fairfield Place, Vict., 1913 (ext.); William Scowcroft Res., 1050 Southgate St., Vict., 1913 (ext.); California Bungalows for the Bungalow Construction Co. Ltd.: 1316, 1320 and 1324 Carnsew St.; 1019 Clare St.; 413, 421, 423, 443 and 451 Durban St.; and 443 Kipling St., Vict., 1912-13 (ext.); Leach Res., 953 Empress Ave., Vict., 1913-14 (ext.); Cottage, 1132 Topaz Ave., Vict., 1914 (ext.). **Green & Aiken:** J. McKay Res., 1237-39 Oscar St., Vict., 1912 (ext.).

GREEN, Frederick Walter

Tender calls and council minutes in the *Colonist* (Cary Castle tender call, Oct. 4, 1862, p.1); partnership with Oakley in the *Chronicle*, Jan. 1, 1865, p.2; Colonial Correspondence [BCA GR-1372], F. W. Green and Green & Oakley; Cotton, *Vice-Regal Mansions*; H. Barry Cotton, BCLS, "Frederick Walter Green, C.E., L.S.: The Original Surveyor of Gastown," published in *Link*, Jan. 1997, pp.8-11. See also Ruggles, *A Country So Interesting*. Information on Cary from James E. Hendrickson's entry in the *Dictionary of Canadian Biography* (University of Toronto Press, 1976), Vol.IX, pp.114-

115. **PROJECTS**: Cary Castle, Belcher Rd., Vict., 1862 (alt. 1865; dest. by fire 1899); Stamp's Sawmill and engine/boiler house, Burrard Inlet, 1865 (demo.).

GREENE & GREENE

Edward R. Bosley, *Greene and Greene* (London: Phaidon Press Ltd., 2000). Plans in Columbia University, New York: Greene & Greene collection in the Avery Architecture & Fine Arts Library; Van. Bldg. Permit #886: May 26, 1904. Further references: William R. & Karen Current, *Greene & Greene: Architects in the Residential Style* (Fort Worth: Amon Carter Museum of Western Art, 1974); Randell L. Makinson, *Greene and Greene: the Passion and the Legacy* (Layton UT: Gibbs Smith Publisher, 1998); *Greene and Greene: Architecture as a Fine Art* (Salt Lake City and Santa Barbara: Peregrine Smith, Inc., 1977); *Greene and Greene: Furniture and Related Designs* (Salt Lake City and Santa Barbara: Peregrine Smith, Inc., 1979); Bruce Smith, *Greene and Greene Masterworks* (San Francisco: Chronicle Books, 1998); Janann Strand, *A Guide to Greene and Greene* (Pasadena: Castle Press, 1974). Information on the Green Res. from Stephen H. Green, North Van. **PROJECT**: Green Res., 1919 Robson St., Van., 1904 (demo. 1969).

GRIFFIN & BYRNE

Town plan for Vanderhoof, and designs for individual bldgs., are reproduced in Brian A. Spencer, *The Prairie School Tradition: The Prairie Archives of the Milwaukee Art Centre*, pp.136-39 (New York: Whitney School of Design, 1985). See also the *Nechako Chronicle*, Historical Supplement, Apr. 12, 1970, and Vanderhoof Board of Trade, *The Town that Couldn't Wait*, 1914, which includes Byrne's preliminary report.

GRIFFITH, Henry Sandham

AIBC; Vict. plans, bldg. and plumbing permits; *CA&B*, Jan., 1897, pp.4-5, *Who's Who in Western Canada, 1911*, and *Who's Who in British Columbia, 1931*. A picture of Griffith's Reservoir Hill house appears in the *VDC*, Apr. 18, 1909, p.16. Records of the construction of *Fort Garry* are held at the BCA MS-1281, which also includes office account information and family information, and a letter from his daughter, Alice Pearson, to Madge Hamilton [Oct. 24, 1981] with personal reminiscences. Manitoba and Saskatchewan references from Barry Elmer; other information from Frank Korvemaker. Information on the asylum competition in *British Columbia Sessional Papers*, Report for 1909 [Public Accounts, p.B102] and from F.G. Consultants, *Riverview Heritage Evaluation*. Specifications for Female Chronic Wing, dated 1912, at BCA GR-0070 Box 2, File 36. UBC Competition documents held at University Archives, UBC. Information on the Stobart-Pease Bldg. is available in the Gladding, McBean & Co. Records, Job #1027, California State Library, Sacramento. Many of Griffith's bldgs. are identified in invento-

ries. **PROJECTS**: The Times Bldg., 660 Fort St., Vict., 1909-10 (demo.; facade rebuilt as part of the Eaton's Centre redevelopment); YMCA, 1203 Blanshard St., Vict., 1910 (demo.); Landsberg Res., 106 Medana St., Vict., 1910 (ext.); Sweeney & McConnell Bldg., 1010-1012 Langley St., Vict., 1910 (ext.); Working drawings and specifications for the Male Chronic Wing, Essondale, 500 Lougheed Hwy., Coquitlam, 1910-13 (ext.); Cliff Block, 28 6th St., New West., 1910-11 (ext.); Empress Bldg. (now the Strathcona Hotel), 919 Douglas St., Vict., 1911 (ext.); Henry Esson Young Res., 1208 Oliver St., Vict., 1911 (ext.); Board of Trade Bldg., 402 W. Pender St., Van., 1912 (ext.); Fairfield Hotel, 1601-1609 Douglas St., Vict., 1912 (ext.); Female Chronic Wing, Essondale, 500 Lougheed Hwy., Coquitlam, 1912 (unbuilt project); YMCA Bldg., 1040 W. Georgia St., Van., 1912-13 (demo.); *Fort Garry* (now known as *Spencer's Castle*), 2906 Cook St., Vict., 1912-14 (ext.); Stobart-Pease Block, 745 Yates St., Vict., 1914 (demo.); T.W. Paterson Res., 3150 Rutland Rd., Oak Bay, 1914 (alt.); T. Edwards & Co. Undertaking Parlour, 2586-2596 Granville St., Van., 1928 (ext.); Fumerton's Department Store, 411-437 Bernard Ave., Kelowna (alt.); Furber Res., 1935 Queens Ave., West Van., 1940 (ext.); Chatsworth Apts., 1950 Robson St., Van., 1941 (demo.); Barrymore Apts., 1131 Barclay St., Van., 1941 (ext.).

GROB, T.

Advertisement in *The Daily Press* [Victoria], Mar. 21, 1861, p.2; *Colonist*, Apr. 16, 1861, p.3 and June 18, 1861, p.3.

GUENTHER, Emil

Scattered references from *The Columbian*, Souvenir Exhibition Supplement, Oct. 4, 1899, p.4; 1901 Canadian Census; the *New Westminster Heritage Resource Inventory*; Van. bldg. permits; *CA&B*; and *Contract Record*. Sherdahl Block citations in *CA&B*, Apr., 1900, p.82. The Canada Hotel is illustrated and described in the *Province*, Oct. 12, 1912, p.23 and *AB&E*, Dec. 20, 1912, p.11. Eagles Fraternity Van. Aerie No. 6 from the *Province*, Dec. 19, 1913, p.28 and *The Contract Record*, Jan. 14, 1914, p.55. Canada Hotel CVA Plans AP-312 and Regent Hotel CVA Plans AP-288. Information on Guenther's activities from outside B.C. from various city directories; Brandes, *San Diego Architects*, p.187 (listed as Emil Guenther von Swartzenberg); Harvey Kimball Hines, *An Illustrated History of the State of Washington* (Chicago: Lewis Publishing Co., 1893), pp.278-279; and *PB&E*, 7.vi.1913, p.354. Correspondence from Seattle, 1922-1923 in CVA Add.MSS.326 540-C-6 File 1. **PROJECTS**: **E. Guenther**: Sherdahl Block (now Dominion Hotel), 92 Water St., Van., 1900-01 (ext.); Regent Hotel, 160 E. Hastings St., Van., 1912 (ext.); Canada Hotel (now Marble Arch Hotel), 518 Richards St., Van., 1912-13 (ext.); Apt. Bldg., Nelson and Howe Sts., 1913 (unbuilt project); Van. Aerie Lodge No.6 for the Eagles Fraternity, 531-537 Homer St., Van., 1913-14 (unbuilt project). **Guenther & Van Aken**:

Windsor Hotel, 738 Columbia St., New West., 1898-99 (demo. 2006); Hotel Fraser, Front St., New West., 1898-99 (demo.); Opera House for the Westminster Opera Co., cor. Lorne and Victoria Sts., New West., 1898-99 (demo.).

HARRIS & HARGREAVES

Directories; census records; tombstones; and B.C. Vital Events. References from the *Colonist*: Union Club (June 5, 1884; Jan. 1, 1885), Redfern's Bldg. (Apr. 12, 1884), Galpin Bldg. (July 28, 1884), Hamley Bldg. (May 28, 1885), Leneveu Res. (Nov. 15, 1884 p.3), and Pooley Res. (June 18, 1885; Jan. 1, 1886); Information on William Fisher from Letter of Jas. E. Nesbitt, Jan. 11, 1965 to J.S. Matthews CVA OUT.P. 957.N.509. **Dennis Harris:** "Married" and "Fashionable Wedding," *Colonist*, Mar. 21, 1878; "The Island Railway-'Eureka,'" *Colonist*, Aug. 10, 1875; "Mr. Dennis Harris," *Colonist*, July 8, 1898, p.4; "A Generous Gift," Apr. 22, 1879, p.3; "Harris V. Douglas," *Colonist*, Nov. 18, 1890, p 2; "Death Removes Mrs. D. R. Harris," *Times*, Jan. 31, 1933. Dennis Harris Collection (VCA PR26). Telephone interview with Denise McAvity, granddaughter of Dennis Harris, Apr. 18, 2000. **George Hargreaves:** Hargreaves Diaries [BCA Add. MSS.443]; Letters of Harold B. Vanstone to BCA Sept. 11, 1987, and to the author, June 18, 1997. Directories; 1881 census; B.C. Vital Events. Newspaper articles include "C.P.R.S.," *Colonist*, Feb. 17, 1875, p.3; "Mr. Hargreaves Mission," *Colonist*, May 1, 1875, p.3; "From Bute Inlet to Cassiar," *Colonist*, May 26, 1875, p.3; "Division R.C.P.R.S.," *Colonist*, Oct. 11, 1876; "George Hargreaves Died This Morning," *Times*, Nov. 10, 1910, p.4; "Hargreaves," *Colonist*, Nov., 11, 1910, p.7. Pierre Berton, *The National Dream: The Great Railway 1871-1881* (Toronto: McClelland & Stewart, 1970). Bissley, *The Union Club of British Columbia*. Additional information from Dorothy Mindenhall and Christopher J.P. Hanna. **PROJECTS**: Galpin Bldg., 1017-21 Government St., Vict., 1884 (ext.); Redfern's Bldg. (now known as the Greenwood Bldg.), 1009-13 Government St., Vict., 1884 (ext.); Union Club, Douglas and Courtney Sts., Vict., 1884 (demo. 1950); Leneveu Res., 634 Michigan St., Vict., 1884 (demo.); Hamley Bldg., 1001-1105 Government St., Vict., 1885 (ext.); *Fernhill*, Pooley Res., 620 Lampson St., Esquimalt, 1885 (demo.).

HARGREAVES, Lord Wilfrid

AIBC; BCA (Public Accounts Annual publications); Vict. plans, bldg. and plumbing permits; Hallmark Society files; *PB&E*; *AB&E*; CVA list of demo. bldgs.; Nanaimo inventories; and reminiscences of his granddaughter, Pamela E Crisp, Vict. **PROJECTS**: Prince George Hotel (now Douglas Hotel), 1450 Douglas St., Vict., 1911-12 (ext.); Andrew Wright Bldg. (now Leland Apts.), 2500-2506 Douglas St., Vict., 1912 (ext.); Scott Bldg., 2659 Douglas St., Vict., 1912 (ext.); Yen Wo Society Bldg., 1713 Government St., Vict., 1912 (ext.); Hargreaves Res., 2378 Pacific Ave., Vict., 1913 (ext.); Pineo Res.,

339 Foul Bay Rd., Oak Bay, 1924 (ext.); Government Liquor Store, Prince George, 1949 (ext.); Government Liquor Store, 25 Cavan St., Nanaimo, 1949 (ext.).

HARVIE, Robert
AIBC; B.C. Vital Events; CVA Plans; and obituary in the *Province*, Mar. 11, 1932, p.21. **PROJECTS:** Mount Pleasant Presbyterian (now Van. Korean Presbyterian) Church, 205 W. 10th Ave., Van., 1926 (alt.); Kerrisdale Presbyterian Church, 5500 Blk. Trafalgar St., Van., 1926 (demo.); Metal Crafts Bldg., 765 Beatty St., Van., 1926 (demo.).

HATCHARD, Otto Beeston
AIBC; and a full page advertisement for Hatchard in the Vernon *News*, Special Holiday Number, 1912, p.77. Additional information from the Greater Vernon Museum & Archives. Obituary in *The Builder*, V.69, Nov. 23, 1945, p.418. **PROJECTS:** Spice Res., 2302 25th Ave., Vernon, 1911 (ext.); Hatchard Res., 2502 23rd St., Vernon, 1912 (ext.); Connaught Gate for Polson Park, Vernon, 1912 (partly ext., located at Greater Vernon Museum & Archives); Urquhart Res., 2501 23rd Ave., Vernon, 1913 (ext.); Res. at Patricia Ranch, 9058 Kalamalka Lake Rd., Coldstream, 1914 (ext.); Kinloch Res., 12803 Kinloch Dr., Vernon, 1919 (ext.).

HAYES, Warren Howard
Withey & Withey, *Biographical Dictionary of American Architects (Deceased)*, pp.274. Plans for St. Andrew's Presbyterian Church in Nanaimo Community Archives. **PROJECT:** St. Andrew's Presbyterian (now United) Church, 315 Fitzwilliam St., Nanaimo, 1892-93 (ext.).

HAZELTINE, Louis R.
Research by Anita Fownes; directories; *AB&E*; Vict. plans, bldg. and plumbing permits; inventories; and Ritz, *Architects of Oregon*. Quote on court case from *VDC*, Sept. 13, 1913. Alkazar Apts. in *AB&E* June 25, 1913, p.14. Philadelphia Architects and Buildings Project website. **PROJECTS:** Res. for Ford & McIntyre, 109 St. Andrews St., Vict., 1912 (ext.); Morrison Res., 1368 Rockland Ave., Vict., 1912 (alt.); Alkazar Apts., Fairfield Rd. cor. Linden Ave., Vict., 1913 (demo. 1977).

HELYER, J.S & Son
Maurice Helyer's AIBC application and army service record; Van. bldg. permits; B.C. Vital Events; and an interview with John Y. McCarter and William G. Leithead by Harold Kalman, 1972, transcription by the CAA, Calgary. **PROJECTS: J.S. Helyer & Son:** Dominion Trust Bldg., 207 W. Hastings St., Van., 1908-10 (ext.); Board of Trade Bldg. (also known as the Trustee Co. Bldg.) 318 Homer St./334-350 W. Cordova St., Van., 1909 (ext.); Exchange Bldg., 144 W. Hastings St., Van., 1909 (alt.); Metropolitan Bldg., 837 W. Hastings St., Van., 1911-12 (demo.). **Maurice Helyer:** Medical Arts Bldg., 823-29 Granville St., Van., 1922-23 (ext.).

HENDERSON, Alexander Ernest
AIBC; CVA plans; Howay & Schofield, *British Columbia: Biographical*, 1914, Vol.IV, pp.283-284; City of Nanaimo plans; B.C. Vital Events; and obituary in the *Province*, Nov. 3, 1927, p.32. Citation for the Bank of Hamilton, Port Hammond, is from *The British Columbian*, Oct. 7, 1919, p.21. **PROJECTS:** Imperial Cannery, Moncton St., Richmond, 1902-03 (demo. 2001); Bank of Hamilton, Port Hammond Branch, 20617 Maple Cres., Maple Ridge, 1919 (ext.); Masonic Hall Ashlar Lodge, 101 Commercial St., Nanaimo, 1923 (ext.); Sheffield Apts., 1325 Comox St., Van., 1925 (demo.).

HENDERSON, John Baptist
AIBC; B.C. Vital Events; BCA vertical files; unpublished manuscript "Story of an Old Timer of B.C." (BCA E/E/H382); marriage notice, *Colonist*, Jan. 4, 1876, p.3; and his obituary in the *Province*, Nov. 22, 1931, p.17. General information from the Alice Arm & Anyox *Herald*, 1920-22. Additional information from the Revelstoke Museum & Archives and the Boundary Museum, Grand Forks. Citations from the Grand Forks *Gazette* for the Grand Forks School (Dec. 7, 1901); Central School, Revelstoke (July 26, 1902); Trout Lake saw mill (Apr. 28, 1903); and Mrs. Henderson (Nov. 21, 1903). **PROJECTS:** Province Hotel, Bridge St. (now Market Ave.), Grand Forks, 1899 (dest. by fire 1986); School, 1200 Central Ave., Grand Forks, 1901-02 (demo. 1972); Central School, Pearson and Second Sts., Revelstoke, 1902 (dest. by fire 1959); Henderson Res., 863 Central Ave., Grand Forks, 1903 (alt.).

HENDERSON, William
Meetings with Mrs. Gordon Henderson, who provided family history; *Who's Who in Western Canada*; Howay & Schofield, *British Columbia: Biographical*, 1914, Vol.III, pp.931-932; Henderson's diaries for 1916-19 [BCA Add. MSS.547]; Archibald, *By Federal Design*; *AB&E*; Barr, *Saanich Heritage Structures*; Stark, *Oak Bay's Heritage Buildings*; *VDT*; *VDC*; Municipality of Oak Bay; and the Records of Oak Bay United Church. Gordon Fulton provided information regarding the Federal Department of Public Works. **PROJECTS:** *Inverallochy* (Henderson Res.), 2150 Oak Bay Ave., 1910 (ext.; damaged by fire 2002); Post Office, Union Bay, 1913 (ext.); St. Columba Presbyterian Church (now Oak Bay United), 1369 Mitchell St., Oak Bay, 1914 (ext.).

HENNELL, Alexander Robert
Information from granddaughter Valerie Hennell, Nanaimo; Col. Pat Paterson; *AB&E*; *VDT*; *Directory of British Architects 1834-1900*; Alex Koch, ed., *Academy Architecture & Architectural Review*, 1900 (London: Academy Architecture, 1900). Partnership with Wilson: *VDC* Aug. 7, 1914, p.13. **PROJECTS:** Paterson Res., 1372 Victoria Ave., Oak Bay, 1913-14 (ext.); Marshall Res., 3475 Upper Terrace Rd., Oak Bay, 1913-14 (ext.); Memorial Bridge to Emily Carr, Beacon Hill Park, 1952-53 (ext.).

HODGINS, Arthur Edward
Nelson: A Proposal for Urban Heritage Conservation; B.C. Vital Events; research from the Nelson Museum; Whittaker, *Early Land Surveyors of British Columbia*, p.69; *Who's Who in B.C.*, 1933; and his obituary, Victoria *Times*, Dec. 19, 1939, p.5 and the *Colonist*, Dec. 22, 1939, p.3. References in the *Colonist*, Oct. 22, 1907, p.7 and Apr. 19, 1914, p.3; and R.J. Taylor, *Report of the Proceedings of the Dominion of Canada Rifle Association*, p.ix (Ottawa: 1905) provided by Professor John F. Bosher, Ottawa. **PROJECTS:** Mara & Barnard Block, 419-421 Baker St., Nelson, c.1897 (ext.); Madden Hotel, 525 Ward St., Nelson, c.1898; London & B.C. Goldfields Block (later the Nelson Daily News office), 266 Baker St., Nelson, 1899-1900 (ext.); *Hochelaga* (Buchanan Res.), 810 Hendryx St., Nelson, 1899 (ext.).

HODGSON, Hugh Astley
Personal interviews with his daughter, Ms. Beatrice Hodgson (deceased Jan. 31, 2004); AIBC; CVA; and WVMA Hodgson Family fonds. Specifications for Burnaby Prison Farm Buildings in BCA GR-0054 Box 36 File 516. W.R. Lort shared his memories of Hodgson. **PROJECTS:** Billiard parlour (now the Only Seafood Restaurant), 22 E. Hastings St., Van., 1911 (ext.); Burnaby Prison Farm (Oakalla Prison), Burnaby, 1911-12; and later bldgs. (demo.); Moore Res., 1498 Laurier Ave., Van., 1912 (ext.); Howard Hotel (now the Brandiz Hotel), 122 E. Hastings St., Van., 1913 (ext.); Hodgson Res., 2355 Marine Dr., West Van., 1913 (relocated); Pauline Johnson School, 1150 22nd St., West Van., 1922 (ext.); Harrison Res., 2587 Kings Ave., West Van., 1923 (ext.); Church of St. Peter & St. Paul, 1426 W. 38th St., Van., 1923 (ext.); St. Stephen's Anglican Church, West Van., 1925 (demo.); Inglewood High School, 1735 Inglewood Ave., West Van., 1927 (demo. 1995 by the West Van. School Board).

HOFFAR, Noble Stonestreet
There are short biographies of N.S. Hoffar in the *Biographical Dictionary of Well-Known British Columbians* (1890), the *VDW Souvenir Edition* of 1889, and the *Van. Daily News-Advertiser* Sept. 29, 1891, p.4. Many of his bldgs. are briefly described in the *VDW* (Dec. 31, 1888; Mar. 9, 1889; June 4, 1889). Metropole Hotel from *VDW*, July 24, 1891, p.8 and Apr. 4, 1892, p.3. Hoffar's descendants (N.H. Hoffar, Sechelt and Helen Jones, Vict.) have copies of letters written by Hoffar in his early years away from Washington, D.C., as well as a short biography written by a family member. Obituaries appeared in the *Province*, Nov. 12, 1907 and the Prince Rupert *Empire*, Nov. 16, 1907, p.1. Bell's Hotel reference from the Seattle *Post-Intelligencer*, Nov. 11, 1883, p.4. Further information from the Prince Rupert City & Regional Archives, including transcription of a letter home, Nov. 25, 1906 [984-19 MS #243]. **PROJECTS:** Hospital Addition, Franklyn Ave., Nanaimo, 1883 (demo. c.1925); Hoffar Res., northwest cor. Georgia and Seymour Sts., Van., c.1886-87 (demo.); Springer-Van Bramer Bldg., 301 W. Cordova, Van.,

1888 (ext.); Competition entry for Van. City Market Bldg., Main St., Van., 1889 (unbuilt project); Horne Block, 311 W. Cordova, Van., 1889 (ext.); Dunn Residence, Georgia and Thurlow Sts., Van., 1889 (demo.); Dunn-Miller Block (also known as Lonsdale Block), 8-28 W. Cordova, Van., 1889 (ext.; restored 1973, with interior alts.); Thomas Dunn Residence, Georgia and Thurlow Sts., Van., 1889 (demo.); New Horne Block, 315-325 Cambie St., 1891 (ext.); Hotel Metropole, Abbott St., Van., 1891-92 (demo.); Court House Addition, southwest cor. Hastings and Cambie Sts., Van., 1893-95 (demo. 1912).

HOLLAND, Sylvia Grace

Interviews with Theo (Holland) Halladay, Sylvia's daughter. Holland's life and career have been covered in Women in Architecture, *Constructing Careers*, pp.26-33. AIBC; Robin Allan, "Sylvia Holland: Disney Artist," *Animation Journal* (1994); Gwen Cash, "Something about Sylvia," *Sun*, Oct. 14, 1933, p.2; Charles Solomon, *The Disney That Never Was* (Hyperion, 1995); John Canemaker, *Before the Animation Begins: The Art and Lives of Disney Inspirational Sketch Artists* (Hyperion: 1996); and various websites relating to Disney, animation and the Cat Fanciers Association. Plan by Day & Holland, UVIC Special Collections File Drawing AP-2079. PROJECTS: **Holland & Holland:** Holland Res., 1170 Tattersall Drive, Saanich, 1926 (ext.). **Day & Holland:** Collinson Res., 640 St. Patrick St., Oak Bay, 1935 (ext.); Tysoe Res., Arbutus Rd., Saanich, c.1936 (unidentified).

HONEYMAN & CURTIS

AIBC; B.C. Vital Events; Boam, *British Columbia*; the *Province*; the *Daily News-Advertiser*; *CA&B*; and the City of North Van. *Heritage Inventory Update*, 1994. Kalman, *Exploring Vancouver*; Wynn & Oke, *Vancouver and Its Region*; and Kluckner, *Vancouver: The Way it Was* provided valuable context and cross-references. Fernie Court House from BCA GR-0054 Box 23 File 402. **G.D. Curtis:** *Nelson: A Proposal for Urban Heritage Conservation*, p.95; and Curtis's granddaughters, Bronwen Souders, Virginia, USA and Mareth Warren, Seattle. Curtis's retirement from Richard and Alexander Mackie, "Roughing It In the Colonies." (*The Beaver*, Apr./May, 1990, pp.6-13). **J.J. Honeyman:** *Who's Who & Why*, 1913 Vol.3; NVMA notes from descendant Florence Riechtel; and Jennifer Nell Barr, *Cumberland Heritage*. Further information from Mrs. Aileen McLellan, a Honeyman descendant. For *Fintry* see David Falconer, "Dun-Waters of Fintry," *Okanagan Historical Society* 38 (1974). Information on Honeyman's uncle, Scottish architect, John Honeyman, is from the *Charles Rennie Mackintosh Society Newsletters* No.62, 63 & 64; he is also mentioned in many of the Mackintosh biographies. PROJECTS: **G.D. Curtis:** Reisterer's Brewery, Nelson, 1897; St. Saviour's Anglican Church, 723 Ward St., Nelson, 1888-90 (alt.); Cathedral of Mary Immaculate, 813 Ward St., Nelson, 1898-99 (ext.);

Public School, Greenwood, 1899; St. Joseph's Catholic School, 523 Mill St., Nelson, 1901 (ext.); Court House, 127 Government St., Greenwood, 1902-03 (ext.); Curtis Cottage, 865 Balmoral Ave., Comox, 1912, additions in 1932 (ext.). **J.J. Honeyman:** A.R. Johnstone Block, Nanaimo, 1893 (demo.); School, Dunsmuir Ave., Cumberland, 1895 (demo.); Central School, Nanaimo, 1895-96 (demo. 1968); Rossland Court House, 2288 Columbia Ave., Rossland, 1898-1901 (ext.); William Wadds Cottage, Rossland, 1902 (ext.); *Warriston* (Charles Dempster Res.), Rossland, c.1908 (ext.); *Kildavaig*, (Honeyman Res.), 3522 W. 47th Ave., Van., 1913 (ext.); *Fintry Proper* (Capt. J.C. Dun-Waters Res.), Fintry, 1919 (dest. by fire; rebuilt 1924; ext.); Honeyman Cottage, Bowen Island, 1929. **Honeyman & Curtis:** Fernie Court House, Fernie, 1907-08 (dest. by fire 1908); Fire Hall No.6, 1500 Nelson St., Van., 1907-9 (ext.; additions by **A.J. Bird**, 1929); Kamloops Court House, 7 Seymour St. W., Kamloops, 1907-09 (ext.); St. John's Presbyterian Church, 1401 Comox St., Van., 1909 (dest. by fire); Logan Res., 2520 Point Grey Rd., Van., 1909-10 (ext.); Addition to the second Hotel Vancouver, Robson and Howe Sts., Van. 1911 (demo.); Imperial Rice Milling Co. Warehouse, 335 Railway St., Van., 1911(ext.); Canadian General Electric office/store/warehouse, 1065 W. Pender St., Van., 1913 (demo.); First Church of Christ Scientist, 185 Keith Rd. E., North Van. City, 1925 (ext.); Shaughnessy Heights United Church, 1550-1590 W. 33rd Ave., Van., 1928, additions 1930 (ext.); Fleck Res., 1296 The Crescent, Van., 1929 (ext.); Bank of Montreal (now Four Corners Community Savings Bank), 390 Main St., Van., 1929-30 (ext.).

HOOPER, Thomas

The information on Hooper is the result of an intensive study of his life and career over a number of years. Biographical data is from English and Canadian sources, including Vital Events in B.C. and England, published references, and numerous interviews with surviving family members in several countries. Citations are from plans, permit records, inventories from many jurisdictions. Hooper's AIBC application contains a list of over one hundred bldgs., which was the starting point of a project list which now contains over three hundred confirmed projects. Further citations from Robert G. Hill. The confirmation of Carrère & Hastings's involvement in the design of the Royal Bank, Vict., comes from the Royal Bank Archives, Toronto. UBC Competition documents held at University Archives, UBC. The existence of the Edmonton office is contained in the reminiscences of J.Y. McCarter, and confirmed by his daughter, Joan McCarter. PROJECTS: **Thomas Hooper:** Hooper Res., 571-573 Homer St., Van., 1888 (demo.); Homer St. Methodist Church, 400-block Dunsmuir St., Van., 1888-89 (demo.); Chinese Mission Church, Pender St., Van., 1889 (demo.); Commercial Block for R.V. Winch, 62-66 Cordova St., Van., 1889 (demo.); Wallace St. Methodist Church, cor. Wallace and Franklyn Sts., Nanaimo, 1889 (demo.); Metropolitan Methodist Church,

1411 Quadra St., Vict., 1889-91 (ext.); Protestant Orphans' Home, 2691 Cook St./1191 Kings Rd., Vict., 1893 (ext.); Colonist Bldg., E. side of View St., Vict., 1897 (demo.); Thomas Earle Warehouse, 530-534 Yates St., Vict., 1899-1900 (ext.); *Hycroft*, A.D. McRae Res., 1489 McRae Ave., Van., 1909-12 (ext.); Royal Bank, 1108 Government St., Vict., 1909-10 (ext.); E.A. Morris Tobacco Shop, 1116 Government St., Vict., 1909 (ext.); Dominion Stock & Bond Bldg., Van., 1910 (unbuilt project); Chilliwack City Hall, 45820 Spadina Rd., Chilliwack, 1910-12 (ext.); Van. Court House Wing, 800 Robson St., Van., 1910-12 (ext.); Van. Labor Temple, 411 Dunsmuir St., Van., 1910-12 (ext.); Vernon Court House, 3001 27th St., Vernon, 1911-14 (ext.); Revelstoke Court House, 1123 Second St. W., Revelstoke, 1911-13 (ext.); Ice Arenas for the Patrick Brothers, Van. and Vict., 1911-12 (demo.); *Greencroft* (McLean Res.), 3838 Cypress St., Van., 1912 (ext.); Royal Bank, Mount Pleasant Branch, 2349 Main St., Van., 1912 (ext.); Winch & Co. Bldg., 670 Fort St., Vict., 1912 (only facade retained); Campbell Bldg., 1025-1029 Douglas St., Vict., 1912-13 (demo.); *Lyndhurst*, P.R. Brown Res., 1182 Old Esquimalt Rd., Esquimalt, 1913 (ext.). **Hooper & Reid:** David Spencer Ltd. Arcade Bldg., Victoria Cres., Nanaimo, 1891 (demo.). **Hooper & Watkins:** Vict. Public (Carnegie) Library, 794 Yates St., Vict., 1904-05 (ext.); Odd Fellows Hall, 300 W. Pender St., Van., 1905-06 (ext.); Winch Bldg. (now part of Sinclair Centre), 739 W. Hastings St., Van., 1906-09 (ext.); B.C. Permanent Loan Co. Bldg., 330 W. Pender St., Van., 1907 (ext.); Additions to Coqualeetza School, 7201 Vedder Rd., Chilliwack, 1907 (demo.); University Schools Ltd., 3400 Richmond Rd., Saanich, 1908 (ext.); George Jay School, 1118 Princess Ave., Vict., 1908 (ext.); St. Ann's Academy, Additions, 835 Humboldt St., Vict., 1908-13 (ext.). **Hooper & Wilson:** Vladimir Apts., 1305 W. 15th Ave., Van., 1928 (alt.).

HOPE, Archibald Campbell

AIBC; application for RIBA membership; F.G. Consultants, *Langley's Heritage*; correspondence with T. Bryan Campbell-Hope, who provided family records such as marriage and death certificates; and *The West Riding at the Opening of the 20th Century* (Scott & Pike, 1902) regarding Thomas Campbell Hope. Gavin Res. in *Province*, June 8, 1912, p.8. PROJECTS: **Pearce & Hope:** Provincial Normal School (**W.F. Gardiner**, supervising architect), 524 W. 10th Ave. (now 501 W. 12th Ave.), Van., 1908-10 (only facade retained); Simon Fraser School, 3185 Manitoba St., Van., 1908-09 (demo. 1981). **A.C. Hope:** Lonsdale School, 2151 Lonsdale Ave., North Van., 1910 (with H.M. Barker, ext.); Masonic Temple, 1140-1144 Lonsdale Ave., North Van. City, 1911 (alt.); Delta Municipal Hall (now Delta Museum & Archives), 4858 Delta St., Ladner, Delta, 1912-13 (ext.); Gavin Res., southwest cor. Buckingham St. and Sperling Ave., Burnaby (demo. 1950s); Postal Station C (now Heritage Hall), 3102 Main St., Van., 1914-15 (ext.); Roxborough (now The Brambly) Apts., 1595 W.

15th Ave., Van., 1928 (ext.); Fort Langley Community Hall, 9167 Glover Rd., Fort Langley, Township of Langley, 1930-31 (ext.).

HOPE, Charles Edward

F.G. Consultants, *Langley's Heritage*; *VDW* Dec. 30, 1893, p.8; *British Columbian Saturday Magazine*, May 14, 1949; Langley *Advance*, May 5, 1949; *Sun*, Apr. 28, 1949; *Early Land Surveyors of B.C.*, pp.74-78; and correspondence with T. Bryan Campbell-Hope, Edmonton. **PROJECTS**: Coronation Block, 9048 Glover Rd., Fort Langley, Township of Langley, 1911 (ext.); *Illahie* (Hope Res.), 23155 96 Ave., Fort Langley, Township of Langley, 1912 (demo.; Coach House ext.).

HOPKINS, John W. & E.C.

McTavish, Newton. *The Fine Arts in Canada*; Weir, *The Lost Craft of Ornamented Architecture*; CAC Accession No. 18, McGill University, Montreal; and City of Edmonton Archives. Lord Elphinstone Block and Opera House in *VDW*, Dec. 31, 1888, p.4-5; Opera House in *VDW*, Mar. 29, 1890, p.1. **PROJECTS**: Lord Elphinstone Block, Granville St., Van., 1888-89 (demo.); Van. Opera House, 751-775 Granville St., Van., 1888-91 (demo. 1969).

HORSBURGH, Victor Daniel

B.C. Vital Events; CVA plans; obituaries and citation for Nanaimo CBC Bank from Robert G. Hill; Vault Bldg. from AIBC Minutes; and W.F. Gardiner collection [courtesy Gardiner family]. **PROJECTS**: Canadian Bank of Commerce (now the Great National Land Co. Bldg.), 5-17 Church St., Nanaimo, 1913-14 (ext.); Canadian Bank of Commerce (**W.F. Gardiner**, supervising architect), 501-509 Main St., Van., 1914-15 (ext.); Canadian Bank of Commerce Bank Vault Bldg. (**W.F. Gardiner**, supervising architect), 1943 E. 1st Ave., Van., 1915 (alt.).

HORTON, Hoult

Vict. plans; bldg. and plumbing permits; city directories; inventories; *Province*, Oct. 12, 1912, p.23; *AB&E*; and BCA visual records. **PROJECTS**: **Hoult Horton**: D.G. McBeath Res., 614 Seaforth St., Vict., 1911 (ext.); John D. Hallam Res., 988 Newport Ave., Oak Bay, 1913 (ext.). **Horton & Phipps**: Belmont House, 600-620 Humboldt St./801-807 Government St., Vict., 1912 (ext.); C.B. Schreiber Res., 930 Foul Bay Rd., Vict., 1912 (ext.); Misses O'Brien Res., 65-67 Wellington Ave., Vict., 1912 (alt.); J.R. Matterson Res., 1016 Verrinder Ave., Vict., 1912 (ext.).

HOUGHTON, Edwin Walker

Essay by J.K. Ochsner & D.A. Andersen in Ochsner, *Shaping Seattle Architecture*, pp.46-51; *Construction*, Oct., 1907, p.64; CVA Plans AP-69, AP-235 and AP-1592; *Province*, Mar 31, 1977, p.23; *Sun*, Mar. 22, 2002, p.B5; and Van. bldg. permits. **PROJECTS**: **E.W. Houghton**: Hotel and Theatre, cor. Columbia and Church Sts., New West., 1907 (unbuilt project); Leigh-Spencer Office

Building, 551-553 Granville St., Van. 1909-10 (demo. 1990s). **E.W. Houghton & Son**: Kinemacolor (Colonial) Theatre (renovation of the Van Horne Block), 601-603 Granville St., Van., 1912-13 (demo. 1972); Theatre and Apt. Bldg. for the Van. Opera House Co., 1023 W. Pender St., Van., 1913 (unbuilt project).

HOY, Henry

F.G. Consultants, *Langley's Heritage*, p.27; Howay & Schofield, *British Columbia: Biographical*, 1914, Vol.IV, pp.103-104; and B.C. Vital Events. Portrait and additional information available at New West. Museum & Archives. Contracts for the Armstrong Scoullar Block and the Masonic/Odd Fellows Block are from the *Mainland Guardian*, July 16, 1887, p.3. **PROJECT**: St. Andrew's Presbyterian Church, 9025 Glover Rd., Fort Langley, Township of Langley, 1885 (ext.).

HUDSON'S BAY COMPANY

Local inventories, and Minaker, *The Gorge of Summers Gone*. Additional information from John Adams. **PROJECTS**: Bastion, 98 Front St., Nanaimo, 1853 (ext.); Craigflower School, 2755 Admiral's Rd., Saanich, 1854-55 (ext.); Craigflower Manor, Island Hwy. at Admiral's Rd., View Royal, 1856 (ext.).

HUNTER, John Douglas

Information from nephew, Stuart Tarbuck.

HUTCHINSON, George Edgar

AIBC; Maud Rosinski, *Architects of Nova Scotia: A Biographical Dictionary 1605-1950*, pp.211-212; additional information from Garry D. Shutlak and Frank Korvemaker; interview with Father Bernard Hanley, Queen of Peace Church, Esquimalt; B.C. Vital Events; and his obituary. Quotes about Hutchinson from the Sydney *Record*, Nov. 2, 1903. A collection of Hutchinson's plans and books are in the possession of Bruce M. Forster. **PROJECTS**: Duchess St. Fire Hall, Vict., 1913 (claimed on AIBC application but not yet identified); Our Lady Queen of Peace Church, 851 Old Esquimalt Rd., Esquimalt, 1931 (alt.).

INDIAN AFFAIRS

Technical Services, Indian & Northern Affairs Canada, Hull, Quebec, maintains the historical collection of plans prepared by in-house Indian Affairs architects and private contractor architects; the departmental annual reports between 1867 and 1972 record the projects undertaken by the various agencies and departments, including costs and payments to architects.

IRVING, David W.

VDC; *AB&E*; and Vict. plans, bldg. and plumbing permits. **PROJECTS**: St. Paul's Evangelical Lutheran Church, 1161 Princess Ave., Vict., 1912 (ext.); Sumner Res., 2614 Avebury Ave., Vict., 1913 (ext.); Emery Res., 1555 Gladstone Ave., Vict., 1913 (ext.).

ISLAND INVESTMENT COMPANY LTD.

Oak Bay plans; Vict. plans; bldg. and plumbing permits; BCA; directories; *VDC*; *VDT*; and inventories. **PROJECTS**: Res., 902 Foul Bay Rd., Vict., 1911 (ext.); Res, 1275 Roslyn Rd., Vict., 1911 (ext.).

JAMES, Douglas

AIBC; Family memorabilia; research at the Cowichan Valley Museum & Archives; Ginnie Beardsley, "An Interview with Douglas James" regarding Hatley Park; Geoffrey Castle, ed. *Hatley Park: an Illustrated Anthology* (Friends of Hatley Park, 1995); *This Old House*; Stark, *Oak Bay's Heritage Buildings*; Ellen Mackay, *Places of Worship*; and his war records in the National Archives of Canada, Ottawa. Information on the bldgs. at Shawnigan Lake School provided by the School Archives. **PROJECTS**: **James & James**: St. Mary's Church, Elgin St., Oak Bay, 1911 (demo.); I.O.O.F. Bldg., Vict., 1911 (unbuilt project); Municipal Hall, Hampshire and Oak Bay Ave., Oak Bay, 1912 (demo.); Oak Bay Grocery (now The Blethering Place), 2250 Oak Bay Ave., 1912 (ext.); Haynes Bldg., 731 1/2 Fort St., Vict., 1911 (demo.); Federal Bldg. (now P.L. James Place), 1230 Government St., Vict., 1946-48 (ext.). **Douglas James**: King's Daughters Hospital, Duncan, 1917 and 1938 (demo.); James Res., 1033 Herd Rd., Maple Bay, 1922 (ext.); Nanaimo Motors, 20 Front St., Nanaimo, 1924 (alt.); Bazett Block, 1924 Craig St., Duncan, 1924 (ext.); School, Cairnsmore St., Duncan, 1925 (ext.); *Stonehaven*, 3069 Gibbens Rd., Duncan, 1926 (ext.); St. Edward's Roman Catholic Church, Coronation Ave. at Brae St., Duncan, 1926-27 (ext.); Structures at Shawnigan Lake School, 1926-34 [Main Bldg., 1926-27 (ext.); Chapel, 1928 (alt.); Classroom Bldg., 1929 (dest. by fire 1958); Copeman's House (Student Res.), 1929 (dest. by fire 1968); Hobbies Bldg., 1934 (dismantled and rebuilt 1995); Cricket Pavilion, 1934 (relocated); several other structures attributed]; Knights of Pythias Hall, Brae St., Duncan, 1930 (ext.); Queen Margaret's Anglican Church, Duncan, 1934 (ext.); Memorial Arena (with **H. Savage** & **D.C. Frame**), 1925 Blanshard St., Vict., 1947-48 (demo. 2003).

JAMES, Percy Leonard

See *The Life and Times of Victoria Architect P. Leonard James*, by Rosemary James Cross (Dear Brutus Publishing, Victoria BC, 2005). James's work is well-documented in his personal papers, deposited in the Chad Evans Collection at the BCA; and an extensive collection of his working drawings is in the VCA. Other information drawn from AIBC; Vict. plans, bldg. and plumbing permits; family memorabilia; and an unpublished manuscript, *Percy Leonard James, Architect* by Rosemary James Cross. See also Alastair Kerr entry in *The Crystal Gardens: West Coast Pleasure Palace* (Vict.: Crystal Gardens Preservation Society, 1977), pp.78-90; Ellen Mackay, *Places of Worship*; *This Old House*; Barr, *Saanich Heritage Structures*; Stark, *Oak Bay's Heritage Buildings*; and Howay & Schofield, *British Columbia:*

Biographical, 1914, Vol.IV, pp.585-86. Information on the Royal Colwood Golf Club from John Ronald. Recollection of James by John Wade from a personal interview with Donald Luxton, on Oct. 2, 1984. **PROJECTS**: *Stonehenge Park* (John Lysle Res.), 1179 Munro St., Esquimalt, c.1909 (ext.); *Bannavern*, 914 St. Charles St., Vict., 1910-11 (ext.); *Durlston* (Jameses Res.), 2385 Tod Rd., Oak Bay, 1910 (ext.); First Royal Colwood Golf Course Clubhouse, Colwood, 1922 (dest. by fire 1929); Provincial Royal Jubilee Hospital East Wing (with **K.B. Spurgin**), 1900 Fort St., Vict., 1921-25 (ext.); Capt. W. Hobart Molson House 1663 Rockland Ave., Vict., 1930 (ext.); E.W. Griffiths House, 235 Dennison Rd., Oak Bay, 1936 (ext.); The Deanery, 930 Burdett Ave., Vict., 1937 (ext.); Chapel of the Peace of God, west side of Vancouver St., between Rockland and Burdett Aves., 1939 (ext.).

JAMESON, Reyburn

City of North Van. bldg. permits; NVMA; and North Van. inventories. **PROJECTS**: Pythian Castle Hall, 177 W. 4th St., North Van. City, (demo. 1989); Sicot Res., 621 W. 15th St., North Van. City, 1912 (ext.); Diplock Res., 404 Somerset St., North Van. City, 1912 (ext.).

JOHNSON, Harry G.

AIBC; directories; California Death Index; and obituary in the San Jose *Mercury*, Sept. 15, 1970, p.25.

JOHNSON, J. Graham

AIBC; B.C. Vital Events; inventories; *VDC* and *VDT* references; *Comox District Free Press*; *Comox Argus*; Vict. plans, bldg. and plumbing permits; Oak Bay permits and plans; directories; VCA files; *AB&E*; Segger & Franklin, *Exploring Victoria*, BCA files; *VDT* July 19, 1941, p.9 (Wavell Apts.); *Home Building in Canada: Small Homes*, 1947 Edition; and *Western Homes & Living*, Nov. 1958 (Hastings House). **PROJECTS**: **J.G. Johnson**: Norton-Taylor Res., 2415 Lansdowne Rd., Vict., 1935 (ext.); Pfender House, 3150 Tarn Place, Vict., 1935 (ext.); Johnson House, 620 Rockland Place, Vict., 1936 (ext.); Cross Residences, 720 and 728 Selkirk Ave., Vict., 1938 (ext.); Townhouses, 2302-2310 Oak Bay Ave. and 1521 Clive Drive, Oak Bay, 1939 (ext.); Dods House, 3096 Cadboro Bay Rd., Oak Bay, 1945 (ext.). **Spurgin & Johnson**: C. Walden, Patio Court Residences, Oak Bay, 1927 (ext.). **Johnson & Stockdill**: Hastings Res. (now Hastings House Country House Hotel), 160 Upper Ganges Rd., Salt Spring Island, 1940 (ext.); Wavell Apts., 1677 Hollywood Cres., Vict., 1941 (ext.); Sandholme Apts., 2450 Quadra St., Vict., 1941 (ext.); Safeway Store, 506 Esquimalt Rd., Vict., 1941 (ext. as Universal Sheet Metal); Safeway Store, 1809 Douglas St., Vict., 1941 (demo.); Safeway Store, 1594 Fairfield Rd., Vict., 1941 (alt.).

JONES, Claude Percy

Who's Who in Western Canada, 1909 and 1911; directories; Van. bldg. permits; and CVA plans. Scott-Allan Res. from Hobson, *This is Our Heritage*, p.91. Magee School competition prizes from

AB&E, Mar. 10, 1913, p.16. St. Barnabas from *AB&E*, Apr. 25, 1914, p.16. See Imbi Harding, *Sun*, Aug. 24, 2001, p.B5. **PROJECTS**: **Claude P. Jones**: Pendrell Apts., 1419 Pendrell St., Van., 1910 (ext.); Stock Judging Pavilion at Hastings Park, 2901 E. Hastings St., Van., 1911 (demo.). **Jones & Beatson**: Magee School, 1975 W. 49th Ave., Van., 1913-14 (demo.); St. Barnabas Church, cor. Cook and Caledonia Sts., Vict., 1914 (unbuilt project).

JONES, Morley Oscar

AIBC; Point Grey permit records; City of North Van. *Heritage Inventory, 1994*; directories; and B.C. Vital Events. **PROJECTS: Jones & Aspell**: St. Edmund's Catholic School and Rectory, 535 Mahon Ave., North Van. City, 1911-13, (ext.); Baxter Res., 2740 Yukon St., Van., 1913, (alt.).

JONES, William Francis

AIBC; directories; B.C. Vital Events; *Who's Who in British Columbia, 1940-1941*, and interview with W.R. Lort. Plans for Point Grey Municipal Hall at CVA. Information on Richmond Municipal Hall from Mary Keen, *Meeting Places: Richmond's Town Halls 1879-1995* (Richmond Archives, 1995). Arundel Mansions in *The British Columbian*, Nov. 4, 1913, p.4. **PROJECTS**: **Thornton & Jones**: Felix Apts., 652 Jervis St., Van., 1910 (ext.); Arundel Mansions, 48 Begbie St., New West., 1912-13 (ext.). **W.F. Jones**: Point Grey Municipal Hall, 5851 W. Boulevard, Van., 1909 (demo.); Richmond Municipal Hall, Richmond, 1919 (demo.).

JULIAN, Thomas Ennor

B.C. Vital Events; *VDW* July 13, 1894 supplement p.4; Scott, *Once in the Royal City*, and the Van. bldg. permit registers. Information on his Calgary practice and relocation to Van. from Barry Elmer; quote from the Calgary *Tribune*, Vol.IV, No.20: Feb. 13, 1889, p.3. Information on New West. bldgs. from *The Daily Columbian* Supplement, Sept. 1899 and *The Columbian*, Souvenir Exhibition Supplement, Oct. 4, 1899, p.4 provided by Jim Wolf. **PROJECTS**: Kwong On Wo & Co., 525 Front St., New West., 1898-99 (demo.); BCER Station, 728 Columbia St., New West., 1898-99 (demo.); BCER freight shed, Columbia St. near 8th St., 1898-99, (demo.); Dr. Drew Res., Carnarvon St., New West., 1898-99 (demo.); B.W. Shiles Res., Carnarvon St., New West., 1898-99 (demo.); Dr. Boggs Res., Agnes St., New West., 1898-99 (demo.); St. Patrick's & Young Mens' Institute Hall, New West., 1898-99 (demo.); Addition to the Electric Light Powerhouse, Tenth St., New West., 1898-99 (demo.); the Queen's Ave. Methodist Church, Queen's Ave., New West., 1898-99 (demo); Holy Rosary Cathedral, 646 Richards St., Van., 1899-1900 (ext.); Wing Sang Bldg., 51-69 E. Pender St., Van., 1901 (ext.).

JULIEN, Phillip

Directories; CVA plans; Van. bldg. permits; and Stark, *Oak Bay's Heritage Buildings*. Rex Theatre from *Province* Dec. 15, 1913, p.2 and Dec. 19, 1913, p.28. **PROJECTS**: Kensington Apts., 1386

Nicola St., Van., 1912 (ext.); *Riffington* (Wright Res.), 3175 Beach Dr., Oak Bay, 1913 (ext.); Rex Theatre, 23-27 W. Hastings St., Van., 1913 (demo.).

KAUFMANN, Gordon Bernie

CVA Plans; Van. bldg. permits; directories; Kamloops Museum & Archives; Kamloops inventories; Avery Index of Architectural Periodicals; archival records of the American Institute of Architects, Washington, D.C.; Jay Belloli et al, *Johnson, Kaufmann, Coate: Partners in the California Style* (Santa Barbara: Capra Press, 1992); and James Ross Moore, *Gordon B. Kaufmann* (American National Biography Online). Information on Archer's American career provided by the American Institute of Architects, Washington, D.C. Kaufmann's work in America is documented in numerous published sources. **PROJECTS**: **G.B. Kaufmann**: Two duplexes for C.N. Ecclestone, 3317-3323 W. 3rd Ave. (demo.) and 3537-3563 W. 3rd Ave. (alt.), Van., 1911; Le Patourel & McRae Drug Store and Apts., 2600-2610 W. 4th Ave., Van., 1912 (demo.); Iona Court Apts., 1125-1131 W. 11th Ave., Van., 1912 (alt.); Apt. Block for E.E. Crandall, 1089 W. 15th Ave./3048 Spruce St., Van., 1912 (ext.); Acadia Block, Seymour St., Kamloops, 1912 (alt.); Ecclestone Res., 1351 Laurier Ave., Van., 1912-13 (alt.); Killam Res., 1947 W. 19th Ave., Van., 1913 (ext.); Bingham Res., 1690 Angus Dr., Van., 1913-14 (demo. c.1973). **Kaufmann & Phillips**: Grubbe Res., 157 Nicola St. W., Kamloops, 1912; Hibbert Res., 171 Battle St. W., Kamloops, 1913 (ext.); Busteed Res., 171 Nicola St. W., Kamloops, 1913 (ext.).

KAYLL, Swinburne Annandale

AIBC; CVA plans; directories; and B.C. Vital Events. **PROJECT**: Salvation Army Grandview Citadel, 1648 E. 1st Ave., Van., 1957 (ext.).

KEAGEY, James W.

Directories and Van. bldg. permits. **PROJECT**: Van. Rowing Club, Park Drive, Stanley Park, Van. 1911 (ext.); William More Res., 3057 W. 39th Ave., 1913 (ext.); A.D. Wilson Res., 3075 W. 39th Ave., 1913 (ext.).

KEITH, John Charles Malcolm

AIBC; Vict. plans, bldg. and plumbing permits; inventories; Robin Ward, *Echoes of Empire; Victoria and its Remarkable Buildings*, Harbour Publishing, 1996; Segger & Franklin, *Exploring Victoria's Architecture*; Brandes, *San Diego Architects*, p.96; Miles Glendinning, ed., *A History of Scottish Architecture*; Stark, *Oak Bay's Heritage Buildings*; Mackay, *Places of Worship*; *Who's Who in British Columbia* (Vict.: S.M. Carter, 1931); *CA&B*, June 1895; the *Colonist*, the *Sun*, the *Province*; *Victoria Architecturally*, 1911; Howay & Schofield, *British Columbia: Biographical*, 1914, Vol.III, pp.566-569; Gray, *Edwardian Architecture*, p.229; McIntosh, *A Documentary History of Music in Victoria, Vol.I*; obituary in the *Colonist*, Dec. 20, 1940, p.2; and B.C. Vital Events. Information on the asylum competition in *British Columbia Sessional Papers*, Report for 1909 [Public Hospital for the

Insane Report & Public Accounts, p.B102]; and F.G. Consultants, *Riverview Heritage Evaluation*. Confirmation of *Hesket* from the J.E. Wilson Journals & Accounts [VCA]. Other citations and information from Jennifer Nell Barr. Citations for the second and third All Saints' Anglican Church, Vernon, from the Greater Vernon Museum & Archives (Second: Vernon *News*, June 6, 1907, p.1; Third: Vernon *News*, Nov. 10, 1932). Other references from Robert G. Hill. **PROJECTS: Evers & Keith:** Christ Church Cathedral, 951 Quadra St., Vict., 1892-1994 (ext.); *Hochelaga* (Galletly Res.), 1715 Rockland Ave., Vict., 1892 (ext.); *Highlands* (Macauley Res.), 950 Terrace Ave., Vict., 1893 (ext.); Two Houses for Anglican Synod, 943 and 947 Meares St., Vict., 1893 (ext.). **J.C.M. Keith:** Hibben Res., 614 Marifield Ave., Vic., 1893 (alt.); Power Station for the Victoria Electric Railway & Lighting Company, 450 Swift St., Vict., 1894-5 (ext.); St. Mary's Anglican Church, Mayne Island, 1897-98; *Hesket* (J.E. Wilson Res.), 811 St. Charles St., Vict., 1905 (ext.); St. John the Baptist, Anglican, Duncan, 1905 (ext.); Second All Saints' Anglican Church, 3205 27th St., Vernon, 1907 (dest. by fire 1931); Winning competition entry for the 'Hospital for the Mind at Mount Coquitlam,' Coquitlam, 1908 (one bldg. completed, working drawings and specifications by **H.S. Griffith**); Nurses' Res., Royal Jubilee Hospital, 1900 Fort St., Vict., 1908 (demo. 1985); Pemberton Memorial Chapel, Royal Jubilee Hospital, 1900 Fort St., Vict., 1909 (ext.); Sir James Douglas School, 401 Moss St., Vict., 1909 (demo. 1997 by the Vict. School Board); New English Evangelical Grace Lutheran Church, 804 Queens Ave., Vict., 1910 (alt.); Dodds Res., 1241 Monterey Ave., Oak Bay, 1912 (ext.); Victoria Steam Laundry (with **Hutchinson & Ford**), 943-947 North Park St., Vict., 1912 (ext.); First Presbyterian Church, 1701 Quadra St., Vict., 1912-15 (ext.); Ryan House, 651 Battery St., Vict., 1912-13 (ext.); Enke Res., 572 Island Rd., Oak Bay, 1912-13 (demo.); Police Station, 625 Fisgard St., Vict., 1914 (demo. 2002; facade retained as part of new development); Beacon Hill School, 120 Douglas St., Vict., 1914 (ext.); *Dunmora*, 8100 McPhail Rd., Central Saanich, 1922-23 (ext.); St. Paul's Anglican Church, Nanaimo, 29 Church St., 1931 (ext.); Third All Saints' Anglican Church, 3205 27th St., Vernon, 1932 (ext.).

KELLY, James

Mills, *Architectural Trends in Victoria*; Nanaimo Community Archives files; City of Nanaimo File 6800-40-H02; Van. bldg. permits; directories; and tender calls in the *Colonist* (May 18, 1895, p.6 and May 1, 1900, p.2). References from Robert G. Hill: Wolfe Block, Nanaimo *Free Press*, May 13, 1895, p.4; Women's Ward, City Hospital, *Contract Record* [Toronto], vol.8, April 22, 1897, p.1; tender call for additions to Union Brewery, *Contract Record* [Toronto], vol. 12, Feb. 20, 1901, p.2; tender call for Catholic Church, Vancouver, *Contract Record* [Toronto], vol. xvi, May 10, 1905, p.6. **PROJECTS:** Davidson Block (Queen's Hotel), 34 Victoria Cres.,

Nanaimo, 1892 (alt.); *Haslam Hall*, 15 Wallace St., Nanaimo, 1893 (dest. by fire 1977); Two small houses for Haslam, Hecate St., Nanaimo, 1893; Wolfe Block, cor. Commercial and Bastion Sts., Nanaimo, 1895 (demo.); Women's Ward for City Hospital, Nanaimo, 1897 (demo.); Canadian Bank of Commerce, 5-17 Church St., Nanaimo, (demo. 1913); Union Brewery Additions, Nanaimo, 1901; Catholic Church, Vancouver, 1905.

KENNEDY, James

Howay & Schofield, *British Columbia: Biographical*, 1914, Vol.III, pp.551-552; obituary in *The Weekly British Columbian*, Nov. 25, 1902. p.2; information in the Delta Museum & Archives; and Colonial Correspondence, [BCA GR-1372 B-1335 and 1336, File 868]. Bldg. citations in *The Daily Columbian* Supplement, Sept. 1899; Powell Block citation in *VDW*, Dec. 31, 1889, p.6; Penitentiary Workshops tender call in the *Colonist*, Sept. 19, 1881, p.2; Colonial Hotel fire from the *British Columbian*, Dec. 15, 1883, p.3 "Fire Fiend." *B.C. Sessional Papers* 1877, Report for 1876, p.xxx confirms Kennedy as superintendent of the Asylum. Other citations from Robert G. Hill and Jim Wolf. **PROJECTS:** Second Colonial Hotel, Columbia St., New West., 1875-76 (dest. by fire 1883); British Columbia Penitentiary Workshops, New West., 1881 (demo.); Webster Block, Front St., New West., 1887 (dest. by fire 1898); Powell Block, Columbia St., New West., 1889 (dest. by fire 1898); Bldg. for The Columbian Printing Co., New West., 1898-99 (demo.).

KENWAY, Balston C.

Advertisements; directories; and newspaper references from Barry Elmer, Calgary.

KERR, Robert Claud

AIBC; B.C. Vital Events; and CVA Plans. Information on Honeyman's uncle, Scottish architect John Honeyman, is from the *Charles Rennie Mackintosh Society Newsletters* No.62, 63 & 64; he is also mentioned in many of the Mackintosh biographies. **PROJECT:** Third Church of Christ Scientist, 1075 Burnaby St., Van., 1927 (converted to apartments; extensively alt.).

KERR, Thomas Logan

AIBC; B.C. Vital Events; Townley & Matheson records [CVA Add.MSS.1399]; obituary in the *Province*, Jan. 15. 1941, p.19; and information from Robert Close, Scotland. **PROJECTS:** Plaza Theatre, 881 Granville St., Van., 1936 (alt.); Lux Theatre, 59 E. Hastings St., Van., 1939 (demo.).

KING, William

Revelstoke *Mail-Herald*, Apr. 6, 1910; *Kootenaian*, June 22, 1911; *VDC* Sunday Magazine, Dec. 22, 1912, p.5; Bradley residence in the *Observer* [Revelstoke], Mar. 5, 1909; Selkirk School in the *Herald* [Revelstoke], Mar. 6, 1909, Observer [Revelstoke], Mar. 19, 1909 and *Contract Record* [Toronto], Apr. 27 1910, p.28 (tender call); Bairne

Warehouse from *Contract Record* [Toronto], xxv, Sept. 6, 1911, 63 (tender call); and additional information provided by the Revelstoke Museum & Archives. **PROJECTS:** Bradley Residence, 818 Second St. W., Revelstoke, 1909 (ext.); Selkirk School, 300 Blk. Sixth St. E., Revelstoke, 1909-10 (demo. by School Board 1983); King Edward Hotel, 112 Second St. E., Revelstoke, 1910 (dest. by fire 1995); Howson Block, 211-217 Mackenzie Ave., Revelstoke, 1910-11 (ext.); Warehouse for F.H. Bairne Co., Revelstoke, 1911 (unbuilt project); Court House, 312 4th St., Kaslo, 1911-12 (ext.).

KING, William R.

Kerr, *Biographical Dictionary of Well-Known British Columbians*, pp.212-213. For the Baptist Church: tender call in the Van. *Daily News-Advertiser*, Sept. 22, 1888, p.1; described and illustrated in the *VDW*, Sept. 14, 1889, p.3. The Anglican Bishop's Palace is described in the *VDW*, Dec. 31, 1889, p.6. New West. references from Jim Wolf: Rousseau Res. tender call, *The Daily Columbian* Sept. 19, 1888, p.3; Railway Co. Bldg. tender call, *The Daily Columbian*, Sept. 25, 1888; *The Truth* (New West.) *Building Operations*, Oct. 13, 1889, p.4; McInnes cottages in *The Daily Columbian*, Mar. 27, 1890, p.4. Financial embarrassment in *Weekly News-Advertiser* [Van.], Oct. 28, 1891, p.4. **PROJECTS:** Rousseau Res., Royal Ave., New West., 1888 (demo.); Commercial Bldg. for the New West. Southern Railway Co., Lytton Sq., New West., 1888 (unbuilt project); Trapp Res., New West., 1889 (dest. by fire 1898); Armstrong Block, Columbia St., New West., 1889 (dest. by fire 1898); Five cottages for McInnes, St. Andrews St., New West., 1889; Anglican Bishop's Palace, Blackwood St., New West., 1889 (dest. by fire 1898); First Baptist Church, 600 Hamilton St., Van., 1888-89 (demo. 1941).

KISHIDA, Isaburo

Toyo Takata, *Nikkei Legacy*, p.75; Toyo Takata, "Victoria's Community that Vanished," *Colonist*, Apr. 23, 1972, p.2; and Linda Brown, "Gardens on the Gorge," *Colonist*, Islander, Apr. 19, 1998, pp.8-9.

KÖRNER, Theodor Frederick

AIBC; B.C. Vital Events; and the International Genealogical Index. Allan C. Kelly, of **Townley & Matheson**, remembered Körner as coming from Seattle. Other information from Mrs. Maida Kirk-Owen, daughter of H.W. Postle. West Van. Memorial Arch from *Province*, Mar. 15, 1925, p.15. Ruskin Power Plant from Van. *News-Herald*, Architectural & Building Edition, Feb. 27, 1939, p.7. A copy of the Van. Civic Centre competition results is held at UBC Special Collections [SPAM 23275]. The information on the Day & Körner lawsuit is on file at the AIBC. The West Van. bldgs. are described in the *West Vancouver Heritage Inventory, 1988-1989*. Wiley House destroyed during relocation; *Seattle Times* June 4, 2003. **PROJECTS:** West Van. Memorial Arch, Marine Dr., West Van., 1925 (ext.);

Bay St. Sub Station, 637 Bay St., Vict., 1928 (ext.); Ruskin Power Plant, Mission, 1930 (ext.); Wiley Res., 124 31st St., West Van., 1937 (demo.); Finqueneisel Summer House, 6043 Gleneagles Dr., West Van., 1938 (ext.).

LAMB, Thomas White

Russell, *All That Glitters*; and Withey & Withey, *Biographical Dictionary of American Architects (Deceased)*, pp.360-361. **PROJECTS**: Capitol Theatre, 805 Yates St., Vict., 1920-21 (demo. 1980); Capitol Theatre, 820 Granville St., Van., 1920-21 (demo. 1974).

LAND SURVEYORS

Information provided by the Corporation of Land Surveyors of British Columbia and their current publications. The Hudson's Bay Co. surveys are covered in Ruggles, *A Country So Interesting*. Biographical information from John A. Whittaker, BCLS, comp. & editor, *Early Land Surveyors of British Columbia*; the *Cumulative Nominal Roll*; issues of *Link* magazine; BCLS Annual Reports; and provincial directories. Additional information provided by H. Barry Cotton, BCLS, and Robert W. Allen, BCLS.

LAW, Alexander

Law's niece has deposited a hand-written memoir with the NVMA [#86-24]. Information on his bldgs. from City of North Van. bldg. permits and the City of North Van. *Heritage Inventory, 1994*. **PROJECT**: Law Block, 123 E. 3rd St., North Van. City, 1913 (ext.).

LAWRENCE, R. Farror

Grand Forks Court House plans (BCA CM-B1670: Mar., 1911); *Victoria Architecturally*, 1911, and the Boundary Museum, Grand Forks. **PROJECT**: Court House, 524 Central Ave., Grand Forks, 1911 (ext.).

LEE, Robert Henry

B.C. Vital Events; Kamloops Museum & Archives (including extensive newspaper references and History Article #219 by Leslie Mobbs); Balf, *Kamloops: A History of the District up to 1914*; and the B.C. Land Surveyors Annual Report, 1936, pp.32-33. Other information from Kamloops inventories. **PROJECTS**: Catholic Church, Second Ave. and Battle St., Kamloops, 1887 (dest. by fire 1919); St. Andrew's Presbyterian Church (later Calvary Temple), 185 Seymour St., Kamloops, 1887 (ext.); Bank of British Columbia, First Ave. and Victoria St., Kamloops, 1887 (demo); Young Res., 133 Battle St. W., Kamloops, 1910 (ext.).

LEECH, Norman Austin

Who's Who in Western Canada, 1912, pp.313-314 and *Who's Who & Why in Canada*, 1913, p.439. References in the *Van. World Progress & Building Edition*, Jan. 6, 1912, p.39; *Province*, Nov. 30, 1912, p.27; *The Contract Record*, Feb. 25, 1914, p.246; CVA plans; California Death Index; and funeral notice in the Los Angeles *Times*, Apr. 2,

1945, p.8. See also Franklin & Fleming, *Early School Architecture*; Saunders, *School Architecture*; and Luxton, *Taming the West*. **PROJECTS**: General Gordon School, 2896 W. 6th Ave., Van., 1911-12 (alt.); Hastings School, 2625 Franklin St., Van., 1912 (addns. 1925; alt.); Hotel for the Ramsay Hotel Co., Burrard & Dunsmuir Sts., Van., 1912 (unbuilt project); Shipyard, Van., 1914 (unbuilt project).

LESLIE, H.H.

Tender calls and news items in the *Colonist*; city directories, assessment records, Maps, and file on J. McB. Smith in VCA; Vertical File at BCA for D. W. Higgins. **PROJECTS**: Drake Res., cor. Pakington and Cook Sts., Vict., 1884 (demo.); Smith Res., Birdcage Walk and Superior St., Vict., 1884 (demo.); *Regents Park* (Higgins Res.), 1501 Fort St., Vict., 1885 (ext.).

LEWIS, Richard

The chief sources of information on the life and works of Richard Lewis are: the author's examination of every newspapers published in Victoria 1858-71; the author's examination of every edition of the Victoria *Daily Standard* 1870-73; Dorothy Mindenhall's examination of the *Colonist* 1871-75; B.C. Vital Events; 1881 Canadian census; BCA photographs, newsclippings, vertical files and Richard Lewis Colonial Correspondence file [GR-1372]; miscellaneous letters in City Clerk series, VCA; Ross Bay Cemetery registers, VCA; and the 1887 Fire Insurance Map of Victoria. **PROJECTS**: St. James Building, 817 Government St. at Courtenay St., Vict., 1860 (demo.); Southgate & Mitchell Bldg., Wharf St., Vict., 1860 (northern half, attributed) and 1864 (southern half) (demo. by City of Vict. in 1980s to create a park); Rithet Bldg., 1117-1125 Wharf St., Vict., 1861 (ext.; additions 1885 and 1889); Bldg. for Backus the Auctioneer, 1109 Wharf St., Vict., 1861 (alt.); Brick stores for Captain James Murray Reid, Wharf St., 1205-1213 Wharf St./8-10 Bastion Sq., Vict., 1862-63 (alt.); Two Stores for Thomas Golden, 1105 Wharf St./500-502 Fort St., Vict., 1862 (alt.; additions for IOOF Hall, 1865); Commercial Bldg., 1129 Wharf St./15 Bastion Sq., Vict., 1862 (ext.; second floor added 1884-85); White Horse Tavern, cor. Humboldt and McClure Sts., Vict., 1865 (demo); Stamp (a.k.a. Masonic) Bldg., Government St., Vict., 1866; Stores for J.J. Southgate, 1102 Government St./530 Fort St., Vict., 1869 (alt.); Brick Store, Fort St., Vict., 1871.

LIGHTHEART BROTHERS

Greater Vancouver - Illustrated, p.208; B.C. Vital Events; CVA plans; and Van. bldg. permits. **PROJECTS; Lightheart Brothers**: Lightheart Apts., 540 Helmcken St., Van., 1910-11 (alt.); Royal Alexandra (now Strathmore Apts.), 1086 Bute St., Van., 1909 (alt.). **O.R. Lightheart:** Marlborough Apts., 1111 Jervis St., Van., 1928 (ext.). **J.R. Lightheart:** Vallejo Court Apts., 1009 West 10th Ave., Van., 1929 (ext.).

LORT, Ross Anthony

Lort, *Old Houses and Old Buildings in Vancouver*; Van. Heritage Register; Bingham, *Samuel Maclure*; Stark, *Oak Bay's Heritage Buildings*; Windsor Liscombe, *The New Spirit*; AIBC; *Sun*; and CVA plans. Ross A. Lort, Architect, Fonds CVA Add. MSS.1015. Lort Fonds, VCA PR.127. Information on the Art Gallery from Doreen Walker, ed. *Dear Nan* (Van.: UBC Press, 1990); and President's Reports, 1947-48 and 1950. Lort Res. in "Old House – New Look," *Western Homes & Living*, May 1952, pp.16-17. Interviews with W.R. Lort. Information on Barber from his obituary, *Sun*, Nov. 15, 1955, p.15. **PROJECTS: R.A. Lort:** Lort Res., 811 Linkleas, Oak Bay, 1913 (ext.); Queen Anne Garden Apts., 1235 Nelson St., Van., 1930 (ext.); Park Lane Apts., 975 Chilco St., Van., 1931 (ext.); *Casa Mia* (G.C. Reifel Res.), 1920 S.W. Marine Dr., Van., 1932 (ext.); Barber Res., 3846 West 10th Ave., Van., 1936 (ext.); Maxine Beauty School, 1215 Bidwell St., Van., 1938 (ext.); Prince of Wales Fairbridge Farm School Chapel, near Duncan, 1939-40 (ext.); Western Society Physical Rehabilitation Centre, 4255 Laurel St., Van., 1947 (alt.); Augustana Lutheran Church, 5 W. King Edward Ave., 1947 (ext.); Alterations to the Van. Art Gallery, 1145 W. Georgia St., Van., 1950-51 (demo.); Lort Res. Renovations, 7250 Oak St., Van., 1952 (demo); Ebenezer Baptist Church, 6850 Fraser St., Van., 1954 (ext.); Additions to the Schara Tzedeck Synagogue, 3476 Oak St., Van., 1955 (alt.); St. Matthias Anglican Church, 680 W. 49th Ave., Van., 1959 (ext.).

LYON, Robert

Personal information on Lyon generously provided by his son, Stewart Lyon, Penticton. Information on family background from Robert Close, Scotland. Lyon's obituary appeared in the *Penticton Herald*, Oct. 16, 1963. Extensive history on B.C. Electric Co. bldgs. provided by Bill Whitehead, Substation Designer, B.C. Hydro. Further information on Lyon's bldgs. is from Henry Ewert, *The Story of the B.C. Electric Railway Company*; the collection of the Penticton Museum & Archives; AIBC; *AB&E*; and directories. Penticton Post Office in *The British Columbian*, Sept. 4, 1935, p.2. **PROJECTS**: Earles St. Substation, 4590 Earles St., Van., 1912 (alt.); Deep Bay Hotel (now Deep Cove Chalet), 11190 Chalet Rd., Sidney, c.1913 (alt.); BCER Station, south side of Granville Bridge, Van., 1913 (demo.); BCER Men's Quarters, 901 Main St., Van., 1913 (ext.); BCER Quebec St. Car Barns (superintendent), Van., 1913-14 (demo.); Central Park Ornamental Gates, Kingsway, Burnaby, 1913-14 (ext.); Buntzen Power House #2, Indian Arm, 1913-14 (ext.); Point Grey Substation (now Sperling Annex), 4003 Maple Cres., Van., 1914 (ext.); Horne-Payne Substation, Lougheed Hwy. at Boundary Rd., Burnaby, 1916 (alt.); Brentwood Bay Steam Plant, Van. Island (demo.); Packing Houses at Penticton, Creston, Salmon Arm, and others; Leir Res., 220 Manor Park Ave., Penticton, 1927-29 (ext.); Three Gables Hotel, Main St., Penticton, 1931 (dest. by fire); Post

Office, Main St. and Nanaimo Ave., Penticton, 1935-37 (ext.); Post Office, Kelowna, 1937 (demo.); G.D. Loane Res., 1858 Abbott St., Kelowna, 1937 (ext.); Badminton Halls at Penticton (ext.), Kelowna, Summerland, and Coldstream; Judge Colquhoun Res., 524 Lakeshore Dr. W., Penticton, 1939 (ext.); Hughes-Games Res., 2094 Abbott St., Kelowna, 1939 (ext.); Penticton *Herald* Bldg., 186 Nanaimo Ave., Penticton, c.1939 (alt.); Penticton Municipal Hall, Main St., Penticton, 1940 (demo.).

McARRAVY, Thomas Black

AIBC; B.C. Vital Events; his obituary in the *Sun*, Sept. 20, 1979; and Nanaimo inventories. **PROJECTS**: **T.B. McArravy**: Addition to Globe Hotel, 25 Front St., Nanaimo, 1936 (ext.), Tom Brown's Auto Body, 28 Front St., Nanaimo, 1937 (ext.); Nanaimo City Hall, 455 Wallace St., designed starting 1940, built 1950-51 (ext.); Wardill Res., 755 Terminal Av. N., Nanaimo, 1945 (ext.). **McArravy & Barley:** Van. Island Regional Library, 580 Fitzwilliam St., Nanaimo, 1961 (ext.).

McCARTER & NAIRNE

There is a large amount of information on this firm at the CVA; this includes clippings files and an interview with daughter, Joan McCarter about her father's practice. Personal communications with Joan McCarter were also of great help. A thorough obituary of McCarter appeared in the AIBC *Architect's Forum* (Sept./Oct. 1981). Nairne's obituary appeared in the *Province*, Apr. 25, 1953. Several of their bldgs. were reviewed in the RAIC *Journal* at the time of their construction. The firm's architectural drawings have been deposited in the CAA, Calgary. Further information from AIBC files. Some of these bldgs. have been extensively covered in Linda M. Fraser, compiler, *McCarter & Nairne: Significant British Columbia Projects* (Calgary: University of Calgary Press, 1995). Information on the role of John Douglas Hunter in the office from Stuart Tarbuck. **PROJECTS**: **J.Y. McCarter**: Patricia Hotel, 403 E. Hastings St., Van., 1911-12 (ext.); Alcazar Theatre, 639 Commercial Dr., Van., 1913 (alt.); Morton Res., 522 E. 12th St., North Van. City, 1914 (ext.). **McCarter & Nairne:** Devonshire Apts., 885 W. Georgia, Van., 1923-24 (demo. 1974); Harrison Hot Springs Hotel and Bath House (with **Townley & Matheson**, associated architects), Harrison, 1925-26 (alt.); Spencer's Department Store (now Simon Fraser University at Harbour Centre), 515 W. Hastings, Van., 1925-26 (alt. 1990); City Market, Columbia St., New West., 1926, (alt.); Richmond High School, 3751 Sexsmith Rd., Richmond, 1927 (demo.); Royal Anne Hotel, 348 Bernard Ave., Kelowna, 1928 (dest. by fire 1971); Medical-Dental Bldg., 925 W. Georgia, Van., 1928-29 (demo. 1989); Marine Bldg., 355 Burrard, Van., 1928-30 (ext.); Post Office Extension (now part of Sinclair Centre), 325 Granville St., Van., 1934-37 (alt.); Seaforth Armoury, 1650 Burrard St., Van., 1935-36 (ext.); Grandview Substation, 2466 W. 1st Ave., Van., 1937 (ext.); McLennan McFeely & Prior Ltd. (now Salvation Army Store), 811 Columbia St.,

New West., 1938-39 (ext.); Livestock Bldg., 2901 E. Hastings St., Van., 1939 (ext.); YMCA, 955 Burrard St., Van., 1940 (ext.); General Post Office, 349 W. Georgia St., Van., 1953-58 (ext.).

McCARTNEY, Alan Edward

B.C. Vital Events; CVA Major Matthews topical files; Matthews, *Early Vancouver*, Vol.IV, p.162 and Vol.V, pp.161-162; Louise Parker's *History of All Saints' Anglican Church* (Ladner 1881-1985); All Saints' Church Committee Meeting Minutes, Nov., 1881 (Anglican Archives, Diocese of New Westminster); *Vancouver Voters*, 1886, p.482; occasional references in the *VDW*; an obituary published in the *News-Advertiser*, May 9, 1901, p.5; and directories. Church of Our Lady of the Rosary from the Vancouver *News*, Oct. 20, 1886, p.4 and Feb. 27, 1887, p.4. Information regarding the City Hospital Commission in Van. City Council Minutes [CVA]. Reference to the City Hospital's use by McGill University is found in A. M. Ross, *The Romance of Vancouver's Schools* (1911), reprinted in James Sandison, *Schools of Old Vancouver*. McCartney's professional career and civic service in North Van. has been extensively researched by Roy J.V. Pallant; we thank both Robert W. Allen, BCLS, and William Chapman, BCLS, Chapman Land Surveying Ltd., for the use of this information. There is confusion over the spelling of McCartney's first name, which appears variously as Alan, Allan and Allen; the most common use of his name in contemporary sources has been adopted. **PROJECTS**: All Saints' Anglican Church, 4755 Arthur Dr., Ladner, Delta, 1881 (alt. 1985); Christ Church Anglican (attributed), 16603 Old McLellan Rd., Surrey, 1884-85, (ext.); City Hospital, Cambie and Pender Sts., Van., 1887-88 (demo.); Condell Block, Homer and Cordova, Van., 1888 (demo.); Alterations and Additions to the Church of Our Lady of the Rosary, Richards St., 1889 (demo.). **McCartney & Marmette:** Church of Our Lady of the Rosary, Richards St., 1886-87 (demo.)

McCOSKRIE, Edward

Tender calls and obituary in the *Colonist*; Information from Family and from his gravestone; B.C. Vital Events; Vertical File at BCA; directories; numerous citations and other information from Barry Elmer in Calgary, who has been compiling a biography of McCoskrie. **PROJECTS**: Six Houses for William Jensen, Superior St., Vict., 1890; Three Stores, Dallas Rd., Vict., 1891; Hotel Dallas, cor. Dallas Rd. and Simcoe St., 1891 (dest. by fire 1928); Conlin Res., Quadra St., Vict. 1891; Hotel for A.R. Johnston & Co., Nanaimo, 1891 (unbuilt project); St. Andrew's & Caledonian Society Bldg., Blanshard St., Vict., 1892 (demo.).

McCRIMMON, Alexander

Vict. plans, bldg. and plumbing permits; *VDT*; inventories; and B.C. Vital Events. **PROJECTS**: 136 Medana St., Vict., 1908 (ext.); 512, 516, 532 and 539 Linden Ave., Vict., 1911 and 1909 (ext.); Porter Res., 543 Linden Ave., Vict., 1911 (ext.) 161 S.

Turner St., Vict., 1911 (ext.); 75, 77, 78, 93 and 94 Linden Ave., Vict., 1911-12 (ext.); Alteration to Holroyd Res., 1028 Craigdarroch Rd., Vict., 1957 (ext.).

MacDONALD, James A.

Nelson: A Proposal for Urban Heritage Conservation; Dogterom, *Where Was It?*; directories; and information from the Sir Alexander Galt Museum & Archives, Lethbridge, Alberta. Obituary in the Calgary *Herald*, March 11, 1926, p.11. **PROJECT**: **Cane & MacDonald**: Strachan Res., 924 Observatory St., Nelson, 1900 (ext.).

McINTYRE, John

AIBC; B.C. Vital Events; the Powell River *Digester*, May/June 1947, p.1 and July/Aug. 1957, p.8; and newspaper references from the Powell River Historical Museum & Archives Association. **PROJECTS**: Brooks School, 5400 Marine Dr., Powell River, 1926 (demo. 1993 for a new school); Dwight Hall, 6247 Walnut St., Powell River, 1927 (ext.); Bank of Montreal Bldg., 5813 Ash St., Powell River, 1931 (ext.).

MacKAY, Donald

David A. Rash's essay in Ochsner, *Shaping Seattle Architecture*, pp.10-13. Subsequent research provided by Dennis A. Andersen and David Rash has confirmed that the Donald MacKay, architect in Seattle and Van., was a different person than the contractor in Portland. Johnson Residence from Vancouver *News*, Mar. 13, 1887, p.4. **PROJECT:** Johnson Res., Seymour St., Van., 1887 (demo.).

McKAY, Thomas

BCA GR-0080 Box 1 File 25: Contract to build Asylum: Thomas McKay and Alexander Robert Kennedy. References from the *Mainland Guardian* (New West.): Aug. 18, 1877, p.3 "Laying of the Cornerstone of the New St. Ann's Convent;" Apr. 28, 1886, p.3 "Consecration of the Roman Catholic Church;" Jan. 19, 1887, p.3 "A Funeral," "The Inquest" and "A Dreadful Calamity." *Daily Columbian*, Jan. 15, 1887, p.3 "Terrible Calamity." **PROJECTS**: St. Ann's Convent (credited to both McKay and **William Turnbull**), Albert Cres., New West., 1877 (demo. 1968). **McKay & Turnbull:** St. Peter's Catholic Church, Blackwood and Columbia Sts., New West., 1886 (demo.); St. Louis College, Agnes and Blackwood Sts., New West., 1886 (demo.).

MACKENZIE, James Clark

AIBC; District of North Van. inventories; *Who's Who in Western Canada, 1911*; information from Roy J.V. Pallant from an interview with Mackenzie's son, Peter; and an interview with the daughter of William Bow, Clara S. Coles. There are several different spellings of Mackenzie's name in these sources. Information on A.N. Paterson from Andor Gomme & David Walker, *Architecture of Glasgow*. 2nd Edition, p.2 (London, 1987). **PROJECTS**: **J.C. Mackenzie:** Municipal Hall, Taylor Rd. (later 17th St. and Esquimalt Ave.), West Van., 1912 (demo.);

Mackenzie Res., 494 Windsor Rd. E., North Van. Dist, (ext.); Gibson Res., 114 Windsor Rd. W., North Van. Dist., 1915 (ext.). **Mackenzie & Ker:** *Iowa* (Buckley Res.), 3498 Osler Ave., Van., 1913-14 (ext.).

McKENZIE, Robert Alexander McKay
AIBC; B.C. Vital Events; Van. bldg. permits; and CVA plans. **PROJECTS:** Frontenac Apts., 2645 Quebec St., Van., 1910 (ext.); Chin Wing Chun Society Bldg., 158-160 E. Pender St., Van., 1925 (ext.).

McLUCKIE, John Macfarlane
CVA Plans; Van. bldg. permits; B.C. Vital Events; *Vancouver Voters 1886*; and *Greater Vancouver - Illustrated*, pp.81-82. **PROJECT:** Malkin Co. Warehouse, eastern half, 55-65 Water St., Van., 1911-12 (ext.) [western half by **Parr & Fee**, 1907].

MACEY, Frank William
AIBC; notice in the *CA&B*: Jan. 1907, p.xi, and brief obituary in *The British Columbian*, Aug. 15, 1935, p.5. Personal interviews with Macey's daughter-in-law, Anne E. Macey of New West., who also has a small collection of Macey's published books. The author is indebted to David Birch of St. Helen's Church, Surrey. **PROJECTS:** Macey Res., 1823 Comox St., Van., 1906-07 (demo.); J.R. Waghorn Res., 1673 Beach Ave., Van., 1907 (demo.); St. Oswald's Anglican Church, 19016 96th Ave., Surrey, 1911 (ext.); St. Helen's Anglican Church, 10787 128th St., Surrey, 1911 (ext.); *Avalon* (Hart House Restaurant), 6664 Deer Lake Ave., Burnaby, 1912 (ext.); *Altnadene* (William J. Mathers Res.), 6490 Deer Lake Ave., Burnaby, 1912 (alt.); Robert F. Anderson Res., 6490 Deer Lake Ave., Burnaby, 1912 (ext.).

MACLEAN, Charles B.
Revelstoke Museum & Archives. Citations from the Revelstoke *Herald*: Imperial Bank (June 26, 1897); Down Res. (July 7, 1897); Taylor Res. (Sept. 8, 1897); and the Court House (Jan. 27, 1897, May 1, 1897, Oct. 6, 1897 and Oct. 9, 1897). **PROJECTS:** Imperial Bank, 300 First St. W., Revelstoke, 1897 (extensively alt.); Downs Res., 917 Second St. W., Revelstoke, 1897 (extensively alt.); Taylor Res., 1118 Second St. W., Revelstoke, 1897 (ext.); Court House and Jail (located at site of current Court House), Revelstoke, 1897 (demo. prior to 1912).

MACLURE, Samuel
Information on Maclure abounds in many sources with, unfortunately, many errors and omissions regarding the operational dates of his offices and partnerships. Primary sources were consulted to confirm and corroborate the write-ups. The list of partnerships and associated architects represents only those commissions that have been confirmed with extant plan sets or tender documents. The major public sources for information on Maclure's commissions are plans held in two collections: Ross A. Lort, Architect, Fonds CVA Add.

MSS.1015; and the Samuel Maclure Collection, UVIC Library Special Collections (transferred from the office of Lort & Lort in 1968), catalogued in David Chamberlin, *Samuel Maclure: Architectural Drawings in the University of Victoria Archives*. Many commissions can be found in numerous tender notices and descriptions printed in *The Daily Columbian* (New West.); AIBC; *VDW*; *VDC*; and *CA&B*. Primary biographical information on Maclure: *Colonist*, Aug. 9, 1929, p.1 "Architect of Many Famous Homes Passes" and p.4 "A Noted Architect;" *Colonist*, Aug. 25, 1929, p.10 "Noted Architect Passes;" Howay & Schofield, *British Columbia: Biographical*, 1914, Vol.IV, pp.1063-1064; "Samuel Maclure, MRAIC, 1860-1929" RAIC *Journal* No.392, Vol.35, No.4, 1958 (B.C. Centennial Edition) pp.114-115 by Ross Lort, MRAIC. *Hatley Park* from *CA&B*, Apr. 1908, p.26. Peter Res. from *British Columbian Weekly*, Dec. 3, 1912, p.19. McAllister Res. from Point Grey bldg. permit #2843. The major published sources are Janet Bingham, *Samuel Maclure Architect*, 1985; Martin Segger: *The Buildings of Samuel Maclure*, 1986; and Leonard K. Eaton, *The Architecture of Samuel Maclure*, 1971. Tender call for Flumerfelt Res., *Colonist*, Mar. 5, 1895, p.5. Strathcona Lodge references from the *Colonist*: tender call, Jan. 18, 1900, p.2; contract awarded, Jan. 27, 1900, p.5; "Hotel Burned at Birth," May 15, 1900, p.5; "To Rebuild," June 13, 1900, p.5. A postcard in the possession of the Soule family indicates C.J. Soule's involvement. **PROJECTS: Samuel Maclure:** Temple Bldg., 519-525 Fort St., Vict., 1893 (ext.); *Ruhebuhne* (A.C. Flumerfelt Res.), 835 Pemberton Ave., Vict., 1895-97 (demo.); Maclure Res., 635 Superior St., Vict., 1899 (ext.); Strathcona Lodge, Shawnigan Lake, 1900 (demo.); *Gabriola* (B.T. Rogers Res.), 1523 Davie St., Van., 1900-01 (ext.); Bank of Montreal Manager's Res., 39th Ave. and 18th St., Vernon, 1902 (demo.); *Hatley Park* (Dunsmuir Res.), Colwood, 1907-25 (ext.); Hall Res., 906 Linden Ave., Vict., 1910 (ext.); *Miraloma*, (W.C. Nichol Res.), 2328 Harbour Rd., Sidney, 1924-26 (ext.). **Maclure & Fox:** BCER Station, 774 Columbia St., New West., 1909 (alt.); *Overlynn* (Charles J. Peter Res.), 401 North Esmond St., Burnaby, 1909-10 (ext.); Dockrill Res., 3351 The Crescent, Van., 1910 (ext.); Huntting House, 3689 Angus Dr., Van., 1911-13 (ext.); Nichol Res., 1402 McRae Ave., Van., 1912-13 (ext.); Jones Bldg., 717-727 Fort St., Vict., 1912 (demo. 1977). *Southlands* (W.H. Malkin Res.), 3269 S.W. Marine Dr., Van., 1912 (demo. 1960); Van. Golf Club, Coquitlam, 1914 (demo.). **Maclure & Lort:** Gibson Res., 1590 York Pl., Oak Bay, 1919-20 (ext.); McAllister Res., 5087 Connaught Dr., Van., 1920 (ext.).

MALLANDAINE, Edward, Jr.
Rev. William Cochrane, *The Canadian Album: Men of Canada or Success by Example in Religion, Patriotism, Business, Law, Medicine, Education and Agriculture* (Brantford: Bradley

Garretson & Co., 1895), Vol.IV, p.74; *British Columbia Pictorial & Biographical* (S.J. Clarke Publishing, 1914) pp.765-766; CVA 0054.013.03061; Matthews, *Early Vancouver*, Vol.V, p.359; *Who's Who in British Columbia*, 1940-41, p.160; *VDW* Mar. 9, 1889, p.4; BCA MS-1214 and MS-2565. Van. City Hall additions CVA Plans AP-2000 and CVA 10-A-1 File 16 p.927. **PROJECTS: Mallandaine & Sansom:** Byrnes Block addition, 2 Water St., Van., 1888 (ext.); City Morgue, Pender St., Van., 1888 (demo.); Additions to Van. City Hall, 137-141 Powell St., Van., 1888 (demo.); School, Main St., Van., 1888 (demo.); James Harney Res., Barclay St., Van., 1888 (demo.); Granville Block, Pender and Main Sts., Van., 1888-89 (demo.).

MALLANDAINE, Edward, Sr.
The main documentation of Mallandaine's career is in the BCA, comprising intermittent accounts and a rambling, gap-filled reminiscence from 1897 [BCA E/E/M.291] and diaries [MS-470]. Cedar Hill School, *VDC*, July 3, 1872. See *B.C. Sessional Papers*: 1876, Report for 1875 of Public Works, p.436, and 1877, Report for 1876, p.250 (teacher's res., Cedar Hill). Almost all his architectural plans were privately destroyed in 1940. **PROJECTS:** T.J. Burnes Bldg., Store St., Vict., 1864 (demo.); Plan for Ross Bay Cemetery, 1872; Cedar Hill School, Saanich, 1872; Asylum, Vict., 1872 (unbuilt project); Nanaimo Public School, 904 Crace St., Nanaimo, 1872-73 (demo.); St. Mary the Virgin Church, 4354 Metchosin Rd., Metchosin, 1873 (ext.); Anglican Church, Comox, 1876 (ext.); Teacher's Res., Cedar Hill, Saanich, 1876; New Wing to Nanaimo Public School, 904 Crace St., Nanaimo, 1878 (alt.); Ward, Royal Hospital, Vict., 1878 (demo.); Chapel, Naval (now Veterans) Cemetery, Esquimalt, 1878 (ext.); Fawcett Res., James Bay, Vict., 1880 (demo.); Mallandaine Res., Simcoe St., Vict., 1880 (demo.); Plan for the churchyard at St. Stephen's, Saanichton, Central Saanich, 1880 (alt.); Chinese Theatre, Cormorant St., Vict., 1884 (demo.); St. Mary's Cemetery, Metchosin, 1884 (ext.); *Marifield*, for Bishop and Mrs. Cridge, James Bay, Vict., 1884 (demo.); Skene Lowe House, cor. Simcoe and Government Sts., 1886 (alt.); St. Luke's Anglican Church, 3821 Cedar Hill Cross Rd., Saanich, 1888 (ext.); London Block, 1315-1317 Broad St., Vict., 1892 (ext.); Res., 528 Simcoe St., Vict., 1890s (ext.); Res., 126 S. Turner St., Vict., 1890s (ext.); Res., 131-33 S. Turner St., James Bay, Vict., c.1905 (ext.).

MALLORY, John Wesley
Province Aug. 6, 1898, p.2; directories; *CA&B*; and information from Robert G. Hill.

MAREGA, Charles
Information from D'Acres & Luxton, *Lions Gate*.

MAWSON, Thomas Hayton
Howay & Schofield, *British Columbia: Biographical*, 1914, Vol.IV, pp.1098-1099; and

Felstead et al, *Directory of British Architects 1834-1900*, p.609. CVA Add.MSS.886; Nickle Arts Museum, *Building A West*; and Ring, *Urban Prairie*.

MAXWELL, Edward

Newton McTavish, *The Fine Arts in Canada*, p.173; Kalman, *A History of Canadian Architecture* (Vol.2), pp.489, 493, 496. The Van. Station is described in the *Province*, Aug. 6, 1898, p.2. Collection of Maxwell's drawings, and biographical information, on McGill University website. **PROJECTS**: Second Van. CPR Station, north foot of Granville St., Van., 1897-99 (demo. 1914); Additions to Glacier House, Glacier, 1897-99 (demo. 1929); Hotel and Station at Sicamous Junction, 1898 (demo.); New West. CPR Station, 800 Columbia St., New West., 1899 (ext.).

MELLADO, Bruno

Peggy Nicholls, *From the Black Country to Nanaimo 1854*, Volume II, 1992; and Barr, *Cumberland Heritage*. See *Colonist*, Aug. 23, 1871, p.3 re the elopement. McKay's hotel in *Colonist*, Oct. 12, 1871, p.3. Further confirmation from directories and B.C. Vital Events. The Mellados' wedding license is in the collection of the BCA. **PROJECTS**: Identical Hotel, Victoria Cres., Nanaimo, 1872 (demo.).

MELLISH, Frederick William

B.C. Vital Events; CVA plans; Van. bldg. permits; and information from Robert G. Hill. **PROJECTS**: A.R. Williams Machinery Co. Warehouse, Foot of Jackson St. at Railway Ave., Van., 1909 and alterations 1913 (alt.); St. Saviour's Church, 1690 Semlin Dr., Van., 1910 and additions 1918 (alt.); Mellish residence, 2325 E. 1st Ave., Van., 1919 (ext.); St. Saviour's Parish Hall, 1690 Semlin Dr., Van., 1920 (ext.).

MESHER, George Charles

Vict. City tax assessment rolls, Vict. plans, bldg. and plumbing permits; B.C. Vital Events; company records and voters lists (held at BCA); and interviews with his grandson, John R.H. Ley (1990), grand niece, Kathleen Johnston (1993) and Pheona Hislop (2001). Published sources include directories; *Colonist* references and tender calls; obituaries and local news items. Also *This Old House*; *AB&E*; *Victoria Architecturally*, 1911; *Pemberton Building*, 1910; Segger & Franklin, *Exploring Victoria's Architecture*; Mills, *Architectural Trends in Victoria*; and Graeme Chalmers, *British Columbia Houses: Guide to Styles* (UBC: Centre for the Study of Curriculum & Instruction, 1981). Additional information provided by Carey Pallister, Jennifer Barr, Dorothy Mindenhall, and Christopher J.P. Hanna. **PROJECTS**: George Mesher Sr. Res., 60 Second St., Vict., 1888 (demo.); George C. Mesher Res., 50 Second St., Vict., 1890 (demo.); Mesher (later Briggs) Res., 154 South Turner St., Vict., 1897 (ext.); George C. Mesher Res., 630 Dallas Rd., Vict., 1904 (demo.); October Mansion, 1010 Cook St., Vict.,

1910 (ext.); Pemberton Building (now Yarrows Bldg.), 625 Fort St., Vict., 1911 (ext.); Sayward Block, 1201-1213 Douglas St., Vict., 1911 (ext.); Savoy Mansion, McClure St., Vict., 1911 (demo. 1973); Metropolis Bldg., 706-716 Yates St., Vict., 1913 (alt.); Hampton Court, 159 Cook St., Vict., 1913 (ext.). **Designed by Charles King; working drawings by H.C. Ferree:** Goulding Wilson Res., 610 St. Charles St., Vict., 1912 (ext.).

MICHAUD, Father Joseph

Little has been published concerning Michaud. One source is a booklet in French by François Lanoue, pte., *president de la Societé d'histoire de Joliette, P. Joseph Michaud, Clerc de Saint Viateur architecte* (1822-1902). There are archival resources, particularly plans and correspondence, deposited with the Sisters of St. Ann, Vict. and Lachine, the *Services des archives, Les Clercs-de-Saint-Viateur*, Montreal and Joliette, Archives of the Diocese of Montreal, and the CCA, Montreal. The Provincial Capital Commission, Vict., contains research notes by Dianne Carr and Jennifer Nell Barr. See MacDonald, *Historical Number of British Columbia Orphans' Friend*; the *British Colonist* [Victoria], Nov. 23, 1860; Harold Kalman, *A History of Canadian Architecture*, Vol.1; Alan Gowans, *Looking at Architecture in Canada* (Toronto, 1958); and Martin Segger (ed.) *St. Andrew's Cathedral, Victoria: A Guide* (Vict., 1990). **PROJECTS**: Old St. Andrew's Cathedral (1858-60) and St Ann's Academy (1871-86), 835 Humboldt St., Vict. (ext.); Bishop's Res., Humboldt St., Vict., 1858-59 (demo.).

MIDDLETON, William

AIBC; William Middleton Fonds, BCA [Add.MSS. 761]; and obituary in the Victoria *Times*, Feb. 16, 1951 p.13.

MILLS & HUTTON

City of North Van. plans, permits and heritage inventories; North Van. *Express*, Nov. 25, 1910: and information from Robert G. Hill. Original drawings for the Bank of Hamilton in the Souter & Lenz Collection, Roll 677, Ontario Archives, Toronto. **PROJECTS**: Bank of Hamilton Chambers, 92 Lonsdale Ave., North Van. City, 1910-1911 (ext.); Keith Block (Aberdeen Block by 1912), 78-90 Lonsdale Ave., North Van. City, 1910-11 (ext.).

MILNER, Warren H.

Ochsner, *Shaping Seattle Architecture*, p.345; Kluckner, *Vanishing Vancouver*, p.81; Thirkell & Scullion, *Vancouver & Beyond*, pp.110-114; and Van. *Daily Province*, Dec. 19, 1908, p.13. **PROJECT**: Horse Show Bldg., W. Georgia and Gilford Sts., Van., 1908-09 (dest. by fire 1960).

MITCHELL, Henry

Tender calls and news items in the *Colonist*. Tender call for work at Ross Bay Cemetery in *VDC*, Sept. 20, 1872, p.2. **PROJECTS**: Christ Church Cathedral School House and Lecture Room, Rae and Quadra

Sts., Vict., 1882 (demo.); Heisterman Res., Douglas St., Vict., 1875 (demo.); Moss Res., Yates St., Vict., 1882 (demo.).

MITTON, Edward Stanley

Vict. plans, bldg. and plumbing permits; Copies of the *Mitton Home Builder*, held at NVMA; Howay & Schofield, *British Columbia: Biographical*, 1914, Vol.III, pp.618-619; directories; newspapers, including the *Portland Canal Miner; Who's Who in Western Canada*, 1911; and Van. bldg. permits. Quote about the opening of the Vict. office from the *VDC*, July 30, 1911, p.19. A copy of The E. Stanley Mitton Co. (Mitton & Gillingham), *Modern Homes for Modern People*, c.1914, was provided by Fred Sigurjonsson. **PROJECTS**: **E.S. Mitton:** Heisterman Res., 1521 Shasta Place, Vict., c.1912 (ext.). **Mitton & Whitehead:** Lineham Res. (now Dashwood Manor Bed & Breakfast), 1 Cook St., Vict., 1913 (ext.).

MOBERG, Otto

Van. bldg. permits, and citations in *CA&B* and the *Province*. Hotel for Walsh in *Province*, Nov. 2, 1912, p.32. Manufacturer's Bldg. in the King Edward High School *Matric Annual* 1913, p.33 and Imbi Harding, *Sun*, Aug. 31, 2001, p.B4. **PROJECTS**: Stanley Park Tea House, Van., 1911 (ext.); Hotel for William Walsh (now the Ramada), 435-439 W. Pender St., Van., 1912-13 (ext.); Manufacturers' (Transportation) Bldg., Hastings Park, 2901 E. Hastings st., Van., 1913 (demo. by the Van. Board of Parks & Recreation).

MODERN HOMES LIMITED

Vict. plans, bldg. and plumbing permits; Oak Bay plans; *AB&E; VDC; VDT*; directories; and inventories. **PROJECTS**: **Jennings & Boulanger:** Res., 3025 Cadboro Bay Rd., Oak Bay, 1913 (ext.); Res., 3280 Ripon Rd., Oak Bay, 1913 (ext.); Uplands Gates, Oak Bay, 1913 (ext.).

MOORE & HENRY

CA&B, Vol.12 (1899) Issue 1, p.5; and information from Robert G. Hill. Plans for the McClary Bldg. in the Moore Collection, D.B. Weldon Library, University of Western Ontario. **PROJECT**: McClary Manufacturing Co. Bldg., 305 Water St., Van., 1897 (ext.).

MORRIS & EDWARDS

Directories; and Vict. plans, bldg. and plumbing permits. **PROJECT**: Edwards Res., 135 Beechwood Ave., Vict., 1912 (alt.).

MOTHER JOSEPH OF THE SACRED HEART

Sisters of Providence Archives, Seattle, Washington and the Sisters of Providence, Provincial Administration, Edmonton. Her life and architectural career are covered in an essay by Cheryl Sjoblom in Ochsner, *Shaping Seattle Architecture*, pp.6-9; Women in Architecture, *Constructing Careers*, pp.10-17; *The Good Work*, Vol.7, #1, Mar. 1980, p.11; and Wilfred P. Schoenberg, S.J., *A History of the Catholic Church in the Pacific*

Northwest: 1783-1983 (Washington, D.C.: The Pastoral Press, 1987). **PROJECTS: Projects built with Mother Joseph's involvement:** St. Mary's Hospital, Agnes and Merrivale Sts., New West., 1886-87 (demo.); St. Eugene Indian School, Kootenay, 1890; St. Paul's Hospital, Burrard St., Van., 1894 (demo. in 1912); St. Eugene Hospital, Cranbrook, 1900 (demo.); Providence Ste. Geneviève Orphanage, New West., 1900-01 (demo.).

MOUNTAIN, Francis

AIBC; B.C. Vital Events; CVA; and plans held at Van. City Hall. **PROJECTS:** Melton Court Apts., 2310 Cornwall Ave., Van., 1923 (ext.); Allen Res., 1096 W. 10th Ave., Van., 1922-23 (ext.).

MUIR, Alexander Maxwell

Vict. newspapers; directories; VCA; BCA; *Victoria Illustrated*, 1891; 1901 Canadian Census; and B.C. Vital Events. For information specific to Muir's involvement in the inquiry involving **F.M. Rattenbury**, refer to Reksten, *Rattenbury*, pp.63-71 and Barrett & Windsor Liscombe, *Francis Rattenbury*, pp.113 & 120. Information about Park School from Saunders, *School Architecture*, p.22. Chemainus Hospital from VCA PR251 Box 28 F4 Folder 3 [McKillican & McCalman, contractors estimates]. Burnside fire Hall from *VDC* July 25, 1909. Muir's grandchildren, Rodney Maxwell-Muir and Bernice Kiehl, have been very generous in sharing their family memories as has Ron Weir, who is a descendent of Muir's wife's family. **PROJECTS:** Board of Trade Bldg., 31 Bastion Sq., Vict., 1892 (ext.); East Fernwood Mission Sunday School, 1602 Redfern St., Vict., 1892 (ext.); Court House, Vernon, 1892-93 (demo. c.1960s); Court House, Ward and Vernon Sts., Nelson, 1893 (demo. c.1956); Nairne Res., 642 Battery St., Vict., 1893 (ext.); Vernon Public School (now the Interior Space & Science Centre), 2704 Hwy. 6, Vernon, 1893 (ext.); Kamloops Jail, Kamloops, 1897 (demo.); Hotel Texada, (Marble Bay Hotel), Texada Island, 1898 (demo); *Bremhill* (Muir Res.), 1828 Oak Bay Ave., Vict., 1901 (alt.; relocated to 1511 Bank St. in 1947); *Hartley Hall*, Metchosin, 1903 (demo. 1956); Hospital, Chemainus, 1903; Burnside Fire Hall, Douglas St., Vict., 1908 (demo.).

NELSON, Horatio Elmer

Vict. plans, BCA plans; bldg. and plumbing permits; directories; and voters lists. **PROJECTS:** Sweeney Res., 521 Linden Ave., Vict., 1911 (alt.); Sooke Harbour (later Belvedere) Hotel, Sooke, 1912 (dest. by fire 1934).

NEWBOLD, H. Bryant

Research by Robert G. Hill and Charlene Gregg; directories; Vict. plans, bldg. and plumbing permits; Oak Bay bldg. plans; *AB&E*; *The Ideal House* (loaned by Geli Bartlett): *House and Cottage Construction*; *The Modern Carpenter and Joiner*; *The National Builder*; *Official Architect*; *VDC*; *VTC*; Hallmark Society files; the Library of the Royal Institute of British Architects, and Newbold's

application for RIBA membership 1925. Ad from *Colonist*, June 9, 1912, p.10; **PROJECTS:** Denny Res. by British Canadian Home Builders Ltd., 2722 Avebury Ave., Vict., 1912 (ext.); Res. by British Canadian Home Builders Ltd., 2161 Fair St., Oak Bay, 1913 (ext.); Alford or Redpath Res., 369 King George Terrace, Oak Bay, 1913, (relocated to Saturna Island); Payn Le Sueur Res., 3570 Beach Drive, Oak Bay, 1913 (ext.).

NEWLANDS, William

Directories; and the Boundary Museum. **PROJECTS:** Cottage Hospital, 9th St., Grand Forks, 1899 (demo.); Almond Res., 7258 12th St., Grand Forks, 1900 (ext.).

NORGATE, Thomas Burroughes

1881 British Census; directories; and Canadian census records. *Colonist* references from Dorothy Mindenhall: dwelling on Chatham (Nov. 19, 1889, p.1); tender call for National Electric Tramway & Lighting Co., Ltd. (July 29, 1890 p.1); and St. Saviour's Church (Norgate's plans accepted, Nov. 20, 1890, p.5; tenders called, Feb. 19, 1891, p.5; Corner stone laid by Bishop, Apr. 2, 1891, p.5). See also Anglican Archives, Diocese of B.C., Vict. Reference to the car barns in Douglas V. Parker, *No Horsecars in Paradise: A History of the Street Railways and Public Utilities in Victoria, British Columbia before 1897* (Van.: Whitecap Railfare Book, 1982). References to Futcher residence in the *Colonist*, Apr. 24, 1890, May 2, 1890, and Jan. 1, 1891. Information on Province Exploring Expedition BCA MS-2777; Norgate's photographs and water-colours from the Expedition are also in the BCA. **PROJECTS:** Frame Dwelling, Chatham St., Vict., 1889; Futcher Res., 1029 Pakington St., Vict., 1890 (alt.); National Electric Tramway & Lighting Co. Car Barns, Vict., 1890 (demo.); St. Saviour's Church, 310 Henry St., Vict., 1890-91 (ext.).

NORTHWOOD & CHIVERS

AIBC; *Who's Who in Western Canada*, 1911; Northwood's obituary, Winnipeg *Free Press*, Dec. 15, 1959, p.38. Information from son, John Chivers, Mill Bay, and grandson, Doug Chivers, Van. **PROJECT:** Hall Bldg., 466 Howe St., Van., 1929 (ext.).

OKAMURA, Paul Louis (Tsunenojo)

Okamura's story has yet to be told in full and as a result sources of his biography remain elusive. Identification of Okamura advertising as an architect was documented by Robert G. Hill's correspondence to Lucy Chambers, May, 1982. Confirmation of his attendance at Tokyo University was found in: K. Kaneko, *Study of the Education System in Meiji Art Institutes* (Tokyo: Central Fine Art Discussion Group, 1993). Okamura's activities in New West. and Van. are documented in local directories; *The Daily Columbian*, Oct. 3, 1901 p.1; "Big Day at the Exhibition;" *The Daily Columbian*, May 27, 1902 p.4; "City News;" *The Daily Columbian Special Supplement*, Dec., 1903

p.73 "P.L. Okamura;" *The British Columbian*, Aug. 25, 1938, "New Catholic Church." Grace E. Thompson, Curator, Reiko Tagami, Reference & Public Programs Coordinator, and Tetsuya Takahashi, volunteer, of the Japanese Canadian National Museum identified a number of obscure Japanese sources about Okamura and provided translation services. Dr. Victor Banno provided much information regarding his grandfather in a telephone interview in 2001.

OSITHE, Sister Mary

Collection of the Archives of the Sisters of Saint Ann, Vict., B.C., including biographical data and her obituary. Several drawings and designs have her name affixed as "architect.," and an oral history survives that attests to her ability and service as an "architect." **PROJECTS:** Gymnasium at St. Ann's Academy, 835 Humboldt St., Vict., 1922 (demo.); Foundress Hall, Little Flower Academy, 4195-4221 Alexandra St., Van., 1931 (demo.); Bulkley Valley District Hospital, Smithers, 1932-33.

OWEN, Frank Ifor Moran

AIBC; B.C. Vital Events; Vict. plans, bldg. and plumbing permits; BCA GR-0054 Box 22 File 384; and directories. **PROJECT:** Provincial Home for Old Men, Kamloops, c.1911 (demo); Provincial Government Temporary Bldg., Government and Superior Sts., Vict., 1912 (demo.); Payne Res., 2701 Forbes St., Vict., 1944 (ext.).

OWEN, William Arthur

AIBC; *AB&E*; Nanaimo bldg. plans and permits; B.C. Vital Events; Nanaimo Community Archives; Cumberland Archives; Courtenay Museum & Archives files; *Cumberland Islander*; *Comox District Free Press*; Bill Owen's 1927 notebook from Richard Graham. **PROJECTS:** Nanaimo Agricultural Bldg. (later High School), Nanaimo, 1912 (demo.); Fire Hall addition, 34 Nicol St., Nanaimo, 1914 (ext.); S&W Apts., 403-09 Fitzwilliam St., Nanaimo, 1910-11 (ext.); Newcastle Hotel, 105 Comox Rd., Nanaimo, 1913-19 (dest. by fire 1990s); Owen Res., 2792 Maryport Ave., Cumberland (ext.); Holy Trinity Anglican Church Parish Hall, 3287 Third St., Cumberland, 1919-20 (ext.); Great War Veterans' Memorial Hall and Arch, 2770 Dunsmuir Ave., Cumberland, 1920-22 (hall demo., arch ext.); Cumberland Literary & Athletic Association Bldg., Dunsmuir Ave., Cumberland, 1920 (demo.); Soldiers' Settlement Houses, Cumberland, 1921 (ext.); Merrifield Res., 2767 Allen Ave., Cumberland, 1936 (ext.); Owen Cottage, *Royston*, near Cumberland, 1940s (ext.); Courtenay City Hall, Cliffe Ave., Courtenay, 1952 (ext.); Park Royal Hotel, 540 Clyde Ave., West Van., 1955 (demo.).

PAINTER, Walter Scott

Kalman, *A History of Canadian Architecture*, p.497-498; Heritage Banff, *Banff Historical Walking Tour*, 1998; Barrett & Windsor Liscombe, *Francis Rattenbury*; and information from Robert G.

Hill. **PROJECT**: Additions to the Empress Hotel, 721 Government St., Vict., 1909-14 (ext.).

PALMER, Bernard Cuddon

AIBC; B.C. Vital Events; directories; CVA plans; and an interview with William Bow's daughter, Mrs. Clara S. Coles, in 1998; and Palmer, *Development of Domestic Architecture in British Columbia*. St. Joseph's Convent is described in the *Sun*, Aug. 22, 1931. **PROJECTS**: *Knoll* (Blythe Rogers Res.; later Goolden residence), 2206 S.W. Marine Dr., Van., 1918-19 (ext.); St. Joseph's Convent (now St. Patrick's Parish Centre), 125 E. 12th Ave., Van., 1927 (ext.); *Fairweather* (Rogers Family Lodge), Bowen Island, 1929-30 (ext.); *Rio Vista* (Harry F. Reifel Res.), 2170 S.W. Marine Dr., Van., 1929-30 (ext.).

PARLETT & MacAULAY

MacAulay's AIBC application and B.C. Vital Events; Boam, *British Columbia*, p.335; Kamloops Museum & Archives; and inventories. Kamloops *Standard*, Apr. 11, 1911, p.5; Kamloops *Inland Sentinel*, Oct. 11, 1911, p.7; and Aug. 15, 1919, p.5. **PROJECTS**: **J. Parlett:** Queen's Hotel [later Hotel Patricia], 235 Victoria St., Kamloops, 1911 (demo. 1919); Fremont Block, 248 Victoria St., Kamloops, 1911-12 (alt.). **Parlett & MacAulay:** Kamloops High School (later Allan Matthews School), 543 St. Paul St., Kamloops, 1912 (demo. 1990); *Dundurn Place* (Costley Res.), 7 St. Paul St. W., Kamloops, 1912 (ext.); Fulton Res., 63 Nicola St. W., Kamloops, 1912 (ext.); Gill Res., 467 Battle St., Kamloops, 1914 (ext.); Sacred Heart Cathedral, 255 Nicola St., Kamloops, 1921-25 (ext.).

PARR & FEE

Parr & Fee's bldgs. are discussed in many sources, and a number are listed on the Van. Heritage Register. A primary source is *Vancouver of Today Architecturally*, a vanity publication from 1900 by Parr, Fee, **William Blackmore**, **W.T. Dalton** and **G.W. Grant**. Information on Parr is from AIBC; B.C. Vital Events; the 1881 British Census; obituary; *VDW* Souvenir Edition, June, 1896, p.30; and *Who's Who & Why*, 1913. Ross Lort's recollection of Parr is from *Old Houses in Vancouver*, pp.18-19. Information on Samuel Parr from Felstead et al, *Directory of British Architects 1834-1900*, p.692. Information on Fee from AIBC; his obituary; and B.C. Vital Events. Fee's retirement was noted in *AB&E*, Aug. 15, 1912, p.7. Robert G. Hill provided an extensive list of bldg. citations. Harold Kalman generously shared research that he has undertaken on Parr & Fee, including family interviews undertaken in the 1970s. Further information from members of the Fee family, including Olga Johnson, Thomas Fee's daughter, interviewed at the age of 102; Tom Johnson, grandson; and Douglas Johnson, great-grandson. *VDW* citations for the Harvey's Chambers, July 11, 1896, p.2 and March 13, 1897, p.3. Earliest mention of partnership in *Province*, Aug. 6, 1898, p.2. Sullivan Block and the Green Bldg., Mar. 13, 1897, p.3; and for the McDowell,

Atkins & Watson Co. Bldg., Mar. 2, 1899, p.8. Mole Res. in *Sun*, July 20, 2001, p.B2. Information on the Van. Block from the Gladding, McBean & Co. Records, Job #935, California State Library, Sacramento. Other citations from CVA plans. **PROJECTS: J.E. Parr:** Sullivan Block, Cordova St., Van., 1896 (demo.); Green Bldg., Nanaimo, 1896 (demo. or heavily alt.); Harvey's Chambers, 399 W. Hastings St./300 Blk. Homer St., Van., 1896-97 (demo.); Apt. Block, Beach Ave., Van., 1923 (unbuilt project). **Parr & Fee:** Thomson Block, 339 W. Hastings St., Van., 1898 (alt.); McDowell, Atkins & Watson Co. Bldg. (Cambie Hotel), 300-320 Cambie St., Van., 1899 (ext.); Ralph Block 126 W. Hastings St., Van., 1899 (ext.); Chinese Methodist Mission, Carrall St., Van., 1899 (demo.); Mole Res., 3350 S.W. Marine Dr., Van., 1901 (demo.); Fee Block, 570 Granville St., Van., 1903 (demo.); Thomas Fee Res., 1119 Broughton St., Van., 1903-04 (ext.); Speculative House for S.J. Steeves, 1122 Comox St., Van., 1904 (ext.); Buscombe & Co. Block, 25-27 W. Hastings St., Van., 1906 (alt.); Thomas Fee Res., 1025 Gilford St., Van., 1906-07 (demo. 1961); Malkin Co. Warehouse, western half, 55-65 Water St., Van., 1907 (ext.) [eastern half by **J.M. McLuckie**, 1911-12]; Manhattan Apts., 784 Thurlow St., Van., 1907-08 (ext.); Dunsmuir Hotel, 500 Dunsmuir St., Van., 1908 (ext.); Hotel Europe, 43 Powell St., Van., 1908-09 (ext.); Stadacona Apts., 601 Bute St., Van., 1909 (ext.); Morin Res., 410 W. 12th Ave., Van., 1909 (ext.); Mount Pleasant Presbyterian Church, 2525 Quebec St., Van., 1909-10 (ext.; gutted for conversion to condominium units); Dufferin Hotel, 536-540 Smithe St./900-918 Seymour St., Van., 1910 (ext.); *Glen Brae*, 1690 Matthews St., Van., 1910 (ext.); Van. Block, 736 Granville St., Van., 1910-12 (ext.); **Parr, Mackenzie & Day:** Port Coquitlam City Hall, 2272 McAllister Ave., Port Coquitlam, 1914 (alt.). **T.A. Fee:** Johnson Res., 4511 Beverley Cres., Van., 1920-21 (ext.).

PATTERN BOOK HOUSES

Sources included copies of pattern books; Margaret Culbertson, *American House Designs: An Index to Popular and Trade Periodicals 1850-1915* (Westport, Connecticut: Greenwood Press, 1994); Margaret Culbertson, *Texas Houses Built by the Book: The Use of Published Designs 1850-1925* (College Station: Texas A&M University Press, 1999); Massey & Maxwell, *House Styles in America*; Stevenson & Jandl, *Houses By Mail*; essay by Dennis A. Andersen & Katheryn Hills Krafft in Ochsner, *Shaping Seattle*, pp.64-71. **PROJECTS**: *Roslyn* (Gray Res.), 1135 Catherine St., Vict., 1890 (ext.); Captain Jacobson's House, 507 Head St., Esquimalt, 1893 (ext.).

PAUW, John Adrian

AIBC; inventories; and correspondence with Delft Technical University, The Netherlands. Quote from "100 Years of B.C. Living," *Western Homes & Living*, Jan. 1958, p.40. **PROJECT**: Lea Res., 4051 Marguerite St., Van., 1930 (ext.).

PEARCE, John S.

Revelstoke Museum & Archives; Barrett & Windsor Liscombe, *Francis Rattenbury*; and CVA Plans. Information on the North Van. Hotels from *The Express Empire Day Prosperity Edition*, May 24, 1912. Notice of partnership with Shand in *CA&B*, June 1905, p.96. **PROJECTS**: P. Burns & Co. Meat Market (now Mackenzie Place), 201 Mackenzie Ave., Revelstoke, 1906-07 (ext.); Holt Res., 302 E. 5th St., N. Van., 1909 (ext.); Canyon View Hotel, North Van. Dist., 1909 (demo.); Lynn Valley Tourist Hotel, Rice Lake Rd., North Van. Dist., 1912 (unbuilt project).

PEARSE, Benjamin William

Richard Mackie's entry in the *Dictionary of Canadian Biography*, Vol.XIII, pp.822-824 (Ramsay Cook, ed., Toronto: University of Toronto Press, 1994). See also Howay & Schofield, *British Columbia: Biographical*, 1914, Vol.IV, pp.1070-1073; Ruggles, *A Country So Interesting*; Cowichan *Leader*, Nov. 29, 1967; *VDT*, Nov. 29, 1967; and B.C. Vital Events. Marine Hospital mentioned in the *Report of the Minister of Marine & Fisheries for the Year Ended 30 June 1873*, pp.xl-xlv; Janet Wright, *Crown Assets*, p.30; and references in the *Colonist*: "Pearse preparing plans," Apr. 3, 1873, p.3; "Instructions from Ottawa to have it started," Sept. 16, 1873, p.3; "Completed & accepted," July 3, 1874, p.3. Typed manuscript, B.W. Pearse, *Reminiscences* (BCA File E/B/p31). Additional information from H. Barry Cotton, BCLS. **PROJECTS**: Marine Hospital, Songhees Reserve, Vict., 1872-74 (dest. by fire 1914); Vict. Post Office, 1200 Blk. Government St., Vict., 1873-74 (demo.; replaced by present Post Office).

PEARSON, Lawrence Lewis

AIBC; directories; Vict. plans, bldg. and plumbing permits.

PELTON, Arthur F.

Kelowna Heritage Walking Tour; Kelowna Heritage Register; directories; Kelowna Voters List 1915; Robert G. Hill; and the Penticton Museum & Archives. **PROJECTS**: Incola Hotel, 100 W. Lakeshore Dr., Penticton, 1911-12 (demo. 1981); Willits-Taylor Bldg., 375-387 Bernard Ave., Kelowna, 1913 (ext.).

PERKINS, Frank H.

Directories; and Van. bldg. permit. #3011. **PROJECT**: Ferrera Court, 504-508 E. Hastings St., Van., 1911-12 (ext.).

PERRY, Richard Thomas

AIBC; B.C. Vital Events; CVA Plans; Kluckner & Atkin, *Heritage Walks Around Vancouver*; Kalman, *Exploring Vancouver*; *Who's Who in Western Canada*, 1911; *Province*, Aug. 26, 1932, p.2 and June 14, 1935, p.7. Further information from the Bessborough Armoury. **PROJECTS: R.T. Perry:** Hall, Dunbar Heights United Church, 3527 West 24th Ave., Van., 1926 (ext.); Hospital Pavilion for T.B. Patients, Shaughnessy Hospital, 800 Blk. W. 28th Ave., Van., c.1926 (demo.); Tatlow Court, 1820

Bayswater St., Van., 1927-28 (ext.); Bessborough Armoury, 2025 W. 11th Ave., Van., 1932-34 (ext.); Randall Bldg., 555 W. Georgia St., Van., 1929 (ext.). **Perry & Nicolais:** Sam Kee (Main) Hotel, 645 Main St., Van., 1911 (demo.). **Perry & Fowler:** City of Vancouver Old People's Home, 951 Boundary Rd., Van., 1914 (ext.); Cashman Res., 4686 W. 2nd Ave., Van., 1914 (ext.). **Perry & Kerr:** Second Church of Christ Scientist, 1900 West 12th Ave., Van., 1926 (ext.); Ryerson United Church, 2205 W. 45th Ave., Van., 1927-28 (ext.).

PETERS, Wesley A.
Anglican churches from the Anglican Archives, Diocese of the Kootenay. Description of the history of St. Andrew's from Primrose Upton, *The First Fifty Years: A History of St. Andrew's Church*, 1961. Other information from Robert G. Hill; the *Kelowna Heritage Walking Tour*; and the *Kelowna Driving Tour*. **PROJECTS:** Presbyterian Church (now First United), 721 Bernard Ave., Kelowna, 1909 (ext.); St. Andrew's Anglican Church, 4619 Lakeshore Rd., Kelowna, 1910-11 (ext.); St. Michael's & All Angels Anglican Church (now cathedral), 1876 Richter St., Kelowna, 1911-13 (ext.); St. Stephen's Anglican Church, 9887 Cameron St., Burnaby, 1913 (ext.).

PHIPPS, Paul
Janie Hampton, *Joyce Grenfell* (London: John Murray, 2002); Joyce Grenfell, *Joyce Grenfell Requests the Pleasure* (London: Futura Publications Limited, 1980); Mary Lutyens, *Edwin Lutyens* (London: Black Swan, 1991); Gray, *Edwardian Architecture*, p.240; obituaries in *The Builder* [London], Aug. 28, 1953, p.311 and the *RIBA Journal*, Vol.61, Nov. 1953, pp.38-39; and city directories. Plans for the Johnson Res. are in the possession of the current owners. **PROJECT:** Johnson Res., 1526 Angus Dr., Van., 1912 (ext.).

POSTLE, Harry Walter
AIBC; Interviews with Mrs. Maida Kirk-Owen, Postle's daughter; Postle's obituary in the *Province*, Aug. 10, 1955, p.5; and B.C. Vital Events. Information on the South Okanagan Secondary School is from the Oliver & District Archives; and the School's archival collection. **PROJECTS:** *H.W. Postle:* Van. Technical School, 2600 E. Broadway, Van., 1928 (ext.; additions 1940 and 1954); Lord Byng addition, 3939 W. 16th Ave., Van., 1938 (ext.); Queen Elizabeth Elementary School, 4102 W. 16th Ave., Van., 1939 (ext.); Southlands School No. Two, 5351 Camosun Dr., Van., 1939 (ext.); The Church of St. Edward the Confessor Anglican, 350 Ave. and 103 St., Oliver, 1949-51 (ext.). **Postle & Körner:** South Okanagan High School, 10532 350 Ave., Oliver, 1946-49 (ext.).

POTTER, Joseph Walter
AIBC; Prince Rupert City & Regional Archives; and Brandes, *San Diego Architects*, p.134. **PROJECTS:** City Hall, Prince Rupert, 1912 (demo.); Fire Hall, Prince Rupert, 1912; St. Joseph's Convent, Prince

Rupert, 1917; Booth Memorial School (Hays Cove School), Prince Rupert, 1920.

POWNALL, Guy Frank
National Archives of Canada Dominion Land Grants, File reel number C-6070; Calgary *Herald Daily*, Dec. 23 1892; BCA Reg. Number 1896-09-201781; 1898 census report and Voter's Lists; Calgary *Herald Daily*, Apr. 28 1899; Calgary *Herald Weekly*, May 4, 1899; directories; Vict. *Times*, Nov. 20, 1939: announcement, p.12; obituary, p.11.

PRATT & ROSS
Entries in *Who's Who in Western Canada*; and Manitoba Culture, Heritage & Recreation, *Neepawa: An Architectural Walking Tour* (Winnipeg: Historic Resources Branch, n.d.). Information from Donald R. Pratt, grandson of R.B. Pratt. **PROJECT:** Canadian Northern Station (now Pacific Central), 1150 Station St., Van., 1916-19 (ext.).

PRICE, Bruce
International Dictionary of Architects (Detroit: St. James Press, 1983), Vol.1, p.697-698; Withey & Withey, *Biographical Dictionary of American Architects (Deceased)*, pp.487-488; *Who's Who in American Art* (available on the Society of Architectural Historians website); Alan Gowans, *Building Canada: An Architectural History of Canadian Life* (Toronto: Oxford University Press, 1966), p.187; CAC Accession No. 9, McGill University, Montreal (includes plans for an office bldg. for William C. Van Horne in Van.); and Arnold Lewis, *American Country Houses of the Gilded Age* (Don Mills: Dover Publications, 1982). Price's Van. bldgs. are identified in "$1,350,000 Spent," *VDW*, Dec. 31, 1888, p.4-5. **PROJECTS:** CPR "Double Cottage B," Georgia St., Van., 1886-88 (demo. 1932); Van Horne Block, 601-603 Granville St., Van., 1888-89 (demo. 1972); New York Block, 658 Granville St., Van., 1888-89 (demo.); Crewe Block, 622 Granville St., Van., 1888-89 (alt. 1948; demo. 2001); Sir Donald A. Smith Block, Granville and Georgia Sts., Van., 1888-89 (demo.).

PRITECA, B. Marcus
Miriam Sutermeister's essay in Ochsner, *Shaping Seattle Architecture*, pp.180-86. **PROJECTS:** Second Pantages Theatre, 20 W. Hastings St., Van., 1916-17 (demo.); Orpheum Theatre (with Frederick J. Peters, Associated Architect), 884 Granville St., Van., 1926-27 (ext.).

PROCTOR, G.L.
Kalman, *The Prince Rupert Heritage Inventory and Conservation Programme*, and the Prince Rupert City & Regional Archives. **PROJECTS:** Roman Catholic Church of the Annunciation, 637 5th Ave. W., Prince Rupert, 1909-10 (ext.); St. Andrew's Anglican Church, 200 4th Ave. W., Prince Rupert, 1912-1925 (architects Gordon & Helliwell, Toronto, ext.).

PROVINCIAL LAND SURVEYORS
Information provided by the Corporation of Land Surveyors of British Columbia and their current publications. Biographical information from John A. Whittaker, BCLS, comp. & editor, *Early Land Surveyors of British Columbia*; the *Cumulative Nominal Roll*; issues of *Link* magazine; BCLS Annual Reports; and provincial directories. Additional information provided by H. Barry Cotton, BCLS, and Robert W. Allen, BCLS.

RATTENBURY, Francis Mawson
Rattenbury's life and scandalous death have been extensively covered. The chief sources of information on his life and career, both documentary and bibliographic are Barrett & Windsor Liscombe, *Francis Rattenbury*, and Terry Reksten, *Rattenbury*. There are also a number of books that cover his murder, and the subsequent sensational trial of his wife's lover, that tangentially refer to his colonial career. Details of his Klondike trip have recently been published in W.H.T. Olive's memoir, *The Olive Diary: The Gripping Tale of W.H.T. Olive's Adventures in the Klondyke of 1898* (Surrey: Timberholme Books, 1998). Further information and photographs provided by Leonard G. McCann, from an unpublished report on Rattenbury prepared in 1967, and based in part on correspondence and interviews with Rattenbury's daughter, Mary Burton. See also AIBC files. **PROJECTS: F.M. Rattenbury:** Parliament Buildings, 501 Belleville St., Vict., 1893-98; Court House, 35 Front St., Nanaimo, 1895-96 (ext.); Bank of Montreal, 1200 Government St., Vict., 1897 (ext.); *Iechinihl* (Rattenbury res.), 1701 Beach Dr., Oak Bay, 1898 (ext.); Burns Bldg., 556 Baker St., Nelson, 1899-1900 (ext.); Bank of Montreal, Columbia and Church Sts., New West., 1899-1900 (demo.); Bank of Montreal, 286-298 Baker St., Nelson, 1899-1900 (ext.); Lyman Duff House, 1745 Rockland Ave., Vict., 1900-02 (ext.); Government House (with **Samuel Maclur**e, associated architect), Belcher Rd., Vict., 1901-03 (dest. by fire 1957); Mount Stephen House, Field, 1902-03 (demo.); Court House, 320 Ward St., Nelson, designed 1903, built 1906-09 (ext.); Empress Hotel, 721 Government St., Vict., 1904-08 (ext.); Court House, 800 W. Georgia St., Van., 1906-11 (ext.); Parliament Buildings Library and Additions, 501 Belleville St., Vict., 1911-16 (ext.). **Rattenbury & James:** Crystal Gardens, 701-711 Douglas St., Vict., 1921-25 (ext.); CPR Steamship Terminal, 396-468 Belleville St., Vict., 1924-26 (ext.).

REA, Kenneth Guscotte
AIBC; and CAC Accession No. 8, McGill University, Montreal. **PROJECTS:** Royal Bank, 205 Victoria St., Kamloops, 1911-13 (alt.); Bank of Montreal, Prince George, 1919-1920 (alt.); Additions to the Bank of Montreal (originally the Merchants' Bank designed by **Somervell & Putnam**, 1915-16), 500 Granville St./640 West Pender St., Van., 1924-25 (ext.).

REES, George Stanley

Fernie & District Historical Society; Fernie *Free Press*, June 18, 1909; *British Columbia Sessional Papers*, Report for 1909 (Fernie Court House rebuilding, $25,000); BCA GR-0054 Box 23 File 402. **PROJECT:** Fernie Court House, 401 4th Ave., Fernie, 1908-1909 (ext.).

RICHARDS, William Austin S.

Kamloops Museum & Archives; and Van. bldg. permits. Kamloops *Inland Sentinel*, May 20, 1912, p.4; May 22, 1913, p.1; and May 23, 1913, p.1. Kamloops *Standard*, Oct. 17, 1913, p.5. **PROJECTS:** Commercial block for Mrs. E. Gould, 752 Robson St., Van., 1910 (demo.); Exhibition Bldg. for Agricultural Association, Kamloops, 1913 (unbuilt project).

RIXFORD, Loring Pickering

California vital statistics (Deaths 1940-1997 from Ancestry.com); websites for Page & Turnbull, Historic Courthouse Buildings, and Carnegie Libraries of California; directories; Vict. plans, bldg. and plumbing permits; Bissley, *The Union Club of British Columbia*; directories; *AB&E*; Barrett & Windsor Liscombe, *Francis Rattenbury*, p.220; BCA MS-0502; David Gebhard, *Guide to Architecture in San Francisco and Northern California*. See *VDC*, July 30, 1911, p.19 for announcement of the Union Club. **PROJECT:** Union Club, 805 Gordon St., Vict., 1911-13 (ext.).

ROCHFORT, William D'Oyly Hamilton

Vict. plans, bldg. and plumbing permits; VCA Demolished Bldg. Plans; death and marriage certificates and notices; and VCA PR 112 Rochfort/Switzer family Fonds. Bldg. citations from *This Old House* and the *Jubilee Neighbourhood Heritage Resource Review*. References from the *VDT*; *VDC*; *Portland Canal Miner* newspapers; *AB&E* 1912-15; *PB&E* 1915 UBC Competition documents, University Archives, UBC; and Seattle Department of Neighborhoods, Landmarks Preservation Board. Kinemacolor Theatre from *VDC*, Apr. 27, 1913, p.8. Terry Reksten, *Royal Victoria Yacht Club 1892-1992* (Vict.: Orca Book Publishers, 1992), and Terry Reksten's personal interviews with Phyllis Rochfort and Rocky Rochfort. **PROJECTS: William D'Oyly H. Rochfort:** Vict. Yacht Club, foot of Kingston St., Vict., 1908 (demo.); Hartman Res., 1009 Cook St., Vict., 1908 (ext.); Three houses for the Bevan Brothers, 1023, 1063 and 1077 Davie St., Vict., 1908-09 (ext.); Mount Edwards Apts., 1002 Vancouver St., Vict., 1910 (ext.); Billings Res., 1528 Cold Harbour Rd., Vict., 1910-11 (ext.); Bechtel Res., 1385 Rockland Ave., Vict., 1911 (ext.); St. John's Church Memorial Altar, Vict., 1919; 1400 and 1405 St. Patrick St., Oak Bay, 1922 (ext.). **Rochfort & Sankey:** New Royal Vict. Yacht Club, 3475 Ripon Rd., Oak Bay, 1912 (alt.); *Purcell* (Cameron Res.), 1320 Purcell Pl., Vict., 1912 (ext.); Royal Theatre, 805 Broughton St., Vict., 1913 (ext.); Kinemacolor Variety Theatre, 1600 Government St., Vict., 1913 (alt.); Levy Res.,

2667 Empire St., Vict., 1913 (ext.).

ROYAL ENGINEERS

A large amount of research has been done over the years on the history of the Royal Engineers in B.C.: Howay & Schofield, *British Columbia: Historical*, 1914, Vol.II, pp.55-68, has an accurate overview of their activities. A focused account is provided by Frances M. Woodward, "The Influence of the Royal Engineers on the Development of British Columbia," *B.C. Studies*, No.24, Winter 1974-75, pp.3-51. Useful for its research and an extensive bibliography is Beth Hill, *Sappers: The Royal Engineers in British Columbia* (Ganges: Horsdal & Schubart, 1987). An article specifically on the history of the Royal Engineer's architecture and town planning is Barry V. Downs, "The Royal Engineers in British Columbia," *Canadian Collector*, 11:3 (May/June 1976). See also H. Peter Oberlander, "...And In the Beginning...," RAIC *Journal*, No.392, Vol.35, No.4 (Apr., 1958); Ormsby, *British Columbia*; and Cotton, *Vice-Regal Mansions*. A copy of Lemprière's diary is held at UBC Special Collections. See BCA Colonial Correspondence, for Lemprière [BCA GR-1372 B-1343 File 985a] and J.C. White [B-1373 File 1860c]. References to the Hyack Fire Co. Engine House in *The British Columbian*, Nov. 28, 1861, p.2; Dec. 12, 1861, p.2; and Feb. 20, 1862, p.1. Quote about the 1864 additions to Government House is from the *Colonist*, Nov. 11, 1864. New West. School from *The British Columbian*, Aug. 26, 1865, p.3 and Nov. 22, 1865, p.2. The BCA has a large collection of maps, drawings and watercolours by J.C. White [including plans CM-D 58; CM-A 1950; and CM-A 1951]; plans also exist for Holy Trinity [BCA CM-B2086]. **PROJECTS: Rev. W.B. Crickmer (attributed):** St. John the Divine Anglican Church, Derby, 1859, relocated to Maple Ridge in 1882, now 21299 River Rd., Maple Ridge (alt.). **John Grant:** Christ Church, Park and Fraser Sts., Hope, 1861 (ext.). **A.R. Lemprière:** Holy Trinity Anglican Church, New West., 1860 (dest. by fire 1865). **J.C. White:** Government House (Col. Moody's House), Sapperton, New West., 1861, additions, 1864 (demo. 1889); Museum for the Exhibition of British Columbian Produce, Columbia St. near Sixth St., New West, 1861 (demo.); Hyack Fire Co. Engine House, Columbia St., New West., 1862 (dest. by fire 1898); St. Mary the Virgin Church, 121 E. Columbia St., New West. (originally Sapperton), 1865 (alt. 1921-22); New West. School, Royal Ave. and Sixth St., New West., 1865 (relocated to 126 Second St.; alt.).

RUSSELL, BABCOCK & RICE

Information from David A. Rash and Thomas Veith, verified through directories; CVA plans; and Van. bldg. permits. See Norman J. Johnston's essay on Harlan Thomas in Ochsner, *Shaping Seattle Architecture*, pp.126-131, and Woodbridge & Montgomery, *Guide to Architecture in Washington State*. **PROJECTS:** Van. Club Competition entry,

1912 (unbuilt project); Weart Bldg. (now the Standard Bldg.), 510 W. Hastings St., Van., 1912-14 (ext.).

RUSSELL, John Hamilton Gordon

Biographical information from Robert G. Hill; Monk & Stewart, *A History of Coquitlam and Fraser Mills*; inventories. **PROJECT:** Canadian Western Lumber Co. Ltd. Head Office, Fraser Mills (now Coquitlam), 1908 (demo.).

SAIT, Edwin George William

Directories; B.C. Vital Events; Cotton, *Vice-Regal Mansions*, pp.72-73; Scott, *Once in the Royal City*; and the *New Westminster Heritage Resource Inventory*. Previous research by Lucy Chambers, including a number of references from *The Daily* and *Weekly Columbian*. Sait is listed in *CA&B*, Vol.12, Jan., 1899, Issue 1, p.5 as one of the architects in New West. rebuilding after the fire. Horse Arena in *The Daily News* ("Would Lease New Arena for Ice," Oct. 1, 1912, p.1; and "Horse Show Credit to City," Oct. 2, 1912, p.1); and *The British Columbian* ("Arena is OK," Jan. 28, 1913, p.8). Lillooet Hospital reference in *The Columbian*, July 23, 1910; Hotel Fraser reference in *The Columbian*, Mar. 13, 1912. Information on the asylum competition in *British Columbia Sessional Papers*, Report for 1909 [Public Accounts, p.B102]. **PROJECTS: Byrnes & Sait:** Government House, Vict., 1900-01 (unbuilt project). **E.G.W. Sait:** Carnegie Library, Carnarvon and Lorne Sts., New West., 1902-04 (demo.); Maternity & Nurses' Home, 1907, and three Isolation Buildings, 1908, Royal Columbian Hospital, 330 E. Columbia St., New West. (demo.); *Eldora* (H.T. Kirk Res.), 321 Fourth Ave., New West., 1908 (ext.); Fisheries Exhibition Bldg., Queen's Park, New West., 1909 (alt.; relocated); King Edward Hotel, 425 Columbia St., New West., 1909 (demo.); Dean Block, 441-447 Columbia St., New West., 1910 (alt.); Public Hospital, Lillooet, 1910; Land Registry Office, 648 Carnarvon St., New West., 1910-11 (ext.); Horse Show Buildings, Queen's Park, New West., 1912 (dest. by fire 1929); Burnaby Municipal Hall, competition entry, 1911 (unbuilt project); Apt. Block for E.J. Fader (now Queens Court), 115 Second St., New West., 1911 (ext.); Hotel Fraser, Front and Begbie Sts., New West., 1912 (demo.); Barbaree Res., 105 Third Ave., New West., 1912 (ext.).

SANKEY, Eben W.

Vict. plans, bldg. and plumbing permits; (www.scn.org/neighbors/montlake/mcc_history.Jim_Gould.html); *AB&E*; *PB&E*; *VDC*; and directories.

SANSOM, C. Wyndham H.

Limited references available in CVA plans; *VDW*; and directories. City Market competition information from Van. City Council minutes, July 22, 1889, v.3, p.72 [CVA]. Information on J.W. Dawson from directories. Calgary references from Barry Elmer. **PROJECT: Sansom & Dawson:** Van. City Market Bldg., 423 Main St., Van., 1889-90 (demo. 1958).

SAVAGE, Hubert

AIBC; Vict. plans, bldg. and plumbing permits; Collection of Savage drawings at VCA; Esquimalt Archives; Hallmark Society files; interviews with Savage's daughter, Ethne Barth; and an unpublished MS by Rosemary James Cross. Esquimalt drill hall and administration bldg. from *The British Columbian*, July 31, 1935, p.2. **PROJECTS: H. Savage:** Harvey House, Knapp Island, Swartz Bay, 1913 (ext.); Savage Res., 3862 Grange Rd., Saanich, 1913 (ext.); War Memorial, Esquimalt, 1923-27 (ext.); W. A. Patterson Res., 2580 Cotswold Rd., Oak Bay, 1937 (ext.); Royal Oak Inn, 4509 W. Saanich Rd., Saanich, 1939 (ext.). **Maclure & Savage, Associated Architects:** Solarium, Mill Bay, 1926 (demo.); Cridge Memorial Hall, 626 Blanshard St., Vict., 1928-30 (alt.). **James & Savage:** *Queenswood* estate for Col. F. Sharland, Saanich, c.1928: Main House, 2494 Arbutus Dr., (dest. by fire), Gamekeeper's Cottage, 2330 Queenswood Dr. (ext.); Royal Colwood Country Club House, Colwood, 1929 (demo.); Laws Res., 2451 Queenswood Drive, Saanich, 1930 (alt.). **Spurgin & Savage:** Drill Hall and Admin. Bldg., Esquimalt, 1935 (ext.).

SCHALLERER, August B.

GedCom Internet site; directories; Vict. plans, bldg. and plumbing permits; *AB&E*; inventories. **PROJECTS:** House for **Ward Investment Co.**, 1069 Joan Cres., Vict., 1912-13 (ext.); House for the **Ward Investment Co.**, 352 Moss St., Vict., 1913 (ext.); Barnes Res., 1897 Monteith St., Oak Bay, 1914 (ext.).

SCHLOMER, Herman H.

Advertisements in *Modern Architecture* and *Victoria Architecturally*.

SCHOFIELD, John

Information provided by Robert G. Hill; Cyndi Smith, *Jasper Park Lodge: In the Heart of the Canadian Rockies* (Canmore, Alberta; Coyote Books, 1985); and Glenbow Archives.

SCOTT, Adrian Gilbert

Reeve, *Every Good Gift: A History of S. James' Vancouver, 1881-1981*. **PROJECT:** St. James' Church (**Sharp & Thompson**, Associated Architects), 303 E. Cordova St., Van., 1935-36 (ext.).

SCOTT, T. Seaton

Dana Johnson, "Thomas Seaton Scott," *Dictionary of Canadian Biography* (Toronto: University of Toronto Press, 1990), Vol.12, pp.957-59; Archibald, *By Federal Design*; Wright, *Crown Assets*; MacTavish, *Fine Arts in Canada*; Janet Wright's entry on Scott in the *Canadian Encyclopedia*; and *Sessional Reports*. Detailed information from an appendix to the Architect's report in the annual departmental report for 1882, prepared by George-Frederick Baillairgé describing every structure built or acquired by DPW to that date. Custom House information from the

Downtown Victoria Heritage Register. Information from *Colonist* tender calls and articles. First reference to the DPW is in the *Colonist*, Aug. 6, 1872, p.3. Further information provided by Gordon Fulton. Langevin's diary that records his trip to B.C. is part of the Chung Collection, Special Collections, UBC. New West. Post Office described in 1882-83 directories. See also Jacqueline Adell, *Architecture of the Drill Hall in Canada, 1863-1939* (Ottawa: Report prepared for the Historic Sites & Monuments Board of Canada, June 1989). **PROJECTS:** Custom House, 1002 Wharf St., Vict., 1873-75 (ext.); Drill Shed (from a standard plan prepared by Walter Moberly), Menzies St., Vict., 1874 (demo. 1892); Federal Bldg. and Post Office, Columbia and Sixth Sts., New West., 1881-83 (dest. by fire 1898).

SEDGER, Thomas Dealtry

AIBC; B.C. Vital Events, Vict. plans and bldg. permits, references in *AB&E*; VCA; Esquimalt Archives; newspaper references and obituaries. Personal information from Patricia MacDonald Sedger. Information on The English Church from Dorothy Stranix, *A Brief Historical Record of Colwood*; and *The Diocesan Gazette*, 1912-15, Anglican Archives, Diocese of B.C., Vict. **PROJECTS: T.D. Sedger:** *Bracondale* (Sedger Res.), 476 Lampson St., Esquimalt, c.1908 (demo.); Res. for A.R. Wolfenden, 812 Dunsmuir St., Vict., 1908 (ext.); Masonic Temple, Cranbrook, 1909; Res. for A.R. Wolfenden, 622 Head St., Esquimalt, c.1910 (ext.); Rectory for St. Saviour's Church, 512 Catherine St., Vict., 1911 (ext.); A.E. Evans Res., 1470 Rockland Ave., Vict., 1912 (ext.); Municipal Hall, Esquimalt, 1912-13 (unbuilt project); The English Church, St. John the Baptist Anglican (now St. John's Heritage Church), Glencairn Lane, Colwood, 1913 (ext.); Scott Res., 1354 Craigdarroch Rd., Vict., 1914 (ext.); Commercial Bldg. for A.R. Wolfenden, 904 Esquimalt Rd., Esquimalt, 1914 (ext.); *Cedar Chines* (Palmer Res.), Cherry Point Rd., Cowichan Bay, 1914 (demo.); Esquimalt High School, now L'école (Victor) Brodeur, 637 Head St., Esquimalt, 1926 (ext.). **Guy F. Pownall & T.D. Sedger:** Robertson Res., 1564 Rockland Ave., Vict., 1906 (ext.); Noder Res., 1015 Cook St., Vict., 1907-08 (ext.); J.T. Redding Res., 822 Catherine St., Vict., 1907-09 (ext.); Chadwick Res., 215-217 Government St., Vict., 1908 (ext.).

SEMEYN, William Jacobus

Information on the Semeyn and Cross families was provided by son, William Semeyn; other information was gained from AIBC; B.C. Vital Events; Vict. plans, bldg. and plumbing permits; *AB&E*; *VDT* references; directories; inventories; Vict. plans, bldg. and plumbing permits; Hallmark Society files; Segger & Franklin, *Exploring Victoria*; and Sherrill MacLaren, *Braehead* (Toronto: McClelland & Stewart, 1986). Tweedsmuir Mansions from *VDC*, Mar. 29, 1936, p.3. **PROJECTS: W.J. Semeyn:** Brown Res., 1210 Tattersall Drive, Saanich, 1912-13 (ext.); Main Res., 3680 Craigmiller Ave.,

Saanich, 1922 (ext.); Crowe Res., 1382 Craigdarroch Rd., Vict., 1923 (ext.); Herman R. Brown Res., 3895 Hobbs St., Saanich, 1927 (ext.); Jameson Motors Bldg., 740 Broughton St., Vict., 1928 (demo. except for fountains); Tweedsmuir Mansions Apts., 900 Park Boulevard, Vict., 1936 (ext.); Rainbow Mansion Apts., 805-811 Academy Close, Vict., 1947-48 (ext.). **Spurgin & Semeyn:** Oak Bay Secondary School, 2101 Cadboro Bay Rd., Oak Bay, 1929 (ext.); Howell Res., 627 Falkland Rd., Oak Bay, 1930 (ext.); Bowden Res., 2809 Burdick Ave., Oak Bay, 1930 (ext.).

SHARP & THOMPSON

AIBC; CVA plans; Clippings files at the CVA, and large collections of architectural drawings and textual information at the CAA, Calgary, and in the University Archives, UBC. The CAA has taped interviews with Sharp, Berwick and Pratt by Harold Kalman from the early 1970s. The UBC collection focuses on the campus bldgs. and postwar work of Thompson, Berwick & Pratt, and includes an institutional history written by Jane Bellyk at the time of the accession. The UBC competition has been analyzed by Douglas Franklin in *West Coast Review* (Spring 1981); the campus bldgs. were illustrated in the *JRAIC* (Sept. 1925). Sean Rossiter has published a useful, if idolatrous, historical overview of the firm in *Vancouver* magazine (Sept. 1983). Sharp's name is sometimes spelled as 'Sharpe' on earlier plans, which may have been the correct spelling of his family name. **PROJECTS: Sharp & Thompson:** A. Desbrisay Res., 3989 Angus Dr., Van., 1910 (ext.); Gilford Court Apts., 1901 Pendrell St., Van., 1911 (demo.); First Congregational Church, 1100 Thurlow St., Van., 1911-12 (demo.); R.S. Lennie House, 1737 Matthews Ave., Van., 1912 (ext.); Van. Club, 915 W. Hastings St., Van., 1912-14 (ext.); St. Mary's Kerrisdale, 2498 W. 37th Ave., Van., 1913 (alt.); Sharp Res., 2427 W. 37th Ave., Van., 1912 (ext.); Science Bldg. (now the Chemistry Bldg.), 2036 Main Mall, UBC, Van., 1914-25 (ext.); Ceperley-Rounsfell Bldg., 846 W. Hastings St., Van., 1921 (ext.); UBC Library (now Main Library), 1956 Main Mall, UBC, Van., 1923-25 (ext.) (with additions 1948 and 1960); Powerhouse, UBC, Van., 1925 (alt.); St. James Clergy House, 303 E. Cordova St., Van., 1927 (ext.); Wyman Res., 1844 Allison Rd., Van., 1927-28 (ext.); Union Hall (now part of Van. School of Theology), 6000 Chancellor Blvd., Van., 1927-34 (ext.); Van. Art Gallery, Georgia St., Van., 1931 (demo.); Chown Memorial Church, 3519 Cambie St., Van., 1936 (alt.). **G.L.T. Sharp:** St. John's Shaughnessy Anglican Church, 1490 Nanton Ave., Van., 1949 (ext.).

SHARP, Kendrick

Vict. plans, bldg. and plumbing permits; local newspapers *The Weekly News, Nanaimo Free Press, Cumberland News, The Enterprise, VDT* and *VDC*; inventories, tax assessments in B.C.; Land Titles; B.C. Vital Events. **PROJECTS:** Holy Trinity Anglican Church (later Cumberland Community

Church), 2732 Penrith Ave., Cumberland, 1895 (alt.); Sharp Res., 2749 Penrith Ave., Cumberland, 1895 (ext.); Bennett Res., 2698 Penrith Ave., Cumberland, 1896 (alt.); Sharp Res., 1716 Fort St., Vict., c.1905 (demo. 1988); Gillespie Res., 528 Trutch St., Vict., 1907 (ext.); Bennet Res., 608 Trutch St., Vict., 1909 (ext.).

SHARP, Richard Prior

The only known biographical sources are the 1881 British Census and the *Vancouver World* supplement of June, 1896. See also Felstead et al, *Directory of British Architects 1834-1900*, p.822. Information on his bldgs. and partnership with Samuel Maclure are found in numerous tender notices and bldg. descriptions in New West. and Van. newspapers. Notice of his participation in the Parliament Bldg. competition is found in *The Daily Telegram*, Sept. 28, 1892, p.5. Plans and specs. for All Saints' Anglican Church, Agassiz, at the Anglican Archives, Diocese of New West. Confirmation of Sharp's departure is in *CA&B* "Personal" Vol.9, 1896, p.133. **PROJECTS**: **R.P. Sharp**: Anglican Parish Rooms for the Bishop of New West., 1890 (demo.); Corbould, McColl & Jenns Block, Lorne St., New West., 1890 (demo.); Mission School, New Wing, Yale, 1890; Central School "Closets," New West., 1892 (demo.); All Saints' Anglican Church, 6906 #7 Hwy., Agassiz, 1894-96 (alt.); St. Thomas Anglican Church, 46040 Gore Ave., Chilliwack, 1895 (ext.). **Sharp & Maclure**: Church of St. Alban the Martyr, Nanaimo, 1891 (demo.); *Norland* (the Misses Schou Res.), Burnaby Lake, Burnaby, 1891 (demo. 1971); M.M. English Res., 119 Royal Ave. New West., 1891-92 (ext.); Van. World Bldg., 426 Homer St., Van., 1892 (alt.); Thomas Cunningham Res., 307 Fifth St., New West., 1892 (ext.); *Rosslynn*, Third Ave. and Seventh St., New West., 1892 (demo. 1932).

SHEWBROOKS, Samuel Bernard Dean

AIBC; B.C. Vital Events; *Who's Who in British Columbia* (Vict.: S.M. Carter) 1937-39, p.135 and 1940-41, p.209; and directories.

SIMMONDS, Henry Holdsby

Simmonds's career has been poorly documented, and it was necessary to trace his work through primary sources, including AIBC files. His sole credit for the Forum Bldg. at the PNE has been confirmed through the CAA, Calgary. Jones Res. from Point Grey Bldg. Permit #6823. Specifications for the Patricia Theatre, Powell River in the McLeod (Scanlon) Amusements Fonds, Powell River Historical Museum & Archives Association. Little was known about Simmonds's personal life until contact was made with his nephew, Geoff G. Simmonds, of Yandina, Queensland, Australia, who has generously shared his biographical research, including family correspondence. Confirmation of some details of Simmonds's life and career were provided by W.R. Lort. **PROJECTS**: **H.H. Simmonds**: W.H. Murphy, 329 Powell St., Van., 1912 (demo.); Jones Res., 4987 Connaught Dr., Van., 1924 (ext.);

Livestock Bldg., 2901 E. Hastings St., Van., 1929 (ext.); Stanley Park Manor Apts., 1915 Haro St., Van., 1929 (ext.); Stanley Theatre, 2750 Granville St., Van., 1930 (ext.); Pure Foods Bldg., 2901 E. Hastings St., Van., 1931 (demo. by the Van. Board of Parks & Recreation, 1998); Women & Fine Arts Bldg., 2901 E. Hastings St., Van., 1931 (ext.); Simmonds Res., 2080 W. 35th Ave., Van., 1931-32 (ext.); BCER Power & Gas Bldg., South Foot of Carrall St., Van., 1932 (demo.); Automotive & Ice Rink Bldg., 2901 E. Hastings St., Van., 1933 (ext.); St. Margaret's Church (now West Coast Christian Fellowship), 3198 E. Georgia St., Van., 1937 (ext.); Studio Theatre, 919 Granville St., Van., 1948 (alt.); Fraser Theatre, 6924 Fraser St., Van., 1948 (demo.); Odeon Theatre, 780 Yates St., Vict., 1947-49 (ext.). **Hodgson & Simmonds**: Collingwood United Church Hall, 5588 Joyce St., Van., 1926 (alt.); British Columbia Electric Railway Co. Showroom, 600 Granville St. (**McCarter & Nairne**, Consulting Architects), Van., 1927-28 (ext.); Patricia Theatre, 5848 Ash St., Powell River, 1928 (ext.).

SMITH, Andrew Johnston

BCA GR-0080 Box 1, Files 20 & 25; *Victoria Illustrated*, 1891 p.76; also "The New Cathedral," *Colonist*, Oct. 20, 1872, p.3 identifies Smith as the contractor for Christ Church. Additional references in the *Colonist* on Oct. 16, 1873, p.3; July 22, 1873, p.3 and Dec. 20, 1874, p.3. B.C. Vital Events for Smith and Clark. Yale Court House reference from New West. *Mainland Guardian*, Aug. 1, 1874, p.3 from Jim Wolf. *B.C. Sessional Papers* 1876, Public Accounts, p.528 and Supplementary Report of Public Works for 1875, p.xxv, identifies Smith as receiving payment of $300 for preparing plans for the Asylum. Additional information from Carey Pallister. **PROJECT**: Provincial Lunatic Asylum, 9 E. Columbia St., New West., 1875-78 (alt.).

SMITH, Sholto

Gordon Fulton, *Sholto Smith: In Search of Dreamwold*, in the Society for the Study of Architecture in Canada *Bulletin*, Vol.15, no. 3 (Sept. 1990), pp.68-82. About two dozen of his Van. commissions, mostly houses, are listed in the Van. bldg. permit records 1909-12. Additional information on Smith's New Zealand career can be found in "Sholto Smith: Stylistic Stride," a research report prepared by Dean B. Burke in Oct. 1993 while a student in the School of Architecture, University of Auckland; and Chris Brockie & Rod Smith, "Site Visit: Two Houses," in *AAA* [Auckland Architectural Association] *Bulletin*, no. 83 (June 1977), pp.16-18. Terry Hitchcock, an architect in Auckland, has assembled a dossier on Smith's New Zealand commissions. **PROJECTS**: Apt. Bldg. (later the Elysium Hotel), 1140 W. Pender St., Van., 1909 (demo.); Sholto Smith Res., 2216 W. 14th Ave., Van., 1910 (demo.); Wigwam Inn Lodge, Indian Arm, 1910 (ext.). **Smith & Goodfellow**: Addition to Woodward's Department Store, 101 W. Hastings St., Van., 1910 (ext.); Woodward's Warehouse and Stable, 1226 Hamilton St., Van., 1911 (alt.).

SOMERVELL & PUTNAM

David A. Rash's essay in Ochsner, *Shaping Seattle Architecture*, pp.120-125, 127 & 307; CVA Plans; Van. bldg. permits; and numerous contemporary newspaper and journal references, including biographies in *Pacific Builder & Engineer*, Nov. 28, 1914, p.286. Additional information from William H. McCarroll, Lawrenceville, New Jersey. The correspondence relating to the Burnaby Municipal Hall competition is in the Burnaby Clerk's Department Records, Box 11, File 252; Somervell & Putnam's plans for the Hall are in the collection of the Burnaby Historical Society. *PB&E*, Mar. 12, 1912, p.100, office notice in Van.; states Putnam was from New York. Information on *Shannon* from John Schreiner, *The Refiners: A Century of B.C. Sugar* (Vancouver: Douglas & McIntyre, 1989). Somervell's essay, *The Architect*, was published in the B.C. Society of Architects *Year Book*, 1913, and reprinted in *AB&E*, Jan. 25, 1914, pp.6-7. **PROJECTS**: **W. Marbury Somervell**: The Bauer Bldg. (later the Pacific, now the Pemberton, Bldg.), 738-744 W. Hastings St., 1910-12 (ext.); B.C. Electric Railway Co. Bldg., 425 Carrall St., Van., 1911-12 (ext.). **Somervell & Putnam**: Burnaby Municipal Hall, Kingsway and Edmonds, Burnaby, 1911 (demo. 1970s; tower preserved at Burnaby Village Museum); Bank of Ottawa, 602 W. Hastings St., Van. 1911-12 (demo.); Birks Bldg., 700-718 Granville St., Van., 1911-12 (demo. 1974); Yorkshire Guarantee (now the Seymour Bldg.), 525 Seymour St., Van., 1912-14 (ext.); Merchants' Bank, 1 W. Hastings St., Van., 1912 (ext.); Bauer Res., 3751 Cypress St., Van., 1912 (ext.); London Bldg., 626 W. Pender St., Van., 1912-13 (ext.); Merchants' Bank, 500 Granville St./640 West Pender St., Van., 1915-16 (enlarged 1924-25 by **K.G. Rea** for the Bank of Montreal; ext.); *Shannon* (B.T. Rogers Res.), 7255 Granville St., Van., 1913-25 (ext.); Union Bank of Canada (now the Morris J. Wosk Centre for Dialogue), 560-580 W. Hastings St./410 Seymour St., Van., 1919-20 (ext.).

SORBY, Thomas Charles

Records in the United Kingdom (particularly the Public Record Office) and Canada (particularly the CPR Archives and the BCA) as well as early periodicals (including *CA&B*). Recent published sources were chiefly books containing incidental references to individual bldgs. References to the Begbie Block in *The Daily Columbian*, Dec. 9, 1890, p.1 & 4. For St. James Church see *Van. News* Aug. 5, 1886 and Reeve, *Every Good Gift: A History of S. James' Vancouver, 1881-1981*. Bank of B.C., *VDW*, Oct. 3, 1891, p.2. Obituaries in the *VDT*, Nov. 17, 1924, p.1 & 18, and the *VDC*, Nov. 19, 1924, p.5. References to *The Laurels* in the *VDC*, Nov. 20, 1890, p.3. School competition covered in the *VDC*, July 18, 1893, p.6. **PROJECTS**: Glacier House, Glacier, 1886 (demo. 1929); Mount Stephen House, Field, 1886 (demo.); Fraser Canyon Hotel, North Bend, 1886 (demo); Second St. James' Church, Gore Ave. at E. Cordova St., Van., 1886-87 (demo. in 1935); first Hotel Vancouver, Granville and Georgia Sts., 1886-87 (demo. in 1914); Lady Stephen Block,

409-413 W. Hastings St., Van., 1887 (ext.); First Abbott House, W. Hastings St., Van., 1887 (demo.); Hudson's Bay Co. Store, Cordova St., Van., 1887 (demo.); Van. Court House, W. Hastings and Cambie Sts. (now Victory Sq.), Van., 1888-90 (demo. 1912); Christ Church Parsonage, 900 Blk. Burdette St., Vict., 1888 (demo.); Bank of British Columbia, 490 W. Hastings St., Van., 1889-91 (ext.); *The Laurels*, Belcher Ave., now 1249 Rockland Ave., Vict., 1890 (alt.); Weiler Block, 921 Government St./609-615 Broughton St./920 Gordon St., Vict., 1898-99 (ext.). **Sorby & Wilson:** Begbie Block, Columbia St., New West., 1890-91 (dest. by fire 1898); Five Sisters Block, Government and Fort Sts., Vict., 1890-91 (dest. by fire 1910).

SOULE, Cornelius John

Newspaper articles in the Port Hope, Guelph and Vict. newspapers. A short article on C.J. Soule appeared in *Victoria Illustrated 1891*. B.C. Directories also provided information about where he lived and worked. Entry in M. Bixbie, *Industries of Canada*, p.102 (City of Guelph, Ontario: 1886). Conversations with family members, especially his son, Rupert, and his grandchildren. Point Comfort Hotel, *Colonist*, Jan. 1, 1893, p.14. Other references from Dorothy Mindenhall, including: Notice of partnership, *Colonist*, Sept. 4, 1891, p.1; Notice of dissolution, *Colonist*, Jan. 28, 1894, p.1. For further information refer to website (wwwsouleweb. ca). **PROJECTS: C.J. Soule:** Claxton Res., 1517 Fernwood Rd., Vict., 1890 (demo. before 1957); Dalby Res., 1607 Camosun St., Vict., 1890, (alt.); Clearihue Res., 1500 Fort St., Vict., 1891 (demo. 1970s); St. Paul's Presbyterian Church, cor. Mary and Henry Sts., Vict., 1891 (demo. c.1965); Willows Agricultural Exhibition Hall, Fair St., Oak Bay, Vict., 1891 (dest. by fire 1907); Additions to *Stadacona* (Major Dupont Res.), Vict., 1891 (demo.); Rock Bay Hotel, cor. Bay and Bridge Sts., Vict., 1891 (demo. 1995). **Soule & Day:** Point Comfort Hotel, Mayne Island, 1892-93 (demo. 1958); North Ward School, 2621 Douglas St., Vict., 1893-94 (demo. 196). **Maclure & Soule:** *Parkside*, Sir Charles Hibbert Tupper Res. (design attributed to Soule), Barclay and Chilco Sts., Van., 1899 (demo.).

SPROAT, William Edwardes

AIBC; directories; inventories; directories; Van. bldg. permits; and California Death Index. **PROJECT:** Chinese Nationalist League Bldg., 284-296 East Pender St./525-545 Gore Ave., Van., 1920 (ext.).

SPURGIN, Karl Branwhite

Interviews with son, Robin Spurgin. Professor John F. Bosher, Ottawa; Margaret Browning and Jill Sewell for research on Soldiers' Settlement Act Housing in Saanich; AIBC; Hallmark Society files; directories; B.C. Vital Events; BCA photos; Vict. plans, bldg. and plumbing permits; Oak Bay permits and plans; *AB&E*; *VDT* and *VDC* references; inventories; War Records, National Archives of Canada; 1881 British Census; Saanich Municipal Archives files; Segger & Franklin, *Exploring Victoria*. **PROJECTS: K.B. Spurgin:** Spurgin Res., 785 Island Rd., Oak Bay, 1912-19 (ext.); Cowper Bungalow, 523 Davida Ave., Saanich, 1920 (ext.); Soldiers' Housing Scheme Houses, Saanich, 1919-20 (most ext.); Smith Res., 767 Transit Rd., Oak Bay, 1921 (ext.); Sidney Roofing & Paper Co. Saturator & Motor House, 47 Songhees Rd., Vict., 1921, (demo.); Fairfield United Church, 303 Fairfield Rd., Vict., 1926 (ext.); Colonel Phillips Res., *The Bourne*, 2745 Beach Drive, Oak Bay, 1927 (ext.); Preston Res., 1590 Despard Ave., Vict., 1927 (ext.); Hunter & Halkett Res. and Doghouse, 1126 Dallas Rd., Vict., 1929 (ext.); Second Spurgin Res., 1908 Waterloo Rd., Saanich, 1928 (ext.); Prince of Wales Fairbridge Farm School, near Duncan, 1935-36 (ext.); Qualicum College School (now Qualicum College Inn), 427 College Rd., Qualicum Beach, 1935-37 (ext.). **Spurgin & Wilkins:** Power Plant, Qualicum Beach; Qualicum Beach Hotel for the Merchants Trust & Trading Co. Ltd., Qualicum beach, 1913 (demo.); Margaret Jenkins School, 1824 Fairfield Rd., Vict., 1913 (ext.). **Spurgin & Rice:** Saanich War Memorial Health Centre, 4353 West Saanich Rd., Saanich, 1920 (ext.). **Spurgin & Johnson:** Patio Court Houses, Oak Bay, 1927 (ext.); Mount Baker Block, 1220 Newport Ave., Oak Bay, 1932 (ext.). **Spurgin & Savage:** Drill Hall, HMCS *Naden*, Esquimalt, 1936 (ext.).

STEVENS, H.L. & CO.

CVA plans; *AB&E*; *Province*; and Van. bldg. permits. **PROJECTS:** Duncan (now Shelly) Bldg., 117-123 W. Pender St., Van., 1911-12 (ext.); Molson's Bank (now Roosevelt Hotel), 150-166 E. Hastings St., Van., 1912 (ext.); Shaughnessy Lodge Apt. Bldg., 1298 W. 10th Ave., Van., 1912 (ext.).

STONE, Howard Colton

Information from Robert G. Hill; CVA plans; Royal Bank Archives, Toronto. **PROJECT:** Royal Bank, East End Branch, 400 Main St., Van., 1910 (ext.).

STROUD, Allan B.

Directories; Van. bldg. permits; CVA plans; and *Who's Who in Western Canada*, 1911, p.354. Lee Bldg. in the *Province*, Apr. 13, 1912 and Apr. 20, 1912. **PROJECT: Stroud & Keith:** Lee Bldg., 2431-2451 Main St./151-57 E. Broadway, Van., 1911-12 (ext.).

STUART, Bertram Dudley

Van. bldg. permits; CVA plans; and directories. See references to Stuart in Ochsner, *Shaping Seattle Architecture*. Notice of Dudley's move to Seattle in *PB&E*, Dec. 25, 1915, p.251. See Imbi Harding, *Sun*, Aug. 31, 2001, p.B4. **PROJECTS: B. Dudley Stuart:** Palace of Horticulture, 2901 E. Hastings St., Van., 1911 (demo.); Campbell Court, 2505-2517 Fraser St., Van., 1914 (alt.). **Stuart & White:** B.C. Wood Products (Forestry) Bldg.; 2901 E. Hastings St., Van., 1913 (demo.).

SWALES, Francis S.

Gray, *Edwardian Architecture*, pp.70-71 & 343; Service, *London 1900*, p.114; *Who's Who & Why*, 1915-16 Edition, p.1318 and 1921 Edition, pp.1517-18; Kalman, *A History of Canadian Architecture*, p.497-498; and Barrett & Windsor Liscombe, *Francis Rattenbury*. See Francis Swales, "American Architecture, with special reference to work at Washington," *Journal of the RIBA*, 26 (20 Mar. 1909), pp.325-355; response by Ernest George, Ibid., p.355. Information on the second Hotel Vancouver from *Contract Record*, Apr. 8, 1914, p.436; *The Architect*, Vol. XII, No.2, Aug. 1916, pp.81-113; and Imbi Harding, *Sun*, Oct. 12, 2001, p.B5 and Oct. 19, 2001, p.B6. **PROJECT: Painter & Swales (superseded by Swales alone):** Second Hotel Vancouver, Granville and Georgia Sts., Van., 1912-16 (demo. 1949).

SWAN, Hamilton Lindsay

Interviews with son, Denis Lindsay Swan, Vict. and grand-daufgter Valerie Hallford, Kelowna. Other sources include his obituary published in the *Sun*, Aug. 26, 1938, p.15; AIBC; a more extensive obituary in *The Engineering Journal*, Nov. 1938, p.522; and Penticton Museum & Archives. **PROJECTS:** Kettle Valley Lakeshore Station, Lakeshore Dr., Penticton, 1912 (demo.); Kettle Valley Engine House, Penticton, 1912; B.C. Growers Warehouse, Penticton, 1919; Municipal Power House, Penticton, 1919; Swan Res., 2474 McNeil Ave., Oak Bay, 1930 (ext.). **Swan & Augustine:** Maternity Hospital, Penticton, 1920-21 (alt.); Addition to Central School, 220 Cranbrook St. N., Cranbrook, 1922 (ext.).

SYME, James

H. Keith Ralston's entry in the *Dictionary of Canadian Biography*, Vol.XI, pp.866-867. Brief references to Syme may be found in various sources relating to the fishing industry, including George North & Harold Griffin, *A Ripple, A Wave: The Story of Union Organization in the B.C. Fishing Industry* (Van., The Fisherman Publishing Society, 1974) and Cicely Lyons, *Salmon: Our Heritage, The Story of a Province and an Industry* (Van., British Columbia Packers, 1969). Thanks to Brian Stauffer, University of Northern British Columbia Graduate Student, for sharing information on early canning from his yet unpublished thesis. Tender call information for fifteen projects identified by Dorothy Mindenhall. Biographical information from death certificates and obituaries for both James and Janet Syme. Information on the Irving House from *The British Columbian*, Apr. 25, 1865; Irving House attribution from Irving Collection, New West. Museum & Archives, letter from Elizabeth Briggs to Naomi Briggs, Nov. 8, 1950. **PROJECTS:** Irving House, 302 Royal Ave., New West., 1865 (ext.); First St. Joseph's Hospital, Collinson St., (now Fairfield Rd.) Vict., 1875 (demo.); *Barossa Lodge* (John Graham Res.), 441 Simcoe St., Vict., 1876 (demo.); St. Peter's Catholic Church, Wallace St. between Fitzwilliam and Wentworths Sts., Nanaimo, 1877-78 (dest. by fire 1910); A.B. Gray House (later the Chief Justice Gordon Hunter Res.), 327 Belleville St., Vict., [tender call May 31, 1877] (ext.).

TAYLOR, John Smith Davidson

AIBC; biographical information from Robert Close, Scotland; B.C. Vital Events; and his obituary. Bldg. citations from CVA plans; Van. permit records; Jack Scott, *Once in the Royal City*; and Bond, *University Endowment Lands Architecture 1940-1969*. Rae Res. from *Province*, July 6, 1912, p.25. **PROJECTS**: Hall (later Seymour St. Gospel Hall), 1181 Seymour St., Van., 1909 (demo.); Beaconsfield Apts., 884 Bute St., Van., 1909-10 (ext.); Canada Permanent Mortgage Corp. Headquarters, 432 Richards St., Van., 1911-12 (ext.); Rae Res., 3490 Cedar Cres., Van., 1912 (ext.); Willingdon Lodge, 1591 W. 16th Ave., Van., 1927 (ext.); Gloucester Court, 1565 W. 16th Ave., Van., 1928 (ext.); York Manor, 1575 W. 16th Ave., Van., 1928 (ext.); Regal Court, 1565 Harwood St., Van., 1930 (ext.); J.L. Hindin Res., 1961 Acadia Rd., Van., 1952 (ext.).

TAYLOR & GORDON

Susan Wagg's entry on A.T. Taylor in the *Grove Dictionary of Art*, 1996, Vol.30, p.385; and CAC, Accession No. 7, McGill University, Montreal. Citations for the Bank of Montreal from *Contract Record*, tender call, Mar. 12, 1892, p.1; for the Molson's Bank (under construction) in *CA&B*, May, 1898 and an illustration, Oct., 1899. Wickenden listed as supervising architect for the Bank of Montreal in *VDW*, Dec. 30, 1893, p.8. Dalton listed as supervising architect for the Molson's Bank in *Vancouver of Today Architecturally*, 1900. **PROJECTS**: Bank of Montreal, cor. Granville and Dunsmuir Sts., Van., 1892-93 (demo.); Molson's Bank, 597 W. Hastings St., Van., 1897-99 (demo.).

TEAGUE, John

The sources used for researching the life and career if John Teague are diverse with varying degrees of accuracy. Biographies appear in Kerr, *Biographical Dictionary of Well-Known British Columbians*; *The Canadian Album: Men of Canada* by Rev. Wm. Cochrane D.D. (1890); and *Victoria Illustrated 1891*, all of which are relatively inaccurate. His obituaries appeared in both the *VDT* and the *VDC* on Oct. 25, 1902 and provide limited information. An article in the *Colonist* on Apr. 2, 1950 by James K. Nesbitt is taken mostly from aforementioned sources. Kalman, *A History of Canadian Architecture*, was consulted, as were records held at the VCA including bldg. permits; tax assessment rolls; city directories; plumbing plans; cemetery records; and CRS 120 & 104. Tender calls from the *Daily Chronicle*, the *VDC* and the *VDT* helped to paint an accurate picture of the number of bldg. projects which Teague was involved in. The *Chronicles of St. Joseph's Hospital* (1875); plans at the Sisters of St. Ann's Archives; plans and government records at the BCA; and the Madge Hamilton Collection were also of great value. We are indebted to Dorothy Sweet, Christopher J.P. Hanna, and

Brad Morrison for numerous contributions. Attribution of the Cameron Bldg. in Vernon from the Vernon *News*, July 7, 1892. Dennis Minaker and Ronald Soule provided additional information. **PROJECTS**: Audit Office, Government Reserve, Vict., 1874 (demo.); Reformed Episcopal Church of Our Lord, 626 Blanshard St., Vict., 1875-76 (ext.); Vict. City Hall, #1 Centennial Sq., Vict., 1875; south wing completed 1878; additions to 1891 (ext.; enlarged); Public School, School Reserve, Fort St., Vict., 1876 (demo.); Shotbolt Drug Store, 585-587 Johnson St., Vict., 1876 (extensively alt.); Sisters of St. Ann Convent, Nanaimo, 1879 (dest. by fire 1910); Odd Fellows Vict. Lodge No.1, 1315 Government St., Vict., 1879-80 (ext.); Oriental Hotel, 550-554 Yates St., 1883, addition 1888 (ext.); *Rose Villa* (Teague Res.), 1902 Cook St., Vict., 1884 (demo. in 1959 for the expansion of Royal Athletic Park); Bldg. for Look Den, 534-534 1/2 Pandora Ave., Vict., 1884 (ext.); Storekeeper's House, now the Admiral's House, Royal Naval Dockyard, Esquimalt, 1885 (ext.); Law offices for the Honourable Theodore Davie, 69 Bastion Sq., Vict., 1885 (ext.); Chinese Consolidated Benevolent Association Bldg., 554-562 Fisgard St., Vict., 1885 (ext.); Addition to the Sisters of St. Ann Convent, 835 Humboldt St., Vict., 1886 (ext.); Occidental Hotel, 432 Fitzwilliam St., Nanaimo, 1886 (ext.); Masonic Hall, Columbia St., New West., 1887 (dest. by fire); Provincial Royal Jubilee Hospital, Vict., 1887 (demo.); Additions to St. Joseph's Hospital, Vict., 1888 (demo.); Seven bldgs. at the Naval Hospital, HMCS *Naden*, Esquimalt, 1888-91 (five bldgs. ext.); Reynolds Block, for the Canadian Pacific Land & Mortgage Co., 1300-1306 Douglas St., Vict., 1889 (alt.); Buildings for Michael Hart, 532-536 Fisgard St. and 529-539 Herald St., Vict., 1891 (ext.); *Burleith* (James Dunsmuir Res.), Craigflower Rd., Vict., 1891 (demo.); Driard Hotel, 1151 Broad St., Vict., 1891-92 (demo.; facade rebuilt as part of the Eaton's Centre redevelopment); City Market, Cormorant St., Vict., 1891-92 (demo); Res., 1012 Richardson St. (one of eight houses designed for the B.C. Land & Investment Agency Ltd.), Vict., 1892 (ext.); W.F. Cameron Store, Vernon, 1892 (demo.); Masonic Hall, Commercial St., Nanaimo, 1894 (demo.).

TEGEN, Robert F.

CVA Plans, Van. and New West. bldg. permits; and Ritz, *Architects of Oregon*. Plans for St. Mary's Hall are in the McCarter & Nairne Fonds, MCA 00H64, CAA, Calgary. Information on St. Paul's in *AB&E*, Aug. 15, 1912, p.5 and May 25, 1913, p.7; and Gladding, McBean & Co. Records, Job #1005, California State Library, Sacramento. Information on Tegen's American career from the Oregon Historical Society; Gideon Bosker & Lena Lencek, *Frozen Music: A History of Portland Architecture* (Portland: The Oregon Historical Society, 1985); the *Portland Daily Abstract*, May 5, 1909, p.5; and the United States National Register of Historic Places website. For unknown reasons his name is consistently spelled in the United States as Tegan and in

Canada as Tegen. **PROJECTS**: **R.F. Tegen:** St. Paul's Hospital, 1081 Burrard St., Van., 1912-13 (alt.); Addition to St. Mary's Hospital, Agnes and Merrivale Sts., New West., 1912-13 (demo). **Tegen & Vezina:** St. Mary's Hall for Holy Rosary Parish, Van. 1913 (unbuilt project).

THORNTON, Walter M.

Directories; and Van. bldg. permits.

TIARKS, John Gerhard

Sources of information for Tiarks included a personal meeting with his daughter-in-law, Evelyn Tiarks, who provided family history and a photograph of the family home in Victoria; and with Henry Tiarks who kindly provided the Tiarks genealogy. Newspapers consulted included the Weston-Super-Mare *Mercury*; *Nanaimo Free Press*; *The Daily Columbian*; the *VDC*; and the *VDT*. Other sources included the BCA; VCA; city directories; *Debrett's Illustrated Peerage*; the 1891 Census; Property Assessment rolls; Records for the Parliament Buildings Competition at the BCA; City of Vict. letter books; Stark, *Oak Bay's Heritage Buildings*; and correspondence to Madge Hamilton from C.C. Pemberton. *Clovelly* from *VDC*, Nov. 9, 1894, p.7. Additional information from Christopher J.P. Hanna; Colin Barr; Donald Luxton; Dorothy Harvey; Robert G. Hill; Ronald Soule; Patricia Taylor; and Dennis Minaker. **PROJECTS**: T.W. Carter Residence, 681 Herald Street, Vict., 1891 (alt.); *Kelston Wood*, Gorge Rd., Vict., 1893 (demo.); *Clovelly* (A.W. Bridgman Res.), Esquimalt Rd. (later 701 Sea Terrace), Vict. West/Esquimalt, 1894 (demo. 1960); Additions to Keating House, Kosilah, 1894 (ext.); George M. Leishman Res., 508 Dallas Rd., Vict., 1896 (alt.); *Annandale*, 1587-95 York Pl., Oak Bay, 1897-98 (ext.); *Garrison House*, York Pl., Oak Bay, 1897-98 (dest. by fire 1930s); Skene Lowe Res., 132 S. Turner St., Vict., 1897-98 (ext.); J.B.H. Rickaby Res., 148 S. Turner St., Vict., 1897-98 (demo.); *Dalzellowlie*, Old Esquimalt Rd., Esquimalt., 1898 (demo.); Hotel for the Kamloops Hotel Co., 1899 (unbuilt project). **Rattenbury and Tiarks, Joint Architects:** Bank of Montreal, 511 Columbia St., New West., 1898-99 (demo.); Bank of British Columbia (Ellis Block), 548-554 Columbia St., New West., 1898-99 (alt.); Hamley Block, 622-626 Columbia St., New West., 1898-99 (alt.).

TIEDEMANN, Hermann Otto

Colonist and *Gazette* newspaper reports and tender calls; directories; census data; B.C. Vital Events; original letters of Tiedemann and J.D. Pemberton; George Hargreaves's Journal of the 1872 Bute Inlet Canadian Pacific Railway Survey [BCA Add. MSS.443]; and marriage from the *Colonist*, Aug. 16, 1861, p.3. Research into his birth place by Brad Morrison; Dr. Thomas Bredohl, Dept. of History, UVIC; and Sebastians Siebel Achenbach, University of Waterloo. Ruggles, *A Country So Interesting*; James Nesbitt's article *Germania Sing Verein*, *Colonist*, mag. sect. Sept. 25, 1949, p.6; McIntosh, *A Documentary History of Music in Victoria, Vol.I*;

The Kirk That Faith Built: St. Andrew's on Douglas Street, 1890-1990 by The Session of St. Andrew's Presbyterian Church (1989); G. Edward Mills, Historical Building Report, Nov. 1976 for the Canadian Inventory of Historic Buildings on the Vict. Court House; Dept. of Energy Mines & Resources, Geographical Branch. The Gazetteer of Canada: British Columbia (Ottawa: Govt. of Canada, 1966); U.S. Dept. of Commerce, The United States Coast Pilot: Southeast Alaska Formerly Alaska. Part 1: Dixon Entrance to Yakutat Bay. (10th ed.; Washington, DC.: U.S. Government Press, 1952). Dr. Allan S. Arnell, archivist for St. Andrew's Presbyterian, provided material and summaries on their first church. Great grandson, Tudor H. Tiedemann, Connecticut, USA, provided some family history. Tender calls for St. Andrew's Presbyterian, Colonist, May 13, 1867, p.2 and July 9, 1868. References to Christ Church, Colonist: Jan. 21, 1872; Feb. 6, 1872 (tender call); and "The New Cathedral," Oct. 20, 1872, p.3. Quotes on the Birdcages from the Colonist, Sept. 19, 1859 and the Gazette, June 23, 1859; on Holy Trinity Anglican Church, New West. from the Colonist, Jan. 1, 1867 and May 13, 1867, p.2; and on St. Andrew's Presbyterian Church from the Colonist, Mar. 29, 1869. Sehl Factory elevator from Colonist, "City Improvements," Dec. 4, 1874. **PROJECTS**: Colonial Administration Buildings (the "Birdcages"), Vict., 1859-63 (demo.); Fisgard Light House (draftsman), Fort Rodd Hill Historic Park, Colwood, 1860 (ext.); Second Holy Trinity Church, 514 Carnarvon St., New West., 1867-68 (dest. by fire 1898 and church rebuilt incorporating the surviving walls; ext.); St. Andrew's Church, Gordon and Courtenay Sts., Vict., 1868 (demo.); Second Christ Church Cathedral, orig. Church Way (now Blanshard St.), Vict., 1871-72 (demo.); Sehl Factory, 1110-1112 Government St., Vict., 1874 and later additions (demo. c.1906); William McNiffe offices and Saloon, Government St., Vict., 1875 (demo.); Tiger Fire Co. bell tower, Johnson St., Vict., 1874 (demo.); John Wilson Bldg., 1150 Government St., Vict., 1878 (alt.); Bossi & Giesselmann Store, 632 Yates St./1303 Broad St., 1878 and later alterations (alt.); R. Rocke Robertson's Law Offices, 1150 Langley St., Vict., 1878 (ext.); Vict. Post Office, new facade, 1200 Blk. Government St., Vict., 1879-80 (demo.); E.H. Anderson Store, 565 Johnson St., Vict., 1881 (ext.); Warehouse for R. Finlayson, 1202-14 Wharf St., Vict., 1881-2 (ext.); Indian Department Bldg., southwest cor. Douglas and Courtney Sts., Vict., 1882 (demo.); Sidney J. Pitts Store, 516 Yates St., Vict., 1882 (ext.); R.P. Rithet's Outer Wharves, Shoal Point, Victoria Harbour, 1882 (demo.); R. Finlayson's Building, Cormorant St., now 538-32 Pandora Ave., Vict., 1882 (ext.); Addition to Driard Hotel, View and Broad Sts., Vict., 1883 (replaced. by 1892); Canadian Pacific Navigation office, Wharf St., Vict., 1884 (demo.); Vict. Court House, 28-30 Bastion Sq., Vict., 1887-89 (ext.); Angel Hotel, Langley St., Vict., 1890 (demo).

TOTTY, Elliott

AIBC; B.C. Vital Events; and Vict. plans, bldg. and plumbing permits. **PROJECTS**: **Totty & Semeyn**: Grace Lutheran Church Parsonage, 2307 Dowler Pl., Vict., 1922 (demo.). **Elliott Totty**: Jones Res., 1505 Bywood Pl., Vict., 1958 (ext.).

TOWLE, Arlen H.

Brandes, San Diego Architects, p.177; and Ochsner, Shaping Seattle Architecture, pp.352-353 for the early history of Towle and his partner Wilcox in Seattle. The Ledger (New West.), Apr. 12, 1890, p.3, Towle & Wilcox Advertisement; establishment of an office, May 1, 1890 p.4. The Daily Columbian, Jan. 8, 1892 p.1 notes the arrival of Towle and his wife to New West. from Seattle. The Weekly News-Advertiser, Mar. 30, 1892 p.6 "Westminster News" comments on Towle's plans for the Odd Fellows Block. The VDC, May 31, 1892, p.1 has the tender call for the Hotel Guichon. The Daily Columbian, Apr. 13, 1892 p.4 "Local & Provincial" notes the awarding of the First Presbyterian Church to Towle, and The Daily Columbian, July 9, 1892 p.4 "A Handsome Edifice" describes his plans. Gladding, McBean & Co. Records, Jobs #183 & #184, California State Library, Sacramento. Additional information from Dennis A. Andersen. **PROJECTS**: Duncan-Batchelor Block, Columbia St., New West., 1891-92 (dest. by fire 1898); Odd Fellows Block, Columbia St., New West., 1891-92 (dest. by fire 1898); Curtis-Burns Block, Columbia St., New West., 1891-92 (dest. by fire 1898); Hotel Guichon, Columbia and McKenzie Sts., New West., 1891-92 (dest. by fire 1898); Two brick duplexes, 1002-1008 Third Ave., New West., 1892 (ext.); First Presbyterian Church, E. Hastings St. at Gore Ave., Van., 1892-93 (demo. 1963).

TOWNLEY & MATHESON

Interviews with Esmée Townley Mansell, daughter of Fred Townley, who graciously provided information about her father and his practice; Mrs. Mansell's collection of photographs is now in CVA Add.MSS.1417. Mrs. Mansell identified a number of her father's residential designs. Further information from Mrs. B.J. Warner and Claudia Paton, daughters of Robert Matheson. Telephone interview with the late Allan C. Kelly, who began work in the office in 1928, was the project architect for Van. City Hall, and remained involved with the firm until its closure; after his death in 2001 the large collection of Townley & Matheson plans in his possession were donated to the CVA [Add. MSS.1399] and further information will surface as they are catalogued. Other biographical information and bldg. citations from AIBC; CVA; and plans held at Van. City Hall. Information on the Mathesons is held in CVA Add.MSS.491. The story of Van. City Hall is covered in David Monteyne, "From Canvas to Concrete in Fifty Years: The Construction of Vancouver City Hall, 1935-6," B.C. Studies 124 (Winter 1999/2000), and in David Ricardo Williams, Mayor Gerry: The Remarkable Gerald Grattan McGeer (Van.: Douglas & McIntyre,

1986). Information on De Guerre from B.C. Vital Events. **PROJECTS**: **Fred L. Townley**: Benwell Res. (later Lort Res.), 7250 Oak St., Van., 1912 (demo.); Deerholme, 6110-76 Price St., Burnaby, 1913 (ext.); Great Northern Railway Terminus, Station St., Van., 1913-17 (demo. 1960s). **Bryan & Townley**: Van. Club Competition entry, 1912 (unbuilt project). **J.P. Matheson & Son**: North-West Trust (now the Lumberman's) Bldg., 509 Richards St., Van., 1911-12 (ext.); Caroline Court Apts., 1058 Nelson St., Van., 1912 (ext.). **Matheson & De Guerre**: First Church of Christ Scientist, 1160 W. Georgia St., Van., 1918 (ext.). **Townley & Matheson**: Frederick M. Kelly Res., 1398 The Crescent, Van., 1921 (ext.); Hugh MacLean Res., 1264 Balfour Ave., Van., 1924 (ext.); W.A. Akhurst Res., 1354 Balfour Ave., Van., 1924 (demo.); Fred Townley Res., 1636 Avondale Ave., Van., 1926 (ext.); Buckerfield Res., 2040 S.W. Marine Dr., Van., 1926 (ext.); Grouse Mountain Chalet, North Van. Dist., 1926 (dest. by fire 1962); Columbia (now Burr) Theatre, 528-538 Columbia St., New West., 1927 (ext.); Tudor Manor Apts., 1311 Beach Ave., Van., 1927-28 (only facade retained); Dick Bldg., 2516 Granville St., Van., 1928 (ext.); Stock Exchange, 475 Howe St., Van., 1928 (ext.); Point Grey Secondary School, 5350 E. Boulevard, Van., 1928-29 (ext.); J.A. Collins Res., 5326 Connaught Dr., Van., 1929 (ext.); Matheson Res., 5234 Connaught Dr., Van., 1929 (ext.); Renovations for Gilbert & Cohen and Permanent Investment Co. (later the Canadian Imperial Bank of Commerce), 817-819 Granville St., Van., 1929 (ext.); Sir Alexander MacKenzie School, 960 E. 39th Ave., Van., 1929-30 (ext.); Bldg. for B.C. Leaseholders, 555 Granville St., Van., 1930 (facade ext.); Causeway Tower, 812 Wharf St., Vict., 1931 (alt.); St. Louis College, 1002 Pandora Ave., Vict., 1931 (ext.); McLuckie Bldg., 797 W. Georgia St., Van., 1931-32 (demo.); Canadian Linen Supply, 1200 Richards St., Van., 1932 (ext.); Van. City Hall, 453 W. 12th Ave., Van., 1935-36 (ext.); Van. General Hospital, 700-800-blocks W. 12th Ave., Van., 1937-60s (ext.); Educational Bldg. (now the Garden Auditorium), 2901 E. Hastings St., Van., 1939-40 (ext.).

TOWNSEND & TOWNSEND

Extensive searches of British, Canadian and American sources has not confirmed where they came from before 1909 or where they went after 1913. Quote from Lort, Old Houses and Buildings in Vancouver. Information on bldgs. from Van. municipal records; references in AB&E; Contract Record citations from Robert G. Hill. Reference to Thompson's Hotel in the Contract Record of Mar. 31, 1909. **PROJECTS**: Hotel for Mrs. P. Thompson, Columbia St., New West., 1909 (alt.); James Goldie Mutch Res., 2646 Yukon St., Van., 1910-11 (ext.); Mount Stephen Block (now Quebec Manor), 101 E. 7th Ave., Van., 1911-12 (ext.); Tamura Bldg., 394-396 Powell St., Van., 1912-14 (ext.).

TRIMEN, Leonard Buttress

Colonist tender calls; B.C. Vital Events; BCA files; VCA photographic collection; International Genealogical Index; UK census data. *Ashnola* from VDC, Jan. 1, 1889, Supplement, p.2. Brackman-Ker from *VDC*, Apr. 10, 1889 and Apr. 27, 1889. Flouring Mill from *VDC*, Apr. 11, 1890. **PROJECTS:** Vict. City Hall, north-west wing, #1 Centennial Sq., Vict., (1888, ext.); Caton Residences, James Bay, Vict., 1888; Hamley Block, 622-626 Columbia St., New West., 1888-89 (dest. by fire 1898); Bushby Block, 630-638 Columbia St., New West., 1888-89 (dest. by fire 1898); *Ashnola* (Snowden Res.), Gorge Rd., Vict., 1888-89 (demo. 1971); Brackman-Ker Bldg., 1407 Government St., Vict., 1889 (alt.); St. Andrew's Presbyterian Church, 924 Douglas St., Vict., 1889-90 (ext.); *Mount Adelaide* (Henry Croft Res.), 819 (847) Dunsmuir Rd., 1890 (demo.); Colonial Metropole Hotel, 547-561 Johnson St., Vict., 1890 (central bldg. and east wing ext., west wing demo.); Saunder's Groceries, 561-563 Johnson St., Vict., 1890 (alt.); Five stores on Johnson St. and two on Oriental Alley for E. H. Anderson (567-569 Johnson St., 1890, ext.; remainder unknown); Flouring Mill, 1824 Store St. Vict. 1890 (ext.); Elworthy Res., James Bay, Vict., 1890; Brick Bldg. for Powell & Currall, near Johnson St., 1891; Lodge and Gateway for *Craigdarroch Castle*, Vict., 1891 (demo.).

TROUNCE, Thomas

Photographs, newspapers; directories; BCA; VCA; and the Nanaimo Community Archives. Newspaper citations from the Vict. *Daily Standard*; *The Chronicle*; the Vict. *Times*; the *Cariboo Sentinel*; and the *Colonist*. Additionally, Voters' Lists; Death Registration Indexes; the 1891 Census Records; Cause Books for Civil Pleas for the British Columbia Supreme Court; his obituary in the *Colonist*, July 1, 1900, p.2; and Letter Books of the City of Vict. were consulted. Contract for bldg. Holy Trinity, New West from Cariboo *Sentinel*, July 1, 1867 and the *British Columbian*, June 19, 1867 p.3: Local Briefs. Additional information from Christopher J.P. Hanna and Donald Luxton. Notes from Madge Hamilton's Collection in the author's possession. Additional primary research by Dorothy Mindenhall on Trounce's activities at Royal Naval Dockyard. **PROJECTS:** Trounce Res., Kane St., Vict., 1859 (demo.); *Tregew*, 436 Menzies St., Vict., 1861 (demo. 1967); St. Paul's Anglican Church (originally the Naval & Garrison Church), 1379 Esquimalt Rd., Esquimalt, 1866 (ext.); "Church & Day School for the use of the Indians," Herald St., Vict., 1874 (demo.); *Armadale*, James Bay, 241 Niagara St., Vict., 1876-77 (demo. 1940s); Hirst Warehouse and Docks, Front St., Nanaimo, 1875 (partially ext., alt.); Weiler Warehouse (The Counting House), 1005-09 Broad St./636 Broughton St., Vict., 1879 (ext.); Morley's Soda Works, 1315-1317 Waddington Alley, Vict., 1884 (ext.).

TURNBULL, William

"Laying the corner stone of the new St. Ann's Convent," from the New West. *Mainland Guardian*, Aug. 18, 1877, p.3. Biography in *The British Columbian* Mar. 18, 1912, p1 "Death of A Pioneer."

TWIZELL & TWIZELL

Personal communication with Mrs. Barbara Speirs, the daughter of R.P.S. Twizell. Other information from AIBC; B.C. Vital Events; Felstead et al, *Directory of British Architects 1834-1900*; *MacMillan Encyclopedia of Architects*, The Free Press, New York, 1982, Vol.3, p.1982; *AB&E*, Aug. 15, 1912; CVA Plans and Add.MSS.166; photograph and biography in *Museum Notes*, June 1926 (CVA 'Museum' file); *Province*, Apr. 13, 1912, p.30; RAIC *Journal*, May 1926, p.130, Jan. 1927, p.39, Jan. 1934, pp.2-5 and Feb. 1957, p.64; Van. bldg. permits, and city directories. See Kluckner, *Vanishing Vancouver*, p.126. **PROJECTS: Twizell & Twizell:** *Fairacres* (now the Gallery at Ceperley House), 6344 Deer Lake Ave., Burnaby, 1911 (ext.); St. George's Anglican Church, 2960 Laurel St., Van., 1911 (demo.); Christian Science Church, 796 E. 17th Ave., Van., 1911 (alt.); St. John the Divine Anglican Church, Quesnel, 1912 (ext.); J.W. Kerr Res., 1575 Laurier Ave., Van., 1912 (ext.); Dr. A.L. Johnson Res., 2395 Balsam St., Van., 1912 (demo.); Twizell duplex, 3036 W. 8th Ave., Van., 1913 (ext.); Walter Walsh Res., 1646 Laurier Ave., Van., 1913 (ext.); W.L. Coulthard Res., 1511 Marpole St., Van., 1913 (ext.); M.P. Morris Res., 1950 Cedar Cres., Van., 1913 (ext.); Queen Mary Elementary School, 2000 Trimble St., Van., 1914 (ext.); Shaughnessy School (now Emily Carr Elementary School), 4070 Oak St., Van., 1917 (ext.); Edith Cavell Elementary School, 500 W. 20th Ave., Van., 1919 (ext.); Prince of Wales High School (now Shaughnessy Elementary School), 4250 Marguerite St., Van., 1920 (ext.); David Lloyd George Elementary School, 8370 Cartier St., Van., 1920 (ext.); William More Res. 1629 W. 29th Ave., Van., 1921 (ext.); Van. College, 1356 W. 38th Ave., Van., 1924-27 (ext.); Canadian Memorial United Church, 1806 W. 15th Ave., Van., 1927 (ext.); Mount St. Joseph's Hospital, 3080 Prince Edward St., Van., 1927 (ext.); St. Saviour's Anglican (Episcopal) Church, Penticton, 150 Orchard Ave., Penticton, 1929-30 (ext.); Willoughby Elementary School, 20766 80th Ave., Township of Langley, 1931 (ext.); St. Augustine's Roman Catholic Church, 2015 W. 8th Ave., Van., 1931 (ext.); St. Andrew's-Wesley United Church, 1012 Nelson St., Van., 1931-33 (ext.); St. Michael & All Angels Anglican Church, 2498 Prince Edward St., Van., 1932 (ext.); Christ Church Cathedral (chancel), 690 Burrard St., Van., 1934 (ext.); Richmond High School addition (now Cambie Junior Secondary School), 3751 Sexsmith St., Richmond, 1937 (ext.); St. Peter's Roman Catholic Church, Royal Ave. and 4th St., New West., 1939 (ext.); St. Phillip's Anglican Church, 3737 W. 27th Ave., Van., 1941 (ext.); West Point Grey United Church, 4595 W. 8th Ave., Van., 1941 (ext.); Burnaby Lake United Church, now Deer Lake United, 5135 Sperling Ave., Burnaby, 1941 (ext.); Blessed Sacrament Roman Catholic Church, 3050 Heather St., Van., 1948 (ext.); Knox United Church, 5600 Balaclava St., Van., 1948 (ext.); St. Giles United Church, 305 W. 41st Ave., Van., 1949 (ext.); West Burnaby United Church, 6050 Sussex Ave., Burnaby, 1948 (ext.); Dunbar Heights United Church, 3527 W. 24th Ave., Van., 1950-51 (ext.); Kimberley United Church, 10 Boundary St., Kimberley, 1951 (ext.); Willingdon Heights United Church, 4304 Parker St., Burnaby, 1952 (ext.); Chilliwack United Church, 45835 Spadina Ave., Chilliwack, 1954 (ext.); Vernon United Church, 2602 Barnard St., Vernon, 1954 (dest. by fire); Windsor United Church, 4720 Elgin St., Van., 1956 (ext.). **Twizell, Birds, & Twizell:** David Lloyd George Elementary School, 8370 Cartier St., Van., 1920 (ext.); William More Res., 1629 W. 29th Ave., Van., 1921 (ext.); Mrs. W.E. Blair house, 1550 Harwood St., Van., 1921 (demo.); Wright Res., 2039 W. 35th Ave., Van., 1921 (demo.); Kerrisdale Elementary School, 5555 Carnarvon St., Van., 1921-24 (ext.).

UNDERWOOD, Percy C.

AIBC; Aero Club project from the *Sun*, Mar. 12, 1938. **PROJECT**: Proposed Aero Club Headquarters, Sea Island Airport, Richmond, 1938 (unbuilt project).

VAN NORMAN, Charles Burwell Kerrens

AIBC; CVA Add.MSS.755; Sean Rossiter, "House That Charlie Built Rests on Shaky Ground," *Sun*, Apr. 9, 1994, p.D7; Powell River Co. Store from the Powell River *Digester*, Mar./Apr. 1947. **PROJECTS**: Revelstoke City Hall, 216 Mackenzie Ave., Revelstoke, 1938-39 (ext.); Company Store, 5831 Ash St., Powell River, 1940-41 (ext.).

VAN SICLEN, William Doty

Van. bldg. permits and directories; and Edmonton Municipal Heritage Resources Inventory. Biographical information from Ochsner, *Shaping Seattle Architecture*, p.353. Information on Lewis E. Macomber from Ritz, *Architects of Oregon*.

VERHEYDEN, Charles

Tender calls and news items in the *Colonist*; Colonial Correspondence [BCA GR-1372]; and the Archives of the Sisters of St. Ann. **PROJECTS:** Theatre, Douglas St., Vict., 1859-60 (demo.); New Hotel de France, Government and Broad Sts., Vict., 1869 (demo.).

VULLINGHS, Father Adrian Joseph

Photographs and notebook pages of Vullinghs, along with a brief biography, are published in Charles Lillard, *Paths Our Ancestors Walked, Father Vullinghs & the Saanich Peninsula 1893-1909* (Vict., 1977). Documentation concerning the St. Ann's Academy garden is held by the Provincial Capital Commission, Vict.

WARD INVESTMENT COMPANY

Vict. plans, bldg. and plumbing permits; directories; inventories; *VDT*; and *VDC*. **PROJECTS: Ward Investment Co.:** Res., 124 Linden Ave., Vict., 1912 (ext.); residence, 436 Kipling St., Vict., 1914 (ext.). **Alex G.L. Lindsay:** Res. for **Ward Investment Co.**, 120 Linden Ave., Vict., 1912 (ext.).

WARREN, Jesse Milton

Directories; *PB&E*; *AB&E*; Vict. plans, bldg. and plumbing permits; Esquimalt Archives; 1913 *Year Book of the B.C. Society of architects*; *The Contract Record*, June 3, 1914, page 731; inventories; Segger & Franklin, *Exploring Victoria's Architecture*; California Death Index; California obituary in the Santa Barbara *News*, Sept. 2, 1953, p. B2; local obituaries in *VDT*, Sept. 2, 1953, p.2, and Sept. 3, 1953, p.15. **PROJECTS:** Central Bldg., 620 View St., Vict., 1911-13 (ext.); Bungalows, 2018 and 2024 Stanley St., Vict., 1912 (ext.); Little Res., 1022 Chamberlain St., Vict., 1912 (ext.); Belbeck Res., 1124 Dallas Rd., Vict., 1912, (ext.); First Baptist Church, Fisgard and Vancouver Sts., Vict., 1912 (unbuilt project); Pantages Theatre (now McPherson Playhouse), #3 Centennial Sq., Vict., 1912-14 (ext.); Hudson's Bay Block House for Vict.-Van. Island Exhibit, 1913 (demo.); Station (later Comus) Hotel, 501 Pandora/1441 Store Sts., Vict., 1913 (ext.); Office Bldg. for R.T. Elliott, Vict., c.1913 (unbuilt project); Sands Funeral Home (now an apartment block), 1612 Quadra St., Vict., 1915 (ext.).

WATKINS, Charles Elwood

Information provided by son, Thomas Watkins, and grandson, David Watkins; other information from Watkins's obituary. Other citations from AIBC; *AB&E*; *PB&E*; Douglas Franklin; *Early School Architecture in B.C.*; inventories; citations provided by Robert G. Hill; and Vict. plans, bldg. and plumbing permits. Information on the Watkins's summer property is from Ursula Jupp, *Gordon Head: From Cordwood to Campus in Gordon Head 1852-1959* (Victoria: Ursula Jupp, 1975), and Saanich Municipal Archives. **PROJECTS:** Watkins Res., 1117 Rockland Ave., Vict., 1904-05 (demo.); Vict. High School, 1260 Grant St., Vict., 1910-14 (ext.); Lee Block, 1618-1628 Government St./565 Fisgard St., Vict., 1910 (ext.); Hook Sin Tong Charity Bldg., 658-66 Herald St., Vict., 1911 (ext.); Lee's Benevolent Association, 612-14 Fisgard St., Vict., 1911 (ext.); P.A. Babbington Res., 1135 McClure St., Vict., 1911 (ext.); Walter Luney Res., 1566 Hampshire Rd., Oak Bay, 1916, (ext.); William Luney Res., 630 Foul Bay Rd., Vict., 1916 (ext.); Royal Oak Burial Park Crematorium Chapel and Retort, 4673 Falaise Dr., Saanich, 1937 (ext.); Saanich Pioneer Society Museum, 7910 East Saanich Rd., Central Saanich, 1932-33 (ext.).

WATSON, Henry Barton

Attributions come from a variety of period newspapers and magazines; B.C. Hydro Archives; BCER Company Records, UBC; and F.G. Consultants, *Langley's Heritage*. Short biographical entry in

Who's Who in Canada 1925-26, p.1612; California Death Index; and funeral notice in the Los Angeles *Times*, Feb. 5, 1946, p.8. Further information from Robert G. Hill. See Imbi Harding, *Sun*, Aug. 17, 2001, p.B2. **PROJECTS:** Queen Alexandra School, 1300 E. Broadway, Van., 1908 (ext.); Florence Court (now Banff) Apts., 1201 W. Georgia St., Van., 1909 (ext.); St. Patrick's Catholic Church, Main St. and 12th Ave., Van., 1909 (demo. 2002); Industrial Bldg., Hastings Park, 2901 E. Hastings St., Van., 1909-10 (demo. 1930s); B.C. Electric Railway Substations at Cloverdale (Surrey), Langley (6835 256 St., ext.), Clayburn (Abbotsford), Sumas (Abbotsford, ext.) and Central Chilliwack (Young St., demo. 1961), 1909-10; Kitsilano Presbyterian Church, 1855 Vine St., Van., 1910 (alt.).

WATSON, Joseph Francis "Doc"

AIBC; B.C. Vital Events; *Who's Who in British Columbia, 1940-1941*; Howay & Schofield, *British Columbia: Biographical*, 1914, Vol.III, p.172; his war records in the National Archives of Canada, Ottawa; and an interview with John Y. McCarter and William G. Leithead by Harold Kalman, 1972, transcription by the CAA, Calgary. Further information from Joan McCarter. Tudor Inn from *The British Columbian*, Nov. 18, 1938, p.6. St. Alban's from Anglican Archives, Diocese of New West. Further information provided by Joan McCarter. **PROJECTS:** Kwong On Wo Stores & Apts., New West., 1913 (demo.); Shakespeare Memorial, Stanley Park, 1935 (ext.); Elks Bldg., 435-439 Columbia St., New West., 1936 (demo. 1980s); St Alban's Anglican Church, 7260 St. Albans Rd., Richmond, 1949-50 (ext.). **Watson & Blackadder:** Empire Stevedoring Bldg., 395 Railway St., Van., 1940 (ext.); Tudor Inn, 187 176 St., Surrey, 1938 (ext.). **Watson & Baxter:** Collier's Ltd. Automobile Showroom, 450 W. Georgia St., Van., 1948 (ext.).

WENYON, George H.

Directories; Van. bldg. permits; and B.C. Society of Architects *Year Book*, 1913. **PROJECT:** Addition to Woodward's Department Store, 101 W. Hastings St., 1913 (alt.).

WHITBURN, James Boulton

AIBC; Scott, *Once in the Royal City*; the *New Westminster Heritage Resource Inventory*; and *The Daily News*, Sept. 25, 1912, p.1: "Burnaby Welcomes Duke of Connaught." **PROJECTS:** Trapp Technical School (later John Robson School), 120 Eighth St., New West., 1928 (ext.); Richard McBride School, 331 Richmond St., New West., 1929 (ext.); Spanish Colonial Revival Seaman's Institute Bldg., 533 Clarkson St., New West., 1929 (demo.); Whitburn Res., 217 Fourth Ave., New West., 1927 (ext.).

WHITE, William P.

Entry by Dennis A. Andersen & Katheryn H. Krafft in Ochsner, *Shaping Seattle Architecture*, p.353. Local attributions from period newspapers; bldg. magazines; and inventories. **PROJECTS:**

Bonaventure Apts., 1041 Comox St., Van., 1910-11 (ext.); Engelsea Lodge, 2046 Beach Ave., Van., 1911 (dest. by fire 1982); Allen Bldg. (now the Highland Apts.), 1932-1938 Commercial Dr./1707 E. 3rd Ave., Van., 1911 (ext.); Port Manager's House, 7620 No. 2 Rd., Richmond, 1911 (ext.); Sylvia Court Apts., 1154 Gilford St., Van., 1912 (ext.); Buchanan Bldg., 1124-1126 Robson St., Van., 1912 (ext.); Store & Apts., 2296 W. 4th Ave./2011-15 Vine St., Van., 1912 (ext.); Leonard Apts. (now Wenonah Apts.), 2703-2707 Main St./156 E. 11th Ave., Van., 1912 (ext.); Del Mar Hotel, 555 Hamilton St., Van., 1912 (ext.).

WHITEHEAD, Edwin A.

Vancouver Heritage Resource Inventory, Phase II; directories; *CA&B*; and information from Robert G. Hill. **PROJECT:** Seymour School #1, 1130 Keefer St., Van., 1900 (ext.).

WHITEHEAD, Herbert Thomas

Directories; B.C. Vital Events; *AB&E*; obituary in *VDC*, Mar. 10, 1936, p.3; inventories; VCA; Vict. plans, bldg. and plumbing permits. **PROJECTS:** Wilkerson Res., 1392 Rockland Ave., Vict., 1913 (ext.); Alderton Res., 1119 Princess St., Vict., 1913 (ext.); Wightman Res., 213 St. Charles St., Vict., 1913 (ext.); Whitehead Res., 1318 Prillaman Ave., Saanich, c.1913 (ext.); Apt. Bldg. for Frederick C. Pink, cor. Cook and Mackenzie Sts., Vict., 1914 (demo.).

WHITEWAY, William Tuff

AIBC; Van. bldg. permits; *CA&B*; Brandes, *San Diego Architects*, p.159 & 199; and contemporary newspaper and journal references. Tender call for the Duck Block, *Colonist*, Feb. 21, 1892. Biographical information provided through ongoing correspondence with Whiteway's grandson, Herbert A. Layfield, Whittier, California. Additions to Van. City Hall from original contract [CVA 10-A-1 File 7, p.163-166] and City Council Minutes [CVA]; quote from the Van. *Herald*, Nov. 19. 1886. Other information from the Public Archives of Nova Scotia; Maud Rosinski, *Architects of Nova Scotia: A Biographical Dictionary 1605-1950*, pp.179-180; Mills, *Architectural Trends in Victoria*; and *Vancouver Voters 1886*. Plans for the Kamloops Public School in the collection of the Kamloops Museum & Archives. **PROJECTS:** Ferguson Block, 6 Powell St., Van., 1886-87 (ext.); Fire Hall No.1, Water St., Van., 1886 (demo.); Additions to Van. City Hall, 137-141 Powell St., Van., 1886-87 (demo.); Duck Block, 1314-1322 Broad St., Vict., 1892 (ext.); Van. High School, 951 W. 12th Ave., Van., 1903 (dest. by fire); Woodward's Department Store, 101 W. Hastings St., 1903 (alt.); Kelly Douglas Warehouse, 316 Water St., Van., 1905 (ext.); Woods Hotel, 412 Carrall St., Van., 1906 (ext.); MacDonald School, 1950 E. Hastings St./1955 E. Pender St., Van., 1906 (ext.); City Market, Main St., Van., 1906-08 (dest. by fire 1920s); Kamloops Public School (now Stuart Wood School), 245 St. Paul St., Kamloops, 1906-07 (ext.);

Admiral Seymour School, 1130 Keefer St., Van., 1907 (ext.); Lord Roberts School, 1100 Bidwell St., Van., 1907-08 (ext.); Commercial Hotel, Hope, B.C., 1910; Holden Bldg., 12 E. Hastings St., Van., 1910-11 (ext.); Storey & Campbell Warehouse, 518 Beatty St., Van., 1911 (ext.); World Bldg., later the Sun Tower, 100 W. Pender St., Van., 1911-12 (ext.); Hotel for Leon Melikov (now the St. Regis); 602 Dunsmuir St., Van., 1912 (ext.); Duncan Elementary School, 1035 Nagle St., Duncan, 1913 (ext.); St. Margaret Apts., 1104 Haro St., Van., 1927 (alt.); The Normandie Apts., 1425 Haro St., Van., 1927 (ext.); Viola Court, 1206 Haro St., Van., 1927 (demo.).

WHITTAKER, Henry

AIBC; inventories; *Riverview Heritage Evaluation*; CVA Add.MSS.315; BCA Add.MSS.651; B.C. Vital Events; and BCA Photograph HP-83643. Numerous sets of plans and specifications in Government records at BCA; including Point Grey School GR-0054 Box 36 File 519; and Ocean Falls School GR-0054 Box 46 File 600. Plans of the Powell River Provincial Bldg. are in the possession of the current owners; the bldg. was described in the *Powell River News*, Aug. 3, 1939, p.6. Plans for the Printing Bureau are in the possession of BCBC. For the Tranquille Sanatorium see Norton, *A Whole Little City by Itself*; copies of plans for the Tranquille Buildings are held at the Kamloops Museum & Archives. Whittaker's personal collection of 1,800 photographs is held by the VPL. **PROJECTS: Provincial Department of Public Works, H. Whittaker, Chief Architect:** Point Grey School, 4055 Blenheim St., Van., 1914 (ext.); Ocean Falls School, Ocean Falls, 1918; Boys' Industrial Training School, Essondale, 500 Lougheed Hwy., Coquitlam, 1920-22 (ext.); Prince Rupert Court House, 401 Market Place, Prince Rupert, 1920-23 (ext.); Acute Psychopathic Wing, Essondale, 500 Lougheed Hwy., Coquitlam, 1922-24 (ext.); Bungalows (H.E. Nelson, Project Architect), Tranquille, 1922 (ext.); Farm Boarding House (G.S. Ford, Project Architect), Tranquille, 1923 (ext.); Printing Bureau (now Queen's Printer), 563 Superior St., Vict., 1926-27 (ext.); New Sanatorium (also known as the Greaves Bldg.; G.S. Ford, Project Architect), Tranquille, 1927-28 (ext.); Female Chronic Wing, Essondale, 500 Lougheed Hwy., Coquitlam, 1928-30 (ext.); Salmon Arm Provincial Bldg. and Court House, 3715 Hudson St., Salmon Arm, 1929-30 (ext.); Veterans' Unit, Essondale, 500 Lougheed Hwy., Coquitlam, 1930-34 (ext.; additions in 1949); Powell River Provincial Bldg. and Court House, now the Old Courthouse Inn & Hostel, 6243 Walnut St., Powell River, 1938-39 (ext.); B.C. Power Commission Bldg., 780 Blanshard St., Vict., 1939-40 (ext.); Mount St. Mary's Hospital, 999 Burdett Ave., Vict., 1940 (ext.); Recreational Bldg. (C.D. Campbell, Project Architect), Tranquille, 1940 (ext.); Addition to the Nurses' Home, 841 Fairfield Rd., Vict., 1942 (demo. 2000); Maternity (later Richmond) Pavilion at the Royal Jubilee Hospital, 1900 Fort St., Vict., 1944-46 (alt.); Douglas Bldg., 617 Government St., Vict., 1949-51 (ext.). **Whittaker**

& Wagg: Federal Bldg. and Custom House, 816 Government St., Vict., 1956 (alt.).

WICKENDEN, Charles Osborn

References from *CA&B*; B.C. Vital Events; *Van. Daily News-Advertiser* Sept. 27, 1891, p.4; obituary in *Province*, Dec. 8, 1934, p.2; Margaret Archibald, *By Federal Design*; and Mills & Sommer, *Vancouver Architecture*, p.246 & p.278. Information on the Kalamalka Hotel provided by the Greater Vernon Museum & Archives; Bank of British North America, Van. Club and other citations from *VDW*, Dec. 30, 1893, p.8. BNA Bank from *VDW*, Oct. 15, 1891, p.8 and *VDW*, Dec. 31, 1892, p.6. Arcade Building from *Contract Record* [Toronto], vol.v, June 21, 1894, p.2. Quote about BNA Bank from *CA&B*, B.C. Letter II, July 1899, p.137. Specifications for Bank of British North America, Rossland, in BCA MS-1424. Competition drawing for Presbyterian Church published in *CA&B*, July, 1903, Vol.16, No.7. **PROJECTS:** Lefevre Block (also known as the Empire Bldg.), 601 W. Hastings St., 1888 (demo.); Innes-Thompson Block, 518 W. Hastings St., Van., 1889 (demo.); Christ Church Cathedral, 690 Burrard St., Van., 1889-95 (ext.); Kalamalka Hotel, 3004 30th Ave., Vernon, 1891 (radically alt.); Hudson's Bay Co. Store, Granville and Georgia, 1891-93 (demo. 1926); Bank of British North America, 501 W. Hastings St., Van., 1891-93 (demo. 1925); Van. Club, Hastings St., Van., 1893 (demo.); HBC Warehouse, 321-325 Water St., Van., 1894 (ext.); The Arcade, 201-207 W. Hastings St. at Cambie St., Van., 1894-95 (demo.); Bank of British North America, Rossland, 1897 (demo.); Municipal Hall, E. 1st St. and Lonsdale Ave., North Van. City, c.1906 (demo.).

WILKINS, Edmund O.

Directories; BCA photos; Vict. plans, bldg. and plumbing permits; *AB&E*; inventories; and Saanich Municipal Archives.

WILLIAMS, Warren Heywood

Extracted from "In Search of Craigdarroch's Holy Grail," *Castle Quarterly* 43:2 (Spring 2000), the Newsletter of the Craigdarroch Castle Historical Museum Society, and printed with their permission. Additional information from Ritz, *Architects of Oregon*. Gladding, McBean & Co. Records, 1889, California State Library, Sacramento. The bank is described in *VDC*, Jan. 1, 1886. See Fred DeWolfe, *Heritage Lost: Two Grand Portland Houses Through the Lens of Minor White* (Portland: Oregon Historical Society in collaboration with The Portland Art Museum, 1995). **PROJECTS:** Bank of British Columbia, 1020-1022 Government St., Vict., 1885-86 (ext.); *Craigdarroch Castle*, 1050 Joan Cres., Vict., 1887-90 (ext.).

WILLIAMS, William Frederick

Information from daughter, Joan Thomas, Kaslo; AIBC; B.C. Vital Events; Elspeth Cowell, *W.F. Williams (1904-1947): On the Edge of Modernism*, Master's thesis, Carleton University, 1993; Elspeth

Cowell, "The Canadian Pavilion at the 1939 New York World's Fair and the Development of Modernism in Canada," *Journal of the Society for the Study of Architecture in Canada*, 19:1 (Mar. 1994), pp.13-20; "Australian Brings Fame to B.C.," *Province*, Saturday Magazine, Mar. 1, 1941, p.2; *Western Homes & Living*, Jan., 1958, p.39; obituary from Royal Victorian Institute of Architects [Australia] *Quarterly Bulletin*, April 1948, p.12; telephone interview with Chris Fairbanks, Nelson; and information from Sherry Nicholson, Cominco Mines, Trail. Collections of Williams's plans held by the CAA, Calgary, and Cominco, Trail. Further information on Ilsa Williams from Julie Willis, *Women in Architecture in Victoria 1905-1955*, pp.227-229. (PhD thesis, University of Melbourne, Australia, 1997). Renovation of Palm Dairies from Victoria building permit #10101, May 26, 1937. **PROJECTS**: Renovation of Palm Dairies, 930-932 North Park St., Vict., 1937 (demo.); Masonic Temple, Trail, 1937-38 (ext.); Tadanac Hall for Cominco Ltd., Trail, 1938 (demo.); Consolidated Mining & Smelting Co. Workers Housing, Warfield, 1938-39; Cafeteria & Pattern Storage Bldg. for Cominco, Trail, 1940-41 (ext.).

WILLS, Herbert Winkler

Gray, *Edwardian Architecture*, p.386.

WILSON, Henry

AIBC; directories; B.C. Vital Events; and biographical information from Robert Close, Scotland. **PROJECTS**: City Hall, Prince George, 1917; Hospital, Prince George, 1918; Bank of Montreal, Prince George, 1919; Soldiers' Housing Act Houses, Prince George, 1919.

WILSON, J. Lennox

Directories; Vict. plans, bldg. and plumbing permits; and Kluckner & Atkin, *Heritage Walks Around Vancouver*. **PROJECT:** Burgess Res., 1251 Victoria Ave., Oak Bay, 1912 (ext.).

WILSON, John R.

Directories; *Seattle Post Intelligencer*; *AB&E*; *PB&E*; *VDC*; Howay & Schofield, *British Columbia: Biographical*, Vol.III, p.540-543; *Victoria Architecturally*, *The Week*; inventories; VCA; Vict. plans, bldg. and plumbing permits. Emily Carr's comments from *The House of All Sorts*, first published 1944. **PROJECTS**: Douglas Hallam Res., 671 Beacon St., 1909 (alt.); Heisterman Res., 1521 Elford St., Vict., 1910 (ext.); Cane Res., 1527 Coldharbour Rd., Vict., 1911 (demo.); Wilson Res., 140 (originally 136) St. Andrews St., Vict., 1911 (ext.); Harvey House, St. Michael's University School, 3400 Richmond Rd., Saanich, 1911 (dest. by arson); "House of All Sorts" (Emily Carr Res.), 642-646 Simcoe St., Vict., 1913-14 (ext.).

WILSON, Robert

AIBC; B.C. Vital Events; CVA plans; and Van. bldg. permits. **PROJECT**: Huntley Lodge Apts., 3050 Oak St., Van., 1927 (alt.).

WILSON, William Ridgway-

Biographical sketch in the 1892 *Williams' B.C. Directory*; contemporary published accounts; marriage in *VDC*, April 25, 1889; and his obituary in the *Colonist*, Feb. 23, 1957, p.18. Other information from the VCA; Madge Hamilton Collection; Vict. plans, bldg. and plumbing permits; *AB&E*; references in the *Colonist*; B.C. Vital Events; 1904 city directories; family members; and interviews by Dennis Minaker with surviving family members. Buildings identified through tender calls; inventories; *Victoria Architecturally*, 1911; Segger, *Exploring Victoria's Architecture*; and Underhill, *The Iron Church*. Nanaimo Opera House citation from John Cass File No.2/2, Nanaimo Community Archives. Information on the Provincial Asylum from BCA GR-0070 Box 1, File 15; and the *Colonist*, June 9, 1897, p.5. The description of Sir Horace Jones is from Colvin, *Biographical Dictionary of London Architects*. Wilson's name is most consistently not hyphenated, although appears in some sources as Ridgway-Wilson, which was his favoured spelling. **PROJECTS: W.R. Wilson:** Opera House, Nanaimo, 1889 (demo.); *Gyppeswyk* (A.A. Green Res.), Belcher Rd., now 1040 Moss St., Vict., 1889 (ext.); Loo Tai Cho Bldg., 549-55 Fisgard St./25-29 Fan Tan Alley, Vict., 1893 (ext.); *Schuhuum* (Bostock Res.), 1322 Rockland, Vict., 1894 (ext.); Isolation Hospital, Royal Jubilee, 1900 Fort St., Vict., 1893 (demo.); South Park School, 508 Douglas St., Vict., 1894 (ext.); Charles Spratt Res. (later *Glenelg*), 219 Gorge Rd. E., Vict., 1894 (demo. 1932); Porter Block, 1402-06 Douglas St., Vict., 1897 (ext.); Provincial Asylum alterations and additions, 9 E. Columbia St., New West., 1897-98 (alt.); Ridgway-Wilson Res., 31 Gorge Rd. E., Vict., 1899 (demo.); Mahon Block, 1110-12 Government St., Vict., 1907 (ext.); Newcombe Res., 138 Dallas Rd., Vict., 1907-08 (ext.); Vict. West School, 750 Front St., Vict., 1907-08 (demo. in 1968); Dr. Jones Res., 1171 Rockland Ave., Vict., 1908 (ext.); *Lotbinière* (C.V. Spratt House), 548 Lotbinière Ave., Vict., 1909 (ext.); W. & J. Wilson Bldg., 1221 Government St., Vict., 1912 (ext.); St. John the Divine Anglican Church, 1611 Quadra St., Vict., 1912 (ext.); Additions to Lampson St. School, 670 Lampson St., Esquimalt, 1913 (ext.); Vict. Drill Hall, now the Bay St. Armoury, 713 Bay St., Vict., 1913-15 (ext.); Colquitz Gaol (now Wilkinson Rd. Gaol), 4216 Wilkinson Rd., Saanich, 1914 (ext.).

WOLFE, James E.

Harold Kirker, *California's Architectural Frontier*; Randolph Delehanty, *In the Victorian Style* (San Francisco: Chronicle Books, 1997); *The Victoria Gazette*; *Colonist*; *California Architect & Building News*, v.5, No.1, Jan. 1884, p.3; Wolfe's obituary in the *San Francisco Call*, Jan. 8, 1901, p.3; and the San Francisco Public Library, History Center. **PROJECT**: Bldg. for J.D. Carroll, 500 Blk. Yates St., Vict., 1860 (demo. by 1882).

WRIGHT & SANDERS

Contemporary summaries of John Wright's career appear in the *California Architect & Building News*, Jan. 1884, p.10; and his obituary in the San Francisco *Examiner*, Aug. 30, 1915, p.30. Ronald B. Reiss, AIA, has generously shared his extensive research undertaken in the 1980s on the San Francisco career of Wright & Sanders. Further information from Norman J. Ronneberg Jr., who is related by marriage to the Wright family; information on Wright's early years in Guelph from correspondence between Ronneberg and L. Kearns, reference librarian, Guelph. Maltwood Art Museum and Gallery exhibition catalogue by Norman Ronneberg & Martin Segger, *John Wright, Grandfather of West Coast Architecture* (Oct. 14-Nov. 25, 1990). Information on Sanders from California Vital Events; directories; census records; his death certificate and his obituary in the Oakland *Tribune*, Jan. 25, 1920, p.B1. Contemporary descriptions of Wright & Sanders's work can be found in newspaper and professional journal accounts; in Victoria, the *Colonist* newspaper; and in California, the *California Architect & Building News*. For detailed descriptions see Segger & Franklin, *Exploring Victoria's Architecture*; Segger & Franklin, *Victoria: A Primer for Regional History*; and Cotton, *Vice-Regal Mansions*. For a background to the California work of Wright & Sanders see Kirker, *California's Architectural Frontier* and Withey & Withey, *Biographical Dictionary of American Architects (Deceased)*, pp.673-674. Other citations in Gebhard, *Architecture in San Francisco and Northern California*. Additional references from Dorothy Mindenhall, including Wesleyan Methodist Church (Vict. *Gazette*, July 23, 1859 and *Colonist*, Aug. 17, 1859, p.3); First Methodist Church, Nanaimo (*Colonist*, July 7, 1860); St. Paul's Anglican Church, Nanaimo (*Colonist*, Oct. 21, 1861); St. Nicholas Hotel (*Chronicle*, Nov. 15, 1862, p.3 and *Colonist*, Dec. 25, 1862, p.3); store for Searby (*Colonist*, Sept. 16, 1862, p.3 and Dec. 4, 1862, p.3); and the Canada Western Hotel (*Colonist*: Jan. 18, 1890, p.4; Mar. 25, 1890, p.1; July 11, 1890, p.1; Jan. 15, 1891, p.5; Apr. 12, 1893, p.3; and Apr. 25, 1893, p.8). First Presbyterian Church from BCA Vertical Files #2356-2436. Hook & Ladder Bldg. from Dave Parker, *First Water, Tigers!* (Vict.: Sono Nis Press, 1987). Information from the Nanaimo Community Archives. Citation for St. John the Divine, Yale from Bufo Inc., *St. John the Divine Church* (Vict.: Heritage Properties Branch, 1989). Plans by Wright & Sanders in BCA include the Ince Cottages [CM-C 815] and Fairfield [CM B1554]. **PROJECTS: John Wright:** Wesleyan Methodist Church, Broad St. and Pandora Ave., Vict., 1859 (demo. 1907); Fire Co.'s Hook & Ladder Bldg., Bastion Sq., 1859 (demo.); *Cloverdale*, 3498 Lovat Ave., Vict., 1859-60 (demo. 1963); Weslayan Methodist Church, Chapel St., Nanaimo, 1860 (demo. 1947). **Wright & Sanders:** *Ince Cottage*, New West., 1861 (demo.); St. Paul's Anglican (Episcopal) Church, Church St., Nanaimo, 1861 (demo. 1907); *Fairfield*, 601 Trutch St., Vict.,

1861 (alt.); *Woodlands*, 138-140 Government St., Vict., c.1861 (ext.); St. Nicholas Hotel, Government St. between Yates & Johnson Sts., Vict., 1862 (demo.); Brick store for W.M. Searby, east side of Government St. between View and Fort Sts., Vict., 1862 (demo.); Original wing of Point Ellice House, 2616 Pleasant St., Vict., c.1862 (ext.); St. John the Divine Church, Yale, 1862 (ext.); First Presbyterian Church, cor. Blanshard and Pandora Sts., Vict., 1863 (demo.); Temple Emanu-El, 1461 Blanshard St., Vict., 1863 (ext.); Richard Carr House, 207 Government St., Vict., 1863-64 (ext.); Angela College, 923 Burdett St., Vict., 1865-66 (ext.); Alterations to Cary Castle, Belcher Rd., Vict., 1865-66 (dest. by fire 1899); *Ince Cottage*, New West., c.1867 (unbuilt project); Canada Western Hotel, Government St. at Broughton St., Vict., 1890-91 (unbuilt project).

WRIGHT, RUSHFORTH & CAHILL

Directories; Van. bldg. permits; Withey & Withey, *Biographical Dictionary of American Architects (Deceased)*, pp.104-105, 532 and 673; Ritz, *Architects of Oregon*; and Bernard J.S. Cahill Collection, Environmental Design Archives, University of California, Berkeley. Holly Lodge in *Pacific Coast Architect*, Vol.7, No.3, May 1914, p.109. **PROJECT**: Holly Lodge, 1210 Jervis St., Van., 1913 (ext.).

YELLAND & RILEY

Directories; *AB&E*; Vict. plans, bldg. and plumbing permits; and inventories. **PROJECTS:** *Tanhaven* (Coon Res.), 1740 Fort St., Vict., 1913 (alt.); German-Canadian Trust Co. Bldg., cor. Douglas and Fort Sts., Vict., 1913 (unbuilt project); Perks Res., 1311 Moss St. (now Franklin Terrace), Vict., 1913 (ext.).

YOHO, Jud

Ochsner, *Shaping Seattle Architecture*; *Craftsman Bungalow Catalogue*; *Bungalow Magazine*; a lecture given by Erin Doherty to Historic Seattle Arts and Crafts Guild members on Jan. 14, 1998, culled from her master's thesis on Jud Yoho and the Craftsman Bungalow Co.; Vict. plans, bldg. and plumbing permits; Van. bldg. permits; inventories; and Ancestry.com internet site. **PROJECTS**: Res. for W. Bownass, 24 Douglas St., Vict., 1911-12 (alt.); Res. for W. Bownass, 27 Olympia Ave., Vict., 1911-12 (ext.); Strange Res., 1549 West 12th Ave., Van., 1911 (demo.); Seabourne & Co. Ltd. Houses, 1226 and 1238 Hampshire Rd, Oak Bay, 1912 (ext.).

Adams, John. *Old Square-Toes and His Lady: the Life of James and Amelia Douglas*. Victoria, B.C.: Horsdal & Schubart, 2001.

Andrews, G.S. *Professional Land Surveyors of British Columbia: Cumulative Nominal Roll*. 4th edition. Victoria: The Corporation of Land Surveyors of the Province of British Columbia, 1978.

Archibald, Margaret. *By Federal Design: The Chief Architect's Branch of the Department of Public Works 1881-1914*. Studies in Archaeology, Architecture in History, National Historic Parks & Sites Branch, Parks Canada, Environment Canada, 1983.

Atkin, John. *Strathcona: Vancouver's First Neighbourhood*. Vancouver: Whitecap Books, 1994.

Balf, Mary. *Kamloops: A History of the District up to 1914*. Kamloops: Kamloops Museum, 1969.

Balf, Ruth. *Kamloops: 1914-1945*. Kamloops: Kamloops Museum, 1975.

Ball, Norman R., sr. ed. *Building Canada: A History of Public Works*. Toronto: University of Toronto Press, 1988.

Barman, Jean. *The West Beyond the West: A History of British Columbia*. Toronto: University of Toronto Press, 1994.

Barr, Jennifer Nell. *Cumberland Heritage: A Selected History of People, Buildings, Institutions & Sites 1888-1950*. Corporation of the Village of Cumberland, 1997.

Barr, Jennifer Nell. *Saanich Heritage Structures: An Inventory*. The Corporation of the District of Saanich, 1991.

Barrett, Anthony A. and Rhodri Windsor Liscombe. *Francis Rattenbury and British Columbia: Architecture and Challenge in the Imperial Age*. Vancouver: University of British Columbia Press, 1983.

Bawlf, Carole. *Historic Buildings Inventory of Central Saanich*. Saanich Pioneers Society, 1987.

Bell-Irving, Elizabeth. *Crofton House School: The First Ninety Years 1898-1988*. Vancouver: Crofton House School, 1988.

Bentall, Shirley F. *The Charles Bentall Story: A Man of Industry and Integrity*. Vancouver: The Bentall Group Ltd., 1986.

Berton, Pierre et al. *The Crystal Gardens: West Coast Pleasure Palace*. Victoria: The Crystal Gardens Preservation Society, 1977.

Beautiful Homes: Vancouver, British Columbia. Vancouver: Saturday Sunset Presses, Undated (c.1912).

Bingham, Janet M. *Samuel Maclure, Architect*. Ganges, B.C.: Horsdal & Schubart Publishers Ltd., 1985.

Bissley, Paul L. *The Union Club of British Columbia: 100 Years 1879-1979*. Second Edition. Vancouver: Evergreen Press, 1979.

Bodnar, Diana. *Vancouver Schools Inventory*. Vancouver: City of Vancouver Standing Committee on Planning & Development, 1982.

Boam, Henry J. *British Columbia: Its History, People, Commerce, Industries and Resources*. London, England: Sells Ltd., 1912.

Bond, Janine. *University Endowment Lands Architecture 1940-1969*. Vancouver: Heritage Vancouver Society, 1993.

Brandes, Raymond S., ed. *San Diego Architects: 1868-1939*. Second Edition. San Diego: University of San Diego, 1991.

Brettell, Richard R. *Historic Denver: The Architects and the Architecture 1858-1893*. Denver, Colorado: Historic Denver Inc., 1973.

Canada Mortgage & Housing Corporation. *50 Years of Innovation 1943-1993: The Canadian Housing Industry*. Ottawa: CMHC, 1993.

Canadian Pacific Railway. *The Canadian Pacific: The New Highway to the East Across the Mountains, Prairies & Rivers of Canada*. Montreal: 1887.

Carroll, Ann. *Guide to Pre-1940 Architectural Records of Vancouver*. Vancouver: City of Vancouver Archives, 1986.

Carpenter Pensioners' Association of British Columbia. *Building British Columbia: The Story of the Carpenters' Union and the Trade Union Movement since 1881*. Vancouver College Printers Ltd., 1979.

Chamberlin, David R. *Samuel Maclure: Architectural Drawings in the University of Victoria Archives*. Victoria: University of Victoria Archives, 1995.

Chamberlin, David R. *Maltwood Museum Architectural Plans Series Comprising The Work of Samuel Maclure and Other Architects*. Victoria: University of Victoria Archives, 1993.

Chuen-yan David Lai. *Arches in British Columbia*. Victoria: Sono Nis Press, 1982.

Cirker, Blanche, ed. *Victorian House Designs in Authentic Full Colour: 75 Plates from the Scientific American - Architects and Builders Edition 1885-1894*. Mineola, N.Y.: Dover Publications Inc., 1996.

City of Victoria Heritage Advisory Committee. *This Old House: An Inventory of Residential Heritage*. Victoria, B.C., 1979 (reprinted 1984 and 1991).

City of Victoria Heritage Advisory Committee. *This Old Town: City of Victoria Central Area Heritage Conservation Report*. Victoria: City of Victoria, 1983.

Claydon, Peter S.N., Valerie A. Melanson and members of the British Columbia Genealogical Society. *Vancouver Voters 1886*. Richmond: British Columbia Genealogical Society, 1994.

Robert Close. *Ayrshire & Arran: An Illustrated Architectural Guide*. Edinburgh: Royal Incorporation of Architects in Scotland, 1992.

Comstock, William. *Directory of Architects in North America*. New York: 1892 to 1914.

Colvin, Howard. *A Biographical Dictionary of British Architects 1600-1840*. 3rd Edition. New Haven & London: Yale University Press, 1995.

Cornwell, John. *Earth to Earth: A True Story of the Lives and Violent Deaths of a Devon Farming Family*. London: Allen Lane, 1982.

Corporation of the City of Victoria. *Victoria Illustrated*. Victoria: Ellis & Co., 1891.

Corporation of Land Surveyors of the Province of British Columbia. *Professional Land Surveyors of British Columbia: Cumulative Nominal Roll*. 7th Edition. Victoria, B.C.: 1998.

Cotton, Peter Neive. *Vice-Regal Mansions of British Columbia*. Vancouver: Elgin Publications, 1981.

Crossman, Kelly. *Architecture in Transition: From Art To Practice, 1885-1906*. Kingston: McGill-Queen's University Press, 1987.

D'Acres, Lilia and Donald Luxton. *Lions Gate*. Vancouver: Talonbooks, 1999.

Daily World, Vancouver. *The A.Y.P. Book of Vancouver, B.C.* 1909.

Davies, Glyn. *A History of Money from Ancient Times to the Present Day*. Rev. ed., Cardiff: University of Wales Press, 1996.

Dempster, Eleanore. *The Laughing Bridge: A Personal History of the Capilano Suspension Bridge*. Maple Ridge: Impressions in Print Enterprises, 1988.

Denhez, Marc. *The Canadian Home: From Cave to Electronic Cocoon*. Toronto: Dundurn Press, 1994.

Dogterom, Irma. *Where Was It? A Guide to Early Lethbridge Buildings*. Occasional Paper #35. Lethbridge: Lethbridge Historical Society, 2001.

Downing, Andrew Jackson. *The Architecture of Country Houses*. Toronto: Dover Publications Inc., 1969.

Downing, Andrew Jackson. *Victorian Cottage Residences*. Toronto: Dover Publications Inc., 1981.

Downs, Barry. *Sacred Places*. Vancouver: Douglas & McIntyre, 1980.

Eaton, Leonard K. *The Architecture of Samuel Maclure*. Victoria: The Art Gallery of Greater Victoria, 1971.

Ewert, Henry. *The Story of the B.C. Electric Railway Company*. Vancouver: Whitecap Books, 1986.

Fairley, Jim. *The Way We Were: The Story of the Old Vancouver Courthouse*. North Vancouver: James Scott Fairley, 1986.

Felstead, Alison, Jonathon Franklin and Leslie Pinfield. *Directory of British Architects 1834-1900*. London, England: Mansell Publishing, Ltd., 1993.

F.G. Architectural & Planning Consultants. *Langley's Heritage*. Langley: Township of Langley, 1995.

F.G. Architectural & Planning Consultants. *Riverview Heritage Evaluation*. Victoria: British Columbia Buildings Corporation, 1995.

F.G. Architectural & Planning Consultants. *Jubilee Neighbourhood Heritage Resource Review*. City of Victoria, 1996.

Field, Dorothy. *Built Heritage In Esquimalt, An Inventory*. Victoria: Hallmark Society, 1984.

Fitzsimmons, Josephine, ed. *Heritage Kamloops: Historic Buildings Inventory*. Kamloops: Kamloops Heritage Advisory Committee, 1983.

Foundation Group Designs Ltd. *Ambitious City: The City of North Vancouver Heritage Inventory*. City of North Vancouver, 1988.

Foundation Group Designs Ltd. *The District of Chilliwack Heritage Inventory*. District of Chilliwack, 1991.

Foundation Group Designs Ltd. *Downtown Victoria Heritage Registry*. City of Victoria, 1989 (Revised 1996).

Foundation Group Designs Ltd. *Heritage Maillardville Report*. Coquitlam: District of Coquitlam, 1986.

Foundation Group Designs Ltd. *The Nanaimo Heritage Gateways Inventory*. Nanaimo: City of Nanaimo Heritage Advisory Committee, 1986.

Foundation Group Designs Ltd. *Richmond Heritage Inventory Phase II*. Richmond: Richmond Heritage Advisory Committee, 1989.

Franklin, Douglas. *The Competition for the Design of the University of British Columbia*. West Coast Review, Vol. XV/4, Spring 1981, pages 49-57.

Franklin, Douglas. *Victoria's Third Giant*. Canadian Heritage Magazine, May 1979.

Franklin, Douglas and John Fleming. *Early School Architecture in British Columbia: An Architectural History and Inventory of Buildings to 1930*. Victoria: Heritage Conservation Branch, 1980.

Gebhard, David et al. *Architecture in San Francisco and Northern California*. Salt Lake City: Gibbs M. Smith Inc./Peregrine Smith Books, 1985.

Glendinning, Miles, ed. *A History of Scottish Architecture*. Edinburgh: Edinburgh University Press, 1996.

Gomme, Andor and David Walker. *Architecture of Glasgow*. 2nd Edition. London: Lund Humphries, 1987.

Gray, A. Stuart. *Edwardian Architecture: A Biographical Dictionary*. London: Wordsworth Editions, 1985.

Greater Vancouver - Illustrated. Vancouver: Dominion Publishing Company, c.1907.

Greater Vernon Museum & Archives Staff. *Valley of Dreams: A Pictorial History of Vernon and District*. Vernon: Greater Vernon Museum & Archives, 1992.

Green, Valerie. *Excelsior!: The Story of the Todd Family*. Victoria: Orca Book Publishers, 1990.

Guter, Robert P. and Janet W. Foster. *Building by the Book: Pattern-Book Architecture in New Jersey*. New Brunswick, New Jersey: Rutgers University Press, 1992.

Hallmark Society. *Inventory of Heritage Buildings*. Victoria: Hallmark Society, 1978.

Harris, Richard. *Unplanned Suburbs: Toronto's American Tragedy, 1900 to 1950*. Baltimore: Johns Hopkins University Press, 1996.

Henry, James Leslie. *Catalogue Houses: Eaton's and Others*. Saskatoon: Henry Perspectives, 2001.

Heritage Conservation Branch. *Nelson: A Proposal for Urban Heritage Conservation*. Victoria: Queen's Printer for British Columbia, 1981.

Hobson, Robert. *This is Our Heritage*. Vernon: Greater Vernon Heritage Advisory Committee, 1987.

Home Builders Lumber Company Ltd., The. *Plan Book and Catalogue: Practical and Artistic Homes, Farm Buildings etc., Specially Designed for the West*. Vancouver: n.d.

Howard, Fred P. and George Barnett. *The British Columbian Victoria Guide and Directory for 1863*. Victoria: Office of the British Columbian, 1863.

Howay, F.W. and E.O.S. Schofield. *British Columbia: From the Earliest Times to the Present*. Vols. I-IV. Vancouver: S.J. Clarke Publishing Company, 1914.

Imredy, Peggy. *A Guide to Sculpture in Vancouver*. Vancouver: Self-published, 1980.

Jackson, Sydney Wayne. *The Men at Cary Castle*. Victoria: Morriss Printing Co., 1972.

Johnson, Patricia M. *Nanaimo, A Short History*. Nanaimo: Trendex Publications & Western Heritage, 1974.

Johnston, Patricia L., and Paul R.L. Chénier. *Index of Canadian Architect & Builder, 1888-1908*. Ottawa: Society for Studies of Architecture in Canada, 1984.

Jordan, David A. *Working-class Suburbs in Turn-of-the-Twentieth-Century Victoria, British Columbia*. University of Victoria, M.A. thesis, 2000.

Kalman, Harold. *A History of Canadian Architecture*. Toronto: Oxford University Press, 1994.

Kalman, Harold. *Exploring Vancouver*. Vancouver: University of British Columbia Press, 1974.

Kalman, Harold. *Exploring Vancouver 2*. Vancouver: University of British Columbia Press, 1978.

Kalman, Harold, Ron Phillips and Robin Ward. *Exploring Vancouver: The Essential Architectural Guide*. Vancouver: University of British Columbia Press, 1993.

Kalman, Harold. *The Prince Rupert Heritage Inventory and Conservation Programme*. City of Prince Rupert: Heritage Advisory Committee, 1983.

Kalman, Harold. *Railway Hotels in Canada*. Victoria: University of Victoria, Maltwood Museum Studies in Architectural History, 1968.

Kamloops Heritage Advisory Committee. *Heritage Kamloops: A Collection of Historical Buildings and Sites*. Kamloops: City of Kamloops, 1993.

Kerr, John Blaine. *Biographical Dictionary of Well-Known British Columbians, with an Historical Sketch*. Vancouver: Kerr & Begg, 1890.

Kirker, Harold. *California's Architectural Frontier: Style and Tradition in the Nineteenth Century*. New York: Russell & Russell, 1970.

Kluckner, Michael. *M.I. Rogers 1869-1965*. Victoria: J. Gudewill, B.C., 1987.

Kluckner, Michael. *Vancouver: The Way It Was*. North Vancouver: Whitecap Books Ltd., 1984.

Kluckner, Michael. *Vanishing Vancouver*. North Vancouver: Whitecap Books Ltd., 1990.

Kluckner, Michael. *Victoria: The Way It Was.* North Vancouver: Whitecap Books Ltd., 1986.

Kluckner, Michael and John Atkin. *Heritage Walks Around Vancouver.* Vancouver: Whitecap Books, 1992.

Kostof, Spiro, ed. *The Architect: Chapters in the History of the Profession.* New York: Oxford University Press, 1977.

Kreisman, Lawrence. *Made to Last: Historic Preservation in Seattle and King County.* Seattle: The Historic Seattle Preservation Foundation/University of Washington, 1999.

Logan, Harry T. *Tuum Est: A History of the University of British Columbia.* Vancouver: UBC, 1958.

Lort, Ross. *Old Houses and Old Buildings in Vancouver.* Address to the Tuesday Club of the Vancouver Public Library (March 1960). Privately Printed, 1960.

Luxton, Donald. *Deco and Moderne in Vancouver.* Vancouver: 1982.

Luxton, Donald. *Capital Regional District Art Deco and Moderne.* Victoria: The Hallmark Society, 1984.

Luxton, Donald. *Taming the West: the Thirty Year Struggle to Regulate the Architectural Profession in British Columbia.* Society for the Study of Architecture in Canada Journal, Vol. 22, No. 4, 1998, pp.108-123.

Luxton, Donald & Associates. *The City of Port Moody Heritage Inventory.* Port Moody: The City of Port Moody, 1999.

Luxton, Donald & Associates. *Delta's Rural Heritage.* Delta: Corporation of Delta, 1999.

Luxton, Donald & Associates. *Delta's Urban Heritage.* Delta: Corporation of Delta, 2000.

Luxton, Donald & Associates. *The Heritage Resources of Maple Ridge.* Maple Ridge: District of Maple Ridge, 1998.

Luxton, Donald & Associates. *The Heritage Resources of Nanaimo.* Nanaimo: City of Nanaimo, 1998.

Luxton, Donald & Associates. *The Modern Architecture of North Vancouver, 1930-1965.* North Vancouver: The District of North Vancouver, 1997.

Macdonald, Bruce. *Vancouver, A Visual History.* Vancouver: Talonbooks, 1992.

MacDonald, Rt. Rev. Alexander. *Historical Number of British Columbia Orphans' Friend.* Victoria: 1913.

Mackay, Ellen. *Places of Worship in the Cowichan and Chemainus Valleys.* Victoria: Sono Nis Press, 1991.

McDonald, Robert A.J. *Making Vancouver 1863-1913.* Vancouver: University of British Columbia Press, 1996.

McDowall, Duncan. *Quick to the Frontier: Canada's Royal Bank.* Toronto: McClelland & Stewart, 1993.

McGeachie, Pixie. *Burnaby: A Proud Century: A Historical Commemoration of Burnaby's Centennial.* Vancouver: Opus Productions Inc., 1991.

McIntosh, Robert Dale. *A Documentary History of Music in Victoria, Vol. I: 1850-1899.* Victoria: University of Victoria, 1981.

McTavish, Newton. *The Fine Arts in Canada.* Toronto: The Macmillan Company of Canada Ltd., 1925.

Maddex, Diane, ed. *Master Builders: A Guide to Famous American Architects.* New York: John A. Wiley & Sons Inc., 1985.

Mallandaine, Edward. *First Victoria Directory.* Victoria: E. Mallandaine & Co., 1860.

Maitland, Leslie. *The Queen Anne Revival Style in Canadian Architecture.* Ottawa: National Historic Parks & Sites, Parks Service, Environment Canada, 1990.

Massey, James C. and Shirley Maxwell. *House Styles in America: The Old-House Journal to the Architecture of American Homes.* New York: Penguin Studio, 1996.

Matthews, Major J.S. *Early Vancouver.* Seven volumes, Privately Printed, n.d. [Collection City of Vancouver Archives].

Mills, G. Edward. *Architectural Trends in Victoria, British Columbia, 1850-1914.* Ottawa: Parks Canada Manuscript Report Number 354, 1976.

Mills, G. Edward. *Buying Wood and Building Farms: Marketing Lumber and Farm Building Designs on the Canadian Prairies.* Ottawa: Minister of Supplies & Services Canada, 1991.

Mills, G. Edward. *The Early Courthouses of British Columbia.* Ottawa: Parks Canada Report Number 2881, Ottawa, 1977.

Mills, G. Edward and D.W. Holdsworth. *The B.C. Mills Prefabricated System: The Emergence of Ready-made Buildings in Western Canada.* Ottawa: Canadian Historic Sites No. 14, 1974.

Mills, G. Edward and Warren Sommer. *Vancouver Architecture 1886-1914.* Report Number #405. Ottawa: Parks Canada, 1975.

Minaker, Dennis. *The Gorge of Summers Gone: A History of Victoria's Inland Waterway.* Victoria: 1998.

Monk, H.A.J. and J. Stewart. *A History of Coquitlam and Fraser Mills.* Coquitlam, 1958.

Nanaimo Community Heritage Commission. *Columns, Cornices & Coal: The Heritage Resources of Nanaimo.* City of Nanaimo, 1999.

National Film Board. *Stones of History: Canada's Houses of Parliament.* Ottawa: Queen's Printer, 1967.

Newspaper Cartoonists Association of B.C. *British Columbians As We See 'Em, 1910 and 1911.* Vancouver: 1911.

Nicholls, Peggy. *From the Black Country to Nanaimo 1854.* Nanaimo Historical Society, Vols. I-V, 1991-1995.

Nickle Arts Museum, *Building A West: Works from the Canadian Architectural Archives.* Calgary: 1990.

Noel, Thomas J. and Barbara S. Norgren. *Denver: The City Beautiful and its Architects, 1893-1941.* Denver, Colorado: Historic Denver, Inc., 2nd printing 1993.

Norton, Wayne. *A Whole Little City by Itself: Tranquille and Tuberculosis.* Kamloops: Plateau Press, 1999.

Ochsner, Jeffrey Karl and Dennis Alan Andersen. *Distant Corner: Seattle Architects and the Legacy of H.H. Richardson, 1880-1895.* Seattle: University of Washington Press, 2003.

Ochsner, Jeffrey Karl, ed. *Shaping Seattle Architecture: A Historical Guide to the Architects.* Seattle: University of Washington Press, 1994.

Oliphant, John. *Brother Twelve: The Incredible Story of Canada's False Prophet.* Toronto: McClelland & Stewart Inc., 1991.

Opportunities Publishing Co., The. *Modern Architecture.* Vancouver, 1911.

Ormsby, Margaret A. *British Columbia: A History.* Vancouver: The Macmillan Company of Canada Ltd., 1958.

Palmer, Bernard C. *Development of Domestic Architecture in British Columbia.* Journal of the Royal Architectural Institute of Canada, 5 (November 1928), pp.405-416.

Parker, Allen & Associates. *Vancouver Heritage Resource Inventory, Phase II.* Vancouver: City of Vancouver, 1986.

Parr & Fee et al. *Vancouver of Today Architecturally.* Vancouver, 1900.

Pethick, Derek. *Victoria: The Fort.* Vancouver: Mitchell Press Limited, 1968.

Pethick, Derek. *Summer of Promise: Victoria 1864-1914.* Victoria: Sono Nis Press, 1980.

Pethick, Derek. *Vancouver Recalled: A Pictorial History to 1887.* Hancock House Publishers, Saanichton, B.C., 1974.

Petrie, Blair. *Mole Hill Living Heritage.* Vancouver: Mole Hill Living Heritage Society, 1995.

Pratt, C.E. *Contemporary Domestic Architecture in British Columbia.* Journal of the Royal Architectural Institute of Canada, 24 (June 1947), pp.179-198.

Record Publishing Company. *The Architect, Builder & Engineer.* Vancouver, 1912-1914.

Reed, S.B. *Village & Country Residences and How To Build Them.* First publication 1878. New York: Lyons Press, 2000.

Reksten, Terry. *The Dunsmuir Saga.* Vancouver: Douglas & McIntyre, 1991.

Reksten, Terry. *The Empress Hotel: In the Grand Style.* Vancouver: Douglas & McIntyre, 1997.

Reksten, Terry. *The Illustrated History of British Columbia.* Vancouver: Douglas & McIntyre, 2001.

Reksten, Terry. *More English than the English.* Victoria: Orca Book Publishers, 1993.

Reksten, Terry. *Rattenbury.* Victoria: Sono Nis Press, 1978.

Report by Plans Committee, 8th April, 1915. *Vancouver Civic Centre.* Vancouver: News-Advertiser Printers, 1915.

Reeve, Phyllis. *Every Good Gift: A History of S. James' Vancouver, 1881-1981.* Vancouver: St. James' Church, 1981.

Ring, Dan, curator. *The Urban Prairie.* Saskatoon: Mendel Art Gallery/ Fifth House Publishers, 1994.

Ritz, Richard Ellison. *Architects of Oregon: Biographical Dictionary of Architects (Deceased) in the 19th and 20th Centuries.* Portland: Campbell & Dempsey Printers, 2003.

Robinson, Sherri K. *Esquimalt Streets And Roads: A History.* Municipality of Esquimalt, 1995.

Rosinski, Maud. *Architects of Nova Scotia: A Biographical Dictionary 1605-1950.* Province of Nova Scotia, 1994.

Ruggles, Richard I. *A Country So Interesting: The Hudson's Bay Company and Two Centuries of Mapping, 1670-1870.* Montreal: McGill-Queen's University Press, 1991.

Russell, Hilary. *All That Glitters: A Memorial to Ottawa's Capitol Theatre and its Predecessors.* Canadian Historic Sites: Occasional Papers in Archaeology & History No.13. Ottawa: National Historic Parks & Sites Branch, Parks Canada, Indian & Northern Affairs, 1974, pp.5-125.

Sandilands, R. et al. *Architecture of the Fraser Valley.* An Opportunities for Youth Project. 1972.

Sandison, James M., ed. *Schools of Old Vancouver.* Vancouver: Vancouver Historical Society, Occasional Paper Number 2, 1971.

Saskatchewan Association of Architects. *Historic Architecture of Saskatchewan.* Regina: Focus Publishing Inc., 1987.

Saskatchewan Association of Architects. *An Interactive History of Architects in the Province of Saskatchewan.* Regina: 1997.

Saturday Sunset Presses. *Beautiful Homes: Vancouver, British Columbia.* Undated.

Saunders, Ivan J. *A Survey of British Columbia School Architecture to 1930.* Parks Canada Research Bulletin No. 225. Ottawa: Ministry of Supply & Services Canada, 1984.

Scott, David Jack. *Once In The Royal City.* North Vancouver: Whitecap Books, 1985.

Segger, Martin, ed. *The British Columbia Parliament Buildings.* Vancouver: Arcon, 1979.

Segger, Martin. *The Buildings of Samuel Maclure: In Search of Appropriate Form.* Victoria: Sono Nis Press, 1986.

Segger, Martin and Douglas Franklin. *Exploring Victoria's Architecture.* Victoria: Sono Nis Press, 1996.

Segger, Martin and Douglas Franklin. *Victoria: A Primer for Regional History in Architecture.* Watkins Glen, New York: The American Life Foundation & Study Institute, 1979.

Service, Alastair. *The Architects of London and their Buildings from 1066 to the Present Day.* The Architectural Press (London) & the Architectural Book Publishing Co. (New York), 1979.

Service. Alastair. *London 1900.* Toronto: Granada Publishing Ltd., 1979.

Shoppell, R.W. et al. *Turn-of-the-Century Houses, Cottages and Villas: Floor Plans and Line Illustrations of 118 Homes from Shoppell's Catalogs.* Mineola, N.Y.: Dover Publications Inc., 1993.

Short, C.W. and R. Stanley-Brown. *Public Buildings: A Survey of Architecture of Projects Constructed by Federal and Other Governmental Bodies Between the Years 1933 and 1939 with the Assistance of the Public Works Administration.* Washington, D.C.: United States Government Printing Office, 1939.

Sleath, Eleanor. *New Westminster Heritage Resource Inventory.* New Westminster Heritage Advisory Committee, 1984.

Smeins, Linda E. *Building an American Identity: Pattern Book Homes & Communities 1870-1900.* Walnut Creek, California: AltaMira Press, 1999.

Soward, Frederic H. *The Early History of the University of British Columbia.* Unpublished Manuscript, 1930.

Stark, Stuart. *Oak Bay's Heritage Buildings: More Than Just Bricks and Boards.* The Corporation of the District of Oak Bay, 1986.

Sterett & Butler. *The Frazer River Thermometer: Great Gold Discoveries of 1858.* San Francisco: Sterett & Butler, 1858.

Stevenson, Katherine Cole and H. Ward Jandl. *Houses By Mail: A Guide to Houses from Sears, Roebuck and Company.* Washington, D.C.: Preservation Press, 1986.

Strickland, Major Samuel. *Twenty-Seven Years in Canada West or the Experience of an Early Settler.* Edmonton: M.G. Hurtig Ltd. Booksellers & Publishers, 1970.

Swankey, Ben, ed. *Building British Columbia: A History of Union Carpenters 1883-1978.* Carpenter's Pension Association of British Columbia, 1979.

Taylor, G.W. *Builders of British Columbia: An Industrial History.* Victoria: Morriss Printing, 1982.

Taylor, W.A. *Crown Land Grants: A History of the Esquimalt and Nanaimo Railway Land Grants, the Railway Belt, and the Peace River Block.* Victoria: Crown Land Registry Services, Ministry of Environment, Lands & Parks, 4th Edition, 1997.

The 1999 Canadian Encyclopedia: World Edition. Toronto: McClelland & Stewart Inc., 1998.

Thirkell, Fred and Bob Scullion. *Vancouver & Beyond: During the Golden Age of Postcards 1900-1914.* Surrey: Heritage House Publishing Co. Ltd., 2000.

Turner, Jane, ed. *Grove Dictionary of Art.* New York. Macmillan Publishers Ltd., 1996.

Underhill, Stuart. *The Iron Church: 1860-1985.* Victoria: Braemar Books Ltd., 1984.

Vancouver and Victoria Architecturally, 1913.

Vancouver Art Gallery. *Vancouver Art & Artists 1931-1983.* Vancouver: Vancouver Art Gallery, 1983.

Vancouver Daily World. *Souvenir Edition – Vancouver City: Its Wonderful History and Future Prospects, a Historical and Statistical Review of the Pacific Terminus of the C.P.R.* Vancouver: Daily World, 1891.

Vaux, Calvert. *Villas & Cottages.* Toronto, Dover Publications Inc., 1970.

Veillette, John, and Gary White. *Early Indian Village Churches.* Vancouver: University of British Columbia Press, 1977.

Victoria Architecturally, 1911.

Wade, Jill. *Houses For All: The Struggle for Social Housing in Vancouver 1919-1950.* Vancouver: University of British Columbia Press, 1994.

Walker, Elizabeth. *Street Names of Vancouver.* Vancouver: Vancouver Historical Society, 1999.

Weir, Dr. Jean B. *The Lost Craft of Ornamented Architecture*: Canadian Architectural Drawings, 1850-1930. Halifax: Dalhousie Art Gallery, Dalhousie University, 1983.

Western Homes & Living. *100 Years of B.C. Living*. Vancouver, January 1958.

Wetherell, Donald G. and Irene R.A. Kmet. *Homes in Alberta: Buildings, Trends and Designs 1870-1967*. Edmonton: University of Alberta Press, 1991.

Whittaker, John A., BCLS, comp. & ed. *Early Land Surveyors of British Columbia (P.L.S. Group)*. Victoria: The Corporation of Land Surveyors of the Province of British Columbia, 1990.

Windsor Liscombe, Rhodri. *The New Spirit. Modern Architecture in Vancouver 1938-1963*. Vancouver: Canadian Centre for Architecture and Douglas & McIntyre, 1997.

Withey, Henry F. and Elsie Rathburn Withey. *Biographical Dictionary of American Architects (Deceased)*. Los Angeles: Hennessey & Ingalls, Inc., 1970.

Wolf, Jim. *Deer Lake Park Heritage Resource Inventory*. Burnaby: City of Burnaby, 1998.

Wolfenden, Madge. *The Early Architects of B.C.* Western Homes & Living, September 1958, pp.17-19.

Women in Architecture Exhibits Committee. *Constructing Careers: Profiles of Five Early Women Architects in British Columbia*. Vancouver, 1996.

Woodbridge, Sally B. *California Architecture: Historic American Building Survey*. San Francisco: Chronicle Books, 1988.

Woodbridge, Sally B. and Roger Montgomery. *A Guide to Architecture in Washington State*. Seattle: The University of Washington Press, 1980.

Woodward, George E. *Woodward's Country Homes*. Watkins Glen, New York: The American Life Foundation.

Wright, Janet. *Crown Assets: The Architecture of the Department of Public Works 1867-1967*. Toronto: University of Toronto Press, 1997.

Wynn, Graeme and Timothy Oke, eds. *Vancouver and Its Region*. Vancouver: University of British Columbia Press, 1992.

Year Book of the British Columbia Society of Architects, Vancouver Chapter. Vancouver: Privately Published, 1913.

Zuehlke, Mark. *Scoundrels, Dreamers & Second Sons: British Remittance Men in the Canadian West*. North Vancouver: Whitecap Books, 1994.

ARCHIVAL AND PUBLIC COLLECTIONS

Architectural Institute of British Columbia: 18, 172 top, 272 top, 273 top, 306 top, 311 top, 348 top left, 370 top left, 374 top left., 394 top left, 396 top left, 411 top right, 428 top left. **Archives of the Anglican Diocese of British Columbia, Victoria:** 26 top, 42 bottom, 134 top left, 180 bottom right, 187 bottom, 202-203. **Bessborough Armoury, Vancouver:** 296 top, 296 bottom. **Boundary Museum, Grand Forks:** 247 top [BM 986-236-001]. **B.C. Archives:** 2 [BCA F-09372], 12 [BCA F-06571], 21 (Holy Trinity Church, New Westminster) [BCA A-01672], 22 [BCA F-07453], 24 [BCA A-05962], 25 [BCA A-02776], 27 background [BCA G-09199], 32-33 background [BCA A-03330], 34 bottom [BCA CM-A 1950], 35 top right [BCA A-07734], 36 top [BCA F-01711], 36 bottom [BCA B-04812], 37 top [BCA H-00838], 37 bottom [BCA C-09022], 38 [BCA B-05459], 39 top [BCA C-03805], 39 bottom [BCA CM-C 815 sh.3], 41 top [BCA G-02350], 42 top [BCA A-04649], 44 top [BCA A-01866], 44 bottom [BCA A-06687], 46 (S.A. Spencer, photographer) [BCA G-05736], 47 top [BCA A-03849], 47 bottom [BCA I-67646], 48 top [BCA G-05372], 48 bottom [BCA A-01660], 49 top [BCA G-00248], 53 [BCA B-04712], 61 (British Columbia Penitentiary, New Westminster; Maynard, photographer) [detail from BCA A-03358], 62 [BCA C-03860], 66 [BCA C-08977], 70 bottom (Maynard, photographer) [BCA A-03358], 72 [BCA C-06771], 74 top [BCA A-08339], 74 bottom [BCA D-02918], 80 bottom [BCA A-04164], 81 [BCA B-03572], 82 top [BCA G-03588], 92 top [BCA G-09190], 92 bottom [BCA D-03646], 93 top [BCA G-07930], 95 [BCA B-01502], 99 (The Last Spike) [BCA E-02200], 107 bottom [BCA G-07936], 107 background [BCA G-08797], 109 [BCA C-08987], 111 [BCA F-07746], 114 [BCA F-02171], 115 [BCA CM-14991B], 124 top [BCA F-07410], 124 bottom [BCA A-04619], 139 (Richard Maynard, photographer) [BCA E-01296], 168 bottom [BCA CM/A831], 179 top [BCA F-00217], 179 bottom [BCA E-02659], 180 top [detail from BCA D-00346], 180 bottom left [BCA H-05541], 197 (Bailey Bros., photographers) [BCA NA-42022], 208 [BCA G-04366], 215 [BCA D-00638], 230 [BCA F-07199], 231 [BCA D-04531], 246 (Campbell Studios, photographer) [BCA G-09566], 267 [BCA A-04632], 280 [detail from BCA F-09372] 286 top [detail from BCA F-09372], 305 [BCA PDP-00577], 367 [detail from BCA F-09372], 393 top, [BCA H-06801], 393 bottom [BCA I-28381], 409 [BCA I-01938], 429 top [BCA A-05281], 430 centre [BCA F-04743], 429 bottom [BCA F-04742], 444 top left [BCA I-32112]. **B.C. Hydro Archives:** 176 [B-0402], 295 top [B-1372], 384-385 bottom [B-0393], 408 bottom [C-0315], 417 top right [B-1245]. **B.C. Packers Ltd.:** 242. **Burnaby Village Museum:** 293 top [BV.985.57.1]. **California History Section, California State Library, Sacramento, Gladding McBean & Company Collection:** 262 [Job Order #1008BD1 (Neg. #27,422)], 263 [Job Order #1019A (Neg. #27,421)], 264 [Job Order #1045FD3 (Neg. #27,423)], 265 top [Job Order #1025HLIO (Neg. 27,424)], 331 (Job Order #998 (Neg. 27,420)]. **California Institute of Technology, Courtesy of the Archives:** 404 top left: [30.16.1-4]. **Canadian Architectural Archives, University of Calgary:** 285 [McCarter Nairne Collection, Accession 71A/80.06, Project MCA 29V25]. **City of Burnaby:** 317. **City of Burnaby Archives:** 85 top and bottom (Bailey & Neelands photographers), 103 (Bailey & Neelands, photographers), 110, 113 bottom (Bailey & Neelands photographers), 164 bottom, 165 top, 167 centre right [#33-2], 187 top [#22], 292 bottom (Stride Studios, photographers), 361 top left [#209-1], 368 top left [#989.22]. **City of Vancouver Archives:** 6 [CVA 647-1], 51 (French, photographer) [CVA 677-452], 86 bottom [CVA Matthews Collection Map. 18], 88 top [detail from CVA AP-2001], 89 [CVA Bu.P.420 N.404], 100 (Charles S. Bailey, photographer) [CVA SGN.4], 102 [CVA City P.50 N.33], 112 bottom [LGN.483], 113 top [CVA Matthews Collection Map. 18], 120 [CVA #1158-123], 121 [CVA Bu.P.85], 130 bottom [CVA Bu.P.116], 151 bottom [CVA 677-4], 154 [CVA 99-5126], 158 top [CVA P.Port.552], 159 bottom right [CVA Bu.P.315 N.196], 160 top left [CVA Bu.P.283 N.176], 171 [CVA Ch.P.6 N.131], 175 [CVA Port.P.67], 177 top [CVA Bu.P.446.1], 229 (The Western Klondike Outfitters, Vancouver) [CVA LGN.1021], 248 left [CVA SP.P.115 N.75], 248 right [CVA St.Pk.P.277 N.167], 249 bottom [CVA SGN.302], 251 top [CVA Bu.P.707 N.622], 253 (Second Hotel Vancouver under construction) [CVA Hot.P.55 N.80.1], 320 top [CVA 1417-3], 322 [CVA 1417-1], 348-349 bottom (Robert Lyon, photographer) [CVA Add.MSS.624 File 7, Temp.1], 355 [CVA OUT P.725], 362 (W.J. Moore, photographer) [CVA SGN 1028], 371 bottom (Stuart Thomson, photographer) [CVA 99-1519], 371 (Stuart Thomson, photographer) [CVA 99-2419], 381 [CVA Und. 831], 389 bottom left (W.J. Moore, photographer) [CVA Bu. N.90], 410 top left [detail from CVA Bu.P.87 N.583], 410-411 bottom (W.J. Moore, photographer) [CVA Bu.P.588 N.249], 424 top left [CVA 371-1368], 425 top [CVA Add.MSS.214 609-G-6 file 4], 425 bottom [CVA Add.MSS.214 609-G-6 file 3]. **City of Vancouver (Plan Collection):** 347 bottom, 363 top. **City of Victoria Archives:** 23 [CVA PR252-6474]; 35 bottom [CVA 98202-16-6469], 45 [CVA PR254-881], 67 [CVA 98110-05-738], 75 [CVA 96604-01-2757], 76 bottom left [CVA PR86-6673], 77 top [CVA 96604-01-3720], 79 top [detail from CVA PR 234-1711], 82 bottom [CVA 98401-13-2512], 93 [CVA PR252-4128], 123 [CVA PR252-4117], 125 bottom [CVA PR132-621], 126-127 [CVA PR-109], 182 [CVA PR-17-5709], 183 [CVA 98302-02-4338], 188 top [CVA 99811-05], 189 bottom [CVA PR132-1211], 213 [CVA 98403-12-768], 265 bottom [detail from CVA #2-0625], 268 top [CVA 98904-23-2892], 282 bottom right [CVA 98710-04-2386], 356 top [CVA 2112-3638], 358 top [CVA 2112-01-2142], 389 centre [CVA PR252-7823], 414 top left (H.U. Knight, Photographer) [CVA PR73-6024]. **City of Victoria (Plan Collection):** 134 bottom, 140 top, 188 bottom, 283 bottom, 330 bottom left, 396 top right, 398 bottom right, 444 bottom. **Corporation of Land Surveyors of the Province of British Columbia:** 43. **Craigdarroch Castle Historical Museum Society, Victoria:** 49 bottom. **Cumberland Museum & Archives:** 227 top [C50-10], 278 top [CMA C192.17], 278 bottom left (Leonard Frank, photographer, 1922) [CMA C30-21], 278 bottom right [CMA C30-111], 279 bottom (Leonard Frank photo, 1922) [CMA C30-139]. **Delta Museum & Archives:** 84 bottom [#1971-26-2]. **District of Oak Bay:** 219, 237. **Greater Vernon Museum & Archives:** 144 top [#981.60.2], 144 centre [#2433], 144 bottom [#4058], 152 bottom [#8686], 161 top right [#3432], 161 top left [#8536], 205 [#16225], 224 top [#16999], 224 bottom [#3587], 225 top [#198], 225 bottom [#3638], 377 [Vernon News, Special Holiday Number, 1912, p.77]. **Hastings School, Vancouver:** 286 bottom right. **Kamloops Museum & Archives:** 119 bottom [#7321], 160 bottom [#487], 177 bottom [#8611], 209 [#7328], 260-261 bottom [#8753]. **Kelowna Centennial Museum:** 281 [#5667], 364 [#10528], 387 centre [#11352]. **Maine Historic Preservation Commission:** 112 top. **Maple Ridge Museum & Archives:** 56 bottom [P.01859], 361 [P.00551], 389 bottom right [P.04328], 445 [P.00555]. **Nanaimo & District Museum:** 87 top [C2-11], 279 top [#C5-14]. **National Archives of Canada:** 28 (George M. Dawson, photographer) [PA-037756], 65 [PA-210578], 71 [PA-116162], 232 [PA-129119], 256 top [PA-021917], 256 centre

[PA-021918], 260 top [C-030620], 261 top [C-030621], 440 [PA-095043].
Nelson Museum: 214 top, 214 bottom. **New Westminster Museum & Archives:** 32 [IHP-4304], 33 [IHP-0622], 34 top [IHP-0086], 50 [IHP-0627], 55 bottom [IHP-0369], 83 bottom left [IHP 2544], 129 top [IHP-0217], 129 bottom [NWPL 1976], 170 bottom [IHP 0172], 195 [IHP-1246], 240 [IHP-0062], 330 bottom right [IHP-0579]. **New Westminster Public Library:** 26 bottom, [NWPL #2277], 41 bottom right [NWPL #614], 50 top [NWPL #2688], 69 (S.J. Thompson, photographer) [NWPL #373], 70 background [NWPL #258], 79 bottom [detail from NWPL #258], 83 bottom right (Maynard, photographer) [NWPL #637], 97 top (Leonard Frank, photographer) [NWPL #1218], 146 top, 146 bottom [NWPL #1368], 147 centre [NWPL #521], 147 bottom [NWPL #2375], 157 top [NWPL #1365], 157 bottom [NWPL #518], 196 top [NWPL #1045], 196 bottom [NWPL #3155], 220 top [IHP-0275], 221 [IHP-1004], 234 top [IHP-4110], 234 bottom [NWPL #3123], 241 top right [NWPL #809], 275 [NWPL #1231], 310-311 bottom [NWPL #1827], 312 top [NWPL #2543], 319 [NWPL #1513], 410 bottom left [NWPL #1254], 411 bottom right [NWPL #1671]. **North Vancouver Museum & Archives:** 207 bottom left [#4221], 323 bottom (Lindsay Loutet, photographer) [#7219], 324-325 (Lindsay Loutet, photographer) [#7216], 389 top [#4704], 394 bottom right [#10010A], 395 bottom [#3900], 422 bottom [#5339]. **Oblate of Mary Immaculate Archives, Vancouver:** 83 top, 316 bottom. **Port Moody Station Museum:** 167 bottom left [#984.103.1]. **Powell River Historical Museum & Archives Association:** 376 top left [No Neg.], 376 bottom [No Neg.], 407 bottom left [Neg. 25005c], 407 bottom right [Neg. 25040], 429 bottom [Neg. 3658], 436 [Neg. #62], 437 [Neg. #2083]. **Prince Rupert City & Regional Archives and the Museum of Northern British Columbia:** 383 centre [JRW No.2498]. **Public Archives of Nova Scotia:** 397 [Map of North Sydney, July 1901, Location 3.1.1]. **Revelstoke Museum & Archives:** 140 bottom [P.1289], 247 bottom [P.264], 433 (Revelstoke City Hall; George Stocks, photographer) [P.151]. **Royal British Columbia Museum:** 29 top (Richard Maynard, photographer) [PN-9074], 29 centre [PN-701], 29 bottom [PN-4450], 30 top [Wilson Duff, photographer] [PN-2429], 30 centre (F. Dally, photographer) [PN-1459], 31 [PN-329]. **St. Helen's Anglican Church Archives, Surrey:** 293 bottom. **Shawnigan Lake School Archives, Shawnigan Lake:** 302 bottom, 303 top, 303 bottom. **Sisters of Saint Ann Archives, Victoria:** 35 top left, 141 top, 418 top left, 418 bottom(Ken Pattison, Photocraft, photographer). **Sisters of Providence Archives, Seattle, Washington:** 96 top. **Trail City Archives:** 297 top [#6499], 297 bottom [#5529]. **University of British Columbia Special Collections:** 142-143, 258, 320 bottom, 349 top right [detail from 1.1/816], 350 bottom [1.1/1502], 351 top [1.1/1331], 351 bottom [1.1/816], 416 bottom. **University of Washington Libraries, Manuscripts, Special Collections, University Archives:** 122 [UW2609; from *A General Historical and Descriptive Review of the City of Seattle*, 1890], 366 top left [UW7250; from *Pacific Builder & Engineer*, November 28, 1914]. **Vancouver Port Authority:** 335. **Vancouver Public Library:** 54 [VPL #6988], 135 bottom [VPL #19860], 192 bottom [VPL #16134], 193 top [VPL #8956], 211 [VPL #6849], 244 [VPL #55287], 249 top [VPL #4997], 251 bottom [VPL #23945], 269 [VPL #22215], 274 [VPL #11977], 276 top [VPL #14953], 295 bottom [VPL #11492], 299 top (Photo by Stuart Thomson) [VPL #16252], 312-313 bottom [VPL #24799], 323 top (Leonard Frank, photographer) [VPL #5054], 326 (Leonard Frank, photographer) [VPL 71054], 327 (Leonard Frank, photographer) [VPL #4634], 350 top [VPL #13797], 353 [VPL #23389], 379 bottom [VPL #4638], 383 bottom (Leonard Frank, photographer) [VPL #5118], 391 bottom (Leonard Frank, photographer) [VPL 11276], 419 [VPL #12447], 423 top (Leonard Frank, photographer) [VPL #5055], 423 bottom (Leonard Frank, photographer) [VPL #5068]. **Victoria Heritage Foundation:** 57 (photographer Norm Spanos). **West Vancouver Archives:** 372 top left [03.001.WVA.HOD], 373 top left [02.006.WVA.HOD]. **Yukon Archives:** 233 top [#4713], 233 centre [#2037], 233 bottom [#2025].

PRIVATE COLLECTIONS

Margaret Bambrick: 138. **Dave Banks:** 241 top left, 241 bottom, 254. **Jennifer Nell Barr & Colin Barr:** 8. **Robert Baxter:** 352. **Irene Berchtenbreiter:** 446 top left (Irene Berchtenbreiter, photographer), 446 bottom left, 447 top right. 447 bottom. **Elizabeth Brooks:** 96 bottom, 97 bottom. **John Bumpus:** 226 top. **Mary Burton** (courtesy Len McCann): 152 top, 169 centre, 216, 218 top, 218 bottom, 220 bottom. **Sally Carter** (courtesy Janet Bingham): 148. **Joyce Clearihue:** 181 bottom (collection Ronald Harold Soule). **Clara S. Coles:** 422 top left. **Sheila & Jim Colwill:** 153. **Pamela Crisp:** 365 top. **Rosemary James Cross:** 302 top left, 304 top left, 414 bottom right (Rosemary James Cross, photographer). **Marjorie Cullerne-Koers:** 167 top right, 438 top left, 438 bottom left, 439 top right. **Curtis Family:** 207 top. **Anita Tong Der** (courtesy Jennifer Nell Barr & Colin Barr): 341. **Robin Dole:** 282 top. **Doreen Draffin:** 255, 257. **Olive Egdell:** 290 top, 290 bottom, 291 top, 291 bottom. **Henry Ewert:** 155. **Janet (Hall) Flanagan:** 333. **Gardiner Family:** 19, 307 bottom, 308 top, 308 bottom, 309 top, 309 bottom. **R. Michael Garrett:** 310 top, 313 top. **Genné Family:** 212 top, 212 bottom. **Maurice Guibord:** 441 bottom left. **Theo Halladay:** 441 top left, 441 bottom right, 442 top left, 442 bottom, 443. **Madge Hamilton Collection** (Stuart Stark): 90 top (C.H. Banks, photographer). **Doria Hawker** (courtesy Janet Bingham): 150 bottom. **Valerie Hennell:** 332, 426 top left, 427 top, 427 bottom. **Hoffar Family:** 86 top. **Douglas Johnson:** 191 top. **Elizabeth & Philip Keatley:** 4-5 (Major J.R. Grant, photographer), 162 (Major J.R. Grant, photographer), 392 bottom right (Major J.R. Grant, photographer). **Maida Kirk-Owen:** 378 top left, 378 bottom right, 379 top, 416 top left, 417 centre, 417 bottom. **Herbert A. Layfield:** 116 top. **John R.H. Ley Family:** 238 top. **Williams R. Lort & Lort Family:** 150 top, 298 top, 298 bottom, 299 bottom (courtesy Robert Lemon & Robert Ledingham), 301 bottom. **Donald Luxton:** 227 bottom. **Stewart Lyon:** 384 top left (George Stocks, photographer), 385 top right, 386 top left, 386 top right, 386 bottom, 387 bottom, 400 bottom (Robert Lyon, photographer). **Jack McBeath:** 400 top right. **William H. McCarroll:** 368 right. **Anne Macey:** 292 top. **Madoff Collection:** 178 top (courtesy Ron Weir), 178 bottom. **Esmée Townley Mansell:** 321 bottom, 328 centre, 328 bottom. **Roz Mellander:** 132 top (Peter Mellander, photographer; courtesy Rosemary James Cross), 133 bottom right (courtesy Rosemary James Cross), 134 top right (courtesy Dennis Minaker). **Bill Murphy:** 77 bottom. **Patricia MacDonald Sedger:** 243 top. **Anne Macey:** 292. **Eric Pattison:** 329 (Ken Pattison, Photocraft, photographer). **Private Collections:** 268 bottom, 334, 438 bottom right. **Gwen D. Rodger:** 420 top left. **Geoff G. Simmonds:** 406 top left, 408 top. **Smith Family** (courtesy Gordon W. Fulton): 354. **Ronald Harold Soule:** 181 top (Jones & Co., Victoria, photographers), 184 top, 184 bottom, 185 bottom. **Barbara Speirs:** 314 top, 314-315 bottom, 315 top. **Robin Spurgin:** 392 top left, 393 centre. **Stuart Stark:** 58, 59, 91 bottom, 90 bottom, 91 top, 92 bottom, 169 top, 170 top, 337. **Denis Lindsay Swan:** 403 top left, 403 bottom right. **Stuart Tarbuck:** 10, 276 bottom, 277, 375 left, 375 right. **Joan Thomas:** 434, 448 top left, 448 bottom right, 449 bottom. **John Thompson:** 147 top, 198. **Jacqueline Tupper** (courtesy Janet Bingham): 185 top. **Walker/Eveleigh Family:** 73 background and bottom, 88 bottom, 105, 108, 165 bottom, 166 bottom, 172-173 centre, 174 bottom, 190-191 centre, 222-223, 236. **Mrs. B.J. Warner:** 321 top. **Jim Wolf:** 56 centre.

PUBLICATIONS

Academy Architecture & Architectural Review, 1900, p.26: 426 bottom left. **Architect, Builder & Engineer:** 117 bottom left (August 31, 1912, p.8), 145 (April 25, 1913; p. 10), 194 centre left (August 15, 1912, p.7), 245 (December 20, 1912, p.11), 304 bottom (March 10, 1913, p.15), 306 bottom (December 10, 1913, p.9), 342 (August 25, 1913, p.4), 356 bottom (November 20, 1912, p.9), 361 top right (November 25, 1913, p.7),

400 top left (August 15, 1912, p.4), 415 (December 20, 1912, p.13). **A.Y.P. Book of Vancouver, B.C. 1909:** 194 bottom right (p.73), 294 bottom (p.81). **Birks Building, Vancouver, B.C.** (courtesy AIBC): 369 bottom. **Boam, Henry J. British Columbia:** 343 centre, 343 bottom. **Bresemann's Brochure: Selections from the Work of E.J. Bresemann Architect, Perkins Building, Tacoma, Washington:** 402 top left. *British Columbian*: 439 bottom right (January 13, 1936, p.3). **British Columbians As We See 'Em, 1910-1911:** 294 top left, 347 top. **Builder, The:** 259 centre (March 25, 1899). **Calgary Daily Herald:** 390 (September 28, 1906, p.1). Vaux, **Calvert. Villages & Cottages:** 55 top. **Canadian Architect & Builder** (courtesy Thomas Fisher Rare Book Collection, University of Toronto): 52 (October 1894, vol.7 no.10), 84 top (October 1894, vol.7 no.10), 137 bottom (May, 1902, vol.xv, supp. p.x), 158 bottom (December, 1895 supp.), 159 bottom left (July, 1895, vol. viii, supp.), 161 bottom (August, 1894 supp.), 164 top (October 1894, vol.7 no.10), 168 (October 1894, vol.7 no.10), 186 (October 1894, vol.7 no.10), 206 top (October 1894, vol.7 no.10), 287 top left (January 1897, p.5). **Craftsman Bungalow** (courtesy Larry Kreisman): 340 centre. **Eidelberg, Dr. Martin. E. Colonna:** 199 top. **First Congress of Canadian Architects & First Annual Convention of the Institute of Architects of Canada: Programme, Montreal, Aug. 19-24, 1907:** 250 top. **Greater Vancouver - Illustrated:** 192 top (p.196), 193 bottom (p.207). **Hampton, Janie. Joyce Grenfell** (London: John Murray, 2002): 401. **Henderson's Vancouver Directory, 1908:** 194 top right, 284, 338 top left. **Henderson's Victoria Directory, 1914:** 344. **Howay & Schofield, British Columbia Biographical** (courtesy Donald Luxton): 27 top (Vol.IV, p.35), 27 bottom (Vol.IV, facing p.1062), 107 top (Vol.III, p.153), 166 top (Vol. III, between pp.92-95), 200 (Vol. III, facing p.566), 318 top (Vol.III, between pp.552-555), 359 (Vol.III, between pp.540-543). **Industrial Progress & Commercial Record:** 117 right (October 1915, p.34), 369 top right (colour plate, May, 1914), 380 (July 1914, p.48). **Frazer River Thermometer:** 24. **Lort, Ross. All Creatures Great and Small:** 300 top left, 300 top right (courtesy Donald Luxton). **Mitton, E. Stanley. Modern Homes for Modern People** (courtesy Fred Sigurjonnson): 338 bottom, 339 top, centre and bottom. **Modern Architecture:** 116 bottom left, 116 bottom right, 118, 131 bottom, 141 bottom left, 210, 259 bottom, 345, 366-367 bottom, 388 bottom left. **Morning Star [Vancouver] Rotagravure Edition, December 11, 1926** (courtesy Walker/Eveleigh Family): 272-273, 396 bottom right. **Nanaimo Free Press Jubilee Edition, 1924:** 250 bottom. **Revelstoke Herald & Railway Men's Journal:** 391 top (August 21, 1902). **Royal Architectural Institute of Canada Journal:** 449 top (15, No.4, Apr. 1938, p.78). **Short, C.W. & R. Stanley-Brown, Public Buildings::** 405 (p.111). **Souvenir Album of West Vancouver, British Columbia 1930** (courtesy West Vancouver Museum & Archives): 372 bottom, 373 bottom right. **Wallace Shipbuilder, September, 1943** (courtesy North Vancouver Museum & Archives): 395 top. **West Shore:** 14 (December, 1885), 76 bottom right (April, 1880), 128 bottom (June, 1889). **Vancouver Daily Province:** 316 top (April 13, 1912, p.30), 363 bottom (July 6, 1912, p. 25). **Vancouver Daily World Souvenir Edition, 1891:** 87 bottom, 165 centre. **Vancouver Sun:** 435 (March 12, 1938). **Vancouver of Today Architecturally:** 130 top, 131 top left, 131 top right, 135 top, 136 bottom, 137 top right, 159 top right, 159 centre right, 173 top, 174 top, 190 top, 239 top, 239 bottom right. **Victoria Architecturally** (courtesy AIBC): 132 bottom, 133 top, 133 bottom left, 136 top, 151 top, 189 top, 204 top, 204 bottom, 220 centre, 238 bottom, 283 top, 287 bottom left, 287 bottom right, 288 top left, 289 top, 289 bottom, 357, 358 bottom right, 359 bottom left and bottom right, 365 bottom right. **Victoria Daily Colonist:** 201 (January 1, 1893), 239 bottom left (June 13, 1913), 397 top left (August 16, 1942, p.5), 421 bottom (March 29, 1936, p. 3). **Victoria Daily Times:** 125 top (November 17, 1924, p.1), 243 bottom (May 31, 1913, p.7), 431 bottom right (July 19, 1941, p.9). **Victoria Illustrated** (courtesy David Watson): 40, 41 bottom left, 76, 78, 104, 156 top, 156 bottom left, 157 bottom right, 163. **Wellcome, Henry S. The**

Story of Metlakahtla: 80 top. **Western Homes & Living:** 448 bottom left (January 1958, p.39). **Who's Who & Why, 1912:** 346. **Who's Who & Why, 1913:** 128 top. **Who's Who & Why, 1921:** 382. **Year Book of the British Columbia Society of Architects, Vancouver Chapter** (courtesy AIBC): 1, 119 top, 141 bottom right, 288 bottom left, 360 centre and bottom, 369 bottom left, 388 bottom right, 398 bottom left, 399, 412 top, 412 bottom, 413. **Yoho, Jud. Craftsman Bungalows, c.1913** (courtesy Jennifer Nell Barr): 340 bottom.

John Adams is a historian and museologist. He is Regional Manager for B.C. Heritage and an active member of the Old Cemeteries Society of Victoria. Areas of research have included documenting brick companies in B.C., particularly the Clayburn Company, the Douglas family, B.C. cemeteries, ghost stories and Victoria neighbourhood history. He is the author of *Old Square-Toes and His Lady: the Life of James and Amelia Douglas*, published in 2001.

Dennis A. Andersen is a Lutheran clergyman in Seattle. He was formerly in charge of photographs and architectural drawings at the University of Washington Libraries Special Collections Division, and has served as a member of the Seattle Landmarks Preservation Board. He has written a number of articles on aspects of Seattle architecture, including contributions to *Shaping Seattle Architecture*. His latest publication, co-authored with Jeffrey Karl Ochsner, is *Distant Corner: Seattle Architects and the Legacy of H.H. Richardson, 1880-1895*.

John Atkin is a longtime heritage advocate in Vancouver, where he lives in a century-old house. He is the author of three books and numerous articles about Vancouver. John also creates and presents unique walking tours of the city.

Fiona Avakumovic is a Community Planner with the City of Burnaby. Her special heritage interests are the role of environmental colour and the social life of the piazza. She lives in Vancouver with her husband and two daughters.

Catherine Barford studied art and architectural history at the University of British Columbia and has been active in several heritage organizations. She was a contributor to *Welcome to Heritage: An Introductory Guide to Heritage in Vancouver* and is a granddaughter of Ross Lort.

Colin Barr has been a genealogical and heritage researcher for over thirty years, working in both Canada and England. He was the editor of *The City of Victoria Downtown Heritage Registry*. In his other life, Colin is a pyrotechnician at The Butchart Gardens. He and his wife,

Jennifer Nell Barr, live in a house designed by Elmer Ellsworth Green.

Jennifer Nell Barr has worked on many heritage inventory projects. Since 1987 she has been the Administrator, then Executive Director, of the Victoria Heritage Foundation (VHF), which funds exterior restoration work on the city's hundreds of designated heritage houses. With the VHF's enthusiastic Education Committee volunteers, she is currently cataloguing the house plans held by the City of Victoria, working on a revised and expanded edition (600 buildings, including schools, churches, etc., and over 600 pages with thousands of photographs and elevations) of the city's heritage inventory, *This Old House: Victoria's Heritage Neighbourhoods*, and (slowly but surely) developing heritage walking tours for Victoria's numerous and delightful old neighbourhoods.

Scott Barrett completed his B.A. in "History in Art" at the University of Victoria in 2000. After travelling in Europe he has returned to Vancouver. Scott is now the Senior Coordinator, Heritage Preservation Services for the City of Toronto..

Paul Bennett, following a diplomatic career, completed his M.A. in Community & Regional Planning at the University of British Columbia. His thesis focused on the economic rejuvenation of Vancouver's Victory Square, including its heritage assets. Paul has written and edited various publications, and is currently working for the federal government in Ottawa.

Janet Bingham is the author of *Samuel Maclure Architect* and *More Than a House: The Story of Roedde House and Barclay Heritage Square*. Both reflect her interest in architectural history which led her to heritage advocacy. In 1998 she received Heritage Canada Foundation's Gabrielle Léger Award for her volunteer efforts in preservation.

Edward R. Bosley, a native of California, is the Director of the Gamble House in Pasadena, and a recognized authority on the work of Greene & Greene. He has written and lectured

extensively on California Arts and Crafts architecture. A recent publication is *Greene & Greene* (London: Phaidon Press Ltd., 2000).

Nancy Byrtus (Master of Arts: Heritage Conservation, Carleton University, 1995) freelances predominantly in the areas of research and conservation in Toronto. After working for two years at E.R.A. Architects Inc., she is currently occupied by the preparation of property designations and heritage easement agreements for the City of Toronto Heritage Preservation Services Department. Nancy also serves as the Editor of *Forum*, the newsletter of the Canadian Association of Professional Heritage Consultants.

Sister Margaret Cantwell, born in Massachusetts, is a Sister of Saint Ann and has ministered since 1944 in British Columbia and Alaska. She spent many years in Alaska and researched material for a book, *North to Share: the History of the Sisters of Saint Ann in Alaska and the Yukon*. Her major studies have gained her both a B.A. from Gonzaga University in English and an M.A. from the University of Alaska. Her appreciation of research materials led her to become an archivist in 1993.

Robert Close is an architectural and local historian and editor based in Ayr, Scotland, and the author of a number of publications including Ayrshire & Arran: An Illustrated Architectural Guide and Street Names of Ayr. He has been involved with a number of Scottish and local architectural and conservation groups, and was one half of the Scottish Handicap Croquet Doubles winners for 1995 and 2002.

Janet Collins is a freelance writer, and was previously the editor of AWARD Magazine, a trade publication aimed at architecture, construction, interior design and landscape architecture professionals from B.C. to Ontario. A former director of communications for Heritage Ottawa, Janet is currently undertaking work for Parks Canada and the Federal Heritage Buildings Review Office, has written entries for the *Canadian Encyclopedia*, and is a contributor to *Canadian Interiors*, *Cottage Magazine*, and *Canadian Architect*.

Elspeth Cowell has a Master's degree in architectural research from Yale University. She currently works for the Canadian Centre for Architecture, Montreal.

Jenny Cowell is a member of the Trail Historical Society.

Rosemary James Cross, the daughter of P. Leonard James, has always been very interested in architecture. She was an indentured architectural student in her father's office for almost three years. Later she worked for Fleury & Arthur, Architects, and Deacon, Arnott & Murray, Architects & Town Planners in Toronto in the 1950s. Although she is known as an artist who paints houses, she hasrecently completed a bography of her father's life and work.

Marco D'Agostini is a planner with the City of Vancouver who has worked in the heritage field for over thirteen years. He is a founding member of the DOCOMOMO.BC working party and is the Coordinator for the local organization. Marco has written and co-authored several articles on the post-1930 period of architecture in Vancouver and was a researcher for the New Spirit exhibition and publication by Rhodri Windsor Liscombe for the Canadian Centre for Architecture.

Mary E. Doody Jones, originally a classicist, has volunteered for twenty-five years as a heritage activist. She has applied her research and documentary skills to a number of projects: "Heritage Report" in the *Fairfield Observer*, 1982-88; "From Cabbages to Concrete," a video on the history of the Central School site, 1984; and three conservation reports on St. Ann's Academy for the St. Ann's Rescue Community Coalition, 1993-1995. She received the Hallmark Society's Award of Merit, 1988 and served on the City of Victoria's Heritage Advisory Committee, 1991-95. She graduated from the University of Victoria with a Diploma of Cultural Conservation, in November, 1996. She co-edited a book published by the Hallmark Society, *Ross Bay Villa: A Colonial Cottage 1865-2000*.

Helen Edwards has been an active volunteer in the heritage preservation field for over twenty years. She is a former president of Victoria's Hallmark Society and has worked as the Society's Office Manager for seventeen years. In 1996, she was elected a Director of the Heritage Society of British Columbia and served as President 2000-02. Helen presented a paper analyzing the urban design theories of Frank Lloyd Wright to the Society of Architectural Historians conference in Toronto in April 2001 and graduated from the University of Victoria

with a B.A. (with distinction) in "History in Art" in June 2001.

Barry Elmer was born and raised in Moose Jaw, and has lived in Calgary since 1982. It has been his hobby since 1977 to research Moose Jaw's older buildings and their architects, and he is now doing the same for Calgary and the western prairies.

Bruce M. Forster is an interior designer in Vancouver, specializing in residential and heritage interiors. Bruce has a long-standing interest in local heritage architecture, and has a collection of G.E. Hutchinson's plans and books.

Gordon W. Fulton, Ottawa, is director of Historical Services for the National Historic Sites Directorate of Parks Canada, a sessional lecturer in the schools of Architecture and Canadian Studies at Carleton University, and a consultant in architectural conservation and downtown revitalization. He holds a M.Sc. in historic preservation (Columbia University), and is a member of the Royal Architectural Institute of Canada. He has written widely on architectural conservation and history, including the *Standards and Guidelines for the Conservation of Historic Places in Canada*, and edited and published the Society for the Study of Architecture in Canada's *Journal* from 1988-99.

Rick Goodacre is a native British Columbian. He completed school in Duncan, and then studied anthropology at the Universities of Victoria, Calgary and Washington. In 1987 he began working in the heritage field, and for the past sixteen years has been the Executive Director of the Heritage Society of B.C.

D. Bruce Grady was born and raised in the East Kootenays, and has lived in Fernie, Cranbrook, Victoria, Courtenay, Williams Lake and Maple Ridge. A school administrator by profession, he has been interested in heritage issues for the last fifteen years.

Maurice Guibord, harbouring a passion for history and museums, has served on the boards of several organizations related to these fields in B.C. and Alberta. He has a background in translation and archaeology, and has also been responsible for museum collections, exhibitions and programmes in both Calgary and Vancouver. He is an enthusiastic supporter of Heritage Vancouver's activities.

Madge Hamilton joined the British Columbia Provincial Archives in 1914, and stayed for thirty-nine years before retiring in 1953. She then continued to research and write about

British Columbia's history, especially focusing on her main interest, the early homes of the province, and their owners and architects. Miss Hamilton died in 1992 at the age of 98.

Christopher J.P. Hanna is a professional historical researcher and writer.

Robert G. Hill is a registered architect and an architectural historian who lives and works in Toronto. He is the author and editor of the forthcoming *Biographical Dictionary of Architects in Canada 1800-1950*, a major scholarly undertaking which has received substantial support from the Social Sciences & Humanities Research Council, the Canada Council, the Bronfman Foundation, the Massey Foundation, the Ontario Heritage Foundation and the Ontario Arts Council.

Dana H. Johnson is an Ottawa-based writer, editor and consultant in heritage. For twenty years he worked as an architectural historian for the Historical Services Branch of Parks Canada, where he specialized in the history of all types of governmental buildings, especially in the 19th century.

Harold Kalman is a heritage consultant and architectural historian living in Vancouver. His interest in T.C. Sorby began with an introduction to a rich album of sketches and photographs, held in a private collection in British Columbia. He is a principal of Commonwealth Historic Resource Management Limited. A recognized national authority on architecture, Kalman is the author of *A History of Canadian Architecture* and co-author of *Exploring Vancouver*.

Michael Kluckner is a native Vancouverite and has been an active participant in neighbourhood and heritage issues for many years. His publications include *Vancouver the Way it Was*, *Paving Paradise*, and *Vanishing Vancouver*. Past-Chair of the Heritage Canada Foundation, Michael has also served as the Chair of the City of Vancouver Heritage Conservation Foundation.

Joel Lawson was, until recently, with the West Vancouver Planning & Development Department where among other duties he administered the Municipality's heritage programme. In a previous life, he worked for the Heritage Architecture Division of Parks Canada in Winnipeg and the Yukon, and in this life is now employed by the City of Washington, D.C. While he promotes the conservation of old buildings, he has not yet actually chained himself to a wrecking ball.

Donald Luxton is a native of Vancouver, has degrees in Fine Arts History and Architecture, and is a fellow of the Royal Architectural Institute of Canada. He has practised as a consultant in the field of heritage conservation and historic resource management since 1983. His interest in the preservation of architecture has led to his involvement with a number of heritage societies, and he has been active in the field of public education through the teaching of heritage conservation courses. With Lilia D'Acres, he was co-author of *Lions Gate* (TalonBooks, 1999) which won numerous awards including the Lieutenant-Governor's Medal for Historical Writing and the City of Vancouver Book Prize.

D.E. MacKay has been a resident of Vancouver since 1985, and has a passion for heritage issues. He is descended from the MacKays of Woodstock, and may or may not be a relative of Donald MacKay.

Donna Jean MacKinnon is a librarian with a background in journalism and public relations. She is past president of the Vancouver Historical Society, and founded Phase I Historical Investigations, an environmental business that researches past uses of industrial sites. Other historical projects have included published articles, and the development of a Historical Researcher Referral Service.

Pamela Madoff has been a member of Victoria City Council since 1993, where she has responsibility for planning Arts & Culture and Parks & Recreation. She is a past president of The Hallmark Society, an organization dedicated to the preservation of Victoria's built heritage and served as Vice-President of the B.C. Heritage Trust. As a consultant she writes and lectures on preservation, planning and design issues. She is the owner of a designated heritage house which was designed by Alexander Maxwell Muir in 1893.

Edward Mills is a Victoria-based consultant in history. He is the author of *Buying Wood and Building Farms: Marketing Lumber and Farm Buildings on the Canadian Prairies* (Environment Canada, 1991) and *Rustic Architecture in Canada's National Parks* (Parks Canada, 1994) and has written on various aspects of architectural history and settlement in western Canada. His fascination with R. Mackay Fripp was kindled during the mid-1970s when he documented the early architecture of Vancouver and Victoria for the Canadian Inventory of Historic Buildings.

Dennis Minaker, writer and artist, has lived in Victoria since 1978, and is a registered nurse by profession. He is the author of *The Gorge of Summers Gone: A History of Victoria's Inland Waterway*.

Dorothy Mindenhall has a Ph.D. from the Institute of Cornish Studies, University of Exeter, U.K; her thesis concentrated on the life, work, and immigrant experience of the Cornish architect, John Teague. She lives in Victoria where she pursues local, architectural and heritage building research.

David Monteyne holds a Master's degree in architectural history from the University of British Columbia, where his thesis concerned the Hudson's Bay Company department stores in western Canada. He has taught courses on the history of Vancouver architecture, worked as a heritage researcher, and after pursuing a PhD. in American Studies at the University of Minnesota, is now an Assistant Professor of Architecture and Urban Design at the University of Calgary.

Carey Pallister grew up in Europe where she developed an interest in architecture and art. She has a B.A. in Art and Architecture History from the University of Victoria and has worked at the City of Victoria Archives for over eighteen years.

Terry Reksten was a full-time writer and lecturer. In addition to *Rattenbury*, which won the B.C. Book Award in 1979, she wrote *More English Than The English: A Very Social History of Victoria*. Victoria, 1986; *Craigdarroch*, 1988; *The Dunsmuir Saga*, 1991; *A Century of Sailing*, 1992; and *The Empress Hotel: In the Grand Style*, 1997. Terry passed away in 2001, shortly after the publication of her last book, *The Illustrated History of British Columbia*.

Martin Segger is the director of the Maltwood Art Museum and Gallery at the University of Victoria. He has written and contributed to numerous books and journals on British Columbia architecture including *The British Columbia Parliament Buildings* (Vancouver, 1979), *In Search of Appropriate Form: The Buildings of Samuel Maclure* (Victoria, 1986), *The Development of Gordon Head Campus* (Victoria, 1988) and *Exploring Victoria's Architecture* (Victoria, 1996). His articles have appeared in *Canadian Collector Magazine*, *Bulletin of the Society for the Study of Architecture in Canada* and *West Coast Review*. He teaches cultural resource management in the Faculty of Fine Arts, University of Victoria.

Warren F. Sommer is currently principal in his own consulting business, providing services to clients in the arts, heritage, and community development sectors. He held a number of positions with the Township of Langley over an eighteen year period, including those of Director/Curator of the Langley Centennial Museum & National Exhibition Centre, Manager of Community Recreation Services, Project Manager, and Deputy Director of Parks & Recreation Services. He has authored numerous books and articles on various aspects of British Columbia's heritage, including *Vancouver Architecture 1886-1914*, (with Edward Mills), *Langley 125: A Celebration* (with Kurt Alberts), and *From Prairie to City: A History of the City of Langley*. He holds Bachelor and Master of Arts degrees from the University of British Columbia. Warren's latest publication is *The Ambitious City: A History of the City of North Vancouver* published in 2007.

Ronald Harold Soule is a restired Senior Planning Analyst having worked with the British Columbia Buildings Corporation from its inception in 1978 to its demise in 2006. His research into the life and works of his great-grandfather, Cornelius John Soule is an ongoing labour of love, and he welcomes any additional information that can be offered. He dedicates this chapter to the memory of Rupert Frederick Soule, youngest son of C.J. Soule, who shared Ron's interest in his father's life.

Jean Sparks is a Fourth year History in Art student at the University of Victoria, with a special interest in Canadian Art and Architecture. She is a member of the Oak Bay Community Heritage Commission and the Tod House Management Committee. She is currently Acting Archivist with the Oak Bay Archives. Her home was designed by D.C. Frame.

Allen Specht is a professional archivist who worked for the B.C. Archives for twenty years and now is a contract archivist. While with the B.C. Archives he was a contributing author to *Voices: A Guide to Oral History*. He wrote *Skeena Country* (SHS), was co-author of *Front Street, New Westminster*, and has written articles for various professional journals. Currently Allen is researching the history of the Hampton Court apartment block with a view to possible publication.

Stuart Stark, B.F.A. B.Arch., is a heritage building restoration consultant based in Victoria. In 1986 he authored the heritage inventory, *Oak Bay's Heritage Buildings: More than Just Bricks and Boards*. He has both researched and directed restoration projects on many heritage buildings throughout British Columbia and the Yukon. He also frequently lectures and writes for magazines. Stuart has served as the Vice-President of The Land Conservancy of British

Columbia. He resides with his family in Oak Bay, in a restored 1892 house, designed by S.C. Burris.

Gwen Szychter is a Delta, B.C. historian and author, with an interest in social history, as well as heritage. Gwen has researched, written and published a series of four books on Ladner, with plans for an additional series to cover the remaining areas of Delta. She holds an M.A. in Canadian history from Simon Fraser University, and is active in heritage issues in the community.

Julia Trachsel spent her formative years living at island and coastal lightstations in Nova Scotia with her lightkeeper parents and siblings, carrying on a tradition started by her maternal grandparents in the 1920s. Her interest in architects and Victorian and Edwardian architectural design became a passion after she and husband Derek purchased a 1906 Arts and Crafts home in Victoria. The research into its original designer and owner led to heritage designation and most recently a Hallmark Award of Merit for restoration. Joining the Victoria Heritage Foundation's Education committee in 2000, and working on their many worthwhile projects only increased her interest in all things heritage and continues to give her a focus for continuing house research.

Jana Tyner works at the University of British Columbia School of Architecture. She holds an M.A. in architectural history from UBC.

Rhodri Windsor Liscombe is Professor and Acting Head of Art History, Visual Art and Theory at the University of British Columbia, and Chair of the Individual Interdisciplinary Studies Graduate Program. He has published extensively on the history of British and European art and architectural history and the history of art and architecture in Canada and the United States. His main books are *William Wilkins R.A.* (Cambridge University Press, 1980), *F.M. Rattenbury and British Columbia* (with A.A. Barrett, 1983), *Robert Mills Architect and Engineer* (Oxford University Press, New York, 1994, and *The New Spirit: Modern Architecture in Vancouver 1938-1963* (1997). He is a fellow of the Society of Antiquaries of London and Past President of the Society for the Study of Architecture in Canada. He was awarded the J.S. Guggenheim Memorial Fellowship in 2000-2001 for his work on Modernist Architectural Theory and Practice in the British Empire and Commonwealth.

Robin Ward is an artist, writer and architecture critic. He was born in Glasgow, where he studied graphic design, photography and typography at the Glasgow School of Art, wrote about and drew Victorian buildings for the Glasgow Herald and published three books on the architecture of Glasgow and Edinburgh. In 1988, after working as a designer with the BBC in London, he settled in Vancouver. He is the author of *Robin Ward's Vancouver*; *Robin Ward's Heritage West Coast*; *Echoes of Empire: Victoria and its Remarkable Buildings*; and occasional articles in Canadian and British periodicals. He also co-wrote, photographed and designed *Exploring Vancouver*. Ward has received Alcuin Society book design awards, two City of Vancouver Heritage Awards, and a 1995 Heritage Canada Achievement Award. In 1996 he was a prize winner in the *Architectural Review* centenary drawing competition in London. From 1988-1999, he wrote a weekly column on architecture and urban design for the *Vancouver Sun*.

Drew Waveryn is a volunteer at the Craigdarroch Castle Historical Museum Society.

Jim Wolf serves as heritage planner for the City of Burnaby. As an historian and author he has written and researched extensively on British Columbia's heritage and history. Jim is currently completing a monograph on Henry Bloomfield & Sons, British Columbia's first art glass studio. A resident of New Westminster, Jim has been actively involved with heritage conservation. He has served as President of the New Westminster Heritage Preservation Society, member of the City's Community Heritage Commission, and as a Director of the Heritage Society of British Columbia. He was a founding, and current, Director of the New Westminster Heritage Foundation. Jim has a passion for heritage homes, previously restoring and designating the 1888 Thomas and Elizabeth Turnbull Cottage, and currently restoring the 1907 Herbert Harrison House, both in New Westminster. He is the author of *Royal City: A Photographic History of New Westminster 1858-1960*, published in 2005.

Telling the stories of British Columbia's early architects has been an immense undertaking, and a project of this magnitude can only be accomplished with the assistance of many, many people.

There is a common public perception that there were exactly two architects who worked in British Columbia before the time of Arthur Erickson – namely Samuel Maclure and Francis Rattenbury. As is evident in this book, nothing could be farther from the truth. We began this project with a mutual desire to broaden our understanding of who these early architects were, and how they were able to design and build such an astonishing legacy of beautiful and unusual buildings, in a province that was still essentially at the edge of the frontier. Clearly, these early architects were an intriguing bunch, and following a telephone conversation between Donald Luxton and Stuart Stark in 1992, we began to pursue the idea of a collaborative publication. When we started, we had no real idea of what it would take to unravel this puzzle. The magnitude of the problem quickly became apparent. As we started to compile lists of those described, or self-described, as architects, it became evident that the term was very loosely applied, especially in the pioneer years.

We were certainly not prepared for how much interest this project would generate, and how explosively it would grow. Fellow researchers and historians indicated their willingness to be involved in a seminar or conference where we could all share information that we had gathered on architects and their careers. Obviously there was far more information available than we ever expected; often, someone had become intrigued by a single architect, and was already researching their career. We were taken unawares by the variety and number of researchers who expressed interest, especially family members. After much further discussion, the line of inclusion in the book was drawn at 'deceased,' practising before 1938, and of some demonstrable significance or interest, and for years the working title of the project was *Great Dead Architects*, or at one point, *Shhhh – They're Only Sleeping!* Eleven years, thousands of Post-It notes, and innumerable e-mail messages later, the "Architects-R-Us" network has solved many, but not all, of our mysteries.

From the onset, we were determined to present the most accurate possible research. Over the course of many years, numerous errors have crept into published works, and we have been extremely cautious in making building attributions. This project has reconciled numerous inaccuracies and inconsistencies, and every attempt has been made to verify the accuracy of this information. Time and again our tireless researchers went back to comb through primary sources to confirm or disprove contentious attributions. We are truly indebted to a number of people who so generously provided ongoing assistance with fact-checking and searches through primary material. Despite their best efforts, however, certain landmark structures could not be definitively attributed, and have been left out rather than perpetuate inaccuracies. This work will be ongoing, and we hope that any additional information or corrections will be brought to our attention.

This process has been a collaboration, and all of the contributors to this book have given generously of their time and knowledge. We would be remiss, however, if we did not single out some of the people who made this project possible. Jim Wolf was the third person into the project, and from the very beginning generously shared his seemingly inexhaustible supply of research material. Among the other early supporters, who stuck with us throughout the process, were Jennifer Nell Barr, Colin Barr, Pam Madoff, Janet Bingham and Carey Pallister. Rick Goodacre, Executive Director, Heritage Society of B.C., has provided support and assistance throughout. Dozens of other people submitted both individual entries or gathered research material that has been worked into the fabric of the book. As can be imagined, the variety of formats in which the contributors submitted their write-ups was as varied as the architects they described. David Monteyne undertook the mammoth task of compiling the submissions into a coherent first draft, editing them together and confirming research material, and couldn't even escape us by moving to Minneapolis. Our sincerest thanks and appreciation go to Gwen Szychter, who took on the mammoth job of proof-reading the manuscript, and was instrumental in ensuring consistency in the grammar and spelling. Dorothy Mindenhall, in addition to sharing her unparalleled knowledge on all matters pre-1900 in British Columbia, most graciously undertook the indexing. Scott Barrett has continued the final fact-checking, worked tirelessly organizing and scanning the images, and dealing with graphic production. Leon Phillips provided the outstanding book design which has finally given coherent expression to our collection of words and pictures.

A debt to the late Dr. Margaret A. Ormsby must be acknowledged, for the structure of this book is substantially based on her pioneering work, *British Columbia: A History*, first published in 1958. Throughout the course of the project we have benefitted from the efforts and generosity of many professional researchers and historians, who have shared willingly and also responded to a staggering number of inquiries. Research assistance was provided by Gordon W. Fulton, Ottawa, Dana H. Johnson, Ottawa, Dennis Minaker, Victoria, and Barry Elmer, Calgary, who generously shared many attributions and references with us. Carey Pallister provided enthusiastic support from the Victoria Archives. Dorothy Mindenhall generated an astonishing number of references, based on her extensive research into tender calls and news items published in early Victoria newspapers. Jim Wolf slogged through a huge number of research questions, and tracked down New Westminster and Burnaby references. Harold Kalman generously shared his personal research files on Vancouver architects, compiled 1970-74, that contained many invaluable references. Dr. Philip M. Sestak identified obscure Victorian diseases listed on death certificates. Robert J.R. Faulkner provided a comprehensive database of North Vancouver building permits. Katrin Grossman provided translations from German. Roger Young of the Legislative Library first drew our attention to their collection's copy of the *Architect, Builder & Engineer*, published from 1912-14 and truly an invaluable reference. A surprising number of our early architects emigrated from Scotland, and we were especially fortunate to enlist Scottish author and researcher Robert Close, who tracked down primary biographical information; his contribution to our research has been invaluable. Margaret Posehn, Posehn Genealogy Research Services, North Highlands, California, tracked down funeral notices and obituaries in California newspapers. Robert G. Hill, author and editor of the forthcoming *Biographical Dictionary of Architects in Canada 1800-1950*, has helped many of us over the years, sharing research material not otherwise available. We particularly acknowledge Robert for his generosity in sharing his extensive research on these early architects, and his ongoing contribution to the study of Canadian architecture.

Undertaken on a volunteer basis, this project bogged down more than once. At times we were just plainly overwhelmed, however, the publication of *Shaping Seattle Architecture* in 1994 gave us a boost at a low point by proving that such a project could happen; the editor, Jeffrey Karl Ochsner, and his contributors have since provided invaluable ongoing assistance in helping trace the movement of some of our peripatetic architects. And just when we thought we would never reconcile all the missing puzzle pieces, *voilá*, along came the miracle of the internet and email. Suddenly we could see the way to finish this project – by driving archivists all over the world crazy with even more requests! We were also greatly assisted by the digital access policies of the British Columbia Archives; their on-line Vital Events has been one of our most valuable sources of biographical information.

The cornerstone of this project has been the membership files held by the Architectural Institute of British Columbia. In addition to ongoing support and encouragement, the AIBC generously allowed access to these files and other records in their holdings. We extend our sincerest thanks to Dorothy D. Barkley, Executive Director, Donna Dykeman, Director of Communications, and present and past staff members: Joanne Charron; Janet Christenson; Diane Gendron; Tammy Shewchuk; Andrew Sinclair; Erin Stone; and Jim Taggart.

There was a strong and fluid overlap between the professions of surveying and architecture, and a number of those covered in this book practised both. Generous assistance was provided by Robert W. Allen, BCLS, Sechelt, Chair of the BCLS Historical and Biographical Committee, and H. Barry Cotton, BCLS (retired), Salt Spring Island, who shared their extensive research. Assistance was also provided by Gordon M. Thomson, BCLS, Secretary-Treasurer and Registrar, and Brenda Tayler, Administrator, Corporation of Land Surveyors of the Province of British Columbia. This information helped us understand the hardships involved, and the rugged nature of the work undertaken by many pioneer architects. The Trustees of the British Columbia Land Surveyors Foundation have allowed the reproduction of H.O. Tiedemann's 1859 Map of Victoria on page 43. Photographic reproductions of the plan in full colour are available in two sizes for a charitable donation to the Foundation: $125 for a 16" by 20" print; and $250 for a 30" by 38" print. Full charitable receipts for these donations will also be provided; for further information please contact the Corporation's office in Victoria.

Our contributors and researchers would also like to acknowledge the assistance of the many archives, libraries and professionals that they consulted, without whom their research would not have been possible. We would like to personally thank: **BRITISH COLUMBIA: Anglican Archives, Diocese of Caledonia, Prince Rupert:** Cliff Armstrong. **Anglican Archives, Diocese of the Kootenay, Kelowna:** Bert Billesberger. **Anglican Archives, Diocese of New Westminster, Vancouver:** Doreen Stephens, Diocesan Archivist; Rita Baldwin, Volunteer. **Archives of the Anglican Diocese of British Columbia:** Mary Barlow, Archivist. **Bessborough Armoury, Vancouver:** Hon. Lt.-Col. Vic Stevenson. **Boundary Museum Society, Grand Forks:** Joan Miller, Curator/Administrator. **British Columbia Archives, Victoria:** ongoing assistance provided by many present and past staff members, including: David Mattison; Kathryn Bridge; Michael Carter; Katy Hughes; Jennifer Mohan; Trevor May; James Cline; Kelly Nolin; and others. **B.C. Confederation of United Church Archives, Vancouver:** Bob Stewart, Archivist. **B.C. Hydro [Edmonds], Burnaby:** Patricia Crawford, Information Specialist, Information Centre; Bill Whitehead, Substation Designer. **Canadian Forces Base Esquimalt, Naval & Military Museum:** Joseph Lenarcik. **Chilliwack Museum & Archives:** Ron Denman, Director; Kelly Harms, Community Archivist. **Central Okanagan Heritage Society:** Peter J. Chataway, President. **City of Burnaby, Parks, Recreation & Cultural Services:** Debbie Strong, Graphic Designer. **City of Kelowna:** Greg Routley, Planner, Long Range. **City of New Westminster:** Leslie Gilbert, Assistant Director of Planning. **City of North Vancouver:** Karen Russell, Development Planner; Gary Penway, City Planner. **City of Penticton Museum & Archives:** Randy Manuel, Director; Suzanne E. Haverkamp, Displays/Collections. **City of Richmond:** Lynn Waller, Archivist. **City of Vancouver Archives:** Sue Baptie, Former City Archivist; Angela Schiwy, Archivist; Ann Carroll, Archivist; Carol Haber, Archivist; Megan Schlase, Archival Assistant; Jeannie Hounslow, Administrative Assistant; Evelyn Peters McLellan, Archivist; Heather M. Godon, Acting City Archivist and Director of Records & Archives. **City of Vancouver Facilities Design & Management:** David Peddle, Project Coordinator. **City of Vancouver Heritage Group:** past and present staff: Robert Lemon; Jeannette Hlavach; Gerry McGeough; Yardley McNeill; Marco D'Agostini; Jim Wolf; Terry Brunette; Hugh D. McLean. **City of Victoria:** Steve Barber, Heritage Planner. **Comox Museum & Archives:** Shirley McLoughlin, Archivist; Janice Leffler. **Corporation of the District of Oak Bay:** Jean Sparks, Volunteer Archivist; Steven Garner, Information System Officer. **Courtenay & District Museum & Archives:** Deborah Griffiths, Curator/Director; Catherine Siba, Curator (Interim). **Cowichan Valley Museum & Archives, Duncan:** Priscilla Davis, Curator/Manager. **Craigdarroch Castle Historical Museum Society, Victoria:** Bruce Davies, Curator. **Cranbrook Archives, Museum & Landmark Foundation:** Garry W. Anderson, Executive Director **Delta Museum & Archives:** Laura Cheadle, Archivist. **District of North Vancouver:** Trevor Holgate, Senior Urban Design Planner; Kathleen Larson, Planning & Development Services. **District of West Vancouver**: Colette Parsons, Community Planner, Urban Design. **Esquimalt Municipal Archives:** Sherri Robinson Dave Parker. **Fernie & District Historical Society & Museum:** Randal Macnair. **Fort Rodd Hill & Fisgard Lighthouse National Historic Sites, Colwood, B.C.:** Dale Mumford, Outreach & Community Relations Officer. **Greater Vernon Museum & Archives:** Ron Candy, Director/Curator; Linda Wills, Archivist. **Kamloops Museum & Archives:** Cuyler Page, Museum Technician; Elisabeth Duckworth, Curator/Archivist; Susan Cross, Archivist. **Kelowna Museum:** Celeste Ganassin, Educator. **Kootenay Lake Historical Society & Archives:** Elizabeth Scarlett, Volunteer Archivist. **Maple Ridge Museum & Archives:** Val Patenaude, Curator. **Nanaimo Community Archives:** Christine Muetzner, Archivist; Dawn Arnot, Archives Assistant. **Nanaimo District Museum:** David Hill Turner, Curator. **Nelson Museum:** Shawn F. Lamb, Director. **New Westminster Museum & Archives:** Jacqueline O'Donnell, Curator. **New Westminster Public Library:** Wendy Turnbull, Reference Librarian. **North Vancouver Museum & Archives:** Francis Mansbridge, Archivist; June Thompson, Assistant Archivist; Cecil Halsey, Photography Technician; John R. Stuart, Curator. **Okanagan Historical Society:** Peter Tassie, President. **Oliver & District Archives:** Lynn Alaric, Archivist. **PAN Productions, Victoria:** Julie Warren, B.C. Archives & City of Victoria Archives Licensing. **Parks Canada, Western Canada Service Centre, Vancouver:** Lyle Dick, West Coast Historian, Cultural Resource Services. **Powell River Historical Museum & Archives Association:** Teedie Gentile, Co-ordinator. **Prince Rupert City & Regional Archives:** Barbara J. Sheppard, Archivist; Carol Hadland, Assistant to the Archivist. **Revelstoke Museum & Archives:** Cathy English, Manager/Curator. **Royal British Columbia Museum, Victoria:** Dan Savard, Collections Manager, Audio-Visual, Anthropology Department; John Veillette, Ethnological Collections Manager. **Salmon Arm Museum & Heritage Association:** Dorothy Chapman, Curator/Archivist. **Shawnigan Lake School:** Maureen Connolly, Publications; Lynn Rolston, Archivist. **Sisters of St. Ann Archives, Victoria:** Sister Margaret Cantwell, Archivist; Mickey King, Assistant Archivist; Debbie Peters, Assistant. **Sooke Region Museum:**

Joyce Linell, Archivist/Registrar. **Township of Langley:** Sue Morhun, Manager of Community & Heritage Services. **Townsite Heritage Society, Powell River:** Nicole Balmer. **University of British Columbia Special Collections & Archives:** George Brandak, Head; Frances Woodward; Chris Hives, University Archivist; Leslie Field, University Archives Assistant. **Vancouver Public Library Special Collections:** Thanks to the "Belles" of Special Collections: Kate Russell, Librarian II; Wendy Godley, Librarian; Mary-Anne MacDougall; Sue Camilleri Konar; Melina Bowden; Donna Meadwell; Corinne Sam; Shirley Sexsmith. **Victoria City Archives:** Carey Pallister, Reference Archivist. **West Vancouver Archives:** Preben Mortenson: Former Community Records Archivist; Lois Enns, District Archivist; Carol Howie, Archives Assistant. **CANADA: Canadian Architectural Archives, University of Calgary:** Linda M. Fraser; Barbara Helen Macleod; Kathy Zimon. **Canadian Architecture Collection, McGill University, Montreal:** Daniella Rohan, Assistant Curator & Architectural Consultant. **Canadian Centre for Architecture, Montreal:** Françoise Roux, Reference Librarian. **Canadian Heritage, Parks Canada, Canadian Inventory of Historic Buildings, Ottawa:** Colin Old, Information Analyst. **Federal Heritage Buildings Review Office, Ottawa:** Jacqueline Hucker, Acting Manager. **Glenbow Archives, Calgary:** Jim Bowman, Reference Archivist. **Oxford University Press Canada, Don Mills, Ontario:** Ann Checchie, Rights & Permissions Editor. **Parks Canada, Western Canada Service Centre, Calgary:** Janet Wright, Historic Site Planner. **Public Archives of Nova Scotia:** Garry D. Shutlak, Head, Graphic Materials Division. **Royal Bank Corporate Archives:** Kathy Minorgan, Archivist. **Saskatchewan Association of Architects:** Leona Schock. **Saskatchewan Municipal Affairs & Housing:** Frank Korvemaker, Senior Historian. **Sir Alexander Galt Museum & Archives, Lethbridge, Alberta:** Greg Ellis, Archivist. **Sisters of Providence, Provincial Administration, Edmonton, Alberta:** Eloi deGrace, Archivist. **Thomas Fisher Rare Book Library, University of Toronto:** Sarah Sung; Katharine Martyn. **University of Washington Libraries, Manuscripts, Special Collections, University Archives:** Kristin Kinsey, Photographs & Graphics Specialist; Nicolette Bromberg, Curator of Photographs & Graphics. **Yukon Archives, Whitehorse:** Suzanne den Ouden, Reference Assistant. **UNITED STATES: The Athenaeum of Philadelphia, Philadelphia Architects & Buildings Project:** Sandra L. Tatman, Principal Investigator. **American Institute of Architects, Washington, D.C.:** Sarah H. Turner, Archivist & Records Manager. **Architectural Archives of the University of Pennsylvania:** William J. Whitaker, Collections Manager. **Avery Architecture & Fine Arts Library, Columbia University, New York:** Janet S. Parks, Curator of Drawings. **Benton County Genealogical Society, Philomath, Oregon:** Gene Newcomb. **Benton County Historical Museum, Philomath, Oregon:** Mary Gallagher. **California Institute of Technology, Pasadena:** Bonnie Ludt, Institute Archives. **California State Library, Sacramento:** Gary F. Kurutz, Principal Librarian, Special Collections Branch. **Carnegie Mellon University Architecture Archives, Pittsburgh, Pennsylvania:** Martin Aurand, Architecture Librarian. **The Heinz Architectural Center/ Carnegie Museum of Art, Pittsburgh, Pennsylvania:** Lu Donnelly, Project Director, Buildings of Western Pennsylvania. **Historic Seattle:** Lawrence M. Kreisman, Program Director. **Maine Historic Preservation Commission, Augusta, Maine:** Earle G. Shettleworth, Jr., Director. **Oregon Historical Society Library:** Bob Kingston, Reference Librarian; M.-C. Cuthill, Special Projects Manager. **Pasadena Foothill American Institute of Architects, Pasadena:** Diana Barnwell, Executive Director. **Pittsburgh History & Landmarks Foundation, Pittsburgh, Pennsylvania:** Albert Tannler, Historical Collections Director. **San Francisco Public Library, History Center:** Timothy Wilson, Librarian. **Seattle Public Library, Seattle, Washington:** Jodee Fenton, Manager, Arts, Recreation & Literature Department. **Sisters of Providence Archives, Seattle, Washington:** Loretta Zwolak Greene, Archivist; Peter F. Schmid, Visual

Resources Archivist. **University of California, Santa Barbara:** Kurt G.F. Helfrich, Curator, Art & Design Collection, University Art Museum. **University of Nevada, Las Vegas, School of Architecture:** Professor Michael Alcorn. **University of Oregon, Eugene, Architecture & Allied Arts Library:** Christine L. Sundt, Visual Resources Curator; Ed Teague, Head. **University of Pittsburgh, Archival Services Center:** Marianne Kasica, University Archivist. **Watkin Museum of History & Art:** Jeff Jewel, Photo Archives. **Wolfsonian-Florida International University:** Francis X. Luca, Associate Librarian. **ENGLAND: Gotch, Saunders & Surridge Architects, London:** Roy Hargave, Historian. **Royal Institute of British Architects, Library & Information Unit:** Nicholas Cleary; Rachel Pownall. **University of Bristol Theatre Collection:** Frances Carlyon. **AUSTRALIA: University of Melbourne, Victoria, Faculty of Architecture, Building & Planning:** Dr. Julie Willis. **NEW ZEALAND: Department of Architecture, University of Auckland:** Professor Michael Milojevic.

Many people provided information on specific architects, provided the attribution of individual buildings, submitted images, connected us with people who we would not have otherwise met, or just helped us out. For their contributions to this project we would like to thank: **BRITISH COLUMBIA: Burnaby:** Brian Elder. **Colwood:** John Ronald, Royal Colwood Golf Club. **Cowichan Bay:** Richard Somerset Mackie. **Cranbrook:** Tom Kirk, Tembec Industries. **Denman Island:** Sheila Tully. **Esquimalt:** Father Bernard Hanley, Queen of Peace Church. **Kelowna:** Leigh-Ann Carter; Dave Dendy; Alice Lundy. **Langley:** Michael Kluckner. **Maple Ridge:** Fred Braches. **Mission:** Eric LeBlanc. **Nelson:** Dan McGauley, Blaylock's Bed & Breakfast; Chris Fairbanks, Fairbanks Architecture; R.J. (Ron) Welwood, Assistant Librarian, Public Services, Selkirk College, Castlegar Campus. **New Westminster:** Dave Banks; Archie Miller, A Sense of History Research Services Inc. **North Vancouver:** Stephen H. Green; Fred Thornton Hollingsworth; A.L. "Dick" Lazenby; Roy J.V. Pallant; Fred Sigurjonnsson. **Oak Bay:** Dr. Len McCann. **Powell River:** Lilia and Ian Gould, Old Courthouse Inn & Hostel. **Prince George:** J. Kent Sedgwick. **Saanich:** Sheila and Jim Colwill. **Sechelt:** Gordon McLeod. **Surrey:** David Birch, St. Helen's Church, Surrey; Terry Shaw.. **Vancouver:** Sue Bennett; Cameron Cathcart; Tom Cox; Beverly Cramp; Chuck Davis; Gerry Eckford; Don Erb; R. Michael Garrett; Imbi S. Harding; Elizabeth and Philip Keatley; Robert Lemon; Leonard G. McCann; Donna Jean MacKinnon; John Mackie; Eric Pattison; Jo Scott-B; Tom Taylor; Peter Vaisbord; Suzi Webster; Floris van Weelderen; John Wellwood; Margo Keate West; Jodi Wigmore. **Victoria:** Geli Bartlett; Robert Baxter; Edith Bradley; Ron Green; Jennifer Iredale; Alastair Kerr; Diane Morriss, Sono Nis Press; Jim Munro, Munro's Books; Bill Murphy; Tim O'Connor; Esther Parker; Robert Patterson; Peter Scott; Christopher A. Thomas; David Watson. **West Vancouver:** Lilia D'Acres; John Mawson. **CANADA: Calgary, Alberta:** Lorne Simspon, Simpson Roberts Architecture & Interior Design Inc. **Whitehorse, Yukon:** Helene Dobrowolsky; Rob Ingram. **Toronto:** Stephen Otto. **Ottawa, Ontario:** Professor John F. Bosher; Charles A. Osborne. **UNITED STATES: Lawrenceville, New Jersey:** William H. McCarroll. **Miami, Florida:** Michael Kinerk; Dennis Wilhelm; Mitchell Wolfson, Jr. **Rochester, New York:** Donald S. Hall. **San Francisco, California:** Edan Milton Hughes; Philip Rossetti and Katherine Petrin, Architectural Resources Group Architects, Planners & Conservators Inc. **Seattle, Washington:** Dennis Alan Andersen; Jeffrey Karl Ochsner; Sidni Sobolik, J. Kingston Pierce, David A. Rash; Thomas Veith. **Portland, Oregon:** William John Hawkins III, AIA. **Ogden, Utah:** Ronald B. Reiss, AIA, Senior Vice President, Case, Lowe & Hart Inc. **ENGLAND: Oxford:** Janie Hampton. **London:** Karen Mann.

We were especially delighted with the ongoing assistance provided by many family members and personal associates of these architects, who provided a great deal of fascinating biographical information, including: **BRITISH COLUMBIA:** Margaret Bambrick, Sidney; Irene

Berchtenbreiter, Mission; Jamie P. Brown and Phyllys Dalton Brown, Summerland; John Bumpus, Victoria; Douglas A. Campbell, Victoria; Kay Carter, North Vancouver; Doug Chivers, Vancouver; John Chivers, Mill Bay; Clara S. Coles, West Vancouver; Pamela E. Crisp, Victoria; Jeannette Dawson, Burnaby; Olive 'Dolly' Egdell, Sidney; Gloria Fleck, Vancouver; J. Gordon Ford, Victoria; Robert Frame, Victoria; Lindsay W.F. Gardiner, Victoria; Elizabeth Genné, W. Thomas Genné, Margaret R. Genné and Susan S. Genné, Corvallis, Oregon; Theo (Holland) Halladay, Victoria; Valerie Hallford, Kelowna; Rosemary Hathaway, Qualicum Beach; Mrs. Gordon Henderson, Oak Bay; Valerie Hennell, Nanaimo; Pheona Hislop, Victoria; Beatrice Hodgson, West Vancouver; N.H. Hoffar, Sechelt; Helen Hurley, Vancouver; Joy Jackson, Shawnigan Lake; Olga Johnson, Vancouver; Kathleen Johnston, Victoria; Helen Jones, Victoria; Linda Jury, Victoria; Allan C. Kelly, West Vancouver; Diana King, Vancouver; Mrs. Maida Kirk-Owen, West Vancouver; Marjorie Cullerne-Koers, Parksville; R.H. Ley, Victoria; Jack Lort, Victoria; Williams R. "Bill" Lort, Vancouver; Stewart Lyon, Penticton; Denise McAvity, Vancouver; Joan McCarter, Victoria; Mrs. Aileen McLellan, North Vancouver; Anne E. Macey, New Westminster; Esmée Townley Mansell, Vancouver; Andrew H. Mercer, Vancouver; Jane Merry, Trail; Claudia Matheson Paton, West Vancouver; Donald R. Pratt, West Vancouver; Gwendoline D. Rodger, Sidney; Patricia MacDonald Sedger, Victoria; Barbara Speirs, Vancouver; William Semeyn, Victoria; Robin Spurgin, Vancouver; Denis Lindsay Swan, Victoria; Stuart Tarbuck, Mission; Joan Thomas, Kaslo; Jans Visscher, Vancouver; Robert Eveleigh "Buzz" Walker, Surrey; William R. Walker, Surrey; B.J. (Matheson) Warner, West Vancouver; David Watkins, Victoria; Thomas Watkins, Victoria; Ron Weir, Victoria; Pam Birley Wilson and Rob Wilson, Saanich. **CANADA:** Barbara Bishop, Calgary; T. Bryan Campbell-Hope, Edmonton. **UNITED STATES:** Peggy Dole, Gig Harbour, Washington; Tom Johnson, Port Townsend, Washington; Douglas Johnson, Seattle; Bernice Kiehl, San Diego, California; Herbert A. Layfield, Whittier, California; Rodney Maxwell-Muir, Chinook, Washington; Alastair Nairne, Ferndale, Washington; Norman J. Ronneberg Jr., San Francisco; Bronwen Souders, Virginia; Tudor H. Tiedemann, Connecticut; Mareth Warren, Seattle, Washington. **AUSTRALIA:** Geoff G. Simmonds, Yandina, Queensland, Australia. We thank everyone who participated for their unfailing generosity, and hope that this publication reflects the efforts that these kind people put into it.

This publication received financial assistance from several cultural grant programmes. The Canadian Art Deco Society acted as our sponsoring agency for this project. Primarily, we would like to acknowledge the generous financial assistance of the Canada Millennium Partnership Fund, and thank Bruce Finlay, Rosaire Cauchon, Natacha Flanagan, and Molly Roberts for their support. We were also very fortunate to receive a grant from the British Columbia Heritage Trust, and thank John Stephenson, Preservation Consultant, for his efforts on behalf of this project. Additional funding was provided by the Leon and Thea Koerner Foundation, and we thank Susan Holmberg Currie, Executive Director for her assistance. In this era of diminishing government support for arts, culture and heritage initiatives, every dollar we received was gratefully accepted and squeezed as hard as possible, and we hope that the quality of this publication reflects our sincerest gratitude.

We also enjoyed the unfailing support of our publisher, Talonbooks, without which this project could not have been realized; we humbly thank Karl H. Siegler, President and Publisher, for his thoughtful, probing and intelligent editing, that questioned our assumptions and pushed us to achieve nothing less than the finest results, a test of our abilities for which we are extremely grateful. Our sincerest thanks go as well to Christy Siegler, Production Manager; Erin Williams, former Marketing Manager; Alexandra Siegler, Office Manager and Customer Service, Vancouver; and Chris Gatchalian, Editorial Assistant, for their ongoing assistance with this challenging project.

And finally, we would like to thank the individual contributors to this book, for their kind offers to undertake this work without compensation other than to help us in our quest to tell the stories of the early architects who built British Columbia. We were pleasantly surprised by the unfailing generosity of our contributors. Not only were they willing to provide their hard-won research *gratis*, they were willing to share whatever information they had with each other! One of the most pleasurable aspects was the friendly competition that grew up among our 'Dead Architects Society.' When we first started circulating lists of available architects, there was a frenzy of phone calls and faxes, with researchers trading architects like baseball cards. Our contributors' meetings, both in Victoria and Vancouver, were genial and informative, and allowed us to have some of the discussions, arguments and even disagreements that we had been waiting for years to have. And we were thoroughly delighted with the 'Victoria Ladies Auxiliary,' which mined the Uplands on Sunday afternoons for previously unidentified houses by James, Savage, Spurgin and Berrill. We could not ask for a more productive or cooperative way to achieve the goals of this project.

It has been a fascinating journey – thank you all!

INDEX OF BUILDINGS

Port Simpson:

Indian Mission School, 140, 502.

Powell River:

Bank of Montreal Bldg., 376, 510.

Brooks School, 376, 510.

Company Store, 437, 522.

Dr. Dave's Smoke House, 497.

Dwight Hall, 376, 510.

Federal Bldg., 436, 440, 497.

Old Courthouse Inn & Hostel, 524.

Patricia Theatre, 407, 518.

Provincial Bldg. and Court House, 428-430, 524.

Prince George:

Bank of Montreal, 515, 524.

City Hall, 524.

Fort George church and houses, 73.

Government Liquor Store, 365, 503.

Hospital, 524.

Soldiers' Housing Act Houses, 524.

Prince Rupert:

Besner Block, 383, 501.

Booth Memorial School, 515.

Church of the Annunciation, 515.

City Hall, 498, 515.

Court House, 331, 428, 429, 496, 524.

Custom House, 256.

Federal Bldg., 498.

Fire Hall, 515.

Grand Trunk Pacific Railway buildings, 89;

Hanson Block, 440, 498.

Hays Cove School, 515,

Post Office, 256.

Prince Rupert Exhibition Bldg., 501.

St. Andrew's Anglican Church, 481, 515.

St. Joseph's Convent, 515.

Princeton:

Swanson, Peter (hotel), 402, 494.

Qualicum Beach:

Lowery (Major James R.) Summer Res., 309, 501.

Power Plant, 392, 519.

Qualicum Beach Hotel, 392, 519.

Qualicum College Inn, 519.

Qualicum College School, 393, 519.

Quesnel:

St. John the Divine Anglican Church, 316, 522.

Revelstoke:

Bairne (F.H.) Co.,Warehouse, 508.

Bradley Res., 508.

Burns, P. & Co. Meat Market, 514.

C.B. Hume Block, 390, 391, 498.

Central School, 246, 247, 504.

City Hall, 433, 522.

Court House, 140, 141, 231, 273, 505, 511.

Downs Res., 511.

Howson Block, 508.

Imperial Bank Bldg., 175, 497, 511.

King Edward Hotel, 508.

Lawrence Hardware, 175, 497.

Mackenzie Place, 514.

Molson's Bank, 498.

Queen Victoria Cottage Hospital, 173, 497.

Selkirk School, 508.

Taylor Res., 511.

Richmond:

Airplane Hangars, South Terminal, Vancouver Airport, 347, 492.

Cambie Junior Secondary School, 316, 522.

General Currie School, 167, 494.

High School, 275, 316, 510, 522.

Imperial Cannery, 242, 504.

Municipal Hall, 507.

Phoenix Cannery, Steveston, 130, 502.

Port Manager's House, 523.

St Alban's Anglican Church, 374, 523.

Sea Island Airport, Aero Club Headquarters, 522.

Rossland:

Bank of British North America, 165, 524.

Court House, 207, 231, 505.

Wadds (William) Cottage, 207, 505.

Warriston (Charles Dempster Res.), 207, 505.

Royston:

Owen Cottage, 278, 513.

Saanich:

Babbacombe Farm (Burbidge Res.), 383, 501.

Brown (Herman R.) Res., 421, 517.

Brown (J. & C.) Res., 421, 517.

Cedar Hill School, 53, 511.

Cedar Hill School and Manual Training Hall, 280, 496.

Colquitz Gaol, 134, 525.

Cordova Bay Rd., (nos. 4920-22), summer cottages, 499.

Cowper (Hector) Bungalow, 392, 519.

Craigflower School, 23, 46, 506.

Holland Res., 442, 505.

Johns (C.C.) summer cottages, 396, 499.

Kennedy (Ernest) Res., 342, 494, 495.

Koble Hurst, Newbury Res., 491.

Laws (HG.W.) Res., 414, 517.

Main Res., 517.

Maltwood Museum, 414.

Morrow Res., 491.

Mount View High School, 444, 495.

Queenswood estate, 414, 517.

Royal Oak Burial Park Crematorium Chapel and Retort, 523.

Royal Oak Inn, 414, 517.

Saanich War Memorial Health Centre, 392, 519.

St. Luke's Anglican church, 53, 511.

St. Michael's University School, Harvey House, 359, 524.

Saumarez-Duke Res., 280, 496.

Savage (H.) Res., 414, 516.

Soldiers' Housing Scheme Houses, 519.

Spurgin (K.B.) Res., 393, 519.

Tattersall Dr., (nos. 1238 & 1244), 497.

Teacher's residence, Cedar Hill, 53, 511.

Tolmie School, 280, 496.

Tysoe (J.E.) Res., 442, 505.

University Schools Ltd., 140, 505.

Vowles Res., 497.

Whitehead Res., 523.

Wilkinson Rd. Gaol, 134, 525.

Wilkinson Rd. Methodist Church, 495.

Salmon Arm:

Packing House, 509.

Provincial Bldg. and Court House, 428, 524.

Salt Spring Island:

Hastings Res. (now Hastings House Country House Hotel), 431, 507.

Sechelt:

Boarding school, 73.

Shawnigan Lake:

Shawnigan Lake School, 302, 303, 506.

Strathcona Lodge, 152, 511.

Sicamous Junction:

Hotel and Station, 236, 512.

Sidney:

Deep Bay Hotel, 385, 509.

Deep Cove Chalet, 385, 509.

Miraloma, (W.C. Nichol Res.), 155, 511.

Smithers:

Bulkley Valley District Hospital, 418, 513.

Sooke:

Sooke Harbour (later Belvedere) Hotel, 344, 513.

Spallumcheen:

Cornelius O'Keefe Res., 224, 492.

Thomas Greenhow Res., 224, 492.

Summerland:

Badminton Hall, 386, 509.

Surrey:

BCER Substation, Cloverdale, 294, 523.

Christ Church Anglican, 84, 510.

Municipal Hall, Cloverdale, 147, 374, 495.

Odd Fellows Hall, Cloverdale, 147, 495.

St. Helen's Anglican Church, 293, 511.

St. Oswald's Anglican Church, 293, 511.

Tudor Inn, 374, 523.

Swartz Bay:

Harvey House, Knapp Island, 414, 516.

Tadanac:

School, 491.

Cominco Machine and Electrical Buildings, 494.

Cominco Munitions Plant, 297, 494.

Terrace:

Military Hospital, 300.

Texada Island:

Hotel Texada, (Marble Bay Hotel), 178, 513.